THE

Ocean Sailing

Yacht

Photo by Stanley Rosenfeld

THE
OCEAN SAILING YACHT

by Donald Street

Introduction by
Carleton Mitchell

Drawings by Morgan MacDonald

DAVID & CHARLES: NEWTON ABBOT

0 7153 6434 0

© Donald Street 1973 & 1974
First published by David & Charles 1974

DEDICATION

THIS BOOK is dedicated to all cruising yachtsmen and yachtswomen—those who go down to the sea in ships and sometimes go down in the sea—and particularly to "Cheever" Rogers, John Schwarz, Peter Van Ness, Aulin Baird, Robert Bockius, George Hoag, Chris Lundal, Bob Post, Chris De Gabrowski, Mike Flint, Sam Lane, Harvey Conover, R. H. "Bobby" Sommerset, and others who have been lost at sea.

When Cheever Rogers and John Schwarz, of South Freeport, Maine, were lost with three others aboard *Windfall,* they left behind them two wives and five children. One of Rogers' close friends, John Muench, wrote a letter, which appeared in *Yachting* in May, 1963, expressing the sentiments we should have for those who have been lost: "We in South Freeport shall miss "Cheever" Rogers and John Schwarz, but we can, to a degree, console ourselves with the thought that the men aboard *Windfall* were not ordinary men, but men with the courage to go down to the sea in a tall ship, to do what they had to do, and to die once, while most men die many times in the boredom of conformity."

To men like this, the book is dedicated.

Contents

DRAWINGS

10 CONTENTS

PHOTOS

14 CONTENTS

ACKNOWLEDGMENTS

THIS BOOK has been a long time in the writing. It could not possibly have been completed without the encouragement of Eric Swenson, of W. W. Norton; the editorial criticism of my father, Donald M. Street; and the assistance of Jon Repke, who did the entire refrigeration section, and was the major contributor in the electrical and mechanical sections. Also of tremendous help with the electrical and mechanical sections were Cis Roper, probably the only Cherokee Indian who sails yachts, and George Gould, of *Lascar*. My wife, Trich, patient and long-suffering through my early-morning typing hours, gave me encouragement and also helped in the proofreading. Advice on naval architecture was freely given by the only female naval architect in the world, Timi Larr. H. Marvin Berning, of Virgin Islands Engineering and Surveying and *Cantellina*, made up the navigational tables in the Appendix. Thanks are due also to Lee Ward, of Norseman Ropes, for allowing me to use tables from Norseman catalogs, and to Pat Black, of Merriman Holbrook, for his similar service.

I am grateful as well to Laurie Le Gay, of *Eclipse*, who gave me major help in taking the photographs, and of course, to my nephew M. B. McDonald II, who did all the drawings. The topsail section, which for a long time had me completely stumped, was contributed at the last minute by Roger Fothergill, of *Tern IV*. Other yachtsmen, too numerous to mention individually, contributed ideas, corrections, and encouragement.

Mrs. Esther Jacobson spent long, hard hours editing the manuscript. It was a difficult job of cross-checking drawings, photos, glossary, appendixes, and, most difficult of all perhaps, correcting my spelling.

David Noyes, Jr. kindly read the text and offered many helpful suggestions. Finally, as the great mass of written material, photos, and drawings were assembled for the printer, David Noyes III checked, cross-checked, numbered, and assembled the final manuscript.

Finally, we must acknowledge the good ship *Iolaire*, sixty-eight years young. She has taken excellent care of me for the past sixteen years, and during that time has given me a thorough education on the maintenance, handling, rerigging, and sailing of a good wooden boat. Under her five different rigs, she has been the best schoolroom and schoolmistress that a man could ever have.

PREFACE

THIS BOOK is not directed at the absolute beginner, who knows nothing whatsoever of sailing. Rather, it is a more advanced text, intended for the person who has sailed small boats, raced small boats, and now—caught by old age, an increase in family size, or simply a change in desires—wishes to cruise. This book is designed to enable him to pick a good cruising boat, to equip her, and to cruise with safety, enjoyment, comfort, and also a fair degree of speed. Rod Stephens states that one should cruise at 90 percent of racing efficiency, but I believe that 70 or 80 percent of racing efficiency is enough.

Good old boats, like good wine, improve with age. Witness the fact that *Iolaire,* after sixty-eight years, is still going strong; we not only cruise in her but also frequently race, with some success. Her hull is little changed from its original form, though her rig, interior, and deck layout have been vastly altered. An old hull, refitted in the light of modern practice, may give many years of wonderful cruising and occasional racing at a cost that is minimal when compared to the price of a brand-new fiber-glass boat. Furthermore, many a new fiber-glass boat is not designed for serious cruising, but rather is designed to be tied up to a marina each night. Sometimes such a boat can be altered and made into a proper cruising boat.

A final point to remember is that if you sit down and study this book and then insist that everything recommended here be installed on your boat before you set out, you will never go cruising. All life is a compromise, and boats are a tremendous compromise—what is gained in one direction is lost in another. Of course you will wish to make your boat as perfect as possible for the cruising you plan to do, bearing in mind the limitations of the boat, your own time, and your finances, but the essential thing is to get moving. To go cruising is far more important than to spend a lifetime equipping the perfect boat.

J. P. Morgan said, "Young man, if you have to ask how much it costs to keep a yacht, you cannot afford to have one." To this I would have replied, "Mr. Morgan, if I had to wait till I could afford a yacht, I would probably die of a heart attack first, or be too old to enjoy her. I believe I shall buy the yacht, enjoy her, and then figure out how I can support her."

INTRODUCTION

The Ocean Sailing Yacht is a book long overdue. Years ago a publisher who was also a yachtsman suggested I tackle a volume along similar lines, there being nothing of the sort in existence, but I replied I had neither the knowledge nor patience for such a monumental task.

To compile the information in a book like this it is not enough to have spent a lifetime sailing, or to be a go-fast racing skipper, or even a cruising man who has put astern many thousand miles of blue water. These elements are important, but more essential would be experience in a great variety of unfamiliar crafts, some indifferently built and maintained, under widely differing conditions, plus the necessity of being ship's husband year round in an area where repair facilities—and skilled help—were virtually nonexistent.

Don Street combines all these attributes. Not only did he undergo the usual indoctrination of a boy brought up on Long Island Sound with a passion for boats, but the way of life he chose as an adult has kept him always afloat. For almost twenty years with the West Indies as his base, he has been living aboard and chartering a 45-foot yawl built of wood in 1905, except for forays to deliver other people's yachts north or south—or even east and west, across the Atlantic. From my viewpoint, nothing could teach more lessons a harder way: it is one thing for an owner to take his carefully prepared boat to sea, or to act as crewman in such circumstances, but to come aboard a totally unfamiliar vessel, spend perhaps a day checking the obvious between sorties to provision, and then shove off for a long passage . . . well, it takes a special type of individual, and certainly forms the ultimate test of seamanship and make-do. But what better way to evaluate different kinds of gear, from hatches to rigging, from steering devices to anchoring tackle?

The Ocean Sailing Yacht is truly an encyclopedic work, right through the appendix, and I do not see how anyone interested in boats and the sea would not profit by reading it—and keeping it aboard (along with other more specialized reference books mentioned in the text, as Don Street does not hesitate to state his recommendations, down to brand names). Withal, due to anecdotes and flashes of dry wit, it is a pleasant book to browse through, and I predict it will become standard equipment aboard small vessels making long passages—but it should be required reading for anyone contemplating either the purchase or outfitting of such a craft, before venturing offshore.

The discussion of refrigeration by Jon Repke deserves special mention. When *Sans Terre* arrived in St. Thomas in 1969, I had a record of woe and food spoilage beginning on the coast of Mexico and running through the Galapagos to the Caribbean, despite listening to a generator some sixteen hours a day. After Jon ripped out the Mickey Mouse equipment and installed the type compressor and hold-plates described herein, generator time went down to one hour per twenty-four—although I usually ran it another half hour in the evening—with nary a defrosted steak or lobster for the next three seasons of tropic cruising.

This has been an easy introduction to write, as I found myself agreeing with Don Street on every item or situation covered by my own experience, from his comment on the proper fuel for the galley stove ("I would rather risk getting blown up by a gas stove than die a slow torturous death fighting with an alcohol or kerosene stove") to the size a head should be ("not like the one on a famous ocean racer that was so small some of the larger members of the crew had to remove their trousers and back in because they couldn't remove their trousers once the door was closed").

Throughout this volume runs the story of Don's love affair with his venerable *Iolaire,* a deep, narrow hull whose keel runs full length. If I disagree with the conclusions in any part of the book it would be the chapter on cruising hulls, as he takes a few swipes at vessels like my own beloved fat girl, *Finisterre.* Although he cites examples of the type coming to grief which I cannot refute, I remain convinced that a properly designed, built, ballasted, and handled centerboarder, of the era preceding current monstrosities, which seemingly have ignored all lessons of the past, makes the most comfortable small boat afloat. *Finisterre* never gave me a bad moment, in one instance during a Bermuda Race driving to windward when larger yachts nearby were hove-to, or even running off under bare poles. Cruising, she rode everything like a resting gull and was a joy to handle under any circumstances. But discussions of relative merits of boats and gear among sailors are among the fascinations of the sport, as this book amply demonstrates.

Carleton Mitchell

Aboard *Land's End*
Cat Cay, Bahamas
June 8, 1973.

I

~~~~~~~~~~~~~~~~~

Construction

Boats have been constructed of almost every material known to man, including wood, steel, fiber glass, and aluminum. Today, ocean racers are being built of ferro-cement; in the distant past, canoes of unbelievable strength and lightness were made of papier-mâché.

WOODEN HULLS

Despite the huge boom in the plastics industry, the majority of boats afloat today are of wood construction. One of the results of the popularity of fiber glass is that a great many good wooden boats have been put on the market at reasonable prices. Well-constructed wooden boats will last practically forever. My own boat, built in 1905, is in excellent shape. Many of the old Herreshoff boats are in use even today; indeed, I would guess that the majority of the New York Yacht Club 30's built in 1904 are still afloat.

But indestructibility is more characteristic of wooden boats in Europe than in the United States. A look at the American *Lloyd's Register* for all the boats built before 1905 shows that relatively few builders are represented, notably Herreshoff and Lawley. In general, as far back as Colonial days, American-built ships have been regarded as fast, cheap, but not long lasting. No United States yards can compare in experience to Samuel White of Cowes, Camper and Nicholsons, Plym, and the like. These yards, some almost two hundred years old, have a tradition of quality in materials and workmanship. They even own stockpiles of wood that they age themselves. It is worthy of note that *America* had to be rebuilt in Cowes when she was scarcely ten years old. By contrast, when *Cutty Sark* was reconditioned in Greenwich the hull was found to be in excellent condition, and in fact it was lamented that not enough money could be raised to keep her afloat and sailing; she was a far cry from the oft-rebuilt American sailing ships.

British boats tend to last longer both because of heavier construction and because of the difference in climate. In the United States, each year boats are removed from the water after the season's sailing; during the long, dry fall and spring their bottoms dry out and the wood checks. The wettest American springs would be considered dry in Europe. When I was in Ireland in 1966, in the last week of May, I spotted a beautiful little Watson-designed cutter, *Peggy Bawn,* built in 1898, which had been out of the water since the middle of October, and her bottom was tight, as were the bottoms of all the other boats in the area. In the United States in the last week of May, boats ashore are so dried out that most seams are showing and on the older boats one can crawl through the seams. In the same way, secondhand Scandinavian boats, several years old, arrive in the United States with glued seams smooth as a bottle, yet within a few seasons thereafter, the glue joints at the seams start to crack.

Now that so many yards, marinas, and yacht clubs have established bubble systems, there is little reason not to leave a boat afloat in the winter, thus putting an end to the danger of drying out. The come and go of the planking is, I feel, the greatest cause of the death of old boats.

The great advantage of wood construction is that we know what we are dealing with. When buying a secondhand boat, one can consult books, and hire a surveyor to examine the boat under consideration, and thus one can determine whether or not she is a good buy. There are numerous books on wooden-yacht construction, and various rules have been formulated for the construction of wooden boats; the most commonly used are the Lloyd's rules, next are Herreshoff's, lastly Nevins'. The first set of rules can be obtained from Lloyd's Underwriters, the next two are included in Francis S. Kinney's revision of Norman L. Skene's extremely useful *Elements of Yacht Design.* L. Francis Herreshoff, son of Nathanael Herreshoff, who was known as the "wizard of Bristol," has written his own book, *The Common Sense of Yacht Design,* and his sections on construction are excellent. It is worthy of note that Herreshoff's rules produce a lighter hull than the Lloyd's rules.

In a paper read on November 14, 1963, before the Seventy-first Annual Meeting of the Society of Naval Architects and Marine Engineers, Robert Henry and Richard Miller gave the following figures for hull weights applicable to the thirty-foot-waterline Naval Academy yawls.

Type of Construction	Weight per lineal foot Hull only
Wood construction as designed	182
Wood—Lloyd's rules	190
Wood—Herreshoff's rules	159
Steel	210 estimate
Fiber glass	144
Aluminum	132

Though I am a great lover of wood, I question the advisability of building with wood today. The old rule of thumb was that oak should age one-half inch per year. Where today can one find oak that has been aged for twenty years? Herreshoff stated that planking must be at least seven years old, air dried. Where is that available today?

In years gone by, the timber merchants of Rangoon cut the teak in the forest, aged it until it would float, floated it down river, sold it, and let it age for years in Rangoon before they shipped it to England. But today in Burma, with nationalization, this practice is no longer followed.

Today the vast majority of boat-building wood is kiln-dried, and in fact many of the big European yards have kilns to dry their own timber. Certainly, a boat made of this wood cannot be expected to last as well as one of Samuel White's yachts built of timber aged for twenty or thirty years.

It is possible to improve the situation slightly. Usually a substantial period elapses between the time a dream is conceived and the time the keel is laid. There are years of sketching on the backs of envelopes, consulting with designers, and checking designs before one is finally chosen. Even then, many months go by before a contract is firmed up with a builder, and still more time passes before the keel is laid. Once the approximate size of the boat has been determined, any good builder can estimate the amount of timber that will be needed. The timber can be bought immediately, and stored until the contract for the actual building is let. When the timber is shipped to the builder's yard, it will have had two or three extra years to season. If it was first-class wood to begin with, it will be even better by the time construction is started.

But although it is thus possible, with effort and planning, to obtain fairly well seasoned wood for new construction, the individual interested in a wooden boat will often find it preferable to buy a second-hand one. Whole books have been written on wood construction; in the sections that follow, I discuss only some of the high points that may prove useful to those contemplating the purchase of a secondhand wooden boat.

HISTORY

Once a likely-looking boat has been located, the first and most important step is to check the designer's and the builder's reputation, the age of the boat, and purpose for which she was built. Many boats afloat today are truly amazing, iron fastened, built in small Down East yards on speculation. These originally sold for a price that now seems unbelievable, and though they are pretty and sail well, all too often they are full of rot, with keels that show a strong desire to part company with the garboard. Other boats can be found, by the same designer, which were built at first-rate yards without regard to expense and are still today in excellent shape. Similarly, some of Herreshoff's boats were better built than others: some, though otherwise well constructed, were strapped with iron, as if they too were made to meet a price.

In the secondhand market, a prospective buyer should ascertain the original intended use of a boat, since this will determine her present suitability for various functions. If a boat was originally a day racer, her scantlings will be too light for her to be changed into a successful offshore cruising boat. Further, tracing the history of a boat, and if possible, securing the original design, may enable one to put a boat back on her designed lines, so that she sails much better than when first inspected. One of my friends purchased a nice little Casey ketch, and discovered several oddities, like three hundred pounds of lead ballast stowed under the forecastle sole. Further checking showed that while the original engine was a little Gray Sea Scout, the present engine was a big 42-h.p. lugger in none too good shape. He eventually switched engines, and the performance of the boat improved radically. Frequently, a change of engines, and the addition of generators, batteries, refrigeration, or the like, have so increased the weight of a boat that she may be down four to six inches below her designed lines.

Another reason for tracing the history of a boat is to find out what work has been done on her. If the boat is thirty years old and has never had a recaulking, possibly that is all that is needed to put her into top shape, or perhaps she has never been refastened, or the keel bolts and scarf bolts have never been tightened or replaced. If the price is right, a boat needing some work may be a good buy; much can be done to make her a good boat that will last for many more years.

CONSTRUCTION WOODS

There are so many different types of wood suitable for boat building that their description alone would practically fill a book, so one of the books on wood construction should be consulted. However, the older texts speak only of the standard woods used in yacht construction prior to World War II. Many of these are no longer obtainable; others are difficult to get. Meanwhile, new lumber markets have opened up, making available an unprecedented variety of woods eminently suitable for yachts. Both the American and British governments put out booklets analyzing the many woods suitable for marine construction.

When I first came to the Lesser Antilles I was amazed at the number of woods to be found here that are highly suitable for boat construction. West Indian cedar is more like oak than anything else. Greenheart is almost impervious to worms, as is pitch pine from the nearby Guianas. In St. Thomas, a local wood called gegrie is black and hard, won't float, and makes wonderful rudderstocks. Worms can only dull their teeth on it. Mahogany comes in all grades and weights, depending on where the tree was grown. This wide choice of suitable woods holds true of other areas; in the Bahamas, for example, are to be found horseflesh and other strange timbers. The fact that a timber is not what the designers and the builders in the United States or England are using does not mean that it is undesirable.

If the wood is sound and hard, and an ice pick won't penetrate anywhere, half the battle is over. But here a word of warning: all too many surveyors are elderly men who cannot possibly get to some of the places that should be checked—all the way up in the forepeak, back in the lazaret, under the cockpit; they may be unable to remove the tanks and get into the very depths of the bilge. The more inaccessible the place, the more important it is to check, for the inaccessible place is the one that gets no air and receives no maintenance in the way of good preservative and paint.

If the wood is sound, the quality of the actual design and construction should next be checked.

FRAMES

Roughly I would classify the types of yacht construction as American, British, and work-boat. The usual American construction relies on light steam-bent frames, or ribs; British construction relies on grown frames with light steamed frames between them; while what I refer to as work-boat construction relies on massive sawn or grown timbers. Today, laminated wood frames and steel frames are also in use. When inspecting a boat, one may find it helpful to consult books that deal with her particular type of construction. For an older boat, books that appeared about the time she was built are desirable. Yacht-building practices have changed drastically in the last fifty years, and inspection of an old boat in the light of modern construction practices can only result in confusion and erroneous conclusions.

Steam-Bent Wood Frames

Steam-bent wood frames were almost universally used in the construction of round-bottom American yachts before World War II. Given a good yard and a large steam box, there is almost no practical limit to the size of frame that can be steam bent, although with timber above 3 by 3 inches the process becomes somewhat of a major project. Small frames can be bent without damage into almost any shape, but when purchasing an old boat one should examine the frames carefully, especially at the point aft where there is a sharp turn from the bilge down to the keel. Here frames often break either during construction or after the boat has been used for a number of years. Cracked frames are not necessarily as serious as one would think; many boats with them have sailed for years. The defect is really serious only if all the cracks are in a straight or almost straight fore-and-aft line. Breaks of this type constitute a major structural defect, and the frames must be adequately sistered up to provide the necessary strength.

Laminated-Wood Frames

Laminated-wood frames have become popular since World War II with the advent of really good glues. Normally they consist of layers of oak or elm, though sometimes mahogany is used. However, some frames are now laminated out of fir. The difference in strength between fir and oak is adequately taken care of in the average forty-foot boat by the addition of one extra quarter-inch layer of fir to whatever would have been used were the frame made of oak.

Grown Wood Frames

An old, reliable method of building strong wood frames is to fashion them of suitably shaped natural crooks. Since it is almost impossible to find a single piece of wood which will take the full S curve in the midship section of a yacht, the grown frames are usually made of several pieces, each with a single curve, attached in such a manner that a compound curve results. Where the pieces overlap they are joined with iron or bronze pins.

In cheaper construction, single grown frames are used, consisting of two pieces bolted or drifted together to make the S curve. In more expensive construction, the employment of double grown frames, made of four pieces of wood, results in good appearance, greater strength, and uniform thickness from heel to head.

A word of caution here: when examining an older boat with grown frames, whether single or double, one should be very careful to check the pins holding the frames together. Even on boats that are bronze-fastened, frequently the pins joining the grown frames are made of iron. Down in the bilge these pins may have completely rusted away, allowing the frames to work, and perhaps even to rot.

Sawn Frames

In heavy commercial construction, particularly on the west coast of the United States, one will find sawn frames. Since these are sawn out of straight or almost straight lengths of timber, the line of the grain of the wood does not follow the curve of the frames as it does in grown frames. This method of construction results in a heavy but satisfactory frame, provided it is double sawn, with adequate overlap, and the several pieces are firmly glued and pinned together, as in a double grown frame. Sawn frames are seldom seen in small yachts, except when they are built along commercial lines.

Steel Frames

In Europe it is not uncommon for the larger yards, such as Camper and Nicholsons, Abeking and Rasmussen, Fife, to build yachts of what is known as composite construction—planking and backbone of wood, and frames, shelf, floors, and the like of steel. In semicomposite construction, some frames are made of steel and some of wood. Composite construction is superbly strong, but it does have its limitations. If the boat is well maintained, in northern Europe, hauled every winter, the bilges dried out completely, the frames and floors painted, and so on, this construction will last almost indefinitely. However, if the boat suffers from bad maintenance, perhaps because of staying in the water all year, the frames and floors in the deep part of the bilge, just forward of the rudderpost, are unlikely to remain in really good condition. It is not at all uncommon when surveying a boat to discover the frames and floors in this area completely eaten away by corrosion and hence requiring a difficult, though not impossible, repair job.

Fastenings in boats of composite construction must be very carefully examined, for iron bolts frequently have corrosion problems, bronze bolts tend to dezincify and to cause electrolysis in the deep part of the bilge, and the copper rivets which are sometimes used also may cause electrolysis.

FLOORS

The floors, which hold the frames to the keel, are among the most important parts of the boat. A boat whose floors are insufficient or weak is bound to leak when being driven hard. The keel will begin to work, allowing water to seep in through the garboard seam. It is worthy of note that Herreshoff's rules demand a floor timber at every frame. This is one of the reasons that the boats built by Herreshoff have lasted so long.

In Europe this practice is not universally followed; usually a boat with alternating grown and steamed frames has a floor at each of the grown frames, but not at the steamed ones. One exception is *Peggy Bawn,* designed by Watson, built by Hilditch in 1898, and still in excellent shape, probably because of the floors. She is narrow and deep, with a huge chunk of lead on her bottom; without a really good floor at every frame she would have torn herself to pieces.

When the boats of the International One design class were built, they did not have large floors at every frame, but after one season's racing on Long Island Sound, bronze floors were installed to strengthen them. The alteration was well worth the time and effort involved, for thirty years later the boats are still going strong.

Floors may be constructed of wood, bronze, or steel.

Wood Floors

In America, wood floors are most common. They should be carefully examined, being in many cases the first area of a boat to show serious signs of deterioration; even when the wood is still sound, frequently the bolts holding the frames to the floors are in bad shape. It is also important when checking the boat to find out how the floors are fastened to the keel. On some boats the floors are bolted to the wood keel and the wood keel is bolted to the ballast keel. In a boat of this type, if the floor bolts are gone, it is necessary to remove the entire ballast keel before the floor bolts can be removed.

Bronze Floors

Bronze floors, which are less bulky than wood floors, are frequently used in American boats, particularly in the deep part of the bilge, where space under the cabin sole is needed for water tanks. These floors usually consist of bronze angles or webs bent and welded to the correct shape. They are very expensive, superbly strong, and if no electrolysis occurs, will outlast the boat.

Galvanized Iron or Steel Floors

Many European boats, especially those built before World War II, have composite construction, with floors and frames of steel, and planking decks, backbone, and the like of wood. Even boats of wood construction, built in Europe, frequently have galvanized floors. In older boats, the galvanized floors are often secured by bronze bolts.

Boats with steel floors, if well maintained, will last for many years. I have seen some built by Fife thirty-five years ago and still in perfect shape. In any case, there is seldom a problem in the ends of a boat, where no appreciable amount of water collects. However, if a boat has been allowed to deteriorate, and especially if a lot of water has accumulated in the deep part of the bilge, the floors in this area may be seriously weakened or destroyed.

The installation of the steel floors should be carefully studied. In some boats the floors are bolted to the frames and then the boat is planked; to replace floors on a boat of this type is expensive, since many planks must be removed. However, some builders bolt the floors into place after the planking has been put on; these floors can be easily removed and replaced. *Iolaire* is built on this latter principle, so I have been able to renew the floors without great expense.

BACKBONES

The backbone of the older wooden boat is an assembly of great balks of massive timbers held together with big bolts. As years go by rigs are changed, the boat may run aground, and for one reason or another the bolts become slightly loose. Frequently, leaking results, which is not through the seams but is caused by the failure of a stopwater, most commonly a stem stopwater.

Stopwaters (Drawing 1) are installed while a boat is being built to prevent water from running along the seams, where the timbers are bolted together. Installing a new stopwater correctly is very difficult; since it should go directly into the rabbet under the plank, one must either remove the plank and drive out the old stopwater, so that it can be replaced, or drill through the planking and through the backbone at another location, so that the new stopwater can be inserted there.

On modern yachts, the entire backbone is frequently laminated of numerous thin strips of wood. This method, though expensive, gives a supremely strong backbone and has the added advantage that before

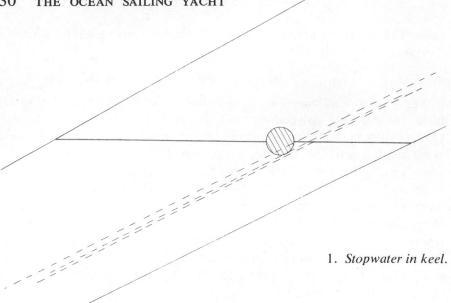

1. *Stopwater in keel.*

lamination the thin, quarter-inch strips of wood air dry in a matter of months instead of having to age ten, fifteen, or twenty years like the wood used in older methods of construction.

BALLAST KEELS

The most common—and most desirable—form of ballast in yachts is a block of cast lead bolted to the outside of the hull. The lead is heavy, and is easy to work in that it has a low melting temperature and can be drilled and planed with normal woodworking tools; paint sticks to it readily; and it has tremendous shock-absorbing powers, very welcome when a boat runs aground.

The next most common material for ballast is iron, which was frequently used in the past when lead was in short supply. Iron keels are satisfactory, but they are difficult to keep painted, and are usually secured with iron bolts which are prone to give trouble. Weight for weight, an iron keel does not give as much stability as does a lead ballast keel.

INSIDE BALLAST

Inside ballast is often used in the older boats built on the lines of the commercial vessels of the past century. On some boats, it takes the form of lead pigs, which should be carefully chocked in place on wood strips laid on the inside of the frames, so that the ballast does not rest on the planking. Shifting ballast in heavy weather can easily loosen the planking and cause the loss of a boat. Other older boats have concrete ballast. Usually the necessary weight is obtained by adding scrap iron or what-have-you to the concrete before it is poured into the bilges.

Many European boats are concreted up to the level of the top of the keel (Drawing 2). It is alleged that rot tends to form on the wood covered by the concrete, but it must be pointed out that when concrete is not used, the space between the side of the keel and the planking generally collects tremendous quantities of dirt, again providing a wonderful place for rot to breed.

MAST STEPS

Since an inadequate mast step can be a source of leaks, one of the first things to check in a secondhand boat is the condition and construction of the mast step. This inspection is especially important if the boat has been converted from a gaff rig to a Marconi rig. In many of the old gaff-rigged boats, the mast step is situated directly on the keel. Though never desirable, this arrangement is acceptable in boats with low sail plans. However, with modern tall, narrow rigs, Dacron sails, and powerful winches, a tremendous amount of strain is put on the head of the mast, and the entire structure pushes straight down, as if trying to force the keel away from the garboard. If one visualizes a sailboat as a bow and arrow, the bow being the keel, the arrow the mast, and the shrouds and stays the bowstring, one realizes the effect. A mast

2. Concrete in bilges up to the top of the keel.

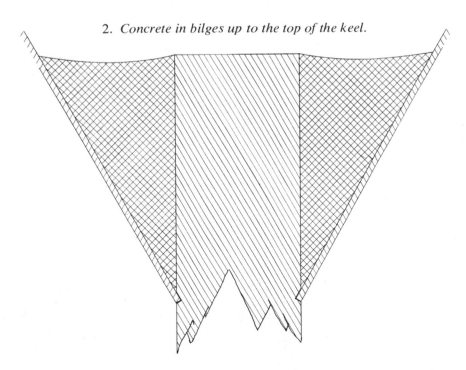

step should be located on top of the floors. It should bridge at least three or four floors, the more the better.

If the mast step does not bridge three or four floors, either it should be replaced or additional floors should be put in; in some cases both of these measures may be necessary. In view of the tremendous strain on the mast step, even where it does bridge a number of floors, one should inspect the installation, checking the size and condition of the bolts holding the floors to the frames. Frequently in older boats the bolts holding the floor timbers to the frames are too small, or are badly corroded, or have long since given up the ghost and cannot even be found.

MAST PARTNERS

Mast partners—the timbers forming the framework around the mast hole in the deck—are a serious source of weakness in older boats. In many of these boats, the mast is wedged tightly at the mast partners. A heavy weight is thus placed on the partners, as they contribute appreciably to the support of the mast. Further, the squeezing action of the mast shrouds tends to bow up the deck beams and the partners. For this reason a tie rod with an adjusting nut or turnbuckle in the middle should be installed between the partners and the mast step; this eliminates the tendency of the partners to bow upward.

Today, ocean racers have taken a page out of the book of the small-boat racers, in that now their mast holes are large enough so that shock-absorbing rubber mast chocks may be wedged in around the mast. This of course takes much stress off the partners, but the nearby deck beams are still under tremendous compression strain and have a great tendency to bow upward.

In fitting out an older wooden boat with a new aluminum mast, it is advisable to open up the mast partners so that the mast is freestanding. Doing so eases the strain on the mast partners and helps prevent the formation of leaks in their vicinity.

DECK BEAMS

Deck beams in older boats are almost always made of a very hard timber—oak, ash, or the' like. In American construction, deck beams are usually quite light and closely spaced—L. Francis Herreshoff urges one deck beam for every frame. The common European practice, also followed by some American designers, is to provide two deck beams for every three frames; this method has the disadvantage that relatively few deck-beam ends match up with the frame heads, and it is therefore not possible to bolt one to the other, although preferably each deck beam should be bolted to the adjacent frame head.

Deck beams are normally sawn out of a single piece of timber. However, there are a few exceptions: for high-crowned cabin tops or high-crowned decks, beams are sometimes laminated or steam-bent over a frame.

SHELVES AND CLAMPS

The shelf and clamp should be good and solid, and the frame heads and deck beams should be securely tied into them. The shelf is a longitudinal timber extending fore and aft at the junction between the frames and the deck beams. The width of the shelf is generally in the horizontal plane. The clamp is a longitudinal timber, extending the length of the vessel, with its width in the vertical plane; it should be firmly bolted to the frame and deck beams and also to the shelf. In American construction, the clamp is commonly placed directly below the shelf, forming an L-shaped unit at the junction of the deck beams and the frames (Drawing 3). However, in European construction the shelf and clamp are frequently combined into one timber roughly square in cross section.

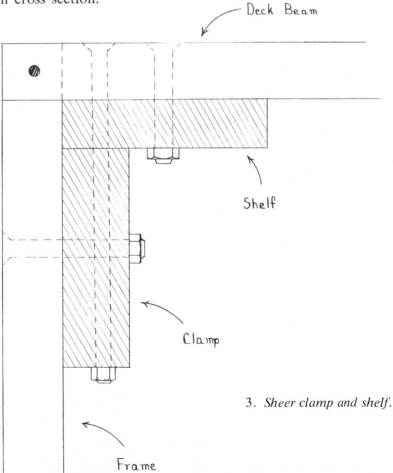

3. *Sheer clamp and shelf.*

FASTENINGS

Plank Fastenings

TREENAILS: In years gone by, in the days of massive construction, planks were put on with treenails—wooden dowels, split and wedged. Though these are seldom seen now, there are a few boats around that are fastened by this method and the fastenings appear to be as good as the day they were put in. Today, however, the costs of this method are prohibitive.

NAILS: Especially on boats built for a price before World War II, iron fastenings were commonly used—square iron boat nails for heavy construction, galvanized iron screws for lighter construction. An iron fastening may be perfectly good for many years, but as the boat gets old, rust begins to bleed through, the fastening deteriorates, and frequently iron rot starts around it. If an iron-fastened boat is thirty years old or older, the maintenance is going to be high, and the purchaser of such a boat is asking for trouble. Even the best Swedish iron boat nails begin to go in time. Admittedly, there are exceptions, but where iron fastenings are concerned, one should be very wary, especially when iron and mahogany are combined, as the mahogany eventually begins to rot around the iron.

For fastening down a deck, bronze or stainless steel is absolutely essential. More good boats have had untold troubles because through the years the decks get thin from scrubbing and water seeps down into the iron fastenings. As they rust, these fastenings make the deck look awful, and are a great cause of rot. The mixture of rust, rainwater, and wood had caused much trouble.

Anchor-fast, or Grip-fast, Nails Occasionally in an older boat one finds the fastenings to be bronze nails of large diameter. These are excellent, as we discovered in rebuilding *Iolaire*. We could not pull them out even with a wrecking bar and had to cut them off flush. There are today on the market nails referred to as anchor-fast, grip-fast, or what-have-you, which are available in a variety of metals. These have immense holding power; once in, they are almost impossible to withdraw. However, unlike the old bronze nails, they are long and slender: a 2½-inch anchor-fast nail has a diameter of about ⅛ inch, where a 2½-inch 20 screw has a shank diameter of $5/16$ inch and a head diameter of ⅝ inch. The diameter of the anchor-fast nail is too small to keep a heavy plank from sliding, and the head is so small that it may pull through the plank. On the other hand, for plywood construction, where the sawn frames are of a deep section but thin, and the plywood planking is thin, the anchor-fast nail is an excellent fastening.

COPPER RIVETS: In European-built boats, one of the most common fastenings is the copper rivet. This is excellent for fastening planks because copper is almost indestructible, the rivets are large in diameter, and the heads are large. The plank does not slide on the fastening, nor does the head pull through the plank. This method is not often used in the United States because it is time-consuming and expensive, requiring the labor of two men. In areas where the apprentice system still exists, riveting is economically feasible because it can be handled by a man and a boy, and the boy is not very well paid. However, if two men must be paid, it gets too expensive.

One must also remember that copper can be of various grades and qualities.

SCREWS: By far the most commonly used method of fastening today is the screw. Modern power drills and power screwdrivers with adjustable torque controls enable one man to set an unbelievable number of screws in a day. Screws must be of the correct size for the job at hand (Table II, Appendix). More than one good boat has been ruined by a builder who tried to save money by skimping on the size of the screws fastening the planks. But screws that are well-proportioned and of good quality are hard to beat as plank fastenings. The planks can be easily unscrewed for repairs. When refastening becomes necessary, one can simple remove the screws one at a time and replace them with larger screws, in the same holes.

Screws are made of various materials: brass, bronze, Monel, stainless steel.

Brass screws may be fine for putting up hinges in a house, but should never be allowed on board a ship, as they fall apart in a relatively short time. Bronze is variable, ranging from alloys that are just barely better than brass, up to some that are almost indestructible. The most commonly used quality bronze screw in the United States is made of a good phosphor bronze with the trade name Evedur. Monel and stainless steel are excellent for fastenings. With all fastenings, care must be exerted to avoid electrolysis. If possible, no dissimilar metals should be used.

Structural Fastenings

IRON: Structural fastenings are the bolts or drifts that hold the structural members of the boat together.

In iron-fastened boats, iron bolts are generally used. For some reason the iron made fifty or more years ago seems to stand up much better in salt water than does modern galvanized steel. Iron bolts well sealed from water penetration seem to last nearly forever, but a water-proof seal is just about unobtainable at the point where the wood and iron keels join, and the water penetration there affects the bolts holding the iron keel in place. More than one boat, heeling well over, has actually lost her keel when the keel bolts let go. Hence any iron keel bolts over twenty years old are suspect, and should be periodically drawn and inspected. Iron assembly bolts holding together the stem, keel, horn timber, and the like, seem to last almost forever and unless there seems to be trouble in the area, I do not think they should be disturbed. Once an iron bolt has been in place for a few years, it is almost impossible to move it. However, stem scarf bolts should be carefully checked. The strain of the head stay is continually trying to tear the stems away from the keel and also open up the stem scarf. Hence the joint works, water enters, and the bolts deteriorate.

BRONZE: Bronze bolts, if they are of good bronze, should last for many years, but they will not, as the advertisements claim, last for the life of the boat, if that life is a long one. Many bronzes tend over the years to dezincify and lose their strength. A rule of thumb is that any bolt over thirty years old that has been in contact with salt water is suspect. A few years ago, I knocked all the assembly bolts out of the stem of my boat and discovered that all of them were soft. I could take what looked like a good bolt and bend it at right angles by swinging it against a post. Being soft, the bolts had stretched and allowed the joints to work. I put in new bolts, cinched everything up tight, and replaced the stopwater, and figure that I am set for another thirty years. One caution, however—bronze bolts can be expected to be durable only if there is no problem of electrolysis. Once started, it can destroy them in a matter of months. Electrolysis will be discussed in detail in Chapter XIII.

MONEL: Monel bolts seem to be indestructible, but because they are very expensive and very hard to work, they are not often found in boats.

STAINLESS STEEL: Stainless steel comes in all types of alloys, some excellent, others not very good. It too is a tricky metal, hard to work and generally expensive, and is seldom found in structural timbers except in boats that have been built in Scandinavia, where it is comparatively cheap.

COPPER: Copper bolts, rather long rods riveted at both ends, are seldom if ever found in boats today. Some older boats have this method of assembly, but it is difficult to drive a long soft copper drift. Either the hole is too small and the bolt bends, or the hole is too large and it leaks.

COLD-MOLDED HULLS

Cold molding is a development of the original hot-molding process used just prior to World War II in the construction of dinghies. In the hot-molding process, thin layers of wood with glue between them were laid up on a mold, an envelope was placed over them, and the air was exhausted from it to build up external pressure. The whole affair was then placed in an oven to bake and cure.

Since that time better glues have been developed, which require little or no pressure, and no heat. First dinghies and then larger boats were cold-molded. Souters of Cowes has developed cold molding to such a high stage of perfection that some people regard the method not as wooden boat building, but rather as engineering in wood.

The cold-molded hulls are built in a somewhat conventional fashion in that first a backbone is laid up; but instead of consisting of great balks of timber bolted together, the backbone is built up of thin strips of wood laminated to the desired thickness. The planking is then molded into place, out of anywhere from five to nine layers of veneer. The hull is usually then removed from the mold, and frames, stringers, and so on, are laminated into place, being made of strips of wood thin enough to obviate the necessity of steaming. The result is a very strong hull of tremendous beauty. The great advantage of this type of hull in my estimation is the fact that thin strips of wood can all be seasoned to the proper moisture content very rapidly; one does not have to wait perhaps fifteen years to get a piece of timber suitable for the keel. The disadvantage, of course, is that if moisture penetrates between the strips, the whole keel may suffer from delamination, and repairs to it are almost impossible. Careful workmanship under controlled conditions is essential. Yachts constructed by this method should be built only at the best yards.

BOTTOM PROTECTION OF WOODEN HULLS

The great terror of people cruising in the tropics is the teredo, or marine borer. The fear is much greater than the actuality. It is true that teredos, once they get into a vessel, can completely ruin it in six months or a year. But with modern methods of protection there is no reason why these worms should even have a beginning chance.

Hull Materials

Teredos have definite preferences in wood. Greenheart is almost impervious to worm damage, teak they do not like very much, and they are seldom found in pitch pine. Instead, they usually seek out some good mahogany or—for their favorite meal—some oak. Once worms get into oak they eat through it in very short order.

Plywood is frequently damaged by worms, but only the outer veneer is destroyed, for the worms will not cross over a line of planking, nor will they cross back into one of their own holes. Instead, they zigzag back and forth, eating along the grain of the wood. This fact was well known to early navigators, and before the days of copper sheathing, really good vessels were clothed from the waterline down in a sacrificial layer of light wood planking. When the worms had finished eating the outer layer of planking, the vessel was cleaned and the sacrificial layer replaced.

Bottom Paints

There are many excellent bottom paints on the market which protect against both worms and fouling. At present I use a paint which costs more per quart than champagne, but I have been going a year between haulings. For the first six months the bottom is absolutely clean; it begins to foul at the end of six months, but just with moss that can be scrubbed off. Fouling along the waterline starts at six to eight months. At ten months it is time to haul; the bottom fouls during the next two months, but still does not suffer any damage from worms.

A few facts about bottom paints should be remembered. First and most important, what works well in one area of the world does not necessarily work in another.

Second, the bottom paint must be fresh. If it is purchased at the home port and applied six months or a year later, its antifouling qualities will be minimal.

Fouling around the waterline is often caused by oil spillage, which appears to choke up the paint so that the poisons will not react and there is danger of worm damage. In the long, flat section of the stern, there is frequently an area of fouling a foot or eighteen inches long where oil has spread along the waterline.

Finally, old wooden boats that have been well cared for are much less likely to have worm trouble than new wooden boats, since the poisons of the bottom paint evidently become absorbed into the wood to a considerable depth. If a new wooden boat arrives down in the tropics with a bare spot, it will have worms in the planking in a matter of months, whereas an older boat may have a bare spot for perhaps six months without suffering worm damage.

Copper Sheathing

Copper sheathing, as the British Navy discovered in the late eighteenth century, is a complete and absolute protection against worms. It became very popular among yachtsmen about a hundred years later, in the days of Claud Worth. Worms are a definite problem in English waters, and at that time bottom paints left much to be desired. The antifouling qualities of copper are none too great, but this was not a problem in England, with the large rise and fall of the tide. If the copper became foul one could berth alongside a wall, at high tide, and as the tide fell, a comparatively large boat could be scrubbed clean in a few hours. It would stay clean for several months in northern waters and for a month even in tropical waters.

However, for a cruising yacht I do not advise copper sheathing. In many areas of the world, and especially in the popular cruising areas in the tropics, the tide is not sufficient to allow the bottom to be scrubbed; instead, one has to dive with an aqualung or snorkel to scrub the bottom, and since copper fouls in about a month in tropical waters, a tremendous amount of time must be spent in scrubbing. Even if the copper sheathing is painted, it fouls much more quickly than wood coated with the same bottom paint. Another disadvantage is that copper sheathing is very expensive. And unless the copper is of a very high grade, it begins to corrode through at the waterline in about two years.

While good bottom paint does provide the best protection against worms and fouling, the teredo can of course enter wherever the paint is scraped off. For this reason, if contemplating cruising in the tropics, one should copper sheathe surfaces which are likely to lose their paint. In my own boat, *Iolaire,* the stem forward of the lead keel is copper sheeted because frequently in exploring she runs aground, so that any paint on the stem is scraped off. Before a trip into tropical waters, a very heavy grade of copper should be applied to the deadwood fore and aft of the ballast heel. Similarly, if the boat has a deep forefoot, the stem must be coppered. The rudderstock should be removed and the rudderpost should be lined with copper. No matter how careful one is, it is impossible to clean adequately between the rudderpost and the rudderstock. If the rudderstock is of wood, its forward edge must be coppered. Also, if it runs on deck through a wooden rudder trunk, the inside of the trunk must be coppered to six inches or a foot above the waterline. Under way, water is forced up the rudder trunk well above the waterline. This frequently makes a feasting place for worms.

Remedying Worm Damage

If, despite all precautions, worms do gain entry, various methods of killing them can be employed. The most reliable method, of course, is to cut out the damaged portions. If the worm damage is really superficial, the worms can be burned out with a welding torch or a hot copper wire.

Though they can exist for a considerable time out of water, the worms do need a free flow of water to survive. Hence, if the damaged area is covered by copper sheeting, the worms will eventually die. Worms are also killed by fresh water; they can be eliminated by anchoring the boat in a fresh-water river for a few days. Or if the boat is placed in one of the new plastic floating "boat baths," loaded with Clorox and fresh water, the worms will be killed.

NONWOODEN HULLS

STEEL

Steel is another common boat-building material. The Dutch, who have always led in this field, first started constructing small yachts of steel back at the turn of the century. Since World War II and the advent of the all-welded steel yacht, they have been able to build quite small yachts of steel with a ratio of ballast to displacement comparable to that of wooden yachts. In the small sizes, this has been done by using very thin plating, which rust can destroy with relative rapidity. But though there seems to be some doubt as to the longevity of the small steel boats, the larger vessels certainly last very well. Many steel cruising boats built by De Vries Lentsch in the 1920's are still afloat and in excellent shape today.

Among the many advantages of steel is its tremendous strength. I know of one yacht that ran into exposed rocks at seven knots, bent in the bow plating terribly, but did not break a single seam. In a steel yacht, one can install watertight bulkheads with watertight doors with the assurance that the vessel will not work and the bulkheads will remain watertight. Integral tanks can be constructed, providing hugh fuel and water capacity. If the tanks are divided so that they remain full a large part of the time, the fuel and water will act as ballast.

Steel construction also gives much more interior space for the same outside dimensions than does wood construction. A sixty-foot steel boat will have six to nine inches of extra interior beam. This does not seem like much, but it adds up to quite a few cubic feet.

At a good yard, all sorts of strange shapes can be constructed of steel with comparatively little difficulty. While some steel boats, though structurally sound, have a very rough appearance, those constructed at the best yards often exhibit unbelievable smoothness and fairness.

Steel is much more easily repaired than most people think. A commercial yard can weld on plates so fast that it has to be seen to be believed. Replacing a number of two-inch planks is far more difficult and expensive than welding on plates or the more common doubler plates.

There are some disadvantages to steel construction. Corrosion is always a problem. Well maintained, steel will last almost indefinitely, but if it is neglected it can go in a hurry and sometimes at the oddest places. In more than one boat the plating under the head has rusted through from the inside out because the head was allowed to leak. The working of turnbuckles in the chain plates is a source of corrosion that is hard to eliminate. One remedy is to insert stainless-steel bushings into the holes in the chain plates; in some cases steel boats have been equipped with stainless-steel chain plates. In most areas, corrosion can be prevented with modern paints; the only problem is that at the slightest break in the paint, the steel starts to rust. Even when this rust doesn't cause structural damage, it is unsightly. For this reason more than one boat has been coated with fiber glass, which seems to be effective in preventing corrosion. Another common method of preventing corrosion is to zinc spray the whole vessel during construction. This method seems to be effective once a year or so has gone by; during the first year a problem exists because the oxidizing of the zinc causes the paint to flake off.

The more cheaply constructed steel yachts tend to afford little protection against heat and cold. One can easily avoid this difficulty by making sure that during construction the inside of the hull was sprayed with an insulating agent. Formerly, chopped cork was used; today, there are various plastic insulation materials available that are far superior to cork.

Electrolysis is a problem but not an insurmountable one, especially now that all-plastic sea cocks and through-hull fittings are obtainable.

In general, though I am not a great lover of steel, I think it is practical for boats of thirty-five feet or more, and excellent for boats of sixty feet or more. The latter can be made at least as light as wooden boats of sixty feet and over. The extra space and the additional fuel and water capacity offered by the steel boats make them appealing to the cruising man.

FIBER GLASS

Fiber glass is without a doubt one of the least attractive materials for a boat. It has absolutely no aesthetic appeal; many fiber-glass boats have the look of a good shiny refrigerator. However, it does have tremendous practical appeal. Like steel, it provides extra interior room for a given dimension. Integral tanks can be installed, and any shape at all can be molded; indeed, whole deck assemblies can be molded in one unit, with no seams to leak. Extra wells can be molded and vented overside for the gas bottles, the elimination of deck beams gives extra headroom, and the complete absence of frames makes it easy to maintain the interior of the boat. Correctly built, the boats are of tremendous strength. While the claim that no maintenance is necessary cannot be taken literally, it is true that a fiber-glass boat requires less continuous maintenance than a wooden or steel boat. Electrolysis is practically eliminated.

But there is another side to the coin. The integral tanks of many fiber-glass boats have turned out to be a rather mixed blessing. Unless the boat is perfectly constructed, there is usually a minute seepage of salt water into the tanks. A few ounces of salt water in the fresh-water tank is not noticeable, but a few ounces of salt water in the fuel tank will raise hob with the engine, especially if it is a diesel.

While the entire deck assembly can be molded in one piece, eliminating leaks around the cabin trunk, all too many builders do not join the deck to the hull in a strong watertight fashion. Numerous boats are famous for the fact that they leak at this joint.

In addition, one of the greatest complaints against fiber-glass boats has been the almost complete inability of the builders to install the bolted deck hardware without causing leaks. These evidently result from bedding down the lifeline stanchions, cleats, winches, and the like incorrectly, and from drilling holes of the wrong size for the hold-down bolts. Often the leaks occur on brand-new boats; sometimes they develop within a few months of delivery, perhaps when the boat is given hard usage in heavy weather. Therefore, when contemplating the purchase of a fiber-glass boat, whether new or secondhand, one should not fail to give her the water test—by taking a fire hose, or a yard's deck pump, and flooding the deck really full of water, to see if she is indeed watertight. If a yard's pump of fire hose is not available, a normal garden hose can be used, or buckets of water can be thrown on the deck and at the closed hatches. However, these substitutes really do not provide enough water.

One of the major complaints against fiber-glass boats has been the slipperiness of the deck. The molding in of so-called nonskid finishes has not been really successful. Many other solutions have been tried, including sheathing the deck in teak, which while satisfactory and handsome, is quite heavy. The best arrangement seems to be the one developed by Molnhyche A.B. in Sweden. Half-inch-thick strips of roughly 1½-inch-wide teak are molded into the deck at intervals of an inch or so. These strips extend a good quarter inch above the deck, and give a firm foothold until ten or fifteen years of deck scrubbing wear them down to the level of the fiber-glass deck.

Some builders are more concerned with profits than with good design and workmanship. Because of the very virtues of fiber glass, inexperienced and unscrupulous builders have been attracted to it. One group of yachts that arrived from Europe promptly began to have a variety of troubles; indeed, the keel of one boat was almost falling off. It turned out that the designer had specified ¾-inch-thick fiber glass at the garboard, but the builders had skimped by using material only ⅜ inch thick. The boats were given a careful survey, all were condemned by the surveyor, and a variety of lawsuits ensued. Boats of another well-known class panted so badly in a seaway that the bunks would come out of the forward cabin. This defect has now been remedied by the addition of bracing.

Some builders install rigging and deck hardware of the cheapest material available. Boats of one popular class are always delivered from the builders with a rub strake of aluminum, which of course begins to corrode almost immediately. Those of another well-known class have stainless-steel fittings that weep rust stains continually. In still another case, the rigging is of the poorest quality and is too light, so it starts straining after one season.

A builder may also find ways to cheat in other aspects of construction. For example, there is the case of one boat that was badly damaged in St. Thomas, but was salvaged. When the crew started to repair the bottom of the ballast keel, which according to the builder's specifications was supposed to be one large block of iron glassed into place, they discovered, instead, miscellaneous bits of iron—nuts, bolts, and sash weights, which dropped out when hit with a sledgehammer.

It is possible to get good fiber-glass boats—some builders do an excellent job—but like good wooden boats, they are expensive. The only way that the costs of fiber-glass construction can be kept in line is by building many boats from the same mold. The owner of a fiber-glass boat must accept the fact that there will be anywhere from twenty to upward of two hundred sister ships. Some people like individuality for its own sake; others have special requirements that the stock boats do not provide. For these people, fiber glass is impractical. The "one-off" fiber-glass hull is difficult to construct except for the man with an unlimited bank account.

The quality of the materials, and also the quantity—the amount of fiber glass, mat roving, and so on—used in the construction, are most important. In England, the best boats are constructed according to Lloyd's rules and under Lloyd's supervision, with the inspector being paid by Lloyd's, not by the boatbuilder. Approval by this inspector, with all of Lloyd's past experience to back him up and form a frame of reference, practically assures the buyer of getting a really good hull constructed to the highest standards. In the United States, quality control is strictly in the hands of the builder and construction can vary from superb to downright fraudulent. It is difficult for the layman to tell excellent from good, indifferent from poor, and even the expert finds it hard to do so once the boat has been completed. The only thing to do is to check with owners of boats previously constructed by the builder under consideration.

Types of Construction

In general, so far we have been speaking of the older methods of fiber-glass construction: fiber-glass cloth and mat resin laid over a mold. In the last few years tremendous advances have been made in the techniques of fiber-glass construction.

BALSO CORE: This method of construction is becoming popular. After the hull has been molded, small square blocks of balsa wood are glued inside it and then sealed over with more fiber glass. This method increases the thickness of the hull to an inch or more, giving it excellent rigidity. Such a hull does not seem to be too difficult to repair, and has good insulating and sound-deadening properties.

FOAM PLANK: This new method of construction is especially popular because only an inexpensive mold is required, so a "one-off" fiber-glass boat can be built at reasonable cost. Basically, long strips of foam are fiber-glassed into place inside the hull, like the blocks of wood in the balsa-core construction. The combination of fiber glass inside and out with the light material in between results in a light but rigid construction with the added advantage of tremendous flotation. Many of the foam-plank yachts are completely unsinkable, as the built-in buoyancy more than compensates for the weight of the engine, ballast, and the like.

FOAM CORE: In another type of foam construction, plastic foam is poured between an inner and an outer hull. The builders have not revealed the details of this process, which has been in use only a few years. It is under development by Whitney Systems, and does show tremendous potential.

A slightly different kind of foam-core construction has recently been developed in Sweden, where it is utilized by Molnhyche A.B. The outer hull is molded of fiber glass with small curlicues sticking out; then the

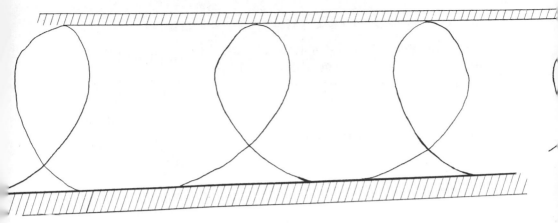

4. *Swedish method of foam-core construction; the inside layer of fiber glass is laid up over curlicues on the outside layer, and the resultant space is filled with foam.*

inner layer of fiber glass is laid on the curlicues, which keep the two shells about two inches apart. The space between them is next filled with plastic foam (Drawing 4).

Location of Ballast

There is a big debate as to whether the ballast should be molded inside the shell or bolted to the outside of the hull. I believe in the latter method, though it is more espensive. It does get the ballast slightly lower, but more important, the lead has a tremendous shock-absorbing capacity, which helps to minimize damage if the boat is run aground and bounces on rocks, and it is easily repaired with normal woodworking tools. If a boat with ballast inside the shell runs aground, the bot-

1. Merlin *ran aground so hard that the lead fell out of the bottom of her fiberglass keel. The entire keel was discarded and a new one ordered. This photo shows the old keel that has been cut from the hull and junked. The hole is where her lead ballast fell out.* (D. M. Street)

tom of the fiber-glass keel may be chewed up, and the resulting repair job is likely to be difficult and expensive.

Photo 1 shows what can happen to a fiber-glass keel once the bottom fails. In this case, the actual lead ballast dropped completely out and remained lying on the reef. A whole new keel had to be shipped from England and glassed into place, at tremendous cost.

Maintenance

Some owners of fiber-glass boats are very vehement in their disagreement with the claim that they require no maintenance, asserting that the maintenance costs are roughly the same for a fiber-glass boat as for a wooden one; the difference is that a fiber-glass boat can be brought back into shape after maintenance has been completely ignored for a year or two, whereas a wooden boat given similar maltreatment could probably never be restored to top condition. On a fiber-glass boat, the rig maintenance is exactly the same as on any other; sail maintenance is the same; engine maintenance is the same; electrical maintenance is the same; below-decks maintenance is the same. If the boat is one on which much wood has been used to avoid that look of a new refrigerator, and varnished trim has been installed on deck, even deck maintenance is roughly the same as for other types of construction. The bottom must be painted just as frequently as that of a wooden or steel boat. Worms will not damage it, but it fouls rapidly.

In actuality, the only real saving on a fiber-glass boat is in topsides maintenance, which probably constitutes only 10 percent of the maintenance bill for any yacht.

The great advantages of fiber glass for boats are that it can be left sitting unattended for longer periods with no serious deterioration and that it makes possible mass production and therefore lower purchase prices.

ALUMINUM

Aluminum is to me the most wonderful of all boat-building materials. It is so light that even small cruising boats of this material can have low weight coupled with plating thick enough to prevent buckling between the frames. It has the advantages of steel with respect to strength, extra interior space, and integral tanks. Aluminum is so light that a very high ratio of ballast to displacement can be achieved—up to 55 percent if desired; if the high ratio of ballast to displacement is not wanted, a tremendously strong boat can be built of aluminum. I sailed over four thousand miles in *Mariann,* a Sparkman and Stephens aluminum ocean racer that had a high ratio of ballast to displacement and extra-large water tanks. She was a wonderful boat. We turned in fabulous runs and during the entire time never really got the rail down. We were firmly convinced that we would fold up the rig before we could get the rail down.

On the debit side, aluminum is susceptible to corrosion and the danger of electrolysis, but with modern paints these problems can be solved, and if local loss of paint and minor corrosion do occur, the resulting aluminum oxide is white, and does not stain adjacent surfaces.

In the past, the major disadvantage of aluminum was its cost. Formerly, an aluminum boat was much more expensive than a wooden one because special tools and welding equipment are needed. Few yards were equipped to handle the material, and those that were, charged a high price. But as time went by, the aluminum boat became cheaper, while the scarcity of good wood and good shipwrights drove the cost of the wooden boat up. Today, the prices of high-quality wooden boats and aluminum boats are just about the same.

FERRO-CEMENT

A few years ago, when yachtsmen sat in front of the fire and someone said he was going to build a stone boat, everyone roared with laughter. When the speaker went on to describe what was not really a stone boat but rather a cement boat, there would be more laughter. However, now experienced yachtsmen are sitting up and taking notice. Ferro-cement, properly used, has proved to be cheap, strong, and long lasting.

In this method of construction, a frame of wire, pipe, reinforcement rod, or a combination of all three is first set up in the shape of the hull. Then cement is forced through and around the frame, either by hand or with the aid of cement guns, which pour cement in under pressure. If correctly built, the cement boat will certainly last. Professor Nervi's schooner, constructed in Italy in 1943, is still going strong. In Australia and New Zealand a number of ocean racers have been built, and Dr. Griffiths, after he lost the first *Anawhi,* retrieved his gear and in a very short time built a cement boat which he has since sailed around the world by way of Cape Horn.

Actually, this is an old method of construction—some cement barges were built by the United States Shipping Board during World War I—but only in the last five or six years has it enjoyed widespread popularity. The Communist Chinese are building sampans and junks of ferro-cement, and commercial docks are built of this material all over the world. Centers of ferro-cement yacht construction are to be found in such widely separated locations as England, Australia and New Zealand, the Victoria area of Canada, and Florida.

Today, the methods of cement construction that are available are legion. Some of the experts are thinking along parallel lines; others have developed diametrically opposed methods of construction. Along with the honest, hardworking people in this new field are others who are nothing but charlatans, making outlandish claims as to how cheaply and easily a cement boat may be built. The result is that some vessels of this type are beautifully constructed, excellent hulls, while others are poorly made and poorly finished, and still others are so bad that they are not even worth launching.

Anyone contemplating the construction or purchase of a boat of this type should write to the various yachting magazines, asking for lists of books and articles published on this subject. After intensive reading, he can examine various ferro-cement boats and draw his own conclusions.

II

Cruising Hulls

All of life is a compromise, and this certainly holds true in the choice of a cruising hull. Josh Slocum's *Spray* and her modern replicas are considered by some to be wonderful cruising boats. They are roomy and comfortable, and can be made to self-steer by adjustment of the sheets only, without fancy, expensive self-steering rigs. A person must have plenty of time, and really love to go to sea, to enjoy this type of stable, comfortable, roomy boat, which always sails on her bottom and is so slow that weeks may be spent making a passage that should only take days. Going to windward, such a boat has all the ability of a loaded sand barge. The replicas of *Spray,* like the Tahiti and Caryl ketches, usually have good big engines.

At the other end of the scale are our modern ocean racers. They are fast in all weathers, never hard on the helm unless very hard driven, but so cut away under water that they seldom self-steer efficiently without the aid of some mechanical or electrical device. I have often experienced this inability to self-steer on delivery passages, and that is the one complaint that Dr. Gifford Pinchot had against his beautiful *Loon* on his Pacific cruise. The crew becomes worn out by the constant attention demanded by the helm, and by the quick motion, which is not at all conducive to sleep. It must be admitted that these boats get you there in a hurry; passages take half the time required by the old slow barges.

Some of the modern centerboarders are fast and easily handled, and can be rigged to self-steer with the helm locked and the course adjusted by regulation of the sails and centerboard. In Percy Chubb's ketch *Antilles,* 46 feet LOA, we twice made fast passages: the first was 920 miles in five days; we told everyone to mark that in the record book—she would never do it again—and on the next trip we did 960 miles in five days. Both times the helm was locked for the greater part of the voyage. As long as the wind was abeam or forward of abeam she sailed beautifully, but of course at this speed her flat bow sections pounded so badly that it was impossible to sleep in the forward cabin and difficult to sleep anywhere else.

There is a midpoint between the modern ocean racer and the old slow barge that makes a good compromise. This is exemplified by my own *Iolaire*. She has a long, straight keel, is narrow and deep, heels over fast but once heeled picks up stiffness rapidly. Her slack bilges and narrow sections with fine entry give easy motion and a good turn of speed, while the long keel gives her the directional stability that many of her modern sisters lack. *Iolaire* was built in 1905.

DRAFT

The first matter to be settled in choosing a cruising boat is that of draft. In some areas shoal draft, provided by a centerboard, lee boards, or twin keels, is absolutely necessary. Thus, it is essential for cruising in Chesapeake Bay, the Bahamas, the rivers and bays inside Hatteras, the Norfolk Broads, the rivers of Europe, or the Zees of Holland. For other purposes, a deep keel may be preferable.

CENTERBOARD VERSUS DEEP KEEL

Of first importance in a centerboard is the construction of the board and trunk. The modern ocean-racing centerboarder with her bronze board and bronze centerboard case firmly bolted to the mast step, keel, and frames is tremendously strong, and the use of metal eliminates the danger of worm damage.

However, these centerboarders do have some troubles. If the board hits bottom, if often bends instead of coming up; also, some boards have been bent flat when the boat dropped off a big wave in rough weather (Drawing 5). The gear for hoisting and dropping the board is a continual source of trouble. Electrolysis between the bronze board and the stainless-steel hoisting pendant frequently causes the pendant to break. It is therefore absolutely essential that the pendant be rigged so that it can be replaced without hauling the boat; this important detail is all too frequently forgotten by the designers and builders. The design of the pivot pin is another source of trouble; more than one centerboarder has lost its board when the pivot pin worked out or broke. Another difficulty is that off the wind the board tends to rattle in the case, making sleep difficult.

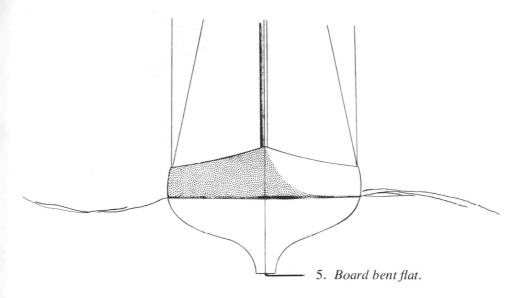

5. *Board bent flat.*

Some of these problems can be avoided by the use of an old-fashioned wooden board. Such a board will come up when the boat runs aground, it seldom bends or breaks, and since it is only made of weighted wood there is rarely any trouble with pendants breaking. However, the case and board can be a feasting place for worms. Furthermore, the designers and builders who really understand the making of a wooden trunk are few and far between. Howard I. Chapelle has written at length and with clarity on this subject in his *Boatbuilding*.

There are also some disadvantages which are common to all centerboarders, regardless of the material used. To be sure, the boat with shoal draft can go to many places where the deep-draft keel boat cannot go. Running aground in three feet of water with a sand or mud bottom presents no danger for a centerboarder, but running aground on a rough bottom leaves the deep-draft boat in better shape, since the rocks or coral heads have no chance to punch a hole in her bilge (Drawing 6). Also, the lead keel can absorb an awful shock without damaging the structure of the boat—unless it has a slot for the centerboard. In that case, it usually closes up, jamming the board.

The centerboarder has tremendous stability at small angles of heel; as a result, the motion is quick, the roll period is very short, and the crew tires rapidly from continually hanging on. The deep-draft slack-bilged boat has little initial stability and a long slow roll which is not nearly so wearing on the crew. Though the centerboarder has tremendous initial stability, its ultimate stability is slight or nonexistent, as a

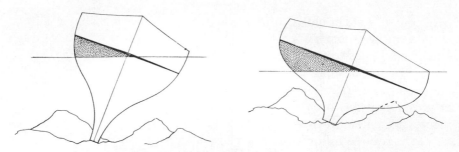

6. *Deep-keel boat versus centerboarder aground on rocks.*

point is reached where the center of buoyancy and the center of gravity interchange. Note the illustration (Drawing 7) of what happens to the stability of a typical centerboarder, in contrast to that of a keel boat, and also note the stability curves (Drawing 8). The keel boat reaches its ultimate stability when it is knocked flat, while in the same position the centerboarder has little or no stability.

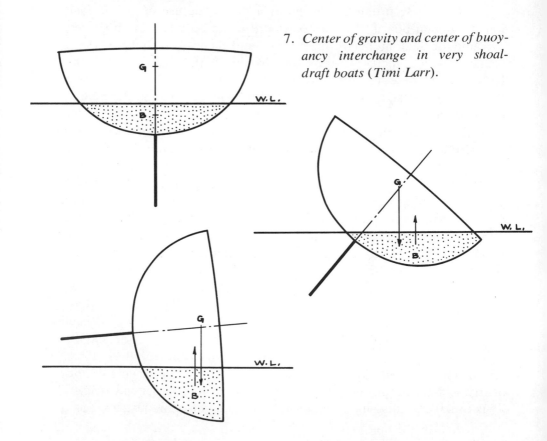

7. *Center of gravity and center of buoyancy interchange in very shoaldraft boats (Timi Larr).*

Sitting at a yacht-club bar and talking to the boys who have had extensive offshore experience with centerboarders, one will hear enough hair-raising tales to make one think twice before venturing offshore or at least before pushing hard offshore in a centerboarder. Knocked flat, the centerboarder just lies there until sheets are cast off or cut, often after the boat has been half flooded through the main companionway hatch. The extent of this danger of flooding is evident from the character of the routine followed by one well-known ocean racer whenever he is racing on centerboard boats. When the spinnaker is up and the breeze is over 8 knots, the lower hatch slide is kept in place; at over 10 knots, both slides are kept in place; at over 14 knots, the hatch is closed, can be opened only with permission of the watch captain, and must be immediately shut again once it is used.

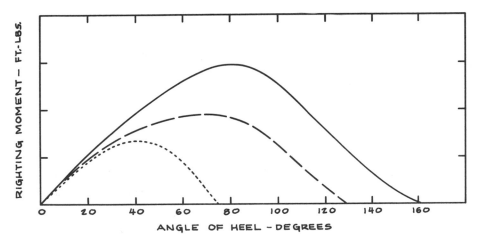

8. *Stability curves for keel boat, ballasted centerboarder, and unballasted centerboarder (Timi Larr).*

In contrast, deep-keeled boats have taken tremendous knockdowns and come right up, as did the old *Ondine* at the start of the 1962 Bermuda race. Sir Francis Chichester reports that shortly after leaving Australia on his solo circumnavigation he was capsized 41 degrees past the vertical and yet came up. *Truzang* twice capsized and twice came back up, admittedly minus rig and deckhouse, but nevertheless back up. *Cimba* capsized off Bermuda in the 1930's, came back up, and even retained her rig. Of course we only hear of those who capsize and live to tell the tale.

There is a popular theory today that in rough weather the centerboarder is safer at sea than the deep-keel boat. It is alleged that when a big wave hits a deep-draft boat the keel tends to trip the boat, where a centerboarder with the board up will just slide to leeward, rolling with the punch as it were. It is a plausible theory, but I am willing to dispute it.

First of all, with the board up, a centerboarder will skid around like a saucer, with little or no directional stability. She will not lie bow on to a sea anchor, because the windage caused by the high bow, pulpit, and mast will continually throw her bow off. Even in a harbor, center-boarders tack around their moorings a great deal. Nor will she be able to run before it with the board up; if she tries, she will only skid around like a top. She may be able to run before it with warps over the stern, but she cannot possibly "lie ahull," beam to the wind and sea, as she does not have the ultimate stability necessary. When *Doubloon* tried it in a northeast gale in the Gulf Stream, breaking crests rolled her over twice.

TWIN KEELS

Those interested in sailing in shoal water may wish to consider an-other method of achieving shoal draft—bilge keels, which are very popular in Europe in areas that have a great rise and fall of tide. Many French and British harbors dry completely at low water, and boats moored there must be strapped alongside the dock or be supported by some kind of legs unless they have twin bilge keels; these enable boats to take the bottom with no difficulty and sit upright. In modern form they stem from Lord Riverside's first *Bluebird,* built in 1923–1924. This was followed by two others, the latest being 50 feet LWL and yet drawing only 5 feet 4 inches upright.

In a twin-keel boat the keels are not vertical, being designed to be vertical when the vessel is heeled; the boat therefore draws more when heeled than when upright. Because the keels can be airfoil shaped and can be toed slightly to the center line, they are very efficient, so effi-cient that their total area can be far lower than that of a conventional keel for a boat of the same size. In the ratio of draft to beam the twin-keel boat compares favorably also with the centerboarders, for all cen-terboarders today used for cruising (as opposed to day sailing) are in reality half keel boats—even with the board up, their draft is at least one-third their beam, which is not particularly less than the draft of a twin-keel boat.

American bilge-board scows, with their toed, angled, and airfoil-shaped bilge boards, are among the fastest sailing boats in the world. It will be very interesting to see what the twin-keel boat develops in the way of speed in the future. The tank tests on twin keels have just been begun, and much data is still to be collected. With further development, perhaps a really fast racing boat may evolve that will also be a good cruising boat.

At present, we do know that a relatively fast cruising hull with twin keels can be built. The runs turned in by *Bluebird of Thorne* on her cruise from England round the world show a fast weatherly vessel. She not only was fast under sail but under power attained a speed that was almost that of a powerboat, while using relatively little horsepower. In boats of this type the propeller can be mounted on the center line in completely unobstructed water, giving great efficiency under power. If a folding propeller is installed, the drag when the boat is under sail is almost negligible. Furthermore, running downwind, the twin keels remove much of the rolling that a single-keel boat is subject to, and give a tremendous directional stability. It is worthy of note that the owner of *Bluebird of Thorne* is a cruising yachtsman with a tremendous number of offshore miles under his belt. He is also the Commodore of the Royal Cruising Club.

In England there are almost thirty recognized classes of twin-keel yachts; they appear in abundance in every English boat show, and it is estimated that there are over three thousand of this type of yacht sailing. As time goes by, more and more designers are going to be designing this type of boat, more and more tank tests will be made, and before very long this type of boat may be among the swiftest of the shoal-draft boats. It certainly does not have the disadvantages of a centerboard boat, yet seems to have all the advantages. Its ease of steering too makes a twin-keel boat a most attractive proposition.

LEEBOARDS

Leeboards, though not the prettiest things in the world, are excellent for shoal-draft boats in that they are easy to build and repair, have no complicated gear, and require no trunk. With leeboards, boats can take the bottom and dry out at low tide, and never worry about sand, mud, or oyster shells jamming the centerboard slot. The boat with leeboards need not necessarily be the round Dutch Boier type; L. Francis Herreshoff designed *Meadow Lark,* long and narrow. I have been told by those who have sailed on and in company with her sister ships that they are very fast and handy.

BEAM

Another controversy arises about the relative advantages of vessels that are long and lean and those that are short and fat. It is possible to have both beam and speed, witness such successful ocean racers as *Anitra, Finisterre, Caribee,* and the like; but these boats have been produced by racing rules, not rules of the sea. A short fat boat may have excellent space for her length but not for her displacement. Both the cost of building and the amount of sail required to drive a boat are more a function of displacement than of length. Further, length is speed. The size of crew needed to handle a boat is a function of sail area more than anything else. This point is well illustrated by comparing a 6 meter and a 30 square meter; with roughly the same overall length, the 30 square has one-third the sail area, one-quarter the displacement, one-half the number of crew, and sails the same course in the same time, given any amount of breeze.

Short fat boats tend to be slow because of their shape and also because of their length. Normally, a yacht's maximum hull speed can be figured by this formula: speed in knots $= 1.5 \times \sqrt{LWL}$.

This is an approximation; for a very short-ended boat the speed factor may be only 1.2 or 1.3, while an extremely light-displacement, long-ended boat, such as a 30 square meter, may have a speed–length ratio of $1.7 \times \sqrt{LWL}$, given perfect conditions. It is true that some of our ocean racers, like *Ticonderoga, Stormvogel,* and *Windward Passage,* under spinnakers have surfed on the face of ocean swells and held speeds well in excess of their supposed hull speeds for long periods of time, but this is surfing on a wave. Probably the best illustration of this is Norris Hoyt's picture showing *Ondine* surfing down the face of a gale-created sea (Photo 2). She is being driven well above hull speed, looks more like a planing motorboat than anything else, and did in fact sail 248 miles in twenty-four hours, giving a speed–length ratio of $1.64 \times \sqrt{LWL}$; for ten hours she averaged 12.2 knots, giving a speed–length ratio of 1.9. But these cases are exceptions.

Going to windward or sailing at any speed that is a ratio of .8 or $.9 \times \sqrt{LWL}$, skin friction comprises 70 to 75 percent of total resistance, while above this ratio, the hull shape becomes important and skin friction is less and less important, until at $1.4 \times \sqrt{LWL}$, 17 percent of the resistance is skin friction and 83 percent is wave-making resistance. Thus, under extreme conditions, an ill-shaped old barge with plenty of sail area will keep up with the well-designed yacht, and given longer length, the large ill-shaped old barge will beat the smaller well-formed yacht under the extreme conditions.

It is worthwhile to stop here and consider the effect of length on speed. Seldom will a boat on a long passage average much more than $\sqrt{LWL}$; motion becomes uncomfortable or sometimes unbearable. This is especially true on the really small cruising boats, those of about 16

2. Ondine *surfing down a swell.* (*David K. Elwell*)

feet LWL. Basically, they are slow; their speed at $\sqrt{\text{LWL}}$ is four knots, where the 25-foot LWL boat will have a comfortable speed of five knots and the 36-foot LWL boat will have a comfortable speed of six knots. Further, the larger boat has inherently slower motion, so that at a hull speed of nine knots, the large boat has an uncomfortable but bearable motion, while the motion of a 16-foot LWL boat at six knots is almost unbearable. I say "almost," as it must be remembered that John Guzzwell sailed the 20-foot LOA *Trekka* around the world. Those west-coast-of-Canada fishermen are tough.

A further disadvantage of the small boat is that it is often all but impossible for her to beat to windward in really heavy weather, especially if there is a current or tide against her. Also, in a small boat, it is very difficult to get anything above minimum accommodation in the hull and still have a pretty hull that will sail. Many of the mini-cruisers around today are suitable for overnight passages, but that is all; except for the yachtsman with an overworked masochistic instinct, they are not suitable for offshore passages.

For those who hate their fellowmen and want to sail single-handed, a boat of 30 feet LOA is about the minimum. At this size she will have acceptable accommodation for one or two persons (most important, those on board will be able to stand up to put their pants on), the sails will be small enough for one person to handle, and the vessel large enough to yield a fair turn of speed without too much motion. Further, if the single-hander decides that he is unhappy being alone, which is often the case, he has room for a mate.

Whole books have been written about hull speed. In brief, there is a transverse wave system which shows itself along the side of the hull in a series of crests. Having measured the distance between crests, either on board or from a photograph, one can obtain a quite accurate estimate of speed by consulting Table III (Appendix). The length of the wave (distance between crests) is the most limiting factor in the speed of a boat. Once the length between crests equals the approximate length of the boat, the bow and stern are supported by the wave crests, but nothing supports the middle of the boat, and she tends to squat. In effect, she digs a hole and sits in it.

At various times, in the West Indies, I have actually experienced extreme squatting. At about 8.6 or 8.8 knots *Iolaire* throws a high bow wave, a deep trough develops amidships, and the stern wave starts to rise higher than deck level. If speed is increased fractionally, the stern wave comes piling on board. She has dug her hole and is sitting in it.

Short fat boats may have nice main cabins because of the beam, but their length leaves room for only two cabins, so there is little privacy. On long narrow boats, the cabins are small but there are more of them, giving more privacy.

Carried to its ultimate, the emphasis on length results in a boat like William Gardner's light-displacement *Oceanus,* sixty feet long, with a twelve-foot beam and only a thousand square feet of sail area. Easily handled by three people, she has a hull speed under sail in the region of ten or eleven knots, and she will easily reach eight knots. Another boat of this type is Eric Tarbley's *Pen Duick II,* certainly the largest single-hander ever built, with potentially great speed.

There is of course a compromise between the extremes, and unless one is going to design and build a boat to one's own specifications, a compromise will have to be reached, much depending upon the use for which the boat is intended. If she is to be used strictly alongshore on the east coast of the United States, with its prevailing light breezes, plenty of sail area is required and little wetted surface. Passages will not be long, so self-steering is not necessary, nor will the boat be required to do much heaving to in a gale, since sheltered waters can usually be reached before the onset of a real gale. A converted 8 meter or boat of similar lines can be a real joy as the example of cruising boats like *Brigadoon, Julie,* and *Caper* indicates. Conversely, if long offshore passages are to be made, a boat with less sail area, heavier gear, and more ability to stay out and take everything the sea can dream up is needed.

It must be remembered that on long offshore passages a well-built and well-equipped boat will stand up to much more rough weather than will the crew. The fast boat with bad motion and erratic steering may have to shorten down because the crew is worn out and incapable of handling her. Thus, some centerboarders, with their flat bow sections, pound so badly that they are miserable at sea, and with respect to one popular ocean racer (in the early models only, now they are strengthened forward), anyone asked how hard she could be pushed on a reach, with the wind high on the beam, was sure to reply, "Until the bunks come out of the forward cabin." The narrow, deep-keel boat, without flat sections or a long overhang forward, will be much more comfortable. Any boat driven to or over its hull speed, however, will be uncomfortable and hard steering.

There is the other extreme. Once when crossing Dominica channel, we were having a rough time of it; with a reefed main and staysail, we were doing hull speed and sticking the bow under, so that waves were washing down the deck. The passage was exciting but rough, and it was most pleasant to reach the calm water in the lee of Dominica. Hours later, a Tahiti ketch that we had passed halfway across came in. Her crew reported a very comfortable passage; they had carried full sail but had only averaged five knots at the most and were so under-rigged that they would only have tied in a single reef for a full gale. In moderate weather, they could not get out of their own way.

DIRECTIONAL STABILITY

On a long trip the activity most wearing for the crew may be steering, unless the boat is fitted with vane self-steering gear or with an electric autopilot. Some boats are continually hard to steer, others easy, others in between. Our modern ocean racers are usually a joy to steer —they are light as a feather on the helm when correctly trimmed, and react instantly to the turn of the wheel or tug of the tiller—but they are a joy to steer for an hour or so only. The keels are so short that the boats have little or no directional stability and must be watched constantly; the helm cannot be locked or lashed. This is not important when there is a big ocean-racing crew, with the helm relieved every hour at the most, perhaps every half hour or even every fifteen minutes.

But on a cruising boat, helm watches often last for four hours, and having to concentrate on steering for all of that time can be most exhausting. If one can lash the helm for only a short while, take a stretch, drink a cup of coffee, life is much more pleasant.

At the other end of the scale is the old Brixham trawler, which once pointed in the right direction and correctly trimmed, will hold her course for days. The keel is long and straight, the bowsprit so long that the jib exerts tremendous leverage, preventing her from rounding up to such an extent that my good friend Jack Carstarphen of *Maverick* reports that his technique for tacking is to "tie the staysail to leeward with a slip hitch, let the jib and jib-topsail sheets go, helm down, go below and have a cup of coffee, come up on deck and sheet the jib and jib topsail, then when full and by on the new tack, let the staysail come over." This is not quite my cup of tea (or coffee!); in between there is a middle road, to be reached through compromise.

Some centerboarders steer very well—*Antilles* for one, though at times on a reach she is very hardmouthed and difficult to hold. We once delivered a centerboarder to St. Thomas from Boston, and she was a joy to steer at first; she had two centerboards, and by adjusting them we could get her to balance under any rig. However, she was hell to steer during the last part of the trip: the forward centerboard jammed all the way down, and the aft centerboard jammed all the way up!

H. Scheel designed an interesting little centerboarder for his own use that was quite successful both for cruising and for racing. He kept the main board in the normal position and added a small trimming board forward. Other designers have put the main board slightly forward of the normal position and then placed a small trimming board aft. Sterling Dunbar is a great advocate of two boards of equal size, and has used this configuration on a number of successful cruising boats. John Illingworth and Angus Primrose have adopted this same idea for some of their small ocean racers, using a small plywood dagger board through the cockpit sole to improve balance when running downwind with a spinnaker up.

The new keel boats with scimitar-shaped keels and spade rudders leave much to be desired for cruising. Their directional stability is often very low, and the absence of lateral planes makes them hard to handle at low speeds or in light airs, as the bow tends to fall off. It is very difficult to sail out a hook or sail off a mooring if the bow falls off until the boat is almost beam to the wind before speed is picked up. Trying to heave to in one of these boats would be, I think, an impossibility.

A moderately long keel is a real asset, as at sea the helm can be

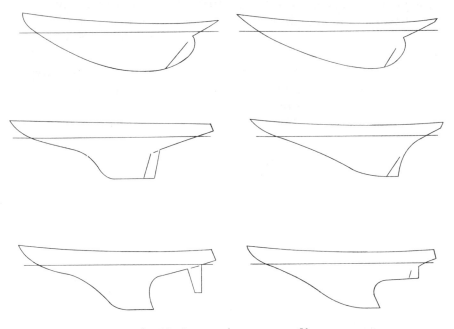

9. *Various underwater profiles.*

lashed, and in crowded water when the mooring is cast off, the boat will gather way without the bow falling off or great amounts of leeway being gathered. *Iolaire* lay for two years to a Mediterranean mooring, bow to the prevailing easterly trades. We would hoist the main, cast off the mooring and stern line, back the mizzen, roll out the jib, and be off, with enough way in three boat lengths to tack to avoid some submerged piles. We had some narrow escapes, but we always succeeded. Drawing 9 shows various underwater profiles.

STEERING

TILLER STEERING

The subject of wheel versus tiller is debated endlessly by sailors. I myself am strongly in favor of the tiller, though of course it does have limitations. I do not advocate going to the extreme of the big British cutters just before the turn of the century which were steered with a twenty-five-foot tiller and four-part relieving tackles and sometimes required three men on the tiller, but I certainly think that until 40 feet LOA is reached, a tiller is vastly superior to a wheel, and a boat of up to 45 feet can be steered comfortably with a tiller.

The great advantages of the tiller are that it is strong, easy to install, inexpensive, and it gives direct linkage and thus perfect feel to the rudder. The disadvantage of course is that the helmsman's position must be close to the rudder, so tiller steering is impossible on a midship-cockpit boat. Further, the tiller certainly takes up much more room in the cockpit than does the wheel, and a tiller of a decent length is essential for handling a boat. For maneuvering in harbor, short tacking, and the like, the tiller should be fairly short, but for a long offshore passage, there should be a second, longer tiller or an extension fitted on the standard tiller, to give more leverage and make steering at sea easier. Actually, the loss of cockpit room is unimportant, as there are not likely to be many people in the cockpit. Going to windward, the longer tiller enables the helmsman to sit at the forward end of the cockpit under the shelter of the doghouse or the dodger.

WHEEL STEERING

One advantage of wheel steering over tiller steering is that the diameters of the wheel, gearing, and quadrants can be adjusted so that a large yacht can be handled easily, without a great expenditure of strength. Further, with some types of gear, the wheel can be located anywhere in the vessel, regardless of the location of the rudder. And with wheel steering one can have two separate steering stations—one out in the breezes for use in good weather, the other under shelter in the doghouse or what-have-you.

Correctly designed, wheel steering can be excellent; incorrectly designed, it can be enough to drive you crazy. It comes in many sizes, shapes, forms, and degrees of reliability. The most basic is the old-fashioned square-rigger style, in which a rope is connected to the end of a short tiller and led through blocks wrapped around a drum directly connected to the wheel. At the other end of the scale are the complicated electro-hydraulic systems. We will here discuss only the most common and the most basic types.

Probably the largest supplier of wheel-steering equipment for yachts and commercial sailing vessels is the Edson Corporation, which has been in the business for almost a hundred years.

Pedestal Steering

Pedestal steering, with wire cables leading from the pedestal through the blocks to a rudder quadrant, is by far the most common type of wheel steering seen on yachts today, perhaps because it is very responsive. Correctly installed, it is excellent. Incorrectly installed, it is treacherous and dangerous. In pedestal steering it is absolutely essential that all lead blocks be lined up perfectly, so that there are no foul leads to cripple the wire. Further, the lead blocks must be of very large diameter—twenty-four times the diameter of the wire. Cables should be of 7 by 19 stainless steel, and should be secured to the rudder quadrant so that there is no crippling of the wire at the eye splice or terminal ending. Even at its best, this type of steering is only fairly reliable. I have yet to see a yacht, no matter how well maintained, that has been in service for four or five years without at some time losing her pedestal steering. Therefore, a full complement of spare parts must be continually carried—sheave pins, set screws, sprocket chain links, and a complete set of cables of the proper length.

The use of a quadrant and cables leading to the steering pedestal means that the wheel can be placed almost anywhere in the boat. Some owners prefer to have the wheel at the forward end of the cockpit. One advantage of this location is that when going to windward in a blow, the helmsman is under or near the shelter of the dodger. Also, the helmsman can get a very good look at the headsails, and during a race he is not affected by the sheet trimmers handling winches, since they are behind him. However, the forward location of the wheel has some disadvantages for cruising: everyone going up or down the companionway has to climb over the helmsman, and if the helm is mounted forward of the winches, it is most difficult for the helmsman to help the sheet trimmer on the sheets, as he often must on a cruising boat.

To my mind the most important consideration—and the one most often ignored—in the location of the steering stand is its position in relation to adequate emergency tiller installation. A functional emergency tiller is absolutely essential for any boat that is to do serious offshore cruising.

Worm Steering Gear

The worm steering gear, often referred to as Edson gear, is undoubtedly one of the most reliable steering systems known to man. Originally it was installed on Gloucester fishing schooners, during the 1870's. Systems of this type are still often seen today; the ships have been wrecked or have rotted out, but the steering gears have been retrieved and installed on other vessels. This type of gear is not particularly popular on yachts, because it is reputed to afford little or no feel. This is not necessarily true. The worm steering gear must be carefully designed so that it is not too powerful for the size of the yacht. I remember one boat that had Edson gear of 7½ turns lock to lock; this was much too powerful and had no feel. Subsequently the pitch of the thread was changed to give 2¼ turns lock to lock and the gear worked beautifully.

The worm gear is absolutely reliable. Its only limitation is that it must be mounted directly on the rudder head; the only variable in the location of the wheel is the length of the shaft. Given plenty of grease, and thread with the correct pitch, the worm gear is an excellent system that can give feel to the helm and has practically no' chance of failure.

Geared Quadrant Steering

Geared quadrant steering is seldom seen today. Like the worm gear it is very reliable because it works by means of a direct mechanical linkage: a gear on the wheel shaft engages directly on a quadrant, secured to the rudder head. Correctly designed and geared, this system is superb, giving almost the same feel as a tiller. Further, since the quadrant is bolted directly to the rudder head, the rudder shaft can be allowed to extend above deck, and an emergency tiller can be easily shipped. Again as with the worm gear, the helm location is limited, being usually quite close to the rudder head, with the length of the wheel shaft the only variable.

Hydraulic Steering

Hydraulic steering is very common in large vessels, especially power-boats. Though sometimes found in moderate-sized sailboats, it is not particularly popular among yachtsmen. The chief complaint against hydraulic steering is that the system gives absolutely no feel. Further, it is prone to failure and none too easy to repair. In general, I would avoid hydraulic steering in a serious cruising yacht.

Wheel-Steering Brakes

Almost every good pedestal-steering stand has at its side a hand-operated brake, which is a great asset, really essential for serious cruising. If one wishes to leave the wheel, one can clamp on the brake, and the rudder is held in place. Some brakes are quick release, operated by excentric cam; in other cases the brake is clamped by tightening a coarse-threaded screw. I prefer the excentric cam for speed of locking and unlocking.

Quadrant and worm steering systems are not usually supplied with a brake, but installation of a brake drum on the shaft, and a brake band which can be set tight against the drum, is relatively simple and well worth the investment.

Steering Wheels

In years gone by, a yacht's steering wheel was usually a thing of tremendous beauty and great cost, made of teak, mahogany, or other exotic wood, and hand carved, frequently with the name of the vessel. The old wooden wheel had hand spokes, for easier gripping. The disadvantages of the spoked wheel were that the diameter was usually too small and that sheets, foul-weather-jacket sleeves, and the like were continually fouling the spokes.

In recent years the so-called destroyer wheel has become popular. This is a wheel of relatively large diameter, made of brass, stainless steel, or aluminum, and absolutely smooth—with no spokes. The diameter of the wheel is limited by many factors, the most important of which arc the location of the wheel and the size of the cockpit. A beamy centerboarder has a cockpit wide enough to permit one to pass around a wheel of large diameter. Also, a large wheel is needed in this type of boat so that one can sit on the lee side of the cockpit and see the headsails. A narrow boat must have a wheel of smaller diameter to leave room for moving fore and aft in the cockpit.

The mechanical advantage of wheel steering—determined by wheel diameter, sprocket-drive diameter, and quadrant size—should be carefully calculated before the installation of the steering gear. It should fit the size of the boat and the size of the rudder. On a boat of forty to forty-five feet, 2¼ or 2½ turns lock to lock on the wheel gives good sensitive steering; additional turns lock to lock would make holding the helm easier, but steering would be much harder because feel would be lost and the rudder could not be turned quickly enough. Conversely, a less powerful wheel would react more quickly but be more difficult to hold. There is a straight mechanical linkage between wheel and rudder, and a designer may define mechanical advantage in terms of tiller size. In this sense a particular wheel may be described, for example, as equivalent to an eight-foot tiller.

WHEEL COVERING: A polished brass, aluminum, or stainless-steel destroyer wheel looks beautiful but is most impractical unless it is covered. An uncovered wheel tends to be slippery, and more important, in cold weather it becomes very cold and freezes one's hands. Some wheels are covered with light rope, which gives a good grip for those with tough hands, but will soon remove the palms of the weekend sailor. More expensive but more suitable for him is elkhide, sometimes referred to as chrome, a soft grayish leather with a rough surface, which gives an excellent grip.

RUDDER DESIGN

While on the subject of steering, we must of course consider the rudder—its size, placement, construction, and so on.

The shape of the conventional rudder, attached to the after end of the keel, has undergone some radical changes recently. In years gone by, the rudder was always broader at the top than at the bottom, but today the rudder blade may be broader at the bottom or may be of uniform width throughout (Drawing 10). The fact that rudders have been made gradually smaller, while boats have been driven harder and harder, seems to be proof that the rudders have become more efficient.

The modern ocean racer often has an independent rudder mounted well aft, which I think excellent if combined with adequate lateral plane. A rudder placed back by the after end of the waterline is most effective, but also very susceptible to damage, especially if it is merely a spade rudder with no skeg. All the strain on the spade rudder is concentrated at the point where the rudderstock comes through the hull. And this strain can be enormous—as, for example, in a boat doing nine knots down a wave with the rudder hard over to prevent a broach. More than one rudder has given up the ghost in this situation and parted company with the boat. When *Firebrand*'s conventional rudder was replaced by a trim tab, and a separate rudder was mounted on a skeg, her steering qualities were vastly improved; but on a transatlantic

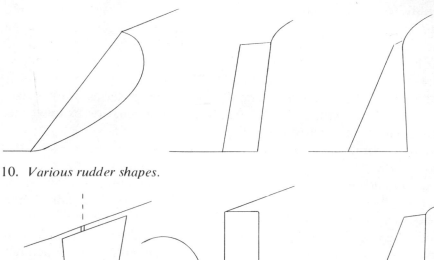

10. *Various rudder shapes.*

race her skeg gave out, and for the last thousand miles the crew had to use the remains of the old rudder to steer. After the race a new and stronger rudder and skeg were installed. Clearly, if there is to be an independent rudder, an effort should be made to attach it very firmly to a good solid skeg, which is none too easy to do on a yacht that is going to be driven hard.

Besides being weak, the independent spade rudder has the disadvantage of frequently stalling out, as it were, when running hard downwind, and becoming totally ineffective. Hence, for heavy weather conditions the separate, completely independently hung spade rudder seems to be losing favor even with racing enthusiasts.

Some of our racing boats are really getting esoteric, with trim tabs on keels, double rudders that can be used independently or coupled together, and the like. These variations are all well and good for round-the-buoys racing, but I do not think they have any place in the cruising boat, especially the offshore cruising boat. Halsey Herreshoff's new rudder is shaped like an airplane wing, with adjustable forward and after edges operating off a central skeg, sort of like the flaps and spoilers on a jet plane. This arrangement too may be fine for racing, but for the average cruising boat, it is inadvisable, as it is just one more thing to go wrong.

RUDDER TRIM TABS

The trim tab on the rudder itself, still only in its earliest stages of development, has a lot to be said for it. In 1960, Jack Carstarphen decided to install a vane self-steering rig on *Shellback,* a heavy forty-foot Block Islander ketch. Since *Shellback* had an outboard rudder, it was simple to install a trim tab on the after edge of it. To try it out, we fastened a pair of vise-grip pliers to the trim-tab shaft, and we discovered that the boat could be easily steered with two fingers: the rudder could be thrown hard right and hard left with absolutely no effort. At that point we wondered why we had been expending so much energy pulling on the tiller for the past few years. Unfortunately, he sold the boat before he had time to get the operation working. I am convinced that the use of a trim tab efficiently coupled with linkage to a small tiller can eliminate nine-tenths of the work of steering.

Installation of a trim tab on an outboard rudder is really no problem; on an inboard rudder, however, a rather difficult engineering job is involved, since there must be a hollow rudder stock with a shaft for the trim tab inside it. Bill Tellier, owner of *North by East,* has this arrangement and says it works perfectly. If the engineers could figure out a simple method of linking a trim tab on an inboard rudder through the shaft of the rudder, more of us would be able to steer with a one-foot tiller attached to the trim tab instead of a seven-foot tiller or a four-foot wheel attached to the main rudder.

RUDDER CONSTRUCTION

Since the rudder is one of the most essential parts of the boat, and is all too often subjected to heavy strains, care must be taken in its construction and design.

Perhaps the most reliable arrangement is the one found in the transom-sterned boat and the double-ender: the outboard rudder firmly set in a heel casting and held to the rudderpost by two or three gudgeons is simple, efficient, and almost foolproof. If anything goes wrong, it is easy to repair.

The next most reliable is the old-fashioned rudder with a wooden stock of large diameter, resting on a heel casting and held to the rudderpost by straps passing around the stock. The top of the stock comes up through a rudder trunk through the deck. This arrangement is simple and strong, but does have disadvantages. Where the straps pass around it, the stock must be coppered and checked regularly to make sure that there are no bare spots that will allow the entrance of worms. Similarly, the rudder trunk must be coppered or fiber-glassed to a level well above the waterline to prevent worms from getting a start when the boat is heavily loaded. The great advantage of this type of rudder is that it is simple and straightforward, easy to repair anywhere in the world, and since the rudder trunk extends up to deck level, there is no stuffing box to bind, leak, or cause trouble.

Our more modern yachts almost universally have a metal rudder-stock with a wooden blade, set in a heel fitting at the bottom of the skeg or keel, and then passing through a pipe with a stuffing box. This is a good arrangement except that all too often no straps are provided to hold the rudderstock to the rudderpost, for essential additional support. It is thought that *Dyna* lost her rudder because the heel fitting let go. There was nothing but the stock to hold the rudder in place, and of course it had not been designed to take that kind of strain. If there had been straps (Drawing 11), the rudder would have stayed on, though it might have become loose.

Often the wooden blade is merely driftbolted to the rudderstock, with no reinforcing plates to hold it in place. Sooner or later the bolts fatigue and the blade comes off. This is what caused the loss of the rudder blade of *Oliver van Nort* in a Fastnet race and the loss of a good part of the rudder blade of *Highland Light* in the 1960 Bermuda race.

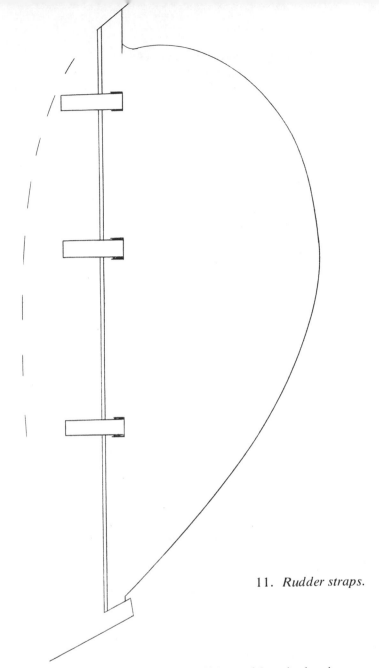

11. *Rudder straps.*

Where there is a stuffing box, another possible problem is that it may leak. Therefore, the stuffing box should be designed so that it can be reached and tightened at sea. Further, one must be careful to keep on board the wrenches to fit the stuffing box.

On steel and aluminum boats the rudder blade too is of metal and is welded directly to the stock. The resulting rudder is strong, simple, and almost foolproof, seldom developing the difficulties found in the rudders of wooden boats. Something is to be said for metal construction.

MULTI-HULLS

So far we have discussed only the single-hulled boat. As years go by, the multi-hull is becoming more and more popular for cruising. This type of yacht has many advantages over the conventional boat in that it provides more accommodation dollar for dollar, it sails relatively level, and if well designed and light, it is tremendously fast. However, all boats are compromises, and to my cruising-oriented mind, the multi-hull, whether catamaran or trimaran, is a compromise in the extreme.

To be fast, the multi-hull must be light; to be light, she must sacrifice some safety. If a very lightly constructed boat hits a log at eighteen knots, the result will be severe damage, perhaps a hole in her hull or a float torn off. Further, multi-hulls are definitely capsizable, and once upside down, are almost impossible to right. More than one ocean-going catamaran and trimaran has the underside of the float, or wing section, painted high-visibility orange, so as to be more easily spotted by aircraft when floating upside down. Further, it should be noted that Bill Howell, of *Golden Cockerel*—certainly a most experienced offshore multi-hull skipper—has built a trapdoor on the underside of his wing section to allow him to reach his life raft and survival gear while the vessel is upside down.

The exact number of people lost in recent years on offshore passages in multi-hulls is not known, but it is substantial. Indeed, underwriters are very reluctant to insure multi-hulls for offshore passages.

It has been pointed out that one of the most dangerous occupations in the world is to design one's own trimaran and take it out to sea. To the best of my knowledge, only three persons have done this extensively—Arthur Piver, Hedley Nichols, and Dick Newick. The first two are dead, lost at sea on their own trimarans; the third is still sailing —I hope his luck continues.

The defenders of multi-hulls often say that the state of the art is still not very advanced, and that in time, catamarans and trimarans will be made as safe as more traditional boats. But multi-hulls are not really so new. The Polynesians were using them to cross great distances of the Pacific back when the Vikings were raiding the coast of Europe. Further, even in the Western Hemisphere, fast catamarans have been known for many years. Captain Nat Herreshoff raced in catamarans as early as 1879—so successfully, in fact, that they were barred from racing and did not reappear in the racing circuit until after World War II.

As cruising boats to be used in sheltered waters, the multi-hulls have much to offer, as their shoal draft allows them to explore out-of-the-way places other yachts could not possibly reach. I would not consider them safe for offshore work.

III

Cruising Rigs

In any of the ports where offshore cruising boats assemble, especially in those that are natural stopping points for round-the-world cruisers, the ubiquitous gaff-rigged Tahiti ketch will be seen. However, the fact that many people have embraced this rig does not necessarily mean that it is ideal for offshore sailing.

Also often present in cruising ports is the schooner with the square yard, but always under the hatches is found a huge diesel and under the stern a large, three-bladed propeller, so heavy that while it is good for powering, it has the effect of a sea anchor when the vessel is under sail. Although the square-sail yard schooner is picturesque, it is highly complicated to sail and maintain.

A most practical little boat that is often seen is the Vertue, designed by Laurent Giles. Hundreds of this class have been built, offshoots of the gaff-rigged *Andrillot* and *Wanderer II,* and not to be confused with the slightly larger Wanderer class (35 feet LOA) that is also much in evidence. These have crossed oceans, rounded both the Cape of Good Hope and Cape Horn, and circumnavigated the globe innumerable times. They are wonderful little boats with a conservative cruising hull surmounted by an excellent rig.

In the United States, Wright Britton has an excellent medium-sized boat, the yawl *Delight,* 40 feet LOA, in which he has successfully raced across the Atlantic, as well as along the coast. He spent many years simply learning to sail the boat well, to handle her with a minimum of effort and a maximum of speed, and now covers vast areas of water in a comparatively short time with an efficient, easily handled rig that is in no way extreme.

He and his wife have probably cruised in more difficult areas of the world than any other persons alive. In recent years, in this normal ocean racer he has cruised the coasts of Nova Scotia, Newfoundland, and Greenland, circumnavigated Iceland, sailed on to Scotland, cruised the coast of Scotland, and circumnavigated Ireland, and as this book goes to print it is rumored that he is preparing to follow the course of the *Manhattan* through the Northwest Passage.

In contrast, ease of handling is not characteristic of the new one-ton class of ocean racers, which should by their size make nice cruising boats. Their rig is too extreme—a very small main and a huge fore-triangle. Admittedly, the main is simple to handle, but trying to douse the genoa alone is really a bit much. The main is so small that to keep the boat moving, one has to change the jibs with exhausting frequency.

Clearly, one should not assume that because a particular type of boat is widely used in offshore racing it will necessarily be a wise choice. In selecting a boat, the individual should consider the various types of boats in terms of his own particular needs, capacities, and expectations. Typical rigs are shown in Photos 3–15 and Drawings 12–24.

VARIETIES OF RIGS

SLOOPS AND CUTTERS

For small cruising yachts, the sloop rig is probably the most popular. The sloop is a fore-and-aft rigged vessel with one mast and one head-sail. In years gone by, sloops were usually seven-eighths rigged, and because the permanent backstay did not meet the mast opposite the jib-stay, they required running backstays or jumper struts. These kept the mast from bending aft and breaking above the jibstay. In recent years, since the advent of the aluminum mast, the masthead rig has gained wide acceptance, especially for sloops of 40 feet LOA and under. This rig is good in that standing and running rigging are kept to an absolute minimum, and it is aerodynamically very efficient. However, it has the disadvantage of inflexibility: when the strength of the wind alters, head-sail changes must be made. Also, if the head stay breaks, there is nothing to hold the mast in the boat; it will fall aft in a hurry.

Many offshore-cruising men prefer the cutter, which—whatever the technical and historical definition may be—I regard in most instances as a double-headsail-rigged sloop. A cutter rig is especially useful in the larger yacht because it avoids the kind of trouble encountered by a masthead sloop when slamming into a head sea—the tendency of the middle of the mast to bow forward. Many boats have broken their masts just below the masthead as a result of this bowing. This is not a problem in a cutter because there is a staysail stay supporting the for-

3. *Gaff-rigged cat.* (*W. Robinson*)

ward face of the mast. Sometimes there are also running backstays leading aft from the point of attachment of the staysail stay, and in most cases these are preventer stays in the truest sense of the word: they are necessary not to hold the mast in the boat, but to tighten the staysail stay and keep the mast straight. The cutter's sails are much more varied than those of the sloop. In light airs or when reaching, the cutter may set a masthead genoa or ballooner, with the staysail stay disconnected for tacking or jibing. As the wind increases, a double-headsail rig may be substituted. This has two great advantages: the individual sails, being smaller, are easier to trim, and when headsail changes are made, the fore-triangle is not dead bare. The staysail remains up when the jib is being replaced by a smaller one. The staysail may be left sheeted and the boat kept moving, or it may be sheeted to weather so that the boat will heave to, helm lashed amidships or to lee-

4. *Gaff-rigged cutter. (Beken of Cowes)*

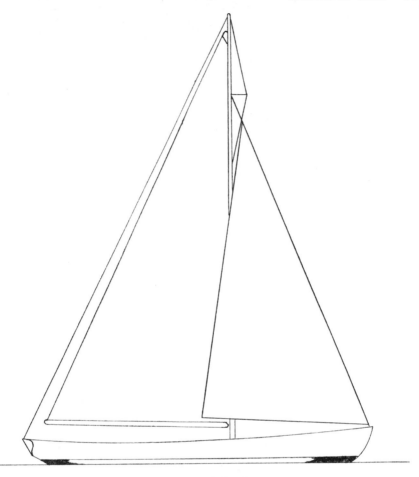

12. *Seven-eighths sloop.*

ward depending on the boat, while the change is made. Further, in heavy weather when beating into a short steep sea, the headsails do not tend to pick up water because the jib is cut high and the staysail is sheeted inside the rail and cannot pick up the bow wave (the latest sloop design also permits the genoa to be trimmed inside the rail). For this reason the double-headsail-rigged cutter is very popular in England, where much of the racing is in the short, steep Channel and North Sea chop, which kicks up when the wind runs against the tide and can raise havoc with low-cut genoas.

The exact proportion of fore-triangle area to mainsail area varies from boat to boat. Much depends upon what is desired. While many cut-

13. *Masthead sloop.*

ters are indeed merely double-headsail-rigged sloops, some will be found, especially among the deepwater cruisers, with their masts amidships or aft of amidships. This type of "cutterish cutter" has many advantages. The main is kept quite small, and the staysail is far enough aft so that the boat will sail in heavy weather under staysail alone, even to weather. Since the mast is out of the bow of the boat, dousing the main and handling halyards is very easy. In light airs, a wonderful light and massively big genoa or ballooner may be set, which will really pull the boat along when nothing else will fill. In a race, the spinnaker is something to behold. MacLear and Harris, a few years back, designed a heavy cruising cutter, *Angantyr,* for James W. Crawford on this con-

5. *Gaff-rigged ketch with yard. (W. Robinson)*

figuration. Just before World War II, Philip Rhodes designed *Kirawan II* along these same lines; as *Hother,* under the ownership of George Hoffman, she became one of the most successful longshore racers on the east coast.

YAWLS

The yawl is very popular today, and in the modern version is often nothing more than a sloop with a mizzenmast stuck sometimes rather

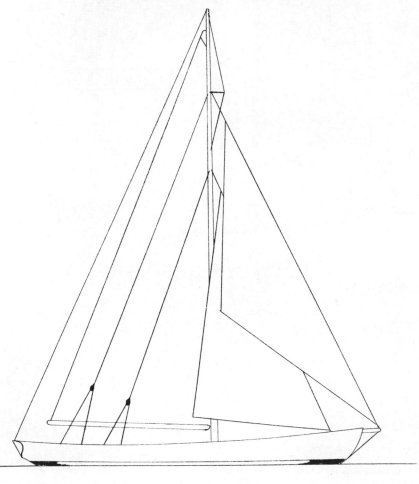

14. *Seven-eighths cutter.*

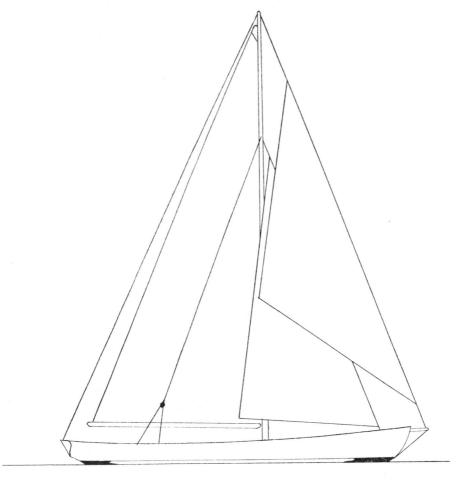

15. *Masthead cutter.*

precariously on the stern. One famous ocean-racing skipper summed up the advantages of a yawl about as follows: "The mizzen is good for the navigator to lean against when taking a sight, and a wonderful handhold for the straphangers offering suggestions to the working crew. At times it will support a mizzen staysail, but most important it is a psychological weapon to be wielded against the owners of sloops and cutters." This is, in my opinion, selling the yawl short.

Single-Headsail Yawls

The seven-eighths-rigged yawl and the masthead single-headsail-rigged yawl suffer from the same disadvantages as the seven-eighths sloop and

6. *Brigantine.* (*Laurie Legay*)

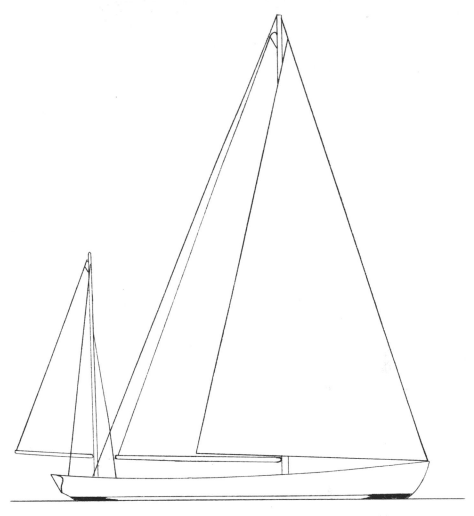

16. *Masthead yawl, single-headsail-rigged.*

the single-headsail sloop with respect to mast strength and the need for headsail changing. However, the yawl does have a decided advantage where balance is concerned. As weather helm builds up with an increase in wind, the mizzen may be dropped. If it blows harder, instead of changing the headsail, one can reef the main and reset the mizzen, and she will still balance. In a hard squall, the main may be dropped and the boat sailed on headsail and mizzen. This of course is only possible if the mizzen is of a decent size and is well enough stayed to re-

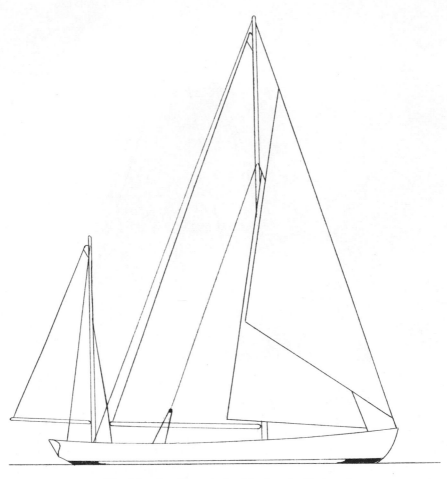

17. *Masthead yawl, double-headsail-rigged.*

main in the boat in heavy weather. All too often, these last two considerations are forgotten when modern yawls are designed, and the mizzen is simply stuck on to beat the racing rule.

Double-Headsail Yawls

The double-headsail-rigged yawl with a good mizzen is to me the ultimate in a cruising rig. She will go to windward almost as well as a sloop or cutter. With the mizzen staysail she will be faster off the wind. In short, she is ultimately flexible. During heavy weather, one can douse the jib and mizzen and hang on to the main and staysail, and she will balance. In a squall, one can douse the main, and she will sail under two headsails and mizzen. In very heavy weather she will sail

7. *Wishbone ketch. (W. Robinson)*

8. *Staysail schooner. (W. Robinson)*

9. *Masthead double-headsail sloop. (W. Robinson)*

10. Seven-eighths double-headsail sloop. (Morris Rosenfeld)

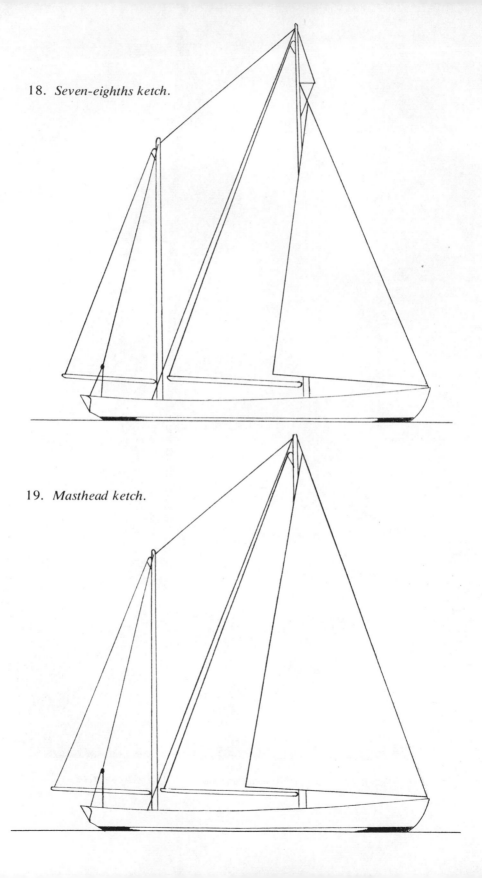

18. *Seven-eighths ketch.*

19. *Masthead ketch.*

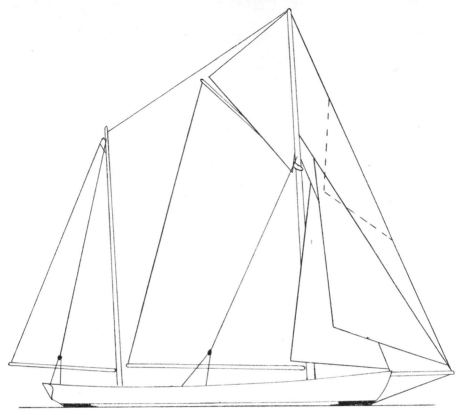

20. *Ketch with gaff main, main topsail, Marconi mizzen, and double-headsail rig; a jib topsail may be set in light airs.*

21. *Wishbone ketch.*

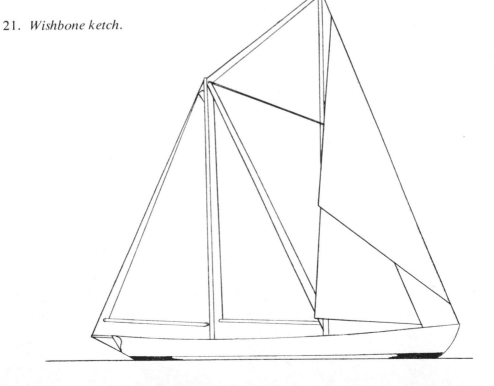

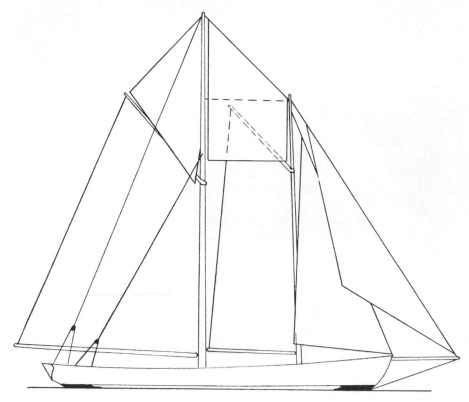

22. Gaff-rigged schooner with main topsail.

under staysail and mizzen, while if the trysail is up, the mizzen can be used or not, as required for balance.

It is essential that the mizzen be properly cut and the mizzenmast properly stayed. All too frequently the mizzen is cut too full, and when the boat is at anchor or going to windward in heavy weather, tries to flog itself to death. For this reason I always specify the installation of a roach (flattening) reef on the foot of a mizzen (see Drawing 85). The mizzenmast must be well stayed because otherwise there is danger of losing it overboard when one is beating to windward in heavy weather.

An additional advantage of the mizzen is that in crowded waters, and when the boat is not moving fast enough to steer, it can be used as an air rudder. By backing the mizzen when dropping off a mooring, one can throw the bow on the desired tack without setting a headsail. When maneuvering in close quarters, sheeting the mizzen flat or backing the mizzen to weather will hold the bow up, while letting the mizzen

*11. Schooner with a Marconi main, gaff foresail, and square-sail yards.
(W. Robinson)*

flop and trimming the jib flat will cause the bow to fall off. When coming into an anchorage, whether under sail or under power, if the mizzen is left up, once the anchor is dropped the mizzen can be backed to port and starboard and the boat backed directly downwind from the anchor without charging all over the harbor. Similarly, when anchoring and trying to back in stern to on a Mediterranean mooring, one can use the mizzen to great advantage to guide the stern to the exact spot desired. And finally, mizzen and headsail, especially if the latter is roller-furling, make a very easily handled rig enabling a husband-and-wife team or even a single-hander to sail right up to the anchorage in a tricky harbor and anchor in complete comfort with no danger to other yachts.

Further, the mizzen makes it easier to rig an awning either at anchor or under sail, and finally, one can eliminate most of the rolling at anchor by setting the mizzen and sheeting it flat. Hence, while most people regard the mizzen as just a rather useless appendage on the stern of the boat, I think it is the most useful of sails.

12. *Masthead yawl with double headsails, both roller-furling. (D. M. Street)*

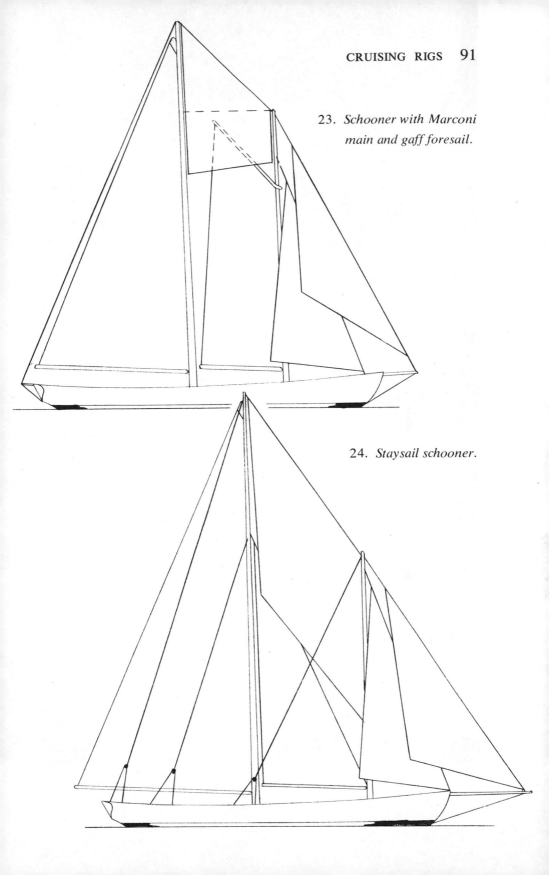

23. *Schooner with Marconi main and gaff foresail.*

24. *Staysail schooner.*

13. *Masthead single-headsail sloop and yawl; note the yawl's*

genoa sheeted to the end of the main boom. (Percy Huggins)

14. Marconi ketch. (D. Hap Veerkamp)

KETCHES

Although the ketch—in which the mizzenmast is stepped forward of the rudderpost or the after end of the waterline—is one of the most popular rigs, I myself do not like it because it seems to me neither fish nor fowl. When *Hurricane* was being constructed by a Biloxi scow schooner builder, Kaufman and Menfred showed the builder the rigging plan; never having seen a ketch before, he looked very puzzled, and when asked his opinion of the rig he said, "Hell man, ain't nothin' but a schooner rigged backwards." A ketch won't go to windward as well as a cutter, sloop, or yawl, and is little, if any, faster off the wind. Nor will she go directly downwind, because once dead before the wind, the mizzen blankets either the headsails or the main, and with the wind on the quarter, the mizzen shoves the stern around to such an extent that in rough weather steering is difficult if not impossible. Unless there is a midships cockpit, the mizzen ends up in the middle of the cockpit and the helmsman goes cross-eyed looking around it. Every time he stands up, he fractures his skull on the mizzen boom. However, I must admit that a mizzen on a ketch makes a really good awning tree.

The rigging of a ketch is complicated because usually the stern is not long enough to permit the installation of a permanent backstay, so running backstays are needed on the mizzen.

On the small ketches, of 35 feet LOA and under, the sail area is so broken up that it loses efficiency, and on large ketches, the mizzen loses its biggest advantage because it is too large to be easily backed when under way in close quarters. However, on the larger boats a ketch rig has the advantage of keeping the area of the mainsail down, thereby making it not too difficult to handle. Further, it gives a man with imagination many ideas to play with.

Wishbone Ketches

The wishbone ketch, originated by Fritz Fenger, has the advantage that all the sails can be comparatively small and handled easily by one or two men. For example, *Wishbone,* a wishbone ketch designed by Uffa Fox, had 2,100 square feet of sail, yet the biggest working sail, the main trysail was only 500 square feet. Admittedly, if *Wishbone* had carried a genoa it would have been immense. Another great advantage of this rig is that there are no running backstays to be set up at any time and all the sails except the jib topsail are self-trimming; also, it is seldom necessary to reef, unless heaving to, because one of the myriad possible sail combinations will suit almost any condition of wind and sea.

Vamarie raced very successfully as a wishbone ketch, winning much more than her fair share of prizes. However, C. Sherman Hoyt, who sailed on her often, hated the rig with a passion. The main difficulty seemed to be in controlling the wishbone and in dousing the sail in rough weather. The wishbone, permanently aloft, is the weak point in this rig. Uffa Fox's *Wishbone* actually lost her entire rig, basically because the sheet from the mizzenmast head to the wishbone parted, starting a chain reaction which caused the whole rig to go overside.

A recent development of this rig allows the wishbone to pivot down almost to deck level when the main trysail is secured. This arrangement seems much more seamanlike but produces many of the same problems in hoisting and lowering the wishbone as are encountered in raising and lowering a gaff.

WISHBONE-KETCH VARIATIONS: There are variations on the wishbone ketch. In one, the main is four-sided rather than three-sided, with the

15. This is the reason masts on ketches and yawls should be independently stayed. (Jerry Holmes)

wishbone functioning like a gaff on a gaff ketch; the advantage is that since the main and the topsail can be one and the same, the area between the main and mizzen masts can be completely filled. On some boats, the boom has been eliminated, so there is much more room on deck. On wishbone ketches of the smaller sizes, greater efficiency may be gained by combining the main staysail and main trysail into one sail. A further variation is to brail the sail against the mast, thereby reducing sail handling to a minimum, as we did on Jim Scott's *Gitana* with great success.

SCHOONERS

In years gone by, the schooner rig—a fore-and-aft rig with several masts and the mainmast at least as tall as the foremast—was by far the most popular among American cruising yachtsmen who wished to make long trips. The gaff schooner with fore and main topsails, three headsails,.and a fisherman is undoubtedly one of the most picturesque of rigs. However, the schooner rig is also one of the most difficult to handle efficiently, and requires an enormous amount of running rigging. It is seldom used today, and then mostly for show. A few people still know and understand this rig. Jim Crawford sailed *Dirigo II* around the world and turned in some fabulous runs; his time of 23½ days for the 3,300 miles from the Galápagos to Tahiti is, I believe, a record—all the more memorable in that there were only four in the crew, the boat was about 60 feet LOA, and she was leaking badly. The great advantage of this rig is that off the wind, acres of sail may be set: there is no substitute for sail area when off the wind, especially when set on a good hull by a crew that is willing to work and knows what it is doing.

Staysail Schooners

The more modern version of the schooner is the staysail schooner, which when well rigged is fast and weatherly—witness the roomful of trophies won by *Nina*. This rig is excellent for the larger cruising boat, for the sail areas are broken up, and if the main boom is kept short, it is not difficult to handle. The fisherman, the sail that everyone fears, really is not as much of a rogue as it is thought to be. If a track is placed on the foremast, this sail can be set and taken in with relative ease, and the addition of a switch on the foremast, with a spur track, makes it possible to stow a fisherman on the main track and a light-weather golliwobbler on the other track (Drawing 25). The small fisherman makes the staysail schooner go to windward, the large golliwobbler makes her go on a reach, and when the wind gets way aft, down comes the main and off she goes. The golliwobbler can be sheeted to the end of the main boom, with a genoa or spinnaker on a pole on the opposite side. The one disadvantage of the schooner is that because of the short foremast, the genoa and spinnaker must be small, so it is difficult to go dead downwind. On a cruising staysail schooner of over 80 feet LOA, the spinnaker will seldom, if ever, be used; instead a combination of square sail and raffe is customary. Irving Johnson perfected this rig on the second *Yankee;* others have copied it. *Westward* is a good

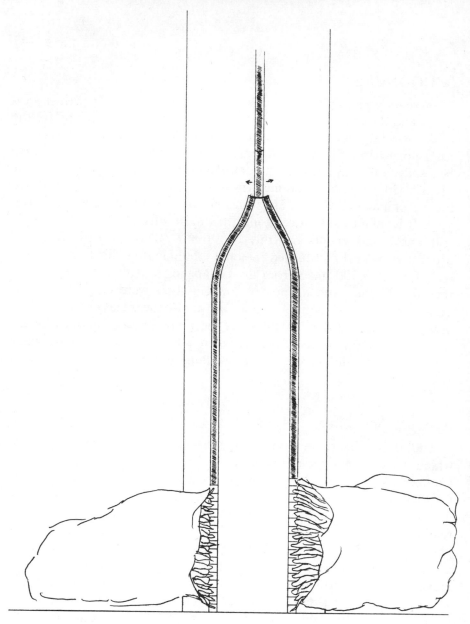

25. *Double-track switch for schooner foremast; the track should reach to the deck to facilitate the stowing of sails.*

example of this type of rig, and *Eyrx* I think embodies the ideal rig for the large schooner used for cruising.

The disadvantage of the schooner rig is that once the wind blows hard enough to necessitate taking off a headsail, the main must be reefed to keep the rig in balance. All too often, the schooner's boom extends over the transom, making reefing difficult. And reefing is hard enough even with a boom that ends flush with the transom, because the trickiest part of the operation, tying in the clew earing, has to be done way back aft where the motion is worst and the boat is narrow. Further, everyone climbs all over the helmsman in the process. (One advantage of a ketch with an aft cockpit is that the crew can reef the main without disturbing the helmsman.)

One reason that the schooner has retained the popularity it has, is that John Alden designed so many good boats of this type in the 1920's and 1930's. Many of them are no longer structurally sound, but if the garboards remain attached to the keel and the stern stays on, they sail like witches. When someone tells me he has an Alden schooner that won't sail, I always maintain that either the rig has been altered or the owner does not know how to sail.

GAFF RIG VERSUS MARCONI RIG

THE GAFF RIG

The old gaff rig does have its advantages. The sails are held at four corners, and a man who knows what he is doing can make even a poor sail set fairly well. Gaff sails are cheap, for several reasons. They can be made of Vivatex, a good waterproof canvas, infinitely cheaper than Dacron. Since the strains on gaff sails are much less than the strains on Marconi sails, they last for many years. Jim Squire, skipper of *Te Hongi,* estimates that his sails last four years—quite a long time for a successful charter boat. Also, small sailmakers, who do not have a large overhead, will make these sails, and make them well. The strains on the rig, too, are less with a gaff sail; the masts, being shorter and stronger, are seldom lost.

However, gaff sails are less than efficient to windward, and they have a tremendous amount of running gear. The old-fashioned gaff rig without winches is expensive in that it requires numerous blocks, tackles, and shackles, and the amount of line required to replace the halyards is unbelievable to a modern sailor. I once saw Victor, skipper of *Tradition,* use up two full 1,200-foot coils of ⅝-inch line to replace the running rigging on a sixty-foot gaff-topsail schooner.

Chafe is a real problem, and one only has to read the cruising books written before World War II to realize what a problem it has always been. When running downwind the chafe problem is intensified; indeed, almost all long-distance gaff-rigged cruising boats switch to square sails when

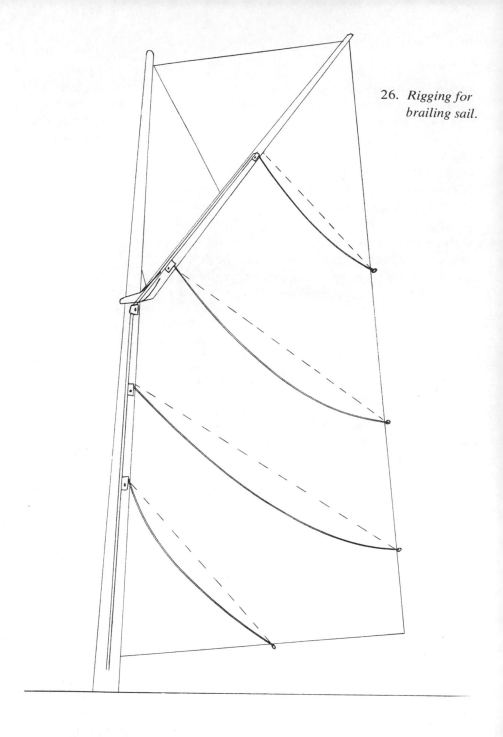

26. *Rigging for brailing sail.*

off the wind. Being becalmed in the open sea is nearly the worst thing that can happen to a gaff-rigged boat. The gaff either crashes back and forth or snubs hard against the vang and the preventer, chafing the mast. Topping-lift blocks seem determined to demolish the sail and the mast. One such experience is often enough to convert a man to the Marconi rig.

When *Integrity* was being fitted out for her trip across the Atlantic, the skipper wanted to put chafe pads around the mast for protection from the gaff. However, he was dissuaded by armchair sailors and armchair carpenters who insisted that the pads would cause the mast to rot. Halfway across the Atlantic, the crew had to cut up the smoke head from the stove, and use it for a chafing sheet to prevent the gaff from chafing through the mast.

Another disadvantage is that the gaffs are difficult to hoist, especially in large boats, where they may be heavier than the man who is heaving them up. It is the big men who love the gaff rig; little guys like myself just don't have the necessary muscle to handle it. To be sure, today one can install winches instead of tackles, wire instead of rope halyards, track instead of hoops, topsails set on tracks, and the like, thereby cutting the work and chafe considerably. The fact remains, however, that the gaff rig was developed in the days of wooden ships and iron men.

Hoisting difficulties can be avoided by rigging a standing gaff, and brailing the sail to the mast and gaff (Drawing 26). A sail is said to be brailed when it is furled by securing it to the mast, gaff, or yard by lanyards rather than by lowering it. On a brailed gaff mainsail, the brail line normally starts on the starboard side of the sail, and passes along the leech of the sail through a polished bronze cringle, back through another bronze cringle, secured to the luff of the sail, and thence down to the deck. Thus, to brail, the sail outhaul is cast off, all sheets are eased, the brail line is hauled in, and the sail is bunched up against the gaff and mast (Drawing 27). On large vessels there are individual brail lines; on smaller vessels, as we have seen, the individual brail lines are spliced together so that only one line need be pulled to brail the entire mainsail.

Rigged with a standing gaff, brailed mainsail, and brailed topsail, a really large gaff ketch can be sailed by a rather small crew. The sixty-foot *Haufrauen*, with her standing gaff and brailed square sail, is easily handled, and off the wind does well. But this type of rig makes it very difficult to go to windward without the aid of an "iron topsail" (engine).

THE MARCONI, OR JIB-HEADED, RIG

Modern rigs can be extremely simple, with winches to do everything but make the coffee. Boats as long as fifty feet may be handled by one man—witness *Gypsy Moth* and the even larger *Pen Duick*. With the ad-

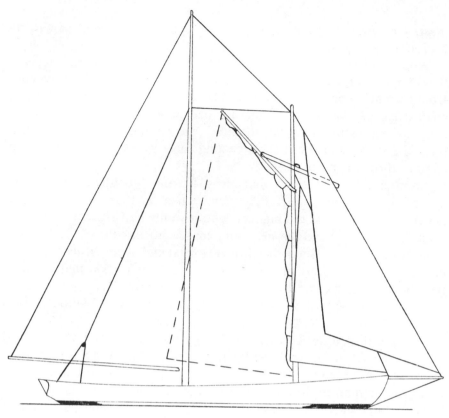

27. *Schooner with a loose-footed gaff foresail that has been brailed.*

vent of self-steering gear, winches so powerful a twelve-year-old child can trim the jib or hoist the main, and modern materials—light aluminum for masts and booms, Dacron for easy-to-handle line and for sails that weigh two-thirds as much as the old canvas sails when dry and half as much when wet—the limiting factor in a design is the size of the mainsail.

A headsail can be rigged with downhauls, roller-furling gear, and whatnot, or replaced by several smaller sails, but the main must be one piece of sail, and its maximum size is governed not only by the number of crew members but also by their size. A small light man in the peak of physical condition is not as useful in dousing a main as a fat man in bad shape. A downhaul can be rigged to the headboard so that the main can be winched down in heavy weather, but once down, it must be furled. The big man can lean over the boom and muzzle it, while the little man when he grabs the leech will be thrown all over the place because he is just too light.

When I first bought *Iolaire* the main was just over 600 feet square, and more than once, trying to douse sail in a squall, I was all but thrown overboard. Now I have a mainsail of 440 square feet, and I find that even in the worst weathers I can handle it without too much difficulty. Older men may have to reduce the size of the main still further, while a six-footer who weighs two hundred pounds and is in top shape may be able to handle a 600-square-foot sail without difficulty. Further, if one expects always to sail with at least two men to handle the main, it can be even larger.

Another limiting factor is the ability of the crew to go aloft. No matter how careful the design and construction of a rig, sooner or later something will have to be repaired or unfouled at sea. If you can climb a mast at sea, and work once you are up there, a taller rig can be carried than if you cannot. Here age catches up with us fast. I have cut six feet off *Iolaire*'s mast, yet every time I climb it I am convinced that it has grown ten feet.

SELECTING A RIG

In choosing a rig, one must keep in mind the purpose for which the boat is intended. A round-the-world cruiser will need a much heavier rig than a boat to be used for weekend or fortnightly cruises. If the boat is to be sailed in an area demanding a lot of windward work, that should be taken into account. Similarly, if extended periods of heavy weather are anticipated, a divided rig that will give flexibility for various strengths of wind is desirable. Further, the availability of repair facilities should be considered. If you are going to an area where the repair facilities are minimal or nonexistent, a plain and simple rig that you can repair yourself is indicated.

The size of the boat and crew should be carefully considered when one is choosing the rig. On a 60- to 70-foot boat, a schooner rig is wonderful and practical, but on a little 30-footer, the sails of a schooner rig are too small, the gear is too complicated, and the windage is too great to allow the boat to sail decently to windward. A 30-foot sloop has sails of a size that may easily be handled by a man and wife. One past 35 feet LOA, a divided rig is usually best, my personal preference being a yawl. If three or four men will always be available as crew, there is practically no limiting size for a yawl rig, but most long cruises are done with a comparatively small crew. At sea for long periods of time, people tend to get on each other's nerves, so a small crew with plenty of elbow room is an asset. Once a yawl gets above 55 feet LOA, the main is too large to be handled by a small crew. When this size is reached, a well-divided rig—ketch, wishbone ketch, or schooner—is preferable, to reduce the size of the individual sails.

For world cruisers of the larger sizes—70 feet and above—a variation of the staysail schooner, such as *Yankee,* is almost invariably preferred because the square sails on the foremast are easy to manage on the long trade-wind passages. In my opinion, the wishbone ketch is the best rig for large boats in that each individual sail is relatively small and easy to handle. Dead downwind, however, the wishbone ketch is difficult to handle. But some ingenious soul will probably prove some day that I am wrong.

The rig must be matched not only to the crew and the weather conditions but also to the boat. It is impossible to set an efficient square sail on a narrow boat with a tall rig. Rod Stephens tried this combination on *Dorade* and it was a total failure, one of the very few failures in his career. The yard could not be braced around, because of the shrouds and spreaders. *Dorade*'s lack of beam meant that the foot of the sail didn't have enough spread; the weight of the yard made her roll terribly. There was nothing wrong with the square rig; it just did not suit the boat. On a heavy boat with a slow roll, plenty of beam, and shrouds led well aft so that the yard can be braced around, the square sail can be a wonderful passage sail.

Similarly, the fact that a hull doesn't have any great sailing qualities, doesn't mean that it should be given an inefficient rig into the bargain. More than one ketch-rigged motor sailer that could not get out of its own way has been vastly improved by the substitution of a really efficient sloop or cutter rig. Laurent Giles in particular advocates installing a really efficient rig on his motor sailers to compensate for the drag of the deckhouse, the propeller, and the overall weight.

Lastly, if a boat has a less-than-satisfactory rig, there is no reason to put up with it forever, even if the boat was designed by an excellent marine architect. The advances in sail design and in materials (aluminum spars, Dacron sails and running rigging) make it possible to revamp or completely rerig an old hull and get a vast improvement—as demonstrated by the almost unbelievable performance of *Cocatoo,* a rerigged New York Yacht Club 30, built in 1904, and *Dolphin,* a Newport 29, designed in 1908 and built in 1917, both strong contenders in every race they enter and often in the prize list, and both designed and built by Herreshoff.

IV

~~~~~~~~~~~~~~~~~~~~~~~~~~~~~~~~~~~~~

Spars and Standing Rigging

After basic hull integrity, the quality of the spars and standing rigging of a cruising boat is most important. If sails are damaged, they can be repaired at sea. If the hull is damaged, the effects can be minimized by pumping, and temporary repairs can usually be made by caulking. When the rig is lost overside, however, it seldom can be retrieved, and only luck will save the boat unless a jury rig can be set up. This has been done, of course, the most fabulous case being the rerigging of *Tzu Hang* by Miles Smeeton, his wife, and John Guzzwill after they had pitchpoled and been dismasted in the Roaring Forties. However, such successful rigging salvages are the exception.

SPARS

MATERIALS

Wood

Spars have changed drastically in shape and material in the last two or three decades. Thirty years ago the typical spar was made of wood, solid or laminated, and was generally round, with almost no taper below the jibstay, but a sharp taper above it. Today, wooden spars are usually oval-shaped, and have little or no taper below the topmost section. Hollow wooden spars are expensive, are difficult to make unless one has an unusually good spar shop at one's disposal, and require materials that are hard to find today.

Sitka spruce, sometimes called airplane spruce, is by far the best material for wooden spars. In years gone by it was available in practically unlimited lengths. At the turn of the century, the great cutter *Octavia* had a solid, one-piece mainmast 110 feet long and 15 inches in diameter. This sort of timber is scarce today, and whatever is available is not well seasoned.

Ordinary spruce is tough, springy, light, and easy to work. However, it has a tendency to rot. Thus there is a continual argument about whether spars should be varnished or painted. Painting undoubtedly gives the spar more protection, but one cannot see what is going on under the paint. The varnished spar needs more frequent attention, but rot is immediately seen. Many builders of cruising boats avoid the problem by making spars of Douglas fir, also called Oregon pine, instead of spruce. This high-grade fir, which is less susceptible to rot, is available in long lengths, and though heavier than spruce, is light enough to be acceptable in a cruising boat.

The most important material in building a hollow spar is of course the glue. Spars built with the old casein glue, used before World War II and still favored by many yards today, should be viewed with suspicion because casein glue is not waterproof and in the tropics tends to deteriorate rapidly, especially if the spar is not perfectly painted or varnished. The resorcinol glues are infinitely better, but because they are black they are often rejected as unattractive. Today many builders are using the epoxy glues, which appear to be completely waterproof, and like casein glue, are colorless.

Metal

Metal spars are not new to the yachtsman. At the turn of the century Herreshoff was designing steel masts for his big cutters, and before World War II, some of the big ocean racers had expensively built-up aluminum spars. They were never used on cruising boats before World War II, and even after the war, aluminum spars were found on few cruising boats until the advent of extruded aluminum.

Today's aluminum spars are economical, especially if one does not bother tapering the upper few feet. This process, which involves cutting a slice out of the side of the spar, heating and bending the forward face back, and rewelding, can be as expensive as purchasing an entire spar, and the saving in weight is relatively small. Hence, many boat owners do not bother tapering the spar, especially with a masthead rig. If one is accustomed to wooden spars, sailing with aluminum spars is a revelation. They are light and yet so strong that many of the stays and shrouds needed by wooden spars can be dispensed with. Today, aluminum spars are offered by many manufacturers, and range from the plain and simple to the most complicated, with internal halyards, fillings of sound-deadening foam, internal shroud anchorages, and other refinements.

One complaint about aluminum spars is that they are noisy. However, a simple set of gilguys will prevent the halyards from slapping. A gilguy is a light lanyard secured to a shroud, passed around the halyard and then back around the shroud, heaved tight, and secured with a rolling hitch. This holds the halyard away from the mast and prevents the noisy *tap, tap, tap*.

Another problem with aluminum spars is that they are subject to corrosion. This can be very serious, especially at the base of the spar, unless proper measures are taken to avoid it. For example, a large drain hole should be introduced at the very bottom of the spar, particularly if there are internal halyards, and it should be checked frequently to insure that it remains clear, for the holes in the mast required by internal halyards allow appreciable quantities of rainwater and seawater to collect inside the spar; if the drain hole becomes clogged, six or eight feet of water may accumulate inside the aluminum mast. This can cause drastic corrosion problems.

An aluminum spar after three years in the tropics is shown in Photo 16. The worst corrosion on this spar, where the hole is actually corroded through, was caused by contact with damp wood. Secondary corrosion, which is also serious, occurred where the aluminum extrusion

16. Iolaire *mast heel.* (*D. M. Street*)

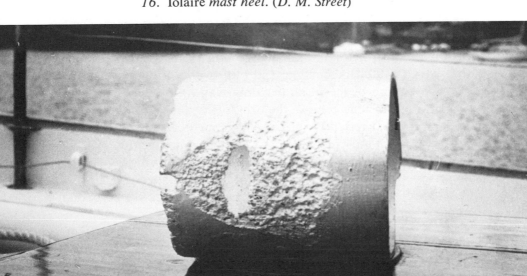

rested in a cast-aluminum heel fitting which was inadequately insulated from the steel mast step. The heel of an aluminum spar should be kept as dry as possible and should be well insulated from the mast step, whether it be steel, stainless steel, or aluminum, to avoid electrolysis.

Corrosion of aluminum also occurs in the air. Most manufacturers do anodize the spars, which appreciably cuts this corrosion. However, anodizing may not be enough, especially in the tropics, where corrosion drastically increases. If the spar is to be given hard and continuous usage, it should be not only anodized but also painted with epoxy paint.

The basic price for a bare aluminum spar is quite low, and making the fittings and installing them on the spar is not difficult if they are so designed that no aluminum or stainless-steel welding is needed. The cost of making the fittings for the spar varies greatly, and since many spar manufacturers tend to ignore special instructions, an owner who wishes to supervise their construction may choose to have the work done to order. Making fittings of mild steel is within the capability of any competent machine shop. The welding of aluminum itself, however, is a tricky job and the amateur is advised to leave it to an experienced yard.

Stainless steel and titanium masts are also available, but these are rather exotic and strictly for the racing man.

ALUMINUM SPARS—HANDHOLE COVERS: In order to bolt fittings to an aluminum spar one must be able to reach inside the spar; hence, at certain appropriate places handholes are made. The fanciest and best-looking covers for these handholes are absolutely flush with the surface of the spar (Drawing 28). However, these have a seam around the edge which allows water to get inside and corrode the fastenings. Further, to remove the handhole cover one must unscrew a set screw in its center, tie a piece of string on it, unscrew the other screws, drop the cover into the spar at a 90-degree angle, and pull it out. If the cover falls down into the bottom of the mast, the only way to retrieve it is to take the mast out of the boat, remove the heel fitting, find the cover, replace the heel fitting, and restep the mast. This can be a very expensive operation, so I much prefer handhole covers which are secured over the hole on the outside of the spar by machine screws (Drawing 29). If someone is careless with one of these, the worst that can happen is that the cover is dropped overboard; it must be replaced, but there is no necessity to remove the spar.

ALUMINUM SPARS—HEEL FITTINGS: Many of the sparmakers cast a heel fitting which enables the spar to be stepped in a normal wooden

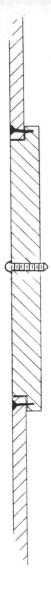

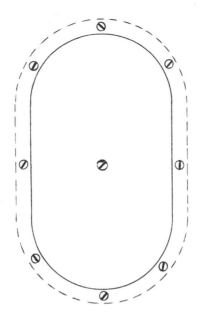

28. *Flush handhole cover.*

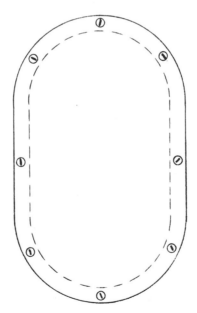

29. *American-type handhole cover.*

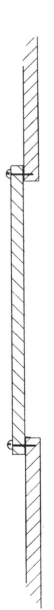

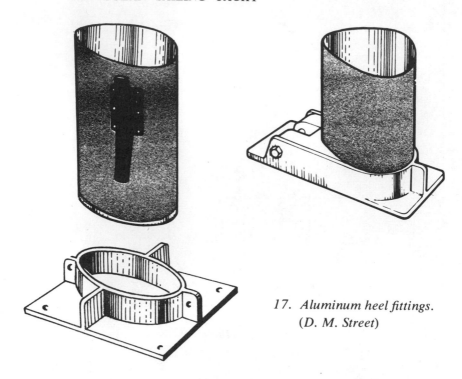

17. *Aluminum heel fittings.*
(*D. M. Street*)

mast step (Photo 17). Others put nothing on the bottom of the spar, and step it onto a stainless-steel plate with a collar around the edge and a large drain hole. These arrangements are equally satisfactory, as long as drainage is adequate.

Fiber Glass

Fiber-glass spars are relatively new on the market, except in Sweden. Experiments were unsuccessful until Oscar Plym, of Vaxholm, Sweden, perfected a process of building them about 1959. During the first two years he had some failures, but from 1961 on, his spars have met with almost complete success. They have almost the same dimensions as equivalent aluminum spars, with slightly thicker walls and the same relative weight. However, because it is easy to taper a fiber-glass spar, they usually have a lower center of gravity than the corresponding aluminum spars. The Plym process is a well-kept secret, but its originator has stated that the most important single facor is the material used, which he calls "unidirectional fiber-glass cloth." In it, 80 percent of the strands go in one direction, in contrast to the usual 50—50 arrangement. Fiber-glass masts have several advantages: they can be made in any size or shape, and they are light, free of corrosion, and much cheaper than aluminum spars. They undoubtedly would have received much wider acceptance had Plym been an American, selling to the huge American yachting market, where his spars have only recently begun to appear.

SHROUD ANCHORAGES

On many of our older boats with wooden masts, the shrouds and stays are secured to the mast by means of wire which has been wormed, served, parceled, spliced, and placed around the mast, resting on wooden cleats glued and screwed to the mast. This method of rigging a mast is very difficult, since shrouds are of varying lengths and require serving, covering with leather, and splicing. Furthermore, once the mast has been rigged, to remove a stay, one must first remove everything above it so that the wire can be lifted up and over the spar. In addition, fitting the track over the splices is an expensive and difficult job. To clear the splices, the track must be bent, or a long feather (a wooden strip underneath the track) must be installed. It is difficult to keep such a rig in tune because the splices tend to sink into the wood, thus altering the tension on the shrouds. This method is seldom used today except in a character boat.

The more common method is to bolt tangs onto the mast and fit the terminal ends of the wire between two plates held by clevis pins. Various arrangements are used to distribute the load and prevent crushing the wood. On hollow spars, a large washer led into the mast around a hollow bolt helps support the tang. Often, additional support is obtained by securing the tang with short, fat wood screws.

There is no reason why a wooden spar, with rigging spliced around it, cannot be rerigged, with tangs instead of wire and cleats.

Tang Materials

Stainless steel appears at first to be the best material for tangs. If they are properly made, polished, and secured to the mast, stainless-steel tangs will last forever. However, there are various reasons why this material is not perfect. First, it is difficult to weld and even when the welding is done by specialists there are occasional failures. If fittings are to be made of stainless, they must be carefully designed so that no shroud, stay, or halyard block will hang on a weld; instead, each should hang on a tang which is bolted to another tang bolted to the mast. Welding a stainless fitting aloft, so that the actual strength of the fitting comes from the weld, is, I think, the height of folly. Further, any flexing of the tang causes it to work harden, become brittle, and fail through fatigue, and even with superior design some flexing is unavoidable.

Monel is also used for mast fittings, though not as often as stainless steel. It is very strong, a superb material, but expensive and hard to work. Like stainless, it is difficult to weld, and no stays should be hung on a weld.

Bronzes come in various categories, beginning where the brasses leave off and running up through various grades to Evedur, which is a trade name for phosphor bronze. This bronze was one of the most common materials used for shroud fittings until the advent of the aluminum spar. Basically, it is not compatible with aluminum, but on wooden spars it is excellent. It is not subject to failure through fatigue, it can be drilled and machined easily, and if the correct welding rods are used, it can be welded without too much difficulty. Although the weld in Evedur is more reliable than a weld in stainless steel, it is still an uncertain factor, and important pieces of gear should not be hung on a weld.

Galvanized mild steel was formerly used extensively in Europe for fittings on deck and aloft. Mild steel was cheap, strong, and easy to work, weld, bend, or drill—anything could be done with it—but then the completed fitting had to be galvanized to prevent rust. Mild steel built up a bad reputation because galvanized fittings on deck last only a short time before they need to be regalvanized. To remove fittings from a boat, regalvanize them, and reinstall them is expensive.

However, aloft they are excellent; well-galvanized fittings bolted to a mast will last twenty or thirty years before needing to be regalvanized. One advantage of mild steel is that any good welder can weld it. Getting good galvanizing is more difficult, but painted with a modern epoxy paint, mild-steel fittings aloft will last for many years.

If mild-steel fittings are bedded with a rubber insulator and secured with stainless screws, they seem to get along well with aluminum spars. Thus, galvanized mild steel makes a cheap fitting, slightly heavier than stainless, which can be easily repaired in any of the out-of-the-way spots a good cruising yacht may visit. Photo 18 shows an *Iolaire* masthead fitting that is four years old.

MAST BOOTS

Making a good mast boot is difficult at best, and only the best of sailmakers seem to be able to put together a really watertight one of canvas. One of the advantages of an aluminum mast is that it can be purchased with a rubber boot which slips into place, is fastened down with a clamp, and is then folded down over an aluminum through-deck fitting, making a completely watertight seal. In the tropics particularly,

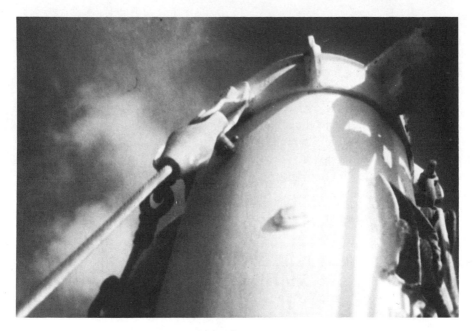

18. Iolaire *masthead fitting.* (*D. M. Street*)

the rubber or neoprene boot tends to deteriorate in the sun, and a canvas boot should be installed over it and painted white.

On some older boats, I have seen wedges so beautifully fitted and caulked in place that they were absolutely watertight and mast boots were unnecessary.

MAST WEDGES

Mast wedges are the subject of much disagreement. In the Western Hemisphere they are almost always made of soft pine, but on the other side of the ocean they are usually made of teak or a similar wood. It is true that the harder teak wedges chew into a soft spruce mast. Indeed, if the spar is of a sufficiently large section, it is preferable to remove the wedges and jam sponge rubber between the mast and the partners. The mast can then assume a single, even curve from step to masthead without being forced out of line by the partners. However, wooden wedges are most common; rubber chocks have been used only lately.

MAST WINCHES

It is seldom possible to have too many winches on a mast; a good idea is to determine the number actually needed, and then add a spare.

The placement of winches will be discussed in the chapter on running rigging, but it should be noted now that halyard winches on wooden masts should be through-bolted if possible. If they are not, they should be secured with heavy wood screws. If a combination of screwing and bolting is used, the bottom two fastenings on the winches should be bolted, while the rest can be screwed; the bottom two bolts take the greatest load when the halyard is trying to pull a winch off the mast. Bronze or stainless-steel winches must be well insulated from an aluminum mast or winch table. A wooden pad under a winch is not sufficient. Beneath it there should be a rubber pad or a heavy layer of rubber seam compound.

Metal Winch Tables

European sparmakers tend to secure sheet-metal winch tables to the mast and in turn secure the winches to the winch tables. Wherever possible, not only the masts but also the winch tables should be anodized. My present mast, which is anodized and painted, is almost completely maintenance-free. However, my winch tables, which are painted but not anodized, require a tremendous quantity of work because they continually corrode.

American spar manufacturers frequently machine the winch bases out of solid aluminum. To prevent corrosion in the area of contact, the pad must be perfectly fitted to the mast, and it should be bedded in some type of rubber composition so that no water can accumulate between the mast and the pad.

Some sparmakers mold their winch pads out of epoxy. These, if well bedded, so that water cannot penetrate beneath them, appear to me to be the best protection against both electrolysis and corrosion.

BOOMS AND BOOM ATTACHMENTS

Booms, like masts, are normally made of wood, aluminum, or fiber glass. The shape of the boom depends upon whether slab reefing or roller reefing is to be used.

Slab-Reefing Booms

If slab reefing is used, the boom can be a boxed section, much deeper in the vertical than in the horizontal. This construction provides stiffness; a flexible boom with complex bending rigs may be desirable for an all-out racing vessel, but is not sufficiently strong for the cruising boat, which may voyage far from a repair shop.

On wooden booms, the gooseneck attachment is one of the sources of trouble. If the boom is to be used with slab reefing, the gooseneck fitting should enable the boom to pivot and line up with the sail (Drawing 30). Further, the gooseneck should be secured to the boom with long metal arms with numerous bolts and/or heavy screws, well staggered so that they are not all on the same line of wood grain. Similarly, at the outer end, the best fitting is not merely bolted on, but consists of a cap set over the end of the boom and equipped with bails for the fore guy, mainsheet, and the like, and with blocks for the outhaul, the topping lift, and so on (Drawing 31). It is also essential, with slab reefing, that cleats and eyebolts be correctly placed to make it possible to reef rapidly.

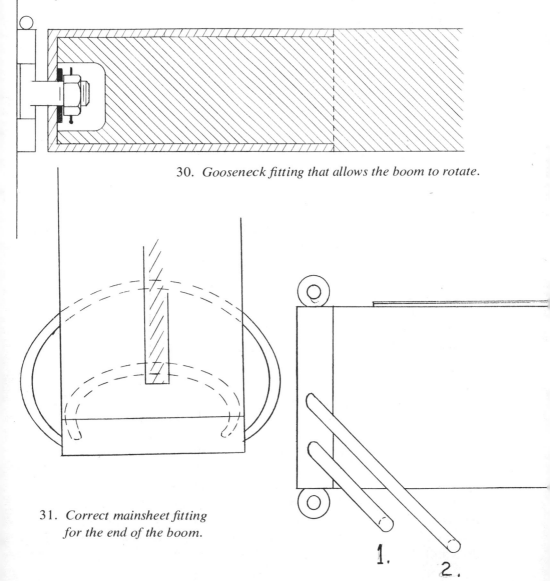

30. *Gooseneck fitting that allows the boom to rotate.*

31. *Correct mainsheet fitting for the end of the boom.*

1.

2.

Roller-Reefing Booms

Since the roller-reefing boom is supported only at the two ends, it should be of large diameter; otherwise, when reefed hard on the wind, the boom will tend to bend upward, throwing a belly into the sail and making it fuller just when it should be flatter. Unfortunately, because a larger diameter means greater cost, few stock boats on the market today have booms of sufficient diameter to prevent this bending upward.

Sliding Goosenecks

In years gone by most boats had fixed goosenecks, and tension on the sail was adjusted strictly by the halyard. However, since World War II most boats have been built with sliding goosenecks; the sail is hoisted up to a mark on the halyard, and tension is regulated by heaving down on a tackle under the gooseneck. These sliding goosenecks are a vast improvement. Formerly, in trying to tighten the lower third of the sail with the halyard one had to overcome the friction of all the slides on the top two-thirds before beginning to put tension on the lower third. Now, in adjusting the tension at the bottom of the sail with a boom downhaul, one only pulls the bottom third; one does not have to overcome the friction of each and every slide, and the weight of the boom helps do the job.

The attachment of the downhaul track to the mast should be very firm. On wooden spars of oval section, the track is usually secured by heavy bands (Photo 19), while on aluminum spars the track is usually machine-screwed, riveted, or bolted to the aluminum mast.

Since the gooseneck track is a big heavy male track, it is best to run the sail track down inside the downhaul track. Then, when the mainsail is furled, the sail slides back neatly on top of the boom, and does not stop at the top of the downhaul track.

SPINNAKER AND WHISKER POLES

If the personality of the owner and the size of the crew permit, a cruising yacht may use a spinnaker pole. Racing rules limit the length of the spinnaker pole to the length of the base of the fore-triangle. However, if one is not racing, it is very useful when winging the jib to have an overlength pole; the exact length will depend on the length of the foot of the jib and of the base of the fore-triangle. In years gone by, with wooden poles, the amount of length that could be added was limited because the pole soon became too heavy for easy handling. With the advent of the lighter aluminum and fiber-glass poles, the extra length does not critically affect their handling.

19. *Sliding gooseneck with mast bands, switch track for trysail, mainsail track running down through the gooseneck slider track.* (*Morris Rosenfeld*)

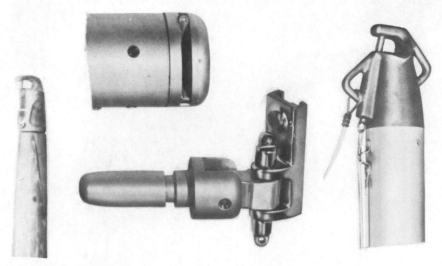

20. *Various spinnaker-pole end fittings.* (*Land's End Catalogue and D. M. Street as marked*)

Fittings and Track

End fittings are of various types (Photo 20). I prefer those with the wide-opening jaw. They make rigging the poles much easier because the genoa sheet may merely be dropped into the jaw and the jaw closed; one does not have to fight to attach the pole directly to the sail. One might expect that the sheet would tend to chafe in the jaw. However, after cruising across the Atlantic in *Antilles,* I was pleasantly surprised to see no sign of chafe on the sheet.

It is essential that the inboard fitting of the pole be carefully and correctly designed. Most important, the pole must be allowed to swivel slightly; otherwise its inner end will be subjected to a bad strain. One of the leading designers of spinnaker poles did not realize this, and one year numerous poles of his design broke within twenty-four hours of leaving the Canary Islands. It is also essential that the spinnaker pole be on an adjustable track, for then the pole can always be kept level and there is little strain on the topping lift and the fore guy; also, the sail can be made to set very well, with a wide latitude of adjustment.

On racing yachts there is a limit as to how high above the deck the spinnaker pole may be carried, but on cruising yachts, the track can be brought well up the mast. If this is done, the track should have a butt-end lift and a downhaul to facilitate the adjustment of the height of the pole. On some boats, the track is carried so far up the mast that the inner end of the pole can be hauled up the mast and the pole stored vertically with the outer end down, clipped to fittings on the bulwark (Photo 21). While this is an effective method of storing the pole, I wonder what it does to the windward performance of the boat. I prefer to see the pole stored alongside the deck, clipped in sockets (Photo 22).

21. Poles stowed vertically. (Laurie Legay)

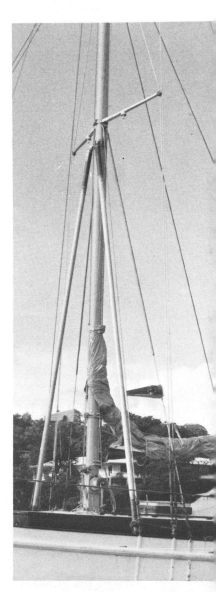

22. Pole stowed in a socket on deck. (D. M. Street)

JIB CLUBS

The advantage of the jib club is that it makes the jib or staysail self-trimming; the disadvantage is that a headsail cannot be set on a club as

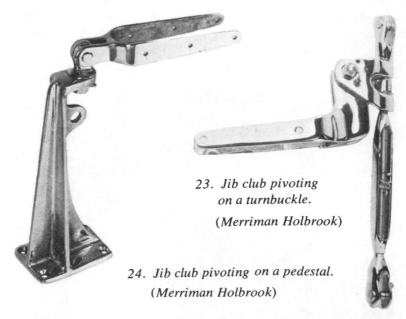

*23. Jib club pivoting
on a turnbuckle.*

(Merriman Holbrook)

24. Jib club pivoting on a pedestal.
(Merriman Holbrook)

25. Jib club pivoting fisherman style. (Uffa Fox)

well as it could be if it were loose-footed. Further, when running downwind or broad reaching, the jib or staysail collapses and the boom comes swinging across and tries to tear the traveler out of the deck. Also, it usually tries to knock overboard whoever comes forward to handle the anchor, and anyone walking across the foredeck must either duck under it or climb over it. Thus the time saved in the hours under sail by having a club for jib or staysail is more than offset by its numerous disadvantages; further, it is a lot cheaper to purchase two medium-priced staysail winches than to have made a staysail boom, traveler, fittings, and attendant blocks. Those nevertheless interested in having a club should review what has been said about booms, since in general it also holds for jib clubs.

A special cause of difficulty in the jib club is the attachment of the forward end. It is sometimes fitted on the turnbuckle, a standard fitting (Photo 23); however, the turnbuckle can be strained or broken. Or it may be placed directly on the stay; this is not a good arrangement since the wire is likely to fatigue at that point. Another alternative is to set the club on a pedestal (Photo 24). This is the method I prefer since it gives the best setting of the club jib or staysail, and if they are correctly designed, the pedestal and club can easily be removed when they are not wanted. The club can then be used as a whisker pole to wing the staysail on a reach or run.

If a jib is set on a club, it is necessary to install a jack line (discussed in detail in Chapter VI). This allows the sail to be dropped without having to slack the outhaul. However, there is a method, known as fisherman style, in which the club jib or staysail is pivoted from two iron bars (Photo 25). Its great advantage is that no jack line need be fitted on the luff of the sail, as when the halyard is slacked, the forward end of the club rides forward, allowing the sail to come down.

SHROUDS AND STAYS

On racing boats, weight aloft is so detrimental to performance that rigging is cut to a bare minimum, and if a single shroud or stay is lost, usually the entire rig comes down. This situation may be acceptable in an ocean race, where other boats are available to tow in the disabled vessel, but it is not acceptable for a cruising yacht alone at sea. On the true cruising boat, the rig should be so designed that the parting of no single shroud or stay can cause the loss of the entire rig. Thus, a double-headsail rig, which offers the staysail stay as double protection, is preferable to a single-headsail rig, because in the latter, if the head stay goes, the whole rig usually is lost overboard.

With a double-headsail rig, a removable staysail stay is advisable, so that in light or moderate wind when sailing with a big genoa alone, one can tack without having to pass the sail between the staysail stay and the head stay. The staysail stay should be of the same or almost the same strength as the head stay. If the head stay fails, the staysail stay must hold the whole rig in the boat.

Similarly, a double-spreader rig is desirable because with it the mast can be kept in the boat despite the loss of either the intermediate shroud or the upper shroud, or even the loss of a spreader (Drawing

32). If a shroud or spreader is lost, the mast will of course be deprived of some support, but total collapse is not inevitable, as it would be with a single-spreader rig. For similar reasons, I dislike panel rigging on a cruising boat (Drawing 33): if the lower panel turnbuckle goes, two-thirds of the mast is unsupported.

Both shrouds and stays help support the mast. A stay supports the mast in the fore-and-aft plane; there are head stays, staysail stays, and backstays. In contrast, a shroud supports the mast athwartships; there are lower shrouds, intermediate shrouds, and upper shrouds.

Backstays should always be brought down on deck and secured to heavy chain plates. The old practice, common in the 1930's, of attaching the permanent backstay to the mizzenmast merely had the effect of tying two whips together. Unless the backstay is brought down to a chain plate on the boat, the head stay cannot be made tight.

It is possible for shrouds to double as stays. In this day and age, with spars of large fore-and-aft dimensions, running backstays should be needed only in very heavy weather. If the lower shrouds are spaced well apart, they will support the lower portion of the mast well. Roughly one inch of drift (that is, distance fore or after the mast) for each foot of mast height is adequate to make a shroud act as a backstay or head stay and help support the mast.

On some boats, an intermediate shroud is used both as an intermediate backstay to keep the staysail stay tight, and as a shroud, but since there cannot be a spreader on this stay and it is difficult to have sufficient spread on it, this rig will only work on a beamy boat. As a general rule, the angle between the mast and the stay or shroud should be at least 7 degrees; every increase in angle eases the strain on the mast and on the stay.

On yawls and ketches, it is imperative that the mainmast be independently stayed (see Drawing 16). Frequently, it is also necessary to add a triatic stay between the mizzenmast and the main to keep the mizzenmast from falling aft when the mizzen is trimmed flat. This situation usually arises because the mizzenmast has been rigged with an upper shroud and two lowers, with little or no spread to the lowers and with the upper shroud secured to chain plates that are not forward of the mast. The main boom often is too long to permit sufficient drift on the lower or intermediate shrouds to support the mast fore and aft. Since it has been shown in ocean racing that a mainsail can be quite small and still remain effective, it is usually possible to shorten the boom so that the mizzen intermediate shroud can be moved far enough forward to support the mizzenmast without the triatic stay. Then, if the mainmast

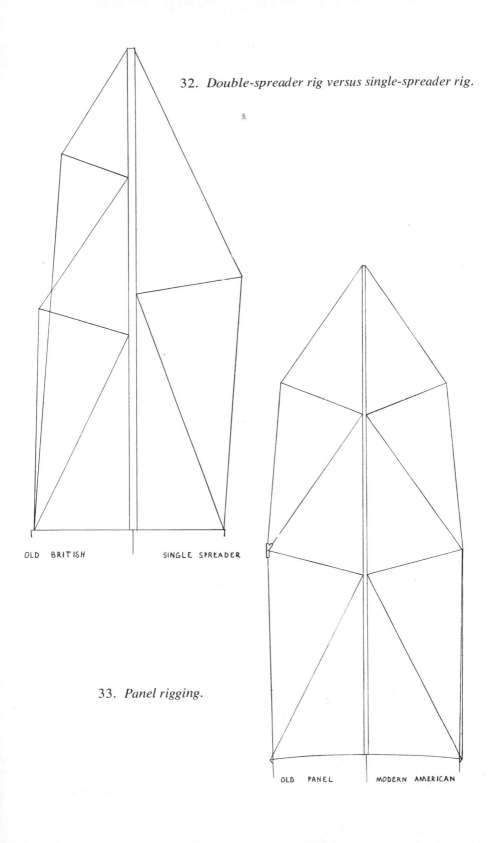

32. *Double-spreader rig versus single-spreader rig.*

OLD   BRITISH   SINGLE SPREADER

33. *Panel rigging.*

OLD   PANEL   MODERN AMERICAN

goes overside the mizzen will remain. But when shortening the boom, and rigging a permanent backstay, one must leave enough space between the end of the boom and the backstay so that the boom does not hook the backstay when jibing. It is not sufficient to have the boom short enough to clear the backstay on a perfect jibe, with the main sheeted flat; the boom should be short enough to clear the backstay even if the mainsheet man is none too good and the boom kites six or eight feet above its normal position. This measurement may be checked either on the drawing board, or by attaching the main halyard to the boom end, and swinging it eight feet above its normal position to see if it still clears the backstay.

The easiest way to achieve independent staying of the mizzenmast is to rig as shown in Drawing 34. Note that the intermediate shroud is led well forward, so that when going to windward it carries the majority of the load. The upper shroud prevents the top of the mizzenmast from falling off to leeward. The middle of the lower section of the mast is supported by the lower shroud. Both the upper and the lower shroud should be led well aft of the mast; on *Iolaire* the height of upper shroud is 24 feet, with a drift of 24 inches; the height of the intermediate shroud is 18 feet, with a drift of 24 inches. Because the spreaders and upper shrouds are rigged so far aft on *Iolaire,* no running backstays are necessary on the mizzen, even when we set a big mizzen staysail. The objection to mizzen spreaders rigged aft is that they try to poke a hole in the mizzen when sailing broad off the wind. However, when the wind is that far aft, the mizzen should be down, with either nothing or just the mizzen staysail set, to provide easier steering; if this is done, the problem is avoided.

Some European designers who no longer tie the two masts together have adopted a contrasting method of supporting the mizzen; they carry the upper shroud well forward over a spreader (Drawing 35). This does support the mizzen well when going to windward; however, as soon as sheets are eased, a running backstay must be set up to take the forward strain. Wishbone ketches and schooners by their very nature must have their masts tied together by means of spring stays and permanent backstays (Drawings 36, 37, and 38).

Usually on well-designed schooners or ketches, there is little or no chance of losing the whole rig. However, schooners, especially those with bowsprits, should be double-headsail-rigged; then if the bobstay or the head stay goes, there is still something to keep the mast on the boat. On schooners, the entire combined load of the main, the fore, and any sail rigged between the masts, is carried by the head stay and/or the staysail stay. On some boats, a backstay is rigged on the foremast, and

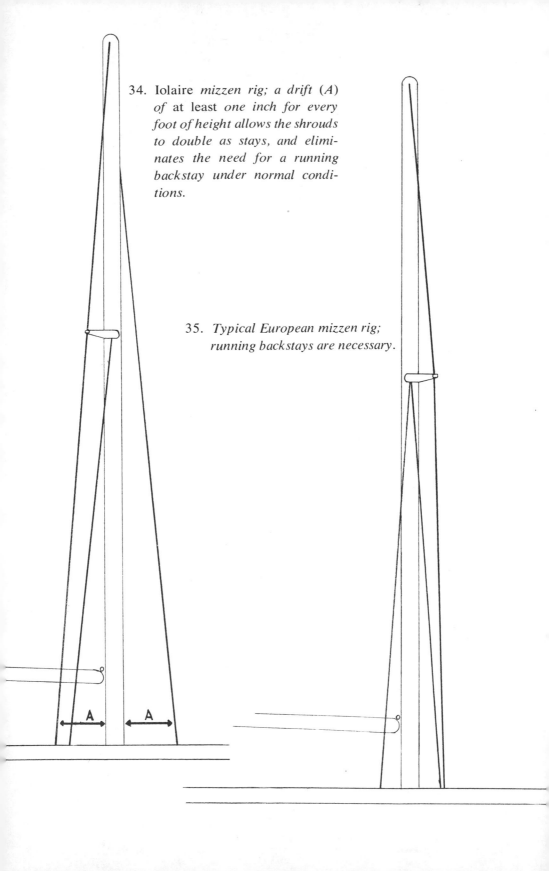

34. Iolaire *mizzen rig; a drift (A) of* at least *one inch for every foot of height allows the shrouds to double as stays, and eliminates the need for a running backstay under normal conditions.*

35. *Typical European mizzen rig; running backstays are necessary.*

A   A

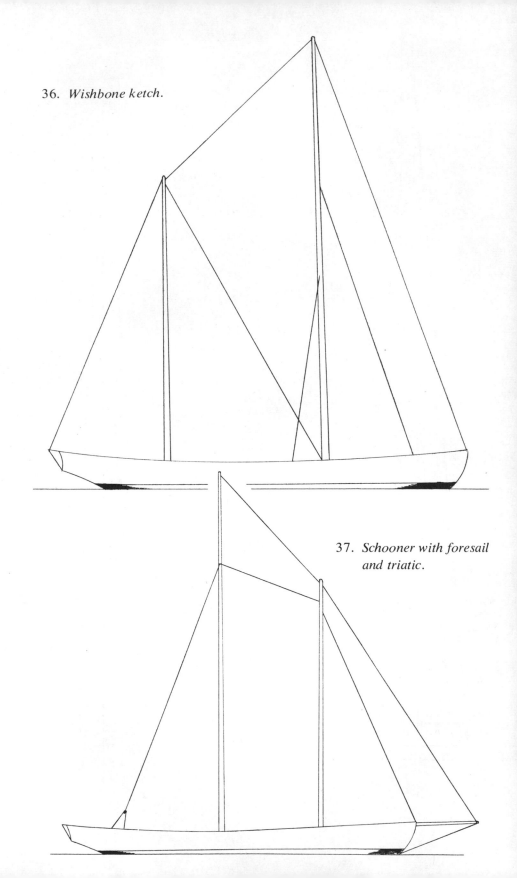

36. *Wishbone ketch.*

37. *Schooner with foresail and triatic.*

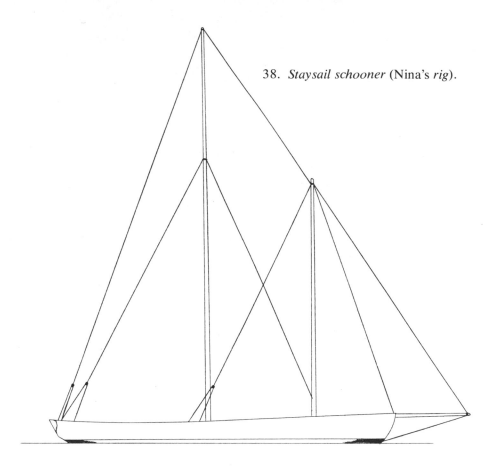

38. *Staysail schooner* (Nina's *rig*).

then the fisherman staysail can tack like any headsail. *Nina* was probably the most famous schooner with this rig. Boats like *Onward III*,
with a comparatively short foremast, have managed to survive without
running backstays on the foremast or triatics between the masts. She
was rigged with a stay from the top of the fore to the top of the main
and then from the top of the main down to a bumpkin on the stern,
carrying the permanent backstay. This rig ties everything up together
very nicely. However, the bumpkin and bowsprit fittings and the various supporting stays and attachments on bow and stern must be in absolutely perfect condition, since a failure in any of these fittings would
leave the entire rig unsupported. For this reason, any schooner with a
permanent backstay secured to a bumpkin should have a heavy, emergency running backstay on the main for use if the permanent backstay
fails. The old-fashioned schooner, with no permanent backstay, has
sailed well for many years, but is difficult to handle—particularly in
jibing, which, with nothing to support the mast other than running
backstays, requires some very fancy backstay handling.

SHROUD-CHAIN-PLATE PLACEMENT

Up to about 1900, sufficient spread to hold the rig aloft was frequently obtained by attaching the shrouds to channels, outside the actual hull of the yacht (Drawing 39). This arrangement was adopted because in view of the narrow beam of the racing boats of that era it was
believed that additional spread was absolutely necessary. More recently, shrouds were almost universally brought to chain plates bolted
either to the inside of the frames on planking, or externally to the
planking, with no channels to spread the base (Drawing 40A).

After World War II, in an attempt to flatten genoas, designers began to
set the chain plates slightly inboard of the rail cap. Also, following the
lead of Sparkman and Stephens (Drawing 40B) they frequently set the
upper shrouds slightly inside the lower shrouds. This was necessary because the lower shrouds led in at an angle, while the upper shrouds led

39. *Channels.*

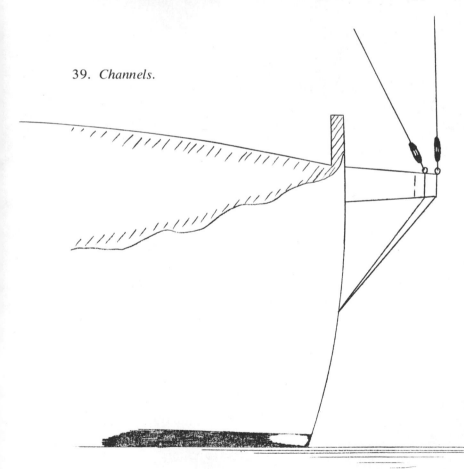

40(C). *Spread between upper and lower shrouds to allow sheeting of stay- sail.*

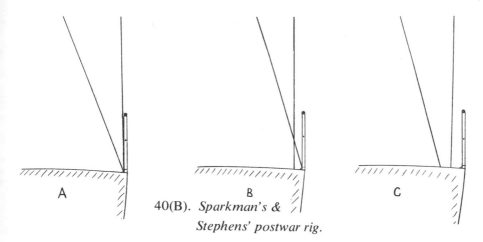

A

40(B). *Sparkman's &
Stephens' postwar rig.*

B

C

40(A). *Normal pre-World War II rig.*

almost vertically to the spreader. Thus if the upper shroud was not set slightly inside the lower, the genoa would fetch up against the upper shrouds while still standing clear of the lower shroud. This installation is more or less standard on modern ocean racers.

However, of late the practice has developed of setting the shrouds well inboard from the rail cap—as much as 1½ to 2 feet—on very beamy ocean racers like the Rancher 41, so the genoa can be flattened going to windward. Failure to set the chain plates well inboard on some beamy boats, for instance the Carib 41, has made them complete dogs to windward. Given enough wind, the Carib 41 will sail on a close reach or a beam reach, but she will do nothing to windward because the genoa cannot be flattened.

The above two methods of shroud placement, while superb for flattening the genoa, are hopeless if one wishes to use a really good genoa staysail. The double-headsail cutter with genoa staysail was originally pioneered in England. John Illingworth was one of the leaders in sheeting the genoa staysail between the upper and lower shrouds. If there is not a gap between the upper and lower shrouds, it is impossible to sheet a genoa staysail unless it is cut fairly high—which is defeating its purpose. The lower shrouds should be set in from 8 inches to 18 inches from the upper shrouds (Drawing 40c), the exact distance depending upon the beam of the boat. With this arrangement, a deck-sweeping genoa staysail can be sheeted flat going to windward. One needn't worry about taking water in this low cut sail, for since it is set back from the bows, the genoa staysail is always well inboard of the bow

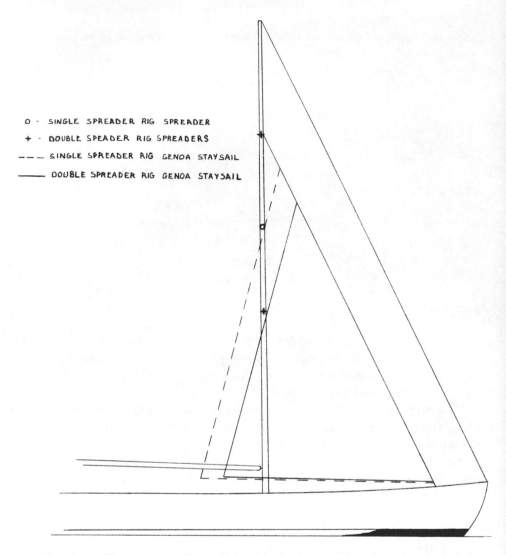

O - SINGLE SPREADER RIG SPREADER
+ - DOUBLE SPREADER RIG SPREADERS
\- - - SINGLE SPREADER RIG GENOA STAYSAIL
_____ DOUBLE SPREADER RIG GENOA STAYSAIL

41. *Area of genoa staysail possible with single-spreader rig and with double-spreader rig.*

wave. Once the sheets are eased, the genoa staysail must be resheeted outside the upper shroud and a tack pendant must be attached to clear the life lines. Similarly, on the aforementioned cutter, the single-spreader rig is infinitely superior for setting the double-headsail rig, as it leaves much more room for a large genoa staysail. Drawing 41 shows the difference in area obtainable with a single-spreader as opposed to a double-spreader rig; with the latter, the leech of the sail must be cut away and the hoist reduced to enable it to clear the lower spreader.

SPREADERS

Spreader failure has caused the loss of many rigs and the abandonment of many cruises and races. Spreaders are an essential part of the rig and should be carefully designed. The debate between the proponents of fixed and of swinging spreaders is endless. I personally prefer the swinging spreader designed so that the swing is limited as the spreader pivots on the bolt (*A* in Drawing 42), while the slot around the bolt (*B*) limits the fore-and-aft movement of the spreader. I also feel that the spreader should be adjustable in the vertical plane, since a spreader carrying only one stay should always bisect the angle of that stay (see upper spreader, Drawing 43); if the spreader does not bisect the angle, it is subject to a bending strain. Once properly adjusted, it must be firmly attached to the stay so that it retains its correct position. With galvanized iron wire, the spreader tip can easily be secured in place.

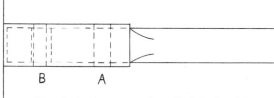

B   A

42. *Swinging spreaders* (Iolaire's *rig*).

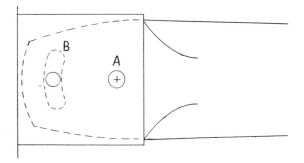

B
A
(+)

43. *Correct spreader angle; theoretically, the lower spreader should follow the dotted line, but with the upper shroud passing over the spreader, it must be at less of an angle.*

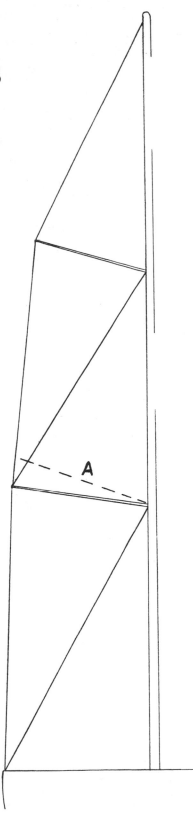

A

However, with stainless wire, the spreader tip tends to slip. The best method is to serve about two feet of the stay in the way of the spreader with marline, then soak the marline in a mixture of half varnish, half linseed oil. Next, a small eye or hook should be secured to the spreader; then marline can be lashed around the serving on the shroud and through the eye or around the hook (Drawing 44).

Further, the stay must be firmly attached to the spreader, so that it will not shake out under any circumstances. When under load, the stay tries to split the wood on the end of the spreader. Therefore, except in the very smallest boats, spreader tips should be lined with metal and another strap should be passed outside the stay and firmly bolted to the spreader tips (Drawing 45).

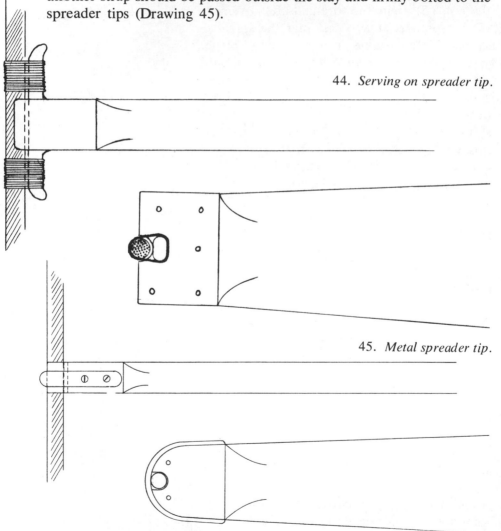

44. *Serving on spreader tip.*

45. *Metal spreader tip.*

ATTACHING THE SAIL TO THE MAST

HOOPS

In the days of gaff rigs, the most common method of attaching the sail to the mast was by hoops. These hoops were usually made of oak or ash bent into circles and riveted together. The sail was lashed to the mast hoops. This method was simple and effective, but was suitable only with a gaff rig, since it was impossible for the hoops to go above the lower shrouds. Hoops began to disappear when the bigger racing yachts arrived on the scene, with light spars supported by numerous stays. The first Marconi masts were not used with jib-headed sails, but were on the big gaff cutters that differed from the old cutters in that the mast and topmast were one unit. Photographs of old cutters taken just before and after World War I often show the gaff above the lower spreaders. This arrangement was made possible by the presence of a hardworking masthead man, who shackled the upper hoops to the sail and the parrels which held the gaff against the spar, once the throat of the sail reached the lower spreaders. Similarly, when the time came to douse the sail, the masthead man had to unshackle the upper hoops and gaff parrels.

Mast hoops have a tendency to jam when the sail is being hoisted or lowered. On commercial vessels the mast is usually "slushed down"—coated with a mixture of grease and tallow. On yachts with varnished masts, it is very difficult to keep the hoops from scarring the mast when they jam. Recently *Boating* described a method of keeping the hoops level, thereby minimizing the tendency to jam (Drawing 46).

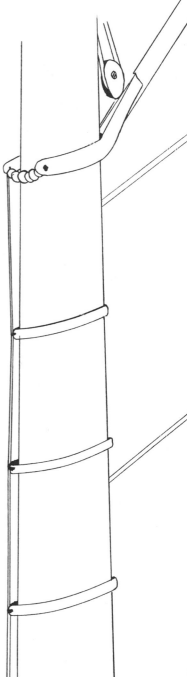

46. *Line on forward side of hoops to keep them from jamming.*

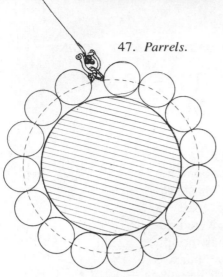

47. *Parrels.*

PARRELS

Parrels—little balls of lignum vitae or other hardwood—are sometimes used to secure the sail to the mast. Each ball has a hole through the center through which a line is threaded. The line has an eye spliced in at either end, and a shackle is passed through both eyes and secured to the sail (Drawing 47). Like mast hoops, parrels are hard to obtain and expensive to make.

LACING

The luff or even the largest gaff sail, especially today, in the age of Dacron, can be secured to the mast with a lacing line. The line should be continuous but zig-zagged—starting on the star-board side of the sail, passing around the spar to the port side, then back to the starboard side, and so on (Drawing 48). It should be kept slack until the sail is set; then it can be adjusted and se-cured back on itself by a rolling hitch.

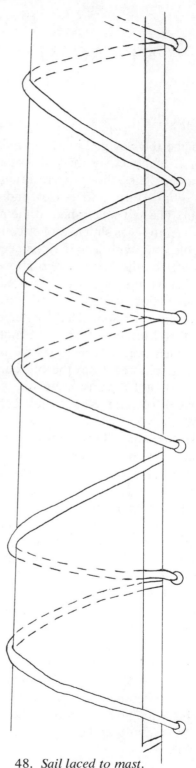

48. *Sail laced to mast.*

26. Iolaire *sail lashed to the boom—a well-reefed main.* (*D. M. Street*)

The advantages of this type of fastening are that it is infinitely adjustable, tension is equalized at each grommet, and it will never jam during hoisting or lowering.

Lacing can also be used to secure the sail to the gaff or the boom. Indeed, this old and common method is much more effective than one might imagine. On *Iolaire* I still have my mainsail lashed to a rail along the top of the boom (Photo 26), even though she is now jibheaded. I have found this arrangement simple and effective, although removing the mainsail is not so simple as it would be with track and slides.

Normally, lacing along the foot of the sail, where it can be kept in view, is done in a continuous spiral, which allows the clew to be adjusted at will. However, on the gaff, the normal practice is to adjust the peak outhaul until the tension appears right and then half-hitch the head of the sail to the gaff with lacing lines (Drawing 49). Because of the half hitches, if the line chafes through in one place, it is unlikely to unthread completely, as it would in a continuous spiral lacing.

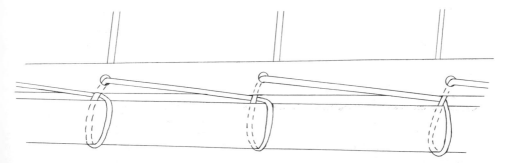

49. Sail laced to gaff with half hitches.

GROOVED, OR SLOTTED, SPARS

Slotted spars have several disadvantages for cruising boats. First, there is no way to hold the sail against the mast when furling, and if the sail is doused in a hurry, it feeds out of the slot, tries to go overside, and can only be controlled by a large crew. This difficulty is to be found also with a grooved head stay. Another disadvantage of the slotted spar is that in heavy weather under sail it is almost impossible to feed the luff rope into the slot. The individual unfortunate enough to have a slotted spar can obtain sail slides specially designed to fit this type of spar.

SAIL TRACK

The great argument with respect to sail track concerns the relative merits of male and female track (Drawing 50). In the past, the American preference for male track seems to have been supported by performance. Female track, which British designers have usually favored, tended to jam if the screws were not set perfectly flush, or worked loose (Drawing 51), while in the male track the screws can work out to a moderate degree without causing jamming. Further, if a slight dent was made in the female track, it was extremely difficult to straighten. Replacement of a section of track was frequently the only recourse.

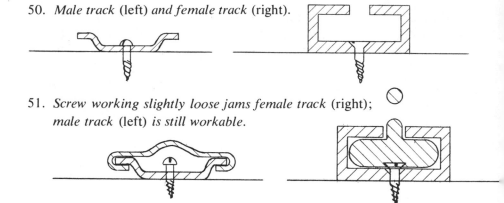

50. *Male track* (left) *and female track* (right).

51. *Screw working slightly loose jams female track* (right); *male track* (left) *is still workable.*

However, in the last few years the whole situation has changed; female track is now available in a wide range of types. One of these (*A* in Drawing 52) has a flange, and the fastenings are on the outside of the track so that a loose fastening does not jam the track. I am firmly convinced that this is the correct type to use in all circumstances.

Female track is especially desirable with aluminum masts. Male track must be machine-screwed in, and the screws cannot be riveted

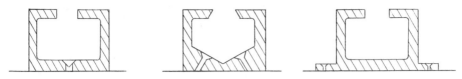

52. *Various types of female track.*

over inside a mast which is made of aluminum. Occasionally a screw works out, causing the slides to jam, something that cannot happen with track of the type labeled *A* in Drawing 52. This type of female track is usually pop-riveted to an aluminum mast. It should be noted that the fastenings should be doubled up where the head of the single-reefed main or the double-reefed main, and the head of the trysail, are secured. Otherwise, in very heavy weather, the track may lift off the mast.

Female track with outside flanges and plastic slides is almost trouble free. A little oil applied occasionally just before hoisting sail keeps the slides operating freely. Coating the entire track with Teflon spray also is effective.

RIGGING WIRE

STAINLESS-STEEL VERSUS GALVANIZED WIRE

The first subject to be considered with respect to rigging wire is the matter of the relative merits of galvanized and stainless-steel products. Quite frankly, except for the large sizes—$7/16$ inch in diameter and over—I think galvanized rigging wire is as dead as the dodo, mainly because of its inferior durability. To be sure, British galvanized wire is superb, far superior to the American product, and especially in Europe, one can find boats with galvanized rigging wire that has lasted for fifteen or twenty years. However, these are usually boats that are laid up for six months of the year, during which the rigging is oiled and gone over very carefully. By and large, now that labor is getting so expensive, it is just not practical to spend the time required for maintaining galvanized wire. Further, if one does extensive cruising, one does not have the time or the facilities to remove the rigging and give it the really good going-over it requires periodically. Finally, in the tropics, even the best galvanized rigging lasts only two or three years. Usually the splices fail underneath the servings, where one cannot see the corrosion at work. Some boats have experimented with galvanized wire covered with plastic. I have seen three, and in each of them the owner reported the experiment to be a dead loss.

It should be noted that in the 12 meters and in some ocean racers the halyards and sheets are still generally of galvanized wire. The reason is that galvanized wire is softer and less likely to kink than is stainless wire. Further, it is less likely to work harden and fatigue. One well-known firm of designers has insisted on galvanized-wire halyards ever since one of its ocean racers broke two stainless-steel halyards shortly after she was built. The theory was that the slight movement of the main halyard wire over the sheave, under load, work hardened the stainless wire and caused it to fracture. However, my guess would be that wire of too small a size had been used, so the slightest weakness in it resulted in a break. I know that the stainless main halyard that I originally installed on *Ondine* in 1954 is still giving good service on *Iolaire* in 1971, whereas galvanized wire, especially flexible wire, seldom lasts more than a year or so.

"Stainless steel" is really an improper term; this metal is merely rustless, not stainless, and when it gets old, its surface becomes dull, perhaps even slightly brown. Occasionally some rust can be found on brand-new wire. What is corroding is not the wire itself, but a hard steel burr coming from the die where the wire was drawn. Although it is unsightly, it does not affect the quality of the wire.

Especially in Europe, stainless-steel wire received a bad reputation right after World War II. Because many ocean racers built with it lost their rigs, for many years after World War II, Lloyd's Underwriters much preferred galvanized wire to stainless wire. Indeed, even today many people in the tropics still do not like British stainless. In one dismasting, the rigging wire failed on a well-designed boat, only four years old, rigged by one of England's top firms. It was not blowing particularly hard when the stay let go. A sample of the wire was sent back to the builder, who admitted that a laboratory examination showed the wire to be fatigued and finished.

I have had long talks with some of England's top men in wire-rope manufacturing, and they state that for years English stainless wire ropes were improperly manufactured—drawn under the wrong pressures, made of the wrong alloys, and so on—but that now the British stainless wire is just as good as the American product. Perhaps they are right, but many people still have a great prejudice against British wire.

American stainless-steel wire from the large manufacturers seems to stand up well. However, among the products of various manufacturers, and even among different runs of wire from the same manufacturer, there may be a substantial degree of variability. I have seen one coil of wire stand up perfectly, while the wire of another coil delivered a few months later from the same manufacturer turned brown, right down to the center.

Further, it must be remembered that stainless wire does not last forever. Flexible rigging is easily checked by bending the wire back and forth where it rests on the sheave; if little strands begin to break off, the wire should be condemned. Standing rigging is more difficult to check, but older wire should be carefully watched where it goes over the spreader tips, for that is the most common place for the wire to begin to strand. One broken strand in 1 by 19 wire means that the rest is about to go, and the wire should be condemned.

WIRE CONSTRUCTION

There are many different types of wire construction, but a number of the older varieties have been discontinued, at least in yacht work. For example, in years gone by, the hemp-core construction with galvanized wire was very popular—the hemp core tends to hold the oil, which would slowly ooze out and give the entire wire a protective shield. Today, this kind of wire is seldom used on yachts.

Almost all wire rope made today is preformed—that is, before being assembled, the individual wires are given the helical shape they will have in the finished product. The result is that when the wire is cut, it does not tend to unlay, becoming difficult to handle, as wire did in the old days. I would question the quality of any rigging wire that was not preformed.

We shall deal exclusively with four types of wire construction found on yachts today: rod rigging, 1 by 19, and 7 by 7, which are used for standing rigging; and 7 by 19, which is used for running rigging.

Rod Rigging

Rod rigging has become of late very popular among members of the ocean-racing fraternity. Normally, rigging wire is made up of many small individual strands twisted to make one large wire. Rod rigging consists of one single rod, which by various hardening processes can be made unbelievably strong. As a result, the diameter of the stay can be substantially reduced, producing a considerable saving in both weight and windage over comparable 1 by 19 or 7 by 7 rigging wire. There is nothing new about rod rigging. The struts that held together the biplane in the 1930's were actually airfoil-shaped rod rigging, and it was frequently found in 12 meter, 8 meter, and R-boats before World War II.

Rod rigging looks beautiful, but it is expensive, and is very unreliable unless regularly checked by X ray, for it tends to fatigue and let go without warning. Further, it is most difficult to handle, and must be stored very carefully, without bending. Therefore it seems to me totally unacceptable on a cruising boat.

1 by 19

For standing rigging, 1 by 19 is the best wire construction; diameter for diameter and weight for weight, it results in the strongest wire available today. It is constructed with a core of one strand, then seven strands rotating around the core counterclockwise, then an outer layer of eleven strands rotating clockwise. The result is a wire that is stiff and has very little stretch because it has little or no tendency to unlay, even under strain. The great difficulty with 1 by 19 is that it is almost impossible to splice. There are a few people who make splices of this wire that are practically works of art, but they are hard to find and expensive to hire. Hence 1 by 19 is usually attached to some sort of special terminal. Terminal ends will be discussed shortly.

7 by 7

The other standard wire construction for standing rigging is 7 by 7. It consists of seven strands, of seven wires each; six outer strands are wrapped clockwise around a center core, which is of course one strand made up of seven wires. Under load, this wire has a slight tendency to unlay, and it has appreciably more stretch than the 1 by 19. Further, it is not as strong (see Table IV, Appendix). However, it does have two advantages; it is slightly more flexible, and it is comparatively easy to splice. This wire is ideally used where rigging must be spliced around the mast or around a deadeye, or indeed wherever it is desired for any reason to splice the ends.

7 by 19

The standard flexible wire construction is 7 by 19. It consists of seven strands, of nineteen wires each—one strand for the core and six strands wrapped around it. Because there are 133 individual wires, it is

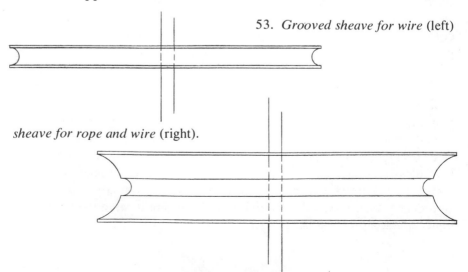

53. *Grooved sheave for wire* (left)

sheave for rope and wire (right).

27. *Spliced shroud anchorages, deadeyes, and lanyards.* (*Norman Fortier*)

impossible to apply a good coating of zinc to galvanize the wire; hence I recommend always using stainless 7 by 19. This wire is very easy to handle, as it bends very readily; it can be spliced into a rope tail without too much difficulty, and an eye splice is no trouble at all. If this wire is to be put over a sheave, the diameter of the sheave should be twenty times that of the wire, or perhaps even slightly larger. Also, the sheave should be grooved to support the wire (Drawing 53).

WIRE END FITTINGS

There are various methods of securing the ends of wire to whatever it must be attached to. The wire can be spliced (Photo 27), socketed, swaged to a terminal, bent around a thimble and held with a compression fitting, or inserted in a cone-type terminal. With whatever method is chosen—poured socket, swage, or cone—either eye fittings or fork (jam) fittings can be used, as circumstances require. It should be remembered that eye fittings are stronger than fork fittings.

Splicing

Wire can be placed around a thimble, mast, or deadeye and spliced back into itself. This is the old standard method of securing the ends of wire. Splicing is considered a great mystery these days, almost akin to black magic, but in reality it is relatively simple. There are probably as many different methods of splicing wire as there are riggers in the world. Descriptions of some of these methods can be found in a book on the subject. Then all the learner needs is a splicing clamp, a good flat spike, a hollow spike, pliers, and some wire, preferably 3/16-inch 7 by 19. After five or six practice splices, the mystery disappears.

The amateur should not attempt to splice 1 by 19 wire, which even the professional finds difficult to work with. On the other hand, 7 by 19 halyard wire should, in my estimation, always be spliced, as otherwise the wire tends to fatigue at the hard spot where it enters the end fitting.

If standing rigging is to be spliced, a good heavy thimble should be used. Solid thimbles, which are preferable by far, are hard to find today and expensive. A bent sheet-metal thimble tends to distort under load, flattens, and bends the end of the wire in too tight a circle, thus crippling the wire. Many splices break right across the head because of this crippling. If solid thimbles cannot be obtained, a common dodge is to use a thimble one or two sizes larger than the wire. Then the wire is served with marline where it touches the thimble. This procedure brings the diameter of the wire up to the diameter of the shoulder of the thimble (Drawing 54), making it fit snugly, so that it obtains the support it should have.

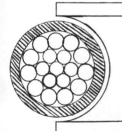

54. *Serving wire to make it fit a thimble.*

Sockets

Poured sockets, also known as hot sockets, constitute the oldest type of wire terminal ever created. I have noted them on the Brooklyn Bridge, built in 1882. They are a staple in the construction industry and were used on yachts extensively until recent times. Galvanized wire requires a galvanized socket; stainless wire requires a bronze socket.

The installation procedure involves several steps. First, the end of the wire is cleaned with a mixture of hydrochloric or nitric acid. The action of the acid is neutralized by rinsing with a base (I generally use ammonia) and the wire is then inserted into the socket. The manufacturers all say it is only necessary to basket, or spread, the wire, but with 1 by 19 I prefer to bend back the outer eleven strands into a good birdcage.

The wire is then pulled down until its end is just flush with base of the socket. In the meantime a pot of zinc has been heated with a blowtorch, a welding torch, a charcoal fire with a bellows, or what-have-you. The socket should then be warmed to 180 degrees with a blowtorch, and a piece of asbestos wicking should be secured around its base. The socket is now filled with the zinc and allowed to cool, and all is well. One should not conduct this operation barefooted or in shorts, as hot zinc can cause a very nasty burn.

The one disadvantage of this type of terminal is that it is a casting, and these castings have been known to crack. A failure of this sort caused me to lose the entire rig of *Iolaire,* when the head-stay terminal broke across the jaws. The possibility of such an occurrence can be minimized if one remembers that an eye terminal is much stronger than a jaw terminal and that some manufacturers make much better terminals than others. Also, terminals should be inspected carefully for imperfections before installation. In any event, this type of end fitting is fast disappearing, as Merriman, the major supplier of this item to the yachting industry, has discontinued making it. Thus in the future, it will probably be used only on large yachts which require the large commercial-size terminals.

Swage Terminals

The swage terminal (Photo 28) was introduced before World War II by American Chain and Cable as the end terminal for rigging wire in yachts and aircraft. Today many other manufacturers of wire, both in America and in Europe, also offer it. Basically, it is a hollow stainless-steel tube which is cold-rolled with tremendous pressure into the wire. For many years it was regarded as the ultimate in end fittings for wire.

The first swage terminals installed in yachts served admirably with very few instances of failure from 1937 or 1938 until the early 1950's. At that point, many of them developed cracks. Bob Hall, then head engineer at Grumman aircraft, tested numerous samples of this type of terminal, new and cracked, to the point of failure, with very inconclusive results. Some of the fittings which appeared to be not too badly cracked failed under a comparatively light load, while others which seemed to be in very bad shape stood almost the full amount of load.

The only thing that can be said about this problem is that when a crack becomes visible, the fitting should be changed. One can find cracks by polishing the fittings and examining them with a magnifying glass. Or the rigging can be sent to a lab to be X-rayed—an expensive undertaking. Or a good machine shop can carry out one of the various spot-check procedures in which the fitting is polished and painted with a special solution that reveals cracks in brilliant color.

The strength of this fitting is also affected by the manner in which it is placed on the wire. Originally this procedure was in the hands of a few licensed representatives of the manufacturer. The fittings were installed with a big expensive hydraulic tool, run by an experienced operator. If an inexperienced person uses this machine, and runs the terminal through the die too often, the fitting is ruined before it is installed on the boat.

Presently, many small yards use small portable swaging machines through which the fitting must be run a number of times. Supposedly they produce just as good a job as does the big hydraulic machine, but my experience leads me to distrust swage fittings put in by these small machines. They appear fine at the time of installation but seem to be much more prone to early cracking than those put on by the big machine.

This type of fitting stands up well in northern climates. Normally, correctly installed, it lasts for eight to ten years and up. However, in the tropics if no protection is given, the ends usually crack within two or three years. If the ends are cleaned out with rust remover and sealed with paint, and if the upper end is protected with a wax seam compound to keep the water out, the fitting will last much longer. However, in the tropics even the best-maintained fittings seldom seem to last more than six to eight years.

The swage terminal is undoubtedly the most popular type of rigging terminal used today, and it does give excellent service, provided that it is carefully installed by competent personnel, and is regularly checked thereafter.

Crimp Fittings

I use the term "crimp fitting" for the type of device in which the wire is bent around a thimble and then a soft metal sleeve is placed around the ends of the wire and compressed under tremendous pressure. There are many varieties of this fitting under many names, among them Nicropress (Photo 28) and Talurit, but all are based on the same essential principle. The crimping is done either mechanically, by a tool that resembles a cutter with grooved jaws, or—for larger sizes—by a hydraulic press. Especially in the small sizes, the sleeves appear to stand

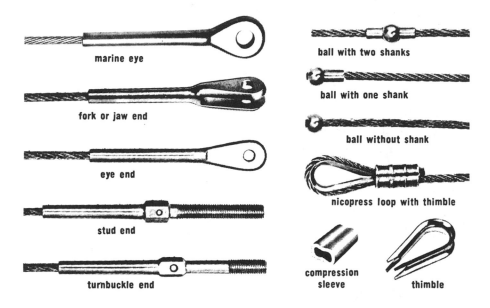

28. *Swage terminals and Nicropress. (D. M. Street)*

up admirably, and the small sizes are easy to install as well. For sleeves of up to ½ inch in diameter, the tool required is no longer than a normal bolt cutter, and in fact the jaws can be purchased and installed in a bolt cutter. Thus a small yacht could carry a coil of wire, sleeves of the correct size, and the tool, and be completely independent of riggers.

However, there is a disadvantage in this type of fitting: the wire must be bent around the thimble, a situation which 1 by 19 wire, because of its stiffness does not like. Bending 1 by 19 wire of sizes larger than 5/16 inch is difficult, and once 7/16 or 4 inch is reached, bending becomes a major project that can be done only with the help of a big specially built splicing vise (rigging clamp). Also, while a heavy sheet-metal stainless thimble seems to be efficient for the smaller sizes of wire, for the larger sizes a solid thimble is absolutely essential, but quite frankly where to purchase solid thimbles today is beyond me. I keep my eyes open for boats being rerigged, and whenever I spot a solid thimble in the old rigging, I purchase the rigging as is, and cut the thimble out, to be put in my emergency goody box.

There have been some cases in which this type of fitting failed because the wire pulled out, and therefore at present many manufacturers recommend that two sleeves be placed on the wire, one behind the other (Drawing 55).

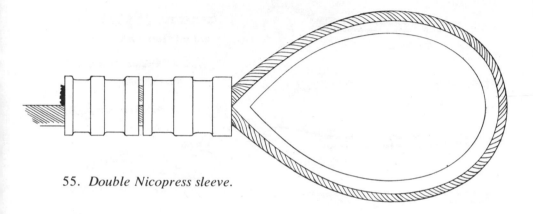

55. *Double Nicopress sleeve.*

Cone Terminals

The end fittings which I refer to as "cone terminals" are manufactured in the United States under the name Electroline and in England under the name Norseman. In these, the wire is first slipped through a stainless-steel cone fitting and then spread, and a soft metal cone is slipped over the core of the wire. The wire is next slipped back into the outer cone and a plug is inserted and screwed up tight. The whole operation is very simple and can be done with nothing more than two wrenches, or better yet, with a wrench and a vise. Even wire as large as ¼ inch can be handled with nothing more than a couple of wrenches and a vise. It is a great advantage to be able to order a bucketful of fittings and a coil of wire and rerig an entire boat.

The British version of these fittings is popular in Europe and will, I think, gain acceptance in the near future in the United States. At present these fittings are not very well liked in the United States. For one thing, there have been a number of failures with the American product, which is made by casting. The lack of popularity of the cone fitting may also be the result of poor marketing, unfamiliarity with the product, and the fact that one of the standard sizes used on large American cruising boats—$7/16$-inch diameter—is not manufactured by the European company, and can be obtained only on special order, which may be expensive and time-consuming. The other sizes can be purchased directly from stock.

The British fittings, which are machined out of solid stainless rolled stock, have had few, if any, failures. The manufacturer supplies an excellent set of instructions with each fitting; if these are followed, there is little danger of the casing exploding or stripping the thread. This is, in my view, an almost foolproof fitting.

Jaw Versus Eye in End Fittings

Basically, a fork (jaw) fitting is weaker than an eye fitting. For one thing, the relatively narrow width of the jaw restricts the size of the fitting it can be connected to. This is especially apparent with the Norseman product; because the opening in the jaw is very narrow, there is a tendency to try to force the jaw over attachments that are too thick for it, thereby stretching the jaw and weakening the installation.

The other disadvantage of the Norseman jaw fitting is that the pin is really a threaded machine screw rather than the clevis pin with a cotter key, normally used in jaw fittings. It is true that the screw should be put in with lock tight, and the threads spread with a center punch, and that if this is done there is little chance of the pin working out. However, if this procedure is effectively followed, how is the rig taken apart in the fall? If it is not correctly followed, the pin works out and rig goes overboard—as happened to one boat in Trinidad, and as almost happened to me with my bowsprit. Thus I would strongly advise using an eye fitting with a clevis pin whenever possible.

TURNBUCKLES (RIGGING SCREWS, BOTTLE SCREWS)

"Turnbuckle," "rigging screw," and "bottle screw" are names used by different people for what is essentially the same device. In years gone by, the cruising yachtsman relied on deadeyes and lanyards, and devoted a tremendous amount of time to tightening them after they had been stretched in a blow. They were picturesque, and good in that practically anywhere in the world one could find a carpenter to carve out another deadeye, and spare lanyard could always be carried; but they were not very efficient, and would be totally useless in holding a modern Marconi rig aloft. Today they are seldom seen except on character boats and in museums.

Before World War II people used whatever was on hand in the way of a turnbuckle, and matching the end of the turnbuckle to the wire terminal end or splice was always a major project. Half of the time spent rigging the boat was devoted to making things fit. In the United States just prior to and after World War II, turnbuckles from most manufacturers became quite standardized, with jaw ends of the correct size to match up with swage terminals and bronze hot sockets. There was still a difficulty in that swage terminals of the aircraft type did not quite match up with marine turnbuckles.

Now that England is planning to go metric, the manufacturers of wire, terminal ends, and turnbuckles, are trying to standardize. They have not yet been successful, and an additional complication is the fact that their standardization does not correspond to American standardization.

Another problem concerning turnbuckles has developed recently. Years ago one could look at the body of a turnbuckle and immediately know its strength. However, there are now so many new alloys on the market, that frequently a bad guess is made. The first time I saw a Superston turnbuckle, I thought someone had made a mistake and selected the wrong size for the boat. However, after much argument the catalog was brought out and I was shown to be in error, as the Superston turnbuckle is roughly 20 percent stronger than the standard good bronze turnbuckle of the same dimensions. Thus one usually chooses Superston turnbuckles that are one size below what one would think of as the correct size.

There are many manufacturers of turnbuckles, and most of them are good. One must be sure to select turnbuckles of the proper size for the end fittings with which they will be used. Otherwise many days will be spent in drilling or bushing. Drilling is the easiest way to reconcile mismatched parts, but also the most dangerous, as frequently if a fitting is drilled out to take a larger pin, there will not be enough material left around the edges to maintain its strength and integrity. Probably a better procedure is to install a smaller pin and bush the turnbuckle as necessary.

The most important thing to remember when installing turnbuckles is that each and every one must be accompanied by a toggle (Photo 29). If the best turnbuckle made by man is installed without a toggle, so that it has universal movement fore and aft and athwartships, it is bound to fail. Sooner or later it will begin to bend and fatigue on its lower half, and eventually, all of a sudden, it will let go.

29. Turnbuckle and toggle. (Lewmar)

Since there are some places in the world where for some reason toggles are scarce, spares should always be carried. They are always useful for making up a few inches if someone has mistakenly made a stay too short. Also, toggles should be installed at both the top and the bottom of the head stay and the staysail stay, to compensate for the athwartship and the fore-and-aft sag of these stays.

V

Running Rigging

While standing rigging is always made of wire, running rigging may be of wire, of line, or of a combination of both. Some European yachtsmen, especially before the days of Dacron, used wire sheets with no rope tails. It proved that they were tough. Standing in a cockpit with his feet among fifty feet of rusty galvanized wire, and wire sheets in his hands, the skipper would sound out "Lee ho," throw the sheet off the winch, and jump clear of the cockpit before a coil of wire wrapped around his leg and tore it off—that was European ocean racing. Happily, with the advent of synthetics, wire sheets have been discarded for all except the largest ocean racers.

Synthetics have replaced manila, Italian hemp, and cotton line almost entirely. Dacron and nylon are the two most popular synthetics; polypropylene is less expensive but also less strong and seems to be self-destructive with age and use. Nylon will stretch as much as 50 percent before breaking. Its stretching qualities make it excellent for anchor or docking line. However, trying to trim or hoist a sail with nylon line would be futile. Hence, Dacron, whose stretch is relatively slight, is usually preferred for sheets.

DACRON

Dacron is so strong that it is used for all sheets and guys (occasionally, large boats will use wire for the spinnaker-pole after guys when carrying it forward in a breeze). On some boats even wire halyards have been replaced by prestretched Dacron, a practice I don't approve of, for reasons given later in the chapter. Dacron is light and flexible, stretches very little under strain (although still too much for some purposes), and does not shrink as it dries, or swell and jam its blocks when wet. Finally, like nylon, it will not rot if stored wet. There are several grades of Dacron, and they vary drastically from manufacturer to manufacturer. Some Dacron is excellent line for sheets, but is of such hard lay that it is almost impossible to splice. Some manufacturers put out soft lay, and some make what is referred to as spun Dacron rather than filament Dacron. Though softer and easier to handle, spun Dacron does not have the strength of filament Dacron.

Dacron line is available in several forms: three-strand, three-strand preformed, braided, and braided Dacron jacket and nylon core, usually sold under the name of Samson Braid. The plain three-strand line is the most common. It is excellent, but tends to unravel when cut. The three-strand preformed is similar to preformed wire in that it has no tendency to unravel and is therefore much easier to splice. It also has a lower stretch factor than the plain three-strand. Regular braided Dacron has no special advantages and is difficult to eye-splice, unless one is experienced at handling it. The splice weakens the line (despite what the manufacturers say to the contrary), and if it develops a chafe spot it cannot be cut and long- or short-spliced. The Samson Braid has the great advantage of being very much stronger, diameter for diameter, than Dacron three-strand. If the strengths of wire, Dacron three-strand, and Samson Braid are compared (Table IV, Appendix), it will be easily seen why so many boats are using Samson Braid for sheets and guys. On my own boat, ½-inch Dacron was too light for my genoa sheets, ⅝-inch was too thick to handle easily, ⁹⁄₁₆-inch too difficult to obtain. I found some ½-inch Samson Braid that has given me years of service with no sign of stretch. Actually, ⅜-inch Samson Braid is strong enough for most jobs on medium-sized cruising boats, but not practical because it is very difficult to pull on a line that has a diameter smaller than ½ inch. For maximum strength, this line should be knotted, since a splice substantially reduces its strength unless perfectly made. On most boats today, the sheets are knotted into the clew of the headsails to allow for ease of handling.

WIRE

Where wire running rigging is required—for halyards, certain guys, and the like—it is folly to use anything but 7 by 19 stainless. Some racing yachtsmen prefer galvanized backstay runners because galvanized wire is softer and less likely to kink than stainless, but it will last one season only. If the sheaves are of sufficient diameter (at least twenty times the diameter of the wire), stainless will last many years. *Iolaire*'s main halyard has been in constant use for eighteen years, win-

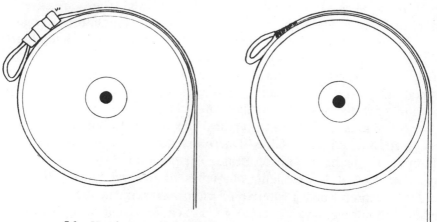

56. *Hard spot where Nicopress runs through the sheave.*

ter and summer, and is still in use. If the sheave is too small, or if the wire is allowed to take a sharp bend because a Nicopress or a splice has been permitted to run into the sheave Drawing 56), the wire will sometimes last only a few weeks.

One or two leading designers refuse to allow anything but galvanized wire to be used for main halyards. Their contention is that under a heavy load, stainless-steel wire work hardens in the halyard sheave and fails. In more than one case the result has been a most embarrassing failure in front of the whole racing fleet on an almost new boat. However, looking at the success *Iolaire* has had with stainless wire, I wonder if perhaps in an effort to save weight they may have cut everything a little too fine and used wire or a sheave, or both, of too small a diameter. *Iolaire*'s halyard is slightly oversize, but seems well worth the weight and windage.

A wire halyard secured to a self-stowing reel halyard winch generally presents no problem if it is just a straight piece of wire, without a rope tail. However, on large boats with two-part halyards this arrangement sometimes results in a rather large drum. One method of minimizing the size of the drum is to long-splice a piece of ⅛-inch wire into a piece of ¼-inch wire, carefully figuring lengths so that the splice and a few turns of ¼-inch wire are on the drum even when the trysail is up.

Self-stowing reel halyard winches are seldom used for jib and spinnaker halyards because such winches are too slow in the initial stages of hoisting; instead, top-action winches are used (see section on winches). As a result, it is necessary to splice a rope tail onto the wire halyard.

There is considerable debate concerning the relative merits of positioning the splice above the winch, so that the splice is not distorted, or below the winch, so that all the strain is taken by the wire on the winch. The latter method seems safer. Whether the rope is spliced to the wire or the wire to the rope is largely a matter of personal preference.

HALYARD SHACKLES

Wire of course cannot be knotted into the head of a sail. There must be a shackle—a key shackle (Photo 30), a snap shackle (Photo 31), or a double-threaded shackle (Photo 32)—to which the wire can be secured.

The Merriman headboard shackle (Photo 32) is exceptionally good because even if during long periods at sea the shackle does become unthreaded from the inner end, it is almost impossible for the second thread, at the outer end, to work its way across the headboard and thread itself out through the side of the shackle.

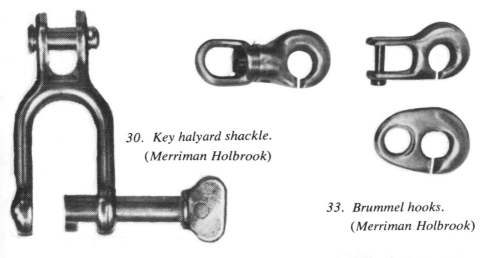

30. *Key halyard shackle.*
(Merriman Holbrook)

33. *Brummel hooks.*
(Merriman Holbrook)

31. *Snap halyard shackle.*
(Merriman Holbrook)

32. *Double-threaded halyard shackle.*
(Merriman Holbrook)

The wire should be run through a thimble (Drawing 57) so that it will not be crippled by taking too great a bend. It can be spliced on a Nicopress or swage, or secured by a Norseman fitting. All three are satisfactory provided the fitting of the splice is not allowed to touch the halyard sheave. If it does, the sharp bend will cripple the wire, as we have seen.

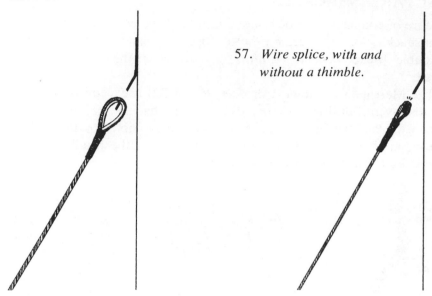

57. *Wire splice, with and without a thimble.*

BRUMMEL HOOKS

On some boats, halyards are secured by brummel hooks (Photo 33). These may be fine for small-boat halyards and for hoisting flags, but they are not satisfactory for headsails that are going to carry a lot of strain. One boat which I sailed on had brummel hooks on the mizzen-staysail halyard; after the third one exploded and put a dent in the teak deck, they were discarded. On one large west-coast ocean racer, they were found to be wonderful in light and moderate weather, but the crew claimed that in heavy weather they put on tin helmets because when the brummel hooks started exploding it was like shrapnel flying around the boat.

WINCHES

Winches have been used for hundreds of years on sailing vessels. In ancient times there was at least an anchor windlass, and it was sometimes used to hoist the yards, but only in recent times did the seamen of the world begin to use winches extensively. Villiers points out that Captain J. C. B. Jarvis, who was active in the late nineteenth century, installed brace winches on the square-rigger *Duntrune,* but succeeding skippers refused to do so despite the fact that one man with a winch could do as much as a number of men with block and tackle. The winch is more efficient than block and tackle because in a well-designed winch, the friction loss is minimal even with maximum power. Modern geared winches almost always have a mechanical advantage of at least 18 to 1. In the fancy new two-speed winches, the ratio often goes up to 48 to 1, or even 96 to 1. With block and tackle it is inefficient to have a ratio of more than 6 to 1, and even then the friction loss brings the effective ratio down to 5 to 1 or less.

As these figures show, winches enable a small individual to develop tremendous power. Even a small woman can apply a pull of 50 pounds if she is braced; thus with a 48-to-1 winch, even allowing for friction loss, she can put more than one ton of pull on the sheet. Similarly, with a large man, whose pull would be about 200 pounds, the winch would develop 9,600 pounds of pull, of which 600 might be lost to friction. Four big men hauling fully braced on four cockpit winches could exert a total pull of 36,000 pounds, which is more than the average forty-foot boat weighs. Thus if the winches and lead blocks are well tied down, a boat could literally pull herself by her own bootstraps!

Yachting World, during the 1969 London boat show, conducted an interesting experiment. An 8CR winch—often used on British ocean racers—was installed on a pedestal, with a strain gauge attached to the end of the ½-inch Dacron line. Individuals and teams were urged to see what power they could develop. The interesting thing was that the big man was not the best man on the winch. The medium-sized man was the best, apparently because not being big, heavy, and able normally to force things, he carefully braced himself and cranked to greater advantage than his heavyweight counterpart. When the two teamed up, it was found to be best to have the big man tailing and the smaller man cranking, as otherwise the sheet tended to slip on the drum.

However, while this arrangement may be desirable for ocean racing, it is less applicable to cruising when the crew consists of husband and wife. The woman is not apt to be strong enough to crank the winch, nor—with a winch of small drum diameter—is she apt to be strong enough to tail up. On the other hand, if the drum diameter is large enough, even a child can tail. *Iolaire* has a Camper and Nicholsons type N winch with a mechanical advantage of 22 to 1, a drum diameter of 6 inches, and a drum height of 6 inches. Once the slack is taken in, six turns can be put around the drum and a six-year-old girl can tail while two men crank to flatten the genoa.

The increase in drum diameter reduces the amount of effort needed to tail up for a given sheet strain because it drastically affects the amount of bearing surface of line against the drum. A winch with a large drum diameter and good height but low power is therefore frequently more useful than a winch with a small diameter, small height, and tremendous power. There are many winches on the market today that will never stall out but need two people to tail up. Even more important, with these winches the strain on the tail is so great that it is difficult to ease the sheet gradually in heavy weather.

In winches for a cruising boat, ease of maintenance is essential. Some of the winches that are most popular for ocean racing must be disassembled, stripped, cleaned, greased, and reassembled after almost every long race. The cruising yachtsman should consider instead some of the older winches, which only need to be oiled every week and torn apart once a year.

For easy use, the largest possible winch should be installed. The limiting factors are space and pocketbook. The space alongside the cockpit of most boats restricts the size of the winch by limiting the base diameter. Further, some of the newest winches cost more than many boats, and there are moderate-sized ocean racers with twenty thousand dollars' worth of winches on deck. For yachtsmen who must watch cost, the secondhand market is a treasure grove. Many owners are removing perfectly good single-speed winches, and replacing them with two-speed winches. The single-speed models can then be bought at a reasonable price, often one-third their original cost. Good winches seem to last forever. The pawls and ratchets may wear, but basically they are repairable. *Iolaire* carriers two winches that were put on her when she was built in 1905, and they still work perfectly.

TOP ACTION VERSUS BOTTOM ACTION

Both top-action and bottom-action winches have advantages. In the bottom-action winch the handle can be kept on all the time, so when hauling is being done fast, the first turn can be thrown on the winch and when it is under tension, more turns can be thrown on while the handle is being cranked. But because only a third or at most a half of a revolution can be made at a time, the heavy hauling is slow. A top-action winch, on the other hand, is faster when the heavy hauling is being done, as the handle can be swung right around through 360 degrees, but the handle cannot be inserted until the turns are all on the winch.

Thus the top-action winch is best where much hauling needs to be done, with a heavy strain on the line—for the genoa sheets, for example, or for the headsail halyards on large boats. However, for backstay runner whips, staysail sheets, and halyards on boats of forty feet or less, the bottom-action winch is best, as the fast easy hauling can be done, more turns can be taken, and one can take in the last six inches or foot of line without having to look for a handle and fit it into place with one hand, while keeping tension on the line with the other. Bottom-action winches for headsail halyards are rare, but nevertheless advisable, in my view.

Geared winches are almost always of the top-action type except in out-and-out racing boats, such as the 5.5, 6, 8, and 12 meters. Once in a while one will see a bevel-drive winch, with the handle protruding through the side of the cockpit coaming (Photo 34). Winches of this type are excellent, having all the advantages of the bottom-action and top-action winches, but they will not fit on all boats, as a deep cockpit is required to accommodate the bevel drive.

34. Camper and Nicholsons level-drive winch. (D. M. Street)

35. *Coffee grinder.* (*Morris Rosenfeld*)

36. *Pepper grinder.* (*Paul Luke*)

There is also the remote-drive winch—the so-called coffee grinder. This type is excellent, giving good power. Further, since the sheet can be cleated on the top of the drum (Photo 35), one man can haul, cleat, and then crank, with no need for someone to tail up. Hence, this is a great winch for a cruising boat, provided one has the room to install it and the wherewithal to purchase this expensive piece of equipment. For those who do not have enough money or space for a coffee grinder, there is a smaller version called a pepper grinder (Photo 36), built by Paul Luke, East Boothbay, Maine.

REEL HALYARD WINCHES

Main halyards are now very commonly secured to reel winches; this arrangement is desirable in that one man can set all but the largest main, and since the halyard consists of one length of wire, there is no splice to pull out, and even with the trysail set there is wire on the drum. Many types of reel halyard winch are available—single-speed, two-speed, holding on ratchets, holding on brakes. Correctly designed, they are all good. The one essential in a reel halyard winch is that it should be designed so that one can lower the sail in the heaviest weather without putting the winch handle in the drum. All too often the winch handle has gotten away from the crew, and arms have been broken, skulls fractured, eyes lost. In one case, on the yawl *Kay* crossing the Atlantic for the 1960 Bermuda race, the main-halyard winch handle flew off; luckily, it did not hit anyone, but it did go through the 1¼-inch teak deck and end up in the main cabin.

One of the most popular of the expensive winches on the market today causes trouble because once the brake is let off, it automatically goes into the high-speed—low-power gear ratio, with the result that more than once the man on the winch has been thrown around the deck. To avoid this problem, on some boats the procedure is to put the handle on the winch, slack the brake, and hand-lower the main the first few feet; otherwise the boom would drop and break the stops off the end of the downhaul track. A better solution is to tie up the gooseneck with a sail stop, then let the halyard run, and lower the boom after the sail is down. A more permanent arrangement is to secure a heavy piece of shock cord to a pad eye on one side of the mast and snap it on to a pad eye on the other side of the mast when the main is set. Then when the main is dropped, the gooseneck slider will land on the shock cord and do no damage.

With all the claims made for the modern halyard winches, it must be remembered that some European yards have been making them on the same pattern for more than half a century. The resulting winch is not as small and clean-looking as its more modern sisters, but it certainly is plain, simple, powerful, and rugged, and it never wears out (Photo 37).

37. Abeking and Rasmussen halyard winch and winch table. (Laurie Legay)

De Vries Lentsch builds what is without a doubt the biggest, ugliest, and most effective halyard winch ever designed for the gaff rig (Photo 38). One man with one handle can hoist a gaff sail, cranking up both the throat and the peak halyards at the same time.

38. De Vries Lentsch halyard winch. (D. M. Street)

LOCATION OF HALYARD WINCHES

Positioning halyard winches is very important and often poorly done. On one forty-foot aluminum yawl which we delivered to Grenada, the main and mizzen halyard winches were placed at exactly the same height as the main and mizzen booms. Therefore, it was impossible to set the main or mizzen on port tack without luffing head to wind. This was especially aggravating because we did 1,700 miles on port tack.

Reel winches should be at a convenient height off the deck to facilitate easy cranking. Headsail winches should be mounted as low as possible. If they are low they are unlikely to foul the headsail sheets, and also, with one or two turns on the winch, the man hauling can be pulling up rather than down. Pulling down from above, a man cannot exert a force that exceeds his own weight, but pulling up, he can apply a force almost double his weight. Besides, the lower on the mast the winches can be mounted, the lower the center of gravity of the mast will be, and the greater the stability of the boat.

Some out-and-out racers have the halyard winches mounted on the deck aft of the mast. This is an excellent place for these winches on cruising boats also, if they have the space. Except in boats of over 40 feet LOA it is not necessary to have geared winches for headsails. The exact size of boat for which a geared halyard winch is necessary is variable, depending largely on the size of the fore-triangle and the size of the crew.

WINCH MATERIALS

Winches are constructed of a variety of materials: some old ones are made of steel; others are made of bronze, Tufnol, or light aluminum alloy.

Steel winches are satisfactory as long as they are simple and well maintained. *Westward* had some mounted on the bulwarks, made by Abeking and Rasmussen, that were of a very old pattern and simplicity itself (Drawing 58). They must be mounted with the axle horizontal, since the ratchet is gravity operated. These winches are ideal on a large boat with deep bulwarks. They are rugged, simple, and inexpensive.

The most common winches are of bronze, and the single-speed version will last forever with only an occasional oiling and an annual tearing down. The same does not hold true for the two-speed winches. One boat was sailed from New York to St. Thomas after her expensive winches had been stripped and greased. They were oiled once en route but received no further care. After arrival, the owner stripped the

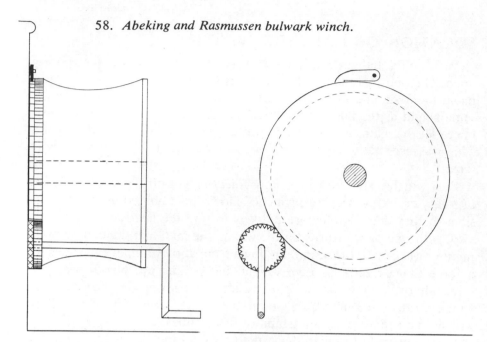

58. *Abeking and Rasmussen bulwark winch.*

winches and found the bearings so badly pitted that many had to be replaced. So check your winches, and learn how to strip them down and reassemble them, making sure, when stripping them, that all cockpit and bulwark scuppers are well plugged—ball bearings have a tendency to roll overboard.

Tufnol winches with bronze sleeves and moving parts have become increasingly popular in the small classes, but except on the smallest of the cruising boats, these winches are not suitable for heavy offshore work. When Tufnol winches are mounted, the winch base pad must be absolutely flat; otherwise the base of the winch will distort and throw everything out of line.

There are on the market today a number of so-called aluminum winches. They actually consist of aluminum drums and baseplates with bronze and/or stainless-steel inserts to take the bearings, gears, and ratchets. They are quite popular among the ocean-racing fraternity as there is a considerable saving in weight. However, aluminum and its alloys do not really like salt water; at best they tolerate it. Hence the aluminum winches must be very carefully maintained—stripped frequently, cleaned, greased, and so on. *Iolaire* has had one such winch for eleven years, and though it is excellent, it has used up more of my time than the other ten winches combined. Unless I were picking up a secondhand winch cheap, I would think twice about getting an alloy winch.

WINCH RATCHETS

Probably the greatest single cause of trouble in winches is ratchets not seating properly, or breaking. As a winch gets old, the ratchets become worn and do not seat properly. Sometimes an owner will discard a winch for this reason. This is folly, for if the springs and ratchets are replaced, and the seats remachined, the winch will be like new. Because of the likelihood of difficulty with ratchets and springs, a spare set of them should be kept on board for every winch. In some cases a piece of neoprene tubing will work in place of a faulty spring.

Occasionally ratchets will shear under load, and many accidents have been caused by this type of failure—broken arms, fractured skulls, and the like. For this reason, on winches of the coffee-grinder type where the sheet is cleated on top of the drum, the sheet should be removed from the top of the drum and secured to a cleat as soon as the sail is trimmed. Then, if the ratchet carries away, the handles will make only one or two turns before the sheet fetches up on the cleat. If it is cleated on top of the drum and the ratchet carries away, the handles will whirl like an airplane propeller.

This problem exists for any winch. Shearing of the ratchets will cause the handle to windmill unless the sheet is cleated, and even if it is cleated, the handle will spin one or two revolutions before snubbing up on the cleat. For this reason, pressure should be kept on the handle until the sheet is cleated. The handle should next be rotated until all the strain is transferred to the cleat, and then should be removed. Because of the danger of the ratchets breaking, the handle should never be left in a winch.

On many of the newer and most expensive winches, the problem of ratchet shearing has been minimized by good engineering. Formerly, on many winches the entire load was carried by a single ratchet. But on modern winches the load is generally carried by two, in some cases three, separate independent ratchets, so the chances of a ratchet shearing and the winch windmilling are minimal.

Some manufacturers are now installing extra-strong, extra-hard, stainless-steel ratchets and pawls. These are a mixed blessing, for though the stainless winch pawls will not break, they are so hard that they cause wear on their seats or gear trains. In time, the replacement of the gear train becomes necessary, and this is a major operation, whereas replacing worn ratchets or pawls is simple and inexpensive. What is gained in one direction is lost in another.

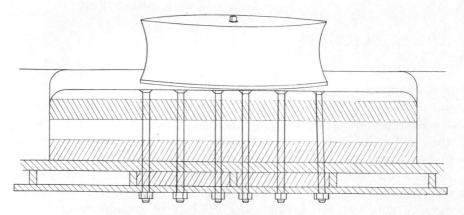

59. *Winch mounting spread across a number of beams, with pad underneath.*

MOUNTING WINCHES

Securing a winch to the deck is an expensive and difficult operation. One can gain some idea of the forces involved by taking the amount of the maximum line pull that can be exerted by a winch and doubling or tripling it. The resulting figure indicates the strain that will be put on the winch when one picks up a sea in the middle of the genoa going to windward in heavy weather. A small winch can be mounted on a pad built up of layers of wood glued together. The pad should be secured to the coaming and the deck, and then the winch should be bolted through the deck and through a pad under the deck. For a larger winch, a metal stand should be welded up, and the winch should be bolted to the stand and the stand bolted through the deck and to a pad that should bridge two or more deck beams (Drawing 59). It is quite a shock to see a winch break loose and a few square feet of deck and coaming come with it.

The winch's mounts must be built up high enough so that the sheet leads up to it (Drawing 60) or there will always be trouble with a riding

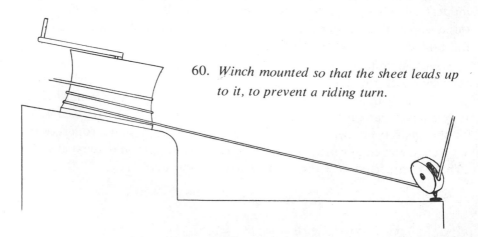

60. *Winch mounted so that the sheet leads up to it, to prevent a riding turn.*

39. *Hold-down block and snatch block secured to lifelines.* (*Laurie Legay*)

turn. Some boats with high bulwarks have a problem in that the winch pads would be high, unsightly, and weak if brought up to the level of the bulwark. Here the solution is to bolt the genoa track and/or pad eyes directly to the covering board alongside the bulwark, or—better yet—to sheet to the rail cap but have a few pad eyes along the covering board so that a snatch block can be hitched to the pad eyes and the sheet can be rove through it and held down (Photo 39).

On wooden masts, all halyard winches should be bolted through the entire mast. If that absolutely cannot be done, they should be secured by the largest screws possible.

On aluminum masts, the winches are usually secured to aluminum or stainless-steel winch tables, but if possible, some of the fastenings should go completely through and be secured on the inside of the mast with nuts and washers. Metal winch tables are better than wooden pads because the underside of the wood tends to remain damp, causing corrosion. One difficulty with metal winch tables is that frequently spar manufacturers will anodize the spar but not the tables, which therefore continually deteriorate. When ordering aluminum masts one must make sure that the winch tables are also anodized and painted with epoxy paint before installation.

To minimize corrosion, wooden and stainless-steel winch tables must be carefully insulated from aluminum spars with rubber gaskets and bedding compound. Many spar manufacturers are not insulating the stainless from the aluminum. This negligence causes some trouble up north, and in the tropics can easily result in a major disaster.

BLOCKS

Blocks come in all shapes and sizes, and are made of many different materials. The old-fashioned rope-strapped wooden block can be left to the collector; it is seldom seen today and is not really practical. The metal-strapped wooden block, which is most frequently seen today, is excellent and will last a lifetime, though if it has iron straps, they will eventually have to be replaced. When they are replaced, stainless-steel or bronze straps should be used. The same holds true for the pins; iron pins do not last very long.

Wooden blocks banging around on deck in a calm are particularly annoying, and also hard on the deck. Some builders design the eyes of their blocks so that they cannot lie flat on the deck; some place wire cages around them to get the same effect. Other solutions are to put a piece of hose around the shackle to hold the block upright, or to place a sword mat around the offending block. One or two manufacturers have a line of rubber-shelled blocks. These are excellent but expensive and not very long-lived, being prone to damage by foul leads. Snatch blocks on the rail for genoa sheets can be secured to the lifelines by short lengths of shock cord which will keep them from banging and also provide fairleads for the sheets (Photo 39).

In years gone by, the size of the block was proportional to the diameter of the line; for every ⅛ inch of line diameter, one inch of block measuring the width of the wooden cheek had to be added. Thus a ½-inch line needed a 4-inch block; a ⅝-inch line required a 5-inch block. These proportions were necessary because the old manila and hemp lines swelled when wet, and if the block was not large enough, the line would not only chafe but sometimes fail to run through the block. With synthetics this swelling is not a problem, and there is a temptation to go to smaller blocks. Careful thought should be given to this before doing so, as many of the blocks were designed in the days of manila lines and their strengths were figured accordingly. Dacron is almost double the strength of manila, so under heavy strain, there is the chance of exploding the block. The largest blocks practical should be used.

In England, Tufnol blocks are becoming more and more popular, and many manufacturers are making them. Some are excellent, others very poor. I have seen Tufnol blocks explode and upon examining them have discovered that what appeared to be a stainless-steel strap was nothing but a chrome-plated brass strap. One difficulty with Tufnol blocks in the tropics is that though they supposedly never need lubrication, they sometimes freeze up if they sit around unused. Freeing them is difficult because the pin bolt is so heavily riveted over that it is almost impossible to undo; oil only expands the Tufnol, making it jam tighter. Perhaps boiling in fresh water might dissolve the salt and free the block?

One of the great annoyances connected with blocks is that when you want a side-shackle block, all you can find is a front-shackle block, and when you want a front-shackle block all you can find is a side-shackle block. For many years it was almost impossible to purchase twisted shackles in the United States, but now these are available; it is possible to rotate a block 90 degrees by using a twisted shackle. Of great help also is the kind of eye which can be unbolted and rotated 90 degrees.

Photo 40 shows many types of blocks, with descriptions of their uses, advantages, and disadvantages.

40. *Various blocks. A. Block with reversible shackle. B. Fiddle block with snap shackle and built-in cam cleat—especially useful for boom vangs, downhauls, etc. C. Fiddle block with snap shackle—useful for light tackles. D. Closed cheek block. E. Open cheek block. F, G. Turning quarter-blocks. G has useful bail for snatch block. H. Low profile, adjustable sheet block. (Land's End Catalogue and D. M. Street)*

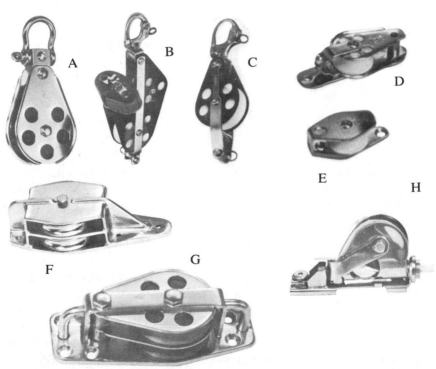

LEAD BLOCKS AND RESULTANT STRAIN

When rigging blocks, one should analyze the strain that is going to be put on them. Drawing 61 shows four different leads—jib topsail, genoa, genoa lead block, and halyard—with the strain for a line pull of 2,000 pounds calculated for each. It is evident that the same line pull results in very different loading on different blocks.

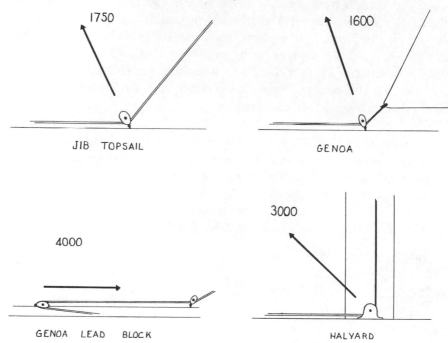

1750

JIB TOPSAIL

1600

GENOA

4000

GENOA LEAD BLOCK

3000

HALYARD

61. *Four different sheet leads, with the strain resulting for each from a line pull of 2,000 pounds.*

The genoa lead block causes much trouble because it must be a snatch block, and this type is inherently weaker than the cheek block. Many of these have exploded, doing damage to both boat and personnel. For this reason it is advisable to position a stanchion as shown in Drawing 62, so that if the block explodes, the stanchion will take the brunt of the force. Often the sheave pin in the lead block is not strong enough, and although it does not break, it distorts under load and increase the friction loss. The genoa lead shown in Drawing 62 is good as it makes it easier to move the sheet lead fore and aft and causes the sheet to lead to the winch at the same angle no matter where the rail-cap snatch block is placed. A rail-cap snatch block occasionally will foul a stanchion if the sheet is led directly to the winch (Drawing 63);

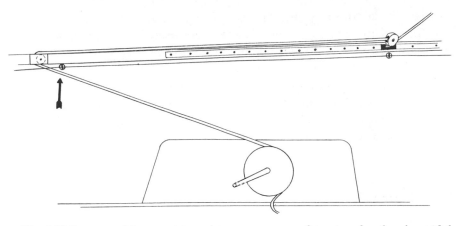

62. *Lifeline stanchion positioned to serve as a safety stop for the sheet if the quarter block fails.*

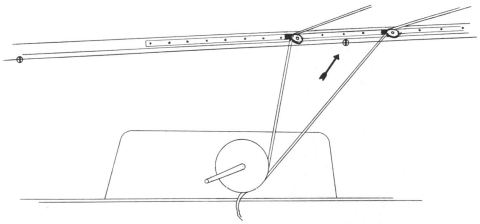

63. *If the sheet lead is moved, it must be passed around the stanchion without a quarter block.*

if the block is moved too far aft, it will tend to twist the bulwark off its mountings.

Often quarter blocks have an eye at the forward end through which a shackle can be secured to take a snatch block. Thus when switching sheets or setting spinnakers or what-have-you, one can lead two sheets to the same quarter block. This arrangement generally causes no problems on a sloop or cutter, but when mounting quarter blocks on a ketch or yawl, one should calculate their position carefully so that when a snatch block is snapped into the forward face of the quarter block it does not foul the intermediate shroud leading to the mizzen— a possibility often overlooked by even good yards.

There is seldom any problem with overstressing the main, mizzen, and foresail blocks and sheets. If the sheet used is of a large size, for ease in handling, the blocks and shackles must be correspondingly large to give an ample margin of safety. Even in ocean racers, booms usually break before the sheet and blocks fail. More and more ocean racers are installing full-width mainsheet travelers. These do increase the performance of the boat, but are so expensive and take up so much room that they are seldom found in a cruising boat.

SHEETS

MAINSHEETS

With roller reefing, the mainsheet must come from the end of the boom, so the entire strain of the mainsheet is placed on one shackle. The strain the shackle will have to withstand can be estimated by the following formula: the number of parts in the mainsheet multiplied by the line pull needed to flatten the main and multiplied by a safety factor of 5. If roller reefing is not used, the mainsheet can be led down from the middle of the boom. This arrangement distributes the strains better and provides support for the boom in the middle, and any bending strain will cause the boom to bend down and flatten the main.

There are arguments as to whether mainsheets should be single- or double-ended. Double ends seem preferable. With these, the point of maximum chafe does not occur at the same spot so frequently, and the mainsheet will last almost indefinitely. If there are two ends to haul on when jibing in a hurry, both ends of the mainsheet can be trimmed at once and the sail flattened quickly. Also, if the ends are cleated on opposite sides of the cockpit, the main can always be trimmed from the windward side of the boat and an end of the mainsheet is always within reach of the helmsman, whether he is sitting to windward or leeward. Drawing 64 shows details of mainsheet leads.

Main sheet cleats should be large, so that both cleating and uncleating can be accomplished with speed and ease.

MIZZEN SHEETS

Mizzen sheets are usually secured at two points near the end of the mizzen boom and then run forward to a cleat under the boom. On larger boats a winch mounted on the boom may be required for hauling in the last few inches of mizzen sheet.

STAYSAIL SHEETS

Staysail sheets are usually single-ended, if the staysail is loose-footed, and rigged to a winch. A winch is needed in even the smallest boats, as

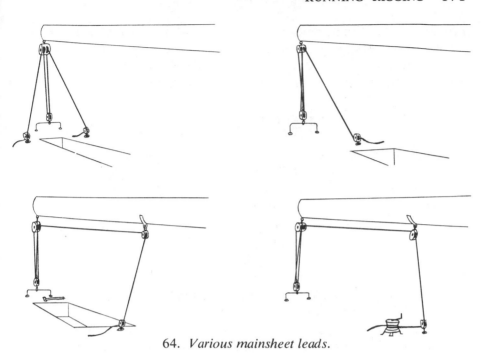

64. *Various mainsheet leads.*

without one it is impossible to get the staysail really flat, and a flat stay-sail is essential for going to windward. Occasionally an older boat will have instead a two-part staysail sheet, with one end to the cleat and a three-part tackle secured to the other end for hauling in the last few inches (Drawing 65). This arrangement is better than nothing, but the friction loss is much greater than with a winch. Also, in heavy weather, with waves washing the ends of the lines, the lee deck soon begins to look like a spaghetti factory. And there is no great saving, since the

65. *Two-part sheet with three-part tackle.*

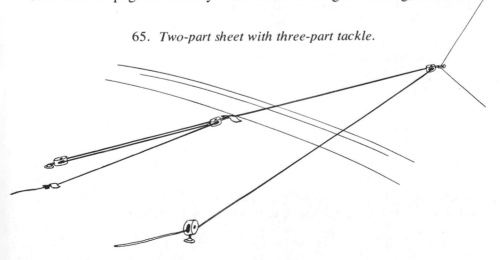

necessary deck fittings, blocks, line splices, and so on will cost nearly as much as two small sheet winches. Similarly, two small sheet winches for the staysail sheet usually cost less than a staysail boom and its fittings—another reason why a loose-footed staysail is preferred.

HALYARDS

All halyards not stowed on reel winches, with the exception of the spinnaker halyard, should be of wire, with rope tails. Spinnaker halyards can be made entirely of rope unless extended offshore passages are planned. In this case a piece of wire should be inserted at the point where they pass through the block, to take the chafe of a long passage.

It has been maintained that prestretched Dacron makes an adequate halyard. This is not so. Even wire has appreciable stretch. A test done by the Sheffield Testing Works shows that under 2,000 pounds of load a $5/16$-inch, 7 by 19 stainless wire fifty feet long will stretch 5 inches; under 5,000 pounds of load it will stretch 7.5 inches. Think of the effect of this stretching in sag and ruination of the genoa shape. The elongation in Dacron under these conditions would of course be much greater.

I sailed on one boat with prestretched Dacron halyards and after eight days came to the conclusion that it was like trying to make sails set by hoisting them with a very strong rubber band. To demonstrate this property in so-called prestretched Dacron, one can secure a length of it to the bow fitting, stretch it down the deck, secure a tackle to the other end, and lead the tackle to a good powerful winch. Next, the line should be placed under moderate tension. and thirty feet should be marked on it with a tape. Then as much pressure as possible should be applied on the winch, and the line should be remeasured to determine the amount of stretch. The result—the end of Dacron halyards for headsails.

Today, reel main-halyard winches are nearly universal on Marconi-rigged boats, but on the small sizes, up to 30 feet LOA, there are other methods that are satisfactory. One method is to end the wire on an open snatch block, such as Merriman's (catalog Fig. 370), and splice a line on the other end. Next the main is hauled up, and when it is almost hoisted, the line is hooked through a deck snatch block, such as Merriman's (catalog Fig. 370B), and then to the snatch block spliced to the wire; the result is a three-part purchase (Drawing 66). This is ample for hoisting a small main, especially if the boom is mounted on a track and has a downhaul. It is much easier to tighten the luff of the

main by taking down on the downhaul than by taking up on the halyard. Only in the largest sizes (about 65 feet luff measurement) is it
necessary to have a two-part halyard (usually rigged as in Drawing 67).

Gaff-rigged boats frequently have double-ended halyards with one
end taken to a tackle to tighten the last few feet. This is a complicated
and crude arrangement that loses most of its power through friction.
The parts necessary to hoist the gaff should be kept to a minimum.
When the gaff is almost up, the throat and peak halyards can be taken
to a winch and the sail sweated up the last few inches. As mentioned
before, the most suitable for this purpose is the De Vries Lentsch reel
winch which takes up both the throat and the peak halyards at the
same time.

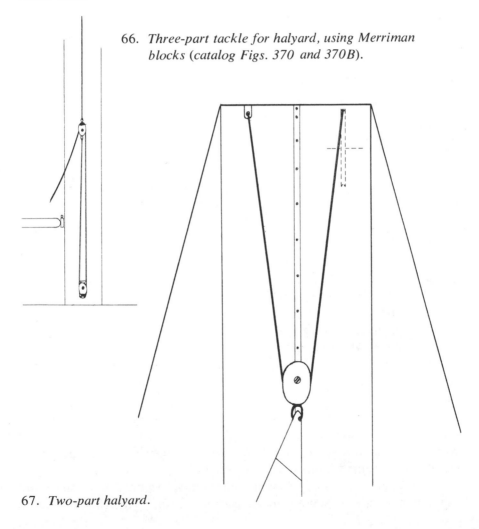

66. *Three-part tackle for halyard, using Merriman
blocks (catalog Figs. 370 and 370B).*

67. *Two-part halyard.*

HEADSAIL HALYARDS

Headsail halyards should be of single-part wire, with a rope tail, for minimum stretch. Every eighth of an inch of stretch means a little more sag in the luff of the jib, and this will hurt, if not ruin, the set of the sail.

For a roller-furling headsail, a two-part wire halyard is necessary. The strength of the halyard must be almost equal to the strength of the head stay because all the strain is carried by the luff of the jib, none by the head stay. The strain is so great that with a jib topsail of 48 feet on the luff, a ¼-inch, 7 by 19, single-part wire halyard stretches like a piece of nylon. If the wire diameter is increased to the point where it is sufficiently strong, the sheave diameter must be tremendous, and more important, the loading on the sheave pin and winch is so great, that it is difficult to keep the pin from bending and the pawls in the winch from shearing.

JIB SECURED TO BOWSPRIT TRAVELER

On some boats the jib is mounted on a traveler that rides around the bowsprit, and the halyard and jibstay are interconnected (Drawing 68). This arrangement is good in that one can hoist and lower the jib without going out on the bowsprit, but the rigging is complicated and the jib flogs around terribly when being hoisted or doused. I have never sailed with this rig, but those friends of mine who have are less than enthusiastic about it.

HALYARD FAIRLEADS

All halyards should be led through fairleads secured to the mast or the spreaders. In a two-spreader rig, there should be fairleads at both spreaders, since otherwise when sail is changed in a seaway the halyards are bound to get fouled of the spreader tips. The fairleads should be smooth and if possible should have plastic inserts to prevent them from chafing the rope tails of the halyards.

On many yachts, the steaming light is mounted on the forward face of the mast, midway between the upper and lower spreaders. This is a poor location, for frequently the halyards hook on the wrong side of the steaming light, and since the halyards are fed through fairleads on the upper and lower spreaders, it is almost impossible to clear this foul without going aloft. To eliminate this difficulty, the steaming light should be mounted at the same height as a spreader.

In the last few years, internal halyards have become more and more popular for ocean-racing yachts. Many cruising yachtsmen too are

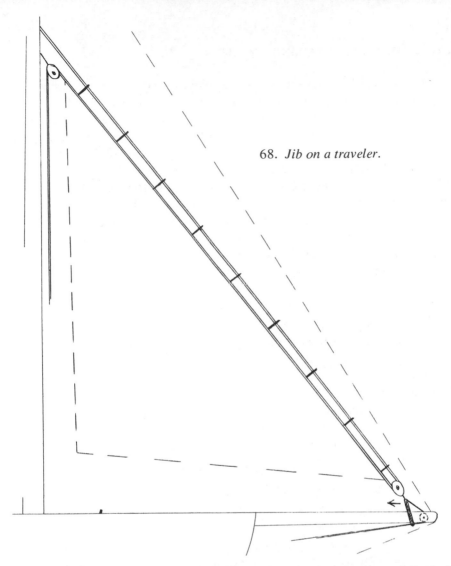

68. *Jib on a traveler.*

using them, as windage is drastically reduced, the chances of fouled halyards are minimized, and the problem of halyards tapping against the mast is almost eliminated. The disadvantage is that if a halyard breaks, it is almost impossible at sea to serve a spare halyard. Thus I believe that a mast with internal halyards should also have on its fitting external pad eyes, to which a block may be shackled and an emergency halyard rigged.

EMERGENCY HALYARDS

Every boat should have a method of sending a man aloft that does not involve the regular halyards, since frequently these may all be in use at a time when someone must go aloft to untangle something or to check for chafe. In the days when most ocean racers were seven-eighths rigged and had wooden spars, the standard Sparkman and Stephens installation was a hole drilled athwartships through the top of the spar above the main-halyard sheave, neatly rounded and lined with copper. A flag halyard was permanently reeved through the hole. If a man had to go aloft, the flag halyard was bent onto a piece of half-inch line, slightly longer than the mast, with a rat-tail eye worked into its end. The flag halyard was used as a messenger to pull the line aloft and feed the eyed end through the hole in the mast. The other end was secured to a block which had a line through it double the length of the mast. Once the gatline was fed through the mast and two-blocked to the masthead, the line was secured, and the block was ready for hoisting a man aloft in a boatswain's chair.

With masthead rigs this is not a very practical arrangement. Instead, a heavy lug is secured to the masthead fitting. This lug carries a large block, suitable for half-inch line, and is normally used as the flag-halyard block; but if a man needs to be sent aloft, all that has to be done is to lower the masthead flag, secure the flag halyard to the previously made-up gatline with the tapered eye splice on the end, and send the line aloft. Since this extra gatline can be used as an emergency main halyard or jib halyard as well as for hoisting a man aloft, a man need not be sent up immediately to rig a new halyard in case of a failure; the whole operation can be done from the deck, and the new permanent installation can be made when the weather calms down.

SECURING HALYARD ENDS

All halyard ends should be permanently secured to pad eyes at the foot of the mast to prevent them from getting lost and going up the mast. Further, there should be strong hold-downs for the snap-shackle ends of the halyards, so that when a halyard is not being used on a sail, it may be secured to a pad eye and set up tight. If poured sockets are used in the rigging, these will serve the purpose, since there is enough room in the socket to snap the shackle to secure the halyard. However, the shackle should not be snapped around the threaded portion of a turnbuckle, as it is bound to ruin the threads.

Antilles has by far the best system: stainless-steel rings secured with serving to the upper-shroud turnbuckle toggle.

GUYS AND VANGS

The terms "guy" and "vang" cause some confusion because they mean different things to different people. In general, in my book, a vang holds a boom down; a guy holds a boom or pole fore or aft.

GUYS

One of the most important lines on the boat, and certainly one that gives great peace of mind, is the main-boom fore guy, rigged when running broad off. On many boats this is a permanent piece of gear shackled to a fitting at the end of the main boom just forward of the mainsheet. If possible, this fitting should have separate bails for the mainsheet and the fore guy; sometimes the bail for the ballooner sheet is also incorporated into it.

These bails are really essential if extensive offshore work is to be done when going dead downwind. One of the things that complicated the jibing of *Antilles,* sailing across the Atlantic in 1969, was that there was only one bail under the boom. Thus on every jibe the boom had to be held amidships, while the snatch block was unsnapped and moved to the other side, so that it would not foul the mainsheet. This job required an extra man and much labor during the three-week passage. Had we had a fitting at the end of the main boom with separate bails for mainsheet, fore guy, and ballooner sheet, life would have been much simpler.

A wire rigged on the bail and secured to the gooseneck makes a fore guy that is always readily available. If it is not permanently rigged, the boom must be trimmed in whenever the fore guy is to be hitched to its end—a fine way to lose someone overboard in heavy weather. With the wire secured to the gooseneck, all one has to do is unhitch the forward end, snap a line onto it, run it forward to the bow chocks, and secure it. An easy technique is to ease the main boom more than desired, secure the fore guy, and then tighten the fore guy by taking in on the mainsheet.

On the mizzen, the mizzen-staysail sheet makes a good fore guy, except on large boats. There, the fore guy should be rigged as described above. The staysail boom often needs a fore guy to keep it from crashing around off the wind. A line should be secured to the after end of the staysail boom and rigged forward to the bowsprit end, or to the stemhead if there is no bowsprit. However, the boat with no bowsprit and a staysail boom that pivots on the stemhead is just out of luck—another reason for discarding the boomed staysail. Spinnaker and twin-jib poles always need a fore guy, preferably rigged to the end of the pole. Rigging the fore guy to the middle of the pole may be acceptable on small boats, but the bending strain is too great on large boats.

On gaff rigs, it is essential at sea to have a guy, or better two guys, to the gaff end. Then one guy can be led forward and the other aft; together they will keep the gaff from slatting around and shaking all the wind out of the sail.

41. Merlin *vang.* (*D. M. Street*)

VANGS

Vangs, kicking straps, go fasts, are all one and the same, all off-shoots of the vangs that were first used in the International 14's before the war to take the twist out of the mainsail. Their use has spread to other classes and they are now even found on ocean racers; their employment on cruising boats, however, is still all too rare. On some of the hot ocean racers, the vang is rigged in the same fashion as it is rigged in the dinghies—to the base of the mast (Photo 41). This arrangement is possible only if the boom is quite high and all the gear is very strong. Its advantage is that once it is set up, adjustments in the mainsheet do not necessitate adjusting the vang.

The more common method of rigging the vang is to fasten a strap around the boom, then bring a tackle down to a pad eye or stanchion on the rail. The pad eye must be through-bolted, and the vang should lead at a 45-degree angle from the stanchion or pad-eye base (Drawing 69). If it is led straight up, the vang may tear the pad eye out of the deck, bend or break the boom, and not flatten the sail. It is important,

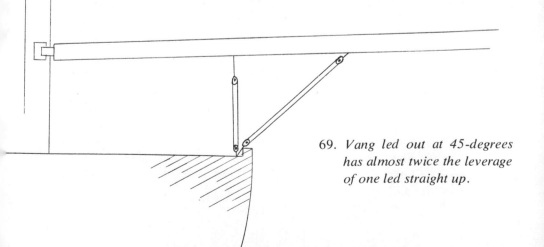

69. Vang led out at 45-degrees has almost twice the leverage of one led straight up.

too, that the vang not be led forward; rather, it should be in the same vertical plane as the boom. If the end of the boom dips on a roll and the vang is holding the boom forward as well as down, the boom will fold up in the middle. Also to forestall this occurrence, a preventer from the end of the main boom should be rigged and set up tight even when the boat is on a reach.

To ease the strains on the rig when sailing with the vang attached, it is best to use a length of very heavy shock cord or one of the standard rubber straps, or snubbers, to secure the boom to the vang tackle (Photo 42). Attachment of the vang to such a strap allows some come and go, and takes the shock loads off the rig. This device is well worth its cost. It can save a broken boom when someone makes a mistake.

Even on a cruising boat, a boom vang is worth the effort when sailing off the wind. By pulling down on the boom, it takes the twist out of the mainsail, thereby easing the strain on the upper spreader, reducing the chafe on the sail, and—since the twist is taken out of the upper portion of the sail—making possible the easing of the boom. This in turn will bring the boat up on her feet, make her go fast, and most im-

42. Rubber snubber. (W. Robinson)

portant, will wither, reduce, or eliminate the weather helm. On a rail-down reach on *Iolaire* the vang set up tight will result in a change from 10 or 15 degrees of weather helm to neutral or slight lee helm.

TOPPING LIFTS

In years gone by, in the days of the gaff rig, topping lifts were a problem. They were rigged from the throat to the boom end. There were two, one on each side of the sail. Once sail was set they had to be slacked off; they always chafed the sail; and when the boat was rolling in a swell, their blocks tried to demolish the mast, sails, hoops, and anything else in the area. With modern Marconi rigs, matters are relatively simple. On boats that do not have roller reefing, a 1 by 19 wire is shackled to the masthead fitting, and a few feet above the boom, is secured to a block. A line is secured to one side of the boom end, rove through the block at the end of the wire, then through a cheek block at the end of the boom, and thence forward to a cleat (Drawing 70). On larger boats a two- or three-part tackle may be installed (Drawing 71).

The booms rigged for roller reefing cause more trouble, and the experts definitely do not agree about what arrangement is best. Rod Stephens refuses to run the topping lift over a sheave at the head of the mast and instead always rigs boats that have roller reefing with a non-adjustable topping lift. It consists of a piece of wire shackled to the head of the mast and lashed to the end of the boom by six or seven turns of light Dacron, which is adjusted so that the topping lift is slacked when the main is flattened hard on the wind. The advantage of this method is that there is no wire going over sheaves aloft and breaking because of fatigue.

However, it has many disadvantages. When the sail is hoisted, the boom cannot be raised out of its gallows frame by the lift, and at one point starts thrashing around and threatening to demolish both the frame and the boom. Also, lowering sail on a reach when the boom has naturally lifted is difficult because when the halyard is cast off, the boom drops three or four feet and fetches up suddenly. Finally, if there is an adjustable topping lift, and a slight strain is taken on it before reefing, the sail rolls up without wrinkles. But if the boom is allowed to droop, as it is with the nonadjustable lift, wrinkles form unless someone is constantly pulling aft on the sail—a difficult process in heavy weather.

Rigging an adjustable topping lift is really not too great a problem. A 7 by 19 flexible wire is extended from the end of the boom to the

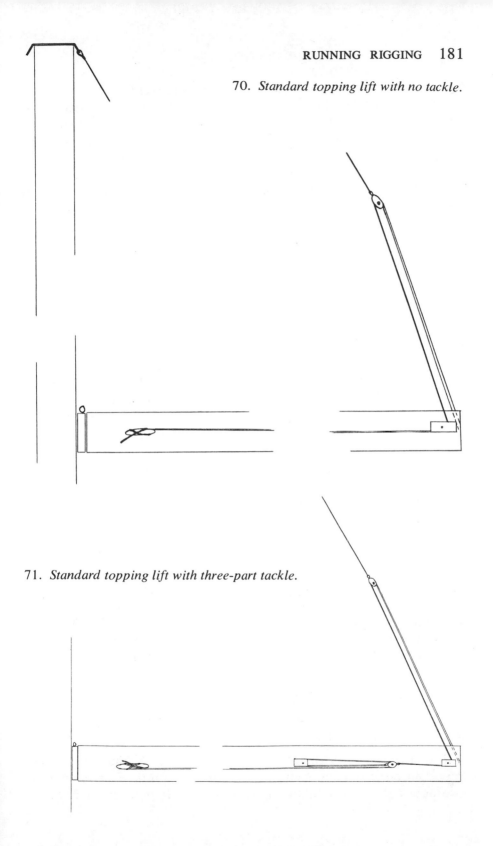

70. *Standard topping lift with no tackle.*

71. *Standard topping lift with three-part tackle.*

top of the mast, where it is passed through a swivel block with a large sheave and then led down to the deck. It can be brought down alongside the mast to a tackle that runs on a track to keep it from twisting. Or the end can be secured to a tackle and the tackle secured out by the rail near the lower shrouds. Another method is to run the wire over the sheave and back down parallel to the backstay and secure the tackle to the backstay pad eye. This has the advantage of putting the mainsheet and the topping lift close together. When the main is flattened, if the lift needs to be slacked, the mainsheet man can reach it without having to go forward.

TOPPING-LIFT CHAFE

If the wire topping lift is allowed to chafe on the leech of the sail, it will soon destroy the sail. For this reason, on many boats plastic-covered wire is used for the topping lift; on others, once the main is set, the lift is disconnected—not a good practice, for the main may have to be dropped suddenly. It is really quite simple to keep the lift away from the leech of the sail. A length of shock cord is fastened to the lower end of the topping lift and stretched until it is about one-third the length of the lift. Under tension, the shock cord is seized to the topping lift in three places. With this rig, as soon as the boom lifts under sail, the shock cord is under tension and makes a straight line from the masthead to the boom end, while the leech of the sail is in an arch to leeward of this line. Tall, narrow sails with considerable roach will still have trouble with the upper part of the leech fouling the topping lift each time the boat tacks. To solve this problem, one should place a thimble around the topping lift, seize a piece of shock cord around the thimble, then seize a polished bronze or stainless thimble to the backstay a fourth of the way down from the masthead. The next step is to slide the thimble up the topping lift until it is level with the eye on the backstay, then run the shock cord down the backstay, about a sixth of its length, pull tight, and serve to the backstay (Drawing 72). The topping lift will be kept tight against the backstay when going to windward but will have enough slack (from the shock cord stretching) to function off the wind.

REEFING GEAR

ROLLER REEFING

The price range for the roller-reefing gear is wide. Since it is a very important piece of equipment, the spending of a little extra money, as insurance against gear failure at an inopportune time, is advisable.

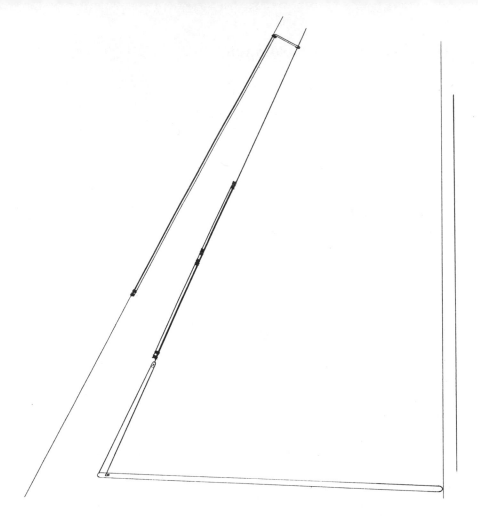

72. *Shock cord on the backstay keeps the topping lift clear of the leech, while shock cord secured to the topping lift under tension takes up slack as the boom is raised.*

One of my pet gripes about the roller-reefing gear is that often instead of a hexagonal stud, a round shaft with pins through it is used. It is said that the pin method is the best because as you slide the handle on, it rotates slightly; thus pins fit in their slots and you cannot lose the handle. True, it cannot drop off, but I have too often seen a strong man shear off the pins; then the handle rotates freely but the shaft does not turn. Admittedly, the handle can be lost if there is a hexagonal head on the stud, but one can always carry a spare handle, and in the engine tool kit there should be a wrench that in an emergency could fit on the head of the reefing gear.

One objection to roller-reefing gear is that the gooseneck must be set back from the mast, resulting in a rub-back dimension. This can be

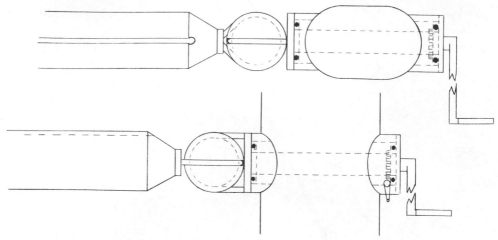

73. *Optimist roller-reefing gear. Since it has direct drive, the length of the handle determines its power; it is controlled by the ratchet assembly at the front end.*

eliminated by the use of what is now referred to as an "Optimist" reefing gear, as designed by Dick Carter. This gear was actually originated by L. Francis Herreshoff before World War II (Drawing 73). With this type of reefing gear the boom is permanently mounted on a universal joint, and a shaft goes through a tube in the mast to a handle forward of the mast. To reef, one pulls the handle out of the hole in the mast, and turns to windward. Once the desired amount of reef has been rolled in, one shoves the handle back into the hole in the mast, thereby keeping the boom from rolling the reef. This method of preventing the reef from rolling out is much simpler than some of those shown in recent boat shows by the popular manufacturers of aluminum spars and roller-reefing gears. The great advantage of this gear is that there is no rub-back dimension, the disadvantages are that one cannot have an adjustable downhaul on a slider, and one cannot reef with this type of gear when broad off. One must be either hard on the wind or almost hard on.

SLAB REEFING

Despite the attractions of roller reefing, there is much to be said for the old-fashioned slab reefing. The reefed sail can be made to set perfectly (Photo 43); two good men can tie in a reef as quickly as they can roll one; slab-reefing booms are infinitely cheaper; the boom can be lighter; and the mainsheet lead arrangements can be more flexible.

If reefing is to be done quickly and efficiently, the correct gear must be installed. A pad eye should be placed on one side of the outer end of the boom and a cheek block on the other, positioned so that they are just a few inches outboard of the clew reef earing. A winch should be on the underside of the boom near the mast, with a cleat. A long line should go from the pad eye, through a clew reef earing, back through the cheek block, and thence to the winch. Another line should run from the tack of the sail through the tack earing for the reef and back down to where it can be reached from the deck. On cruising boats, these lines can be left in permanently; on racing boats, messengers are left in and if it is decided to reef, the messengers are used to pull the lines through.

When the time comes to reef, the procedure is to take up on the topping lift, slack the main-boom downhaul, slack the halyard to a mark previously placed on it, secure the tack earing to the tack of the sail (three or four turns of ⅜-inch Dacron will suffice), then take up on the clew earing by means of the line to the winch under the boom, crank away until it is two-blocked, cleat it down, tie in the reef points, heave away on the main boom downhaul, and slack the topping lift.

43. Iolaire *reefed main; the tied-in reef is just as good as a rolled-in one.* (*D. M. Street*)

Some people prefer reef points that are permanently attached to the sail. They are easier to rig, but it is difficult to get all the points tied with the same tension, and if one reef point is missed when a reef is shaken out, there will be a torn sail. Lacing lines are almost as fast if they are previously made up of the right length. One person starts at the end of the boom, the other at the mast, and the two lengths are joined in the middle. In another method, a red patch is sewn as a marker around the middle reef eye, and a red ribbon is sewn at the mid-point of the lacing line. Half the lacing line is threaded through the middle reef eye, and then one person starts threading the lacing line through the reef eyes working aft toward the clew, while another does the same working forward toward the tack.

However, by far the best method is to keep a lacing line permanently in the sail, threaded from port to starboard through alternate reef eyes (Drawing 74). Hooks are put on the boom. Clew and tack earings are hauled down in the normal fashion, the lacing line that is already rigged is slipped over the hooks and sweated up, and all is finished.

These methods are rapid and practical as long as the gear is there, the lines have been cut to the correct lengths, and the fittings have been installed as necessary.

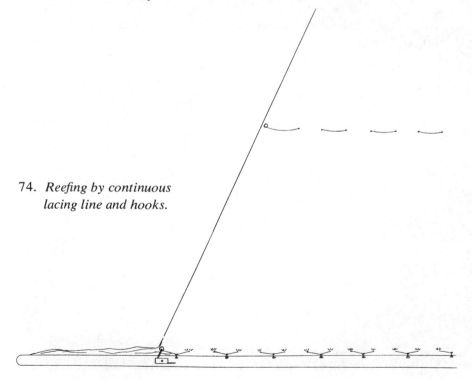

74. *Reefing by continuous
lacing line and hooks.*

TACKLES

In days gone by, a good man had innumerable ways of using tackles. By rigging a tackle on a tackle, and by various other methods, he could do practically everything with them. Now most of this work is done by winches, but tackles still have many functions.

Because of the powerful winches available, many yachtsmen prefer to sheet trysails as they do the genoa—with a heavy sheet going into the clew, through a block, and directly to the winch. However, I prefer to use a four-part tackle leading to the quarters of the boat. With this arrangement, the windward tackle is cinched up tight before tacking and the trysail never flogs when tacking. Even in heavy weather, two men can always control the trysail without the aid of a winch, while if a sheet is led directly to the winch, and the winch man is careless, a turn is lost, and the trysail starts flogging. A flogging trysail is enough to demolish a boat or seriously injure someone.

Tackles are extremely useful in other ways as well. Indeed, every boat should have at least two three-part tackles made up with snap shackles at each end. These can be used, for example, to set up the main-boom fore guy, or they can be snapped on the line attached to the tack of a reaching or running sail to adjust the height. They can be used not only at sea but also in port in the multitude of jobs involved in working on a boat—for hauling people aloft, and lifting engines, gearboxes, tanks, ballast, and so on. Further, unreeving the mainsheet and making a tackle out of it enables one man to haul himself aloft without having someone crank him up and down. On *Iolaire* there are always available gun tackles with snap shackles at each end and two four-part tackles; through the years, these have paid for themselves a hundred times over.

To be used in conjunction with a tackle is the endless strop (Photo 44). This item, in its various sizes, is most useful, as it can be passed around such things as a lifeline stanchion base, through hawsepipes, bulwarks, mooring cleats, or what-have-you, and then back through itself (Photo 45), and then a tackle can be snapped into its end. A strop is easily made by taking a length of ⅜-inch or ½-inch Dacron and short-splicing the ends together.

It is also handy to have a six-foot length of line—⅜-inch spun Dacron, as this will have less tendency to slip than filament Dacron—for use as a stopper, secured with a rolling hitch to another line. An eye splice is made at one end and the other end is whipped; then if a stopper needs to be placed on a sheet, one can secure the spun Dacron onto

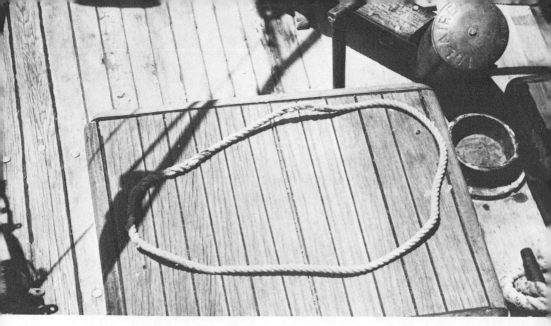

44. Endless strop. (D. M. Street)

45. Endless strop in use. (D. M. Street)

the sheet with a rolling hitch, put a tackle on it, take a strain, cleat it down, and disconnect and move the sheet as necessary (Photo 46).

46. Stopper with tackle. (D. M. Street)

RUNNING BACKSTAYS

The original manuscript of this book was completed when it suddenly dawned on me that I had not mentioned anything about running backstays—it just shows how much I dislike them. Formerly, with the gaff rig, long booms, and topmasts, backstays were common, and indeed on many boats there were upper and lower backstays. These ran on two tackles, making jibing most difficult; hence seamen of two generations ago regarded jibing with much terror. If the backstays were not correctly handled, the result was a broken boom, a lost topmast, or possibly a whole rig overboard.

But even in years gone by, many of the commercial cargo schooners, fishermen, and pilot schooners managed to sail with no running backstays. Instead, they had a heavy mast, in many cases well bowed forward, and sometimes windward-going ability was sacrificed for the ease of handling gained by dispensing with backstays. However, it is worthy of note that whenever they raced, running backstays were rigged.

Running backstays that are continually needed are happily becoming a thing of the past. More and more they are mere preventers, used to strengthen the mast under certain circumstances rather than to hold it up at all times. Today, even for gaff-rigged boats they are not always regarded as essential. Formerly, gaff-rigged boats almost always had running backstays because with a gaff rig there is usually very little spread to the lower shrouds. Now we know that on small gaff-rigged boats, running backstays can be dispensed with if the lower shrouds are well spread and thus also perform the function of a stay—remember, an inch of drift compensates for one foot in height. On larger gaff-rigged boats, where there is a topmast and/or topsail, it was common in the past to have two sets of running backstays, one going to the jib-stay, the other going to the topmast head. Here again, if the lower shrouds are well spread, the lower backstays can be dispensed with; the upper backstay, to the topmast head, will still be needed.

One of the greatest advantages of the Marconi rig (also often referred to as "jib-headed," "Bermudian," or "leg-o-mutton," although strictly speaking each of these terms has a slightly different definition, as noted in the Glossary) is the fact that the upper running backstay can usually be replaced by a permanent backstay to the stern or to a bumpkin. If the boom is so long that a permanent backstay cannot be rigged, it can be shortened. The experience of recent years has proved that the sail area along the leech is not particularly essential even for the performance of racing boats. Further, most of the older boats have a good

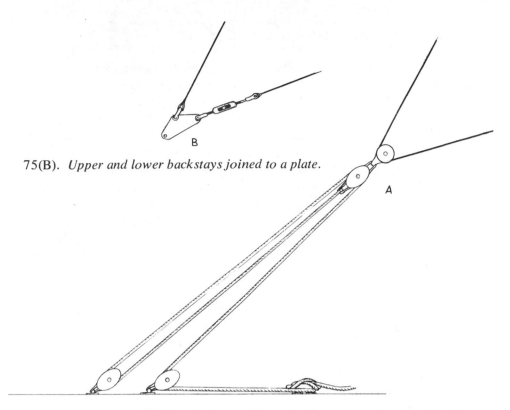

75(B). *Upper and lower backstays joined to a plate.*

75(A). *Upper and lower backstays run through a block.*

deal of weather helm. In a boat of this type, cutting a few feet off the end of the boom, though it sacrifices some sail area, usually results in much better balance. The boat usually sails much better despite the loss of sail area.

DOUBLE RUNNING BACKSTAYS

I dislike running backstays, and double running backstays are an abomination to be avoided at all cost. They are difficult to handle, and they are all too often improperly rigged. Frequently the double-head-sail-rigged seven-eighths cutter or yawl, if racing, will have two independent sets of running backstays. To handle this rig with a short crew is an impossibility, so the two backstays are usually joined—to a block, a clamp, or a triangular plate (Drawing 75).

This is a frequently misrigged operation. For example, the use of a block may result in serious difficulties. Many times the upper backstay is run down through a block, then back up to the mast and secured at a point opposite the staysail stay tang. Tension is applied by a tackle at the bottom end of the block (Drawing 75A). This arrangement makes it very simple to stow the lee backstay, as the block is free to run on the wire and the block can be tied down to the lee rail with a lanyard or shock cord; the equal tension on the upper and lower backstays will keep them from flogging arund loose. However, there is a great disadvantage to such a rig. A running backstay of this type should be very heavily loaded, because the permanent backstay at the top of the mast cannot adequately tighten the head stay and the staysail stay. The backstay wire, under this load, will tend to fatigue where it bends around the sheave on the block. Further, since the upper and lower backstays are one continuous wire passing through the block, their tensions are always equal, which is an incorrect method of rigging because the head stay with its large jib carries much more strain than does the staysail stay and therefore should carry much more strain than the lower backstay. Hence, in my estimation, this rig should not be used.

In other cases the backstays are joined by a clamp. This method has an advantage over the block method in that tension can be adjusted, although with difficulty, and more load put on the upper backstay than on the lower backstay. It has a disadvantage in that when the backstays are run forward and lashed to the lee rigging, the lower backstay will lengthen more than the upper (which is under tension) and therefore will flog around loose.

A better arrangement, if one must have upper and lower backstays, is to secure both to a triangular-shaped plate. The upper backstay may first be connected to the plate and adjusted to the correct tension; then the lower backstay may be connected and adjusted in its turn. On boats of 50 feet and over LOA this is usually done by a turnbuckle attached to the mast by a mast tang which is connected to a staysail stay. On smaller boats, a heavy Dacron lanyard lashing and a snap shackle may be used. When the backstays are lashed forward, the lower backstay can be unsnapped, and snapped on to its own piece of shock cord, which will minimize its flogging around.

Finally, it is best if the lower backstay can be discarded altogether. There are a number of methods for eliminating it. The most common on beamy boats is to lead the intermediate shroud (or an extra shroud installed for this purpose) from the same height as the staysail stay out to the rail cap, far enough aft to act as a stay—with, as always, an inch of drift for each foot of height.

Another method is to build the mast with a deep enough fore-and-aft section so that it can stand without a lower running backstay except in the worst weather. However, if a new mast is being built, this is the time to discard the seven-eighths rig and go to the masthead rig, where only a permanent backstay and one running backstay are required.

SINGLE RUNNING BACKSTAYS

On most modern boats with a double-headsail rig there is a permanent backstay and one running backstay. On racing boats the running backstay is used continually. However, on a boat designed for cruising, the mast should be given so deep a fore-and-aft section that the running backstay will be needed only in extreme circumstances. *Iolaire*'s sixty-foot mast is not supported at the deck, as there are no wooden wedges. Yet with the fore-and-aft dimension of nine inches, I practically never use my running backstay unless I am racing. Occasionally in very heavy weather—beating to windward when it is blowing 35 knots or so —I will break down and rig a running backstay, but it is strictly a preventer, not essential for keeping the mast on the boat. This is the type of rig that a cruising boat should have.

RIGGING RUNNING BACKSTAYS

The simplest rig of a running backstay is that used on a yawl or ketch to secure the mizzen. In this case the function of the running backstay is merely to take the pull of the mizzen staysail and keep the mizzenmast in the boat. The fact that it may bend forward slightly is not important, as one is not trying to keep a tight luff on a jib. Therefore, running backstays on any but the very largest mizzens (forty feet or more on the hoist) can usually be secured by a pelican hook to a pad eye (Drawing 76). In this drawing, *A* shows what I refer to as a lowered-bearing pelican hook. The pin is slightly slack in its hole. When strain is placed on the hook, the shoulder takes the entire load; the ring merely keeps the hook from drawing open. *B* shows a hook in which

76. *Pelican hooks.*

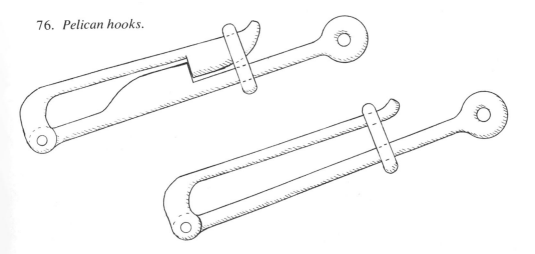

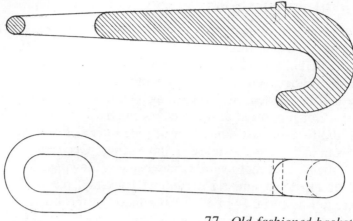

77. *Old-fashioned backstay hook.*

the ring not only holds the device closed, but is an essential part of the arrangement and carries considerable load. The backstay pelican hook should be of type *A*. Also, a hole should be drilled through the top of the hook, and a large cotter pin with a light lanyard should be inserted after the ring has been shoved home. This will make it impossible for a loose sheet to knock the rig off the pelican hook. Were this to happen, with the hook popping open, the mizzenmast would go by the board.

This type of backstay is really only necessary on those ketches and yawls that do not have their mizzen spreaders rigged well aft to serve as backstays, as is done on *Iolaire*.

WHIP ATTACHMENT FOR RUNNING BACKSTAYS

One end of the whip is attached to a tackle or a lever; the other end must be attached to the deck firmly yet in such fashion that the runner can be easily disconnected. For one must disconnect the runner in order to carry the runner block forward to secure it to the lower shrouds. On many boats a normal old cargo hook is used. However, the proportions of a cargo hook make it unsuitable for hooking into a pad eye, and a special eye must therefore be provided. The old-fashioned backstay hook, which was standard for many years, is infinitely better shaped for this job (Drawing 77). Because of the short lip on the hook, it can be hitched onto a normal pad eye, and yet it is so thick across the throat that it is amply strong. The great disadvantage of this type of hook is that in heavy weather, the hook is attached to the pad eye, preparations are made to tack, and just before the helm is put down, the yacht hits a big wave and the hook shakes loose and flies off to leeward; then the tack must be delayed until hook is retrieved. I therefore much prefer a Merriman eye attaching to a hook bolted to the deck (Drawing 78). Drawing 78 shows a Merriman eye and backstay hook (catalog Fig. 542). This is by far the best method for securing the dead end of the running-backstay whip to the deck. As the drawing indicates, the eye must be laid absolutely flat on the deck and slipped under the hook. Once the thimble is drawn upright, it cannot shake out from the hook; it can be disengaged only by being placed flat once again. Thus once the dead end of the runner is hooked into place, one need not worry about its coming loose.

BACKSTAY LEAD BLOCKS

On some boats the lead block for the backstay is merely a wire or rope block secured directly to a pad eye. I dislike this type because it means one more block to bang around on deck, and because it is difficult to maintain. Far more desirable, in my view, is a block obtainable from Merriman (catalog Fig. 541). Especially intended for use as a backstay lead block, it can be bolted directly to the deck. It is made with an offset to allow for the camber on the deck and for the fact that the backstay does not lead straight up, but rather toes inward. The exact angle of this toeing inward depends upon the beam of the boat and the height of the point of attachment of the backstay. If the standard angle on the Merriman block is not sufficient, the block may be

78. *Properly designed backstay hook and eye.*

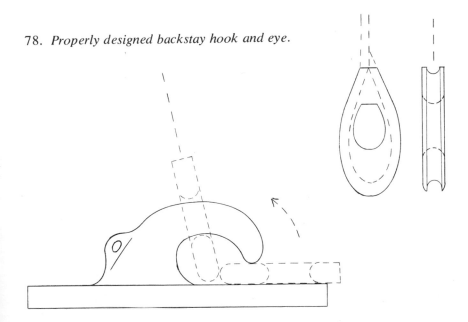

mounted on a wedgeshaped wood pad. Since this block is fixed, with no pivoting action whatsoever, all angles must be very carefully figured so that everything lines up and there are no foul leads to cause chafe on the block or cripple the wire.

BACKSTAY TACKLES

Four-Part Tackles

The four-part tackle is the oldest and the crudest method of tightening a running backstay. When not in use, the tackle is slacked, and the backstay is run forward and secured to the after lower shroud. This requires overhauling a large quantity of line to bring the tackle forward. Further, when the tackle is set up, there is a good deal of line to be coiled and stowed. Therefore, on running backstays a tackle on a whip is preferable.

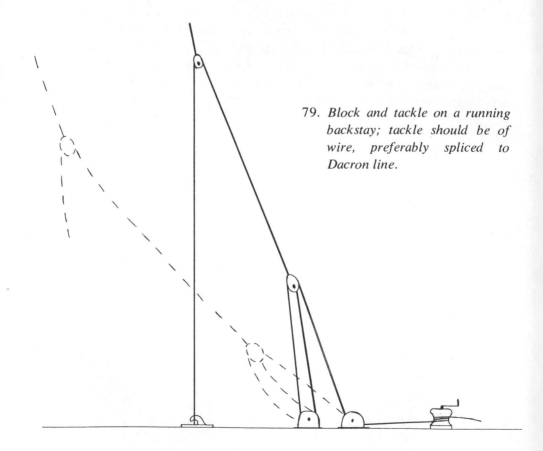

79. *Block and tackle on a running backstay; tackle should be of wire, preferably spliced to Dacron line.*

Backstay Tackle on a Whip

On this rig, the running backstay is secured to a block, and wire is secured to the deck and run up through the block and then to the three- or four-part tackle (Drawing 79). To run the lee backstay forward involves merely slacking the tackle a foot or so, disconnecting the dead end of the whip, and running the block and backstay forward for securing to the lower shroud with lanyard or shock cord.

To determine the height of the backstay block off the deck, one should measure the distance between the after point of securing the whip on the lower shroud, and the mast, divided by 2, and add one or two feet, depending upon the size of the boat. The block should be kept as low to the deck as possible; if it is too high, it is very difficult to reach to secure forward so that it does not slam around in the rigging.

Formerly, the tackle to the whip was made up of hemp or manila line, which would shrink and stretch as it was alternately wet and dry. Thus the watch on deck was continually adjusting backstays. With the advent of Dacron, much of this come and go was eliminated; its length is not affected by its becoming wet. However, maintaining the exact adjustment of the running backstays was still difficult because through the months or years even the Dacron line would slowly stretch. For this reason, the usual practice today is to join the Dacron line by means of a tail splice to a wire of such length that there are three or four turns of wire on the winch drum. Then one can place a mark on the strands of the wire and a mark on the deck, and thereafter one need only tighten the running backstay until the two marks line up. In this fashion the running backstay can be given the same tension each time the tackle is set up.

At one time, the standard medium-sized backstay winch had an 8-to-1 mechanical advantage. If a three-part tackle was placed on a two-part whip, a 6-to-1 mechanical advantage was achieved in tightening the running backstay. Then, if the backstay was secured to the 8-to-1 winch, power was obtainable at a ratio of 48 to 1, sufficient to tighten most backstays. After World War II, on some boats the small backstay winch was discarded and replaced with the standard Merriman No. 6 geared winch, with a mechanical advantage of approximately 18 to 1. Thus with the same rig as used before, roughly 100-to-1 power could be developed on the backstay. If one was not careful, the backstay could be pulled right out of the mast. For this reason, many yachtsmen discontinued the use of the three-part tackle, and took the end of the runner whip direct to the winch, thereby obtaining a mechanical advantage of about 36 to 1, sufficient but not excessive.

With the advent of the expensive two-speed winches, there is no reason why on the average cruising boat a heavy 7 by 19 wire with a rope tail cannot be shackled to the running backstay, and taken directly to a 48-to-1 winch; the result is ample power with perfect simplicity.

LEVERS

Highfield Lever

The Highfield lever was invented in the 1930's by J. S. Highfield, to use on his 15-meter *Dorina*. The original Highfield lever (Photo 47) was a great improvement over the tackles found on most vessels at that time. On *Dorade,* Highfield levers were installed on one side of the boat and the old winch and tackles were kept on the other; the crew almost always decided that the levers were better than the winch and tackles.

However, the original Highfield lever does have various disadvantages. Because adjustments are made by moving to a new hole the bolt on which the splice is secured, the minimum adjustment is approximately one inch; no really fine adjustment is possible. Further, in order to provide sufficient slack to disconnect the hook end of the backstay, the stay must be secured roughly midway between the pivot bolt and the end of the lever, so only a moderate mechanical advantage can be obtained. The Myth lever and the Merriman lever, described below, are superior, but they are much more expensive.

47. Highfield lever. (D. M. Street)

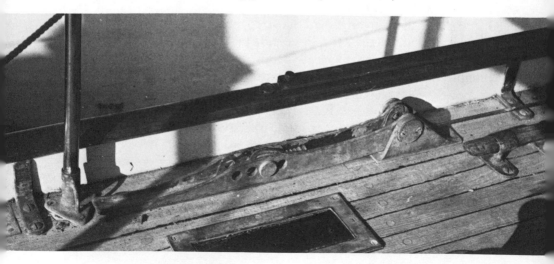

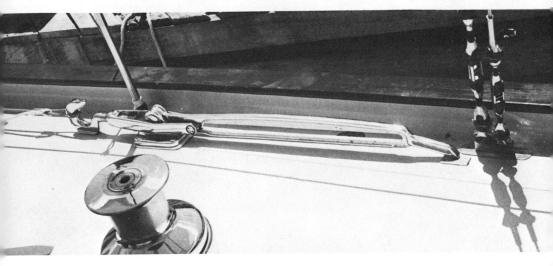

48. Myth lever. (D. M. Street)

Myth Lever and Merriman Lever

The Myth lever (Photo 48) is vastly superior to the Highfield lever in several respects. Since the bar is slotted, once it is thrown forward, the slider can slide its full length, so that the slack is equal to roughly double the length of the bar. Further, this lever is thrown into the vertical position, with the slider shoved to the bottom, and thus the slider taking the strain of the backstay is approximately one-eighth the distance from the fulcrum to the end of the lever, giving a tremendous mechanical advantage. Because the hook is threaded into the slider, adjustments of length can be made by quarter or half turns of the thread; thus much finer adjustments can be achieved than were possible with the original Highfield lever. This lever was originally designed by Laurent Giles and Partners for *Myth of Malham,* prior to World War II. It is still extensively used in Europe today, in various sizes, and is available through Laurent Giles and Partners.

Where the Myth lever has a slot cut in it, with the slider running in the slot, the Merriman lever (Photo 49) represents an opposite approach. It has a channel in which slides a special bronze fitting, threaded to take the wire. Both achieve the same purpose—providing an amount of slack that is double the length of the lever. Also, because the slider slides to the base of the lever arm, both the Myth lever and the Merriman lever give infinite mechanical advantages. In the Merriman lever the runner pendant is secured not to an open hook, but

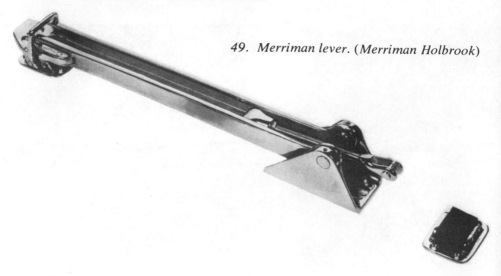

49. Merriman lever. (Merriman Holbrook)

rather to a standard turnbuckle jaw end, a good deal lighter and stronger than an open hook. Both models are held down against the deck. In the Myth lever the slider passes over the center of the pivot bolt and tends to hold the lever down. In the Merriman model, the lever is actually lashed down by a catch operated by a rubber spring. I prefer the Merriman lever, but it is by far the more expensive of the two.

Lever Versus Tackle

It might appear that levers would be invariably preferable for use with running backstays, but actually, this is not so. For a vessel on which the running backstays must be set up each and every time she is tacked, I would definitely say levers are the answer. However, with most modern rigs, the backstays are needed only in heavy weather. Most of the time they are secured forward with shock cord alongside the lower shrouds. If the backstays are set up on tackles, the tackles may be unshackled, coiled, and sent below, leaving a nice clear deck. In contrast, levers and their attendant fittings are always in the way. Hence, they are preferable only if backstays are to be used continually.

OTHER BACKSTAYS ARRANGEMENTS

Before World War II, on some cruising boats, many 6 meters, and numerous other small racing boats, a wire span was used for setting up the backstay. Two heavy bronze eyes were secured to the deck, with a heavy wire stretched between them. Around this wire was placed a U-shaped bronze slider, to which the running backstay was attached. To both ends of the slider was secured an endless lanyard, running through blocks at the ends of the wire span. To tighten the backstay, one pulled the slider aft on the wire span and winched tight; to slacken the backstay, the endless lanyard was thrown off and the slider pulled forward to clear the boom. This method worked, but it required an awful lot of heavy gear bolted along the deck. It is seldom seen today.

Similarly, before the war, on 6 meters and larger, one saw backstays on sliding tracks. This rig was good in that it made possible adjustment for every wind strength; one could alter tension by regulating how far aft the backstay was pulled on the slider. However, this installation too meant an awful lot of gear and weight bolted to the deck. And it was expensive, since stainless-steel or bronze track was advisable. If galvanized track was used, the underside of the track corroded and the resulting friction made it very difficult to tighten the backstay. This type of rig is seldom seen today on cruising boats, though one may find it on small boats—Stars, Comets, and the like.

Recently I have seen one large boat—*Baracuta*—with a variation of this type of rig. Since she has both main and mizzen backstays, all on sliders, one might expect the setup to be very difficult to handle. However, it is not difficult, as the main and mizzen backstay sliders are interconnected by a stainless rod, so that when the main backstays are slid forward, the mizzen backstays also go forward. Further, while it is usually difficult to get the last bit of tension on backstay sliders, to enable them to be set up really tight, this problem is taken care of on *Baracuta* by a big Highfield lever which picks up the last remnants of travel. This rig is very complicated, difficult to comprehend even when one looks at it, impossible to describe. It is specially made up, all of stainless steel, and probably cost thousands of dollars.

REMOVABLE STAYSAIL STAYS

When the genoa first came into use on cruising boats, it was a real man-killer, in that it had to be passed between the head stay and the staysail stay. On a medium-size boat, of perhaps 45 feet LOA, it was quite a trick to pass a genoa that was 30 feet on the foot between a head stay and a staysail stay that were four feet apart. Before long, people began to think of disconnecting the staysail stay in light and moderate weathers so that the genoa could be easily tacked. There are various methods of performing this operation.

SLACKING THE TURNBUCKLE

The earliest method was simply to slack the turnbuckle and pull the pin from the turnbuckle fork to disconnect the stay. This is a slow and

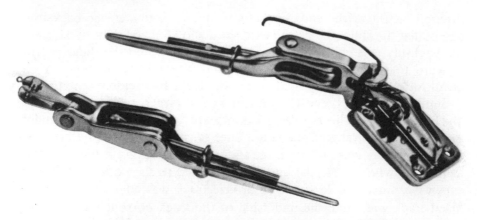

50. *Rhodes-type release lever; it lies up against itself instead of down on deck.* (*Yacht Specialties*)

tedious operation, involving fighting with pliers and split pins; therefore some people inserted a tapered leather thong in the end of the clevis pin, while others installed drop-nose clevis pins. In any case, this procedure could be followed only in light airs because as soon as it began to blow up, the stay had to be kept in place; in moderate weather it was not possible to reconnect the stay at each tack. Hence, people began to investigate a variety of release-type levers.

STAYSAIL-STAY RELEASE LEVERS

The first and simplest of these consists of a Highfield lever connected to a piece of flexible wire which passes through a block. The lever is firmly bolted to the deck, and is attached to the foot of the staysail stay with a backstay hook. This arrangement does make possible the quick connecting and disconnecting of the staysail stay, but is unsatisfactory in that the wire leads over a sheave, and is accordingly subject to fatiguing and possibly failure. People therefore thought a little further. Philip Rhodes designed a quick-operatng release lever which obviated the necessity of leading the wire over a sheave (Photo 50). This lever consists of a piece of channel secured to a pivot. A few inches from the pivot, an open slot is cut to receive a toggle secured to the staysail-stay turnbuckle. On the other side of the pivot is a handle about three feet long. The toggle is inserted into the slot, and the lever arm—heaved up tight—drops over the staysail stay, where it is secured in place with the pin. This is an excellent device in that it is simple and powerful, and takes up little deck space when connected. However, if during this time the staysail is connected to the stay, the staysail has to be snapped on and furled above the release, quite high off the deck. Another disadvantage is that when disconnected, the lever still takes up deck space.

To my mind the best staysail-stay release is Merriman's (catalog Fig. 647). (Photo 51). It is complicated and expensive, but very powerful, fast, and easy to operate. Its great advantage is that the turnbuckle can be secured at the top of the mast, and the sail hanked onto the stay and stowed right down against the deck. Thus when short tacking with the genoa up—on a wooden spar that needs the additional support of the staysail stay—it is a simple matter to disconnect and reconnect the staysail stay after every tack.

51. Merriman release lever. (Merriman Holbrook)

VI

~~~~~~~~~~~~~~~~~~~~~~~~~~~~~~~~~~~~~~~

Sails

In years gone by sails were made of cotton or flax; cotton was used for the working sails, and flax was preferred for the storm sails because it did not mildew and was soft even when wet. The best cotton sailcloth was made in England from long-staple Egyptian cotton. American domestic cotton was not well regarded. Today with few exceptions all sailcloth is made of synthetic fibers, generally either Dacron or nylon, often called by different names in different countries. Dacron was a British invention, manufactured in America under license, but the Americans have so improved it that their Dacron sailcloth is exported all over the world.

Even in the production of canvas sailcloth, the United States has taken the lead—by default rather than by design. Egyptian cotton sailcloth is just not made today, and when cotton is specified for a sail it is usually supposed to be mildewproof, so the sailmaker is likely to use boat-shrunk Vivatex. This is not really good sailcloth in that it is not strong enough and there is too much come and go in it, but it is impervious to mildew and is waterproof. It makes excellent gaff sails or low-aspect-ratio Marconi sails but will not hold its shape well enough to make a good tall narrow mainsail, jib topsail, or genoa.

Dacron has really made sailing a pleasure. It has put an end to the continual fight to get wet heavy canvas dry before it mildews; it does not get heavy and stiff when wet; outhauls and halyards do not change dimensions and have to be adjusted with every patch of fog or rain-squalls. Luff ropes do not break, and sails seldom tear in squalls. Genoas can be carried in stronger winds. Formerly, many stiff boats seldom got their rails down because the canvas would split in heavy weather. These boats today sail well in heavy weather because they can carry Dacron sails through almost any wind. Except in the case of sails that are old, one seldom hears of the material of Dacron sails tearing. Seams may open up, but that is all. Dacron is so hard that in heavy sails, stitching through heavy reinforcement patches is impossible unless a pilot hole is drilled with an electric drill. However, because Dacron is so strong, it no longer protects the rigging by carrying away first. Consequently, extra care must be given to the design, tune, and maintenance of the rigging.

Dacron is tremendously strong, hard, and impervious to rot from mildew. However, it is affected by sunlight. The ultraviolet rays destroy the fabric at a rapid rate, a serious problm on a boat that is used continually in the tropics. Also, the strength and hardness of Dacron works to its disadvantage in one respect: the stitching stands proud on top of the material, and anything that tends to chafe the sail will chafe the stitching first; it is for this reason that so many Dacron sails split along the seams. Most sailmakers now use a triple row of stitching for Dacron sails, while some use a quadruple row for the larger sizes. A few sailmakers do work referred to as half hand stitched, with one side of the seam machine stitched, the second side hand stitched. This is an improvement, but Dacron is so hard that even with this technique it is impossible to get the stitches to pull down into the cloth as they do with cotton. A few sailmakers completely hand stitch very large sails. They are beautiful and long lasting, but very expensive.

CHAFE

Chafe has always been a problem. Prior to World War II, baggy wrinkle was seen in great balls, all over the rigging of cruising yachts and even transatlantic ocean racers. Galvanized-iron rigging caused much chafe, and of course gaff-rigged boats, with their running backstays, double topping lifts, and lazy jacks, were troubled by chafe at all points of sailing. The modern jib-headed yacht, with Dacron sails, does not have this difficulty. The stitching may chafe easily on Dacron sails, but the sails can be restitched time and again.

The worst chafe problem on a Dacron sail occurs when the main chafes on the lee rigging. Running backstays must be brought forward and secured so that they do not chafe the lee side of the main, or they will remove the stitching in a matter of hours. Stainless-steel shrouds do not seem to chafe the sail too badly, unless much time is spent broad off or dead downwind, with the main up against the shrouds and spreaders. Baggy wrinkle will minimize this chafe, but the windage of baggy wrinkle is so great, and it is such a tedious job to rig correctly, that I strongly advise against it. A better solution if one is contemplating long offshore passages, where one will be reaching or running for considerable periods, is to spend a day or so well in advance of your estimated departure sailing broad off; then drop the sail, tie in a reef, and again sail on a broad reach and then a run. When the sail is brought back to the sailmaker, he will be able to see the chafe marks. The material itself will show few signs of chafe; these will be seen mainly on the stitching. Instead of using large, ugly, and difficult-to-install chafe patches, he can then cover the chafe spots and seams where necessary with a narrow strip of Dacron, say 3-ounce Dacron sewed on 8-ounce. These strips will not last forever, but they will increase the life of the seams that are subject to chafe. At the same time, one should cover the spreader tip and after edge of the spreader with soft felt.

Chafe in the mainsail will be minimized if a good fore guy and boom vang are rigged to keep the boom secured. If this is done, the sail does not work itself up and down over the shrouds and spreader tip. Further, on long passages when broad off so that the mainsail is hard up against the shrouds and spreaders, the mainsail should be doused, a medium genoa set to windward on the pole, and a second, larger genoa also set but sheeted to the end of the main boom; these measures will completely eliminate chafe.

ROPING A SAIL

Roping on canvas sails was a real art; and even on Dacron sails it requires skill. To get away from the hand work of roping mainsails, mizzens, and so on, sailmakers now often sew many layers of Dacron tape to the luff and the foot of the sail. If this tape is attached correctly, I think it is better than the old hand-stitched rope. The tape makes roller reefing and furling easier, and appears to be just as strong as rope. Other sailmakers have taken to sewing line to Dacron tape (Drawing 80) and then sewing the tape to the sail; this procedure, properly followed, seems to be eminently satisfactory.

In my view, headsails should have wire luffs, because a headsail luff should have as little stretch as possible. Even steel wire has stretch, and though a sailmaker can demonstrate with facts and figures that a Dacron-taped luff is strong enough, he cannot deny that the tape is stretchier than wire. It is for this reason that there are always more snaps on a headsail with a taped luff than on a headsail with a wire luff.

To be sure, there is a lot of experimentation with genoas with stretchy luffs, which allow the shape of the sail to be varied so that a light, very full genoa can be flattened and used in moderate airs. How-

80. *Boltrope of braided line is sewn to the middle of Dacron tape, which is in turn lapped up on either side of the sail and sewn in place.*

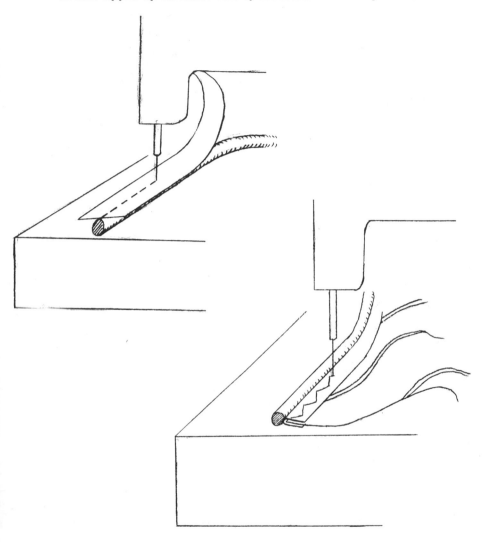

ever, the stretchy-luff genoa, I think, is strictly a racing man's plaything, not likely to be found on an average cruising boat.

When Dacron first came into use, a tremendous amount of trouble resulted from the fact that Dacron and stainless steel do not like each other and react violently. The stainless turns rapidly to a black powder, while the Dacron rots and turns brown. Now all stainless fittings are well insulated with plastic before they are sewn into the sail, and the trouble seems to have been eliminated.

CHOOSING A SAILMAKER

Sailmakers today are in a very competitive business, and their sales and profits strongly reflect their success in making winning racing sails. Going to a top-notch racing sailmaker for a good suit of cruising sails is often the height of folly. Such a man is likely to be unwilling to listen, intent on doing things his way. But what is right for racing sails is not necessarily right for cruising sails. The racing man wants strength and lightness and is willing to sacrifice longevity for a 5-percent saving in weight. The cruising man wants longevity and does not care as much about weight. The cut of the sails will be entirely different, and so will the fittings. Furthermore, while for an important cup defense or for a very expensive ocean racer, the best is none too good and the sailmaker sees that it is delivered; too often the cruising man's sail is fed through the mill and made by apprentices.

These problems may be avoided by going to one of the newer sailmakers, who is working hard to establish a reputation. He is also more likely to show a willingness to sit and listen, which is important if one's needs are out of the ordinary. For this reason I once approached a Hong Kong sailmaker, with exact specifications for sails I wanted made for various yachts in the Caribbean; everything had been worked out for our specialized requirements, as determined by weather and cruising conditions and the vicissitudes of the charter business. This sailmaker accepted all the suggestions and made the sails to my specifications. They were admittedly not the specifications one would want for a racing sail on Long Island Sound, for what I needed were heavy sails that would last.

In an area where there are a number of sailmakers available, the man who will make the best sail is the one who is willing to come down to the boat, go for a sail, and take the measurements himself. Misfitting sails can frequently be traced to the fact that the measurements sent to the sailmaker were insufficient or in error.

SPECIFICATIONS

In measuring for sails one must be sure, first and foremost, not to rely on the builder's or rigger's sail plans: the measurements must be taken directly off the spars. All too often, even in boats from the most expensive yards, the boom may be three inches shorter than shown on the plans, or the mast five inches longer, or the boom four inches higher. Thus, one should measure the luff and foot on the spars, top up

81. Rub-back dimension.

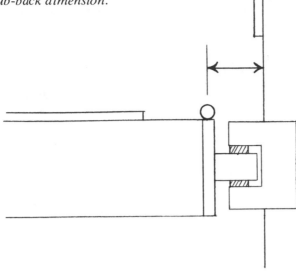

the boom to the level that it will be when sailing for the leech measurement, and send the sailmaker these extreme dimensions; he will allow for stretch.

At the same time, one should note anything special about the head, tack, and clew. If the main-halyard sheave is too small and pulls the head of the sail forward, one should notify the sailmaker. If the gooseneck is set back from the mast (Drawing 81) he should be given the rub-back dimension, and if it is not in line horizontally with the boom, he should be told how much it is out of the horizontal (Drawing 82); similarly, the extent to which the outhaul is out of horizontal alignment with the boom should be ascertained. If the boat has shackles that must pass through the clew and tack, one should measure the shackles and give the sailmaker the minimum inside diameter of the tack and clew cringles.

82. Gooseneck out of horizontal alignment.

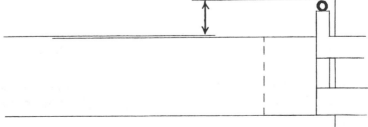

Boats intended for sailing in certain areas demand special treatment. If one plans to sail on the east coast of the United States, or in any of the major yachting areas, one need only tell the sailmaker where and he will know how to cut the sails. However, if one is going to do a lot of offshore work, or sail in the trade-wind belt, this fact should be specified and the working sails should be made of heavier cloth than usual. On a cruising sail, reef cringles, corner patches, and the like can be made heavier than on a racing sail. Even with roller reefing, one set of reef earings should be installed, so that in the event of a failure of the reefing gear, which happens more often than manufacturers like to admit, it will still be possible to reef in the normal fashion. Further, the big roach now seen in racing sails is hard to cut and is unnecessary in cruising sails. Some people have their cruising sails made with no battens; if this is done, and the sails are cut with a straight or slightly hollow leech, they will set quite well but will have a curl to the leech. If battens are desired, special provisions must be made if the sails are to last in a heavy-weather area.

BATTENS

The batten is a strip sewn into a sail at approximately right angles to the leech, to make the sail set flat. Traditionally, the batten has been made of wood. To prevent breaking, one may use several light battens instead of a single heavier one. A single ⅜-inch-thick batten will bend in a small curve and then break, but three ⅛-inch-thick battens, or four ⅛-inch-thick battens laid together in a loose lamination, will bend in almost a complete circle before fracturing. If perchance there is a break, it will probably be in only one of the battens, and if they all break, they usually do so at different points and show little tendency to put a hole in the sail.

There are available on the market today, fiber-glass battens which are very stiff. The batten is cut to the correct length, and a soft plastic cap is slipped over each end. These battens are very expensive, but well worth their cost. In the past three years, using these, I have not broken a single one, while in previous years, I lost a batten a month.

Batten Pockets

Sailmakers at present usually sew one side of the batten pocket directly to the sail, and often they make the pocket with an angled end (Drawing 83) instead of a tie. This arrangement may be fine for Long Island Sound, but it is no good at sea in a squall. When a batten breaks

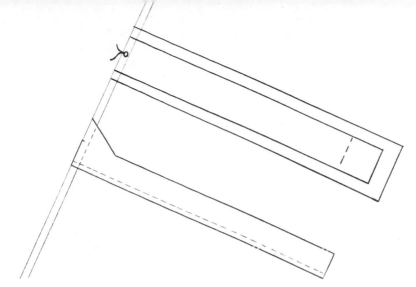

83. *Batten pockets: the lower is incorrect; the upper is properly made—sewn on a patch which is then sewn to the sail.*

—as it is sure to do sooner or later—with the perversity of inanimate objects, it will invariably tear the sail rather than the pocket. In squalls, it will throw itself out of the end of the angled pocket—exactly how, I have never figured out, but that's what happens. Finally, the pocket is usually sewn on top of the seam, so when the seam must be restitched, the pocket first has to be removed.

I highly recommend the following method for installing a batten pocket in a cruising sail. A full pocket should be made, and then sewn to a strip of cloth; then the strip and pocket should be sewn on a panel of the sail, not on top of a seam, and grommets and ties should be provided at the outer end. The pocket should be large enough easily to accommodate three thin battens placed one on top of the other. With this arrangement, there are two layers of Dacron between the battens and the sail; if a batten breaks, it should tear the pocket, not the sail. When the sail is to be restitched, the pocket need not be disturbed. The battens can be tied in and will not shake out in a squall.

ROLL REEF

For extensive offshore cruising, a roll reef is indicated (Drawing 84). It consists of a row of reef earings running diagonally from the tack to the first reef clew earing. Tying in this reef off the wind will keep the boom from tripping in the sea when rolling.

ROACH REEF

Many racing yachtsmen trying to get the best of both worlds—full sail off the wind, flat sail on the wind—install a roach reef along the

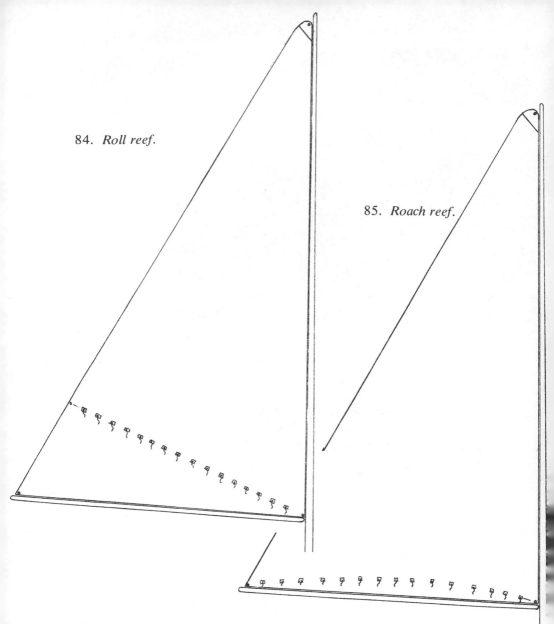

84. *Roll reef.*

85. *Roach reef.*

foot of the main and/or the mizzen (Drawing 85). This roach reef is secured either by a zipper or by a continuously threaded line through eyelets set in the sail.

In this respect, the cruising man can learn from the racing man. Since the mizzen operates in the backwind of the main, it should be cut as flat as possible. In my view, most mizzens are cut too full, and could be drastically improved by the installation of the roach reef, which makes it possible to get the mizzen absolutely flat when using it either going to windward in heavy weather, or resting at anchor as an antiroll measure. Indeed, to me the ideal mizzen would be a piece of $\frac{1}{32}$-inch stainless-steel plate riveted to the mizzenmast and mizzen boom. This metal sail might be difficult to furl, but it would not wear out.

SAIL SLIDES

Sail slides come in bronze, aluminum, and plastic; the exact type to be used depends mainly upon the type of track on the mast (see Chapter IV). There is a good deal of argument concerning the best method of securing the slides to the sail.

Slides Sewn to Sail

SAIL TWINE: A slide can be secured to the sail with a shackle sewn to the luff rope with waxed Dacron twine (Photo 52). If correctly made, such a lashing will last almost forever. The trick is to use very heavy waxed twine, begin the sewing in the luff rope, then sew through the eyes of the shackle, through the cringle, back to the eye, through the cringle again, and so on, until the shackle is firmly attached. Then one must bed the bitter end of the sail twine securely by sewing numerous times back and forth into the luff rope.

52. *Cast-bronze slide secured with a shackle sewn to the luff rope. (Merriman Holbrook)*

LEATHER: Some sailmakers secure sail slides to the sail with rawhide. If properly attached, the slides stay in place forever; if not, they come off the first time it rains really hard. To secure a slide correctly with leather, one first obtains a narrow, flat piece of leather of suitable width to pass through the cringle on the sail and through the slide. This is passed through the slide and the cringle as many times as possible; then, with a small electric drill, two holes are drilled through all the

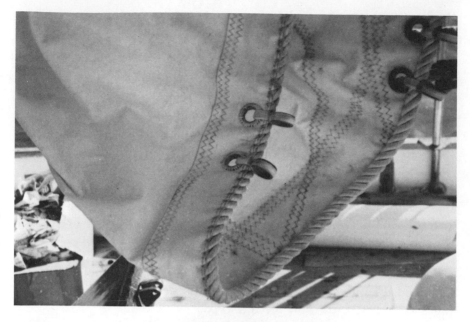

53. Nylon lashing. (D. M. Street)

leather, and waxed Dacron twine is stitched through the holes and around until the entire strap is firmly sewn down.

NYLON: Instead of leather, a narrow strip of nylon cloth of suitable length can be passed back and forth through the clew cringle and the slide. (Photo 53). This too is secured by stitching with waxed Dacron twine.

Shackles

The method that I prefer by far for securing the sail slide to the sail requires a light stainless-steel shackle made out of a flat stainless strap and secured with a screw. A plastic insert must be placed around the sail before the shackle is installed, as otherwise the shackle will rapidly chafe through the luff rope. Shackles of this type, suitable for all sizes of sails, are available from Howe and Bainbridge (Photo 54).

Jack Line

If roller reefing is used, one must disconnect the bottom three, four, five, or six slides to roll down a reef. There are many methods of doing this; for example, key shackles may be installed, which are disconnected as the reef is rolled out. A preferable method, however, is to

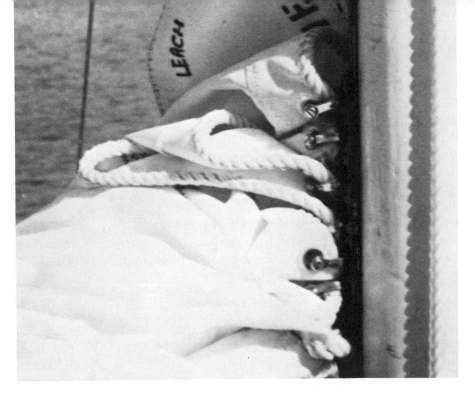

54. Howe and Bainbridge shackle. (D. M. Street)

connect the bottom four or five slides with a jack line. Because the line is infinitely adjustable, it is easy to reeve and unreeve as the reef is rolled in or rolled out.

Even without roller reefing, a jack line on the bottom three or four slides is desirable, for if this line is installed, it is not necessary to slack the outhaul of the sail when the sail is furled. Many people maintain that in any case, when furling a Dacron sail one need not slack the outhaul, but I believe they are mistaken. Whenever a sail is dropped, the boom drops slightly, and the angle between the first slide and the outhaul changes, becoming slightly larger. Therefore, if a sail is dropped and the outhaul is not slacked, tension develops on the bottom two or three —and in some cases four—slides. This strain, which is diagonally across the lay of the cloth, certainly does not do the sail any good. Hence, installation of the jack line will not only make furling easier, but also increase the life of the sail.

CUNNINGHAM HOLES

Cruising-boat owners may acquire secondhand racing sails either from a racing friend or from a dealer. Often these sails almost fit, but not quite, and here again is where the cruising man can learn from the racing man. The racing man has used Cunningham holes to improve the set of his sails for over thirty years (Briggs Cunningham first used them before World War II in 6 meters). If the sail is a little too long on the foot, or on the hoist, the solution is to sew in cringles—the Cunningham holes—at a distance of six to eighteen inches (depending on size of sail) from the tack cringle on both luff and foot. The next step is to secure some ⅛-inch Dacron line to the tack cringle, reeve it through the appropriate Cunningham hole, cinch it up tight, using line as block and tackle, and adjust it carefully. Or one can secure a piece of ⅜-inch Dacron line to the tack, run it up to the luff Cunningham hole, thence to the spinnaker halyard winch. When going to windward the luff can thus be easily tightened under load and draft accurately controlled.

Mainsails

The mainsail is not necessarily the largest sail on a boat, but it is almost always the heaviest and most expensive. Further, since it is used continually, it is the sail that must take the most wear and tear. Hence, the mainsail must be well and strongly made. A cruising mainsail will be appreciably more expensive than a racing mainsail; it is almost invariably one weight heavier, the reinforcement on the corners is heavier, the batten pockets are heavier, and it will probably have reef eyes, a roach reef, and a roll reef—all costing money to install.

The modern racing mainsail is made as light as possible in order to keep weight aloft at a minimum. The headboard frequently consists of two aluminum plates pop-riveted together with aluminum rivets, and these may also be used at the tack and clew. While sufficiently strong for a racing mainsail that will only be used for one or two seasons, this type of construction is totally useless on a sail that is to be used year in, year out, and that cannot be allowed to blow out or split a seam, because it frequently will be up to a thousand miles from the nearest sailmaker.

All three corners of a cruising mainsail should be heavily reinforced, and the luff and foot rope should be extended around the headboard and clew earing and be continued for a foot or so along the leech of the sail. Strong reinforcement patches must be provided at all corners. The clew earing, a bronze or stainless-steel ring sewn into the sail, should on larger sails be reinforced by being secured to two or three small worked eyes set diagonally up the sail; these distribute the strain of the earing over a larger area. Another satisfactory method of reinforcement used by some sail-makers is to sew Dacron tape to the sail, passing the tape through the clew earing prior to the insertion of the brass liner.

One set of reef eyes should be provided, with the tack and clew reef cringles as strongly, or more strongly, reinforced as/than the tack and clew of the sail. One set of reef cringles is sufficient, in my view, as I do not believe a mainsail should be double or triple-reefed. A double-reefed mainsail is not too much greater in area than the trysail. This part of the sail takes a continuous beating, being up in the breeze. Should it split luff to leech one would find oneself with no mainsail at all. Therefore, a trysail the same size as the double-reefed main should be used in very heavy weather.

The tack and clew reef cringles will be very heavily loaded, as that is the portion of the sail taking the strain when it is blowing 35 to 40 knots. Even if a boat has roller reefing, the reef eyes should be provided for two reasons. First, roller-reefing gear can fail, and if the sail has no reef eyes, there is no possibility of reefing. Second, frequently one is anchored in a crowded anchorage, it is blowing very hard, and obviously a reef will be needed, but one does not wish to hoist the full mainsail and charge around the harbor while trying to roll in a reef. It is much easier and better to tie in the reef prior to hoisting the sail.

I specify eyes rather than reef points because it seems to me infinitely better to use a lacing line rather than individual points. Getting the exact same tension on each individual point is most difficult with points, but with a lacing line the tension will equalize under strain, resulting in a smoothly setting reefed mainsail (see Photo 43).

For the boat that is to do serious cruising offshore, and especially one that will be doing a good deal of downwind work, a roll reef is most useful. The modern ocean racer may not need this roll reef, as the boom is so high and so short it is practically impossible to dip it into the sea while going downwind. However, the older boat, with a lower boom and a luff-to-foot ratio of 2.5 to 1 or lower, will almost definitely need a roll reef. A roll reef is most easily installed diagonally from the clew earing to the tack. But the effect of this installation must be checked on board the boat or against the drawings, as a roll reef of this depth may lift the boom so high that it will not clear the backstay, making it impossible to jibe. If this is so, a separate lower clew earing for the roll reef should be installed, once the depth of the reef has been carefully ascertained.

Many modern ocean racers now install roach reefs, and the cruising man can learn from his racing cousin. A cruising boat will, hopefully, spend most of its time reaching and running, and hence a full, baggy mainsail is desired. Unfortunately, all too often the time comes when even the cruising boat must fight its way uphill at a dead slog to windward, trying to reach home, and therefore requires a flat mainsail. A roach reef will enable the sail to be flattened, making the ideal reaching sail into a good windward-going sail. For this roach reef, either a zipper or eyes sewn into the sail may be used. The racing boys prefer the zipper but the cruising men are better off with sewn eyes and a lacing line. A zipper is likely to let go when the boat is far from shore and no replacement is possible. A lacing line with sewn eyes is all but foolproof.

Cunningham holes, which are found in most racing mainsails, are most useful even on a cruising boat, especially the older cruising boat that probably has inadequate, or less than adequate, outhaul and halyard winches. Tightening either the foot or the luff is much easier to do by means of Cunningham holes than by heaving out on the outhaul or up on the halyard. The slight gathering of cloth around the rack of the sail may affect its appearance, but obviously the racing fraternity feels that it does not affect the drive of the sail, and they should know.

A jack line should be installed on the lower five to eight feet (depending on the size of the sail) of all main and mizzensails. This eliminates the need to slack the outhaul when the sail is dropped, as shown early in this chapter.

The racing man always requests the sailmaker to put as much roach in the leech of the sail as the racing rules allow, in order to get the maximum area. This of course demands battens as long as the rules allow. Those who are concerned less about area than about a sail that sets well and will not cause trouble, frequently desire a much smaller amount of roach with shorter battens. Some cruising men go so far as to request a straight or slightly hollow leech and no battens. In some ways this arrangement is very good; dropping the sail off the wind is much easier, and there are no battens to break. However, while going to windward it is very difficult to keep the leech from chattering like a machine gun unless one heaves up on the leech line, which then bags the leech to such an extent that the weather helm is intensified. I myself prefer a sail with battens and a moderate amount of roach. Batten pockets should be heavily reinforced.

When off the wind, the mainsail will of course take chafe from the upper shroud spreader and the after lower shroud. Therefore, chafing strips should be placed on the sail, in accordance with the procedure outlined early in this chapter.

Mizzen Sails

Despite the fact that the mizzen on a ketch or yawl is much smaller in area than the mainsail, it should be only one weight less than the mainsail. Indeed, on a ketch that is to do a large amount of heavy-weather sailing, the mizzen is sometimes made of the same weight as the mainsail, for it will be used in heavier wind conditions than the mainsail.

The comments made with respect to the mainsail about reinforced corners, reef eyes, the roach reef, battens, and the roach of the sail apply also to the mizzen. On a cruising ketch, the mizzen definitely needs reef eyes, as there will be times when one will wish to heave to with nothing up but the reefed mizzen, the full mizzen being too much. Reef eyes are seldom seen on the mizzen of a yawl, but I have come to the conclusion that they are advisable, since there are times, especially when beating to windward, when the full mizzen produces too much weather helm and no mizzen does not produce enough.

A roach reef seems to me absolutely essential for the mizzen whether on a ketch or on a yawl. Since this sail is to be used when going to windward in the backwind of the mainsail, it must be as flat as possible, and a roach reef will help flatten it. Further, one of the big advantages of a ketch or yawl is that at anchor the mizzen may be sheeted flat, the boat will always weathercock into the wind, and if there is a swell rolling in, the mizzen will deaden the roll tremendously. To do this effectively, the mizzen should be almost as flat as a board, necessitating a roach reef. However, a roll reef is not necessary on the mizzen of a ketch or yawl. When running off the wind, the first sail that should be taken down when the wind and sea begin to pick up is the mizzen; hence there is no danger of dipping the mizzen while rolling downwind.

Main Staysails

The main staysail is the staysail set forward of the mainmast, between the mainmast and foremast on a schooner. Since the main staysail is frequently the last sail to be taken in on a schooner, despite its small size it should be the same weight as the mainsail on a serious cruising boat. However, while the necessity for reef eyes in a club staysail is debatable, I would say that any serious cruising schooner should have reef eyes in the main staysail.

Main Trysails

The main trysail is a triangular sail set on the mainmast of a ketch and sheeted to the mizzenmast by means of a wishbone. The main trysail can be one weight lower than one would normally expect for the mainsail of a ketch or schooner of similar size because it is usually one of the first sails taken in when it begins to blow. Because reefing this sail is impossible, because it is one of the largest sails on the cruising wishbone ketch, it is never used in heavy weather. However, it is sometimes overstrained as one tends to hang on to it too long before taking it in. For this reason, it would be worthwhile, on a wishbone ketch, to have not only the large main trysail that is the full length of the mainmast on the luff, but also a smaller flat topped main trysail of heavier weight that is only three-quarters of the length of the mainmast on the luff. Both sails could be stowed at the base of the mast by means of a track with a switch and a spur, in the arrangement sometimes adopted for a fisherman staysail and a golliwobbler. The comments about the reinforcements necessary in the mainsail of course hold also for the main trysail.

Gaff Foresail

The gaff foresail found on a schooner should be the same weight as the mainsail. Like the main staysail it is smaller in area than the mainsail and is frequently the last sail taken in on a schooner in heavy weather. A typical heavy-weather rig on a schooner consists of main trysail, foresail, staysail, and possibly jib, depending on the wind velocity. Further, many schooners will heave to very nicely with nothing up except the gaff foresail. Thus, a gaff foresail should definitely have one row of reef eyes. It goes without saying that the gaff foresail must be heavily reinforced at all four corners in the same fashion as the mainsail.

One objection to the gaff foresail is the difficulty of making it stand properly, which is usually caused by poor rigging and lack of thought. A major difficulty with the gaff foresail is the sagging of the gaff to leeward as soon as the sheet is cracked off the least amount. This is usually caused by a poorly designed traveler, the lack of a boom jack, and the lack of a vang from the end of the gaff to prevent the gaff's sagging to leeward.

These problems can all be surmounted by the installation of a maximum-width traveler for the foresail boom, with adjustable stops so that the boom may be pinned amidships or almost amidships while going to windward but the sheet slider may be slacked well off when reaching. A boom vang like the one used on the mainsail may be installed. Finally, if a vang is rigged from the peak of the gaff to the mainmast, and then down the mainmast to the winch, the gaff may be trimmed and adjusted independently of the boom and thus all the sag and twist may be removed from the sail and the performance of the schooner will be greatly enhanced. When the sag is thus taken out of the head of the sail, the foresail boom is substantially eased; this easing in turn removes the backwind from the mainsail, thereby eliminating much of the weather helm. The weather helm on a reach has always been one of the great disadvantages of a schooner, but this weather helm can be largely removed with the correct trimming of sails, and the correct use of vangs to the fore gaff from the fore and main booms.

HEADSAILS

The racing boat carries so many headsails and spinnakers that there is seldom enough room for the crew. Luckily, sails are not too bad as . mattresses. Often the two biggest genoas will be of the same size but different weights; then there will be a ballooner (also known as a reaching jib), a medium genoa, a heavy-weather genoa, a working jib, and the usual storm sails and spinnakers. Double-headsail-rigged boats usually have a number of different-sized jibs. Many of these sails are unnecessary on the cruising boat, even to cruise at 70 percent of racing efficiency. Rod Stephens likes to cruise at 90 percent of racing efficiency, but that involves a little too much work for most.

PENDANTS

Every headsail should have attached to its head a pendant of such length that the luff of the sail plus the head pendant equals the length of the luff of the largest jib. The tail splice on the halyard will then be in the same position no matter what headsail is to be used. Also, the head pendant should be permanently secured to head of the sail; otherwise it will invariably be lost when one desires to use it. Finally, to keep the head pendant from winding itself around the head stay while being hoisted, a jib snap should be secured to the upper end and snapped onto the stay.

All headsails except the deck-sweeper (the low-cut genoa) should have tack pendants secured to them to lift the foot high enough to clear lifelines and bow waves.

GENOAS

I do believe in using the genoa on a cruising boat. The man who states that he wants only working sails on his boat and turns on the engine whenever the going gets light is missing half the fun of sailing and is well on his way to purchasing his first powerboat. Since on a cruising boat one does not want all usable space filled with spare sails, one should have the sails cut and the weights of the cloth adjusted so that though not quite as efficient as their racing counterparts, the sails will each do the job of two or three racing sails.

The low-cut racing genoa that lies along the deck has no place on the cruising boat. It is hard to handle and is usually so light that as soon as a decent breeze fills in, it must be doused. If the slightest sea builds up, the bow wave dumps into the foot of the sail, straining both the sail and the rigging. The light ballooner cut high at the clew so that on a reach it may be sheeted to the end of the boom is a wonderful sail but can be used all too infrequently. The medium genoa of the racing boat is a wonderful all-round sail, will fill in all but the lightest of breezes, yet is heavy enough to take a good bit of wind to windward and almost any amount of wind reaching and running.

A sail with the weight of the working genoa and the cut of the ballooner is what the cruising man wants (Drawing 86). Off the wind, the clew is high enough to sheet to the end of the main boom; the foot is high enough to remain out of the bow wave in normal weather; and the cloth is heavy enough to allow the sail to be sheeted flat in light-to-moderate going.

Now that the new I.O.R. rule measures the area of the largest headsail by multiplying the length of the luff by the LP (the perpendicular distance from the luff to the clew), low genoas are disappearing from

86. *Genoa cum ballooner.*

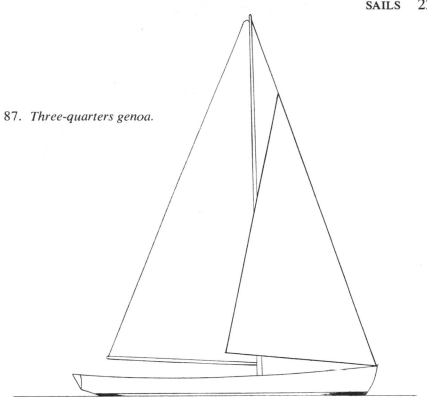

87. *Three-quarters genoa.*

the average man's sail wardrobe. With a high clew, the genoa can also be an effective reaching jib with no loss of area. The racing hotshots operating on a cost-be-damned basis will doubtless continue to have their low-cut, deck-sweeping jib for use in light and moderate airs. However, on a reach even they switch to a high-clewed genoa. The cruising man who does occasional racing can probably make do with a combination genoa-ballooner.

Three-quarters Genoas

When it blows too hard for the big genoa, the single-headsail-rigged boat must shift to a smaller genoa or jib. Here the most useful sail is a bulletproof three-quarters genoa set on a tack pendant and cut high enough to stay out of the bow wave. This sail should be about three-quarters the length of the head stay, and overlap the mast by about one-quarter the length of the base of the fore-triangle (Drawing 87), and it should be of very heavy Dacron. This sail is strong enough to carry to windward in all but the heaviest blows, and off the wind can be used in any weather.

WORKING JIBS

The single-headsail-rigged boat, though it needs fewer headsails than the double-headsail-rigged boat, does have to change headsails more often, and the crew will spend more time on the foredeck. When it gets too heavy for the three-quarters genoa, the single-headsail-rigged boat should switch to the working jib of heavy Dacron. This sail should overlap the mast by not more than a foot or so, preferably not at all. This working jib is the sail one should use when maneuvering in tight places. Because it overlaps the mast only minimally, it can be sheeted instantly on tacking. A good fast man won't need a winch handle.

All too often this sail is made tall and narrow, so that trying to trim it is like trying to trim a ribbon. It is very important that the angle between the luff and the leech at the head of any Dacron jib be at least 20 degrees; 25 degrees is better, and 30 degrees is excellent. Thus in the design of a working jib, once the length on the foot has been decided, the length on the luff depends strictly on the angle between the leech and the luff. To get necessary area, the foot dimension can be increased; under no circumstances should this area be achieved by making the sail long on the luff.

JIB TOPSAILS

The double-headsail-rigged boat should have the same genoa-ballooner that the sloop has, but once it blows too hard for this sail, should switch to a double-head rig of staysail and jib topsail. The biggest jib topsail should be almost the full length of the head stay on the luff, and the clew should reach or slightly overlap the mast.

Like the working jib, the jib topsail is not very effective if it has the shape of a tall, narrow ribbon. Some of the racing classes, such as the 5.5's, have tall, narrow jibs, but to make these jibs stand, the sheet lead is led down below the line from the miter. As soon as the sheet is eased, the head of the jib sags off and begins to chatter. Once again, it is the angle between the luff and the leech at the head of a jib that is critical, and again, somewhere between 20 and 25 degrees is best. If a greater angle can be carried, so much the better (Drawing 88). To achieve this angle the length of the miter may be increased or the luff shortened. The clew should be quite high or it will backwind the staysail.

Illingworth and Primrose perfected the double-headsail rig for racing (Drawing 89), with jibs and staysails for every weather. For the cruising boat, these are not necessary. The cruising boat should carry a big jib topsail of fairly heavy Dacron, to be set in a breeze of 10 knots or

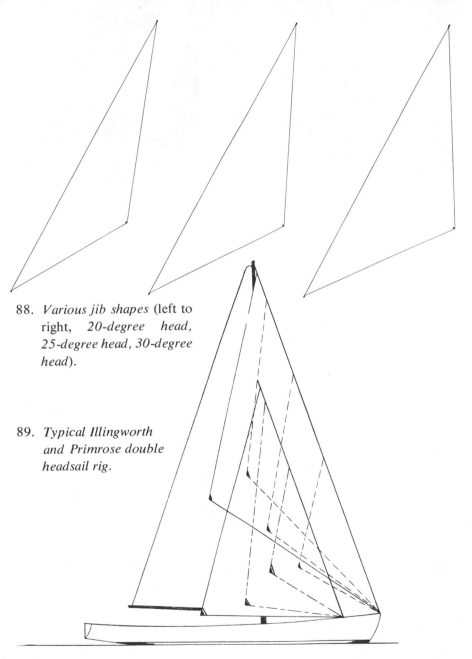

88. *Various jib shapes* (left to right, *20-degree head, 25-degree head, 30-degree head*).

89. *Typical Illingworth and Primrose double headsail rig.*

more, and a smaller jib topsail, the same length on the luff as the stay-sail. In emergencies, the smaller jib topsail can be used as a heavy-weather staysail. This sail should be of heavy Dacron, since it will not be set except in a blow. Under heavy weather conditions, when a sail

55. Merriman heavy weather jib snaps. (Merriman Holbrook)

56. Abeking and Rasmussen staysail snaps. (D. M. Street)

luffs, the flogging will often open the normal jib snap. Hence the heavy weather sail should be secured to the stay with Merriman jib snaps (Photo 55) or Abeking and Rasmussen special staysail snaps (Photo 56) or screw shackles.

CLUB STAYSAILS

Probably most double-headsail-rigged boats have a club staysail. This arrangement is discussed in the section on the club jib in Chapter IV.

If the staysail is boomed, it need not be secured along the foot to the boom; it need only be secured at the tack and clew.

The club staysail should have reef points for rough weather; they may never be needed, but if one should want to reef the staysail, they would be most welcome. The staysail should, of course, be made of heavy Dacron, and if reef points are installed, the clew and tack earings should be of very heavy Dacron, as they will be used in storm conditions.

GENOA STAYSAILS

Illingworth and Primrose are great advocates of genoa staysails, and they really do make a boat go. When they have a big overlap they are difficult to handle, but if they have only a small overlap, they can be sheeted before they fill; only a little cranking on the winch is necessary. They set beautifully in all weathers and points of sailing, and most im-

57. *Forward lower shroud moved inboard to clear the genoa staysail.*
    (*D. M. Street*)

portant, the slight overlap not only produces more area but increases the slot effect. Further, a design which causes the staysail to overlap the mast slightly will also widen the angle between the luff and the leech, thereby making the sail set much better, since, like the other jibs, the staysail should have an angle of 20 to 25 degrees between luff and leech. As noted in Chapter IV, it is absolutely essential that there be a spread between the upper and lower shrouds to allow the genoa staysail to be effectively sheeted (Photo 57).

It should be evident that the double-headsail rig, if the sails are correctly chosen, need not demand too many more sails than the single-headsail rig, and the individual sails (with the exception of the genoa) are smaller and more easily stowed and handled than those of a single-headsail-rigged boat.

ROLLER-FURLING HEADSAILS

So far we have been discussing normal headsails, hanked onto the stay. There is another type of headsail, in use for over seventy years, that has become increasingly popular in the last ten years or so. I have found designs for roller-furling headsails in a book by Linton Hope published in 1902. They have become popular of late because of the improvements in stainless-steel wire, Dacron sails, and so on.

In years gone by, if a roller-furling jib was rolled up wet, it was bound to mildew, and the galvanized-wire luff ropes rusted. Now the only source of concern in a roller-furling jib is that if it is left up month after month, the leech of the sail eventually rots out because of sunburn. If a modicum of care is given to the sail, it will last for many years. I don't leave my roller-furling three-quarters genoa up when in port for long periods of time, and it has lasted nine years.

To make a roller-furling jib last longer, some sailmakers sew an extra layer of cloth on the leech after the sail has been completely made up. This sacrificial layer, made of a lighter-weight Dacron than the sail itself, becomes sunburned and finally begins to disintegrate, but the actual sail is not affected at all. The sacrificial panel is then removed and replaced.

Some people, instead of adding this layer of Dacron, solve the problem by using a kind of long sack, hoisted on the flag halyard, to cover the sail. The sack is usually secured with lanyards or snaps. Eric Swenson, the editor of this book, has come up with what I consider the most brilliant method for securing the edges of the sack; he uses Velcro tape, which is simple and effective.

If roller headsails are to set well, the roller-furling gear must be correctly chosen and rigged. Correctly rigged with a two-part halyard, the luff may be made to stand as straight as that of a hanked-on jib.

Roller-Furling Gear

TRADITIONAL ROLLER-FURLING GEAR: In years gone by, the heavy-duty roller-furling gear most commonly seen on cruising boats was the Merriman gear (catalog Figs. 436–437). This gear was designed back in the 1930's and has remained basically unchanged since then.

This gear gives excellent service, provided the correct size is chosen. All too often people try to save money by buying one size smaller than they should. This is a false economy, for invariably at the worst time there is a huge explosion and the jib is left attached only at its peak and clew, flogging around with a ten-pound roller-furling gear at its tack trying to demolish the boat.

When installing Merriman roller-furling gear one should be sure to place a toggle below the drum so that the drum can pivot in line with the luff of the jib. Unless it lines up perfectly with the luff wire, the jaws at the bottom of the roller-furling fitting are strained, and binding occurs when furling is done in heavy weather.

The one disadvantage of the Merriman roller-furling gear is that the roller bearings, though packed in grease, still tend to corrode and disintegrate, as they are made of hardened steel not stainless steel. Indeed, even where bearings are of stainless steel, over a period of years the ball races will acquire dimples and the balls will tend to flatten, making it very difficult to roll up the jib in heavy weather. Hence, one should carry a spare set of bearings.

The drum of the Merriman gear is so large that to obtain enough turns of wire on the drum to make it possible to roll up the headsail completely in heavy weather, a wire tail spliced to a rope tail must be used.

New Roller-Furling Gear: There are so many new kinds of roller-furling gear on the market today that they cannot all be discussed here. They vary from the most expensive, most beautifully engineered pieces of equipment imaginable, to some cheap pieces of gear that are guaranteed to cause trouble.

When contemplating the purchase of roller-furling gear, one should examine the various kinds that are available. As has been stated, it is essential to buy gear of adequate size. Second, when a tentative choice has been made, one should check the quality of the gear to make sure that it is worth the purchase price. This is best done by taking an engineering friend to the shop and dismantling the gear to its bits and pieces. A beautiful casing can sometimes cover a multitude of sins. Another good test, if the dealer permits it, is to connect the roller-furling gear to a chain block and/or a tension meter, put it under considerable tension, and see if it still turns freely. The Nautical Development Company, of Port Washington, has for many years put on an excellent demonstration of the quality of its gear at the New York Boat Show. A drum and swivel under considerable tension are placed on a stand, and everyone is invited to play with the gear. Despite the considerable tension, it spins freely.

Other equipment on the market is not necessarily anywhere near this good. I note one gear, advertised for use on sails of up to 400 square feet, which is secured to the tack of the sail and the bow fitting with $5/16$-inch stainless shackles; these are grossly inadequate for a sail of 400 square feet.

ROLLER-FURLING LANYARD: On roller-furling gear of relatively small size, used on a small boat, the roller-furling line will be nothing but a piece of Dacron flag halyard. On larger yachts, this kind of line is not adequate. The roller-furling gear is subject to chafe; were the line to break, it would be difficult, perhaps impossible, to furl the sail, and embarrassing or even dangerous situations might result. Further, to be of sufficient strength for the larger gear, this kind of line would have to be of such great diameter that there would not be room enough to stow it inside the drum. On this point, it should be remembered that when a sail is rolled up under strong tension in heavy weather, it rolls much tighter—and therefore requires much more line—than when it is rolled up in light airs or in a calm. Hence, when setting up a roller-furling jib, one should make sure that when the jib is completely rolled up, there are at least eight turns around the drum, to provide the extra length needed in heavy weather.

Some people like to lead the wire from the roller-furling drum direct to a reel halyard winch, which is then used for rolling up the jib. I do not like this method because it is slow, and while the jib is being rolled up it tends to flog, flap, and demolish itself. I prefer to have the wire on the drum spliced to a rope tail. I use forty-five feet of ⅛-inch wire and forty-five feet of ⅜-inch Dacron. The wire runs from the roller drum on the bowsprit back through two fairleads secured on the lifeline stanchions, through a block on the quarter, and thence forward. In moderate weather, one person may sit down and roll up with no problem. If it is blowing harder, two people may heave on the line, or if necessary it may be taken around the cockpit winch and cranked in in the first stages; once the line is partially rolled up, the majority of the sail area has been furled, and it is quite easy to roll up the remaining portion rapidly, hand over hand.

SETTING ROLLER-FURLING JIBS: One reason many people do not like roller-furling jibs is that they tend to have excessive sag in the luff. This is the fault not of the roller-furling jibs, but rather of the gear used to hoist and secure them. Since the roller sail is held at only three corners, tremendous strains develop at these points. The halyard, shackles, and blocks must be tremendously strong, at both the tack and the clew. If the sail is to set right, the luff must take all the strain and the head stay or staysail stay must be slack. No matter what the size of the sail, the luff wire should be ¼ inch or above, to give the sail something to roll on. Further, the wire must be 1 by 19; otherwise it will tend to unlay, and the top and bottom will not roll up at the same rate. If a short tack pendant is needed, it should be made out of stainless steel,

Monel, or bronze rod. A short length of 1 by 19 is inadequate; under heavy strain it will distort, unlay, and fail, usually when one is trying to roll up the jib in heavy weather. Having the jib streaming from the masthead in a squall at two o'clock in the morning is no fun.

Because the roller-furling jib receives no help from the head stay, the gear must be powerful enough so that the entire strain of mast support is taken by the jib. The luff wire of the jib must be of the same diameter as the head stay, and the breaking strength of the drum and swivel must be the same or almost the same as that of the head stay. These requirements are very easy to fulfill; however, to get a halyard the same size as the head stay is quite difficult. For example, a $5/16$-inch 1 by 19 head stay would have a breaking strain of 12,500 pounds; for the same strength, one would need a $3/8$-inch halyard, which would require a sheave approximately $7\frac{1}{2}$ inches in diameter. Further, the load on the sheave pin would be roughly double the load on the halyard, or 25,000 pounds, so a massive sheave pin would be required. The winch taking the halyard, too, would have to be tremendous, since it would have to take a 12,500-pound load.

The solution to this problem is to secure a large block to the top swivel of the roller-furling gear. Then $1/4$-inch 7 by 19 wire halyard is secured to the starboard side of the masthead, brought down through the block, spliced into a rope tail, and brought up through a block on the port side of the mast and down to a winch on the port side. The sail can then be hoisted and winched tight with a normal, moderate-sized winch—preferably a geared winch if the sail has an area of 450 square feet or over.

Rigging a Two-Part Halyard for a Roller-Furling Jib   The standard method of rigging a two-part halyard for a roller-furling jib has been to secure one end of the halyard aloft and then run it down through a wire and rope block which is secured to the head stay by a metal plate to prevent twisting. The disadvantage of this arrangement is that if at the same time a hanked-on headsail has been hoisted on a spare halyard, the metal plate fastening the block to the head stay makes it impossible to lower the roller-furling jib.

Since I frequently like to hoist the genoa behind the roller-furling jib and then roll up the jib, I had to find some other answer to the twisting problem. My first solution was to secure three or four strands of marline from the block to the head stay; these kept the block from swiveling, and once the halyard was two-blocked, the nylon broke, allowing the roller-furling jib to be lowered with the hanked-on jib in place.

After many years, a West Indian crew boy, Zut, came up with a better solution. He suggested securing the dead end of the halyard to the mast with a good swivel, thereby enabling the standing part of the halyard to swivel at the masthead, and eliminating the tendency of the halyard to twist up on itself. Originally, I used the swivel that is mounted at the head of a roller-furling jib. Later, I discovered that it was cheaper to use a good heavy spinnaker-halyard swivel of the type that can be ordered in various sizes from Howe and Bainbridge.

Another objection to the two-part-halyard jib is that when one is not using the roller-furling jib, the two-part halyard is too slow to hoist a normal headsail. This problem too can be solved, for it is relatively simple to transform the two-part halyard into a single-part halyard. An eye splice is placed in the dead end of the halyard, which is then secured to the aforementioned spinnaker swivel, attached to the mast by means of a Gibb shackle (Merriman catalog Fig. 997 or 999), which has a snap at one end and a jaw at the other. Then if one wishes to use a single-part halyard, a man is sent aloft and the snap shackle is undone and brought down to deck. The swivel shackle is removed from the eye splice, the eye splice is passed through a wire and rope block, the snap shackle is reattached to the halyard, and a single-part halyard results. Thus one has the best of both worlds.

The final problem connected with the two-part halyard for the roller-furling jib is the fact that the fall is of course very long; for example, on a fifty-foot spar, once the halyard is two-blocked, a hundred feet of rope line must be coiled and stowed. Since normally ½-inch line is spliced into ¼-inch halyard, the result is a considerable pile of line. To minimize the stowage problem, I use only twenty feet of the ½-inch line, and splice the other end of this ½-inch line into eighty feet of ⅜-inch line, making a relatively small coil to stow.

Similarly, if the roller-furling jib is set on a reel halyard winch, a really good rigger can splice ⅛-inch wire into the ¼-inch wire, appreciably reducing the amount of wire to be stowed on the drum. There must be enough ¼-inch wire so that ten or twelve turns of it are on the drum when the halyard is two-blocked.

Handling Roller-Furling Jibs

When rolling up the jib, one must be sure that the wind is either abeam or forward of the beam. If it is aft of the beam, or dead aft, the head stay is slack, and invariably gets rolled up inside the roller-furling jib and stops it from furling; then one must swing up with the wind abeam, roll the jib out, and start again. Similarly, unrolling the jib is best done with the wind on the beam or forward of the beam. It can be done with the wind at the quarter, but if it is attempted dead down-wind, the jib usually binds against the head stay.

Double Roller-Furling Jibs

Normally, just one sail is secured and rolled on each wire, but some-one always builds a better mousetrap, and Wright Britton saved on sail gear and running rigging by securing both his twins to the same luff wire. He wrote an article for *Yachting* about this rig, which has much to be said in its favor and no real drawbacks, in my view. However, the owner of *Ensis,* who came across the Atlantic with this rig, had very little good to say about it, complaining about the amount of extra gear and the length of the poles. Of course, no two sailors agree. This gear has become so popular that Ratsey and Lapthorn, City Island, New York, is now marketing it.

ROD-LUFF SAILS

In recent years, the rod-luff sail has become very popular. This type of sail is set on a solid steel rod instead of 1 by 19 wire and is claimed to be roller-reefing rather than roller-furling. It is alleged that with a rod luff, one large genoa will do for all sailing conditions, since it can be used completely unrolled, partially unrolled, or as a storm jib, with only a corner sticking out. This assertion is subject to much debate. Most good sailmakers are opposed to the idea, maintaining that a sail used in that fashion will give a lot of trouble: with the sail half rolled up, most of the strain is on the foot and the leech, so the sail is rapidly pulled out of shape and requires recutting. It must also be remembered that as the sail is partially rolled up, the sheet leads must be moved for-ward, if the lead is to be kept correct. Further, I do not believe that any sailmaker can cut a sail that will set perfectly half rolled up.

The rod-luff jib may be good in Long Island Sound, with its basi-cally light airs and short squalls, but it is not advisable for the serious cruising man, planning to sail offshore. The rod-luff sail cannot be stowed on the boat, as is necessary if the weather blows up and a switch to a smaller headsail must be made. It is true that the sail can be coiled, but the coil is so large, that it is impossible to have a hatch on board large enough to permit stowing it below.

LIGHT SAILS

Spinnakers are best left at home under the skipper's bed for any off-shore passage, unless there is a good big crew on board. All too often the result of setting a spinnaker at sea is a torn sail, damaged gear, or a sail wrapped around the head stay. For offshore cruising, the genoa to the end of the spinnaker pole is usually sufficient. I do believe in carrying on board and occasionally setting the spinnaker in alongshore cruising. Alongshore, there are frequently long periods of calm or light airs, and the big spinnaker enables one to ghost along with perfect comfort, safety, and serenity. But this is alongshore, not offshore.

MIZZEN STAYSAILS

Although Eric Hiscock does not like a mizzen staysail on his new ketch, I feel that it is an ideal cruising sail and really earns its money. It can be set with the wind anywhere from one point forward of the beam to dead aft. When the wind gets on the quarter, it is best to douse the mizzen and rely on the mizzen staysail. On a ketch, the mizzen staysail is often actually bigger than the main, and many boats have crossed the Atlantic with headsails, a big mizzen staysail, and an awning rigged under the mizzen staysail.

Mizzen staysails are wonderful passage sails; size for size they are not expensive, they take up no room, and off the wind, especially in light airs, they really make a boat go. Made out of 1.5-ounce rip-stop nylon, they are amazingly strong. They are easy to set; one need only fasten the tack to a pad eye, snap on the sheet and halyard, haul away, and sheet in—being careful not to forget the mizzen backstays. Mizzen staysails of the smaller sizes are easy enough to douse, but on the larger sizes it is imperative to have a jackstay—a light, removable stay from the mizzenmast head to the tack-down point. The mizzen staysail should have three to five hanks. Then when the time comes to douse it in a squall, one man can haul it down the stay. If, instead, it is held only at three corners, when the sheet and halyard are slacked, it just plasters itself up against the main rigging and is all but impossible to douse without tearing.

Mizzen staysails are real pullers in light airs, when the heavier working sails will not draw. The old, heavy *Iolaire*, with a displacement of twenty tons, always does well on a reach or a run during our Thursday-afternoon regattas because of the pulling power of the mizzen staysail.

FISHERMAN STAYSAILS

There are other sails seldom seen on a cruising boat that are very useful and not difficult to handle if they are correctly rigged. The first of these to come to mind is the fisherman, on a schooner. In the days of gaff-rigged schooners, with triatic stays, spring stays, and what-have-you between the masts, and a gaff-rigged foresail, the fisherman was a real mankiller. It was hoisted on a jackstay and had to be brought down on deck and rehoisted every time the vessel tacked. However, this is not true today on the average schooner.

On a staysail schooner, a track which makes handling the fisherman quite simple can easily be mounted on the foremast. With the peak halyard shackled on the head of the fisherman, and the other halyard shackled on the throat, one can heave away: two-block both halyards, heave down on the tack downhaul, and sheet in. When tacking, the fisherman is handled just like a jib; it must be sheeted with each tack. Admittedly this is work, but the normal cruising schooner becomes a very fast vessel indeed when this sail is used, as shown by the fact that the old *Golden Eagle, Onward III,* and *Nina* were consistent winners in races even when they had to go to windward, which is not supposed to be a schooner's forte.

MAIN-TOPMAST BALLOON STAYSAIL

On some staysail schooners the track has a switch and a spur, so that beside the fisherman, the golliwobbler—formerly called the main-topmast balloon staysail—can be stored. This is the sail that really makes schooners go; with the wind abeam it is a real puller, and when the wind is off the quarter, or when going dead downwind, the main may be doused and the golliwobbler trimmed to the end of the main boom. The golliwobbler is seldom seen on cruising schooners, but I feel it is an excellent sail, for it is light, it is not too difficult to control if set on a track, and it produces no chafe problems.

On a long downwind passage on a schooner, I would be inclined to use a reaching jib, a golliwobbler, and no main. If the wind shifted so that the course was dead downwind, I would use the reaching jib to windward on the pole and the golliwobbler to the end of the main boom to leeward. It is roughly with this rig that *Dirigo II,* a heavy cruising Alden schooner, made a record passage from the Galápagos to Tahiti.

TOPSAILS

Topsails are something I know little about, but I do know that if one puts a big topsail on a little, fat gaff cruising boat, she will really get up and go, surprising everyone. In the old days, good runs were turned in by gaff-rigged boats using topsails at every chance. For the person who has a gaff-rigged boat and feels he needs extra sail area, an easy solution is to attach a straight aluminum pipe to the top of the mast and install the necessary rigging to set the topsail. Perhaps an extra topmast should be carried on deck. But it should be remembered that replacing a topmast at sea was not formerly considered, as the West Indian would say, "some big ting." My friend Jack Carstarphen, on *Maverick,* has lost three topmasts, and he reports it is quite easy to replace one in a couple of days; he is even thinking of carrying around a spare with him. In the old days, when the spinnaker pole was longer than the base of the fore-triangle, it was usually a relatively simple job to rig the spinnaker pole as a topmast.

Complete information concerning topsails can best be obtained from British cruising or racing books published before World War II. However, in the following sections may be found some tips and hints by Roger Fothergill, owner of Claud Worth's famous *Tern IV*. Fothergill is such an advocate of topsails that he switched *Tern IV,* then a Marconi yawl, back to her original gaff-cutter rig. He is one of the few men I know who likes and understands the topsail.

GENERAL REQUIREMENTS

There are two principal requirements for a topsail—it must be large enough to be worth setting, and it *must* set well.

As regards size, it should be not less than a quarter the area of the mainsail approximately, but can be up to half the area, as long as it still sets well.

The yachtsman who is sufficiently dedicated carries two topsails, a working one and a ghost. The basic gear needed to control any topsail consists of just a halyard, a sheet, and a tack line. There are, however, numerous minor extras used to achieve a good set or to facilitate hoisting or furling; these include downhauls, brails, jackstays, and so on.

TYPES OF TOPSAILS

There are two main types of topsails—those which are set from the deck, and those which remain aloft when furled, known as standing topsails. Generally speaking, the standing topsail sets best, since it can, and should, always be set on the lee side of the peak halyards. However, it is not practical for small vessels, since a hand working aloft is required both to set it and to take it in. Also, there is a point in size below which a sail of this type becomes not just unsafe but also impossible to handle.

Topsails Set from the Deck

JIB- OR THIMBLE-HEADED TOPSAILS: Of the topsails set from the deck the simplest is the jib-headed, or thimble-headed, topsail. This is a triangular sail with a thimble at each corner, comparatively easy to hoist, sheet out, and tack down. But unless something is done about the luff, it will sag off when on the wind and prove of little use when close-hauled. Various methods have been used to overcome this failing. One common method in quite small yachts has been to have eyelets sewn along the luff of the topsail, to which thimbles are seized. Before hoisting, the hauling part of the halyard is rove through these thimbles, and when all has been set up tight, the halyard itself helps to keep the luff from sagging off. Larger vessels have used a jackstay consisting of a light wire made fast to the topmast or masthead at a point which will lie about halfway along the luff of the topsail when it is hoisted; at that point on the luff, a thimble is seized. Before hoisting, the jackstay is rove through the thimble and its end set up on deck; then when the topsail is hoisted, its luff is brought into the mast as it rides up the jackstay.

YARD TOPSAILS: An entirely different approach to this problem of keeping the luff straight has been to bend the topsail to a yard before hoisting it, whereupon it becomes one of the many varieties of yard topsail. An added advantage of this arrangement is that it provides extra area, as the halyard is usually made fast to the yard somewhere above the center, so that when hoisted, the upper part of the yard extends above the masthead. In any case, this is the only type of topsail that can be set on vessels with short mastheads.

Where the topmast is extremely short, another method is used. A case in point is the Falmouth Quay punts, small cutters which attended the windjammers lying in Falmouth Bay and the Carrick Roads. Since they had to maneuver alongside square-rigged craft, passing under their lower yards on occasion, these cutters had very short mastheads. However, they set large yard topsails. To allow the top of the yard to extend high enough beyond the short masthead the halyard was bent to the yard well below the center point; and to prevent the yard from capsizing as soon as hoisting began, the heel of the yard was clipped or shackled to the after lower shroud. This arrangement kept it on end as it was hoisted and gave it an aesthetic cant forward when fully set, which was very pleasing to the eye.

Jack-Yard Topsails   Just as the head of the topsail can be extended above the mast by means of a yard, so the foot can be extended beyond the end of the gaff by a short yard. This spar, which is laced along the after part of the foot of the sail, is called in England the jack yard. In the days before synthetic fibers, when stretch was a problem, the relationship between the topsail clew and the end of the gaff was always altering, as both mainsail and topsail stretched. This meant that the topsail sheet no longer led fair and the sail ceased to set well. However, if the topsail had a jack yard, the position of the sheet could be moved along it as the sails stretched, and the set of the topsail could be maintained; hence the jack yard was much commoner in those days than it is now. To hoist a topsail equipped with both topsail yard and jack yard on a breezy day, one brings the two yards together and passes a light twine seizing around them and the bunt of the sail; the yards are then hoisted up on the halyard, and when they are fully up, the sheet is manned smartly to break the seizing and sheet home the jack yard. A certain expertise is needed, but the satisfaction, if the operation is successful, is immense.

Gaff Topsails An earlier type of yard topsail is the gaff topsail. This is a four-sided sail with a yard laced to its head which, when the sail is set, crosses the topmast at an angle. It is, in fact, a small lugsail set on the topmast and sheeted to the gaff. This topsail can be made very large; indeed, with the aid of a jack yard one can manage a topsail quite half the size of the mainsail. It is difficult to measure and cut, and tricky to set; also, it is quite useless if not well set. To describe the methods used to ensure a proper set to a gaff topsail is beyond the scope of these notes (one could write a paper on the subject); suffice it to say that once the snags are overcome, it is the most efficient of all the topsails set from the deck, and quite the most splendid to look at.

HALYARD INTERFERENCE WITH TOPSAILS: All the topsails so far described, and any others set from the deck, can only be set on that side of the mast to which their gear is rove. Consequently, on one tack the topsail will be found on the weather side of the peak halyards which, girting across the lower part of the sail, render it less efficient than when on the other tack. To minimize this interference with the topsail, the peak halyard blocks are carried as low down the masthead as is consistent with their being able to fulfill their function.

Standing Topsails

One can avoid this problem altogether, and incidentally ensure a perfect-setting topsail at all times, by using a standing topsail. This sail is bent to mast hoops which run on the topmast; like any other topsail, it is equipped with a halyard, a sheet, and a tack line, but it also carries a downhaul. Of course, it needs a hand aloft for setting or furling, and for this reason it is rather less popular than those set from the deck. To set it, a hand goes aloft and casts off the gasket, then passes the tack line (which is made up with the sail) over the peak halyards to leeward and out over the *weather* side of the gaff, and so down to the deck, where—after the halyard and sheet have been set up taut—it is set up with a purchase. When the vessel goes onto the other tack, the tack line is let go and a hand aloft hauls it up (now on the weather side of the peak halyards), passes it over to leeward of the peak halyards and out to the *weather* side of the gaff again, then tosses it down to the deck to be set up, the sheet and halyard being undisturbed all the time. For a short tack it can be left unaltered, but will not be very efficient.

The standing topsail also has a downhaul which leads from the deck through a small block seized to the head of the topsail, through a thimble seized to an eyelet halfway along the leech, through another seized on one side of the clew, and is finally made fast to an eyelet halfway along the foot of the sail. With halyard and sheet let go and the downhaul manned, the sail is not only hauled down onto the lower mast cap but semi-furled as well, and left in a compact bunch which only requires the gasket passed around it and the lee cap shroud to secure it safely. This type of topsail thus has an added advantage in that should a squall come down, the topsail sheet and halyard have only to be let go and the downhaul manned, and the sail is virtually furled; when the squall eases, the process is reversed and the sail is set once more without any need to go aloft, and without the fuss occasioned by bringing the whole lot down on deck as is necessary with any other type of topsail.

STORM SAILS

STORM HEADSAILS

All boats need a storm jib or staysail if they are to do any serious cruising. This sail should be of very heavy Dacron, with heavy hanks, like those advised for the smaller jib topsail, and should be of Scotch cut (Drawing 91). Scotch cut is very useful for storm sails because the seams run parallel to the leech and the foot of the sail, and therefore if a seam begins to open in heavy weather, the sail will not be split luff to leech. The greatest strain is along the seam rather than across the seam.

The storm staysail should have half to two-thirds the area of the normal staysail. On the double-headsail-rigged boat, the storm staysail will be well aft and off the bows. On the single-headsail-rigged boat, there should be a separate emergency staysail stay that can be set up for the storm staysail (Drawing 92). This arrangement is very common in Europe, where each year many ocean racers get stuck out in a full gale and must be able to beat to windward to keep from being driven ashore.

This stay serves many purposes. It moves the center area of the storm jib back aft, nearer the mast, making it easier to heave to, and it

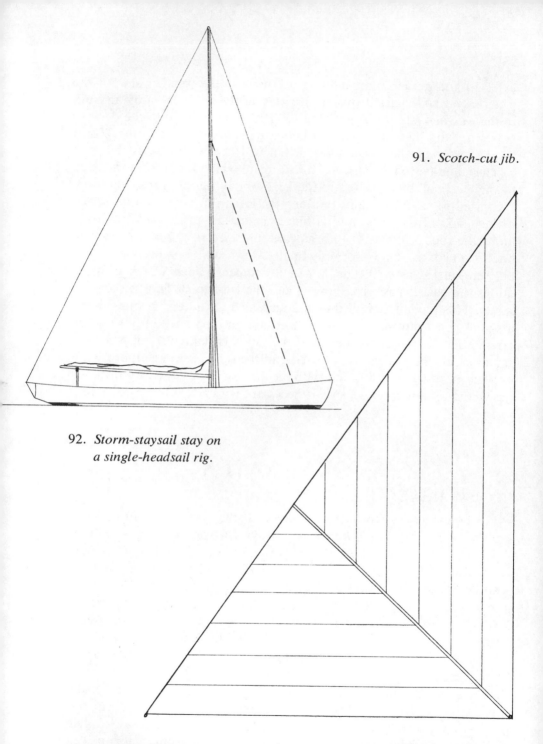

91. *Scotch-cut jib.*

92. *Storm-staysail stay on
a single-headsail rig.*

gives a slot effect between the storm staysail and the storm trysail when
one is trying to claw off a lee shore. The sail is easier to handle, since
the sail handlers are not in the eyes of the boat, disappearing under

93. *Storm trysail.*

every wave. And the stay gives extra fore and aft support to the mast when it is most needed.

STORM TRYSAILS

The storm trysail too should be made of the heaviest grade of Dacron, Scotch cut, and very heavily reinforced at all corners. Furthermore, the cringles should be extra large to allow extra lines to be run through them when necessary. This sail should be cut flat but high at the tack so that it can clear the furled mainsail (Drawing 93). I believe that a large storm trysail, equivalent in size to a double-reefed main, is preferable for use in heavy weather to the double-reefed main. The latter is most likely to be double-reefed at a time when half a gale is blowing. There is an extra-heavy strain on the sail and it is concentrated on the part that is most vulnerable—the upper portion, which chafes on the shrouds and is most likely to have weak seams. However, a large storm trysail, made of extra-heavy material and Scotch cut, suffers little or no wear in these circumstances, and there is no chance of it blowing out. The boom is down in the gallows frame, where it belongs in heavy weather. If the wind increases, it is a comparatively easy operation to reef a loose-footed trysail. Nevertheless, many good sailors do not agree with me and stick to their little trysail, regarding it as a last resort only, rather than as a mainsail for very heavy weather.

VII

~~~~~~~~~~~~~~~~~~~~~~~~~~~~~~~

Deck Layout

The deck layouts of yachts have improved over the years. Thirty years ago few yachts had lifelines, and those were rudimentary; still fewer had bow pulpits; almost none had stern pulpits. It was presumed that anyone going forward to handle headsails or going aft to tie in the clew earing was a well-trained seaman with suction cups on his feet and a grip like a vise.

Fittings were usually of galvanized iron, and were often not well secured. Mass seems to have been more important than design. Ventilators were few and far between, and hatches leaked like sieves, or were prevented from leaking by canvas covers firmly secured over them. Dodgers were unknown, and doghouses, except on European boats, were almost unknown. Happily, today much of this is changed; however, our stock builders still seem completely unable to make watertight hatches.

COCKPITS

A boat should be designed for the climate where it is to be sailed, and cockpit sizes and locations vary accordingly.

Ocean racers on both sides of the Atlantic usually have relatively large cockpits, because even in the smaller classes they will have to contain four to six men cranking winches. However, although these cockpits are usually roomy, frequently their seats are at two levels—a disadvantage in warm climates, where sleeping on deck is desirable, as one cannot stretch out and sleep comfortably unless one has 6½ feet of flat space on one level. If a boat is to be used in the tropics or on the east coast of North America, the cockpit seats should be at least 6½ feet long, to permit comfortable sleeping.

European cruising boats invariably have very short cockpits. It is not at all unusual to see motor sailers and midship-cockpit cruising boats of forty to forty-five feet with cockpits only four or five feet long. These are fine in European waters, where the weather in general is so bad that most of the time is spent below decks.

COCKPIT LOCATION

Until about twenty years ago it was almost unknown to have a cockpit anywhere but at the stern of the boat. Everyone sat aft, out of the spray kicked up when going to windward. However, an aft cockpit means that the helm and crew are in an exposed location going downwind before a gale. Further, when the whole crew sits in the cockpit, a boat is likely to squat by the stern, which does not improve her sailing qualities. In years gone by, in Europe, it was common on boats of fifty-five feet and over to have a small cockpit well aft, but to place the doghouse amidships. Thus in foul weather the owner and his friends would sit amidships, warm and snug in the doghouse, while the professional skipper and crew sat out in the cold and wet.

On the older British yachts the doghouses were most practical. No attempt was made to put the whole saloon on deck; instead, the doghouse was a small, comfortable cabin where three or four people could get out of the weather and still see what was going on. Usually it was narrow enough so that it did not obstruct the fore-and-aft movements of the crew, nor did it obstruct the view of the helmsman, who could see up the deck on either side of the doghouse.

In the late 1940's, a number of designers, in order to provide more privacy, placed the cockpit so far forward that there was room behind it for an after cabin. This layout has a number of advantages: being further forward, the cockpit has much more width, so big sail lockers can be placed under each side; the engine can be installed beneath the cockpit, where access is easy; weight is moved out of the stern; and in heavy weather, with the boat running downwind, the danger of the cockpit being flooded when pooped is reduced to a minimum.

DOGHOUSES AND DODGERS

When a boat is reaching or beating to windward, midship cockpits are wet. Some designers compensate for this by putting a doghouse over the forward end of the cockpit (Photo 58), where everyone except the helmsman can sit comfortably, back against the cabin, fully sheltered.

This doghouse arrangement works admirably in northern climates. However, in southern climates, it leaves a good deal to be desired. On a

58. Midship cockpit with open doghouse. (Doug Terman)

59. Antilles dodger. (D. M. Street)

boat sitting at anchor in hot weather, no breeze can reach the cockpit. For this reason, numerous designers specify full-width dodgers (Photo 59), which give the same shelter as the doghouse, but can be collapsed when not wanted. This arrangement is lighter, cheaper, and more practical in a southern or tropical climate.

If the dodger is merely snapped to a breakwater on the cabin top, water can drive up underneath and between the snaps securing it. This problem can be solved by installation of a wooden breakwater grooved to take a boltrope sewn to the bottom of the dodger (*A* in Drawing 94).

If it is not possible on an existing boat to build in the grooved breakwater, the next best arrangement is to secure an aluminum extrusion (*B*

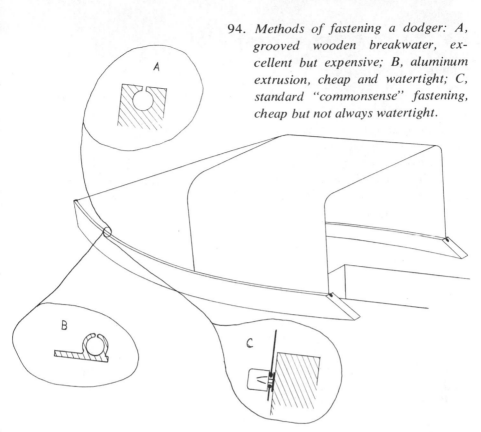

94. *Methods of fastening a dodger: A, grooved wooden breakwater, excellent but expensive; B, aluminum extrusion, cheap and watertight; C, standard "commonsense" fastening, cheap but not always watertight.*

in Drawing 94) along the deck and feed the boltrope through this extrusion. If an aluminum extrusion is unavailable, grooved wooden strips (Photo 60) will suffice. In the same manner, dodgers may be installed over the hatches, allowing them to remain open in all but the very worst weathers.

60. *Grooved wooden strips for hatch covers. (D. M. Street)*

COCKPIT SEATS

Cockpits should be comfortable to sit in not only in port but also at sea. On small boats it is relatively simple to design a cockpit of such width that a person sitting on the windward side can brace his legs comfortably on the lee side.

However, on large or beamy vessels the width of the cockpit often makes it impossible to brace one's legs on the lee side. Hence, when sitting on the weather side of the cockpit with the lee rail down, one must hold on for dear life by wrapping an arm around a winch, cleat, or whatever is handy. This situation may be remedied by installation of a removable bar (Drawing 95) along the part of the cockpit sole where people are likely to need a foot brace. The bar will be wanted only when the rail is down; otherwise it may be removed and stowed.

Cockpit Coamings

Cockpit coamings frequently have a capping, which is fine so long as it is flush with the inside of the coaming. However, the capping often extends ⅜ to ½ inch inside the vertical coaming (Drawing 96), and is therefore extraordinarily uncomfortable to lean against. Cockpit coamings should be smooth and preferably toed outward a few degrees. The minimum height above the seat or cushion for a comfortable coaming is 14 inches; 16 inches is better.

Seat Cushions

There is a long-standing debate concerning the desirability of cockpit cushions. Being skinny, I feel that they are necessary. However, these cushions are often too thick—four inches or more—with the result that they are unstable to sit on, take up too much room, and tend to slide around. Further, thick cushions too frequently are made of foam rubber, which absorbs water like a sponge. In heavy weather they may weigh as much as fifty or sixty pounds. Cockpit cushions should be made of polyfoam, which does not absorb any appreciable amount of water. Further, polyfoam cushions with rings sewn at the corners may be lashed together to form an emergency life raft.

Even polyfoam cushions will absorb moisture if they sit in a pool of water on the lee side of the cockpit. This soaking may be avoided two ways—by the use of duckboards and by the installation of properly designed seat drains. Cockpit cushions should be set on duckboards (Drawing 97) which keep them about ¼ inch or so above the seat, allowing air to circulate underneath the cushions. The duckboards should be made of teak and left unvarnished, so as to be easy to maintain and not slippery. They should have a one-inch lip at the outer edge

95. *Removable footrest for wide cockpit.*

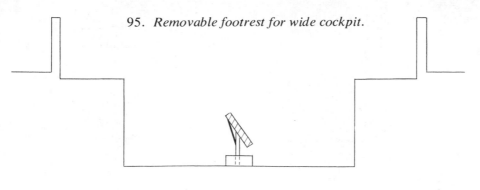

96. *Improper capping on coaming;*
the shaded area should be removed.

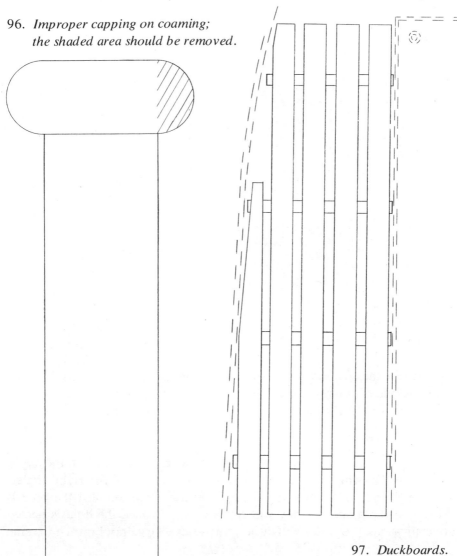

97. *Duckboards.*

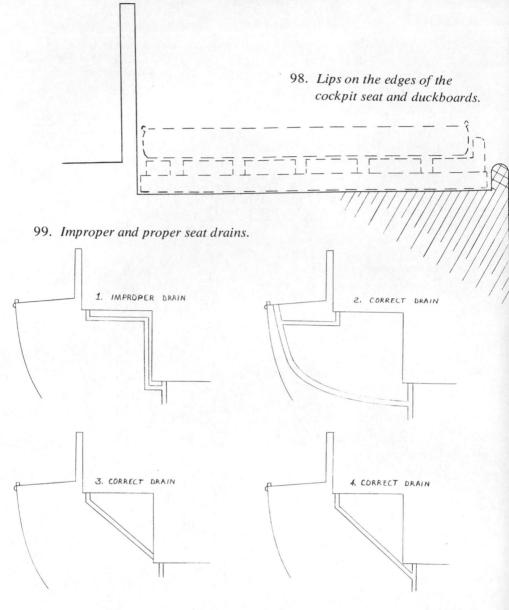

98. *Lips on the edges of the cockpit seat and duckboards.*

99. *Improper and proper seat drains.*

1. IMPROPER DRAIN

2. CORRECT DRAIN

3. CORRECT DRAIN

4. CORRECT DRAIN

to prevent the cushions from sliding off the seat and into the middle of the cockpit. Similarly, the edge of the cockpit seat should have a half-inch lip to keep the duckboards in place (Drawing 98).

Seat Drains

The seat drains should be carefully designed. Drains of the types shown in Drawing 99 are not satisfactory because of the right angles. Although they will empty the cockpit during a rainsquall if the boat is sitting at the mooring, they will not do the job once the boat is heeled over; instead, the water will either collect in a large pool on the lee side of the cockpit or leak below and keep the sail lockers soaking wet. The drains should be led diagonally (Drawing 99), and then they will drain directly overside through the cockpit scuppers.

Cockpit-seat scuppers should be made of plastic hose. Their diameter is so small that they are continually being clogged with matchsticks, cigarette butts, and the like. Scuppers of copper tubing are difficult to clear, but if made of plastic tubing they can be disconnected, cleared with a wire, and reinstalled.

Seat-Locker Latches

In the old days, cockpit seat-locker latches caused much anguish. It is essential that cockpit seat lockers have good latches to hold them closed in heavy weather; otherwise, if the cockpit is flooded, the seat lockers may be thrown open and the boat filled with water in a matter of seconds. In the past, these latches were usually Highfield levers of one pattern or another—expensive, easily damaged, and great catchers of clothes. Recently, however, yachtsmen have obtained from the automotive industry a very effective solution to the problem. This is the rubber hood latch with metal fittings, as used by Mercedes-Benz on

trucks and by Morris on the Mini Moke (Photo 61). The metal fittings, which are of steel in the automotive latches, can be duplicated in brass or stainless steel for marine use. Simple, absolutely foolproof, and easily replaceable, this is by far the best latch. On some boats it is also used to hold down skylights, hatches, and the like.

61. Mini Moke hood latch.
(D. M. Street)

COCKPIT SOLES

Every builder treats the cockpit sole in his own way; I find most satisfactory an unvarnished teak grating made to cover the sole. Such a grating is completely nonskid, requires minimum maintenance, and always looks trim. In port, one can remove the grating and then disassemble the engine, clean parts, and do other dirty, messy jobs in the cockpit without creating a mess elsewhere. Once a job is completed, the sole may be scrubbed out with diesel fuel and the cockpit grating reinstalled, covering any remaining stains.

AVOIDING COCKPIT FLOODING

Where there is a large, comfortable cockpit, the problem arises of what to do when the cockpit is flooded. In the 1950's large cockpits were installed in ocean racers to enable a full working crew to work the winches with plenty of elbow room. However, it was discovered that these cockpits were dangerous under certain conditions. They were so big that when a boat was pooped, the cockpit floor sank below the waterline level, and the flow in the scuppers was reversed.

At present, an ocean-racing rule limits drastically the size of the cockpit by regulating the cubic content of the cockpit as compared with the displacement of the boat. Some boats with high coamings could not race under the rule until large gravity-opening bronzed doors were installed in the sides of the coamings at deck level (Drawing 100), lowering the floodable level and thereby reducing the amount of water that could be held in the cockpit. This arrangement is desirable for a cruising boat as well.

Cockpit Scuppers

Cockpit scuppers should be as large as practical. Admittedly, a twenty-two-foot midget ocean racer needs only half-inch plastic hose, but the sixty-foot yachts should have discharge pipes with a diameter of two inches or more. These discharge pipes should be as straight as possible to facilitate the free flow of water. An owner in doubt about the size of his cockpit drains can perform a simple test. He should moor alongside the dock, and get the yard to set its big emergency pump on the dock, with the intake hose in the harbor and the discharge hose in the cockpit. Then he should fill the cockpit right up to the top of the coamings, turn off the pump, measure the amount of freeboard remaining when the cockpit is full of water, and check the time necessary for the cockpit to drain out completely. If much freeboard is lost with the cockpit filled, at sea in rough weather the next wave will probably come aboard and keep the cockpit full.

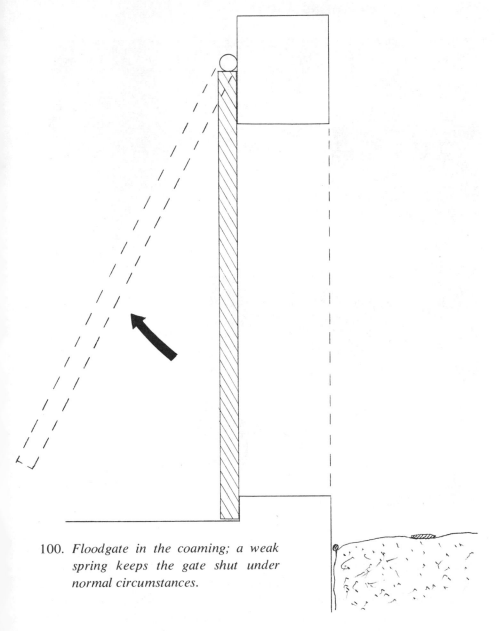

100. *Floodgate in the coaming; a weak spring keeps the gate shut under normal circumstances.*

WINCHES AND
THEIR MOUNTINGS

The size and power of winches is discussed in Chapter V. Equally important, however, is their location and mounting. On ocean racers, the helmsman is frequently stationed so far forward or aft of the winches that he cannot reach them. His function is to give orders and

62. Antilles *cockpit side winch base.* (*D. M. Street*)

concentrate on sailing the boat, and he is not to be distracted by cranking or tailing up on winches. The situation is different on a cruising
yacht. Since a true cruising yacht usually sails shorthanded, the helmsman must.be able to get to all or most of the sheets. As a bare minimum, he should be able to reach the mainsheet and one headsail sheet.
On a single-headsail yacht the problem is minimal, but in locating
winches on a double-headsail-rigged boat one must decide whether the
helmsman is to be able to reach the jib-topsail sheet or the staysail
sheet. On ketches and yawls, it is advantageous for him to have the
mizzen sheet at hand.

Formerly, winches were mounted on wooden blocks secured by long

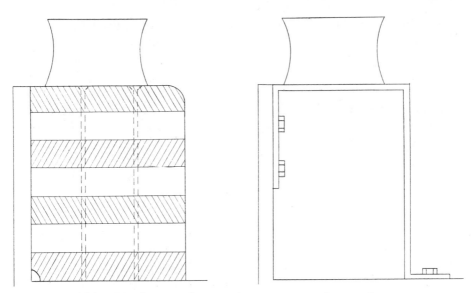

101. Wooden winch mounting versus metal mounting.

bolts to the deck beams and perhaps an underlying pad. This was a difficult installation, for the wooden blocks had to be laminated up and the bolts were frequently twelve to eighteen inches long. Drilling and driving had to be done very carefully to prevent leaks. Further, removal of the winch was a problem because it is difficult to drive out bolts of that length. Even now one finds yards still laminating up blocks for winches, as they have carpenters capable of doing this job, but do not have welders capable of making really finished metal winch brackets. However, today large winches are frequently installed on bases (Photo 62) made of bronze or stainless steel. The winch is secured to the base with relatively short machine screws. The bolts securing the base to the deck and/or cockpit coaming are relatively short. Although the metal base is expensive, when the total cost of the base and hardware is compared with the cost of the old-style wood base and hardware, the additional strength and ease of installation seem worth the small difference in price (Drawing 101).

The more powerful the winch, the stronger must be its base and its fastenings to the deck and cockpit coaming. On a 48-to-1 winch with a double handle, two men can easily develop 18,000 pounds of line pull. This should be remembered when the winch is being installed. Merely screwing the winch into the deck and bolting it to one or two deck beams is not enough. It must be bolted to a pad with a spacer that bridges two or more deck beams. Before mounting the winch, one should calculate what line pull it will develop, then double that figure to determine the strain that will be placed upon the winch when the boat is punching into a head sea in rough weather and the genoa picks up a wave.

Placement of the winches is very important. They must be not only firmly bolted into position but also located so that a man may brace himself and crank to maximum advantage. It does no good to install a very expensive, powerful winch if it is placed so that the winch cranker cannot develop maximum power. Mounting on one side of the cockpit is usual, since a person kneeling in the cockpit, or with one foot in the bulwark and one in the cockpit, can develop good power.

Recently, in order to reduce the number of people in the cockpit, some yachtsmen have mounted two winches port and starboard on the after end of the cabin top, instead of on either side of the cockpit coaming. This setup seems to work well, as the winch cranker can really brace himself in a standing position and crank away. However, in mounting winches on the after end of the cabin top, one must first be sure that the cabin top is strongly built, and one must also sacrifice the dodger across the forward end of the cockpit. Like everything else in a boat, this arrangement is a compromise.

On flush-deck boats, mounting a winch outside the cockpit is a real problem. Winches bolted down in the middle of a vast expanse of smooth teak deck are not particularly efficient, since the cranker and the tailer have no place to brace themselves. There a coffee grinder— or pepper grinder—comes into its own. A man can stand up and really put his back into winch handles which are mounted at waist level. On flush-deck racing boats it is not uncommon (now that ocean racers are no longer required to carry rigid dinghies) to find two coffee grinders mounted amidships, side by side. More usual on cruising boats and older ocean racers is one coffee grinder mounted on the stern, where it can handle both genoa sheets by means of lead and quarter blocks.

Another important, and often neglected, aspect of yacht design and winch installation is the height of the winch base. If riding turns are to be avoided, the winch must be mounted high enough so that the bottom turn on it leads slightly down to the block through which the line is led. On modern boats with only a toe rail or low bulwark this requirement causes no problems; however, on boats with high bulwarks it can be a source of great difficulty. On a standard four-inch snatch block, the distance from the top of the genoa track to the bottom of the sheave is seven inches; thus the top of the winch base should be nine inches above the top of the genoa track. For this reason, blocks are often fitted to hold the sheet down (see Chapter V).

63. Running Tide *winch console.* (*Charles Booz*)

HALYARD WINCHES

At one time, halyard winches were always bolted to the sides of the masts. This arrangement works well on flush-deck boats and those with plenty of nonskid area on the cabin top. However, on some modern boats the high crown on the cabin top makes it difficult to maintain one's footing on the lee side while trying to tail and crank on a halyard winch. On modern ocean racers one frequently finds the halyard winches mounted on the cabin top. Especially on boats with a trunk cabin this is an excellent arrangement, as it brings the halyard winches to a very workable height. On flush-deck boats, if the winches are bolted directly to the deck they are usually low and difficult to work.

A few very expensive ocean racers have mounted a winch console (Photo 63), a massive aluminum plate bolted to the deck, to which are bolted all the halyard winches, in an imposing array. This is a most practical system.

DECK HARDWARE
PAD EYES, SHEET TRACKS, AND BLOCKS

To lead sheets from the sail to the winches, blocks are required at various points on the deck. Before World War II, there were relatively few pad eyes along the side of the deck to take the blocks, and the fine adjustment of sheet leads was made by using a tack downhaul to the headsails: instead of running sheet leads forward, one raised the whole headsail, and instead of leading the sheet further aft, one hauled the headsails further down on the stay. After World War II, it became customary to secure a genoa track along the rail cap as far outboard as possible. Normally the genoa track is placed outside the lifeline stanchions. However, especially on beamy boats designed for racing, a second genoa track is installed inside the lifeline stanchions, so that the biggest genoa can be sheeted inside the stanchions.

Installation of a genoa track along the rail cap requires very long screws going down through the rail cap and into the toe rail, or into the bulwark. The bulwark must be firmly secured to the covering board and sheer strake. In heavy weather there is considerable lifting strain on the track. Further, when adjusting the genoa slider, one must remember that the lead between the sheet lead and the winch must be led from the bulwark to the winch at a right angle, as it is all too easy to twist the genoa track right out of the toe rail or bulwark. For this reason, the use of quarter blocks is becoming more and more common; the sheet leads always go to the quarter block and come to the winch at a constant angle. Also, after experiencing trouble with the genoa-track distortion under load, some boats have been fitted with long stainless-steel or aluminum plates on the bulwark, with numerous holes to take the snatch blocks. Other boats have gone back to the old-style pad eyes.

64. Screw-in airleads.
   (*Merriman Holbrook*)

65. Staysail-sheet blocks with screw-in eyes.
   (*Merriman Holbrook*)

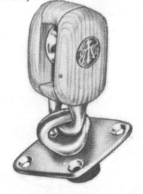

102. Feather on staysail sheet track to prevent fouling and broken toes.

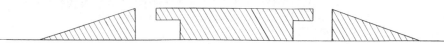

Leads for the staysail sheets are usually screw-in eyes (Photo 64) or wide-mouthed blocks with screw-in eyes (Photo 65). When the sheet leads are not being used, they may be unscrewed, leaving a clear, unobstructed deck. On some boats, however, an adjustable lead is desired for the staysail sheet, as well as the jib-topsail sheet and the genoa-staysail sheet, and a track is installed along the deck. It is, of course, an efficient toe remover. The damage done to the crew's feet can be minimized by installing wood feathers (Drawing 102).

CLEATS

When it comes to cleats, I admit to a strong bias. I believe that the only one that should be installed is the old-fashioned cleat originally designed by Nathanael Herreshoff back in the 1890's, and manufactured by various people ever since (Photo 66). The crossbar stands high, so there is room to take plenty of turns around the cleat; it has four well-spaced fastenings; it is open in the center so a strop or a large snap shackle may be snapped around it if desired. In general, it is superb. Various other cleats are available (Photo 66)—Merriman Truform, wooden cleats, plastic jam cleats—but they are all second-rate in comparison. To be sure, on boats of up to 30 feet LOA, the various types of jam cleats used on the one-design racers will be eminently satisfactory.

Sheet cleats need not be as strongly mounted as the winches, for if sufficient turns are placed around the winch, the pull on the cleat will be only a quarter to an eighth of the line pull on the winch. However, frequently a block, a tackle, or a rope strop will be placed around the cleat in an emergency, and the cleat will have to do a job for which it was not designed. Hence it is a good idea to install cleats which can carry a much greater load than they are normally intended for. When a cleat is attached to the cockpit coaming in the vertical plane it should be secured with machine screws to a bronze or stainless-steel plate on the inside of the coaming to spread the load (Drawing 103). If it is only secured with nuts and washers, the nuts will protrude uncomfortably in the cockpit and not give a sufficient spread to the load. When a cleat is secured to the deck, there must always be a large block or backing plate beneath it.

A cleat that is to take heavy strain should be carefully mounted. Serious damage has often been done to a boat by the departure of a mooring or spring-line cleat. The cleats for mooring lines and anchor lines must be heavily secured to the deck, as they may be used for trying to tow a boat which was unfortunate enough to run aground off

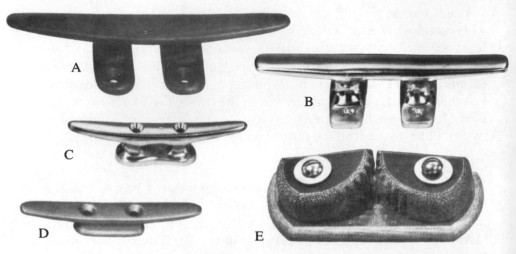

66. *Various cleats. A. Popular modern cleat. B. Similar to, but definitely not, a Herreshoff cleat. C. A type of cleat to be avoided. The ends are too high—will snag the wrong line. Cleat secured by only two screws. D. Good for small lines (³⁄₁₆ or ¼ inch). E. Cam action cleat. Popular on dinghies and small cruisers; unsuitable for large, cruising yachts. F. Herreshoff cleat—still reputed to be the best. (Land's End Catalogue and D. M. Street)*

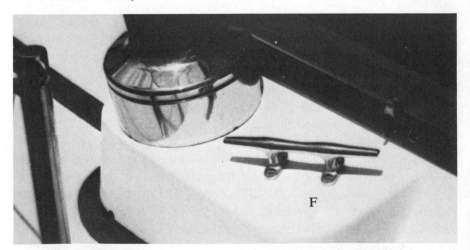

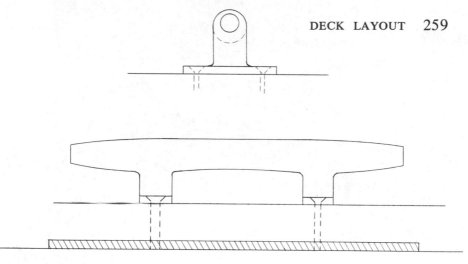

103. *Herreshoff cleat mounted on the cockpit coaming with a metal backing plate.*

a shoal. Mooring cleats should be secured to a heavy block of wood under the deck which bridges at least two deck beams and is firmly attached to them.

CHOCKS

Chocks are often neglected on modern boats; they are generally poorly designed, too small, inadequately placed, and improperly secured. On bow chocks with rollers (Photo 67) almost invariably the rollers are not large enough. Often chocks are provided on top of the

67. *Roller bow chock.* (*D. M. Street*)

68. Antilles *bow chock mounted in the bulwark, opening chocks on top of the bulwark, danforth stowed in the pulpit.* (*D. M. Street*)

rail, or are built into the bulwarks forward, but one seldom sees a chock amidships in the bulwarks. The built-in chocks in the bow (Photo 68) are all very well, but sometimes it is very difficult to reeve lines through them in a hurry, so open or opening chocks should be mounted port and starboard on the bow (Photo 69). For both bow and quarter lines I prefer what is referred to as the Skene type of chock; each chock of this sort is specifically designed either for port or for starboard use, so care must be taken to install it on the correct side of the boat. Amidships, a chock should be placed through the bulwark or on top of the rail (Photos 70 and 71), as that is where the spring lines should be rigged when the boat is coming alongside the dock. If a spring line is rigged from the bow or the stern, as soon as a strain reaches the line, the bow or stern tries to come in. If it is not possible to provide a separate chock in this position, a line can be rigged through a snatch block as a spring; this arrangement, though adequate, is not the best.

Closed bow chocks (Photo 68) are excellent because they give wonderful places through which to reeve the main-boom fore guy, the pole fore guy, and so on. Strops can be rigged through them, to which snatch blocks can be attached for extra fore guys and the like. On numerous occasions, boats which have lost their head-stay fitting on the bow have been brought home with the head stay secured by the anchor

69. *Skene chocks.* (*Land's End Catalogue*)

70. Antilles *bulwark chock.*
   (*D. M. Street*)

71. *Rail-cap chock.*
   (*D. M. Street*)

line rigged through the forward bow chocks and around the bow three or four times. A firmly mounted bow chock is very strong and has no tendency to move even if a foul strain is placed upon it.

GALLOWS FRAMES

Gallows frames are very seldom seen today on yachts. Everyone is now too concerned with wind resistance. However, I refuse to go offshore on a boat that does not have one. Too many people have been injured by a topping lift that let go and dropped the boom into the cockpit in heavy weather. Further, even if the topping lift holds, it seems the height of folly in heavy weather, with the mainsail stowed, to let the boom and the sail hang on the lift with two strong tackles heaving the boom down. No matter how tight the tackles have been set, there is always a little stretch in the topping lift; and each time the boat rolls, the boom works everything a little bit looser. In heavy weather, when the mainsail is doused, the boom should be dropped into the gallows and firmly secured there by mainsheets and/or tackles. Then it cannot get adrift and do damage. At the same time, the gallows provides a good hand hold for people working on deck. But while a main-boom gallows is a must for any boat of thirty feet or above going offshore, a mizzen-boom gallows is a bit of a problem, and is not necessary except on quite large boats.

The gallows must be strongly constructed and braced securely fore and aft and athwartships. Also, if possible, it should be removable for short inshore or round-the-buoy races. On most boats with cabin trunks the type of installation shown in Drawing 104 is preferable. A piece of pipe is welded to a flat plate which in turn is bolted to the cabin trunk. A pipe one size smaller than the pipe welded to the plate is used for the main frame of the gallows. This must slide freely inside the plate. It may be secured in place by set screws. Since the outer pipe is secured for a length of eight to twelve inches to the side of the cabin trunk, it provides firm fore-and-aft and athwartship support.

The gallows secured back aft in the old style or in the middle of a flush deck is most difficult to support. Since reliance must be placed almost completely on its heel fitting, this must have good bolts securing it to the deck. Further, the heel fitting should consist of a large plate with a pipe welded to it. Again, the actual frame of the gallows should drop inside the base plate and be secured with a set screw or large cotter pin.

Gallows have a reputation of being very ugly, and likely to catch sheets, guys, or what-have-you, but if correctly designed, they need not do so. The gallows frame on *Iolaire* (Photo 72) has never caused this

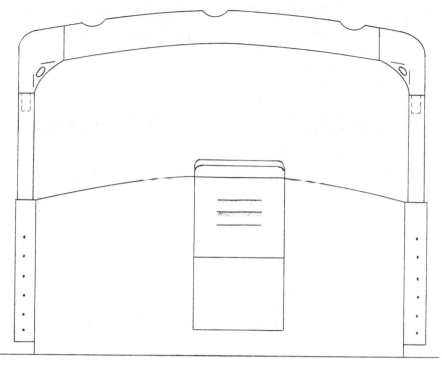

104. *Gallows frame is both adjustable and removable.*

72. Iolaire *gallows frame and sailing awning.* (*D. M. Street*)

kind of trouble, mainly because of the superb end fittings made by Merriman (no longer in the catalog but last carried as Fig. 543). These are simple bronze castings. If Merriman cannot supply them, perhaps you can find an older boat with these fittings; using one of these as a pattern, any foundry can cast a set.

LIFELINES AND PULPITS

Before World War II, lifelines were seldom rigged on boats except in heavy weather. Bow and stern pulpits were practically unknown. A cruising boat or offshore racer had bulwarks—four inches high on the little thirty-five-footer, 2½ feet on the hundred-footer. Lifelines were generally rigged only in heavy weather; in the few offshore boats that did have them, they usually consisted of a line hitched around the main rigging, run aft to somewhere in the vicinity of the cockpit, and run forward to the bowsprit.

Just before World War II, some ocean racers began to install lifelines as standard equipment, and one or two actually installed bow pulpits. After World War II, lifelines became mandatory on all ocean racers. About 1950, bow pulpits became mandatory, but not until recently have stern pulpits ("pushpits" to the British) been required.

Many builders tend to forget that lifelines, stanchions, and bow and stern pulpits are not installed as ornaments. Their purpose is to prevent anyone from falling overside. Therefore they must be firmly bolted to the deck and must be of adequate strength—as they all too often are not in the boats being produced today.

LIFELINES

It is most important that the lifelines be sufficiently strong. When the boat is lying alongside a dock, a two-hundred-pounder is likely to stand on them when climbing on board. In heavy weather, the crew members may clip their individual safety lines onto the lifelines. To assure adequate strength, the lifelines must be made of stainless steel. The plastic-covered galvanized wire is worse than useless, because frequently corrosion occurs under the plastic covering, not to be discovered until a crew member finds himself overboard. Uncovered 1 by 19 wire is acceptable, as the individual wires in this size are big enough so that they do not tend to strand. Uncovered 7 by 19 wire leaves much to be desired because the individual strands are likely to break, catch a spinnaker or mizzen staysail, and tear the sail. By far the best wire for lifelines is 7 by 19 plastic-covered stainless—of the finest quality obtainable. The thick plastic covering is what is needed; the thin plastic coating on cheaper wire is lost all too soon. I know from learning the hard way.

Years ago, lifelines were always spliced, but as we have seen, splicing is rapidly becoming a lost art. Eye splicing, or bending around a thimble and securing with a Nicopress, or the equivalent, leaves something to be desired because it is impossible to pass the eye of the lifeline through the eye of the stanchion. For this reason it is usual to use either a swage (Photo 73) or a Norseman fitting (Photo 74); both of these will allow the lifeline to be unrigged at any time.

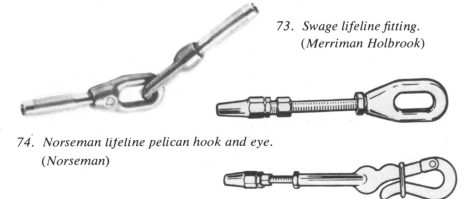

73. Swage lifeline fitting.
(Merriman Holbrook)

74. Norseman lifeline pelican hook and eye.
(Norseman)

Ordinarily, the tension on a lifeline is adjusted by means of a ¼-inch or ⁵⁄₁₆-inch turnbuckle. However, since a turnbuckle of this size, while expensive, is easily damaged, it is preferable to adjust the tension on the lifeline by means of a lashing of ³⁄₁₆-inch dacron, passed through the eye in the pulpit and through the eye on the lifeline six or eight times and heaved tight. The lashing is, if anything, stronger than the wire and cannot be damaged by unfair strains (Photo 75).

75. Lashing lifeline ends. (D. M. Street)

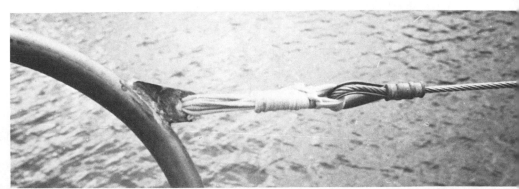

76. *Break in lifeline, with pelican hook.* (*D. M. Street*)

On all but the smallest boats, there should be a break in the lifeline at the gangway stanchions. This is normally made (Photo 76) with a short length of wire and a pelican hook. This is easy to open and close, but it is also all too easy to dislodge the pelican hook accidentally at sea. Therefore, if this method is used, once the boat leaves port the pelican hook should be taped closed. Lifelines made up with no turnbuckles can be so arranged that they include a gangway break that does not require a pelican hook. They are shackled directly to the bow and stern pulpits and reeved through the stanchions; once they have been reeved through the stanchions forming the midship gangway break, the Norseman lifeline end fittings are secured. A ³⁄₁₆-inch Dacron lanyard is spliced to one eye, then reeved back and forth between the eyes, heaved tight, and secured with a rolling hitch (Photo 77). This procedure effectively tightens the lifelines and does away with the turnbuckles and the potentially dangerous pelican hook in the break in the lifeline.

The lower lifeline is a relatively recent addition. Generally, a ³⁄₁₆-inch hole is drilled in the middle of each stanchion, and a piece of ⅛-inch 1 by 19 wire is threaded through the holes and adjusted and

77. *Break in lifeline lashing.* (*D. M. Street*)

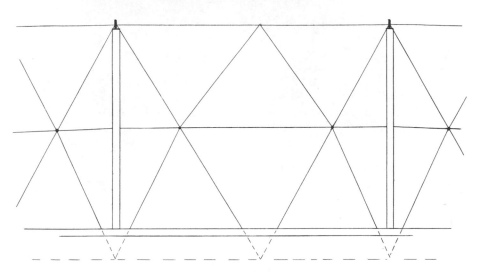

105. Zigzag line in the lifelines to prevent sails from blowing overboard.

secured like the upper lifeline. A few boats have plastic lower lifelines, but these require special stanchions with plastic bushings to avoid chafe. Another refinement found in some boats is a zigzag line secured to the lifelines forward, to help prevent headsails from blowing overboard when they are being changed (Drawing 105).

Lifeline Stanchions

On old, large yachts the stanchions were usually short and placed in the top of a high bulwark, with ½-inch or ⅝-inch line reeved through them, and they protected only part of the boat. When lifelines were first extended the full length of the boat, the stanchions were usually made of cast bronze, and were threaded into a baseplate so that they could be removed for alongshore racing or cruising. These bronze stanchions were beautiful, but very heavy and expensive.

At present, stanchions are almost universally made of stainless-steel or bronze pipe. There was a period just after World War II when British ocean racers were extensively equipped with aluminum lifeline stanchions set in galvanized-iron baseplates—a combination which proved notably unsuccessful. Because of their unreliability in these years, British lifeline stanchions were placed much closer together than American stanchions. Now stanchion spacing seems to have been standardized by the ocean-racing rules, at seven feet. Similarly, stanchion height is standardized at twenty-four inches for all except the small JOG and MORC boats, which are allowed twenty-inch stanchions. The taller stanchions are not advantageous on a small boat because when the

78. *Merriman and Lewmar lifeline stanchions.*
(*Merriman Holbrook and Lewmar*)

boat is heeled over, the space between the cabin and the stanchion is drastically restricted, making it very difficult to move along the weather deck. Further, on a small boat one is likely to crawl, rather than walk, in heavy weather, so the height is not so important.

A stanchion should be strong enough so that it will not bend if a 220-pounder seizes the top, puts his feet on the rail, and leans as far outboard as possible. Lifeline stanchions should be made out of ¾-inch thick-walled stainless-steel pipe; anything lighter is likely to bend. Photo 78 shows standard stanchions by Merriman and by Lewmar.

STANCHION BASES: Stanchion bases should be tested in the same fashion as stanchions. All too many of our stock designs in recent years would not stand this test, being fabricated of light stainless-steel plate. Furthermore, many of these bases are not adequately secured to the deck. A base must be through-bolted with heavy bolts, and in addition a heavy pad must be placed under it to distribute the load over the deck; otherwise, under stress the entire baseplate and six square inches of deck may all come loose in one fell swoop.

The Lewmar catalog (Fig. 1099) and the Merriman catalog (Fig. 672R) show well-designed cast-bronze stanchion bases. These bases not only give proper support of the stanchion in all four directions, but also have eyes on the side which enable one to shackle fore guys, boom vangs, or what-have-you to them. If it is to support a stanchion adequately, a base should be similar to these in design.

Bases of this type have come into popular use because relatively few modern boats have bulwarks of any height. With a fulcrum of perhaps only three inches, the base must be extremely strong. If a boat has bulwarks of six inches or more, additional support can be obtained by placing a bronze plate over the top of the bulwark and around the stanchion (Photo 79; Drawing 106). The base then need not be as strong as if it alone supported the entire stanchion, and if the covering board is

79. Iolaire *lifeline stanchion.* (*Laurie Legay*)

106. *Stanchion supported by bulwark.*

sufficiently thick, the baseplate can be secured by big screws, rather than bolts. A stanchion supported like this will normally bend flat before it will break loose. This is well illustrated by *Iolaire*'s stanchions, which are made of 1-inch thick-walled stainless pipe. Each one is supported not only at its base, but six or eight inches above its base, by a brace to the top of the bulwark. Though one of these stanchions was bent almost 180 degrees, neither the base nor the rail-cap support came loose. A properly secured stanchion base of the type offered by Lewmar and Merriman is also strong enough so that though the stanchion will bend, the base will not come out of the deck (Photo 80).

PULPITS

At one time, pulpits were normally made up of iron pipe and then galvanized. This method was not really satisfactory because every few years the pulpit had to be removed and regalvanized. Also, when it was bent, the straightening process was likely to remove all the galvanizing, making it necessary to regalvanize once again. In recent years, however, pulpits have been made almost exclusively of heavy bronze or stainless-steel pipe, with the latter becoming more and more common.

80. Stanchion bent, but base held. (D. M. Street)

81. Pulpit of correct size (Antilles). (*D. M. Street*)

A well-designed pulpit is a godsend, but is difficult to come by. Many pulpits are not very well designed. The most common error is to place the forward end of the pulpit too close to the head stay, so that there is no room to stand or sit between the pulpit and the head stay. The other error is to make the pulpit too wide, so that when one is chocked in the pulpit, the head stay is not in a convenient position. A man should be able to sit inside the pulpit, firmly braced, with both hands free to work on the jib snaps (Photo 81).

The pulpit must of course be securely bolted to the deck. A 220-pounder should be able to hang from one side of it without shaking it. All too often the baseplate for the pulpit provides support only fore and aft, not athwartships. Also, the pulpit must be designed to take the aft pull of the lifelines; a person standing on the lifelines puts a tremendous strain on the pulpit, and if it bends out of shape, the lifelines are slacked. It should be noted here that the British racing rule requires an intermediate bar in line with the lower lifeline so that one cannot fall through the pulpit. Such a bar makes it very difficult to bring the an-

82. Pulpit of A-frame bowsprit. (W. H. DeFontaine)

chor on board, since the anchor must then be passed over the entire pulpit. To facilitate anchor handling, therefore, a removable lower pulpit bar may be installed. This is excellent, but expensive.

The pulpit not only is a safety aid, but also serves other purposes. Frequently, chocks for the spinnaker pole are installed in the pulpit. Further, running lights are normally placed there, since they are then visible even when a low-cut genoa is used, and are kept out of the worst of the spray. Often, a bail in the pulpit provides a handy place for securing spinnaker halyards and spare jib halyards.

In former years, the bowsprit was referred to as the "widow-maker." With a pulpit at its end, the bowsprit is much less of a widow-maker. However, making a pulpit stay at the end of a bowsprit is difficult. I have spent much money and time redesigning and rebuilding my pulpit in an effort to make it stay on the bowsprit. It is still there, but it shakes and shivers. Boats equipped with an A-frame bowsprit are much better off. The pulpit can be secured to the A-frame solidly, with ample spread; the whole thing can be welded into one unit (Photo 82).

Pushpits, or Stern Pulpits

"Pushpit," the British term, is by far more picturesque than "stern pulpit." Originally, the pushpit was a simple railing around the stern of the boat, usually incorporating the stern light. As years went by, more and more things were included in the pushpit. Frequently today one sees a pushpit that also serves as the support for backstays, the main-sheet horse, dinghy davits. This is particularly likely on transom-sterned boats, where bringing the backstays to the top of the pushpit gives them extra fore-and-aft spread, making it easier for them to clear the main boom and the leech of the mainsail.

AWNINGS

Awnings are a subject of great argument in the tropics, but on one fact everyone there agrees: no sailmaker and no awning maker in the United States or northern Europe knows how to make an efficient awning.

The first error comes in the choice of material. Sailmakers almost invariably make their awnings of nylon or Dacron. These are a nuisance in the tropics because of their chatter when the breeze blows. Also, the reflection from a Dacron or nylon awning is so great that one can sit under the awning in the shade and get a very bad sunburn. Furthermore, though nylon and Dacron do not mildew, they are affected by the sun. Within not too great a time, the awning itself sunburns and falls to pieces.

In *Cruising Guide to the Lesser Antilles,* I strongly recommended the use of boat-shrunk Vivatex for awnings. Since that time many new cloths, fibers, and finishes have come to the market, and some have been promoted as the ultimate awning material. Most of them are expensive, and having watched awnings made, folded, stowed, and used, I still believe that the best material with which to make awnings is this boat-shrunk Vivatex. It is soft, waterproof, mildewproof, easy to sew, and relatively inexpensive.

When it comes to rigging an awning, sailmakers once again seem to be at a nearly total loss. Most awnings require three people and half an hour to rig. They have battens, spreaders, strings, pulleys—the works —all expensive to make and difficult to connect up. A boat awning is frequently close to the size of the mainsail, and in the tropics may be left rigged for days or weeks on end. Hard squalls come through, and unless the awning is made in the same fashion as the mainsail—roped on all sides, with heavy reinforcement patches on the corners, sewn grommets, and so on—it soon departs in long ribbons.

One reason I prefer a yawl to a sloop is that rigging the awning is simpler on a yawl. The awning on *Iolaire* is easily rigged, and remains firm no matter what the wind velocity. It took me a full seven years to design this awning so that it fit the boat to perfection.

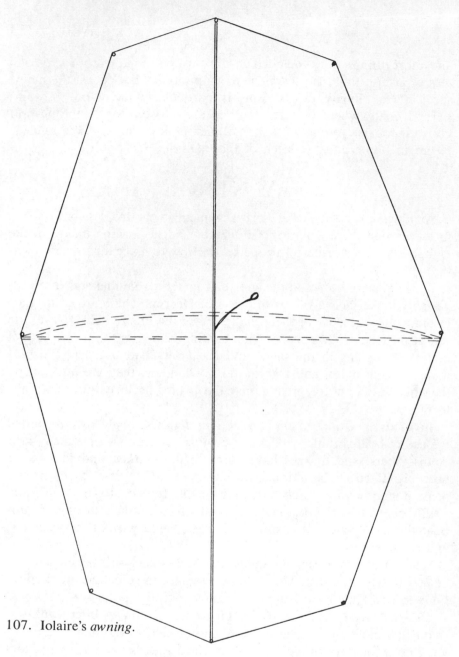

107. Iolaire's *awning*.

Iolaire's awning is simplicity itself (Photo 83; Drawing 107). It is wider in the middle than at the ends, to prevent scalloping in the center when it is stretched tight between the main and the mizzen. It is roped down the center and on all four sides, with heavy reinforcement patches where it is attached to the mainmast and mizzenmast and at the four corners and amidships, where the awning spreader is attached. The awning is thrown over the boom, and secured to the mainmast

83. Iolaire's *awning.* (*D. M. Street*)

with a lanyard; another lanyard, at the center after end, is reeved
through an eyebolt on the mizzenmast and then back through itself,
tightened, and secured with a rolling hitch. The mizzen-staysail halyard
is then secured to the single lift on the ridge rope. Then the two forward corners of the awning are secured to the upper shrouds by jib
snaps. The awning is then secured to the awning spreader by two more
jib snaps, which hook into pad eyes at the end of the spreader. A light
lanyard secures the center of the spreader to the ridge rope, directly
under the lift eye. Each of the after corners is lashed to the mizzen rigging by running a lanyard from the cringle around the mizzen rigging,
back through the cringle, back around the mizzen rigging, and then
down to the lifelines, there to be secured with a clove hitch. The mizzen-staysail halyard is heaved up to lift the spreader to a height where
it clears the tallest member of the crew. Lanyards from the spreader
tips are then secured to midship cleats, and light lanyards leading down
from the forward jib snaps are snapped onto the forward lifelines. All
this can be done faster than one can write about it, and the result is a
completely clear space under the awning. A person 6 feet 2 inches tall
can stand under *Iolaire's* curved awning spreader. This spreader is
stored forward, outboard of the spinnaker pole.

Some people like side curtains on their awnings to give additional shade and keep out rain. This is a matter of personal preference. Side curtains make it impossible for one to see out when standing. Further, side curtains add appreciably to the size and volume of the awning. Many people who dislike the late-afternoon sun insist on having a sun-shade hung vertically from the after end of the awning, since in the tropical northeast trade wind area, the stern will always be to the sun at cocktail time.

VENTILATORS

When the Stephens brothers designed *Dorade*, they invented a type of ventilator which still bears the name, being known as the Dorade vent. Until then, all ventilators fed directly below; they were fine during good weather, but no help just when they were most needed—in a blow, with the hatches dogged down. Basically, the design of the Dorade vent has changed not at all. Its essential feature is a baffle between the downtake from the vent and the downtake into the hull. However, through the years various improvements have been made, the first and

108. *Dorade vent with two intakes and
      adjustable plywood baffle.*

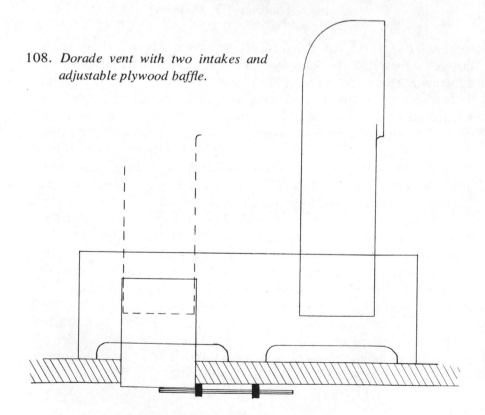

foremost being the introduction of a box with two holes in the top. Thus in hot weather, with no rain or spray flying, one can switch the vent to the after, straight-through hole, and obtain much more air (Drawing 108).

Years ago, Dorade boxes were square wooden boxes with wooden tops. After World War II, the design was changed slightly so that a translucent top could be screwed to the wooden box, giving more light belowdecks. Now many boats have streamlined fiber-glass boxes with no sharp or projecting edges.

The advent of the Dorade vent meant that for the first time in history the belowdecks area could be kept ventilated even in bad weather. However, everything involves compromise: there then arose the problem of damage to ventilators in heavy weather. Until the middle 1950's, ventilators were almost exclusively made out of light sheet metal and were very prone to damage. Further, the old-style ventilator had a lip under which the sheets tended to catch. And if a sheet threw a half hitch around the ventilator, it was almost impossible to unfoul.

In the early 1950's, Moyle came out with a ventilator made of vermalite (a salt-water aluminum alloy), which I think is superb. There is no lip on the forward face for a sheet to catch; it is light; and it is so strong one can stand on it without causing damage. However, getting the aluminum alloy to hold paint requires extra effort. For this reason, when *Djinn* was built, fiber-glass ventilators of similar pattern were used. These are light, strong, and easy to keep painted, and do not corrode.

A few builders, such as Abeking and Rasmussen, mold cast-bronze ventilators, but these have the great disadvantage of being both heavy and expensive.

VENTILATOR SIZE

Ventilators should be as large as possible. People may complain that big ventilators produce too much cold air belowdecks. However, there is the old dodge of putting a sock in the downtake, or better, one can have a baffle made out of $\frac{7}{8}$-inch plywood (Drawing 108). With a baffle of this type, the air flow can be regulated as desired. Ventilators under four inches in diameter are almost useless. Since the amount of air that passes through a ventilator varies with the square of the diameter, increasing the diameter from four to five inches gives a slightly more than 50 percent increase in the volume of air passed; an increase from four to six inches in diameter more than doubles the amount of air into the vessel.

Height is very important, as one can see by observing the increasing motion of a piece of woolen yarn as it is gradually raised from a distance of six to a distance of twenty-four inches off the deck. A height of at least a foot is desirable. Low vents, such as the low collapsible vents placed on the new stock fiber-glass boats, are totally useless. They are expensive ornaments that really do not produce enough air to make them worthwhile.

LOCATION OF VENTILATORS

If ventilators are not properly located, the jib sheet will wrap around them at every tack. Normally, one ventilator is mounted on the foredeck, forward of the midpoint between the mast and the bow, where there is little or no danger of its snagging a sheet during tacking. On some boats, one or two ventilators are mounted three or four feet forward of the mast. These are in a dangerous position; unless a guard of some sort is placed over them, the genoa sheet will foul them continually. One solution is a heavy bronze or stainless-steel hoop (Drawing 109). Another solution is to face the two ventilators toward each other and join them with a piece of heavy, short cord secured to the lashing eyes at their tops (Drawing 110). This method is inconvenient because the ventilators must be faced to each other every time the boat is tacked. If there is only a single ventilator close to the mast forward, it should be faced aft and a lanyard run from its top to the spinnaker-pole slider prior to tacking.

Ventilators placed just aft of the mast usually do not cause much trouble, unless they are mounted too far outboard. If so, they should be faced athwartships and connected by shock cord prior to tacking. However, if they are fairly near the center line, there is little or no danger of their being caught by the genoa sheets. Elsewhere in the boat there are few problems involved in mounting ventilators; one should just check that they do not foul sheet leads. When installing ventilators aft, one should remember that quarter berths and berths in the after cabin are very hot in the tropics. Hence for tropical sailing one must make sure that vents feed into all the quarter berths; otherwise they will be uninhabitable.

It should be remembered that all Dorade boxes and ventilators must be firmly attached to the deck. They are very prone to damage if a heavy man or a spinnaker pole falls against them.

HATCHES

Before World War II, few boats had Dorade vents, so in heavy weather, when the hatches were battened down, the boat in a temperate

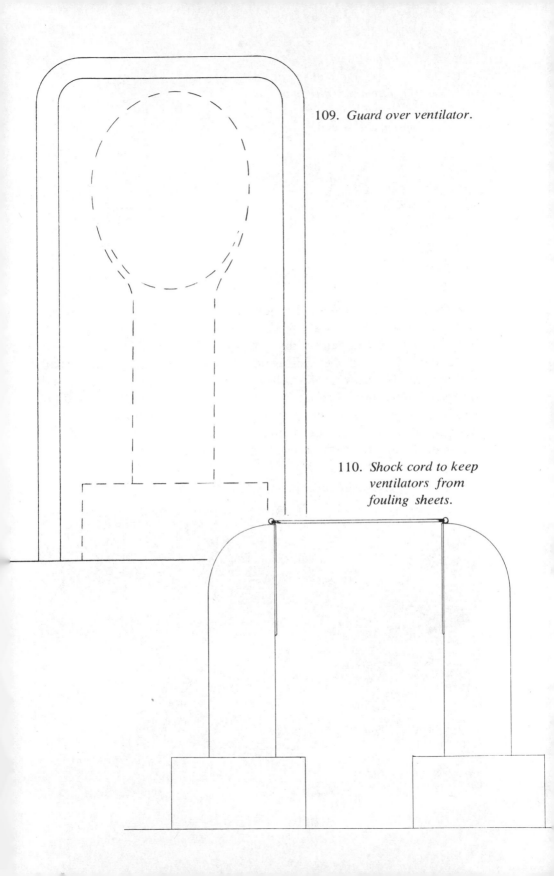

109. *Guard over ventilator.*

110. *Shock cord to keep ventilators from fouling sheets.*

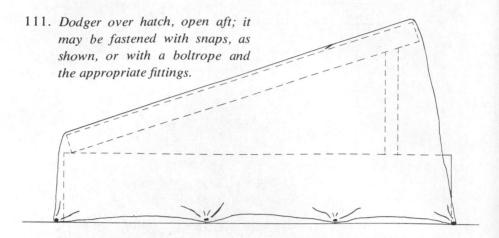

111. *Dodger over hatch, open aft; it may be fastened with snaps, as shown, or with a boltrope and the appropriate fittings.*

area became stuffy and smelly, tending to make the whole crew sea-sick. The boat in a tropical area became an unbearable gigantic sweat-box. Few boats had canvas dodgers over the companionway hatches (Drawing 111), and the old-fashioned fore-and-aft skylights usually leaked like a sieve. The old-fashioned skylight (Photo 84) is a classic thing of beauty, but it belongs in a museum, not a boat. One could pre-vent it from leaking in heavy weather only by placing a canvas cover over it, secured with battens and wedges like the cargo hatch of a freighter. The belowdecks area then became dark and stuffy.

84. Old-fashioned skylight. (D. M. Street)

85. Antilles *submarine-type hatch.* (*D. M. Street*)

Many designers have attacked the problem of hatches. A Sparkman and Stephens design that can be referred to as a submarine hatch (Photo 85) is excellent in that it can be dogged down firmly so as not to leak a drop. However, this type of hatch is expensive and difficult to maintain; also, the fact that it is secured directly to the deck makes putting a baffle around it difficult, so in heavy weather it must be kept closed. Further, its dimensions suggest that it was designed for a small man.

In my estimation, the best hatch is the one designed by Maurice Griffiths (Drawing 112). It is thirty inches square—the minimum size

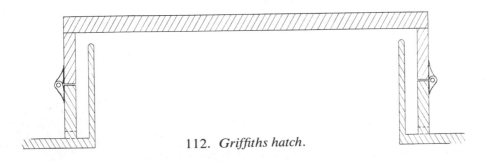

112. Griffiths hatch.

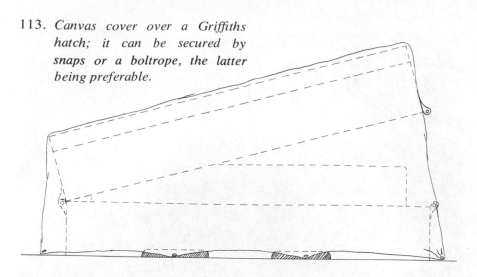

113. *Canvas cover over a Griffiths hatch; it can be secured by snaps or a boltrope, the latter being preferable.*

for a hatch on any boat, for though boats may differ in size, people are pretty much the same. The hatch is hinged at both the forward and the after end, so in port it can be opened forward, and at sea it can be opened aft, with a dodger around it to keep out the spray. Indeed, with its double rim, which acts in the same fashion as the baffle of the Dorade box, and with the canvas dodger secured above it (Drawing 113), this hatch can be left open at its after end in any but the heaviest weather. Further, the cover can be attached to the thwart of a dinghy secured upside down on top of the hatch. Then even in the heaviest weather the hatch in the main cabin can be left open and a free flow of air guaranteed, for the cross-sectional area exposed by a half-opened hatch is infinitely greater than that afforded by a ventilator of four or five inches in diameter. If the boat is to be used extensively in a tropical or subtropical climate, the hatches should be hinged on all four sides. Then when the boat is alongside a dock in a cross wind, or is sailing on a reach in a light or moderate air with no spray, the hatches may be faced to windward.

To allow light to pass freely below, the top of a hatch should be made not of wood but of ¾-inch or 1-inch Lucite. If one desires more privacy than clear Lucite permits, one can take a piece of fine sandpaper and sand the surface, making it opaque—and nonskid—but still permitting light to pass through.

Needless to say, a hatch should be made as large as is practical. This is especially important for the forecastle hatch on a boat that will be extensively raced. Passing sails in and out through a small hatch is discouraging and time-consuming. On a cruising boat too, if the forecastle is to be used as a sail locker, the forecastle hatch should be at least thirty-six inches square, and even larger on the sixty- and seventy-footers, to facilitate the removal and stowage of sails.

SLIDING COMPANIONWAY HATCHES

Because it is likely to leak, the sliding companionway hatch has a very bad reputation. Where there is just a straight sliding hatch on the cabin top, it is all but impossible in heavy weather to keep water from driving up under the forward end of the hatch and dripping down on the chart table or on the cook or bunk underneath. The first improvement on this type of hatch was the addition of a box into which it could be slid. This would appear at first glance to be the perfect solution. However, it generally is not. In most designs incorporating the box, the runners extend up into the box, with the hatch overlapping the runners (Drawing 114). This type of hatch is prone on certain occasions to dump a couple of quarts of water out of its lee side.

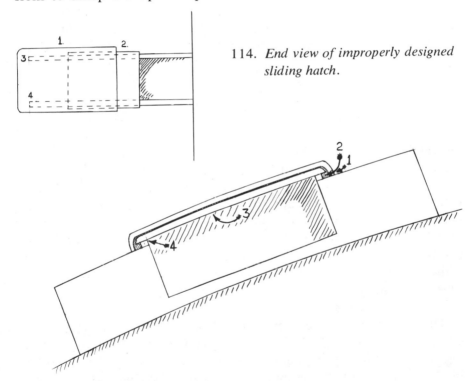

114. *End view of improperly designed sliding hatch.*

What apparently happens is this: with the vessel heeled down on a starboard tack, a heavy wave comes aboard; water pours along the starboard (i.e., windward) side of the hatch runner, and runs forward into the box and over to the lee side of the hatch runner. Then the bow rises, and the water accumulated in the lee side of the box comes running aft and spills out into the cabin. A hatch can be constructed which will minimize this problem (Drawing 115). The sides of the box itself form the runners for the hatch. The hatch slides inside of the two run-

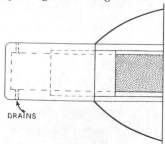

DRAINS

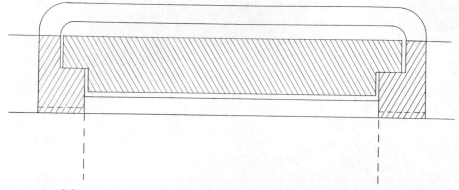

ners and into the box. The box prevents water from driving up under the hatch, and water piling up on the weather side of the box runs either forward of the box or into the cockpit. Since the hatch is flushed with the runners, water tends to run off the top of it and not pour below. Some water may run into the box, but it can be taken care of by drain holes cut in the sides of the box and sealed with little rubber flapper valves; the windward one will be closed by the weight of the water, while the leeward one will be opened by the weight of the water. This type of hatch, given a full-width dodger secured to a firm breakwater, guarantees a dry companionway.

There are those who complain about the windage of the full-width companionway dodger, but by reducing crew fatigue (thereby increasing efficiency) and by helping to preserve valuable equipment, it probably compensates for the additional windage. The chart table and the galley are usually very near the companionway hatch. If the cook gets wet, he is merely annoyed and uncomfortable. However, intermittent dollops of salt water are guaranteed to ruin the best electronic navigation equipment. The effort of manufacturers to produce waterproof equipment for use belowdecks shows only too well how designers and builders have failed in their efforts to make the companionway hatch watertight.

MATERIALS FOR
DECK FITTINGS

Formerly, in Europe almost all deck fittings—bow pulpits, lifeline stanchions, anchor windlasses, cleats, and so on—were made of galvanized iron. In the European climate these stood up well for quite a few years, but in the tropics, they deteriorated very rapidly. A further disadvantage was that although originally inexpensive, they had to be removed periodically from the yacht, cleaned, regalvanized, repainted, and reinstalled.

American yachts on the other hand, very early, even before World War II, were equipped with bronze deck gear, which has stood up fabulously through the years. Before the war, boats built by Lawley, Herreshoff, Nevins, were distinctive for beautiful castings that were true works of art. Such bowsprit fittings, mast bands, winch mountings, and the like will probably never be seen again. Today the patternmaker has become too expensive. Further, castings received a bad name right after World War II, when many yards and manufacturers began designing and casting their own fittings, and did not use carefully controlled virgin-bronze alloys. The difference in strength between a fitting made of controlled casting bronze and the same fitting made of miscellaneous scrap is vast.

As a result of the bad name cast bronze acquired, the preference today is for fittings of stainless steel or bronze plate, fabricated to the shape desired. The great advantage of stainless-steel deck fittings is that if they are well made and well polished they can be kept looking beautiful with relatively little labor. However, as was mentioned in the discussion of mast fittings in Chapter IV, stainless steel is very subject to fatigue, and the strength of stainless-steel welds cannot be relied upon. This difficulty is less crucial on deck than aloft, because on deck, weight is less critical. Thus one can compensate for the unreliability of stainless-steel welds in deck fittings by increasing the mass, to obtain a safety factor of 10 or 12, rather than the 3 or 4 which is acceptable for fittings used aloft.

Stainless-steel fittings on deck have one other disadvantage. Though stainless steel does not rust through like ordinary iron, it is not—despite its name—actually stainless. Over a period of years the stainless-steel bolts and other fittings begin weeping rust stains, which detract from the appearance of the yacht. These are especially troublesome in the tropics, where the progress of corrosion is drastically accelerated.

For these reasons I prefer bronze for deck fittings. However, I will admit that ¾-inch thick-walled stainless-steel pipe is undoubtedly the best material for lifeline stanchions because of its availability, strength, and good looks.

Bronze deck hardware can be made by casting or can be fabricated from bronze plate, which is welded, bent, and riveted in the same fashion as stainless steel. Bronze is easier to cast than stainless steel, but as previously noted, the quality of the castings and alloys must be carefully checked.

Recently, aluminum has come into wide use on board yachts in an attempt to save weight. Deck cleats, ventilators, genoa tracks, and so on are now made of corrosion-resistant aluminum alloy. But while this material may be corrosion resistant, as claimed, it is not corrosion proof. Although it does not turn into a black powder instantly upon contact with salt water, it does slowly corrode. A white powder continually builds up, and eventually the fittings disintegrate. Therefore, aluminum deck fittings are acceptable for a cruising boat to be sailed primarily in a freshwater area—the Great Lakes, Lake Geneva, or some other large inland lake—but not for a cruising boat intended for use at sea, in salt water. I would make an exception for the Moyle ventilators, which are strong and light, and given five or six good coats of anticorrosion paint and a top coat of epoxy paint, seem to stand up quite well. However, were I able to afford them I think I would prefer the Abeking and Rasmussen cast-bronze ventilators, which cost a fortune and weigh a lot, but never need painting. They can be either left to turn a nice seagoing green or polished to impress people in the marina.

VIII

~~~~~~~~~~~~~~~~~~~~

Anchors and Anchoring

Anchors and anchoring have been the subject of prolonged and bitter controversy. The English think that anyone anchoring with anything but chain is out of his mind, while most Americans believe that one can anchor anywhere in the world with nylon line, and often, when racing in Europe, break the racing rules by not carrying chain. Both groups are narrow-minded and wrong. Different boats and different conditions demand different methods of anchoring. A true cruising boat must have a variety of anchors and rodes on board.

The basic mistake in this area is to start at the wrong end of the scale. The temptation is to read the advertisements and strength tables and purchase the lightest anchor and anchor rodes that will hold the boat, rather than the heaviest anchor and rodes that the crew and boat can handle. Also, one should not pay too much attention to price lists. It is false economy to purchase an imitation CQR, Danforth, or fisherman anchor—cheap but of poor design and construction—or to attempt to make do with polypropylene line, rather than the more expensive nylon. Expensive chain is well worth the extra pennies too.

TYPES OF ANCHORS

FISHERMAN ANCHORS

The old-fashioned fisherman is a wonderful and much-maligned anchor. There are many patterns on the market, some not too good, with palms at the ends of the flukes which do not have the necessary

86. (From left to right) *Nicholson, folding Northill, navy, and Herreshoff anchors.* (*D. M. Street, Morris Rosenfeld*)

area to give good holding power, and which constantly foul the anchor rodes when the boat swings on the tide. In Europe the popular variation of this type is the Nicholson anchor, sometimes referred to as a rock pick. Its flukes have rounded inner faces and are narrow in comparison to those of the Nevins or Herreshoff version (Photo 86). This lack of fluke area makes it poor in sand and useless in mud. The Herreshoff anchor will hold well in rock, has the area to be effective in mud, sand, or clay, and has enough weight to enable it in most cases to work its way down through kelp or grass. The Herreshoff is also good in that it can be dismantled into three pieces and stowed in the bilge when not in use on long trips. On *Iolaire,* a 150-pound three-piece Herreshoff anchor is stowed in the bilge, to be used as a storm anchor or "life-insurance policy." It has been needed only four times in fourteen years, but was most deeply appreciated on those occasions.

The one difficulty with the fisherman type is that it is an awkward anchor to get over the side and back on board without banging up the topsides. The average person can handle a fifty-pound fisherman anchor, and a very strong man can manage a seventy-five-pounder. To handle a fisherman above this size, one needs an anchor davit, crane, or some other gear. Another disadvantage of this type of anchor is that it will not stow in the hawsepipe.

NAVY ANCHOR

The navy anchor (Photo 86), the earliest of the stockless anchors, was designed long ago to be stowed in the hawsepipe. The most modern derivative of this type—the Danforth—is excellent, but the old-fashioned navy anchor is worse than useless. Its holding power is so low that it should never be used on a yacht. In one instance a three-hundred-pound navy anchor installed for a permanent mooring was dragged all over the harbor by a fifty-seven-foot schooner.

DANFORTH ANCHOR

There is a high-tensile Danforth, a standard Danforth, and a cast Danforth. The first, once buried, has unbelievable holding power, and it is much more strongly constructed than the standard Danforth. However, it may bend its flukes and shed its stock under heavy strain. The second, which is heavier for the same given fluke area, has a better chance to work its way down through grass and the like than does the high-tensile Danforth, but has even more of a tendency than the high-tensile to shed its stock and to bend its flukes. The cast Danforth is a wonderful anchor to stow in the hawsepipe (Photo 87). It has great holding power and also the weight necessary to force its way down to

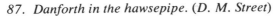

87. Danforth in the hawsepipe. (D. M. Street)

good holding ground despite obstacles. A real find is a cast stainless-steel Danforth of the kind used on nonmagnetic minesweepers.

The Danforth anchor is excellent, provided that it is of sufficient weight. The manufacturers of anchors of this type advertise tremendous holding power for models that are barely bigger than watch charms. But the figures they mention apply only to perfect conditions—a bottom of soft sand, clay, or the like. Frequently, however, the Danforth will refuse to dig in at all if the bottom has weeds, grass, kelp, or really hard sand, or is covered with loose rocks. Under these conditions most Danforths will refuse to function. The heavier the Danforth, the better the chance that it will dig in. A further hazard in crowded waters is that if an old can lodges on a fluke, it prevents the anchor from digging in.

The high-tensile Danforth, with its large flukes, tends to plane like an aquaplane at as little as three knots. Once the anchor is broken out, all way must be kept off the boat until the anchor has been taken aboard; otherwise it will rise to the surface and knock all the paint off the bottom of the boat. Similarly, if one stops a boat in a tideway, drops the anchor, and then eases back on it and snubs it up, holding the boat on the range, the anchor will pop to the surface instead of sinking.

The greatest advantage of a Danforth is that if the heaviest one *that can be handled* is carried and properly used, it will give immense holding power. A further advantage is that a Danforth stows well in a hawsepipe. A fine rig for a cruising boat is a hydraulic windlass and a big, cast Danforth on chain, stowed in the hawsepipe.

If nylon line is used with a Danforth, there must be at least two fathoms of heavy chain at the end of the nylon to hold the stock of the anchor parallel to the bottom. Danforths are very sensitive to scope, requiring a ratio of cable length to depth of water of at least 5 to 1. Consequently, difficulties may arise in crowded anchorages, especially if there is a tide running.

CQR (PLOW) ANCHOR

English yachtsmen are great believers in the CQR anchor, which was designed before World War II, originally as a light anchor for flying boats. It is an excellent anchor, which holds in most bottoms and with great power in sand. One seventy-seven-foot schooner has had a thirty-five-pound CQR as its standard anchor for years. As with the Danforth, if nylon line is used, two fathoms of chain must be placed between the line and the anchor. There is a ring on the back of the CQR to which a buoyed line may be attached to facilitate breaking the an-

88. CQR in the bow chock. (D. M. Street)

chor out if it is fouled. Somehow—exactly why, I don't know—this anchor has given much trouble in the Virgin Islands despite its fine reputation in the rest of the world. There's a reason to always carry at least two different types of anchor.

One of the nicest things about the CQR is that it can be made to stow in the bow roller chock (Photo 88), and this chock is standard in the designs of a number of naval architects, the late Laurent Giles for one. It is a pleasure to be able to just heave up on the anchor and haul it home with no bother. A CQR can also be made to stow in the hawsepipe (Photo 89), as is done on *Pixie,* but this hawsepipe is of a specialized design and not often seen.

89. CQR in the hawsepipe. (D. M. Street)

The main difficulty with the CQR is that many manufacturers have copied the design, often very badly. *Yachting World* ran a series of tests on anchors of the CQR type produced by various manufacturers. Some of the copies were good, but others were not. Thus it is essential to procure a genuine CQR, which can be identified by the name and patent number on the stock.

NORTHILL ANCHOR

This excellent anchor was originated by Northill while he was working for the Northrop aircraft company, designing flying boats and seaplanes. Although the Northill (Photo 86) is neither well known nor much used, long experience has shown its handling qualities and holding power to be excellent. Indeed, it seems to hold equally well in mud, rock, sand, and weeds. Possibly the reason this anchor is not more preferred is that it is difficult to get aboard because the fluke and the stock are at the same end of the shank, and are at right angles to one another. A more probable reason for its lack of popularity is the absence of publicity.

This anchor is well worth consideration, although, being cast, it is not as strong as the high-tensile Danforth. A stainless-steel folding Northill can be obtained, at high cost.

SWEDISH ANCHOR

The Swedish are advocates of the four-pronged rock pick, which is excellent in rocky areas. In the smaller sizes it makes an excellent dinghy anchor, and because it folds up, it is easily stowed. The larger sizes are also stowable, and have no pivot pins to break. One prepares the anchor for stowing by sliding the upper fluke up the shank until it comes to the rounded portion, rotating it 90 degrees, and dropping it down on top of the first fluke.

ANCHOR RODES

MATERIALS

Chain

Chain is beloved by the European yachtsmen because the weight of the chain allows a yacht to ride at substantially less scope than if line is used. They also like it because it will not chafe on a rocky bottom. However, it is hard to handle. Pulling chain up with the bare hands is not my idea of pleasure, a windlass is a nuisance on a small boat, and a really good one for the larger boat is difficult to find. When chain is hauled in, 50 percent of the effort is expended overcoming friction. If a 75-pound anchor hangs straight down on forty feet of ⅜-inch chain, the weight of the chain and anchor is 115 pounds. With a 50 percent loss to friction, a pull of 172 pounds will be required to haul anchor if the boat is lying dead still in calm water. However, in actuality the boat usually has some way on, or a slight current may be running. This added friction will result in a line pull of up to 300 or 400 pounds.

Because the British use chain much more than Americans, they are more skillful at handling it. American chain rollers are usually too small in diameter and frequently are not grooved to take alternate links (chain links lie at an angle of 90 degrees one to another). The weight of chain, while an advantage in anchoring, is a disadvantage in that, unless the chain is stowed well aft, a lot of weight is placed forward, where it should not be. Furthermore, chain is not as strong as many people think, and unless there is an oversized link at each end, a shackle one size smaller than the chain, and correspondingly weaker, must be used. Actually, in view of the weakness of regular shackles, chain should be joined by a chain-joining shackle, such as Simpson Lawrence's (catalog Fig. 1593; Photo 90). This shackle has no thread, but instead an oval-shaped pin held in place by a wooden peg. It is stronger than the ordinary shackle that would be used on the same size of chain, while at the same time it has the advantage of being easy to break if the occasion should arise. To break the shackle, one need not fight with wrenches, pins, and so on. All that is necessary is to knock out the pin with a punch. The wooden peg breaks under a little strain.

90. Simpson Lawrence
    chain shackle.
    (*Laurie Legay*)

The time may come when it is necessary to slip the chain in a hurry. This is only possible if the chain is secured either as just described, or by a nylon lashing that can be cut. As has been justifiably pointed out, trying to dig around to find the nylon lashing in the depths of the chain locker at two in the morning is most difficult. To eliminate this problem, some people splice one end of a ½-inch line to a pad eye or the mast step, and the other end to the bitter end of the chain, making the line long enough so the bitter end of the chain comes up to take the naval pipe. This arrangement enables one to cut free without going below.

In buying chain one should remember that tested chain is well worth the extra expense. However, strength decreases with age. After a few years, even good-quality chain becomes worn, corroded, rusted, and in general untrustworthy. This deterioration is particularly rapid in the tropics.

The chain and windlass must match perfectly. If they do not, the chain will slip and jam in the wildcat. Therefore, when ordering a new windlass one must make sure it matches the chain; better yet, one should order the new windlass and new chain from the same manufacturer.

A disadvantage of chain is that it is difficult to clean after anchoring in mud. One of the best solutions is to have a large-capacity water pump belted off the engine, with a pipe running to the foredeck. Then when the anchor is weighed, the pump clutch can be engaged and the chain can be subjected to a high-pressure stream of water which, with the help of a vigorous scrubbing, will remove the mud and its smells. (Another advantage of this system is that in emergencies the washdown pump can serve as a fire or bilge pump.)

Nylon

Manila, sisal, and other old-fashioned ropes have been supplanted for use with anchors—and properly so—but nylon makes excellent anchor rodes, since it is light and extremely strong, and its immense stretch gives it significant shock-absorbing qualities. Because of its strength there is a tendency to use line so light that it is extremely stretchy. The line gives with the puffs and contracts in the lulls. As we shall see, some people—for example Robert D. Ogg of Danforth and Robert Bavier of *Yachting* magazine—feel this is the correct method of anchoring. However, I believe that heavier anchors and heavier line are preferable. Nylon is so strong that it frequently is stronger than the chain it is secured to. A ¾-inch nylon line secured to a twenty-eight-pound high-tensile Danforth by a $\frac{5}{16}$-inch chain is not an unusual combination. Yet the strength of the shackles and chain is frequently a fraction of the strength of the line. Since the strength of the whole is no greater than that of its weakest part, the ¾-inch nylon line is considered waste. However, there are considerations other than strength to be taken into account. It is difficult to haul hard on any line of less than ½ inch in diameter; ⅝-inch line is a good size for hauling. For anchoring, I would recommend ½-inch line for boats to 25 feet LWL, ⅝-inch for boats of 25 to 40 feet LWL, and ¾-inch for boats of 40 to 50 feet LWL. For boats above that size I feel that chain and a powerful windlass should be used.

Nylon is very sensitive to chafe, and probably because of its stretch it tends to work back and forth across the bow chocks. Therefore, the chocks should be of well-polished bronze and the line should be fitted with chafing gear where it rides in the chocks. Stowage of nylon is no problem. Of course, it should be stowed dry if possible, but in any event, unlike the fiber ropes, it will not rot.

Polypropylene

Polypropylene is beginning to come into favor for anchor line, but I advise strongly against it. It is highly variable in quality and erratic in behavior, breaking when one least expects it to. Its great assets are that it floats and is cheap, but these advantages do not outweigh its unreliability, its proneness to damage by chafe, and its slippery quality,—knots made in it slip and splices don't hold.

Stainless-Steel Wire

At one time, anchor rodes of stainless-steel wire were much used for anchoring large vessels owned by yachtsmen of unlimited finances. The advantages of stainless wire are that it suffers a friction loss of only 10 percent, has great strength, and is easily stowed (on a reel powered by an anchor windlass). Its disadvantages are that it is expensive and lacks shock-absorbing properties. Today, except in specialized applications, it is not much used in yachting circles. However, stainless wire on a reel is standard equipment for the fishermen of the west coast of North America. They carry a heavy-duty rubber snubber to take the shock when anchoring offshore in deep water.

HANDLING AND STOWAGE

In my view—as I have previously stated—every boat should be equipped with both chain and nylon anchor rodes. If chain is indeed carried, there must be adequate means of handling it. The smallest sizes (³⁄₁₆-inch and ¼-inch chain) can be hauled up by hand. But in-

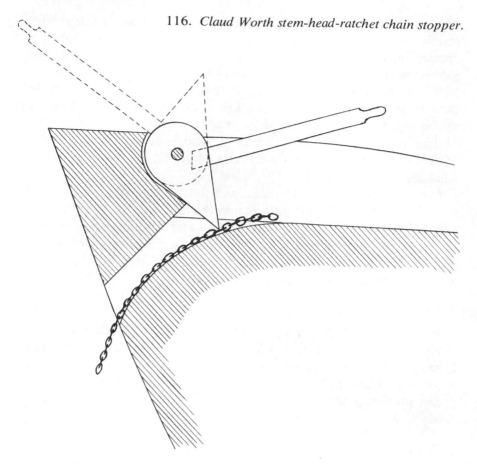

116. *Claud Worth stem-head-ratchet chain stopper.*

stead of trying to grab a turn around a samson post, risking the loss of a finger in the process, one should install a chain stopper of some sort. One of the oldest and simplest is the Claud Worth stem-head ratchet (Drawing 116); also effective is the gravity ratchet (Drawing 117), of the type used on *Iolaire*. Although it does not have an automatic ratchet, the Simpson Lawrence eccentric-cam device (catalog Fig. 582; Drawing 118) is a rugged and efficient design; it has been unchanged in half a century.

Hand-Powered Windlasses and Capstans

The larger sizes of chain require an anchor windlass or capstan. For boats of 25 to 35 feet LWL, a good hand-powered windlass or capstan is advisable. But obtaining one of these today is a problem. Some of the best now in service could easily be sold as museum pieces. I bought a Herreshoff hollow-cast anchor windlass in a junk shop for fifteen dollars; a similar one could not be found in the catalog today at any price.

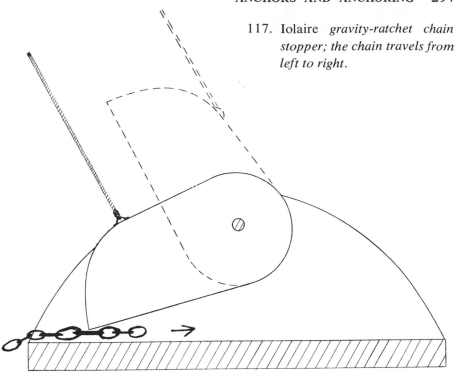

117. Iolaire *gravity-ratchet chain stopper; the chain travels from left to right.*

118. *Simpson Lawrence eccentric-cam brake and chain stopper; the arrow indicates the chain direction.*

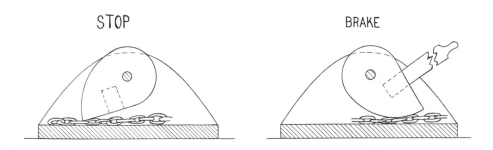

The first decision to be made is whether a windlass or a capstan is preferable. One advantage of the capstan in hauling off is that because the rope drum can take a direct pull in any direction, the use of the bow chock, with its loss through friction, is eliminated (Drawing 119).

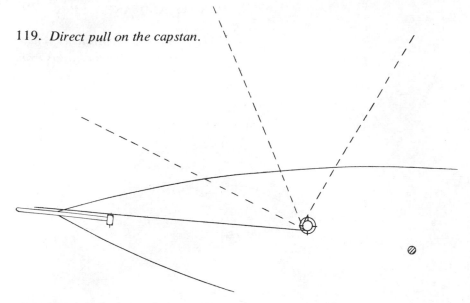

119. *Direct pull on the capstan.*

Another advantage of the capstan is that since the handles can be rotated through a full circle, two men can crank in chain at a great rate of speed. Further, if the handles have ratchets in them, tremendous power can be developed. However, one can operate a capstan effectively only from a kneeling position.

By contrast, a windlass requires the use of anchor chocks, but one can operate it standing up. Windlasses are available in single- and double-action models. A single-action windlass takes up the chain only on the pulling stroke, while a double-action windlass takes it up on both the pulling and the pushing stroke. There are many hand-operated windlasses on the market, varying from crude to fancy.

The homemade windlass installed on *Quandy* is the cleverest, and one of the most powerful, I have seen. The only improvements possible would be for it to have warping barrels on both ends of the shaft, and two handles and two ratchets, as shown in Drawing 120. The two handles would double the possible power and the double ratchets would double the holding strength.

On yachts of over 35 feet LWL, it is advisable to install power windlasses, hawsepipes, and anchors that stow in the hawsepipes. Otherwise, the temptation to use ground tackle that is too light will be great. It is of course possible to anchor and weigh anchor without power: the spritsail barges of England—a hundred feet long, with a crew consisting of a skipper and a mate, without power, without a donkey engine—often anchored on every change of the tide. If handled correctly, their anchoring gear worked; if not, a hand was crushed or a life was lost.

120. Quandy *windlass, improved*.

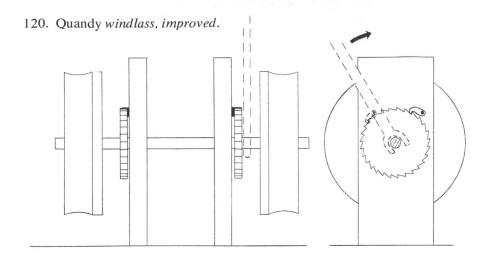

Power Windlasses and Capstans

Windlasses and capstans may have either electric or hydraulic power. Hydraulic power is preferable. An electric motor installed on deck in the wettest part of the boat is apt to be unreliable. Although some electric windlasses installed prior to World War II are still running with minimum maintenance, the electric motor is more usually found in bits and pieces in the repair shop.

Hydraulic windlasses have been on the market for many years. A pump belted off the main motor, or off the generator if it is of sufficient size, pumps hydraulic fluid through pipes and/or hoses to the motor on the windlass. The hydraulic windlass is not susceptible to electrical failure, and its power is unbelievable. A good hydraulic windlass or capstan will depress the bow of a large yacht substantially when straining on a fouled anchor. Another advantage of hydraulic windlasses is that they are likely to have a very efficient back-up hand-power arrangement for use if power fails. This is usually lacking in electric windlasses and capstans.

POWER WINDLASSES—STRANGE RIGS: On the west coast of North America, commercial fisherman power their anchor windlasses directly off the engine by a complicated system of chain drives, universal joints, and a shaft running in the overhead from the engine to the anchor windlass. This contrivance is powerful, and it works, but it is cumbersome and space-consuming. The charter yacht *Georgiana*, formerly a Brixham trawler, had an anchor windlass powered by its own ancient gasoline engine. Why it ever ran, considering that it spent most of its

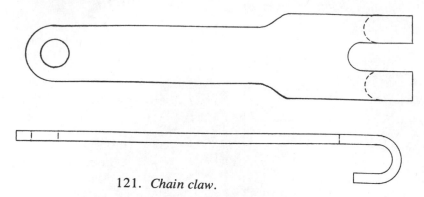

121. *Chain claw.*

time under water, is a mystery, but run it did. Ross Norgrove, on *White Squall,* had a strange but workable rig with a heavy-duty 110-volt electric drill on the drive shaft of the windlass in place of the winch handle.

On one ocean racer that had a grossly inadequate anchor windlass, the chain was hauled up by means of two chain claws (Drawing 121), each attached to a line running aft to a cockpit sheet winch. Employment of the two winches and claws in alternation made possible the hauling of the anchor with moderate efficiency, but four men were required to get it up with any speed.

Location of the Anchor Windlass or Capstan

The anchor windlass or capstan should be as close to the chain locker as possible. Under American racing rules, chain must be stowed forward of the mast. Under RORC rules, chain may be stowed anywhere, and on some boats anchor windlasses are mounted well aft of the mainmast. This arrangement is extreme, but in view of the weight of chain and windlass, it is important to get the chain as far aft as is practical. If the chain does not feed directly from the wildcat into the chain locker, weighing anchor is a time- and labor-consuming operation.

If the windlass or capstan is well aft of the bows, the anchor chain will give the deck quite a beating over a period of time. The oldest remedy, which is still perfectly acceptable, is to attach to the deck a sacrificial strip of teak, perhaps a quarter or a half inch thick, which will take the chafe and can be renewed from time to time. Another method, which requires more labor but results in a better appearance when the anchor is not in use, is to have a wooden trough made up in sections. Whenever the anchor chain is needed, the sections of the trough are assembled and laid on deck and the chain is run through them.

91. Chain brake with buffer. (Morris Rosenfeld)

Securing Anchor Chain

At times, particularly when anchored with chain in a seaway, a boat will fetch up hard, threatening to snap the chain or break out the anchor, or it may seem that the foredeck will be torn from the boat. If the chain has been left on the windlass, once the boat is anchored, heavy surges may bend the shaft, ruining the anchor windlass and making life difficult for all on board. On medium-sized boats the answer to this difficulty is a chain stopper such as was shown in Drawings 116 and 117; heavier boats need a chain brake with coiled-spring snubbers to absorb the shock (Photo 91). Another solution, on some boats, is to lower lead weights on a bow slung over the chain. Perhaps a more seamanlike method is to secure a chain claw to the chain and secure the claw to heavy bitts by means of a nylon line, which will stretch and shrink, acting as a shock absorber (nylon will elongate 50 percent before breaking). Nylon of much lighter size than one would expect may be used (see Table IV, Appendix). If a chain claw is unavailable, one can tie nylon line to the chain with a rolling hitch, veer out another few fathoms of chain, secure the end of the nylon to the anchor bitts, and ride on the nylon.

If the boat has no bowsprit, chain will be a nuisance when she is anchored in a tideway, the chain will chafe the topsides whenever the boat is lying with the tide rather than with the wind. This can be prevented with a bow pad (Photo 92). Even on a boat with a bowsprit the chain is a problem; it will chafe on the bobstay and in time actually break it. Some boats have the anchor chocks out on the bowsprit; this arrangement is excellent so long as the sprit is short and there is not too much sea, but if the sprit is long or a sea is running there will still be an excellent chance that the sprit will break.

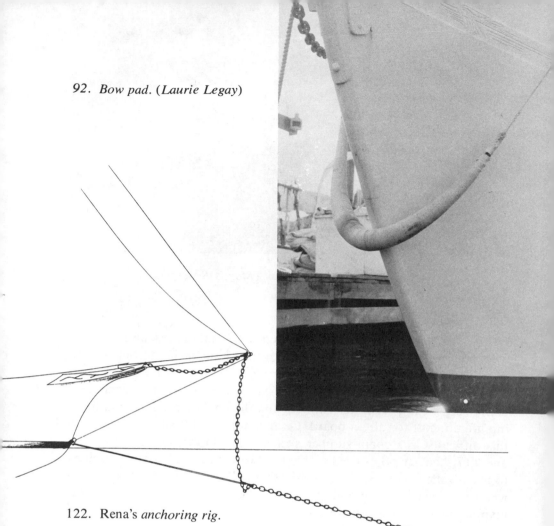

92. Bow pad. (Laurie Legay)

122. Rena's *anchoring rig.*

The solution to the chafe problem, for a bowsprit boat anchored to chain is that of the *Rena* (Drawing 122). An extra eye is included in the bobstay fitting below where the bobstay is attached to the bow of the boat. To this eye is shackled a length of ⅝-inch nylon with a chain claw on the end of it. The line is of such length that the claw hooks onto a fitting on the end of the bowsprit when not in use. When the boat is anchored, the claw is hooked to the anchor chain. An extra two fathoms of chain are veered and the boat rides to the nylon line, which acts as an excellent shock absorber. It also improves the angle of scope without appreciably increasing the amount of chain let out. If the nylon parts, the chain fetches up on the anchor windlass.

On small boats the chain is frequently secured to a samson post, to the great danger of fingers, or is dropped into a groove in a plate bolted to a samson post (Drawing 123).

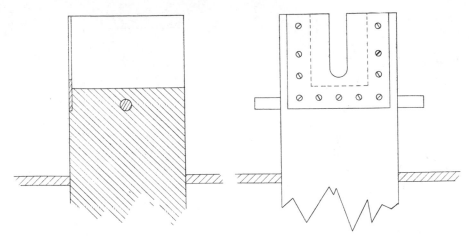

123. *Notched plate for chain, on the after side of a samson post.*

Securing Nylon Anchor Rodes

Securing nylon anchor rodes is not really a problem; two big cleats bolted through the deck and through a pad that spans the deck beams are generally used. Some boats have a good honest samson post stepped on the stem and firmly bolted to a deck beam. *Spookie,* a forty-five foot ocean racer built before World War II, had what may have been the neatest and cleanest samson post ever designed. It consisted of one pipe with flanges top and bottom bolted to the stem and deck, and with its top flush with the deck. Into it was telescoped a second pipe, which when in use, was held in a raised position by a pin. When the pin was pulled, the inner pipe could be dropped inside the outer pipe, leaving a flush foredeck with no obstructions (Drawing 124). With a little

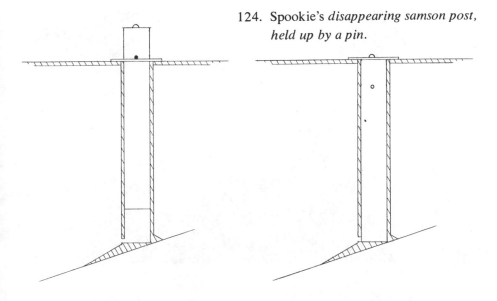

124. Spookie's *disappearing samson post, held up by a pin.*

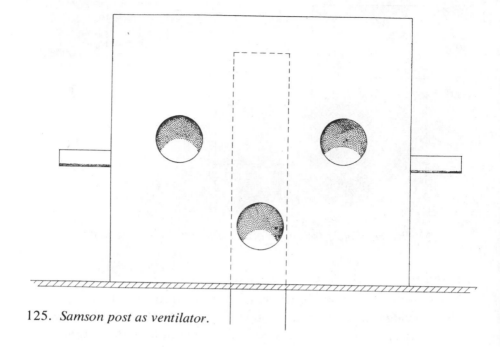

125. *Samson post as ventilator.*

redesigning, this could also be a ventilator in port (Drawing 125). Bitts that can be used as ventilators are useful; the forepeak is the most difficult area of the boat to ventilate. On old-fashioned boats, the bowsprits and bitts to support them also serve as an excellent place to secure the mooring line (Photo 93).

93. Iolaire *bitts. (D. M. Street)*

Chain Stowage

The chain should be self-stowing in its locker. Otherwise a man will have to be sent below to take it down. Some designers run the chain through a pipe from the deck to the chain locker, but all too frequently, when the chain is running fast, it jams at the entrance to the pipe. Since the pipe extends all the way to the chain locker in the bilge, the foul is difficult to clear. On the other hand, if the chain is hanging free between the chain locker and the deckhead, the fouls will usually clear themselves.

Chain is generally stowed as low in the bilge as possible, and if not kept absolutely clean, it causes a foul smell. Ken Goodings on his yacht *Tondemenai,* has an ingenious solution. Instead of stowing his chain in the bilge, he bolts a steel drum with an inspection plate to the underside of the deckhead. A drain pipe leads from the bottom of the drum directly overside. This has some great advantages. Because chain stows compactly, feeding it directly into a drum of the correct size results in a great saving of space. Second, the chain is sealed tight against the deckhead, so any smell from it will not penetrate the forecastle. The overside drain pipe carries off any leakage that otherwise would have entered the forecastle. Also, the chain can be veered, the inspection plate removed, and the inside of the chain locker flushed, cleaned, and painted.

SEALING CHAIN PIPE: Sealing the pipe which leads to the chain locker is always a problem, and unless it is solved, in heavy weather a large quantity of water may find its way belowdecks through the pipe. If the chain can be unshackled from the anchor and dropped into the locker, the pipe may be sealed with Abeking and Rasmussen's standard fitting. The crane can be unscrewed, and in its place a cap can be screwed in (Drawing 126). If the anchor is stowed in the hawsepipe, the chain will have to be broken and the anchor and chain held in place by a chain stopper set up tight with a tackle or turnbuckle. If the chain cannot be broken and sent below, one is reduced to playing unseamanlike games with wooden plugs, rags, corks, and the like.

126. *Abeking and Rasmussen removable*
    chain pipe with screw-in cover.

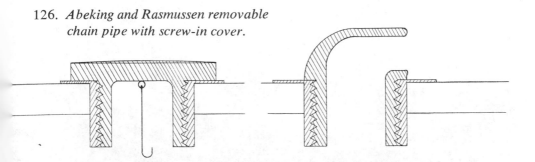

Nylon Stowage

Nylon line is easily stowed. Unlike the old anchor rodes of manila, linen, or other fiber, it is unharmed by being stowed wet. Hence, on some boats nylon line is fed directly into the forepeak through a deck pipe. Some people claim this method works out perfectly, but it does result in dampness in the forepeak; also, when the line is run out in a hurry, a kink may jam in the deck pipe.

For short cruising with daily anchoring, it is preferable to coil the nylon line down on deck and secure it with stops to lifeline stanchions or pad eyes. If the cruise is offshore for any period of time, the anchor rode should be disconnected, dried, and stowed. When the anchor rode is prepared for storage, if it is made of ⅞-inch or ¾-inch nylon, it should be coiled in a large coil, secured with stops, and twisted into a figure eight, which should then be folded down on itself, to give a very small tight coil (Photos 94, 95, 96). Once coiled, nylon can be stowed belowdecks in the forepeak lazaret or the sail lockers, depending upon the weight distribution desired.

For a smaller boat, using ⅝-inch or ½-inch nylon, one can have made up a stainless-steel or wooden frame on which will fit a spool (Photo 97). A drum 18 inches in diameter, with 12 inches between the faces, will hold two hundred feet of ⅝-inch nylon. Or a drum can be made which will fit over one of the mast winches. Line can be rolled onto the plywood spool, which can then be left on deck or removed and stowed below.

94. *Coiling ¾- or ⅝-inch anchor line in large diameter circle. (D. M. Street)*

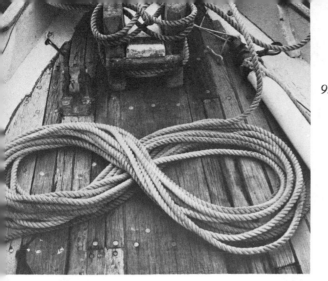

95. *Coiling line in a figure eight. Secure with small bits of marline.* (D. M. Street)

96. *Left hand of figure eight has been folded over right hand. Secure with a couple of sail ties. Anchor line, now stowed in 2 foot diameter circle, by reversing process, can be fed off a large coil and will not foul if fed off small coil.* (D. M. Street)

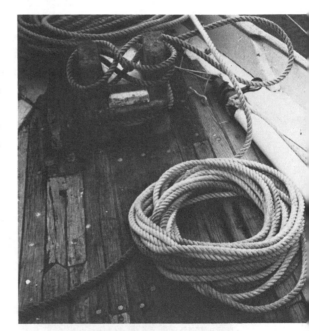

97. Iolaire *anchor-rope stowage.* (D. M. Street)

ANCHOR STOWAGE AND HANDLING

STOWAGE

In years gone by, the commercial sailing ships secured their anchors to a cathead in the bow and never took them up on deck. This was a good seamanlike arrangement that solved the stowage problem, but it is not feasible on a yacht except in the few instances where the yacht has been built on the lines of the old coasters. On a yacht, unless the anchor can be stowed in the hawsepipe or in a specially created bow chock, it usually must be taken aboard. However, there is another method of stowage which may be adopted on a boat with a bowsprit. If the chocks are at or near the end of the bowsprit, the crown of the anchor can be swung aft, dropped over a hook, and secured (Photo 98, Herreshoff anchor; Photo 99, CQR anchor). The advantages of this arrangement are that the anchor cannot dig up the topsides when it is being swung into its chock, and it can be allowed to hang there while the boat is making sail or sailing into a harbor.

If the anchors are taken on board, a place must be found to stow them. On boats with wide cabin houses, they may be set in chocks on

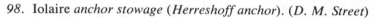

98. Iolaire anchor stowage *(Herreshoff anchor). (D. M. Street)*

99. Iolaire *anchor stowage (CQR anchor). (D. M. Street)*

the cabin top, alongside or under the dinghy, depending on the beam of the cabin top. On many boats they are set in chocks on the foredeck, but stumbling over them in the dark is bothersome and dangerous.

Some of the older boats with high bows forward had an excellent method of stowing anchors. Teak gratings on the side of the inner end of the bowsprit could be removed, providing access to wells in which the anchors could be stowed. When the gratings were replaced, a smooth unobstructed foredeck resulted.

Some other older yachts still pick up their anchors with davits and hold them on deck with arm-overside flukes, secured to the bulwarks (Photo 100). Stowing anchors in this way is an awkward, time-consuming job, difficult to achieve without damaging the topside.

100. *Anchor stowage* (Eudroma). (*D. M. Street*)

101. Danforth stowage (Gitana). (*D. M. Street*)

A Danforth anchor is especially troublesome to stow on deck because the stock projects six inches or more above the deck, with exposed ends which are likely to foul sheets. This difficulty can be avoided by the use of wooden chocks to hold both ends and the plate (Photo 101). On *Djinn,* Captain Ole Bergendal devised a better system. He cut the stocks off the anchors and fitted them with threaded ends (Photo 102). He keeps everything well greased, and unscrews the stocks when the anchors are not in use. Then he can stow one anchor above the other so that they take up little space, and since the stocks are removable, he can stow the anchors in the forecastle bilge, which is the best place possible.

102. Danforth with screw-in stock ends. (D. M. Street)

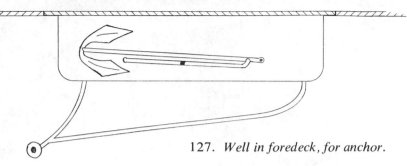

127. *Well in foredeck, for anchor.*

On some of the new boats, especially those built of aluminum or fiber glass, a small self-bailing well is installed in the foredeck. The anchor and rode are placed in it, and a cover is dogged down over them (Drawing 127).

Large storm anchors should if possible be broken down into their component parts and stowed below, preferably in the bilge, where their weight will do the most good. When they are broken down, their weight also is divided, so they can be handled without too much difficulty and assembled on deck.

HANDLING

For yachts which have anchors that stow in bow chocks, bowsprits, or hawsepipes, anchor handling is no problem. However, if the anchor must be brought on deck there may be some difficulty, the degree depending on the size of the boat. The small boat may have an anchor that can be handled with one hand; the seventy-foot schooner may have a two-hundred-pound anchor that must be manhandled on deck. Between these extremes, of course, lie most boats.

A strong bow pulpit is a great asset for the boat without a bowsprit. If a snatch block is attached to the forwardmost part of the pulpit, once the anchor is broken out, the anchor line may be dropped into the snatch block and the anchor two-blocked to the pulpit, brought clear of the topsides, and then easily swung in under the pulpit (Photo 103). This method of course will only work if the anchor does not have a length of chain attached to it. If it does (as it must if it is a Danforth or a CQR) a slightly different technique can be used. A buoy line having been attached to the crown of the anchor, the anchor is broken out, and hoisted until the buoy appears. The buoy is picked up, the buoy line is dropped into the snatch block on the pulpit, and the anchor is two-blocked upside down to the pulpit. Slack can then be taken up on the anchor line, the two fathoms of chain can be taken aboard, and the anchor can be secured on the pulpit, for a short sail, or stowed in its

103. Snatch block and roller in pulpit for handling light Danforth anchors (D. M. Street)

normal place, for a longer sail. When buoying anchors which are to be picked up under power, one should make sure that the distance from the bow of the boat to the propeller is greater than the length of the buoy line; otherwise it is all too easy to wrap the buoy line around the propeller.

Those who have to heave a heavy anchor up on deck must find a way to do so without scarring the topsides or injuring a member of the crew. One method in calm water is to set the main and sail up to the anchor. Once the anchor has been broken out, the procedure is to hoist it until it is two-blocked, tack so that it is hanging from the lee chock, hitch the spinnaker halyard to the anchor, and take a strain on the halyard. When the weight of the anchor is on the halyard, the anchor line should be slacked; the anchor will swing back alongside the mast, but clear of the boat because of the angle of heel. Then one need only hoist the anchor on the spinnaker halyard until it is high enough to clear the lifelines, luff to swing the anchor inboard, and lower away. This maneuver is easy with a good crew, but should not be attempted with an inexperienced one.

On some boats the spinnaker pole is used as a cargo boom. First, the spinnaker pole is placed in the bell in the mast; with the bell as low as possible, the jib halyard is attached to the outer end of the pole, and two lines are secured, to act as guys. Next, a tackle is attached to the end of the pole, and the pole is hoisted until its forward end is directly over the anchor. Then one proceeds to hook the tackle into the anchor, heave up on the tackle with one of the spare halyard winches until it is hoisted high enough to clear the lifelines, top up the pole, swing it inboard, and lower the anchor on the tackle, and the job is done. With this rig, my wife and I have managed to handle a 150-pound anchor complete with $7/16$-inch chain.

Some boats, especially the older ones, have anchor davits. With a quick-release hook, a davit provides an excellent method of handling the anchor. The davit, however, is heavy, hard to stow, and expensive to purchase and mount.

Since any method of taking on deck an anchor of more than seventy-five pounds is time-consuming and laborious, the temptation is to use anchors smaller than is advisable. It is therefore a good safety practice for all boats requiring standard anchors of seventy-five pounds or more to have self-stowing anchors. (It is worthy of note that the German yawl *Kormoran* raced with a Danforth stowed in the hawsepipe.)

ANCHORING

In its simplest form anchoring consists of coming in under power, throwing over the anchor, backing down, giving slack until the scope is sufficient, snubbing up, shutting down the engine, rigging the awning, and having a drink. However, frequently conditions exist that complicate this ideal procedure: a crowded harbor, a large rise and fall of the tide, a strong or reversing current.

Ideally, there should be 5-to-1 scope, especially if a Danforth anchor is being used. Slightly less is acceptable with a CQR, and once a fisherman anchor is set, one can usually ride to 3-to-1 scope without much difficulty. In crowded anchorages, care must be taken not to foul another yacht's berth, whether she be on an anchor or a permanent mooring. One should avoid anchoring close to a mooring buoy; the owner may return in the small hours of the morning, pick up his mooring, and find that his berth has been fouled. The legal situation concerning the rights and privileges involved in prior and subsequent anchoring, permanent moorings, and so on is complicated and contradictory, but common decency and politeness demand that these matters be settled on a first-come first-served basis, with permanent moorings taking precedence.

As we have seen, methods of anchoring vary, even among experienced yachtsmen. In the September, 1969, issue of *Yachting,* Robert Bavier, a most experienced seaman, tells how he has for many years successfully anchored his thirty-seven-foot Apache on a twelve-pound Danforth with two fathoms of chain and ⅜-inch nylon line. He states that this method is effective because the ⅜-inch nylon, which has ample strength for this size yacht under normal conditions, behaves in effect like a strong rubber band: when a puff of wind or a sea hits the boat, the line stretches and absorbs the shock load before it reaches the anchor. However, he believes that when a boat is anchored with a minimum-weight anchor and very light line, scope at least seven times the depth of the water is advisable. If generally followed, this practice would drastically restrict the number of boats that could use a given harbor. Anchoring in thirty feet of water would require 210 feet of nylon plus 40 feet for the boat, or 250 feet. The swinging circle would be 500 feet. Anchoring in twenty feet of water with a twenty- or thirty-foot tide would require 300 to 400 feet of line, creating a swinging circle 600 to 800 feet in diameter. Few harbors could contain many boats thus anchored.

No matter what method of anchoring is used, in an area where there is a large rise and fall of tide, such as the Bristol Channel and the Bay of Fundy, an anchor watch will probably have to be kept so that the anchor rode can be slacked or taken in according to the state of the tide. Under such circumstances, chain is most useful; its weight tends to keep the strain on the anchor parallel to the bottom, and scope can be substantially reduced. If there is a reversing current and other boats are in the area, it is essential to rig a Bahamian moor—two anchors are put out, one up and one down the tidal stream, so that the boat pivots between them. The boat can then lie to the wind or the tide, whichever the shape of the underbody and the windage of the hull dictates, and only the space of a circle whose radius is the length of the boat will be required (Drawing 128).

This type of anchoring or mooring is far superior to lying on one hook, for if the latter method has been followed, when the wind is across the tide it prevents the boat from sailing around her anchor. Since every boat swings at her own time and in her own direction, crowded anchorages can become highly dangerous under such conditions. This situation has arisen during New York Yacht Club cruises at Edgartown, where there is a strong reversing tide. One year, just at cocktail time, when everyone was ashore at a party, the tide reversed and boats started bouncing off one another, causing such widespread

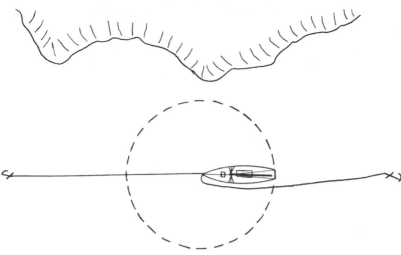

128. *Bahamian moor.*

damage that the next day's racing had to be canceled to give the fleet time to put itself back together again.

Where there is a reversing tide, some yachtsmen anchor bow and stern to the axis of the tide. But then if the wind comes on the beam, the strain on the anchors is immense, since the boat cannot face into the wind and the windage is greatly increased. If it blows hard, the anchors are bound to drag.

However, some areas demand bow and stern moorings. Attempting to anchor under the lee of an island that has a very steep shore, one may find it almost impossible to get enough scope out to let the stock of the anchor lie parallel or almost parallel to the bottom. In this case, one should go right up to shore—or if necessary, send the dinghy ashore with the anchor—drop the anchor in shoal water or tie the bow line to a tree, and put a stern anchor out. Since the bottom drops off very sharply and the stern anchor is pulling uphill, the angle between the stock and the bottom is almost parallel and the holding power will be good. This is not the best method of anchoring, but in certain areas it is the only practical one (Drawing 129).

In some areas, notably the west coast of Mexico, Central America, and some parts of the Lesser Antilles, bow and stern anchoring is made necessary by the swell which runs in from the sea. The wind is off-shore, and if one does not moor head into the swell, the boat will lie beam to the swell and try to roll its masts out.

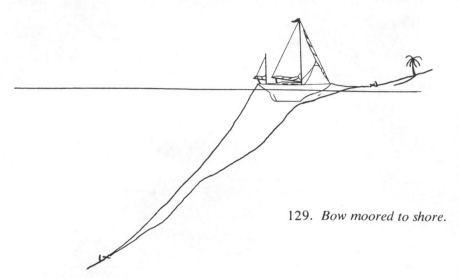

129. *Bow moored to shore.*

Along with anchoring head into the swell there are two other methods used to reduce the amount of roll. Yachtsmen on the west coast of North America have adopted the so-called flopper stoppers. These are paravanes rigged to booms, used on west-coast power fishermen to keep them from rolling too greatly while under way. Yachtsmen have discovered that one flopper stopper rigged to the end of the spinnaker pole when the boat is at anchor will minimize the rolling action.

The third method of reducing the amount of roll—applicable to yawls and ketches—is to set the mizzen. The mizzen should be cut flat and sheeted in as hard as possible. On larger boats it may have to be secured with tackles so that it will not swing back and forth. On sloops, cutters, and schooners the same effect can be achieved by setting the storm trysail or be setting a small flat riding sail hanked on to the permanent backstay.

When one is in strange areas or unprotected anchorages, it is important to lie to two anchors set so as to counter conditions that could cause trouble. Numerous world cruisers have anchored in the lee of an island in an area of supposedly constant wind only to have the wind shift and put them on the beach. The second great cause of unsuccessful anchoring is the breaking of an anchor shackle or the failure of the anchor itself. I once lost my boat when an anchor shackle broke in an exposed anchorage. Had she been on two anchors, all would have been well. When things look the least bit doubtful, two anchors should be used.

Many people anchor by guess, estimating how much chain or line they have out. A much better method is to have the anchor line and chain marked at every five fathoms. There is no standard marking method for yachts; everyone is an individualist, using whatever he finds satisfactory. The commercially sold plastic numbered tags for marking anchor lines are not really adequate because at night a flashlight must be used on deck to read the markings. In the midst of anchoring, one doesn't want to play with flashlights and ruin everyone's night vision. A better method is to sew strips of rawhide through the strands, one strip at 5 fathoms, two at 10, three at 15, and so on. These can be easily seen during the day and can be felt in the dark at night. Chain can be marked in the same way, with galvanized wire instead of rawhide. All markings on anchor rodes must be adjusted for the size of the boat and the area in which one is cruising.

Once the boat is anchored, a few bearings should be taken and noted down for use later in checking for drag. If fog or rain obliterates all reference points, the lead line should be dropped over with a couple of fathoms of slack. If the lead line comes taut, tending forward, the boat is dragging.

Prior to anchoring, the boat should be stopped, and sternway should be gathered as the anchor is dropped. Line or chain should be paid out as the boat drops aft. Slight tension on the line will help hold the head into the wind and prevent the line and/or chain from piling up on top of the anchor and fouling it. This is easy to achieve under power, less easy under sail.

ANCHORING UNDER SAIL

Anchoring under sail, and sailing out the hook, constitute a useful skill as well as a sporting gesture. Continuous practice will teach the yachtsman what he and his boat can do. The individual who can handle his boat under sail in crowded anchorages is indeed a sailor, and if he loses his engine in the midst of a cruise, he need not turn back. Performing these operations under sail alone puts the sport back into sailing, and provides the satisfaction of successfully carrying out a difficult exercise.

In areas where there is no current or where the current is weak and the boat will lie to the wind rather than the current, anchoring under sail is relatively simple. The first step is to get rid of the big genoa. Then a small headsail should be set, if necessary; many boats will handle perfectly well under the main alone. The most useful sail in anchoring is the mizzen. On a yawl, the mizzen can serve as a reverse jib: if it is backed to port or starboard, the bow will correspondingly go to port or starboard. Indeed, the mizzen can be used as an air rudder, and will swing the bow when the boat does not have enough way on to make the rudder effective. When the boat is luffed up, the mizzen can be held aback until sternway is gathered. If the mizzen is sheeted flat, it will tend to hold the head of the boat into the wind.

A strong current requires different techniques. One of these might be called a "flying Bahamian moor." Properly executed, it is a spectacular maneuver; done wrong, it is a shambles. The heavy anchor is hung under the bows; a nylon rode is secured to the second anchor, and double the length of scope needed is flaked out on deck, and secured. The boat is sailed into the harbor with a good head of steam and headed upstream, luffing if necessary but sailing if possible. When an appropriate spot is reached, the on-deck anchor is let go, the line is run out, and the sail is doused. As the anchor snubs up at the end of its double scope and digs in, the other anchor is let go, and the second anchor rode is heaved in until the boat is midway between the two anchors. The boat will pivot from the bow in a circle the radius of which is equal to the length of the boat. If the boat is anchored with chain and nylon, the nylon can be served to the chain to prevent the lines from crossing as the boat swings. If not, the lines probably will cross.

PICKING UP THE HOOK UNDER SAIL

If there are two anchors out, the down-tide anchor should be taken up first. A buoy on the anchor is helpful because it makes it possible for a man in a dinghy to trip the anchor, so that it can be hauled home. If there is no buoy, the down-tide anchor line can be given plenty of slack and one can then underrun the line in a dinghy and break the anchor out—not always an easy job. If this cannot be done, the up-tide anchor line can be slacked until the down-tide scope is short enough to allow the down-tide anchor to be broken out.

If there is a tide rode—that is, the vessel is lying to the current rather than to the wind—once the down-tide anchor is on board it is simple to hoist either the headsail or the main, as the situation dictates, and sail up hard over the anchor, allowing the weight of the boat to break it out. This can be usually done under headsail alone, and the main can be hoisted as soon as the anchor is weighed.

On a ketch or a yawl, if lying head to the wind, one should set the main and mizzen, back the mizzen to make the bow pay off, and tack to windward in a series of tacks until the boat sails over the anchor, again letting the weight of the boat break out the anchor. In a sloop, cutter, or schooner, a headsail will have to be hoisted to kick the bow off. A small headsail should be used, and the foredeck crew must be wary of the sheets.

Specific instructions cannot be given for every situation, but whatever the circumstances, the chances are that a method can be found for sailing the anchor out. Some careful figuring may be necessary, and the crew must be briefed, so that everyone knows his job.

Boats with powerful anchor windlasses, and especially those with self-stowing anchors, are relatively easy to sail off the anchor. The sails are set, the headsails are hoisted in stops, and the boat is wound up to the anchor. When the anchor breaks out, and the boat gathers sternway, she can be steered to fall off on the desired tack, and her jib hoisted or broken out, and the task is done.

IX

~~~~~~~~~~~~~~~~~~~~~~~~~~~~~~~

Dinghies

In years gone by, large yachts had beautiful rowing dinghies that would glide silently across the harbor with a minimum of effort. Even the large steam yachts had their four-oared or six-oared gigs. Yards like Herreshoff, Lawley, and Camper and Nicholsons offered dinghies of standard designs in various lengths, all developed over a period of many years. They were built with unbelievable rapidity and were sold at what today would be unbelievably low prices. Usually lapstrake, though sometimes carvel-built, these boats, given careful handling, might last twenty or thirty years. They were objects of admiration and pleasure. I remember the beautiful Lawley-built dinghy carried by *Victoria;* she performed so smoothly that the crew used to row her along the shore, one mile to town, because rowing her was easier than walking.

This type of dinghy is seldom seen anymore. Yachts are smaller, and it is difficult to build a well-formed dinghy less than nine feet long. Instead of a flush deck or a straight coach roof, today's boat frequently has a doghouse, which reduces the space available for stowing a dinghy. The movement of masts further aft, and the introduction of midship cockpits, have also reduced dinghy stowage space. Besides, the outboard motor has arrived, and with its aid, any old box will do.

Many people never get away from the areas serviced by club launches. They cruise for weeks without having to put the dinghy in the water. Cruiser racers, for example, always start and finish their races at yacht clubs.

When racing rules required a rigid dinghy, the large ocean racers complied by carrying a 7 foot 6 inch Dyer Dhow midget dinghy. Though an excellent dinghy, this boat cannot carry enough people to take care of the comings and goings of a large crew on a large yacht.

Things have changed indeed since the 1930's, when ocean racers frequently carried a dory, or sometimes two dories nested, to serve as lifeboat and dinghy. Dyer made a set of lapstrake dinghies for one ocean racer: a twelve-footer, a ten-footer nested inside, and an eight-foot pram placed upside down on top of the other two.

At present, ocean racers are no longer required to carry dinghies, so most of them do not, but the serious cruising man needs a dinghy of some sort since he will be visiting out-of-the-way places where there will be no launch service. Like the anchor, the dinghy should be not of the minimum size that can possibly carry the necessary load, but of the maximum size that can be fitted on board the boat and lifted by the crew. Many dinghies advertised by their manufacturers as filling minimum requirements really are not even minimally adequate. One story holds that a yachtsman made his cockpit removable and used it as a dinghy. With a small outboard it worked beautifully, but when he was asked, "How does it row?" he replied, "Just like a cockpit."

In former days, the size of a dinghy was limited by the availability of space, but not by considerations of weight. For at the turn of the century, even the smaller yachts had davits. I have photographs of *Iolaire*, 45 feet LOA, taken about 1910, and there hanging in davits is a beautifully formed twelve-foot dinghy (Photo 104). Davits disappeared from yachts of this size in the early 1920's, and thereafter weight became an important consideration in the construction of a yacht dinghy. However, today, with plywood, fiber glass, or a combination of the two, lightness can be achieved without any sacrifice in strength.

104. Iolaire *dinghy in davits. (Beken of Cowes)*

DESIGN

The dinghy should be as long as possible, since it is very difficult to design one less than seven feet long with any carrying capacity at all. Also, the smaller the dinghy, the shorter the run between pulls on the oars, and a short-run boat is difficult to row in any sort of chop. A seven-foot dinghy must be of the pram type to have any capacity. Once a length of nine feet is reached, a decent dinghy, with good shape and capacity, is possible. Once twelve feet is reached, a dinghy can be designed and built, or purchased ready-made, that will be a real joy.

Some boats do not have enough room to stow a decent-sized dinghy. On *Alano* this problem is solved with a ten-foot pram that comes in two pieces for stowage, while one company in England has advertised a twelve-foot dinghy that breaks into three pieces and stows in 4 feet 6 inches of space. Another dodge is to have a removable transom, so that the stern of the dinghy can be placed over the companionway hatch; with this arrangement a larger dinghy is possible and a doghouse is formed. If none of these approaches is acceptable, a folding dinghy or an inflatable dinghy is needed.

Prout, the designer and builder of many famous racing cats, also designs the most ridiculous-looking minimum dinghy man has ever conceived. When some friends of mine bought one for their twenty-one-foot boat, I predicted that the thing would last six weeks and drown them in the process. Three years later they were still using the same little collapsible dinghy, an amazing, minimum means of transportation. An Indian in the Pacific Northwest built and sold a stock fifteen-foot collapsible runabout that looked ridiculous but went beautifully with an outboard and folded flat to a pile about 1 foot thick, 2 feet high, and 15 feet long. *Altura* had one for years and her crew swore by it.

The inflatable dinghies have the advantage that they can be deflated and stowed below. The larger ones with wooden bottoms and transoms can serve as beautiful high-speed launches suitable for water skiing. Moreover, the inflatable dinghies make good life rafts, while normal dinghies most decidedly do not. And they do not scratch up the topsides when lying alongside. However, all inflatable dinghies suffer from the disadvantage of being almost impossible to row in the best of conditions and absolutely impossible to row in heavy weather, so they are nearly useless for rowing out an anchor. Further, they are expensive, and if in daily use, they must be scrapped after about two years, so depreciation is great. And since the process of deflating them and stowing them below is not easy, it is a tremendous time waster on short passages.

If a yacht is big enough to carry two boats, one of these should be a really good rowing and sailing dinghy for relaxing, and the other a whaler-type launch for heavy work on long trips. The whalers are excellent. Just as the advertisements claim, a whaler can be cut in half, and both halves rowed away. These broad, square, foam-filled launches will carry a number of people with ease, and can serve as excellent lifeboats; if two big sweeps with strong oarlocks are installed, they can be rowed in an emergency with a fair degree of efficiency. Their only disadvantage is that fools get their hands on them and start speeding through anchorages, perhaps with water skiers in tow, disturbing the peace and endangering life and limb. The culprits claim that they leave less wake at full throttle, but when they run over a swimmer or small dinghy, they chop the poor unfortunate into little pieces.

STABILITY

It is very important for a dinghy to be stable, and not to fit the description one of my friends gives of his dinghy—"not only able to be capsized, but willing and desirous of doing so." Initial stability is not necessary, but ultimate stability is essential. My Saints dinghy (Photo 105) has little initial stability, but once loaded down with a number of people she is as steady as a rock, and even when she is empty, I can stand on a gunwale and she won't go over. The flared topsides give the ultimate in stability. The lack of initial stability in the fisherman dory scares everyone, but one of my friends used to demonstrate the stability

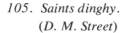

105. Saints dinghy.
(D. M. Street)

106. Fairy Duckling, with one leeboard. (D. M. Street)

of his Gloucester dory by running around the rail standing up. Admittedly he was a bit of an acrobat, but he proved his point.

The Fairy Duckling (Photo 106) is a fine wooden dinghy, her very flat floor giving her excellent stability, and her rounded bow providing great carrying capacity. Another excellent stock wooden dinghy is the Dyer Dhow (Photo 107), which comes in various sizes. Still another is the ubiquitous Sabot-type pram dinghy (Photo 108), originally designed for *Rudder,* then used as the pattern for the El Toro dinghy. Literally tens of thousands of boats have been built on this basic Sabot design,

107. Nine-foot Dyer Dhow, carrying five adults. (Dyer Dhow Comp.)

108. Hagerty pram. (Hagerty)

which in most respects is hard to beat for a really small dinghy. However, the rowing qualities of the basic El Toro dinghy can be improved drastically by the removal of part of the rocker. Further, the newer models, being built out of plywood and reinforced fiber glass, are much lighter than was the original dinghy, made of plywood and wooden frames. George ("Porgy") Rapier of the Grenada Yacht Club builds Sabots that weigh between fifty and sixty pounds.

MATERIALS

Most fiber-glass dinghies on the market today are totally useless for a cruising yachtsman. For one thing, they can only operate with an outboard, so the user risks being stuck on an uninhabited island with a broken-down motor. Situations of this nature, in which the yachtsman cannot return to his boat, or cannot row out from his boat to drop an anchor, have frequently caused the loss of a yacht. The normal modern fiber-glass dinghy is almost impossible to row. The oars supplied with it are generally fit only for a six-year-old child. If a set of long oars is obtained, the oarlocks, and the securing of the oarlocks, turn out to be grossly inadequate. Also, most of these dinghies are very unstable. And almost without exception they have no chafing strips on the bottom. Fiber glass, though very strong, is very sensitive to chafe. Hauling a dinghy up on a beach or dock will rapidly wear holes in the bottom if it is unprotected.

Happily, this situation may not continue forever. In the fall of 1970, Mystic Seaport held a rowing workshop which attracted good rowing dinghies from all over the Northern Hemisphere. The workshop was a tremendous success, and two very encouraging things were discovered. First, a few rugged individuals still build good working rowing dinghies in small shops. They pointed out at the workshop that wood is a wonderful material, that we have roughly four thousand years of engineering experience behind us in building with wood, and that a well-built wooden dinghy will last for a very long time. Further, since a large proportion of the price results from finishing costs, they are delivering wooden dinghies unsanded and unpainted, so that the purchasers can save a great deal by finishing the boats themselves.

The second encouraging aspect is that other individuals have recognized that fiber glass is a good material for dinghies, but that the designs being used at present are not satisfactory. Hence, they are either adapting good proven designs from the old dinghies or are using the old dinghies themselves for molds, and are building boats of fiber glass. These are excellent in that they have the wonderful shape of the older dinghy without requiring the expensive maintenance which was essential for the wooden original, and most important, on a long cruise they will not dry out. However, many of these beautiful, well-formed dinghies suffer from one disadvantage—a lack of carrying capacity. This is the result of their low freeboard. It is regrettable that those who copied the wonderful old rowing dinghies for yacht tenders did not think of raising the freeboard by four to six inches. On a twelve-foot dinghy, such a change would increase the carrying capacity by two or possibly three people. Six persons can be carried in each of *Iolaire's* lapstrake dinghies, which are 10 feet long, 4 feet 1 inch wide, and 19 inches deep.

Those interested in dinghies should subscribe to the *National Fisherman*. In it, frequently appear worthwhile articles by John Garden on dinghies and small boats, and one will find innumerable advertisements for small boat shops that build high-quality dinghies, for firms that supply lumber for building dinghies, and for many other goods and services of importance to the cruising yachtsman.

PROPULSION

ROWING

The ability to row out an anchor in adverse conditions without depending upon an outboard is important for the safety of a vessel. I well remember once lying in the Tobago cays when it began to blow very hard, and obviously two anchors to windward were needed. Though it was tough work, we were able to row out and set an anchor. Our next-door neighbor, with a rubber dinghy, was not even able to start to row out an anchor, and had we not been there he could not have placed his second anchor. In a similar situation, *Passim* was lost on Providenciales island, in the Caicos, because she did not have a dinghy capable of rowing out a second anchor. She slowly dragged ashore, grounded, and sank—merely for want of a good dinghy.

A dinghy loses usefulness· if its oars are inefficient. They may be badly proportioned or of the wrong type of wood. There may be no provision for the rower to brace his feet, or the oarlocks may be improperly designed. An excellent article on oars and rowing by the late W. H. Taylor appeared in *Yachting,* June, 1956.

Oars

Oars should be at least five feet long on even the smallest dinghy; on my daughter Dory's six-foot dinghy, five-foot oars are perfect. In general, one should swing the largest pair of oars that is practical for the size of the dinghy. One of the limiting factors on the length of the oars that can be used is the beam of the dinghy. If the oars are too long, lifting their tips clear of the water during rowing will be difficult. Considerable effort will be expended in doing this, and rowing will be tiring and uncomfortable. The length of the oars is also influenced by the weight of the wood which is used. An old favorite among American yachtsmen has been sassafras. This is light, has a straight grain, and is easy to work, but it is difficult to obtain. More frequently one finds spruce oars; these are excellent, and because of their lightness can be easily handled even when they are quite long.

An oar made of ash will last almost forever and can be very satisfactory. However, ash is very heavy, and unless the oar is very carefully made, it will be too heavy to be easily handled. Most of the ash oars sold today are poorly proportioned and way over strength. A correctly proportioned oar should have considerable spring in it. To test for this spring, one first places one hand on the loom of the oar and the other by the blade. The next step is to place the blade on the dock and lean; if there is no spring, the oar is too heavy and stiff. One should either reject the oar or trim it down to size.

In years gone by, to keep the ends of oars from splintering, copper tips were used. Today, these are difficult to come by. Instead, one can prevent the ends of the oars from splintering when they are used to send off from the rocks, docks, and so on by fiber-glassing the outer six inches. Also, the part of the oar which wears in the oarlock should be covered with leather. The joint in the leather will last if it is kept free from chafe. This is achieved by placing the joint in the leather in line with the vertical blade of the oar. Normally, leather is soaked for many hours, till it is soft and pliable, then cut, and tacked into place around the oar with the proper tacks. But tacks eventually cause rot at the end of the leather, and the oar breaks. One method of avoiding this difficulty is to sew the leather in place with catgut or Dacron sail twine.

When varnishing or painting oars one should be very careful to avoid the looms, for if the looms are varnished or painted, holding on to the oars when pulling hard is most difficult.

Oarlocks

Proper oarlocks are also important. In certain primitive areas two tholepins are used instead of an oarlock ("rowlock" to the British, and "spur" to the Irish). In other areas only one tholepin is used. Most yachtsmen will want to stay with regular oarlocks, but it is worth remembering that if these are lost, hard wooden pegs will suffice. The great problem with oarlocks is that they come in all shapes and sizes, and when they are lost or stolen (small boys the world over are fascinated by oarlocks) replacements of the proper kind seem always to be unobtainable. So one should make it a practice to carry a spare pair. The type that are permanently attached (Photo 109) are wonderful in that they cannot be stolen; a piece of shock cord will keep them in position when stowed.

British oarlocks (Photo 110) are much better than the American type because the longer shank allows them to be secured in two places and they do not subject the gunwale to the wringing strain imposed on it by the short-shanked oarlocks.

109. Nonremovable oarlocks, shown in position (left) *and out of position* (right). (*Wilcox Crittendon*)

110. British oarlocks. (Laurie Legay)

Instead of securing a line to the eye in the bottom, one should secure a clove hitch around the neck of each and tie the oarlocks together with a five-foot length of line. Then they may be used in the forward or aft rowing position, and if additional holes are drilled for the oarlocks in the seats, the oars may be dropped into the oarlocks and secured with shock cord so that nothing will rattle around when the dinghy is towed or placed upside down over the skylight. Oarlocks should never be left in place when not being used; they dig up the yacht's topsides.

Seats, Footrests, Floorboards

In rowing, one's legs should do an appreciable amount of the work; otherwise, if one pulls hard on the oar, one pulls oneself right off the seat of the dinghy, onto the bottom boards. Hence, an adjustable footrest should be provided, where one can brace one's feet. This was always seen in old dinghies, but is practically never seen in modern dinghies.

Another disadvantage of the average modern yacht dinghy is that the seat is made of slick, beautifully varnished mahogany. This is undesirable for two reasons. First, normally, the individual coming aboard the dinghy steps onto the seat, and if it is slippery, he is in danger of a bad fall. Second, when trying to row and pulling hard on the oars, one slides on the seat, and this sliding makes rowing difficult. For these reasons, I feel that the seats in all dinghies should be of bare teak, which is easy to maintain and provides a nonskid surface for the person climbing aboard and the person trying to row.

A similar observation may be made about the floorboards of modern dinghies. All wooden dinghies and most fiber-glass dinghies have wooden floorboards. Most of these are either varnished or painted mahogany, with a bright, glossy surface as slippery as a skating rink. Slipping on the floorboard of a dinghy is a good way to break a leg or go for a swim. Further, the floorboards are difficult to maintain, as they are continually soaked in salt water, and the sun rapidly takes off the finish. For this reason, on all the dinghies I have ever owned I have replaced the standard floorboards with new ones made of bare teak, with no sanding, no painting, no varnishing—and the best nonskid surface in existence. Man has yet to improve on God's creative work when it comes to nonskid surfaces.

Techniques of Rowing

For best results with the least waste of effort, the oarsman should begin by taking his seat in the dinghy, and adjusting the footrest so his knees are slightly flexed. Next, he should pick up the oars, hold them parallel to the water, bend forward, drop the oars in, and start to pull easily; most of the arm, back, and leg pressure should be exerted in the middle part of the stroke, with the oar blades traveling parallel to the boat's course. The rower should ease up and begin to lift the oars as they angle aft, raising the blade no higher than necessary to clear the wave top, then drop his wrist to feather the blades, and take it easy on the back swing. The legs and the back do the vast majority of the work; the arms are used only on the follow-through. With a good dinghy and equipment and a little training, a man can row for hours at a respectable pace. My wife and I swing ten-foot oars (the wide beam at the rail cap of a Saints dinghy makes possible the use of tremendously long oars) to row a thirteen-foot dinghy at the same speed my ten-footer went with a small Seagull on the stern.

Rowing Out the Anchor

A sculling hole in the stern of the dinghy makes rowing out the normal yacht anchor (the fisherman) quite simple. The curved end of the stock is hooked into the sculling hole, and when the correct place is reached, the anchor is merely lifted and dropped. If another type of anchor is being taken out, one can secure a lanyard to the stern ringbolt, through the anchor shackle, and back to the ringbolt, tying with a slip hitch; then one can row out the anchor and slip the line without taking the anchor line into the dinghy. More than one person has been drowned on a cold, dark night, when he capsized the dinghy while trying to throw an anchor overside and caught his foot in the bight of a line. How best to row out an anchor, especially under adverse conditions, is discussed further in the chapter on safety (Chapter XX).

SCULLING

A sculling hole in the stern of the dinghy also has other advantages. If someone steals the oarlocks, one can always scull home. And sculling is the only method of propelling a dinghy under oars that leaves one hand free to hold a beer bottle. Sculling off the stern is an oft neglected method of propelling a boat. Once learned, it is quite simple. When the technique has been mastered, and the wrist developed, it is amazing how fast a dinghy can be made to go. The long sculling oar is sometimes known as the "Bahamian outboard."

SAILING

If a sailing rig can be installed, the dinghy will be much more useful, if only to entertain the small fry. The installation of a centerboard or daggerboard trunk in a sailing dinghy is expensive and not worth the effort. The trunk is a constant cause of leaks. Often when towing, the boat fills through the top of the trunk. Leeboards are good, but a nuisance. One long narrow leeboard will work just as well as two.

The science of naval architecture was put back twenty years when a friend persuaded me to install a single leeboard on my Duckling dinghy. The job took only about two hours. A sailing rig was borrowed and a rudder installed. The result was tested in a race against a proper Duckling with a daggerboard. The one-leeboard Duckling beat the properly designed daggerboard Duckling decisively in a series of races.

The greatest advantage of the single leeboard is its simplicity. All that is needed is one ¼-inch diameter brass bolt through the leeboard (⅜-inch plywood is fine) and through the side of the dinghy and an appropriately placed pad; the bolt is secured with a wing nut, and the angle of the board is regulated by a piece of flag halyard to the oarlock.

It is important that the rigging and spars stow inside the dinghy. A Marconi rig fills this requirement if a jointed mast is used, but this rig has the disadvantage of needing stays, and the dinghy cannot be left with its mast in because a squall is likely to dump it. The sliding gunter rig installed on the old Dyer "D" Dinks was excellent. It had only one stay—the head stay—and the mast could be left in place and all spars stowed inside the boat. Even the head stay could be dispensed with if the halyard was secured to the bow eye. The sprit rig, as in the Optimist pram, is wonderful as there are no halyard, no stays, and in fact no boom; this is by far the simplest of rigs (Photo 111). Another simple rig I have seen used is the lateen rig; one can obtain this from a Sailfish or Sunfish and clap it on the dinghy. Drawings 130a-e show various rigs.

111. Saints dinghy with a simple sail, à la Optimist pram. (D. M. Street)

Now that metal spars have been developed, one can set a jibhead sail, with no stays, on a jointed aluminum spar. If the dinghy is to be towed, one can easily yank the mast out, pull it into its two sections, and place it inside the dinghy.

OUTBOARDS

The subject of outboards causes much bitter argument. I myself am a lover of the Seagull, the engine that everyone either loves or hates. Engineers and mechanics usually point out how old-fashioned and inefficient it is. In truth, it is so old-fashioned and simple that even a non-mechanic can keep one going. My present Seagull has been running for twelve months a year for the past four years. It was assembled out of abandoned parts. The more efficient Evinrude, Johnson, and Mercury, and their European copies, are so complicated that they are almost always giving trouble and must be taken to a repair shop to be fixed. Once they have been in salt water for a year or so, they are almost impossible to take apart; generally in the tropics their maximum life is

130(A). *Loose-footed Marconi rig with jointed mast.*

reckoned to be two years. If high speed is desired, there is no alternative to the big complicated engine. But for low speed, the Seagull with reduction gear is hard to beat. *Iolaire's* twenty tons can be pushed by a Seagull with reduction gear. The Seagull has fewer rpm, but plenty of torque, while the more complicated engines have plenty of rpm but little torque.

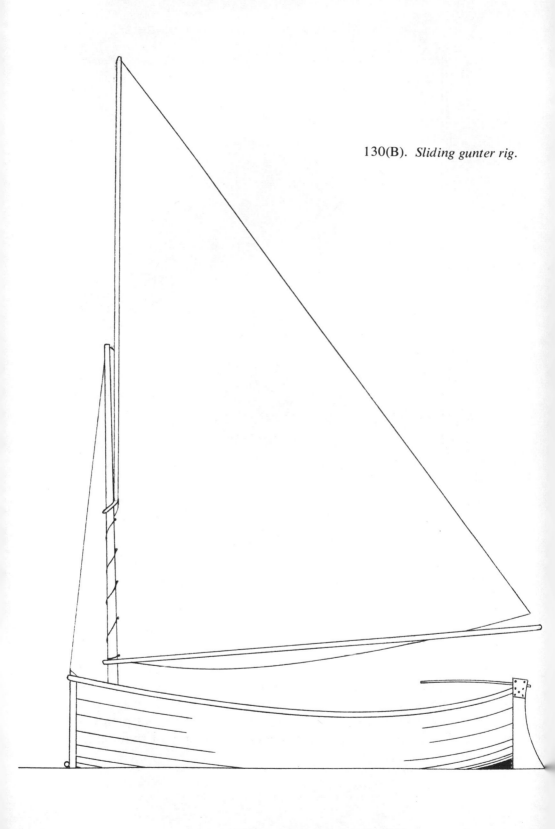

130(B). *Sliding gunter rig.*

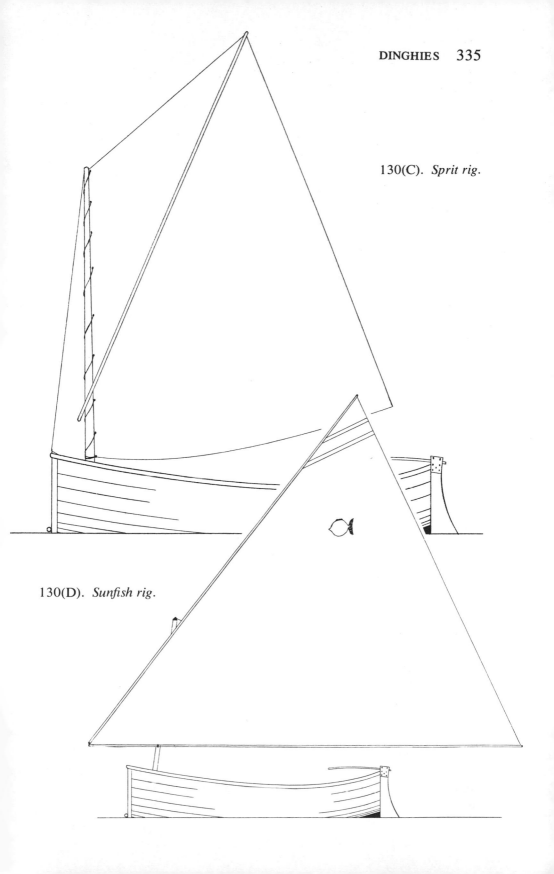

130(C). *Sprit rig.*

130(D). *Sunfish rig.*

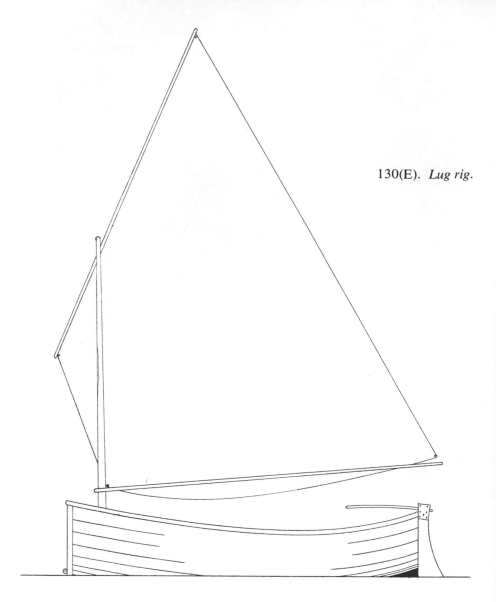

130(E). *Lug rig*.

SECURING

A really good dinghy fender (Photo 112) that will not mar the topsides is essential; large-diameter rope is only a poor substitute. On a wooden dinghy the fender can be secured with copper tacks or with small screws; on a fiber-glass dinghy it must be secured with stainless-steel self-taping screws. Two people are needed to get the fender to stay on, for it must be stretched tight and kept under tension while it is being secured. A dinghy should not be secured on the quarter; passing swells will cause her to swing under the counter, and a long counter coming down on a dinghy will put deep dents in the stern.

112. Dinghy fender. (D. M. Street)

BEACHING AND MOORING

Every dinghy should have good brass-covered skids on the bottom. Then on a shingle beach or on a hard, the dinghy may be skidded along like a sled without damage to the bottom. Admittedly it is better to carry the dinghy, but often carrying is not possible. On a sandy beach, the dinghy cannot be skidded any distance because the friction between the sand and the bottom of the boat is too great. It is instructive to watch a group of West Indians hauling one of their heavy beach boats. They simply put some hardwood sticks in the sand so that the skids of the dinghy do not dig in; then it is comparatively easy to slide the dinghy across the sticks. If worst comes to worst, the oars can be used instead of sticks, but in an area of sandy beaches, it is best to carry about four sticks of the correct length in the dinghy at all times.

If skids are unavailable, the stern can be picked up and the dinghy pivoted on her bow 180 degrees; then the process can be reversed, and the dinghy pivoted on her stern; and thus she can be crabbed up the beach.

The dinghy must be secured above the high-water mark, and note should be made of the surge. The dinghy painter should be tied to a tree, or the anchor should be embedded in the beach. In areas of large tides or steep beaches, special precautions must be taken. It is always embarrassing to return to find the painter secured to the bottom of a pile, the tide now risen, and only the stern of the dinghy above water. Or the reverse may occur: the dinghy secured at high water is found to lie hanging by its painter.

When securing to rough rocks, stone jetties, or the like, one must have a stern anchor out to keep the dinghy from beating herself to death against the dock. The Swedish folding anchor is ideal for this purpose, and a piece of shock cord seized to the stern anchor line will hold the dinghy away from the dock and yet permit her to be pulled close enough so that one can get on board (Drawing 131).

HOISTING

On boats with Davits, lifting the dinghy or launch is no problem, but on a boat that does not have davits, lifting the dinghy can be difficult. Many boats have a short spar (a reaching strut, for example) that can serve as a cargo boom and, with a tackle, be used to hoist the dinghy aboard. Boats that have a reel winch for the main halyard can shackle it onto slings made fast to the bow and stern of the dinghy and hoist away. One person can hold the dinghy away from the side of the boat while the other cranks. Even quite a heavy dinghy, weighing perhaps two hundred pounds, can be hoisted in this manner. If the dinghy is to

131. *Shock cord on the anchor line to keep a dinghy away from the dock.*

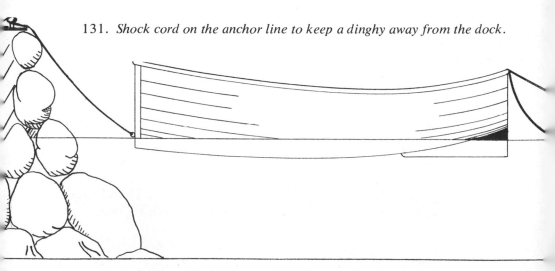

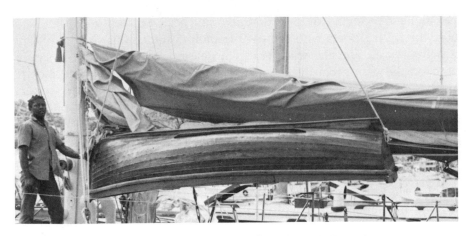

113. Dinghy in slings (Iolaire). (*Laurie Legay*)

be stowed inverted, the slings should be fastened on the outside (Photo 113; Drawing 132), so that the dinghy can be turned upside down while still in the air, and can be lowered into place while still on the halyard. The slings should be as long as possible.

Schooners have an excellent method of hoisting a dinghy aboard. If blocks are placed halfway out on the fore and main spreaders, a Spanish burton can be rigged, and the dinghy hoisted aboard à la Gloucester fisherman. Another technique for the schooner that has the rigging is to use the fisherman throat and peak halyards to lift the dinghy.

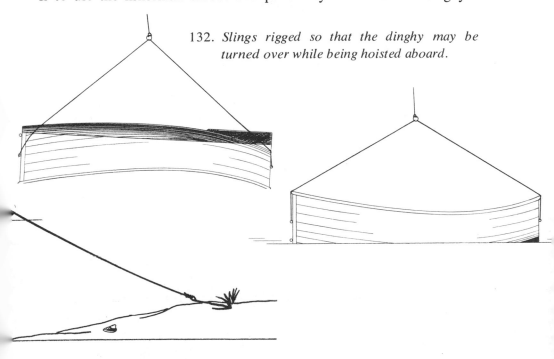

132. *Slings rigged so that the dinghy may be turned over while being hoisted aboard.*

Taking the dinghy on board under sail need not be too difficult—particularly for boats with removable lifeline stanchions. If the dinghy is being towed and the wind rises, the easiest thing to do is to come hard on the wind, then tack and leave the jib sheets alone, letting the headsails be sheeted hard aback; the boat will lie dead in the water, well heeled over. Each boat will have her idiosyncracies—one will want the mizzen eased, to maintain this position; another will want the helm lashed down, and so on. While she is lying there well heeled over and dead in the water, one should remove one or two lifeline stanchions on the lee side, disconnect the lifeline, and then float the dinghy in over the rail. If not absolutely railed down, the boat will be almost so, and not much lifting will be required to get the dinghy aboard.

133. *Dinghy over skylight; the hatch may be left open under the dinghy in all conditions.*

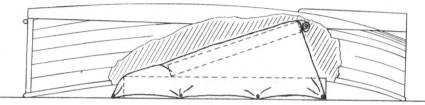

STOWING

A rigid dinghy can be stowed right side up or upside down. I much prefer the upside-down position, for the dinghy stowed in this fashion is much lower, and keeps a good deal of water out of the main skylight (Photo 114). If the main skylight has a canvas cover, open at the aft end, and the dinghy is stowed upside down over it, the skylight can be left open in all but the very worst weather (Drawing 133). *Julie* had an even better arrangement: a canvas cover fitted over the dinghy and snapped down to the deck, keeping water from running under the dinghy and down the skylight (Drawing 134).

134. Julie *arrangement.*

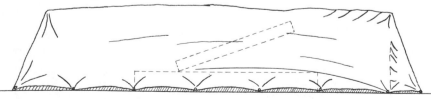

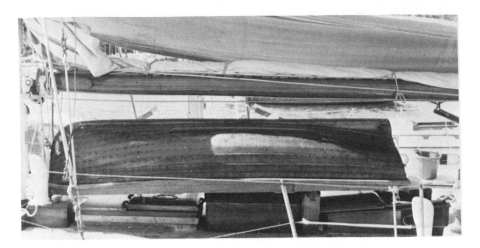

114. Dinghy upside down (Iolaire). (*Laurie Legay*)

If the dinghy is stowed right side up (Photo 115) it becomes a catch-all for miscellaneous gear. Large weights should not be stowed high. A further disadvantage is that frequently the dinghy ends up full of water, which is hard on the dinghy, and affects the stability of the boat. For though a canvas cover provides some protection, it will not keep out a heavy sea breaking aboard. The rounded shape of the bottom of the

115. Dinghy right side up (Iolaire). (*Laurie Legay*)

dinghy presents much less resistance to a wave than does the top of a right-side-up dinghy.

The best place for most dinghies is amidships, just aft of the mainmast, or of the foremast on schooners. Sometimes for various reasons, this is not practical. Stowage off center is not desirable, for there is nothing worse than trying to move sheet leads with the lee rail buried and having to lie on one's belly like a snake to reach a pad eye under a dinghy. Some midship-cockpit ketches have room enough to stow the dinghy aft of the mizzen, and this is an excellent location.

A common European arrangement is to stow the dinghy on the foredeck. This is intolerable. It is better to put up with an inflatable or folding dinghy than to climb over a dinghy on the foredeck, at four o'clock on a cold, dark, and windy morning, trying to douse a headsail. And, of course, a dinghy on the foredeck takes a maximum battering from seas in a storm.

Most important of all, the dinghy must be well secured. There should be straps across the dinghy, set up tight with lashings, and the lashings should be secured to pad eyes that are either bolted through the deck to a pad underneath or bolted through a deck beam.

TOWING

Towing a dinghy is to be avoided; if unavoidable, it should be done with a long nylon line, well secured. The chock through which the line passes must be well polished, and the line well parceled. The towing eye in the dinghy must be strong and should be well down on the bow, almost at the waterline. This location will cause the bow to be raised during towing and prevent the dinghy from sheering around.

Another method of keeping the dinghy from sheering around— suggested by Cis Roper, a Cherokee who spends his time on yachts—is to find the clamp of an old outboard motor and bolt onto it a rudder of ½-inch plywood. Then whenever the dinghy is to be towed, this rudder can be clamped to her stern, and it will help keep her on a straight course.

Regulation of the length of the towing line so that the dinghy is towing downhill on the second stern wave will substantially ease the strain on both the line and the dinghy. Towing in heavy weather in a following sea is a problem. All one can do is veer plenty of line. The old dodge is to tie a bucket to the stern of the dinghy to keep her from riding up, but a wind strong enough to make the bucket necessary will make it impossible to get the dinghy alongside to secure the bucket.

When reaching and beating to windward in heavy weather, one may find it best to tow the dinghy from the lee quarter, where a smooth patch can often be seen. The location of the smooth patch will vary from boat to boat, and with the weather conditions, but it is usually there and worth trying if the dinghy is not towing well astern.

If extensive towing is contemplated, there should be two separate towing lines going to two separate towing eyes on the boat, so that if one fails the dinghy will fetch up on the other. Many yachtsmen with whaler-type launches have taken to towing their boats astern all the time. They put on a heavy towline of great length, open the self-bailers, and are all set—until the towing eye pulls out. To be sure, others have towed their whalers with little difficulty, but there is a risk, and a whaler is an expensive piece of equipment to lose. In any event, I simply dislike towing, which seems to me like sailing with a sea anchor over the stern.

COURTESY

When a number of people live on one boat with one dinghy, someone is always being caught ashore, and borrows the first handy dinghy to get home. Taking such a liberty is fine and dandy, provided the dinghy is returned the same night, not the next morning.

X

Accommodation

There is a vast difference between the requirements for comfortable accommodation on an offshore cruising boat and those for an ocean racer or a weekend cruiser. All the offshore racer needs is enough bunks aft of the mast for the watch below to sleep undisturbed. The racing boat is going flat out; comfortable accommodation is of secondary importance. Standing watch after watch, being called out at times to help with sail changes, the crew members only want comfortably dry bunks and do not care about privacy or a large, well-arranged main cabin.

On the weekend cruiser the aim seems to be to fit as many bunks into as small a space as possible; witness the number of six-berth thirty-footers on the market today. They can sleep six, but where does one stow the clothes, foul-weather gear, food, and so on? They cannot hold equipment for more than a weekend.

For the serious cruising boat the approach is entirely different. She needs only enough bunks for the crew members, who are usually relatively few in number. Each person must have plenty of room to stow working clothes, shore-going clothes, foul-weather gear, cameras, and the like. Further, over a period of time on a small boat, people begin to get on one another's nerves. The more separate cabins that can be provided, the better. If possible, the galley should be apart from the rest of the boat, so that the cook will not disturb the others when cooking.

It is possible to cram immense amounts of gear into a small boat, and people do it, but life in such crowded surroundings is difficult. Displacement—not net, gross, or Thames, but the actual weight of the boat—is a good indication of whether a particular boat will be suitable for comfortable cruising. A man is likely to weigh at least 150 pounds.

For serious cruising in northern latitudes his gear is going to weigh 75 to 100 pounds; food for thirty days, 165 pounds (see Chapter XI); water (and other liquids, like beer), 240 pounds; the total will be about 655 pounds per person. Thus the gear necessary for three people for a long cruise can be crammed on board a thirty-foot boat of the Wanderer class, with her heavy displacement, while in these circumstances a light-displacement thirty-foot boat would be so overloaded that she would hardly sail (see Table XII, Appendix).

Before the advent of the vane self-steering rig, long cruises with only two people could get to be a drag. The routine of watch after watch, with four on and four off, and part of the time off having to be devoted to cooking, cleaning, navigating, and the like, left little time for sleep; and a three-member crew was hardly the solution because crews of three seldom get along. Today, with a good vane self-steering gear, the watch on deck can do the ship's work, and the watch below can sleep undisturbed. With self-steering, boats of thirty to thirty-five feet can be easily handled by two persons; those of thirty-five to forty feet, by three persons; and those of forty to fifty feet, by four; while five persons can handle all but the largest boats.

In planning the belowdecks accommodations of a cruising boat, one must keep in mind the type of cruising the boat will do, the size of her crew, and the climate of what will ordinarily be her home waters. Various layouts are shown in Drawings 135A–K.

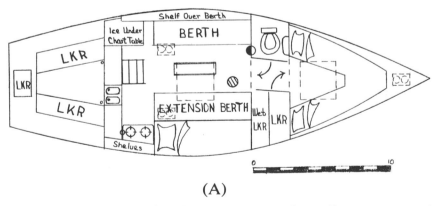

(A)

A thirty-foot boat suitable for offshore cruising. Admittedly, going to windward the two forecastle bunks will frequently be useless. However, a boat of this size is normally sailed offshore by a crew of two or three, with one person on deck and one or two people below. Going to windward, the pilot berth on the starboard side, and whichever settee is to leeward, are available for comfortable sleeping.

Going downwind, both the forecastle bunks will be perfect for sleeping; the forecastle hatch open facing aft will gather in tons of air. Off the wind, with vane steering, the deck watch can cook or navigate keeping watch through the hatch of the main cabin.

The head appears quite small, but because the doors open in opposite directions, it is actually very spacious.

A center hatch in the lazaret gives good ventilation and access to its aftermost part. Cockpit lockers give ready access to any sails or gear stowed there. If the hatch over the main cabin is equipped with a good dodger, it can be left open in all weathers, and the cabin will be cool and habitable even in the tropics.

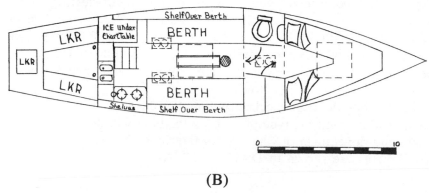

(B)

A narrow thirty-footer. Because of the lack of beam, a boat of this type has no room for a pilot berth. Hence, the berths in the main cabin must be fitted with good lee canvases or, preferably, bunk boards. Cruising to windward, the off watch will have to sleep in the main cabin; only when going downwind will the forecastle be usable. And, of course, this foreward cabin will provide privacy and comfort when the boat is anchored in port.

As in the preceding layout, the forecastle will be fine downwind; its big hatch and Dorade ventilators (see Chapter VII) will provide air. The hatch over the main cabin table can be kept open at all times under the dinghy if a good canvas dodger has been fitted, admitting plenty of air to the main cabin. Also, the Dorade vents with double holes will provide good ventilation by means of the straight-through holes in port and the baffled holes at sea. The gimbaled main cabin table allows eating even at sea. Sitting at the end of the port bunk, the navigator can work at the chart table in a fore-and-aft position. The sinks, mounted quite close to the center line, will be self-draining. A gimbaled stove with an oven vent will make life much more livable both in port and at sea.

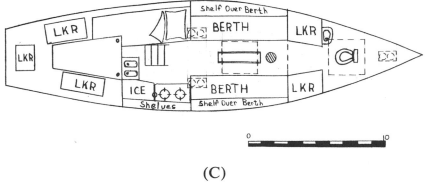

(C)

Another narrow thirty-foot boat, this one most suitable for the person who plans on doing a tremendous amount of offshore cruising and living aboard, rather than just going offshore occasionally. Again, because the boat is narrow, the main cabin has no room for a pilot berth. Instead, there is a portside quarter berth, which provides one good place to sleep in any weather. With self steering, many thirty-foot boats now sail with a crew of two rather than three. The watch on deck then has the entire main cabin, with its gimbaled table, completely to himself. The on-center sinks will drain on both tacks; the gimbaled stove with an oven and oven vent makes cooking easy and does not heat up the main cabin.

Hatches in the forecastle and over the main cabin table, along with Dorade vents, will give plenty of ventilation and the center-line hatch on the stern will give ample ventilation to the lazaret. The roomy head, mounted directly underneath the forecastle hatch, will be beautifully ventilated as well. The extra space around the head can be used for stowing sails, boatswains, stores, and the like. Also, the lockers just forward of the main cabin give generous stowage.

In short, I think, this is a tremendously good layout for a relatively small boat with a small crew; it is not suitable for a family with six children or for four couples out for a weekend sail.

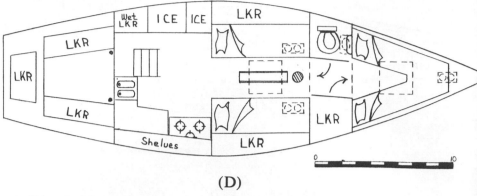

(D)

A thirty-five-footer suitable for short-term cruising. This layout is slightly different from the ordinary in that it provides a gimbaled table in the main cabin, plenty of ventilation by means of Dorade vents, a skylight over the main cabin that can be opened under the dodger in any weather, and a very roomy head, the extra space being provided by doors opening in opposite directions. The galley is much larger than one would expect on a boat of this size. The sinks, being almost on center, will drain on either tack without the aid of a pump. A center-line hatch and cockpit lockers provide ample access and ventilation back aft.

The disadvantage of a layout of this type is that when going to windward, the forward cabin is uninhabitable and everyone must sleep in the main cabin; the deck watch cannot come below and relax there by himself while the boat is sailing with the helm lashed or under self-steering gear. However, this layout is good for weekend cruising with the boat generally anchored at night, since there are two separate cabins, for two couples.

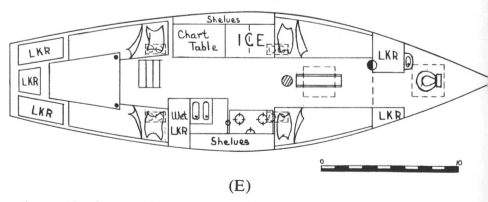

(E)

A very nice honest thirty-five-foot cruising boat. A thirty-five footer is too small to have a proper after cabin, but it can have two big comfortable quarter berths, habitable in any weather, which will be absolutely dry provided one installs a full-width dodger. A Dorade vent is located over each quarter berth. At sea, the baffled holes will provide good ventilation; in tropical areas, the straight-through holes will prove effective.

In port, the two main-cabin bunks may be used at night, but they are seldom required at sea; hence, the main cabin is left free, and when sailing under self steering, the deck watch can come down below, have a cup of coffee, and relax. There is a separate chart table; the navigator has the port-side quarter berth and when he is off watch he may sit in a comfortable fore-and-aft position when using the chart table.

Since the wet locker is directly to starboard of the companionway hatch, wet gear can be put away without fouling up the entire boat. The sinks un-fortunately are off center, to starboard, and possibly may not drain on the port tack when the boat is well heeled down, but as I have said before, all is a compromise. The three-burner gimbaled stove with oven is a cook's de-light. Twin iceboxes, each with a capacity of seventy-five pounds, provide ice for a full two weeks even in the tropics. The lazaret lockers are all quite small, but the forecastle is occupied only by the head and has ample room for the stowage of gear.

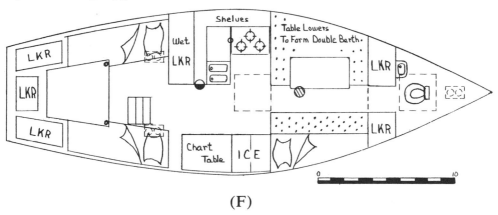

(F)

Another good layout, this one for a beamy thirty-five-footer. Again the stor-age area back aft in the lazaret lockers is restricted, but again there is ample space in the forecastle, which is occupied only by the head. The two quarter berths are always habitable in rough weather, and in addition, a pilot berth usable in all weather has been fitted into the starboard side of the main cabin. The large double-opening hatch with dodger over the galley means that it will be possible to cook in the galley in any weather, as ventilation will always be adequate. Indeed, hatches and Dorade vents provide ample ventilation throughout.

The sinks will drain on either tack. The wet locker is so situated that one may place gear in it immediately upon coming below. The location of the chart table permits the navigator to sit on the head of his bunk, in the fore-and-aft position, to do his job.

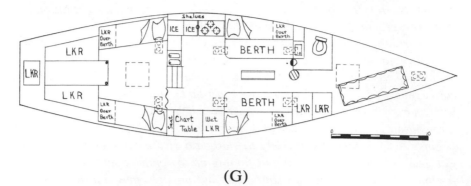

(G)

A very good cruising layout, prosaic but rather difficult to beat on a forty-five-foot boat with a moderate amount of beam. The main companionway hatch is amidships, leading directly to the area occupied by the galley, the chart table, and the wet locker. Foul-weather gear can be stowed immediately upon coming below. The navigator has his own private hole, and can work at the chart table undisturbed.

The galley has on-center sinks that can be drained on either tack, a pair of hundred-pound ice boxes, a gimbaled stove with an oven, and two big Dorade vents with both straight-through and baffled holes, plus ventilation from the main companionway hatch.

Aft of the galley is the after cabin, with its own big hatch, its own big dodger, and Dorade vents making it habitable in all weathers. It has two big berths with large lockers aft of the berths, and is in short a good sea going cabin. The main cabin is as usual ventilated by a double-opening hatch with a dodger, over the gimbaled table. There are two extension berths and two pilot berths, with lockers over each berth giving ample stowage space for those sleeping in the main cabin. A yacht such as this gives four bunks for the off watch in the roughest weathers, without restricting the main cabin and galley. On the port side forward of the mast is a head of adequate size, and opposite it are two large hanging lockers which should easily hold all the cruising gear normally required. If a paid hand is occasionally carried, he can use the folding cot in the forecastle. Also in the forecastle is ample storage space for sails and the like.

Admittedly, this is not a luxurious cruising boat with two or three heads with showers, but I cannot see why a boat of forty-five feet needs more than one head, unless what is desired is a floating home or palace, rather than an honest cruising boat.

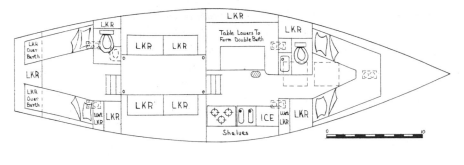

(H)

A center-cockpit layout for a forty-five foot cruising boat favored in the West Indies and by many yachtsmen who spend most of their time weekend cruising, with the boat anchored every night. The great advantage is that when the boat is at anchor, one has the use of two completely separate double cabins—one at the after end and one at the forward end, each with its own head—giving complete privacy for two couples on a weekend cruise. If one can accept a little crowding, a third couple can be accommodated for in a layout of this type, a double bunk can generally be fitted in on the port side of the main cabin. Since a big double bunk is most uncomfortable in a seaway, for seagoing use the mattress should be split so that a bunk board can be slipped in to divide the bunk into two singles. Hatches over the forward cabin, and over the head and passageway, guarantee ample ventilation to the forward half of the boat. The after cabin is superbly ventilated, by means of the companionway hatch, ventilators, and probably ports in the transom.

From a seagoing standpoint, another advantage of this boat is the wonderful full-width cockpit. With the engine mounted underneath the cockpit, and lockers opening to the engine room, there is ample room for sails and gear on either side of the engine and excellent engine accessibility. Frequently this midship-cockpit layout is coupled with a ketch rig. The worst disadvantages of a ketch—that whenever it rains the water pours off the sail on to the helmsman's head, that he gets cross-eyed looking around the mizzenmast, and that when he stands up he usually gets whacked on the head by the mizzen boom—are eliminated in this layout because the mizzenmast is aft of the cockpit. Since the midship cockpit is so far forward that it is subject to plenty of heavy spray when the wind is anywhere forward of abeam, it must have a good watertight dodger.

For a seagoing boat, this layout has both advantages and disadvantages. On long downwind passages, with the big sea rolling in the stern, the security of the midship cockpit is wonderful. Similarly, when going downwind, the forward and after cabins give crew members complete privacy. However, when going to windward, the forward cabin will have to be abandoned, and only the bunks in the main and after cabins will be available.

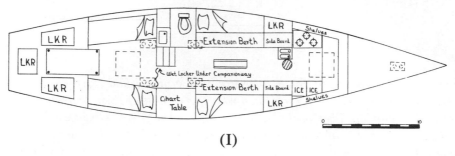

(I)

An excellent layout for a forty-five-footer, which will work well as long as there is a tough crew on board, not bothered by working in the forecastle while going to windward. Basically, this is the layout found in Iolaire, *built in 1905; however, in* Iolaire *we have thrown out the engine that was under the chart table and altered the chart table so that the navigator can sit in the fore-and-aft position, at the aft end of the table.*

Among the desirable features of this layout are the companionway hatch amidships, the location of the wet locker under the companionway ladder, the head to port, and the chart table to starboard. Any water coming down the companionway does little or no damage as there is a teak grating under the ladder. The main cabin has extension berths with lockers, outboard of them. In the after cabin are two comfortable pilot berths with lockers over the foot of each, giving room for almost all the gear one would need; these are good in all weather, amply ventilated by the after-cabin hatch, with its dodger. This forty-five-foot boat thus has four good all-weather berths. In port, both extension berths can be pulled out, for a total of six berths, and at sea the lee extension berth in the main cabin can be utilized as an additional berth. Also, in port two can sleep in the two extra pipe berths in the forecastle.

Needless to say, the location of the galley in the forecastle makes cooking while beating to windward a little less than enjoyable, but it is still possible, although difficult, with the aid of a large Luke stove on gimbals with an oven vent, a big icebox, and plenty of working area. In port, the cook may feel isolated, up forward away from the rest of the crew, but by the same token, the main cabin is very comfortable even in the worst weather because the heat and smells from the galley do not reach it.

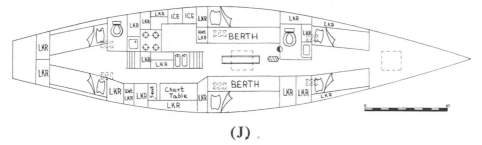

(J)

Once a length of fifty-five feet has been reached, the possible layouts are al-most innumerable. But there are certain essentials for a boat of this length, and these are shown in the sketch. The after cabin with its own head is a must. The navigator and the cook are well treated amidships, with an iso-lated galley off to one side of the boat, and the chart table on the opposite side. Center-line sinks drain on either tack and are accessible from both the passageway and the galley, so that someone may help the cook in dishwash-ing. In the main cabin are pilot berths, with lockers over the foot of each. Extension berths inboard of the pilot berths, provide two extra berths in port. The forward cabin is not so far forward that the berths are toed in drastically, making one feel when in a lee berth going to windward as if one is standing on one's head. Rather, the berths are fore and aft, almost paral-lel to the center line. The forecastle provides plenty of room for the sails, boatswains stores, and so on.

The variations possible on a boat of this size are infinite. For instance, placing the head forward of the forward cabin would mean the cabin would be even farther aft, closer amidships, but then, of course, one would have to walk through the cabin to reach the head. As has been stated hundreds of times, in a boat, compromise is unavoidable.

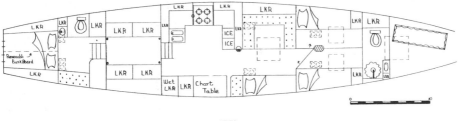

(K)

A narrow sixty-one-footer. As has been stated in my estimation, a long, narrow boat is preferable for cruising to a short, fat one; length means speed, and length makes possible the individual cabin space necessary to as-sure privacy and compatability over a long period of time. A sixty-one-foot boat similar to Garden's **Oceanus,** *with comparatively light displacement* *and narrow beam, can be propelled with a very small engine, a small sail plan, and a very small crew. The few people on board have plenty of room to spread out. On this boat, the after cabin has a comfortable double bunk with a removable bunk board in the middle, and plenty of locker space on each side. The cabin has its own head, a small settee and desk, and a companionway leading to midship cockpit. Under the cockpit is ample room for the engine, with sail lockers on each side. The galley is spacious. Opposite the galley is plenty of room for the wet locker, a hanging locker, and the chart table with the navigator's own private seat. The navigator can sleep in the main cabin in his own pilot berth while the other half of the cabin is free from a big U-shaped settee (usable in emergencies as a single or double bunk) with is own gimbaled table. Forward of the main cabin are two single cabins (or doubles if one wishes to use upper and lower bunks), and forward of them is a good proper head and shower. And there is still space enough for a forecastle with a pipe cot and plenty of stowage for sails and other gear.*

This type of layout provides ample room for a crew of the size needed to cruise with comfort, speed, and efficiency on a light, narrow sixty-one-footer.

BUNKS

LOCATION

Placement of bunks is most important. At sea, any bunk forward of the mast can be eliminated as a place to sleep except when broad off, as the motion is too great when going to windward. Of course, occasionally some old-timer will crawl into a forecastle bunk, tie himself in with a sail stop, and sleep soundly. An ex-coastguardsman of my acquaintance is always comfortable up forward. After twenty years of riding the eighty-three-footers, anything feels comfortable. My late wife, Marilyn, would sit and read in the galley of *Iolaire*, which is in the forecastle, while beating to windward. She was fine, but just watching her made the rest of us seasick.

The normal stock layout, with galley aft, main cabin, head to port, hanging locker to starboard, and forward cabin, is not good for extended cruising. The forward cabin is useless when reaching or going to windward, so one is left with just the main cabin and a head that is usually too small for comfort. For the smaller boat I prefer a layout with the galley aft on one side, a quarter berth with chart table over it on the other side, then the main cabin and some hanging lockers, with the whole forecastle left for storage and the head. If the boat has sufficient beam—nine feet will do—a pilot berth can be built on one side of the main cabin, with a settee in front of it, and a settee on the other side. If only two are sailing the boat, each can have his own bunk, and the main-cabin settees are free for general use. It is aggravating to have to make up a bunk every time one wishes to use the main cabin. If there is a three-man crew, bunks are still available for the off watch, while the man on watch, if he wishes to read, rest out of the gale, and the like, can do so in the main cabin without disturbing anyone.

Once a length of forty feet is reached, the ideal layout, in my view, begins with an aft cabin with two bunks, a chart table in between, and an escape hatch under a dodger to be used in heavy weather. Forward of this, preferably with its own hatch, will be the galley, with a wet-storage locker for foul-weather gear; forward of this will be the main cabin. Forward of the main cabin will be hanging lockers, and a full-width head; and gear and sail storage will be in the forecastle. With this arrangement, the off watch can sleep completely undisturbed by any activities in the main cabin or in the galley. If the boat is too small for this layout, and the main entrance has to be aft, there still can be two quarter berths with a modicum of privacy if the galley is bulkheaded off. The chart table should be aft, because in that position the navigator can most easily communicate with the helmsman.

For boats above forty feet, innumerable arrangements are possible. The biggest advantage of the larger boat is that the layout can include a midship cockpit with an aft cabin completely isolated from the rest of the interior. Here is where the long, narrow boat comes into her own.

SIZE

Bunks are most important, for at least one-third of the day will be spent in them. In America today, a generation of giants is growing, and the last generation is not far behind. A bunk that is too short, especially if it is also narrow, is most uncomfortable. When I rebuilt the interior of my boat, I made four of the bunks six and a half feet long and two of them seven feet long. I now wish that I had made them all seven feet long. Width is not as important as length, but still must be considered. In northern climates a twenty- or twenty-four-inch-wide bunk is adequate, but in the tropics, thirty inches is much better. Double bunks are wonderful in port, but at sea in rough weather they are inconvenient in that the occupants roll around too much in them and must chock themselves into place. The best solution here is to have two separate mattresses. Then a piece of plywood can be slipped between them to form a bunk board in rough weather.

CONSTRUCTION

My favorite bunk consists of a mattress of four-inch polyfoam (which unlike foam rubber does not deteriorate and does not absorb

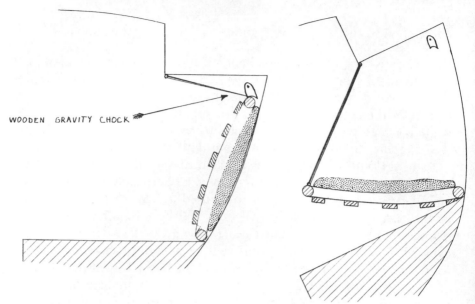

136. *Concordian berth forms backrest when not in use* (left); *berth peaked up when in use under way* (right).

water to speak of) laid on plywood and covered with Vivatex canvas, which is waterproof and mildewproof. The slick coverings, such as Naugahyde, are much too hot to sleep on. A cloth cover may be more difficult to keep clean, but it is comfortable and looks much better.

Concordian Berths.

The Concordian berth was made popular by Waldo Howland, who used it in the Concordia yawls built prior to World War II. A Concordian berth consists of a metal frame, the bottom side covered with wooden strips, the top with a piece of canvas (now Dacron) stretched tight. When the Concordian berth is turned down for use, its angle can be adjusted to the angle of heel, and most people find it comfortable. When not in use, it may be pivoted up against the side of the hull, and the wooden slats make a very comfortable backrest (Drawing 136).

Many yachtsmen are great believers in the Concordian berth. But like the pipe berth and the Root berth, it must be adjusted to the angle of heel. Every time the boat tacks, the berth must be readjusted, and when the boat is rolling badly, it must be peaked up so high that one is sleeping in a corner. Further, no matter how tightly it is lashed, there is some sag, and I for one get a backache.

Pilot Berths

Pilot berths are so called because they were found on the old pilot sailing vessels the world over. They are in effect little cabins, six feet

long and two feet wide, with a locker at the foot of the berth, high
bunk boards, and often, a curtain. There is always a settee inboard of
the pilot berth, for reading, yarning, and the like.

I like pilot berths in the main cabin because the curtain enables the
occupants to sleep undisturbed when the main cabin is in use. Also,
one does not have to make up a bunk in order to sit down to a meal,
and the person who comes down and sits at the main-cabin table in wet
foul-weather gear does not get the bunk wet. Space limits the use of
pilot berths. One may be squeezed into a boat with nine feet of interior
beam; two can be squeezed into a boat with ten feet of interior beam.
In both cases, there is a tight fit; another foot of beam helps a great
deal. Pilot berths also require a certain amount of freeboard. On a boat
with a flush deck, 2½ feet are available between the underside of the
deck and the bunk, but on a boat with a cabin trunk, there will be only
eighteen to twenty inches—enough in the northern climates, but not in
the tropics. One large body crammed in this small space just gives off
too much heat, and sleep is all but impossible.

Getting into a pilot berth, especially the windward one when beating
in heavy weather, can be most difficult, if not impossible. The best solution I have ever seen is the monkey bar installed in *Mariann* (Drawing 137). The ends of the gimbaled table are supported by two aluminum pipes, each two inches in diameter, firmly secured to the overhead
and to the integral tank tops; running fore and aft between these
supports is another pipe of the same diameter, which provides a great
place for one to brace a foot or hand when getting in or out of the
bunk.

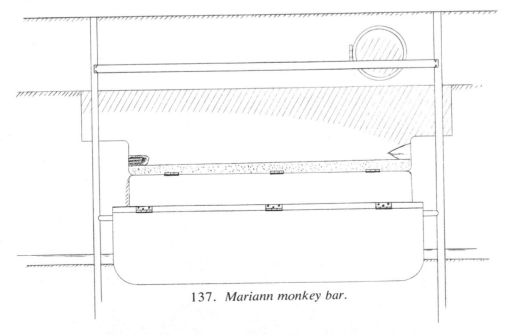

137. *Mariann monkey bar.*

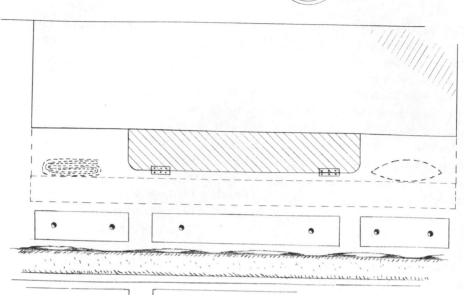

138. *Bunk board; the permanent parts at each end hold in the pillow and blankets.*

Lee Canvases Versus Bunk Boards

There is an everlasting argument about the relative merits of bunk boards and lee canvases. I prefer bunk boards, rising at least eight inches—and preferably twelve inches—above the mattress. Only the middle of the bunk board should pivot (Drawing 138). The permanent pieces at the ends should be eighteen inches long, so that they can hold the pillow and blankets in the bunk when the middle section is down. Some boats are so fancy that the inside of the bunk board is upholstered, making it more comfortable to sleep against; also, in the case of a pilot berth, it serves as a backrest for the settee below.

A lee canvas can simply be a piece of canvas tacked to the bottom of the bunk and secured to the overhead by lanyards. The lanyards must be long enough to form a three-part tackle, otherwise it will not be possible to get the lee canvas to stay permanently and comfortable tight (Drawing 139). The normal lee canvas is a solid piece of canvas, and in the tropics restricts airflow and makes the bunk hot. On some boats the lee canvas is made of two-inch-wide nylon webbing in the form of a net. This is much cooler.

CLOTHES STOWAGE

Clothes lockers on the serious cruising boat must be large and numerous. On *Lutine*, each bunk had at its foot a locker the width of the

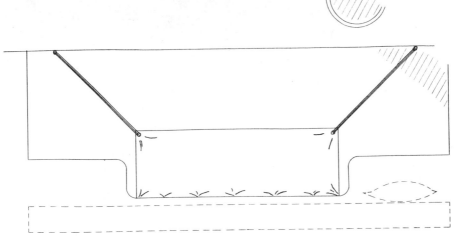

139. *Lee canvas held by three-part purchase at each corner.*

bunk, 1½ feet high and 1½ feet deep, with two shelves, giving a total of 4½ cubic feet of storage space for each bunk. The access hole opened into the bunk, and being athwartships rather than fore and aft, needed no door (Drawing 140).

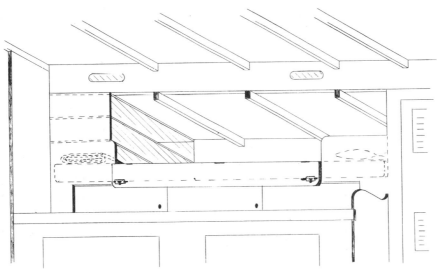

140. *Locker at foot of pilot berth.*

I feel that shelves, behind doors, are preferable to drawers. Though admittedly more convenient, drawers are expensive and difficult to install well, and take up much more space than shelves. If drawers are installed, catches should not be necessary. With the bottom notched (Drawing 141), a drawer will stay in place even when the boat is heeled over.

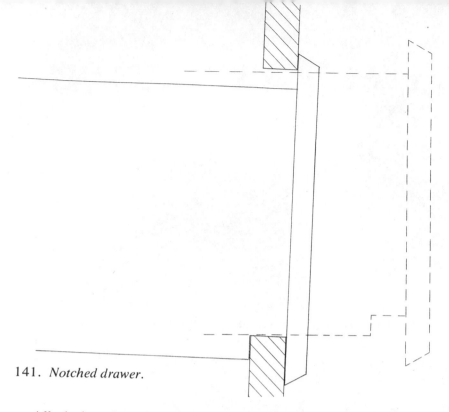

141. *Notched drawer.*

All clothes should be stowed in plastic bags; then, no matter what happens, they will be dry. I remember one time when at the end of a gale, with supposedly not a dry piece of clothing in the boat, I went to my well-soaked clothes locker and pulled out some plastic bags containing a dry sweater, trousers, and socks, much to the envy of the rest of the crew.

Clothes in hanging lockers must be secured with straps, to keep them from chafing with the roll of the boat. Shore clothes should be kept inside plastic hanging bags like those the airlines sell. These reduce chafe damage and assure clean, dry clothes at the end of the cruise. Shoes should be polished before storing, or they will become mildewed despite good ventilation. All lockers should have holes drilled in them so that the air will circulate and prevent both mildew in the clothes and rot in the boat.

WET CLOTHING

No matter how good one's foul-weather gear is, some wetness invariably seeps through. In fine weather, when no foul-weather gear is worn, night dampness soaks normal clothing. Piles of dank, smelly clothes soon turn the best boat into a pigsty. Therefore, enough hooks should be provided so that as soon as clothes are removed, they can be hung up to air and dry. They should never be taken off, balled up, and stuffed into a locker or lodged at the foot of the bunk. In rough weather, especially in cold rough weather, the cabin should be criss-crossed with flag halyard, where one can hang clothes immediately upon coming below.

An accumulation of wet foul-weather gear can rapidly mess up a boat, so proper provisions for it must be made. An open grating at the foot of the companionway hatch, where one can stand and drain off the worst of the water, is especially helpful. Foul-weather gear should then be removed and hung to dry, preferably in a foul-weather-gear locker. This locker should be large enough to hold all the foul-weather gear on board; otherwise the gear ends up all over the boat. The locker should drain into the bilge, be well ventilated, and have a rack on which boots can be dried upside down. Once dried, they can be stowed anywhere convenient.

On the boat with a large head equipped with a shower, the shower makes an excellent place to stow foul-weather gear. When the water supply permits, it is a good practice to rinse foul-weather gear in the shower on a good drying day, to remove the accumulated salt, which will always absorb dampness.

Incidentally, when going on a long cruise, one should invest in a few extra sets of foul-weather gear. If someone tears his own, or if, as frequently happens, the bottom wear out, not only will that person be wet and miserable, but his wet clothes will be all over the boat, making everyone else miserable.

HEADS

The greatest luxury I ever experienced was sailing on *Djinn* to St. Thomas and coming off watch, going to the head, and taking a hot shower. A shower is common enough on large boats, but generally on small cruising boats the only shower obtainable is the one God gives. In the old wooden boats, the keel, planking, frames, floors, and so on left little room for water tanks. But today, with a steel, aluminum, and fiber-glass construction, and integral tanks, one can have the luxury of a shower in a relatively small boat. If there is to be a shower, the head must be of a good size, not like the one on a famous ocean racer that was so small that some of the larger members of the crew had to remove their trousers and back in because they couldn't remove their trousers once the door was closed. One method of getting space is to use the forecastle for the head and for nothing else. Another method is to put the head opposite a hanging locker and have its door and the

142. *Full-width head.*

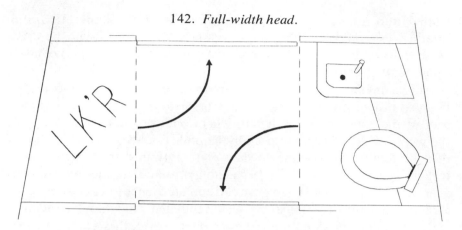

locker door open in opposite directions, so that with both doors open the head occupies the full width of the boat (Drawing 142).

WASH BASINS

If the basin is small and the pumps are hard to operate, there will be little trouble with excessive water consumption. Also, a salt-water tap in the head sink and a supply of soap or detergent effective in salt water (such as Joy, or the pure palm-oil soap available at any copra factory in the tropics) will further reduce water consumption.

In some boats the waste water from the basin is drawn into a sump tank; in others, it is pumped directly overboard. But the simplest disposal method is to let the water run into the head and pump it out from there. With this arrangement the head is sure to be pumped a few extra strokes, which is all to the good.

MARINE TOILETS

The head itself is always a problem. Some people take a violent and drastic approach to the matter by removing the head and throwing it overside; others have no faith. When *Circe*'s owner decided to enter the 1955 Transatlantic race, he called Rod Stephens to ask for advice on preparing the boat for the race. Rod said, "Buy two hundred pounds of good anthracite blue coal, and have a board with a hole ten inches in diameter in it fastened to the transom, and call me back next week." The owner was a little miffed, but at the end of the race, it appeared that the amount of coal had been exactly right for the cabin heaters; and as Rod had anticipated, the head packed up halfway across, and for the remainder of the trip the crew used the board with the hole in it, hung over the stern—cold, public, but foolproof. It seems amazing that though marine heads have been manufactured since 1840 or so, they are still so unreliable. Some people urge a cedar bucket—L. Francis Herreshoff wrote pages extolling its virtues—and in actuality on the twenty- or thirty-footer, it does have its advantages. On larger boats, with ladders to climb up and down, I'm afraid it is just not practical.

Anything I say now on the construction of heads will soon be out of date. For many years the make-up of the head was the most neglected part of yacht-equipment design. However, with the development of plastics, and the increasing popularity of the diaphragm bilge pump, various manufacturers are coming up with completely new concepts for marine heads. Anyone contemplating installing a new head would do well to examine the brochures of the manufacturers, whose addresses may be found in yachting magazines (including the European-show issues) and the *Boat Owners Buyers Guide* issued by *Yachting*.

Heads break down mainly because no one wants to work on them. As soon as one purchases a boat, or a new head, one should separate the head into its bits and pieces; analyze what makes it work; purchase all the spare parts that could possibly be needed; grease all the nuts, bolts, threads, and so on, making sure that they are good bronze or stainless steel, not soft brass, and reassemble the whole. A broken machine screw in a head at sea can be most discouraging.

Next, one must convince everyone that nothing (except toilet paper) that has not been eaten first, should be put into the head. Hair, tissues, paper towels, tampons, matches, cigarette butts, will just bind the head up solid, and it never binds up except right after use.

There is no reason for the head to smell like an old cesspool unless the crew is sloppy and lazy. If the head is well pumped—twenty-five strokes are excellent; twenty, good; and fifteen, a bare minimum—and a few ounces of Clorox are dumped into it every day, it will stay fresh and clean. Periodically, someone must go in with a bucket of water, scouring powder, and Clorox to scrub the compartment. The necessity for this scrubbing will be minimized if the male members of the crew either sit down for all functions or use the lee rail. On one boat there is a sign: "You cannot shoot a hole in one on the golf course and you probably can't shoot one here, so sit down."

When a boat is not in use, there is frequently a horrible smell when the head is flushed. The source of this smell has always puzzled me. My friend John Hazelhurst, of *Paisano*, who has a good inquisitive mind and a fair grounding in chemistry, has come to the conclusion that the smell is caused by algae growing inside the head intake pipe. They are especially likely to flourish if the pipe is made of translucent plastic, which admits enough light for them to really thrive. He therefore recommends that when leaving the boat for more than a day or so, one should shut off the sea cock, disconnect the intake valve before the pipe enters the head, pour a few ounces of Clorox into the pipe, and then reconnect the pipe. The Clorox will kill the algae and eliminate the smell; when one comes back on board one need only open up the sea cock, and all is well.

These days, the question of holding tanks, chlorinators, macerators, and the antipollution laws arises with increasing frequency. I have been lucky enough to have lived and sailed for years in areas of the world where the matter has not yet come up. In the United States, at this writing, the laws are a tangle of confusion, with the various states and the Federal Government all steering different courses. It seems inevitable that some sort of chemical treatment of human waste will be mandatory in many parts of the world, where it is not now required, and probable that holding tanks also will be obligatory. However, as yet there has been no genuinely successful system put on the market. By and large, the ones now available are as frequently out of order as in, tend to smell, and in general stand as poor substitutes for L. Francis Herreshoff's wooden bucket. A further complication is the scarcity of pump-out stations ashore, which causes even boats with holding tanks to empty them into the sea. In short, there is no constructive way for the subject to be dealt with here except to recommend that the reader keep reading his yachting journals to stay abreast of both the law and the new devices that are surely coming.

MAIN-CABIN TABLES

A cruising boat should have a gimbaled main-cabin table. If the table is not gimbaled, the cook must serve each person individually, since he cannot place bowls or platters of food on the table. Furthermore, it is difficult to eat at sea without a gimbaled table. The knife and fork take two hands, and no hands are left to steady the cup and plate. Some of the ocean racers with a high ratio of ballast to displacement no longer have gimbaled tables because the boats are so stiff and their motion is so quick that the tables begin to oscillate and everything falls off. On some boats this situation has been corrected with a brake on the pivot that slows the motion down; if there is no brake, one can tie some shock cord from the bottom of the lead weight to the leg of the table. One may have to experiment a little to get the correct tension on the shock cord, but once adjusted, it will slow down the motion and make everything stay on the table (Drawing 143). Objects can also be kept in place by a correctly designed fiddle rail (Drawing 144). Its in-

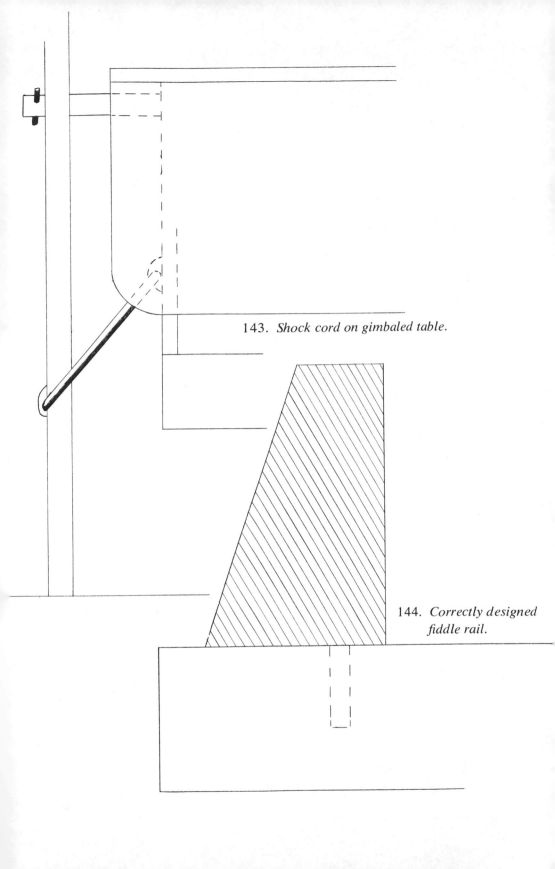

143. *Shock cord on gimbaled table.*

144. *Correctly designed fiddle rail.*

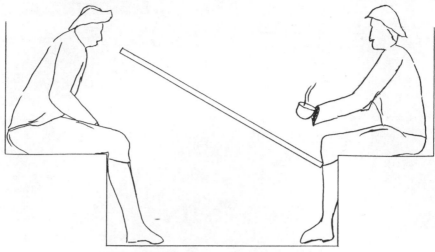

145. *Wide table at extreme angle of heel.*

side edge should form a right angle with the table top, since otherwise a bottle or glass sliding against it will tend to capsize.

Many main-cabin tables are too large. When the boat takes a large angle of heel, the table hits the legs of the people on the windward side (Drawing 145). The corners of the table should be well rounded, so that people can slide around it without upsetting it. It should weigh as much as is practical, fifty pounds being about the minimum. If the boat's hand-powered sewing machine is placed in the ballast box, it serves as ballast and is readily available. The table can be made so that the sewing machine fits into its center. The machine will earn its keep ten times over in making emergency sail repairs, cushion covers, dodgers, and what-have-you.

STOWAGE

CUTLERY

On some boats all the cutlery is stowed in a box in the center of the table. This seems an excellent idea, but once the table is set, if someone wants an additional spoon or fork, he must rummage around in the center of the table under all the food. A good arrangement stolen from *Mariann* is to have a couple of Dacron pockets sewn to an upright monkey bar, and place the most-used knives, forks, and spoons in these.

LIQUOR

A true cruising boat should have an ample liquor locker, since on some trips one may have opportunities to buy liquor in bond at considerable savings. In some areas, customs officials insist on sealing the liquor in a compartment; thus a liquor locker should be a minimum of 22 inches by 12 inches by 13 inches deep. Also, it should be provided with a lock, so that when one hires labor in a strange area, no one can sample the contents. Bottles should be stowed vertically.

When under way, the rattling of liquor bottles not only is disturbing but can cause them to break. To eliminate this problem, on some boats a piece of plywood is placed in the liquor locker, with an individual hole drilled in it for each bottle. Another method is to place at the bottom of the locker a piece of plywood with holes drilled at fairly close intervals and pieces of dowel slipped into the holes to keep bottles in place. On other boats, my own included, we just keep the locker filled, and jam some towels between the bottles to chock them in place and prevent rattling.

WINE

In some areas, wine is unbelievably cheap, and it is well worthwhile to keep a stock on board, especially if the local water is likely to be unpalatable or not safe to drink. If wine is bought in demijohns—large bottles covered with straw—one must give them a very good spray with insecticide before bringing them on board, as the straw is a bed for cockroaches. Demijohns are rather awkward in size, so about the only thing to do is to stow them anywhere they will fit. Regular bottles of wine should be stowed on their sides so that the corks do not dry out. A wine rack may be devised in which an amazing number of bottles can be stowed in a comparatively small space (Drawing 146).

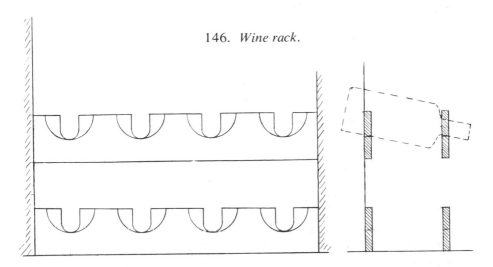

146. *Wine rack.*

147. *Glass rack.*

GLASS

Stowing wine glasses, champagne glasses, any glasses at all, is always a project. The only way to prevent breakage is to have racks made for the individual glasses. In *Iolaire* we have a hanging locker immediately behind the liquor locker, with pieces of plywood secured with small brass angles to the locker door. Holes have been cut in the plywood to fit the individual glasses (Drawing 147).

BOOKS

An important but oft neglected problem is the stowage of books. On a long cruise, many books will be read. I myself average about one book a day; indeed, someone once described *Iolaire* as thirty feet of bookshelves surrounded by a boat. All types of reading matter can now be purchased in small paperbacks—a real godsend to the sailor. On many boats, books are thrown helter-skelter into lockers, shelves, or wherever. It is worthwhile to install numerous bookshelves in accessible locations, so that the books can be neatly stacked and easily found. Most of the shelves can be small, for the paperbacks, but some will have to be large enough for the old standard classics that every yachtsman carries.

RECORD PLAYERS AND RADIOS

Conventional record players are difficult to rig so that they will work at sea. However, a good small tape recorder will work whether it is right side up or upside down, and music of all types is now available on tape. A good tape recorder, mounted in its own locker or on its own shelf, with a library of tapes in a handy position nearby, will be worth its weight in gold. All of these recorders have provisions for plugging in an additional speaker. Such a speaker, with a long wire, will save much wear and tear, since it can be plugged into the recorder, with the wire run through a ventilator or hatch, and placed in the cockpit for the evening sundowner. If a wave drowns everything out, only the speaker will be damaged, rather than the whole set.

Radios are no longer a problem, as quite small ones can now be purchased that will give excellent reception. One year I purchased a small transistor radio for $12.95 at a discount house, as an emergency standby unit. It turned out to pull in WWV better than the big radios I had hitherto been using. The small, cheap transistor radio can be taken on deck to keep the night watch company. Here it can also be used to get the time tick without having to wake the navigator in the middle of the night. Remember, however, that the speaker has a magnet in it, and that it should never be played anywhere near the compass, or the navigator will have nightmares.

Because of their susceptibility to damage, two radios should be kept on board: one to be moved around for general use; another, bolted or strapped firmly in place, for the navigator's use, and as a spare.

LIGHT

Lighting is most important for the comfort of the crew. In the old days, boats were usually dark and gloomy belowdecks; now, with hatches made of clear or translucent Lucite, ample light passes below.

In the northern climates, kerosene lamps are popular and practical for lighting the cabin, though inadequate for reading. Their glow is pleasant, and the warmth given off by the flame takes the chill off the cabin. However, kerosene lamps in the tropics will soon turn the belowdecks area into a sweatbox, so electric lights are essential there.

The lights should be numerous and well placed. A small dim light in the correct location will be much more useful than a bright light badly situated. Each bunk should have a light by which a person can read comfortably in bed. At one end of the main-cabin settee, there should be a good reading light for those who prefer to read sitting up. The galley should be well lit, as it is difficult to cook in semidarkness. Fluorescent lights are suitable for the chart table, galley, and head. They are available in 6, 12, 24, and 32 volts and are not too expensive. They are especially good in the tropics because they do not give off the kind of heat that is produced by other lights. Further, the amperage drawn by fluorescent lights is minimal, so they may be left on for hours without dragging the battery down. They give a very bright light which many people do not like, but which is sure to be welcomed by the navigator, the cook, and anyone in the head trying to shave. Furthermore, a good chart table with a comfortable seat will be a favorite place for the lee helmsman and the second watch keeper to sit and read in the evening. For this reason, there should be a good bright light with a narrow beam over the chart table (Photo 116). Often lights of this type are not bright enough to do the job required of them, so before purchasing, one should check the size and intensity of the bulb, making sure it will give a good bright light, concentrated on one spot. Then those who are up can read to their hearts' content without disturbing anyone else.

At the same time, the navigator normally does not wish to lose his night vision when he comes below at night. There should therefore be a red shielded light that illuminates the chart-table area only. Similarly, at night in the galley, one generally wants only to make a cup of coffee or something equally simple, and especially if the galley is in the main cabin, one doesn't wish to wake people up by turning on bright lights. Hence there should be in the galley a small dim light, so shielded that it does not light the main cabin.

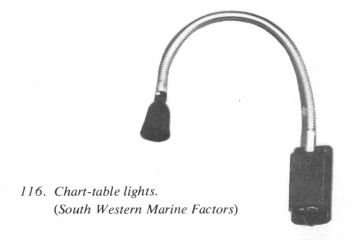

116. Chart-table lights.
(South Western Marine Factors)

VENTILATION

Ventilation sometimes does not receive the attention it deserves. As many ventilators as possible should be installed, located so that air can flow through the entire boat. This is important up north and absolutely essential in the tropics. One ventilator should be placed in the extreme bow of the boat, and another in the stern—two on a broad-sterned boat. When the boat is at anchor, the forward ventilator should face aft and the aft ventilator forward, since on a boat, air naturally circulates from stern to bow. This circulation is easily seen on a boat with curtains instead of doors: when the curtains are closed, their bottoms always tend forward.

Before going to the tropics, one should throw overboard all doors (except the head door) and replace them with curtains that end eighteen inches above the cabin sole. The boat will be much cooler. Some people object to the lack of privacy with curtains, but in any case how much privacy does a ¾-inch plywood bulkhead afford?

Ventilators should be at least four inches in diameter and one foot high—the higher the better. They are discussed in more detail in Chapter VII.

All lockers should have cut in them as many vent holes as possible, and the bulkheads separating the quarter berths from the lazaret and/or sail lockers should have holes of large diameter drilled in them to allow the free passage of air.

HATCHES

On a boat venturing into the tropics, there must be a large hatch over the main cabin, for when five or six people are filling the cabin with hot air, both from their mouths and their bodies, ventilation is essential. Hatches should be hinged so that they can admit air from at least two directions, and preferably all four. It is essential to have hatches which may be opened both into the wind, on quiet days, and facing aft, when the spray is flying.

As noted in Chapter VII, hatches should be at least thirty inches square, to allow a decent amount of air—and a decent-sized person—to get below.

WIND SCOOPS (WINDSAILS, GALLEY STAYSAILS)

The best wind scoop I have ever seen is the one on *Maverick;* it merely needs to be hoisted, and no matter what the direction of the wind, the scoop operates. At the head of the tube conducting air belowdecks, is attached the device shown in Drawing 148. Four pieces of

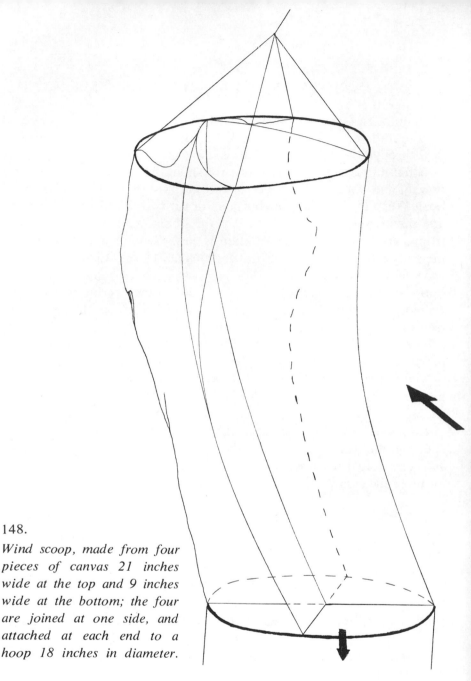

148.

Wind scoop, made from four pieces of canvas 21 inches wide at the top and 9 inches wide at the bottom; the four are joined at one side, and attached at each end to a hoop 18 inches in diameter.

canvas are sewn together in the form of an **X** and attached at each end to a hoop. The canvas panels are trapezoids. At the bottom, each is equal to ½ the diameter of the tube; at the top, to ⅜ the circumference of the tube. Hence if the tube is 18 inches in diameter, each of the four panels forming the **X** should be 9 inches wide at the bottom and 21 inches wide at the top; the height of each panel (and thus of course of the opening of the intake) is 3 feet.

At anchor, one or two wind scoops should be rigged. These will give forced-draft ventilation below in even the hottest weather, provided there is a little wind blowing.

FANS

If the batteries will stand the drain, fans in the bunks are wonderful, even though they cannot be used continuously. By turning the fan on for fifteen minutes when first getting into a bunk, one can dispose of all the hot, stale, dead air.

CABIN HEATING

Those who sail in northern climates may feel that with all the ventilators I have recommended, they will die of the cold. But ventilators make it possible to cool the boat when it does get hot, and in cold weather, one can close off some of them, and bask in the warmth of a good coal stove.

Certainly anyone cruising in northern waters wants some sort of cabin heater on board. There are many types on the market. Some use kerosene or alcohol; others use solid fuel. I much prefer the latter. The kerosene and alcohol stoves are easier to light and provide plenty of heat, but they have no drying power. Indeed, they seem actually to produce moisture. I have frequently seen the interior of a boat sweat when a heater using liquid fuel was going. By contrast, a coal stove dries the atmosphere so much that at times the throat becomes parched.

Solid-fuel stoves are available in many varieties, ranging from the incredibly cheap metal Tiny Tot (an excellent stove), through soapstone fireplaces, beautiful but expensive, to the highly efficient, well-insulated Aga cooker with a hot-water heater. If only a little heat is desired, to take the chill off the cabin in the morning, a small charcoal or wood-chip fire is sufficient, but if the stove or heater is to run all day, good, hard, blue anthracite coal is needed. Such coal is difficult to find, in both the United States and Europe. But surprisingly, there is often plenty of anthracite in out-of-the-way places in the tropics. Both St. Thomas and St. Lucia were coaling ports; the remains of old coal piles are still there, and the coal is free for the taking.

The pipe from the stove to the deck is a source of trouble and has caused the end of more than one boat because it was run through lockers to dry clothes, and the clothes ignited. Similarly, small fires have started in the main cabin when clothes hung to dry there have hit the hot stovepipe. For this reason, I recommend mounting a heavy wire-mesh guard about four inches away from the stovepipe. Behind the

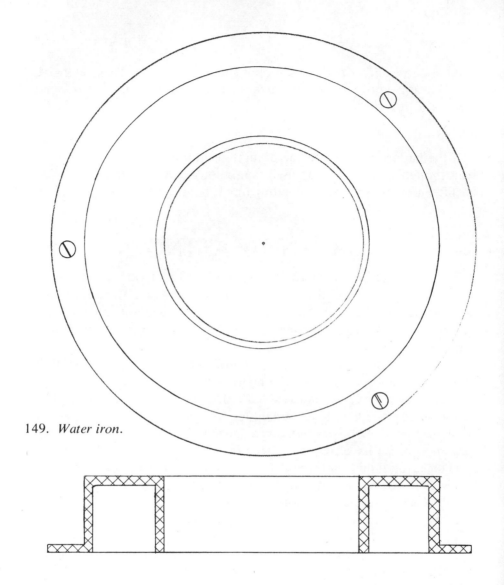

149. *Water iron.*

stove and pipe, the bulkhead must be lined with copper or stainless steel, preferably the latter, and asbestos sheeting must be placed between the metal and the bulkhead. Where the pipe goes through the deckhead there must be some protective arrangement. The old standby was the water iron, a trough filled with water to keep the pipe cool and thus prevent it from charring the planking (Drawing 149), but it is always dirty and rusty. Another possibility is to have the pipe double jacketed as it goes through the deck (Drawing 150).

SMOKE HEADS

Smoke heads (Photo 117) are the subject of much debate and little scientific knowledge. Under certain conditions—when there are high

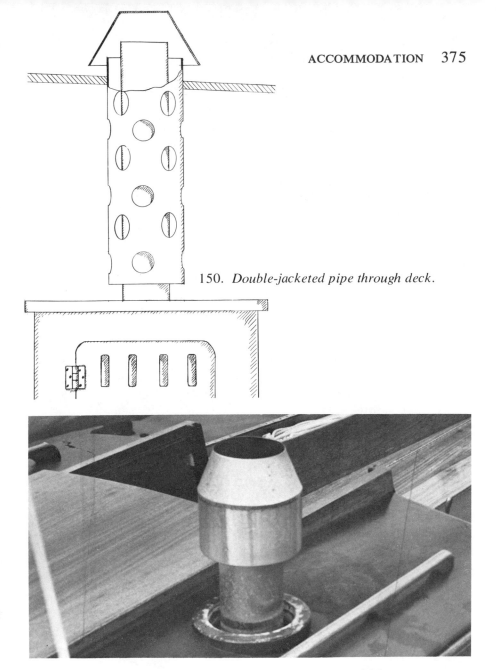

150. *Double-jacketed pipe through deck.*

117. *Modern smoke head.* (*Morris Rosenfeld*)

winds and downdrafts off the sail, for example—it is almost impossible
to get the normal smoke head to work. My good friend Dave Ellis,
who sails in the spring and fall, made a wonderful discovery. If a gutter
elbow of the right diameter is placed over the flue and faced downwind, the harder it blows, the better the smoke head sucks. This arrangement is simple, cheap, and effective.

118. Old-fashioned smoke head. (Elon Jessup)

Another answer is to install the kind of smoke head found on the old-fashioned schooner (Photo 118; Drawing 151). This is likely to work consistently.

Still another solution is based on the fact that the stove will normally draw so long as the smoke head is to windward. Therefore, one can install an L head when needed to maintain this orientation. For example, if the smoke head is all set to port, it will work beautifully on port tack, and on starboard tack the L head may be attached to carry the smoke to the other side of the boat.

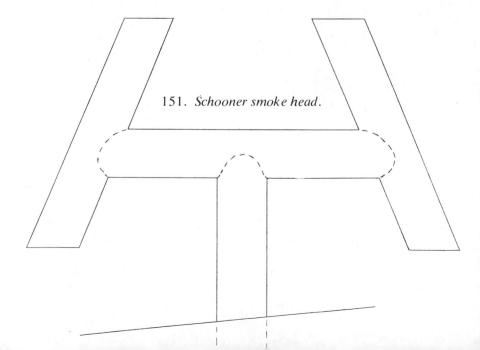

151. Schooner smoke head.

119. Iron coal stove in the galley. (Morris Rosenfeld)

COAL-STOVE LOCATION

If the coal stove is normally used for cooking, of course it will be plunk in the middle of the galley (Photo 119). If it is merely a secondary cooking and cabin-heating unit, it is usually placed at the forward end of the main cabin (Photos 120 and 121). When the head is on the reverse side of the bulkhead against which the stove is mounted, it is a very good idea to cut a hole in the bulkhead and install a metal plate, so that the heat given off by the stove will also warm the head. On some boats, the stove is actually positioned so that one-third of it is in the head and two-thirds in the main cabin, for there is nothing quite so miserable on a cold, wet, and windy night as having to sit down on a freezing-cold head seat.

COAL-STOVE LIGHTING

Lighting a coal stove is always difficult. A cold stove and pipe just do not want to draw, so the first step is to heat the pipe with a bottled-

120. Tile stove in the main cabin. (Morris Rosenfeld)

121. Iron coal stove in the main cabin. (Fasch)

gas torch. Then some newspaper and some dry wood chopped up into tiny pieces can be ignited. As soon as this catches, charcoal can be added, and then good hard coal. If the stove is of a decent size, once the technique is learned, it can be persuaded to run as long as eight hours without feeding, but when sailing, one should stoke the stove at every watch change. A good cabin heater can make cold-weather sailing pleasant, keeping the boat, its occupants, and their clothing warm and dry. Without it, dampness soon gets into everything, and life becomes miserable.

Once the stove is burning brightly, everything is fine—until there is a sudden wind shift, and the sails must be trimmed. By the time the boat is squared away on a new tack, the stove has often been blown out and will not draw, and the fire must be built all over again. For this reason, not only a good supply of coal but also plenty of wood chips and charcoal should be kept on hand. If the kindling has been used up, one can try putting some coal into the wire basket used for preparing French fries, and placing the basket on the galley stove. Once the coal is burning brightly it can be dumped into the stove, and will probably stay lit. This dodge was taught me by Bob Lamson on *Antilles*. Sometimes it worked, but sometimes it didn't. Really, there is no substitute for a good supply of kindling.

The preceding discussion has covered the various standard dodges for making a recalcitrant coal stove operate. However, what I feel is the best method is seldom used. A small engine-room blower is installed, with the discharge connected to a pipe soldered or welded to the coal-stove flue (Drawing 152). Turned on just before the stove is lit, the blower produces a positive flow of air up the pipe, so the stove must draw. Once the pipe is hot, the blower may be switched off, as the natural draft will suffice. If weather conditions are bad, and the stove refuses to draw even with a hot pipe, the blower can be left on. The power consumption of this type of blower is relatively low.

INSULATION AND CONDENSATION

On a wooden boat, insulation is not a serious problem unless one is sailing in very cold areas and the heating system is not adequate. However, the deck fastenings holding in place the cleats, pad eyes, and so on often collect droplets of moisture which will slowly drop down in the middle of the nice dry bunks. Proper heating by coal will take care

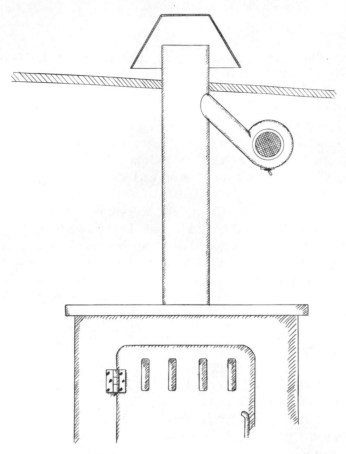

152. *Blower on stovepipe.*

of the moisture problem. The only alternative is to mix up little batches of liquid styrofoam and cover the metal parts to stop the condensation.

On metal boats, condensation occurs on the interior metal at almost every temperature change. The old solution was to coat the interior of the hull with a mixture of cork and bitumastic—a difficult, sticky, and messy job which had to be done while the boat was being built. Now various plastics have been developed that may be sprayed on the interior of the boat; this spraying too should be completed while the boat is being built, since doing it afterward, while possible, is very difficult.

Boats of solid fiber glass have the same sweating problem as metal boats, and should be sprayed to minimize condensation, especially on the underside of the deck and cabin top.

The fiber-glass boat with foam-plank or balsa-core construction has no problem, being in effect a great big icebox. Heating or air-conditioning such a boat is simple, because heat transfer through the hull is very slight.

XI

~~~~~~~~~~~~~~~~~~~~~~~~~~~~~~~~~~~~~

Galley

The galley is one of the most critical areas of a true cruising yacht. The man who uses his boat only for short weekend cruises, taking off on Saturday morning and returning on Sunday night, may be content to get his meals catch-as-catch-can, and to subsist on sandwiches and soup, tea and coffee. However, for extensive cruising, the galley must be well designed and fully equipped. Relatively few yacht galleys are really well designed, probably because the women who will use them are not consulted. To the best of my knowledge, the only female yacht designer is Timi Larr of McCurdy and Rhodes, and even she is seldom found in the galley. The average yacht designer spends most of his time at sea on ocean racers he has designed, and he is too busy worrying about sails, trimming, rigging, weight distribution, and the like to pay much attention to the galley. I think the galleys in yachts would improve immeasurably if every designer were required to stay aboard one of his creations for three months, doing all the cooking, and eating all meals on board.

Cruising-boat galleys vary in the extreme, going from the simplicity of the one-burner Primus of the single-hander, who eats everything out of a lone pot which is sent overboard attached to a string to be cleaned, and who possesses one knife and one fork, to the elaborate installations in luxury cruisers, complete with everything, including a dishwasher. The efficient, comfortable galley lies somewhere between these two extremes. The single-hander's galley almost always changes substantially for the better when the lone sailor decides he needs company, for usually the company is female.

A great many cruising boats are owned by a husband and wife. Generally, after years of planning and saving, the husband has finally managed to purchase a cruising boat, and dreams of sailing to the far corners of the world. However, the dream will not last very long unless his wife is happy in the galley. The galley on a boat will necessarily be different from the kitchen ashore, but some approximation to the shore kitchen should be attempted, to the extent that time, space, and money permit. Some yachts have absolutely fabulous galleys, with electric cooking, electric refrigeration, a freezer, a dishwasher, automatic can openers, electric air conditioning, blowers, the works. The money spent on a galley of this type could buy enough food and supplies to keep a yacht cruising for a year. Further, since all the mechanical equipment must be kept in repair, either the husband or the yacht yard usually works full time trying to keep the galley going, and as a result the boat seldom leaves the dock. Electric galleys are a disadvantage too in that if the generator fails, the boat must cruise from one 220-volt AC plug-in to the next. Outside of the United States, these are few and far between.

A galley can be simple, straightforward, and practical. The exact nature and size of the equipment will depend upon the size of the boat and crew, the location of the galley, and the type of cruising to be done. The basic requirements in a galley are a good stove, a good ice-box or refrigerator, food stowage, work space, and comfortable facilities for washing up. The most important consideration—and one often neglected—is that the galley be comfortable at sea. Many galleys that look superb when the boat is on dead level, are unusable when the boat is rail down. In the planning of one ocean racer, this problem was tackled correctly. A mock-up of the galley was built and tried. It proved to be good, and when it was rotated to simulate a 30-degree starboard-tack heel, everything still seemed satisfactory. However, when it was rotated in the opposite direction to simulate a port-tack heel, the galley was completely useless—and so, back to the drawing board. This experiment was expensive, but changing the actual galley in the boat would have been far more costly.

LOCATION

First of all, the location of the galley should be considered. On boats of 40 feet or less LOA, the galley should unquestionably be aft —either at the after end of the cabin or just forward of the quarter berth and/or the after cabin if there is one. The motion on a forty-footer is just too great to allow the galley to be placed forward. To be sure, in years gone by, in the days of professional crews, a boat as small as thirty-five feet would have a bunk and galley forward for the paid hand who did the cooking. But those days are pretty well gone.

For boats above forty feet, the location of the galley to a great extent depends on the purpose of the boat and the feelings of the cook. On *Iolaire,* which is forty-five feet long, we have the galley in the forecastle, for a number of reasons. The heat from cooking is kept out of the main cabin, and the cook can work in privacy, without everyone leaning over his shoulders to offer suggestions. If a paid crew is carried, its members have the entire forecastle and galley to themselves, and when I am chartering the boat, it gives me a place of refuge from the charter parties. The disadvantage, of course, is that going to windward, the motion is greater forward. Off the wind, the galley forward works out beautifully, and all in all I think in general I prefer it there on a boat of forty-five feet or over.

Many people do not agree with me, and the more normal location of the galley is aft or amidships, until a length of about sixty feet is reached. On larger boats, except for a few ocean racers, the galley is almost always forward, giving the paid crew members the entire forecastle and galley area for themselves.

SIZE

A large galley is to be avoided. When the boat heels well over and drops hard off the waves, the cook goes flying across, fetching up on the other side with a couple of broken ribs, or lands on top of the navigator and gives him a few broken ribs. Some say the answer is to strap oneself in, but when I am cooking I want to be able to dodge any pots that jump off the stove.

A small galley with plenty of work space, everything within easy reach, and a bar, ladder, or counter against which the cook can wedge himself, is excellent, in my view. When the stove, sinks, and icebox are positioned, accessibility to other members of the crew should be kept in mind. I remember one boat in which the galley was fine except that only the cook could reach the icebox. Hence when anyone wanted a beer, the cook had to put down whatever she was doing and reach for it.

SINKS

One of the most-disliked jobs on board boats is dishwashing. For a cruise to be enjoyable, the dishwashing facilities should be as good as the size of the boat permits. Double sinks make dishwashing so much easier that I do not believe any boat should be without them. They should be deep, and if they are oval, will not take up much room. For

122. Oval sink. (South Western Marine Factors)

example, mounted side by side, two oval sinks of the kind shown in Photo 123 (made by South Western Marine Factors) occupy a space of 18 inches by 24 inches. Because sinks like these are narrow, though deep, plates, frying pans, and so on can be placed in them only on their sides, but by the same token very little water fills these sinks to a sufficient depth for easy washing.

SINK DRAINS

If possible, the sinks should be self-draining. All too many boats, my own included (I hope to change it), have off-center sinks. Thus while they drain beautifully in port, or on one tack, they will not drain on the other tack, and installation of a pump is necessary. The old piston-type pumps had continual difficulties; today's diaphragm pumps should work better, but still the pump is just one more piece of equipment to maintain. I therefore strongly recommend that the sink be mounted on or almost on center, so that it will drain on either tack. It need only be two or three inches above the waterline if it is given a good drainpipe, and only 1½ or 2 inches in diameter.

WATER SUPPLY

A serious cruising yacht should have facilities for using salt water for washing. Normally, a salt-water pump is installed in the galley for this purpose. But years ago I decided a pump was really rather silly. Why pump salt water into the sink when it is so much simpler to run a hose through the sea cock to a tap mounted low down, about a foot from the cabin sole (Drawing 153)? Since this is well below the waterline, one need only turn on the tap, collect a couple of gallons of water, close the tap, and put the water into the sink. The whole process is infinitely easier than pumping, and cheaper as well.

If the detergent Joy is carried, there will be no difficulty in washing everything in salt water. Why Joy should work in salt water so much better than any other product, I can't say, but it does. I know many women who use it for shampooing their hair in salt water. Also effective in salt water is the palm-oil soap obtainable at low cost at copra factories in the tropics.

For fresh water, of course, either a pressure system or a hand pump must be provided. These are discussed in Chapter XII.

DISH DRAINING

For comfortable cruising, a drainboard with dish rack is essential, so that the dishes can be washed and stacked, and left for someone else to dry and put away later. This is particularly useful while beating to windward in heavy weather, for in these circumstances trying to pass each individual dish to the dryer to be dried and stowed is a tiresome job.

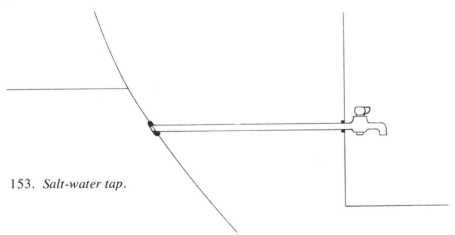

153. *Salt-water tap.*

WORK AREAS

Yacht galleys are often somewhat cramped. But adequate work area is important, and while a new boat can be planned to include sufficient work space, on an older boat one must make do with what is there. Here are a few simple ideas for making the best use of the available area. First of all, a wooden top can be built to fit over the sinks; it will provide a good place for preparing food, and increase the work space tremendously. Another space maker—which also solves the problem of where to put something taken off the gimbaled stove, so that it does not fall over—is the gimbaled sideboard. There is one on *Antilles* that hangs over the foot of the main settee, within easy reach of the cook. This superb arrangement allows the cook to place anything he wishes on the sideboard, knowing it will not end up on the cabin floor in even the heaviest weather.

STOVES

COAL STOVES

The stove is probably the most important piece of galley equipment. Some larger yachts that sail continually in northern waters use a coal stove. As noted in Chapter X, a coal stove will be excellent in cooler areas, since it heats up the cabin beautifully and keeps the whole boat warm and dry. However, once the temperature gets much above 50 degrees, cooking on a coal stove can be a very hot and sweaty proposition. Therefore, a boat with a large coal stove may also have a gimbaled Primus, to be used in hot weather or very rough weather at sea.

ALCOHOL STOVES

The alcohol stove is probably the most commonly used stove in America. I must admit that I hate this stove with an absolute passion. Frequently people (myself included) allow too much alcohol to flow into the burner while priming the stove, so a flare-up results. Or a burner leaks a little alcohol into the oven, and when the top of the stove is lit, a great flame bursts forth. Many a happy cruising family has ended a voyage because the wife just had one alcohol fire too many and refused to go near the stove again.

Although alcohol stoves cause fires, Underwriters' Laboratories considers them safe because the fires can be put out by water, with no fire extinguishers needed, and even if the boat burns up, the crew is seldom killed or injured. By contrast, when a gas stove explodes, it usually blows the boat apart, seriously injuring or killing a couple of people.

Alcohol stoves are liked by many not only because of their safety but because alcohol burns with a clean flame. However, there are also disadvantages. The flame, though clean, is not particularly hot. Also, when the stove is first lit and still being primed, the alcohol gives off an aroma that makes some people instantly seasick. Another disadvantage is that even in the United States, stove alcohol is often expensive. I remember once buying stove alcohol in Bermuda for ten dollars a gallon, which is more than I had to pay there for a gallon of Scotch. My Scottish blood revolts at spending more on alcohol to feed my stove than on alcohol to feed myself.

Those interested in purchasing an alcohol stove will find many versions on the market. The smallest and cheapest are the little camp stoves fed from a small tank. The best are those made by Luke and by Lecomte; they are very expensive, but well worth the money. These stoves are copies of the Heritage stove, originally made in Huntington, Long Island. Made of stainless steel and aluminum, with bronze burners and gratings, and an iron baseplate which serves as ballast so that gimbaling is possible, these stoves will literally last a lifetime. The one I have in *Iolaire,* now converted to gas, works perfectly after eighteen years of use, and looks beautiful. A copy of this stove is made in Europe, but it has two disadvantages. First, it lacks the heavy baseplate; hence, if a big stewpot is placed on it, the center of gravity gets too high and the stove loses stability. Second, it lacks the built-in oven vent found in the original Heritage stove and obtainable with the Luke stove on special request (Drawing 154). Two inches in diameter, this oven vent (which is located on the left side but could probably be

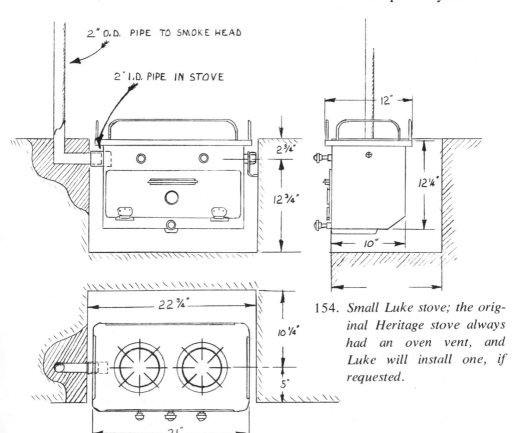

154. *Small Luke stove; the original Heritage stove always had an oven vent, and Luke will install one, if requested.*

placed on the other side on request) also serves as a gimbal. It runs up to a smoke head via a two-inch stainless-steel pipe in which a baffle can be installed in the pipe to adjust the oven temperature. The result is a wonderful stove installation. The smoke and heat produced while roasting in the oven are carried out through the oven vent. If an oven vent is not installed, the galley soon becomes hot and smelly, and the smoke soon turns the overhead brown. This stove comes in two sizes. The larger size has three burners on top and two burners in the oven. I can only think of two improvements to this superb stove: attachment of a grill to the top of the oven, so that things could be grilled as well as baked in the oven; and installation of a manifold on the side of the stove, so that each burner would have an individual shutoff (Drawing 155). In the absence of a manifold, if a burner begins to leak, the fuel line must be shut off and all cooking stopped until the repair has been made. Once a manifold has been installed, one can simple cut off the bad burner and continue to cook on the others while the repair work proceeds.

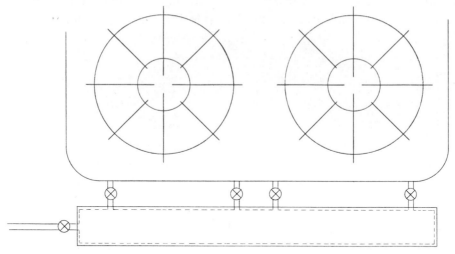

155. *Manifold for a stove.*

KEROSENE STOVES—THE PRIMUS

The Primus is the old reliable that has conquered every ocean. It is inexpensive, and cheap to run. Parts can be purchased almost anywhere in the world. The actual burners are usually the same no matter where they have been manufactured, but when getting either a burner or an entire stove, one must be sure to purchase the self-pricking type. The older type, that is not self-pricking, has to be cleaned with a special little tool which is difficult to use in rough weather. Also, if the burner needs to be cleaned, the stove has to be turned off and then later relit. With self-pricking burners, all that is necessary is to turn the handle all the way clockwise, and then back to its former position.

The Primus does have several disadvantages. I do not know of any manufacturer that makes a really good, proper oven for it. Various makes of Primus have a warming oven, but it cannot be used for baking or roasting. Another disadvantage of the Primus is that even perfectly run, it tends to smoke up the cabin. If anyone is at all careless, the entire galley and main cabin will quickly turn gray. Furthermore, heat regulation is exceedingly difficult. Since the heat can be regulated only by adjustment of the pressure tank, all the burners burn at the same degree of heat. One cannot have one burner red hot and the other just warm.

Vastly superior to the alcohol stove in heat production, the Primus actually melts the pans if one is not careful. Like the alcohol stove, it must be primed, and this is one of the great causes of difficulty. The small cup under the burner must be filled with alcohol, and the alcohol must be lit, and burn off completely, before the burner is lit. This procedure is relatively simple when the boat is anchored in a calm bay, but in heavy weather half the alcohol sloshes out of the cup, the burner doesn't get hot enough and will not light, and the whole sequence has to be repeated before the stove is finally lit. Some people solve this problem by installing a cup which takes double the required amount of alcohol. Then the alcohol doesn't slosh out in rough weather, and the cup always holds enough to prime the burner. Other people have a small metal clip made, which holds a gauze wick. They soak the clip and its wick in alcohol, hook the clip with the wick around the burner, light the wick, and the burner is heated. Still another dodge to make priming the burners easier is to keep handy one of the small bottled-gas torches. The lit torch, aimed at the base of the burner for half a minute or so, does the job. This method appeals to me because it eliminates the sickly sweet smell of burning alcohol.

The normal priming alcohol is commercial stove alcohol, but in an emergency, drinking alcohol can be used. However, strong brandy or 120- to 150-proof rum is necessary; 85- or 90-proof rum or Scotch does not burn hot enough.

To get the best out of a kerosene stove, one must use nothing but the finest grade of kerosene. A poor grade clogs the burners very rapidly and gives off too much smoke. In some areas the kerosene is so bad that people have tried substituting mineral spirits. The result is a nice clear flame, so hot that occasionally the side of a burner burns out.

Then the galley is filled with flames as the blazing fuel starts pouring out from the burner under pressure. This is one of the situations in which an accessible shutoff between the fuel tank and the burner is essential. Also desirable is a manifold enabling one to cut off the individual burner without shutting off the entire stove.

When purchasing the small, standard two-burner Primus stove, one should choose the all-stainless model, even though it costs a little more. The model with the galvanized-iron top will start to rust within six months. One should also purchase spare burners, with the tools necessary for installing them, and asbestos pads. Although the heat of the stove cannot be regulated, the heat reaching the pot can be regulated by means of these pads. Those with asbestos on one side and wire mesh on the other also serve as excellent griddles for making toast.

REMOTE FUEL TANKS—KEROSENE OR ALCOHOL

Except for the smallest models, in which the fuel tank is attached to the stove, kerosene and alcohol stoves have remote tanks. If one is going to the trouble of installing a remote tank, it might as well be a big one that will require filling only once every month or six weeks. Alcohol burns much faster than kerosene. For alcohol, I strongly recommend a ten-gallon tank on a thirty-five-foot boat, a fifteen-gallon tank on a forty-five-foot boat. For kerosene, a five-gallon tank will probably be ample.

Pressure must of course be maintained in the tank, and sometimes fancy, expensive brass pumps are installed for this purpose, but a simpler method is to insert a normal tire valve at the top of the tank. Then a standard bicycle pump can be connected and the tank pumped up whenever necessary. A gauge must be provided, and should be easily visible from the stove. Most important of all is the fuel shutoff, which *must be* in such a position that the fuel to the stove can be stopped even if the stove is completely on fire. Many a boat has been lost because the fuel shutoff could not be reached when the stove caught fire.

DIESEL STOVES

So far, we have been discussing the small kerosene stove fed by fuel stored under pressure. There is another type of stove using liquid fuel, very popular among commercial fishermen on the west coast of the United States, and among yachtsmen. That is the oil-fired gravity type, with a blower to provide the draft. This stove looks like the old-fashioned coal stove but is much easier to run. It has the same disadvantage as the coal stove—giving off too much heat to be suitable for a warm climate. Another disadvantage is that since it burns liquid fuel, it does not dry out the boat. The great advantage over the coal stove is that this stove can be lit, used for a few hours, and turned off, and will cool down quite rapidly. It is used for cooking in the same fashion as a coal stove, and in fact, at first glance, it is difficult to tell the two apart.

ELECTRIC STOVES

Electric stoves are becoming increasingly popular on shore and on big powerboats. There are some sailboats that have electric cooking, but I would not consider it for a true cruising boat. I for one usually get up around four or five in the morning and want to make my cup of coffee. On a boat with electric cooking, that would necessitate starting a diesel generator—which would not be very kind to the other people on board or to those on boats anchored nearby.

Furthermore, many generators will not operate at very great angles of heel. There is a story of one famous racer that had an elaborate galley, air conditioning, water pressure, the works, all operated off electricity. The first race was largely a beat to windward, and although they won the race, it was hard on the crew. Whenever they were going to windward, and it blew hard, they could not run the generator; refrigerators and freezer started defrosting, the air conditioning would not work, and belowdecks became stifling. Worst of all, with the electric stove not functioning, everyone subsisted on sandwiches or cornflakes.

On a cruising boat with electric cooking, two generators are essential, for sooner or later one will either break down or require an overhaul. And with two generators, plus the main engine, the boat becomes a mechanical monster, likely to spend most of its time alongside the repair docks.

BOTTLED-GAS STOVES

Propane, butane, Butta gas, or whatever—gas is in my view by far the best fuel for cooking on a boat. To be sure, one can blow oneself up with a gas stove. But a good stove, properly installed, and used with normal safety precautions and common sense, will not explode. In any event, I would rather risk getting blown up by a gas stove than die a slow torturous death fighting with an alcohol or kerosene stove. One can get killed crossing a street, but one continues to cross streets. I would advise those who want to do serious cruising to take the proper safety precautions and use bottled gas.

Different types of bottled gas are sold in different parts of the world, but they all seem to work in the same stoves. There are sometimes problems in filling the bottles, but these can be surmounted. American and British fittings are completely compatible, and both these fittings are close enough to the French type so that American and British gas bottles can be filled in countries that use the metric system. The fit isn't perfect, but not too much gas is lost in the process of filling. Better yet, a pigtail can be made up with the American fitting on one end and the metric fitting on the other; then there will be no trouble at all. American bottles can be filled abroad, but foreign bottles normally cannot be filled in the United States because the American safety law requires a relief valve built into the valve at the end of the gas bottle, and most European bottles do not have this.

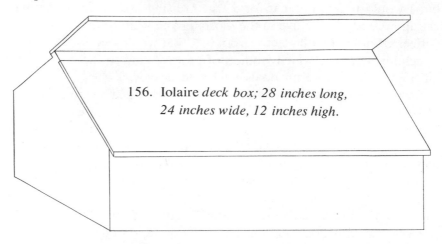

156. Iolaire *deck box; 28 inches long, 24 inches wide, 12 inches high.*

Storage of Gas Bottles

It goes without saying that bottled gas should be stowed on deck or in vapor-proof lockers vented overboard. Many fiber-glass boats are now built with lockers mounted into the deck unit; these have gas-tight fitted lids, and pipes that lead any escaping gas directly overside, not into the boat. This arrangement is by far the best.

Size of Gas Bottles

Gas bottles come in all shapes and sizes. The standard European propane-gas bottle, 21 inches high and 12 inches in diameter, is satisfactory on larger boats, as a deck box of this height is not cumbersome there. However, on the smaller yachts a deck box of this height takes up too much room and looks awful. I much prefer the gas bottles made by Suburban Propane; these arc 10 inches in diameter and 20 inches long; since they lie on their sides, they can be kept in a deck box 28 inches long, 24 inches wide, and only 12 inches high (Drawing 156), which is about the same height and shape as the normal skylight, giving a very nice low profile and taking up very little deck room.

Bottled gas is very economical, although its price varies from place to place. With six persons aboard, and cooking, baking, and roasting being done for two large meals a day, soup being heated for lunch, and coffee being warmed at all hours, a twenty-pound bottle lasts for ten days, sometimes two weeks when not on charter. If only three or four persons are on board and the cooking is not as fancy, it usually lasts a month.

Gas-Bottle Shutoff Valves

It goes without saying that whenever the stove is not being used, the gas bottles should be shut off right at the deck box. However, all too often on a cold, dark, windy night one neglects to do so, because one doesn't feel like putting on foul-weather gear and fumbling around in the dark and rain trying to find the valve.

On some boats the shutoff valve is located at a point on the gas line before it comes belowdecks, and one can reach it by passing an arm through a porthole. On other boats, among them *Iolaire,* the shutoff valve has been installed in the line on deck just before it comes below. The valve is mounted upside down and attached to a long shaft which comes through a stuffing gland on deck and passes into the main cabin. Immediately upon securing the stove, someone in the main cabin need only reach up over his head to turn off the gas. Were there to be a break in the line, or a leaky burner, only the very small amount of gas left in the line itself could leak into the boat. This arrangement is an old one. I first saw it on board John Burr's *Iolanthe,* in St. Croix in 1956. Since it is simple but foolproof, I wonder why it is not seen more often.

Selection of a Gas Stove

To my mind, by far the best choice is a stove of the Heritage type, in stainless steel. Though designed as an alcohol stove, this can be obtained in a gas version. The stove is definitely not a thing to skimp on. Whether a Luke stove or a European copy is purchased, it should incorporate the same features that are desirable in an alcohol stove: the oven vent, the heavy baseplate (weighing at least fifty pounds), bronze burners, and a manifold. Many stoves on the market look like the Heritage type but are really inferior. They do not have the oven vent; they are not sufficiently ballasted; and although they appear to be all stainless, inspection reveals that the burners, gratings, and so on are iron. Within one or two years, such stoves will have rusted and require replacement, whereas the genuine Heritage or Luke stove, with its bronze burners and bronze gratings, will last for the life of the boat. To be sure, eventually the gratings and burners may have to be replaced, but that will be only after the stove has been used for eight or ten years, 365 days a year.

KEEPING POTS ON THE STOVE

As previously mentioned, the stove must be on gimbals if the cook is to be given a fair shake. But even on a gimbaled stove some sort of hold-down is necessary to keep the pots from sliding. All kinds of rigs have been advised to fill this need: stainless-steel springs, bars dropping into notches, adjustable crossbars. Some of these are shown in Drawings 157–160.

Especially in boats with a quick motion, the gimbaled stove—like the gimbaled table—may begin to oscillate, and then the food splashes off the stove. To prevent this excessive swinging, a piece of shock cord should be fastened to the bottom of the stove, run through a small block, and then secured under tension under the stove (Drawing 161). Then if the stove is well ballasted, it will always remain level.

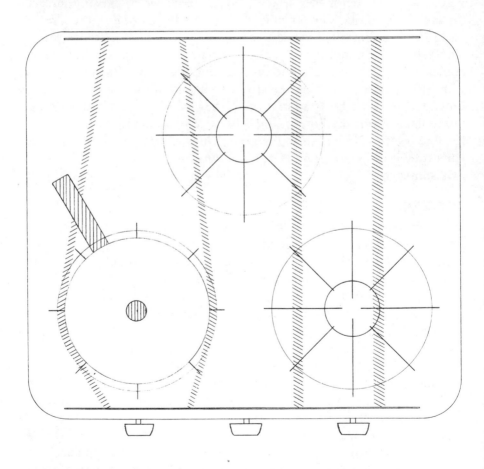

157. *Springs to hold pots on the stove.*

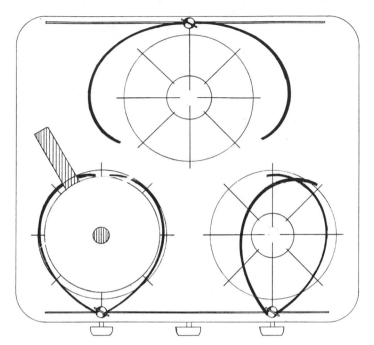

158. *Arms adjust with thumbscrews to hold pots on the stove.*

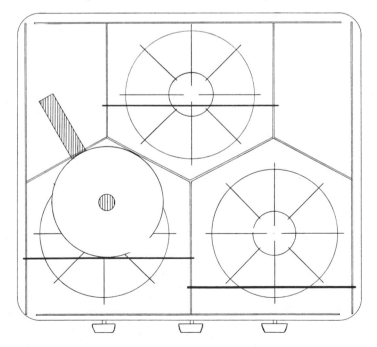

159. *Bars drop into notches on the rails to hold pots on the stove.*

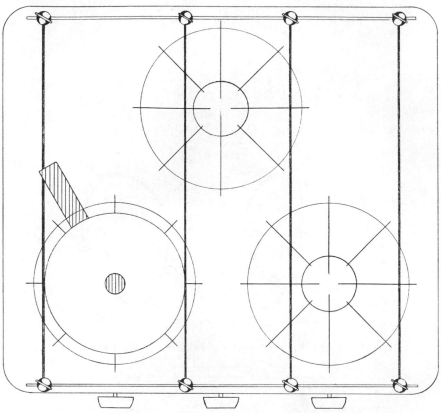

160. *Crossbars adjust with thumbscrews to hold pots on the stove.*

161. *Shock cord rigged to steady the stove.*

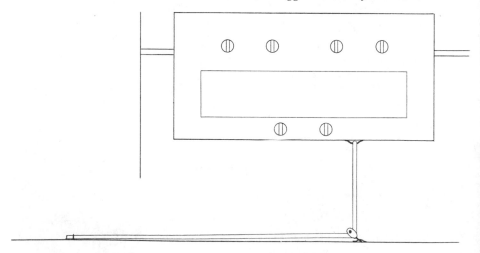

WATER

Water stowage is not as much of a problem as it is usually thought to be. If the crew is well disciplined, salt-water soap is used, dishes are washed in salt water, and other liquids—beer, Coke, fruit juices—are drunk, water consumption will be only about two quarts per man per day. This amount will be adequate even in the tropics. The old-fashioned ration of a gallon per man per day, if used sparingly, actually is sufficient for an occasional fresh-water shower. When cooking, instead of adding salt one can use salt water for approximately 5 percent of the cooking water. Vegetables of course can be washed in salt water, and lobsters, salt fish, and the like are best cooked in salt water. If the pressure system is disconnected at sea, there will be no problem with water consumption.

GALLEY UTENSILS

The choice of galley utensils will depend upon the type of cruising planned. My own preference is for utensils of aluminum—not the thin sheet aluminum, but the heavy cast aluminum used for pots sold under the name Wear-Ever. In particular, I recommend heavy, cast aluminum with a porcelain layer on the outside. This is thick enough to cause even heat distribution, and utensils made of it are handsome and durable. The porcelainized aluminum pots I bought fifteen years ago are still going strong. The disadvantage of aluminum ware is that if the articles are not consistently used, aluminum oxide forms on their surfaces, making them difficult to clean. If a boat is only used on weekends and for a few fortnightly cruises, the cook will have to spend an hour at the start of each trip cleaning the pots before beginning to cook. In these circumstances, stainless-steel pans are best. I don't like them because they are too thin and too hard to use, but they do have the wonderful advantage of staying clean indefinitely in storage.

Actually, my favorite is a tinned copper pot, of a sort nearly impossible to find today except in an antique store. Another favorite is a cast-iron frying pan porcelainized on the outside and painted on the inside with one of the no-stick finishes. This is not to be confused with a Teflon pan. Teflon utensils do not seem to stand up on board a yacht. Perhaps the crew is not careful enough with them. Also, when cruising in out-of-the-way places, one frequently hires some local people to come on board and help with the cleaning up; once they get their hands on a Teflon pan, it's gone. The old standby, the cast-iron frying pan, is impossible to beat when one is continually living on board. If it is just rinsed without scrubbing, rubbed with grease, and left on the stove, there will be no trouble with rusting.

In general, the fewer pots and pans on board the better. They take up considerable space and few are really essential. Deep casseroles to be used in the oven are very useful. They should be made of porcelainized cast iron, and have metal lids. Baking tins of Teflon are wonderful. I generally buy the cheapest ones I can find, use them until they wear out, and then throw away. If Teflon baking tins cannot be found, aluminum tins do well.

Two extra-large pots are needed on a yacht. One of these is the stewpot, which should be big enough to hold a double order of stew for the boat's normal cruising crew. A double order is often a lifesaver, especially on the first day out, when everyone is tired from doing last-minute provisioning, the weather turns rough, and no one feels like cooking a full meal. Similarly, when at sea, if the barometer begins to drop, one can prepare a big pot of stew, to be warmed up as desired. Every yacht should also carry a pot big enough to boil two or three lobsters at a time. Such a pot will be about two feet high and sixteen to eighteen inches in diamter. It takes up a large amount of room, but the space need not be wasted. On *Iolaire,* for example, we coil our dock lines down inside the lobster pot.

All mixing bowls should of course be either stainless steel or plastic. A quantity of small square plastic boxes with tight-fitting lids should be kept on hand for stowing leftovers. A plastic basin with holes in the sides is excellent for stowing food on the ice. The holes allow the cold to get into the plastic, and any drippage from the food remains in the basin, where it can be cleaned out periodically, instead of dropping to the bottom of the icebox.

Spatulas, colanders, eggbeaters, and the like, should be made completely of stainless steel. One should search long and hard, if necessary, for utensils of these materials, for all others will rust almost faster than they can be washed. Then every time someone tries to make a batch of scrambled eggs, for example, the rust will flake off the eggbeater and pepper the eggs. Similarly, can openers, which give trouble enough ashore, are far worse at sea. When a good one has been found it should be permanently mounted, but an old-fashioned hand can opener should be kept for emergency use.

Instead of putting utensils in a drawer, I prefer to stand them vertically in a wooden box with a hole at the bottom. A box measuring 6 inches by 6 inches by 8 inches high will do the job. Similarly, knives should be kept not in a drawer but in a knife rack (Drawing 162). This

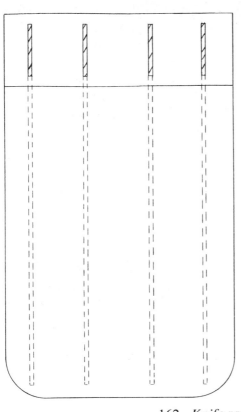
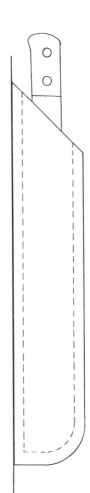

162. *Knife rack.*

should hold at least five different knives: a big French chopping knife, a good carving knife, a bread knife, a filleting knife, and a small paring knife. Many people insist on stainless-steel knives, but I do not agree, as they do not keep their edge. A stainless-steel bread knife is fine, but the others should be of just plain steel that can take a good edge. They will not rust if they are dried each time before being put away, and a wipe with vegetable oil will help.

FOOD

FRESH AND FROZEN FOOD

Food stowage is less of a problem than is generally believed. In a proper icebox, food should stay fresh for at least eight or ten days. On larger boats, with good-sized, efficient iceboxes, food should keep two or three weeks. And on boats with mechanical refrigerators and freezers there is no limit, so long as the power units keep working. Frozen meat placed directly on the ice will last, and does not deteriorate as a result of thawing well before the time it is cooked. However, it should not be refrozen. Frozen vegetables will keep only four or five days after being thawed, so I strongly urge the use of fresh vegetables.

In a temperature climate, fresh vegetables such as peas, squash, and the like will keep almost indefinitely if they are stowed in bins which are dry and well ventilated by louvers or by holes drilled in all sides. Onions and potatoes will last for many weeks even in the tropics if stowed in the coolest possible place and kept absolutely dry. They must be picked over at least every four or five days. If those that go bad are removed and thrown overside promptly, so that they do not contaminate the remainder, the remaining good ones will last even longer. If they have been bought in sealed bags, they should be removed from the bags before stowing.

In a northern climate, fresh fruit will keep for a substantial period —almost indefinitely if it is stored in ventilated bins and regularly picked over. Even in the tropics, fruit stowed in a ventilated bin, or in a straw basket hanging from the overhead, will last. It too should of course be picked over, so that the ripe fruit can be consumed before it rots and ruins the remainder.

Fruits vary in the tropics, so before making purchases one should consult the local people for advice. The old faithful is the banana. Bunches of bananas may be hung from the stern pulpit, gallows frame, or what-have-you; the only trouble is that once they start ripening, everyone must eat bananas steadily for three or four days. One technique for avoiding this difficulty is to hang up one stalk of bananas and stow another stalk underneath the dinghy, where it is cool, in the hope that perhaps the two stalks will not ripen at the same time.

The stowage of eggs is a subject of much debate. Some people coat them with wax, others boil them for ten seconds, others cover them with drinking glasses, others pack them in salt. It is often not realized that eggs purchased direct from the farmer—i.e., eggs that have not been cleaned and refrigerated—will last two or three weeks in the tropics and six or seven weeks in cold-water areas. Therefore even in preparing for a long cruise, one need treat only half the eggs by one of these complicated and time-consuming preservative processes. Eggs may be tested by putting them in a pot of water: good eggs sink; bad eggs float.

CANNED GOODS

Canned goods can be stowed in nooks and crannies from one end of the boat to the other. The problem is to remember where they have been put. Therefore, every locker in the boat should be numbered, and then a log should be kept, recording exactly what is in each locker. As the items are used, the entries should be crossed off in the log. If cans are to be stowed in the bilge, all labels must be removed (since otherwise they would come off in the bilge water and clog the pump), and the cans must be coded. In a dry bilge, cans will last two or three months without rusting through; however, for storage in a wet bilge, they must be dipped in some sort of plastic to prevent rust.

Aluminum cans must be stowed in a dry place. In the bilge, they will corrode through in a few weeks; aluminum beer cans are particularly subject to this difficulty.

DRIED FOOD

Dried food can be stowed indefinitely as long as it is kept dry. Packages of such items as rice, flour, cornmeal, sugar, and salt should be stowed in airtight, screw-top, plastic containers. Other dried foods, such as breakfast food, pancake mixes, and roll mixes, will keep for a very long time if immediately upon purchasing, the boxes are put into plastic bags which are then securely sealed. These will prevent dampness from being absorbed through the cardboard packages and causing mildew. It is desirable to keep on board a variety of mixes for use when the fresh bread runs out. Preparing toast in the morning is a nuisance, but rolls can be made easily and will be greatly appreciated by both the cook and the crew.

Some of the bread sold in America will last two or three weeks, but I think it is baked with formaldehyde. Bread obtained elsewhere will last four or five days, with the exception, of course, of hard German pumpernickel. Wrapped in aluminum foil, a loaf about the size and weight of a brick will last absolutely indefinitely, and it is excellent. The more one cruises, the more one is involved in a continual fight to find fresh bread. Therefore, anyone planning to cruise seriously should learn to make his own bread. Because bread dough will keep, a batch may be made up in advance and baked as necessary, to raise the spirits of the most disheartened crew.

PLANNING FOOD PURCHASES

The experienced yachtsman will look at his chart, figure out how many days he will be at sea, then go to the supermarket and emerge with enough food to last him the proper amount of time, with a surplus for contingencies. However, most yachtsmen need more than intuition to guide them in determining how much food must be purchased for a long trip. In this situation, one should not under any circumstances rely on the judgment of one's wife. Her experience has been gained in shoreside shopping, where if something has been forgotten or runs out, one can easily go down and get it at the market.

In storing a vessel, one should stow enough food not only for the planned cruise, but also for emergencies. In general, provisions should be included for a trip 50 percent longer than the one anticipated. Needless to say, the extra supplies should consist of canned and dried foods which will keep indefinitely. Some boats carry in special stowage a food supply for fifteen days which is never touched except in emergencies.

Years ago, Frederick M. Gardner wrote an article, "Care and Feeding of a Yachtsman," which has been reprinted innumerable times. It includes a food list which has been used as a standard for yachtsmen for the last three decades. Here is his list. The numbers represent ounces per man per day.

Meats, Poultry, Fish
    Fresh, 4.0; canned, 4.0; salted (bacon, etc.), 6.5   14.5
Drinks
    Coffee, 2.0; tea, 1.0; cocoa, 1.0   4.0
Dairy Products
    Milk (fresh and evaporated), 12.0; butter, 4.0; eggs (3),
    4.0; cheese, 2.0   22.0
Cereals and Bread
    Dry cereal, 1.0; cooking cereal, 1.0; bread, 3.2; flour, 4.8;
    pilot bread, crackers, 2.0; cornmeal, 1.0   13.0
Fruits
    Fresh, 3.0; canned, 4.0; dried, 1.0   8.0
Vegetables
    Potatoes, 6.0; onions, 1.0; fresh (green), 2.0; canned, 2.0   11.0
Soups
    Dried, 1.0; canned, 2.0   3.0
Sweets
    Sugar, 6.0; maple syrup, 0.5; sweet chocolate, 2.0; pre-
    serves and jams, 4.0   12.5
TOTAL, standard rations, 88 ounces, or 5½ pounds, per man per day.

To the standard food ration of 5½ pounds per man per day must be added a gallon of liquid (juice, beer, water, and so on) per man per day, weighing 8 pounds, for a total of 13½ pounds per man per day for food and drink. A crew of four will consume 54 pounds of total stores a day. Storing a boat for 40 days—for a 26-day cruise with 14 days' spare supplies—means loading approximately 2,160 pounds of consumable items aboard the vessel. In addition, substantial quantities of fuel, clothing, spare gear, sails, and the like will be required. As stated before, it is for this reason that I regard light-displacement boats as unsuitable for long-distance cruising. By the time all the supplies and equipment have been taken aboard, the light-displacement boat has become a moderate-displacement boat, with a resulting falling off in performance.

In summation, once a boat has been purchased and a cruise is being planned, the first place to be refitted and altered should be the galley. Especially if one is living on board while preparing for a trip, an efficient and comfortable galley is essential. Then one can sit back and enjoy three square meals a day while wearing oneself out working on engines, rigging, sails, deck fittings, and the like. If, however, refitting the galley is left to the end, for many months one will be laboring with poor food, and tempers will get short and people will be unhappy because the inner man is not taken care of.

According to Napoleon, an army marches on its stomach. Similarly, a boat travels on its stomach. I have never seen a well-fed crew that was complaining and uncooperative. No matter how rough the going, it's never really bad if one can get two hot heals a day.

I have discussed the galley, its equipment, and its care, but I have not discussed cooking. That is really the realm of the cookbook.

XII

~~~~~~~~~~~~~~~~~~~~~~~~~~~~~~~~

Plumbing

BILGE PUMPS

In years gone by, the bilge pumps were considered among the most vital pieces of equipment on the entire vessel. One needs only to read the stories of the British frigates station keeping off the coast of France during the Napoleonic Wars to realize that these wooden ships worked tremendously in heavy weather. It was not at all uncommon to have the pumps manned half the time, if not continually, in rough seas.

Stories of the early days of yachting, too, are full of accounts of long sessions at the pump. Today, on a well-found yacht this extensive pumping is unnecessary. There are some well-built wooden yachts that will go for weeks on end without having to be pumped. However, even on the best-constructed yacht, at some time, something will fail, and the survival of the boat will be dependent upon a good bilge pump. Furthermore, since the bilge pump too is likely to fail just when it is really needed, two bilge pumps should be installed on any true cruising boat.

Today, many a boat is equipped only with a small electric pump. I dislike electric pumps for several reasons. First, they are usually so small that they will not move any real volume of water. Second, it is so easy to turn on the electric bilge pump (some have automatic switches) that a leak may go undetected for some time. On the other hand, a manually operated pump calls attention to the problem in short order (a good practice is to pump out at regular intervals and count the strokes required to do the job). Finally, when a boat takes a knock-down, rolls on her beam ends, and recovers half full of water, invariably the electrical system is finished and with it the electric bilge pump.

There are many types of hand bilge pumps, the simplest of course being a bucket (Photo 123). Every pump has some loss of efficiency through friction. The amount of water that may be moved with a given degree of effort is also affected by the distance which it must be lifted. This fact was impressed upon me when I was caught in a gale in late November southeast of Cape Hatteras. Every hour or so a wave would come aboard and fill the cockpit. Though self-bailing, the cockpit had lockers in its side, and with each wave, enough water came through the locker-door seams to fill the boat to an inch or so above the cabin sole. At this point it was discovered that the navy-type bilge pump had

123. The fastest and most efficient method of pumping. (Elon Jessup)

packed up, and things looked grim indeed. However, we found that a half-gallon coffeepot just fit between the floor timbers. Further, the galley sink was offset, and had a straight-through 2½-inch drain. By bailing direct from the bilge to the sink, we were able to dispose of the water in only five or ten minutes.

PISTON PUMPS

The old-fashioned brass navy-type piston pump was very good for its day, and if correctly installed moved a fair quantity of water. However, this type of pump does have many disadvantages. First and foremost, with a large (two- or three-inch) navy pump, by the end of the thirtieth stroke, the pumper's arm is ready to come out of its socket. Second, if in rough weather the pumper is thrown against the handle when the piston is up, the handle will bend and then bind or jam in the guide, effectively destroying the usefulness of the pump. Third, these pumps are built of brass or bronze, and unless torn down to their bits and pieces, and cleaned and greased, two or three times a season, they become impossible to disassemble. Since pumps, like heads, only fail when they are being used, they should be easy to take apart for repairs under the most trying circumstances.

For these reasons, I consider the navy-type pump not particularly useful.

GUTTER-TYPE PUMPS

The gutter-type pump is the old faithful on wooden boats. It was often used in the past as an emergency pump. It is plain and simple, consisting merely of a light tube of galvanized iron, with a leather flapper valve at its bottom, and a cone attached to a wooden stick for a plunger.

This pump is awkward to use because often it is difficult to find a place where one can effectively chock oneself, but it will move tremendous quantities of water. More than one modern boat stows a big one in the forepeak for emergencies.

WOODEN PUMPS

Wooden pumps (Drawing 163) were very popular for many years among the wooden boats of the Great South Bay. In some cases they were made of great length, so that they could be placed in the lee bilge and a man perched on the weather rail could still pump. In other cases, in the West Indies, a square wooden pump was built into the boat, with a foot valve at the bottom, and a handle with a wooden valve for

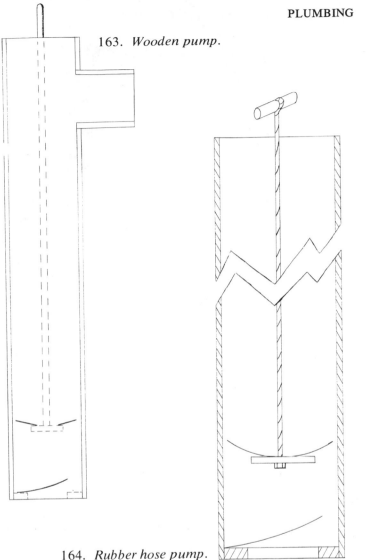

163. *Wooden pump.*

164. *Rubber hose pump.*

pumping. They are simple and cheap, but bulky, and are now seldom seen on yachts.

RUBBER HOSE PUMPS

Rubber hose pumps (Photo 124; Drawing 164) are very commonly used in Ireland, and are wonderful for pumping dinghies and other small boats. They are cheap and absolutely foolproof, and can be bent around corners to allow the deepest part of the bilge to be pumped. They are easy to stow and almost indestructible.

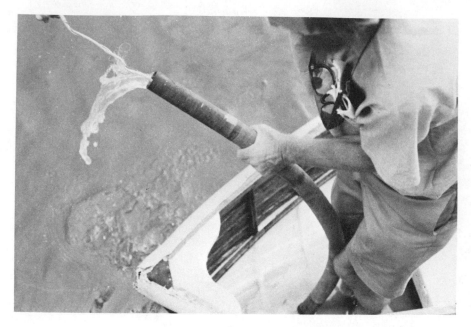

124. *Rubber hose pump (Wykeham Martin type made by Jack Holt). (Laurie Legay)*

VORTEX PUMPS

Some people swear by the vortex pump; others swear at it. This pump is capable of transferring a tremendous amount of water, but will not lift water any appreciable height. Hence it must exhaust out through the side of the vessel under water and must have a sea cock on the discharge. If one neglects to shut the discharge valve when the pump is not in use, water instantly flows back into the boat. Basically, the vortex pump consists of a handle going through a step-up gearbox that revolves at very high rpm. It must be turned very rapidly, and considerable effort must be put into the operation if any quantity of water is to be moved.

DIAPHRAGM PUMPS

Diaphragm pumps have been in use for many years. The old Gloucester fishing schooners had huge galvanized-iron diaphragm pumps made by the Edson Corporation. A new, smaller diaphragm pump has become very popular with yachtsmen as it is only eleven inches in diameter and six inches high, and will operate through a five-inch deck plate. This excellent pump was originally made of either bronze, galvanized iron, or aluminum. The galvanized-iron model, which has been discontinued, was superb. Today, because of its relatively low weight and price, the aluminum model seems to be the most popular among yachtsmen, but as started before, aluminum does not like salt water, merely tolerating it in the best of circumstances. The bronze model is still made and is excellent, though expensive. The parts of these three models are interchangeable.

A boat equipped with this type of pump should carry not only a spare diaphragm but also a spare rocker arm. The rocker arm has been known to fail at the point where the handle is inserted in the shaft. Further, the bolts holding the diaphragm in place should be well greased, so that they are easily removable. One of the great advantages of the Edson diaphragm pump is that its intake and discharge lines, and flapper valves, are so large that a strainer is unnecessary. The pump seems to be able to suck up just about anything (except a cellophane cigarette wrapper, which can place itself across the mouth and stop it completely).

In Europe, the Whale and the Henderson diaphragm pumps are standard. Both are excellent and both have the great advantage over the Edson pump of coming in numerous sizes. The smaller sizes are suitable for the twenty-foot Midget Ocean Racer, while the larger sizes are suitable for the largest cruising boats. A Whale is mounted on *Iolaire,* and I have only two criticisms of it. First, the stock handle should be replaced by one three times as long. Second, there are many nuts, screws, and bolts which freeze up all too easily. The pump must be torn down at least onace a year, cleaned and painted, the screws and bolts encased with grease, and reassembled. The Henderson pump is obtainable in an all-plastic model, which is easier to disassemble and clean the Whale pump. Both are excellent, and their largest, double-acting models can throw a tremendous volume of water.

One great advantage of these pumps is that they may be bolted to the underside of the deck and operated from on deck through a watertight socket (Photo 125). They can therefore be mounted in such a fashion that they are within easy reach of the helmsman. While sailing, he can check the bilges without leaving the helm.

In the United States a new all-plastic pump called the Guzzler is now available. This is an excellent little pump, easy to assemble and disassemble, but at the present time the only model is quite small; in years to come, it will undoubtedly be produced in various sizes.

SEMIROTARY PUMPS

Semirotary pumps were very popular on yachts immediately after World War II, largely, I think, because they could be purchased dirt

125. Watertight deck socket. (R. M. Smith)

cheap since literally millions of them had been made during the war as emergency fuel-transfer pumps.

When operating well, the semirotary pump will throw great quantities of water, but it is likely to develop air locks, causing water to siphon back, and is not easy to disassemble. The difficulty can be overcome by installation of a primer (Drawing 165), which makes it possible to prime the pump without disconnecting any lines. A stopcock is installed in the top half of the pump, and a small line is run from it to an open-top reservoir tank which will hold more water than the interior valve of the pump. Then the reservoir is filled, the stopcock is opened, the pump is filled, the stopcock is closed, and the handle is operated vigorously. If no air leaks on the suction side of the pump, it should work perfectly. However, having fought with semirotary pumps on numerous occasions, I am not enthusiastic about them.

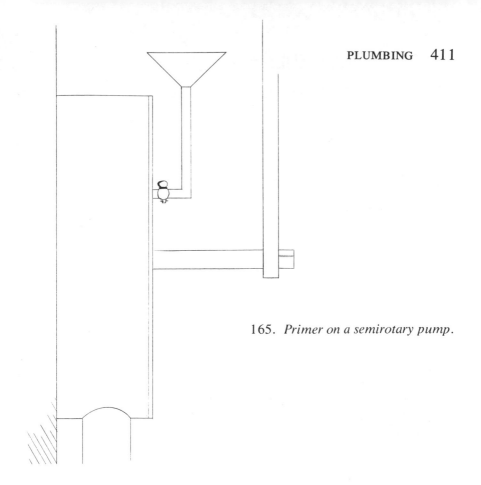

165. *Primer on a semirotary pump.*

MECHANICAL PUMPS

While an electric pump should not be chosen as the main pump for any yacht, it is a great convenience. A pump such as the large-diameter Jabsco, driven from an independent generator or from the main engine, throws a huge quantity of water. For instance, a 1¼-inch-diameter Jabsco will throw 3,600 gph at normal engine revolutions. A pump of this type should be equipped with a manifold, so that it can be used either as a bilge pump or as a deck-wash pump, sucking water in from outside. It is particularly useful on boats that anchor with chain, since it provides a good method for washing down the chain. In an emergency, as long as the vessel is not flooded so deeply that the engine or generator stops, a pump of this type will throw enough water to stay ahead of almost any leak, but there is always that possibility of electrical failure.

EMERGENCY PUMPING

Yachtsmen frequently ignore the fact that in an emergency the engine salt-water pump can be used as a bilge pump. On any boat with a fairly sizable water pump for the main engine, the pumping system should include a tee with a valve and a suction line leading into the bilge. Then if a dangerous leak is sprung suddenly, the engine may be started, the sea cock on the engine intake closed, and the bilge valve opened up, and as long as the engine runs, the pump will operate. Even the standard 40-hp diesel salt-water pump will normally throw 500 gph. The amount of water thrown by an engine pump increases drastically with an increase in the size of the engine—a G.M.6-71 will throw 3,400 gph. Once started, a diesel engine will run until the air intake is submerged, so the pump will continue operating until the boat is well down in the water. It is important in an installation of this sort that a really good strum box be included, and that it be accessible and flexible, so that the line may be cleared easily and regularly when the pump is operating. Also, with this type of rig the valve to the bilge must not be opened while the sea cock is open, or the boat will flood rapidly through the sea cock.

PUMP DISCHARGE

At the New York Boat Show in 1969 the small Guzzler pump was shown to move an unbelievable quantity of water. The reason for its amazing capacity was that an oversized discharge hose, with no sharp bends, was used. Sharp bends increase resistance on the discharge side of the pump to a very marked degree. For maximum efficiency, the discharge line from the bilge pump should be about 25 percent greater in diameter than the intake line. Any increase in discharge-line size, especially when the run is long or goes around corners, will add to the performance of the pump.

On many boats, to eliminate the need for an extra sea cock, the bilge pump is discharged directly into the cockpit. This is a very poor practice, because it means the cockpit must always be cleaned after the bilge is pumped. Further, under certain conditions, it can be dangerous. For example, if an oil leak develops in the engine and the oil gets into the bilge and is then pumped into the cockpit, very soon the cockpit—and the entire boat—will turn into a skating rink.

I much prefer to have the pump discharge directly overboard, either through the side of the boat or by way of a cockpit scupper. The advantage of discharging into an overside cockpit scupper is that the sea cock need not be turned off when the pump is not being used (Drawing 166), as the cockpit scupper leading in to the top of the tee will break any siphon effect. Needless to say, the sea cock should be very large, so that the pump discharge is not restricted. If the pump discharges out of the side of the boat (Drawing 167) a shutoff is necessary. Going to

To Pump ←

166. *Pump discharge leading into a cockpit scupper; this cannot be used in a low or flooding cockpit.*

167. *Pump discharge leading directly overboard.*

windward there will be a tendency for water to siphon back through the bilge pump. If the flapper valve seats perfectly, this cannot happen, but all too often there is a little dirt in the valve, which allows the passage of water back into the bilge.

PUMP SUCTIONS

The pump suction should go to the deepest part of the bilge. However, on a boat with a wide keel it may be worthwhile to have an arrangement by which the suction may be manually switched to the lee side of the bilge, or to install a Y valve so that water can be pumped

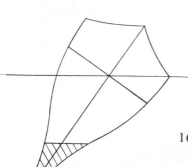

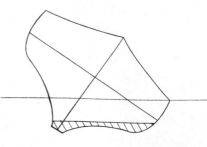

168. Water in the lee bilge of a shallow hull as compared to water in a deep hull.

directly from the lee side of bilge at all times. The producers of the Guzzler pump also make Y valves of various diameters which can be completely disassembled in a matter of seconds, without tools. Wide shoal centerboarders frequently need suction going not to the deepest part of the bilge but rather off to each side of the vessel at the turn of the bilge. When a centerboarder is well heeled, water will tend to go into the lee bilge (Drawing 168).

On some boats, the bilge suction consists of beautifully installed heavy bronze or copper pipe. This arrangement can be dangerous, because if the pipe becomes clogged, a major operation with hammer and cold chisels may be required to disassemble the installation so that the line can be cleared. This kind of situation caused the loss of *Black Dog* off the coast of Venezuela. Although leaking badly, she still might have made port, but the suction line to the big Edson bilge pump clogged, and the complicated piping that went through the deck and into the bilge could not be disassembled.

A noncollapsible hose secured by stainless-steel hose clamps is therefore preferable to bronze or copper pipe. If the hose clogs, one can easily remove it, shove a stick through it to clear the jam, and put it back in place. Formerly, a wire coil was molded into the rubber of the hose to prevent collapsing. Through the years the wire corroded, and eventually the hose either developed leaks or collapsed. Today these difficulties have been overcome; noncollapsible hose is available either made entirely of plastic, with a hard plastic spiral molded in, or made of rubber which has been ribbed to prevent collapsing.

STRAINERS (STRUM BOXES)

The simplest way to keep dirt out of the bilge pump is to cover the end of the intake hose with wire mesh. The problem with this method is that the wire rapidly becomes covered with miscellaneous bilge garbage and seriously restricts the flow of water into the intake pipe.

The most satisfactory strainer is one called by the British a "strum box." This is a large strainer in which the cross-sectional area of the holes is four or five times that of the end of the intake hose. There are some commercially available, designed to fit various types of hose (Photo 126). Or one can make one's own out of a piece of brass pipe the same diameter as the hose. The end of the pipe of course must be welded up, and numerous holes then drilled in the pipe. The total area of these holes should be greater than the cross-sectional area of the hose. This type of strum box is absolutely essential for a navy, semirotary, or vortex pump, and also for any electrical or mechanical impeller pump. These pumps are easily made inoperative by miscellaneous bits of wood.

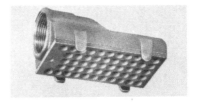

126. Commercial strum boxes.
  (D. M. Street)

One of the great advantages of the diaphragm pump, especially the Edson model, is that it can swallow up and discharge all sorts of miscellaneous junk. But though the bits of junk will pass through the pump, they will lodge wherever there is a corner, so the fewer bends in the discharge line the better.

INTERNAL WATER-
SUPPLY SYSTEMS

Every boat must have some method of getting water from the tank to the sink and/or pots. This may be anything from the most complicated pressure system to the simplest system known to man, as used by Basher Bales in a modified Folkboat in which he made a habit of commuting across the Atlantic. He sailed with minimum equipment and on a minimum budget, and he disliked his crew's using much water. The water was stored in a small fiber-glass tank in the bilge with two small hoses protruding from its top. One was attached to what would normally have been a vent inlet, the other went to the bottom of the tank, where the pump suction would normally have been placed. To get water out of the tank, one took the hose going to the vent inlet into one's mouth, and inserted the other hose into the teakettle. One then blew as hard as possible to build up pressure in the tank; and by the time one had turned purple in the face, there was usually enough water for two cups of tea. Needless to say, Basher had no trouble with excessive water consumption, but I think the average cruising crew would rebel at this system of obtaining water. Basically, water systems are of three types: pumping, gravity, and pressure.

PUMPING SYSTEMS

On most small yachts, water is drawn from the tank by pumping. However, many boats have switched from hand pumping to electric pressure systems because the galley pumps on the market have generally been none too easy to use. The wrist and arm tire, and washing the hands is difficult if one hand must do the pumping. Not many foot pumps are available in America today, but innumerable European manufacturers supply excellent foot pumps, clearly superior to the hand pumps.

GRAVITY SYSTEMS

Gravity water systems were ofen found on larger yachts in years gone by. A large-capacity pump was used to bring water from the water tanks to a header tank on deck, holding twenty gallons or more. This system was simple and foolproof, and gave a flow of water under pressure, but pumping the water up to the header tank was an onerous chore.

PRESSURE SYSTEMS

The pressure systems on the market today vary tremendously in size and price. Especially for small boats, the little PAR pressure pump is hard to beat. It is inexpensive and reliable, and since it is a diaphragm pump rather than an impeller pump, it will not burn out if the tank runs dry. An added advantage of the PAR pump is that it is quiet. Some of the older pumps started up with all the silence of a machine gun. If a PAR pump is installed, the stock cadmium-plated hold-down bolts should be replaced by bolts of stainless steel.

The two disadvantages of pressure systems are that they cause an increase in water consumption and that they are unreliable. A hand pumping system should therefore be installed along with the pressure system. Then if the batteries die or the pressure system fails for some other reason, water will still be obtainable. Further, on a long cruise offshore one may wish to switch to hand pumping to reduce the strain on the pressure system and to keep the rate of water consumption minimal.

SEA COCKS

All through-hull connections must of course be fitted with stopcocks of some sort. Many boats are equipped with gate valves. These are much cheaper than bronze stopcocks, but have several disadvantages. First, it is difficult to ascertain whether a gate valve is made of good bronze, poor bronze, or possibly brass. Valves made of brass may deteriorate rapidly. Second, all too frequently, especially on bilge-pump discharges, the valve will seem to be closed when actually a piece of wood, paper, or the like is jammed under the seat of the valve, holding it partially open so that the pump is siphoning water back into the boat.

Proper, tapered sea cocks, closing with a 90-degree turn, should be installed on all through-hull openings. Admittedly they are expensive, but they are nearly foolproof and can be easily disassembled, greased, cleaned, ground in if necessary, and reinstalled.

Even the best sea cocks should be checked at least once a year, and periodically while the boat is in the water they should be opened and closed to make sure that they have not corroded in place. Further, each sea cock should be installed on a good solid block of wood (Drawing 169); then if the sea cock does jam and a wrench must be used to turn the handle, the wood will distribute the load, and the sea cock will close instead of coming out of the hull. All sea cocks should of course be easily reached. Frequently one discovers sea cocks tucked away in the back of lockers, behind engines, and in various other places where they are nearly inaccessible for use or maintenance. Then for all intents and purposes one has no sea cocks, as one will not be able to shut them off when necessary.

When an older boat is being examined before purchase, the sea cocks should be disassembled. One finds strange objects inside sea cocks. On one very expensive ocean racer, all the sea cocks were frozen. With the aid of a welding torch, hammer and big wrenches we managed to free

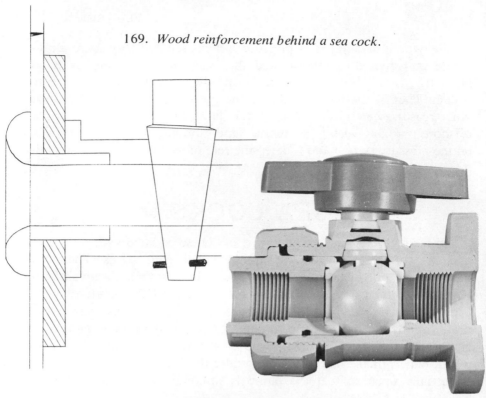

169. *Wood reinforcement behind a sea cock.*

127. *Ball-valve sea cocks. (Photo Illustrators, Inc.)*

them up, and then proceeded to disassemble them. They were big, beautiful bronze sea cocks, but we found that their cone-shaped valves were held in place on the seat by steel springs. When the springs were replaced with phosphor-bronze springs, they gave no further trouble.

PLASTIC SEA COCKS

In recent years, what may be the perfect solution to the sea-cock problem has appeared. A ball valve (Photo 127) is now available, made of high-impact plastic, with seats lined with Tufnol, and O-ring seals. This should end the corrosion problem, and should be particularly useful on a boat of steel or aluminum, since there will be no electrolytic action between the plastic sea cock and the hull.

PIPING

METAL PIPING

In years gone by, either lead or bronze pipe was used on all well-constructed boats. Lead piping stands up for an amazing period of time, but it does deteriorate eventually, so by now boats with old lead piping are headed for plumbing troubles. Bronze piping seems to last almost indefinitely, but on an old boat with bronze pipes, disconnecting or altering anything will probably be difficult because of frozen joints. Installation of bronze or lead piping requires a really good pipe fitter. Some yards still install this metal piping, but in my estimation it is an unnecessary expense.

RIGID PLASTIC PIPING

This type of piping is frequently used in yachts today. It is completely impervious to corrosion, electrolysis, and other forms of deterioration. It is available in almost all sizes, and with a variety of end fittings, and is secured usually with glue. Furthermore, the piping is relatively easy to work with: it is cut to the desired length with a hacksaw; then glue is placed on the pipe and the fitting, and the two are shoved together. The one disadvantage of rigid plastic piping is that, like bronze piping, it must be measured exactly for a good fit.

FLEXIBLE PLASTIC PIPING

Flexible plastic piping varies from the hose made of thin-walled collapsible clear plastic up through large-diameter plastic hose made noncollapsible by a molded-in coil of hard plastic. I much prefer plastic hose for the entire plumbing system, because it is easy to install and repair, and is generally available. Once plastic hose of the proper size has been obtained, along with the correct ribbed-plastic fittings, it is a simple matter to slip the hose over the suitable fitting and clamp the two together with a stainless-steel hose clamp. If the correct plastic fittings are unavailable, brass, bronze, or iron pipe fittings can be used where necessary, the hose being held in place with hose clamps. If the hose end is too small for a particular fitting, one can soften it in boiling water, and then jam a wooden fid into it, expanding it to the desired diameter.

For salt-water use, good stainless-steel hose clamps ("jubilee clips" to the British) are essential. All too often what is sold as a stainless-steel hose clamp turns out to be a stainless-steel strap with an adjusting screw of cadmium-plated steel, which will soon begin to rust and corrode so badly as to become immovable. Stainless-steel hose clamps are expensive, but they are well worth the cost.

WATER TANKS

Water tanks should be placed as low as possible, preferably in the bilge. If they will not fit in the bilge they should be mounted under the

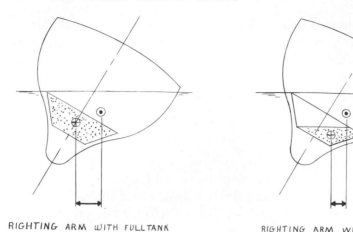

RIGHTING ARM WITH FULL TANK   RIGHTING ARM WITH HALF-FULL TANK

170. *Half-full tank versus full tank.*

lower bunks. Full water tanks in the bilge contribute appreciably to the stability of the boat. Particularly effective in this respect are the immense tanks that may be built into the keel of a steel, fiber-glass, or aluminum boat.

When large water tanks are built into the keel, they should be broken up into as many sections as possible. One large water tank half full of water, even though fairly well baffled, is likely to be very noisy as the water surges back and forth with the roll of the boat. Further, only a full water tank adds stability; in a half-full tank, all the water sloshes to the lee side, giving the same effect as a bilge full of water (Drawing 170). If a water tank is split up fore and aft into four or five sections, each full section contributes to the stability of the boat, and the volume of water in the partially filled tank that is being used is small enough not to affect appreciably the stability.

A further advantage of splitting the tanks fore and aft into four or five separate compartments is the fact that keeping track of how much water is being used is easier, since when one section is sucked dry, one must switch to the next. Also, if the water in one section is contaminated in any way, only a fraction of the supply has been lost, not half or all of it.

MATERIALS

Water tanks have been built of galvanized iron, copper, stainless-steel, and fiber glass. Copper tanks are excellent. They last for many years, but not forever. Eventually, especially if they are deep in the bilge, salt water will corrode holes in the copper and the tank will have to be replaced. The same holds true to a lesser degree for stainless-steel tanks;

many boats will fall apart before their stainless tanks do, but as a boat may last fifty years, and we have had only about twenty-five years' experience with stainless water tanks, it is too early to say exactly how long they will last. I delivered one boat that had fresh-water problems as a result of small rust stains at the bottom of her stainless tanks.

Galvanized Iron

Many older yachts are equipped with galvanized-iron tanks. These appear to last an amazingly long time. A well-built galvanized tank is made of iron of a very heavy gauge, and has a large manhole in the top, through which one may put head and shoulders while cement washing the tank. This process, in which the inside of the tank is given a thin coating of very fine cement, is necessary to prevent the water from becoming contaminated by the iron. As long as the cement is in good shape, the water is pure and has a good taste. When the cement begins to deteriorate, the water of course deteriorates too, containing bits of rust and so on. The main disadvantage of these iron tanks is that they are almost universally placed deep in the bilge, and unless they are frequently removed, cleaned, and painted they rust out, the rust working from the outside in.

Fiber Glass

Fiber-glass tanks can be molded into the vessel, or, as in *Iolaire,* they can be molded separately and installed in the bilge like conventional metal tanks. They work very well. My only problem has been with holes caused by improper chocking of the tanks after they were removed so that the bilge could be cleaned, but this is a minor difficulty, since fiber glass is easy to repair.

Many people complain of the taste of the water carried in fiber-glass tanks. This problem may easily be eliminated in the same way that a similar problem is eliminated from an icebox—by the application of steam, or of boiling water. If the tank is removable, it can be taken to a garage and steam cleaned. If it is an integral tank, the easiest method is to half fill a fifty-five gallom drum with water, attach a hose to the fill hole, and run it down into the empty tank. A good big fire is built under the drum, and the water is kept boiling for four or five hours. All the taste of fiber glass is removed by the steam.

WATER-TANK REMOVAL

All too frequently the water tank is installed in a yacht by the builder as soon as the frame has been set up. The water tank is dropped into place, and then the interior is built. This is a very poor practice, for it is likely to mean that the tank cannot be removed except with the aid of a hacksaw and a cold chisel. And sooner or later, removal of the tank will be necessary, either because it requires repairs or because the bilge must be cleaned.

Wood chips, shavings, and miscellaneous junk that fall into the bilge under the water tank provide a great place for rot to start, which could cause the ruination of the vessel. One reason *Iolaire* has lasted so long is that with only a few hours' work all the floorboards, water tanks, and inside ballast can be removed. Once a year, everything is taken out of the bilge, and it is scrubbed and then coated with Cuprinol or some other wood preservative. This procedure should be followed, if possible, on every wooden boat. Indeed, a similar routine is advisable even for fiber-glass boats with separate rather than integral tanks. The result is a bilge that always smells clean and fresh.

WATER-TANK FILLS

As in so many other matters concerning a boat, the choice of water-tank fills involves compromise. If on-deck fills are used with divided tanks, some difficulties may arise. For example, one may think all the tank sections have been filled and then discover offshore that as a result of a failure to open the correct valves, actually only three of the five sections have been filled. Further, once in a while an air lock will form and the water tank will seem to be filled when it is not. (This happened to me once, and I ran completely out of water while sailing in the Baltic, but luckily, eighteen cases of beer were on board.) Also, if there are on-deck water-tank fills, they should be clearly marked and should not be near the fuel-tank fill. Practically every really experienced yachtsman has at one time or another put water in his fuel or fuel in his water, or has at least been on board a boat where this happened.

The vents on most water tanks are much too small, and some, improperly, are located on deck. If they are on deck they must be small, to prevent salt water from siphoning back through them and into the water tanks. It is far better to have the water-tank vent inside the boat and a good half inch in diameter, so that rapid filling of the water tank is possible.

I prefer to have the water-tank fills themselves belowdecks as well, leading directly into each tank section. Then it is simple to fill each section in turn, until one sees that it has reached capacity. Admittedly this is a more tedious and time-consuming arrangement, but it is foolproof. A further advantage is that it saves the cost of installing much piping from the deck down to the individual tank sections.

EMERGENCY WATER

Extra water, completely independent of the normal supply, should be carried, particularly on a long cruise. In the old days, cruising yachtsmen used steel jerricans for this purpose. These were none too good and very hard to stow. Next, plastic bottles were used. They were excellent, except that they took up too much space. During the bomb-shelter craze, various companies produced inexpensive, collapsible, five-gallon plastic water jugs. These were wonderful, since they could be collapsed when empty, and while in use, and partially full, could be chocked in any old nook or cranny in the boat.

In Europe today even these have been superseded. One can buy plastic water tanks, in various sizes, that will chock in any odd corner. Since these are true tanks, with vent pipes and suction pipes, they can be cross connected to the ship's supply system with no great difficulty, whereas the contents of the individual jugs had to be poured into the ship's main tanks for use. This type of tank is available from Taselaar's in Holland and West Products in the United States.

HEADS

The head was discussed in Chapter X. The only matter to be considered here is whether it should be operated by hand, by electricity, or by a combination of both. The hand-operated head is certainly the most reliable and the easiest to maintain. The electric type is admittedly very convenient, but is very hard to maintain, and one can expect to spend much time upside down in the head working on the electric motor. Further, it is very noisy, it uses appreciable quantities of electricity, and it is expensive. I would say, then, that unless one has a large yacht with a good crew, or is forced by local law to install it, the electric head should be avoided.

XIII

~~~~~~~~~~~~~~~~~~~~~~~~~~~~~~~~~~~~~~~

Electricity

As the years pass, yachts become more and more complicated. The engine which once drove the boat and generated a little electricity for a few lights, must now power all kinds of electrical and electronic equipment, including refrigerators, air conditioners, power-driven anchor windlasses, bilge pumps, automatic pilots, homing devices, and a good deal more.

The first question to arise is whether the power required should be supplied by belting off the main engine or by a separate engine. Size is an important consideration. Few boats of fifty feet or under have sufficient room for a separate generator, and therefore the decision is simple for them.

One should bear in mind, however, that belting off the engine has certain disadvantages. A big heavy-duty compressor for a freezer is likely to draw as much as 1 h.p.; a 60-ampere alternator consumes power, and frequently two alternators are belted off the engine. An anchor windlass belted from the engine by mechanical linkage, a hydraulic pump, a bilge pump—all will draw power. The result will be that while an engine may be rated at, say, 40 h.p., the actual power available to the propeller shaft may be considerably less.

This problem of loss of power can be managed. Albina, and various other manufacturers, make power takeoffs that can be mounted on the forward end of the engine, with a built-in clutch. Thus if maximum power is required, all the auxiliary equipment can be disconnected and full power delivered directly to the shaft (Drawing 171).

The second disadvantage of belting directly from the main engine is that smaller diesels, of 30 to 40 h.p., usually are quite sensitive to side loading. If equipment is belted off the forward end of the engine, the resulting side loading may be enough to burn out the front-end bear-

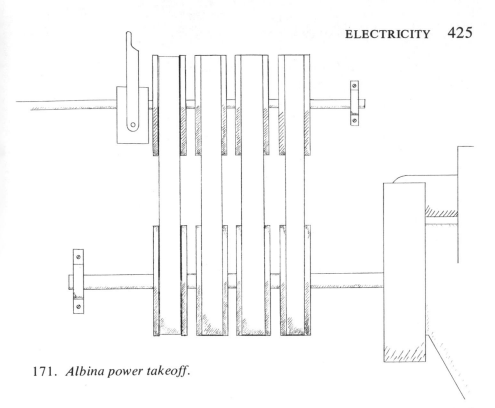

171. *Albina power takeoff.*

ings in a relatively short time. In these circumstances, a short shaft should be installed with its forward end supported by a pillow block, to relieve the side loading on the engine shaft (Drawing 172).

The electrical system causes more trouble, demands more time, gives rise to more anguish, and probably more expense, than any other single component of a boat. Basically, electricity and salt water are incompatible, and a boat—even the best-ventilated one—is never thoroughly

172. *Pillow block to relieve side loading.*

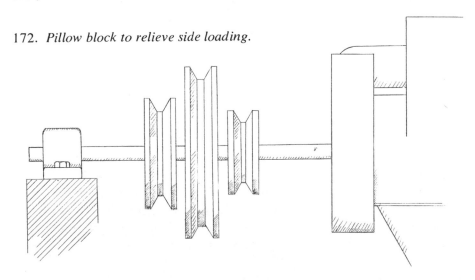

dry. Corrosion tends to form on contacts, and chances for short circuits abound. Interestingly, corrosion in electrical wiring is a greater problem today than it was thirty years ago, probably because the alloy used for copper wire was formerly of much better quality than it is now. When I purchased *Iolaire* in 1956, the wiring system, installed in 1929, and apparently not touched since, worked perfectly. We had no problem with corroding connections in junction boxes or elsewhere, until the boat was rewired.

The copper wire available today tends to corrode as soon as it is exposed to air, doubtless because of impurities in the copper. Tinned copper wire is best; it costs only 10 percent more, and since each individual wire is coated, soldering is easier and corrosion is all but eliminated. Stranded wire is advisable, since otherwise over a period of years vibration may break the wire, producing an intermittent short which is most difficult to trace.

The second reason that electrical installations on boats are likely to give trouble is the fact that unlike those in most buildings on shore, they are not governed by a strict code enforced by independent inspectors. Anyone can wire a boat, and in some cases, even in expensive yards, just anyone appears to have done so.

VOLTAGE

What voltage is to be used on the average yacht is again subject to much debate, but my experience is that much trouble will be avoided if one sticks basically to a 12-volt system. As installations become more complicated with the addition of radar, loran, and sealed 110-volt AC refrigeration compressors, a case can be made for 110 voltage. But even in vessels requiring 110 volts for such equipment, it is still best to step it down to 12 volts for lights, pumps, starters, and the like which will be running off the ship's batteries.

SIX VOLTS

The 6-volt system is practically extinct, and 6-volt equipment is difficult to obtain, now that even American autos have switched to the 12-volt system.

TWELVE VOLTS

The 12-volt system is recommended, except for the very largest vessels, which are really ships rather than cruising yachts. Almost all automotive equipment today is 12-volt, and since millions of trucks and cars are built every year, mass production of 12-volt electrical items, such as motors, fans, starters, cutouts, and relays, has made them available at very reasonable prices.

Formerly, the great objection to the 12-volt electrical system was that the long run needed for the masthead lights and running lights of the larger yachts caused a voltage drop; hence boats in the larger sizes usually had 32-volt systems. Now many top builders in the United States feel that it is much easier and cheaper to minimize the voltage drop by running heavy wire throughout the boat. Furthermore, a 12-volt bulb costs a fifth to a tenth as much as a 32-volt bulb. And while the life of a 12-volt running-light bulb is rated normally at six hundred hours, that of a 32-volt bulb is rated at fifty hours; thus 32-volt running-light bulbs are likely to burn out at the end of four or five nights. Finally, the 12-volt system is by far the safest. A 12-volt system can give one a shock and a scare, but it will not kill, as can a 110-volt or 220-volt system on a boat.

If one needs 110 volts AC for loran or radar, the 12 volts may be stepped up to 110 by means of a solid-state inverter. In the past inverters were none too reliable; now they are regarded as almost foolproof. Solid-state inverters will put out up to 350 watts, enough to operate a ¼-h.p. electric drill. Connected in parallel, they can increase power wattage as much as fourfold.

TWENTY-FOUR VOLTS

The 24-volt system is very popular in Europe and was popular right after World War II in the United States. In that period, the surplus market was flooded with good, cheap 28-volt aircraft equipment which worked perfectly well on a 24-volt system. This equipment has long since disappeared, and the system is not often seen on American yachts. It is still used occasionally, even though surplus aircraft equipment is not plentiful, because some yachtsmen prefer aircraft equipment to marine equipment, believing it to be better made—a subject of some debate.

Some people believe that automobiles are now getting so complicated, and their electric-power demands so great, that before long Detroit may switch to the 24-volt system for all cars. If this happens, 24-volt equipment will be as available and as inexpensive as the 12-volt items are today, and the 24-volt system will again become popular for boats.

THIRTY-TWO VOLTS

The 32-volt system is popular on yachts of fifty feet or over. However, it has serious drawbacks with respect to cost, reliability, and availability of replacement parts. Thirty-two-volt motors are hard to find, 32-volt bulbs are almost unobtainable, and 32-volt compass bulbs are available only direct from the manufacturer. Because 32-volt equipment is used only on boats, and is therefore not produced in vast quantities, it is much more costly. As previously stated, the voltage-drop problem can be minimized by installation of heavier wire, at far less expense than is required for 32-volt equipment. Further, with a 32-volt system it is usually impossible to cross connect the batteries, as almost all engines are supplied with 12-volt starters. Thus, if one has a 32-volt generator, nothing can be cross connected in an emergency except by jumpers.

110 VOLTS

Generator Belted off the Main Engine (Smaller Yachts)

The 110-volt system is often found on yachts today. For lighting, I consider it unseamanlike, dangerous, and not worth the time and trouble. Some yachts have the 110-volt system because it is required for the electric stove. But electric stoves belong in the home, not aboard a boat, since whenever anyone wants to make a pot of coffee, the generator must be started, perhaps at five thirty in the morning in a quiet anchorage.

A second reason for installing a 110-volt system is that it is required by a household refrigerator, household air conditioner, or the like with which the boat has been equipped. But the use of household equipment on a boat is false economy. Though it is initially cheaper, maintenance costs are so high that one would do better to buy really good marine equipment to begin with.

The final reason for having a 110-volt system is that it is required for loran or radar. But this necessity can be met by the installation of an inverter, which converts the 12- or 32-volt DC to 110-volt AC. In the same way, 110-volt current can be supplied for power tools.

A 110-volt system is useful if heavy, hermetically sealed refrigeration and freezer compressors are used. If so, a 110-volt generator is run when necessary to run the compressors. Through a converter, the 110-volt AC can be changed to 12-volt DC to charge the batteries. The difficulty with this system is that it is essential for reliability to have two separate 110-volt generators—a main, and an auxiliary in case of failure. Contrary to popular belief, the belting of a 110-volt AC generator off the main engine is possible. In refrigerator trucks, 110-volt AC alternators have been belted off the engines for years, to run the refrigeration equipment. A variable-speed clutch drive compensates for the varying engine speed. Further details can be obtained from any large trucking company that has refrigerator trucks in its fleet.

In an area where radar or loran is absolutely essential, a backup power supply may be obtained from the batteries by means of a 12-volt–110-volt inverter.

Independent 110-Volt Generators (Larger Yachts)

My good friend Jon Repke, of St. Thomas, has spent the last seventeen years straightening out electrical systems, mechanical systems, and refrigerators improperly installed by various yards all over the world. Since St. Thomas is a yachting crossroads of the world, he sees many types of refrigerators and electrical systems. Like me, he dislikes the all-electric 110-volt boat, with a generator operating continuously. Both he and Cis Roper have pointed out that if the generator must run twenty-four hours a day, and one lives continuously on board, a major overhaul becomes necessary every five or six months, so for reliability, at least two generators are necessary. Indeed, since generators are very hard to overhaul in place, a 110-volt boat should really have three: one sitting in the shop for repairs, one operating, and one as a standby.

This twenty-four-hour operation of the generator can be avoided, as Repke indicates. A 110-volt AC generator can be run either off the main engine or as an auxiliary generator with its own motor; the latter arrangement is by far the better for daily use. This generator will operate the 110-volt sealed-unit refrigeration compressor. If the refrigeration unit is correctly installed (see Chapter XV), the generator should have to work a maximum of one or two hours a day, during which it will run the refrigeration unit and also, through a 110-volt–12-volt converter, charge the batteries. All lighting, pumps, and other 12-volt equipment will be run from the batteries. Radar and loran can be run from the 110-volt generator, or if the generator is shut down, a 12-volt–110-volt inverter can be installed and the radar and loran can be run from the batteries through the inverter. Further, this 110-volt system can be plugged into shore power, so that when the boat is alongside a dock, the batteries can be charged and the refrigeration maintained without the generator being run. Drawing 173 shows a basic installation of this type.

The advantage of this kind of installation is that 110-volt AC generators have no brushes, only slip rings. Thus they are much more reliable and much less likely to give trouble than the standard brush-type generators. The disadvantage is that the system is substantially more expensive to install than a straight 12-volt system with one inverter to produce power for the radar and loran.

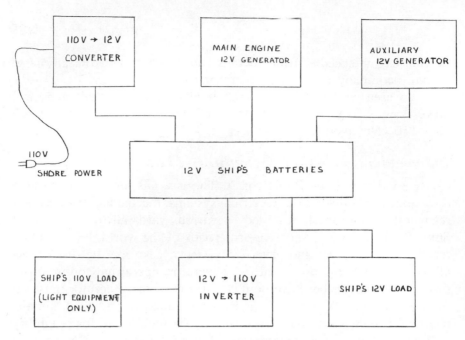

173. *110-volt—12-volt power setup.*

A variety of arrangements can be made for ultimate reliability. First, there can be an independent diesel generator; then, for emergencies, a 110-volt AC generator belted off the engine. The refrigeration unit can consist of two separate 110-volt motor-driven compressors, each with its own independent holding plate, so that if one compressor fails the other will still function. To be sure, it will have to run twice as long, but refrigeration will be maintained. Similarly, two 110-volt–12-volt converters can be installed, so that if one breaks down, the other can carry the load (Drawing 174). While expensive, the installation of enough backup systems makes it practically impossible for a boat to be tied up by electrical failure.

220 VOLTS

The 220-volt system only compounds the errors of the 110-volt system, and provides a good way to electrocute people. Furthermore, leakage from a 110-volt or 220-volt system into a vessel can speed up electrolysis dangerously.

SWITCH PANELS

On many expensive yachts the switch panel is something to behold, big, beautiful, expensive—but inaccessible, and frequently not any where near as good as one would expect for the money spent on it.

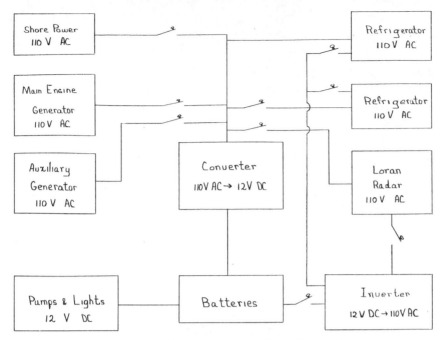

174. *Double 110-volt system to double refrigeration system.*

First and foremost, the switch panel itself should be made of Formica or other plastic. Frequently, switch panels are made of metal, which of course is a good conductor. A short within a metal panel will quickly burn out every piece of electrical equipment across the board. This is less likely to happen with a panel of plastic, a nonconductor.

A second error in installing switch panels is to put a 32-volt and a 110-volt panel right next to each other. In that case, a short in the 110-volt system can easily burn the entire setup. This is especially likely to happen if a leak down the hatch or behind the panels permits water to get to them. A third error, then, is to mount a panel where it may be reached by spray, or other water.

The switch panel should either be removable or be mounted on hinges, and should be held by an easily removable catch. Its back should be instantly accessible. All too often on a beautiful and expensive yacht when an alteration to the electrical system is to be made or trouble is being traced, a good carpenter with a good set of tools takes an hour or so to remove the panel.

When a panel is installed, room should be left for three or four additional circuits. Too often, the installation will just handle the original equipment; when more equipment is acquired, doubling up becomes necessary. After a few years, the electrical system is such a maze, no one can comprehend it.

Whenever a boat is designed or rewired, a schematic diagram of the electrical system should be firmly fastened inside the door to the switch panel. As equipment is added, the wiring may be drawn in on the original schematic, for the information of any strange electrician who may come on board to do repairs. Otherwise, solving a relatively minor problem may take a full day, because the electrician spends the first six hours trying to figure out the system.

For every piece of electrical equipment on the boat, one should have not just the owner's manual, but the manufacturer's schematic. In all sorts of out-of-the-way places one finds electronic technicians, electricians, or what-have-you, who—given the schematic—can fix almost anything, but without the schematic cannot even get started.

A few companies make reasonably priced switch panels for yachts. West Products has numerous standard panels available, can make up nonstandard panels, and also sells the parts so that one can put together one's own. The Crouch Engineering Company, in England, makes switch panels which are almost waterproof, certainly splashproof. West Products uses circuit breakers, while Crouch Engineering uses fuses.

CIRCUIT BREAKERS VERSUS FUSES

Both are acceptable. However, care must be taken that the correct circuit breakers are used. In general, today, AC circuit breakers are installed in yachts. These give little or no protection to the normal 12- or 32-volt DC motors. They do not trip out until the load is so heavy that, in most cases, the motor is already burned out. This error is to be found even in some of the most expensive installations, made by supposedly good yards with good electrical departments. With 12-volt or 32-volt systems, then, DC circuit breakers of the correct amperage are essential.

Circuit breakers are expensive, while switches are cheap; for example, a 32-volt circuit breaker may cost twenty-two dollars, while the corresponding switch costs fifty cents. All too frequently, a switch panel is expensive because circuit breakers have been used throughout the panel as individual switches. Thus to minimize cost, circuit breakers should be installed only for various circuits (such as lighting forward, lighting amidships, running lights, pumps, refrigeration) and individual switches should be used for the items of equipment (such as the various running lights, electronic devices, and so on). Spare circuit breakers must be carried at all times, since if a circuit breaker fails, the system is completely out of order.

Fuses are perfectly acceptable, but difficulties may arise because they have not been standardized. Every country has numerous different types of fuses and fuse holders. Hence, if contemplating extensive cruising, one should have on board a good supply of fuses. The old type of fuse holder was subject to corrosion, but as has been noted, the Crouch Engineering panel is splashproof and is well sealed; in a panel of this type the corrosion problem should be minimal.

PANEL METERS

On the electrical panel, there should of course be meters showing the amount of charge that each generator is producing. Further, an ammeter, which shows the amount of discharge at any time, is very useful. Since it indicates how much current is actually being used, it may explain why a boat continually has dead batteries; they may be just too small for the amount of current pulled from them.

A voltmeter on the same panel is also desirable. The state of the battery is best determined with a hydrometer, but when beating to windward in half a gale no one is going to go down to check the batteries; at such a time one must look to the voltmeter for some indication of the state of the battery. If the boat has auxiliary AC generators, each should have an hour meter and a frequency meter.

ELECTRICAL CIRCUITS

As has been pointed out, a separate circuit breaker is not necessary for each individual electrical circuit. However, judgment must be used in combining circuits. For instance, port and starboard lighting should be on separate circuits, so that a single short will not black out a whole cabin. Similarly, the running lights and the compass light should be on separate circuits, so that the loss of one will not mean the loss of the other. One can exist fairly easily with no running lights, but trying to sail at night with no compass light is a bit of a bore.

In planning circuits one should also consider the relative power demands of various items. Care should be taken to avoid an excessive power drain on any one circuit.

ELECTRICAL POWER SOURCES
ALTERNATORS VERSUS GENERATORS

There is a running argument among cruising sailors concerning the relative merits of the alternator and the low-voltage generator.

The advantages of the alternator are that it is small and light, and will begin to put out at very low rpm. However, there are a number of disadvantages. To begin with, alternators are sensitive to dampness. The 12-volt automotive alternator will not operate with any degree of reliability unless it is absolutely dry.

To dissipate heat, the alternator casing is aluminum, with large air ports cut into it. The internal mechanism of the alternator is copper; the shaft, steel. Aluminum, copper, steel—a look at the galvanic-action table (Table XIII, Appendix) will suggest what is likely to happen.

Marine alternators are expensive, a decent-sized one costing four or five hundred dollars. Also, they draw a tremendous amount of power. They are notorious for wearing out belts, often because a single belt is used where double belting is actually required. Another reason for the short life of belts on alternators is that frequently the pulley on the alternator is very small, to give the alternator the necessary rpm. This bending around a pulley is very hard on the belt. A rough rule of thumb is that the diameter of the pulley should be ten times the width of the belt. Thus a standard belt should not be placed around a pulley less than 5 inches in diameter if it is making a 180-degree turn. A 50-ampere 12-volt alternator charging dead batteries will draw 1½ h.p., a good load for one belt. Use of one of the new wire-cored belts will minimize stretch.

Alternators are very sensitive to mishandling. Running an alternator on an open circuit for even a second will burn out the diodes, which are expensive to replace. A set or two of spare diodes for the alternator should always be kept on board. C. E. Niehoff makes an alternator which seems quite popular with marine electricians. They say one very good feature is the ease with which the diodes can be changed if necessary.

Generators are much bigger and admittedly less efficient than alternators, but they will take much more abuse. Generators will work for years, with normal maintenance and replacement of brushes as necessary. Again, spare brushes should always be carried. Anywhere in the world, one can find people able to work on generators; if worst comes to worst, armatures can be rewound, field coils rewound, and so on. Another great advantage is that rebuilt generators are available in the United States at minimal cost, perhaps thirty to thirty-five dollars for a 40- or 50-ampere 12-volt rebuilt generator. At that price, one can obtain a complete spare generator to keep on board for installation when necessary.

ENSURING CONTINUOUS POWER

It is the height of folly to rely on a single generator or alternator belted off the engine. All too frequently the generator or alternator

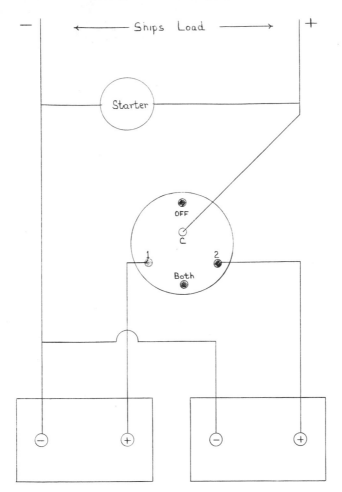

175. Batteries connected for use in parallel or separately.

breaks down, ruining or seriously delaying a cruise. Two separate generators or alternators should be belted off the engine. Two separate banks of batteries, one for starting, one for operating the ship's electrical equipment, are also essential. Wired as in Drawing 175, both batteries can be paralleled for charging if the engine is to be run for a long time. Similarly, if the batteries are both low for some reason, they may be paralleled for starting the engine.

Finally, if wired as in Drawing 176, two 12-volt batteries can be placed in series by throwing switch *A,* giving 24 volts. Even two almost-dead 12-volt batteries should supply enough amperes to turn over and start the engine. However, the starter button must not be held down, since the 12-volt starter might then burn out. Similarly, with a gasoline engine, one must be sure to disconnect *A* immediately upon starting, to avoid blowing the coil and the condenser.

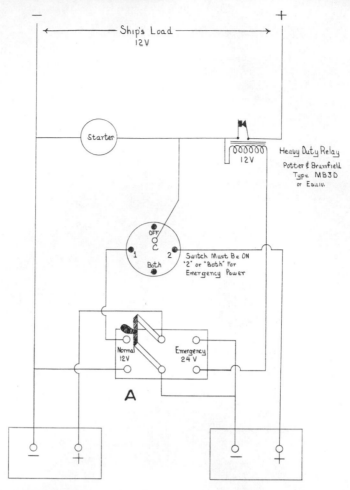

176. *Batteries connected in series for emergency starting; a relay switch protects the other circuits from the higher voltage.*

The battery capacity required by a yacht will depend on the size of the boat and the amount of electrical gear on board. Basically, the house batteries, which run all electrical equipment except the starting motor, should be able to take care of the boat without being recharged for a full forty-eight hours at sea, with the running lights burning as needed, people turning on lights belowdecks, and the navigational equipment given normal use. If the batteries will not last for two full days—or, better yet, three—one takes the risk of encountering heavy weather and not desiring to run the engine, but being forced to do so to keep the batteries charged.

SWITCHING

If the boat has an independent generator, it should be able to charge both the house batteries and the starting batteries. Similarly, the generator belted off the engine should be able to charge both sets of batteries. Thus when the main engine is not being run—as when the boat is moored to a dock for a period of time, or is cruising offshore—the independent generator can be used to charge the batteries. Conversely, when the main engine is running, as in long periods of calm, it can also charge both sets of batteries, and the independent generator need not be used. During day cruising, the engine is usually run for half an hour when the boat leaves the anchorage in the morning and for half an hour as she returns in the evening; this time is sufficient for a decent-sized generator belted off the engine to take care of the normal load and keep the batteries up.

CHARGING RATE

The proper practice will depend on the size of the generator or alternator. A small three-brush generator of 15 to 20 amperes, such as is found on old gasoline engines, usually has a simple cutout, which can be bypassed by a normal 15-ampere switch if any failures occur. Heavier-duty generators and alternators usually feed through a voltage regulator which regulates the output according to the state of the battery. Some boats have a manual rheostat on their generators or alternators. This seems the ideal arrangement, since if the batteries are well up, almost fully charged, the engine or generator must be run for a long time to complete the charge. With the automatic regulator, the output of the 50-ampere alternator is cut back to perhaps no more than 10 or 15 amperes. However, with a rheostat, the desired amount of current can be delivered to the batteries regardless of the state of charge.

A heavy charge can be put into a battery, but only for a very short time. One must either watch the bubbles coming up in the battery or keep track of the temperature, to make sure the battery does not begin to get hot.

BATTERY VENTILATION

The importance of battery ventilation is not always recognized. In my view, the new fiber-glass battery case is totally useless. It gives almost no ventilation to the battery. This means, first of all, that the battery heats up, and second, that there is the danger of hydrogen collecting and igniting.

The importance of ventilation is dramatized by a recent occurrence involving a charter yacht in St. Thomas. The boat had a big set of batteries on deck under the upturned dinghy. The owner's mother came for a visit, and spread the blankets over the dinghy for an airing, effectively cutting off all ventilation. The skipper, unaware of what she had done, was charging his batteries merrily when a short circuit caused a spark. The hydrogen which had accumulated exploded, and blew the dinghy into a thousand pieces; luckily, no one was seriously injured.

Mounting batteries, like so many other aspects of boating, involves compromise. To get the most power to the starter, the batteries should be as close to the starter as possible. Similarly, to avoid voltage drop, the batteries should be close to the generator. However, batteries operate best if they are cool. Diesels run at 185° F., engine rooms are small, and when one is cruising in the tropics, where the water temperature goes up, the engine room becomes an oven. The batteries are hot even before they begin to function. To avoid this situation, the batteries should be mounted outside of the engine room—perhaps under settees in the main cabin or in the after cabin—as close to the engine as possible but separated from the engine room by a bulkhead.

Frequently, on new racing boats one sees batteries mounted in the bilge. This arrangement is objectionable, for if the bilge becomes flooded, the entire electrical system will short out very rapidly. The bilge is always damp, and battery connections will tend to corrode. Placing the batteries down low does increase the stability of the boat, but under the new I.O.R. rule, this means the boat's rating will go up as well. Thus if the batteries are mounted higher, stability will be slightly reduced, but so also will be the boat's rating. At the same time, the safety and reliability of the electrical system will be vastly increased.

Battery Boxes

To ensure proper ventilation, one might make a fiber-glass-lined wooden box, as shown in Drawing 177. This type of box has a two-inch tray around the bottom to catch any dripping battery acid, and a top to keep tools from shorting the terminals, but the sides are cut out to allow ventilation around the battery. If the battery is installed under a cabin settee, ventilation holes must be cut in the front of the settee; better yet, the whole panel can be removed and replaced with screening or lattice work. Of course, the settee must be hinged, to give easy access to the battery for checking with a hydrometer.

HYDROMETERS

Hydrometers are fragile and in many areas, expensive. A good way to minimize hydrometer breakage is to secure to the engine-room bulkhead a piece of rubber steam hose large enough in diameter to contain the hydrometer, the bottom of the hose being filled with a circle of

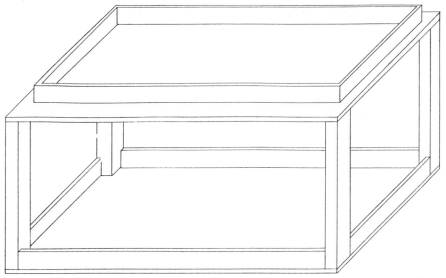

177. *Battery box.*

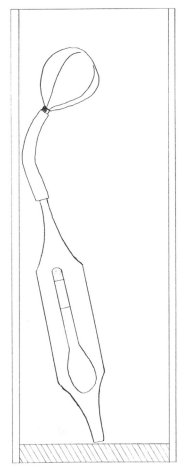

wood (Drawing 178) to prevent any battery acid from dripping from the hydrometer. Also, for proper maintenance of the batteries, a jug of distilled water, the quantity depending upon the size of the boat, should always be carried. Nondistilled water, with its various salts, can ruin a battery in very short order.

ELECTRONIC-EQUIPMENT POWER SUPPLY

Radar and loran of course will have to be powered either off a 110-volt generator or off the ship's battery, with the aid of an inverter. However, anemometers, Fathometers, and the like can be powered either from their own small batteries or from the ship's battery. I prefer to power them from the ship's battery.

178. *Cross section of hydrometer holder.*

This method was disliked years ago, because the Fathometer and the wind indicator, used twenty-four hours a day during cruising, drew a considerable amount of current and would rapidly run the battery down. This is not true today; indeed, since equipment of this type has been completely transistorized, the power drain has been reduced to the point where operation from dry cells is feasible.

But while dry cells are satisfactory for weekend sailing or offshore racing, they are not practical for serious cruising. In certain circumstances—hugging the Mexican coast for instance—the Fathometer will run through dry cells at a great rate. The same holds true for the wind indicator. The problem is not that dry cells are expensive, but that satisfactory replacements may be impossible to obtain. In out-of-the-way areas dry cells are likely to have deteriorated by the time they are offered for sale, so they do not last long once installed. For example, years ago one of the major battery manufacturers started marking the batteries with a date after which they were not to be sold. The batteries shipped to St. Thomas usually arrived about a week before their expiration date, sometimes later.

Another disadvantage of using dry cells is that one must keep several different sizes on hand. Searching around for penlight batteries for the Fathometer, or D cells for the wind indicator, or flashlight batteries for the direction finder, at five in the morning is no one's idea of a picnic. All in all, although there are advantages in having a separate battery for each piece of equipment, I prefer to run everything off the ship's battery, which can be recharged without difficulty.

AUXILIARY GENERATORS

An auxiliary generator must be quiet. Therefore, two-cycle generators and air-cooled generators, both of which are noisy, are unacceptable. On some boats, an insulated box is built around the generator to deaden the sound, but then holes must be made, through which air can reach the engine for both cooling and operating. The generator should be firmly mounted, with a good exhaust; the Aqualift exhaust (Chapter XIV) seems to be the most quiet.

The auxiliary generator must be accessible and easy to remove for maintenance if one is doing serious cruising, and is living on board for extended periods. Running a generator three hours a day for a year, for a total of 1,095 hours, is equivalent to putting 50,000 miles on a car in a year. One representative engine manufacturer recommends the following procedure for maintaining a generator: every 500 hours, the cooling system should be overhauled, the injectors cleaned, and so on; every 1,000 hours, the head should be removed, decarbonized, and so on; every 5,000 hours, the generator should be stripped down to its bits and pieces and given an overhaul. If the generator must run not three but twenty-four hours a day, to power air conditioning and the like, it should be removed about twice a year for a complete overhaul. That necessity alone is enough to convince me that electric cooling does not belong on a serious cruising boat.

GROUNDING SYSTEMS

Whether a positive ground, a negative ground, or a floating system is to be preferred, I will not venture to say. Each electrician has his own theory. However, everyone agrees that stray voltage wandering around —shorting out through the vessel's hull because of bad electrical connections, bare wiring, or what-have-you—causes immense electrolysis problems. The electrical system should be regularly checked to find out if there is a discharge into the vessel which will run down the batteries and cause electrolysis.

ELECTROLYSIS

There are numerous articles and books on the subject of electrolysis prevention, some presenting views which are diametrically opposed.

Some people swear by the induced-current system of electrolysis prevention. This is rather complicated and must be continually adjusted, as different amounts of current are induced when the boat is at rest, running under power, sailing at various speeds. I have seen a few boats with this system, and it seems to work well.

Bonding, a traditional method for preventing electrolysis, is still used by some people. When the yacht is built, all the fittings—chain plates, keel bolts, stem fitting, sea cocks, and the like—are bonded together with a copper strip. As with other methods of electrolysis prevention, its success is not completely predictable. I know of one case where a boat with this system had electrolysis problems which an expert eliminated by cutting all the bonds.

There is only one sure way to be completely free of electrolysis; that is to use only a single kind of metal. However, this solution is just about impossible to carry out in practice, since different makers of, let us say, the same type of bronze may put out slightly different alloys: the manufacturing process does not permit sufficiently close tolerances to keep the alloy absolutely uniform. Hence, a supposedly good bronze nut has been known to fall to pieces while the bolt it was attached to was in perfect shape. Doubtless the problem will remain with us until we reach the day of plastic boats with plastic sea cocks, fiber-glass masts with plastic standing rigging, and even a plastic engine!

Table XIII (Appendix) gives a galvanic series of metals and alloys. The closer that metals are in this series, the fewer the electrolysis problems that will be encountered when they are used together. However, it should be noted that there are many types of stainless steel, and electronic action between them is entirely possible.

The first basic preventive of electrolysis, then, is to avoid mixing metals if at all possible. Another advisable measure is to install zinc anode disks on all through-hull fittings, rudder straps, and the like. A copper strap or wire machine screw should be inserted into the fitting being protected and into the zinc. When 10 percent of the zinc is gone, it should be replaced, for the most active portion of the zinc goes first. Just cleaning the zinc when the boat is overhauled does no good. Leaving old zinc in place can cause the process to reverse. One must also be careful to obtain suitable zinc in the first place. Not all the zinc sold for use as anodes is pure enough to do the job. Special care must be taken in this respect with aluminum boats.

A final preventive, as has been indicated, is to check the electrical system to make sure there are no stray grounds wandering around.

ELECTRICAL CONNECTIONS

The soldered connection is generally regarded as the ideal electrical connection. However, it is beyond the capabilities of many of us, and once made, it is hard to alter or move. Instead, many people use crimp-on connectors, and place the terminals on terminal blocks, such as Manhattan Marine's (catalog Fig. 1865) or Simpson Lawrence's (catalog Fig. 1259). I am told that the United States Navy specifies crimp-on fittings, and what is good enough for the navy should be good enough for the average yachtsman.

An even simpler method is to use a standard British household junction box (Drawing 179). This has the advantage of being made of plastic; it has four poles and a screw-on lid. If it is screwed into place, *a hole cut in the bottom,* and wires run up from the bottom, the occasional dollop of spray will have no effect on it, especially if the hole is sealed with a little grease. Unfortunately, plastic junction boxes are almost impossible to find in the United States. The open terminal-block type is very likely to short, or to perform poorly because of corrosion.

There should be no plug-in connections on deck. Though various types of supposedly waterproof plug-ins are made, none of them are really effective. If a flood lamp is to be used on deck aft or forward,

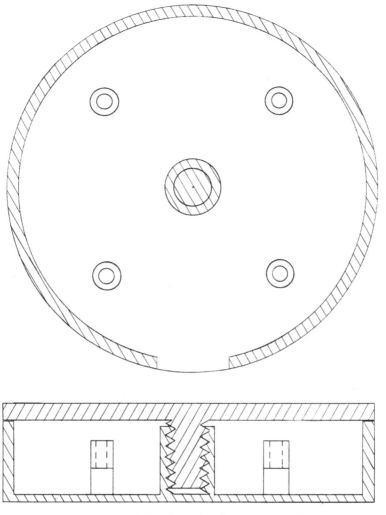

179. *Junction box.*

the wire should be run down through a Dorade box, so that it can be plugged in belowdecks.

All wires for running lights, spreader lights, and the like should be brought through the deck by means of a small bronze stuffing gland, such as Manhattan Marine's (catalog Fig. 1862), made for ⅜-inch OD electrical wire. Wires that go up inside the mast should be brought out of the mast belowdecks, and should there be plugged in at a point two or three feet away from the mast. Mast boots are not supposed to leak, but all too frequently they do, and then dampness shorts out any connections that have been let in flush to the side of the mast.

LIGHTS

Belowdecks lights have been discussed in Chapter X. It should be noted here that one may have too many lights or too many bright lights. A few bright lights are necessary—for the cook, and for people who wish to read—but all others should be dim. One method of evaluating the situation is to turn on all the lights on the boat at once and check the battery drain.

Fluorescent lights, which can now be obtained at a reasonable price, give much less heat and draw much less amperage than incandescent lamps. However, it is difficult to find out which brands should be purchased; many of them have parts made of cheap white metal, rather than plastic, stainless steel, or something else noncorrosive.

Rheostats for lights are difficult to obtain, but if possible they should be placed on the chart-table light and the compass light. Different people like light of different degrees of intensity while steering and/or working at the chart.

The compass light is discussed in detail in Chapter XVI.

ESOTERIC GENERATORS

Lang Syne sailed around the world, and across the Pacific, with no electrical-generating problem, the matter having been taken care of in a very unusual fashion. A low-rpm generator was belted directly off the propeller shaft, which was allowed to turn when the boat was under sail. This gave electric power for both refrigeration and the autopilot. This rig is not often seen, but it obviously works; it has been on *Lang Syne* for the better part of twenty years.

Wind generators have been tried on various boats. I have a wind generator on a tower at my home at Calivigny Point, in Grenada, which is most effective and most reliable, but hardly suitable for a boat; it is too heavy and sets up too much vibration, and the noise would drive one crazy. However, it is interesting to speculate whether a little alternator from a motorcycle, mounted on a swivel on top of the mizzen-mast, would not be useful. Even if it put out only 3 amperes an hour, that would still total up to 72 a day, enough for the batteries of a medium-sized cruising yacht. I would like to experiment with an arrangement of this sort, or to hear the results of anyone else's experiments.

There are a few very small wind-powered trickle chargers on the market, but they produce only 1 ampere an hour at best.

XIV

~~~~~~~~~~~~~~~~~~~~~~~~~~~~~~~~~~~

Mechanical Equipment

Whether an engine is needed on board will depend upon the sailing ability of the owner, his philosophy of life, the type of boat, and the area in which she is sailed. In the Virgin Islands, with the almost ever-present trade winds, and no large islands to block them, an engine can easily be dispensed with. However, if one is sailing on the east coast of the United States, with its long periods of flat calm, or in European waters, where there are strong tidal currents, an engine is indeed an asset. Time and tide wait for no man, and the wind does not necessarily wait for the tide. So in an area of large tidal fluctuations, an engine is almost essential.

Again, if most of one's sailing will be offshore rather than in coastal waters, an engine can probably be dispensed with, unless large areas of calm are to be crossed. And large offshore areas of calm weather are relatively infrequent. The big, heavy cruising boats, and the old commercial square-riggers and schooners, would frequently become becalmed in the doldrums and spend weeks breaking their way free. But a modern, well-sailed yacht seldom has this difficulty. With the aid of the big genoa, the mizzen staysail, and so on, even on the calmest day a yacht is usually able to turn in a run of fifty to eighty miles.

As has been noted, if sailing is to be done in the tropics, electric lights are necessary, since kerosene lights give out too much heat for use in warm weather. If an engine must be installed to generate electricity, it may as well be connected to the shaft and the propeller, in addition to the generator.

The temperament of the owner has much to do with whether or not an engine is to be installed. Some people would much rather work their way up the channel, in light air against the tide, enjoying the sport of making the most of what God has given us, instead of turning on the engine and listening to the noise. One of the fastest around-the-world cruises was made by Peter Tangevald, with *Dorothea*. She was a heavy cruising cutter with an engine. However, he threw the engine overboard at Majorca, took off the propeller, plugged up the aperture, and thereafter visited many harbors in the Pacific that supposedly could not be entered except with an engine. Similarly, for almost twenty years Dr. Gifford Pinchot sailed his first *Loon* on the east coast of the United States with no engine. She was a beautiful and very fast Sparkman and Stephens cruiser that sailed superbly. The ocean-racing version of the boat, which did have auxiliary power, sailed very well, but her performance was improved, particularly in light airs, when the propeller was removed and the aperture plugged.

INBOARD VERSUS OUTBOARD ENGINES

If it is decided that an engine is needed, the question arises of whether an outboard or an inboard is preferable. An outboard has various disadvantages for use as an auxiliary. The outboard intended for this use usually has no electric starter or generator; it is strictly a means of propulsion. Second, if it is not to be dragged all the time, destroying performance, it must be lifted out of place and stowed. Also, a two-cycle outboard is usually not as reliable as a four-cycle inboard.

However, there are many advantages to outboard power for very small yachts. First and foremost, if the outboard is well designed, it can be removed, and a plug can be inserted in the outboard well, leaving a completely clean and unobstructed bottom which makes possible fine performance under sail. Second, if the outboard needs an overhaul, bringing it to the dock or to the engine shop for repairs is very simple. It is not too easy to remove an inboard engine, or to work on it in the depths of the bilge. The dangers of explosion through the use of gasoline are minimal with the outboard, because it is usually run in an open well, and when not in use, it is stowed in a vapor-tight locker. Finally, an outboard in a well is infinitely cheaper than an inboard, with its shaft, clutch, stuffing gland, exhaust pipe, and so on.

TYPES OF OUTBOARDS

Most outboards today are designed for pushing fast, light dinghies. Hence they have high rpm but little torque. They throw a very small propeller at a very high speed. However, for auxiliary power on a sailboat, a large-diameter, slow-turning propeller is needed. Accordingly, a high-rpm engine can be geared down with a 2-, 3-, or 4-to-1 reduction gear; better yet, a slow-turning engine can be geared down. For this purpose, a Seagull Century with a clutch and reduction gear is hard to beat. In calm weather, with no difficulty at all, I have for many years maneuvered my twenty-ton, forty-five-foot yawl with a Seagull Century on the dinghy, which is lashed to the quarter and used as a push boat.

INBOARDS

If an inboard engine is to be installed, a choice must be made between a gasoline engine and a diesel. In the past, most cruising yachts had gasoline engines. Diesel engines were heavy, noisy, expensive, generally slow, and rather difficult to service because most mechanics were not familiar with them. This situation has changed drastically within the last twenty years. Mechanics have become much more familiar with diesels, so that it is usually as easy to have a diesel repaired as a gasoline engine. The price of the diesel engine has dropped sharply in comparison with that of the gasoline engine. Even in small sizes, diesel engines are now available, with a power-weight ratio acceptable for sailboats. A ratio of 1 h.p. to a thousand pounds of displacement gives a fully powered auxiliary; ½ h.p. to a thousand pounds gives adequate flat-calm power but nothing more, while 1½ h.p. to a thousand pounds makes a boat almost a motor sailer.

Diesel Engines

The diesel engine has many advantages. First and most important, it is virtually explosion-proof. Diesel fuel, being nonvolatile, cannot be lit by a spark, and when lit, it will burn rather than explode. However, there can be a fire on a diesel engine, and one should be prepared for that eventuality. An automatic fire extinguisher is highly desirable. A broken fuel line pumping diesel fuel on an exhaust pipe can cause a beautiful fire (a United States Coast Guard cutter was almost destroyed in this fashion in St. Thomas because the heat of the blaze made it impossible to enter the engine room and trip the CO_2 system).

Diesels are economical in their use of fuel. On a power cruiser the resulting savings soon make up for the additional cost of the diesel engine. On a sailboat it might take thirty years to recover the extra cost of the diesel through savings in fuel consumption, but the diesel's economical use of fuel is important for another reason: the fuel tank need not be nearly as large as it would have to be for a gasoline engine. A 40-h.p. gasoline engine will burn at cruising speed just under two gallons of fuel an hour, while a 40-h.p. diesel under the same conditions will burn about seven- or eight-tenths of a gallon of fuel. So for the same tank capacity the diesel has double the cruising range.

Another advantage is that the diesel has amazing reliability. There is no carburetor, and the difficulties caused by the electrical system on a gasoline engine do not arise with a diesel engine. Basically, if the fuel is clean and the starter working, the engine will run. Keeping the fuel clean is important; one must have the correct filters, and change them frequently.

Diesels are to be found in two main types: the big, heavy, slow-turning four-cycle "rock crusher," which can usually be hand started, and the modern, light, high-speed two- or four-cycle engine, which is impossible to hand start.

SLOW-SPEED FOUR-CYCLE DIESELS: The slow-speed four-cycle diesel will usually be found to have been designed for marine use, rather than to be a marine conversion of an engine designed for another purpose. Because it is intended for marine use, it is generally well built, but since the demand for this type of engine is relatively small, and few are built, it is likely to be expensive, and parts may be difficult to obtain, except direct from the manufacturer. However, because it is slow turning, its parts are likely to last, and the engine seldom breaks down completely. Indeed, the heavy old-fashioned diesel frequently runs for just about the life of the boat.

Usually on these slow-turning diesels, the access provided by the various inspection ports enables one to change bearings, pistons, and rods, and basically rebuild the whole engine without removing it from the boat. This of course cannot usually be done with the high-speed diesels, as they are generally designed for nonmarine use, where dropping the pan is easy.

Frequently, the slow-speed diesel is not quite as heavy as it appears on first inspection. In some cases it has a relatively small reduction gear, perhaps 1.5 to 1, or 2 to 1; and often it has direct drive, so the entire weight of a heavy reduction gear is saved. For a given horsepower it has much more torque than a high-speed engine. It swings a big propeller at low rpm, giving smooth—and economical—cruising. Another hidden weight saving thus results from the fact that it requires a relatively small amount of fuel. To compare the two types of diesel accurately, one must consider total weight, including that of the engine, the gearbox, and the fuel required to cover a thousand miles. The heavy rock crusher may turn out to be surprisingly light.

Finally, and most important, except in the larger sizes, the rock crusher is usually independent of mechanical starters. Indeed, even one of the really big engines, the six-cylinder Gardner, can easily be started by one man, because of its big flywheel, compression releases on each cylinder, and an efficient hand-starting mechanism geared to the flywheel. All one needs is almost full headroom and plenty of elbow room.

Slow-speed diesels do occasionally have their problems. For example, crankcase explosions have been known to occur which shattered pans and actually blew pieces of crankcase through the bottom of the boat.

LIGHTWEIGHT DIESELS: Few lightweight diesels of less than 25 h.p. are available. For this reason, many boats under thirty feet use gasoline engines. Such an engine as the Saab HS (459 pounds, 20 h.p.) almost, but not quite, fits into the category of the lightweight diesel. From 25 h.p. up, many lightweight diesels are on the market. They are intended primarily for nonmarine use, in taxis, tractors, and the like. Some of the marine conversions of the engines are cheaply done; some are excellent. While the converted portion of the engine must of course be ordered from the manufacturer, the nonmarine portions—crankshafts, pistons, bearings, and the like—can be purchased locally, if one knows what basic block the engine is assembled from. Many people buy engines which are widely used in their nonmarine versions, because parts for these are easily available. For example, the Ford marine conversion, suitable for fifty- or sixty-foot cruising boats, is in its basic form a tractor engine, so parts are usually obtainable worldwide. Similarly, the Perkins and Mercedes Benz engines are popular for yachts of thirty-five to fifty feet because they are both used in taxicabs all over the world.

Lightweight Two-Cycle Diesles The lightweight two-cycle diesel was made popular by General Motors during World War II. The horsepower-weight ratio is excellent, and since the war, the engine has been highly developed and widely distributed for both commercial and yachting use. The two-cycle does have a number of disadvantages. Because it is a high-rpm engine, parts tend to wear out relatively rapidly. Also, the very high speed makes a large reduction gear necessary. Further, because it is a two-cycle, the engine needs a scavenging air blower, and is sensitive to back pressure. It is famous for its noise, and can often be heard miles away, sounding almost like an airplane engine. The noise does not bother power yachtsmen or commercial fisherman, but it is not particularly attractive to the sailing yachtsman. It has been alleged that if the engine is muffled, its efficiency drops off drastically, but I am told that this is not true. The trouble is just that few of the builders and marine architects have bothered to spend time, money, and energy on the investigation and installation of good quiet exhaust systems on two-cycle diesels. Incidentally, between 1947 and 1950, General Motors put out a complete book on the installation of General Motors diesels, but no one seemed to read it so the company stopped printing it.

Another disadvantage of the two-cycle diesel is that occasionally something goes wrong, and the engine takes off and begins revving up. Even cutting the fuel supply does not necessarily stop the engine, as it will begin to run on the lubrication oil from the oil pump. One answer to this problem is to have mounted a CO_2 fire extinguisher, with the nozzle aimed directly into the air intake. Then in the event of a run-away diesel, one need merely set off the extinguisher, to stop combustion and thus shut down the engine. Better still, the two-cycle General Motors diesel can be equipped at the factory with a valve which automatically shuts off the air intake if it begins to run away.

A further disadvantage of the two-cycle diesel is that it has a much higher fuel-consumption rate than does a four-cycle diesel. This is because the combustion explosion is still going on when the exhaust ports are open. Hence some unburnt fuel, and some of the force of the combustion explosion, are lost through the exhaust pipe.

The two-cycle diesel does, however, have many advantages. It is light in weight, and parts are relatively cheap and superbly distributed. Also, one can pick up a factory- or commercially-rebuilt diesel at a very good price. Indeed, with many of the popular sizes of two-cycle diesels, one may be able to trade in one's engine periodically for a rebuilt model, at one of the commercial rebuilding firms. Doing this would minimize the chances of a breakdown.

Gasoline Engines

In the past, gasoline engines were very popular because suitable diesels for the average cruising yacht were scarce and expensive. This is not true today, except for high-performance power cruisers. Cruising yachts seldom use gasoline engines of more than 40 h.p.

Years ago, it was apparent from reading British yachting magazines that the British were exceedingly wary of gasoline engines. English yachtsmen frequently refer to the number of explosions on the Norfolk Broads. When *Iolaire* was purchased, she was equipped with a well-known British gasoline-driven generator, and its character made clear some of the reasons for the British ill luck with gasoline engines.

The gas tank was mounted on a bulkhead and vented through a cap into the engine compartment. To start the engine one first had to tickle —i.e., flood—the carburetor. If the carburetor was flooded a little too much, gas was spilled around the generator, and the engine space was filled with gas fumes. At this point, with a gas-filled compartment creating an almost perfect combustion chamber, one pulled the starter cord. Of course the engine then sparked; it might backfire, and there was no spark arrester. Luckily, there were no explosions in the three months I kept the engine.

This engine was sold in England until recently, with the old-fashioned tickle carburetor, both as a main engine for small yachts and as the power source for an auxiliary generator. Though popular in England, it is not popular in the United States, because for at least fifteen years it has been illegal here to mount this type of engine belowdecks. The tickle carburetor is illegal, and a flame arrester has been required in all American engines for approximately twenty years.

While there is always some chance of an explosion with gasoline engines, because the fuel is highly volatile, the danger may be minimized by care and thought. The gas flow should be stopped as soon as the engine is secured. If the float sticks, the bilge soon fills with gasoline or gasoline fumes. This possibility can be eliminated by the installation of an electrically operated valve, such as the Fuel/Trol, made by Research Enterprises, which shuts off the fuel supply when the ignition is turned off.

On many boats, electric gasoline sniffers have been installed: an alarm bell rings if an explosive mixture is in the bilge. This device is excellent, but like any mechanical item, it may fail. One of my friends had an experience which only luckily did not end in tragedy. One Sunday morning, he decided the marina at San Juan was much too noisy, bought a newspaper, backed out of the slip, and anchored in the middle of the harbor. He then made himself a pot of coffee and relaxed with the paper. Later he decided to go back to the marina. Luckily he was sitting on the flying bridge.

He turned on his gas sniffer and no alarm bells rang, so he turned on the blowers, let them run for five minutes, then reached over and hit both starter buttons. There was a violent explosion, and suddenly he was flying through the air. He landed with a splash about fifty feet away, shaken, bruised, very sober, and slowly paddled around as his boat burned to the waterline. The moral of this story is—there is no gas detector like the human nose.

Before starting a gasoline engine, one should take a good sniff right near the blower; then if there is no odor of gas, it is safe to start the engine. Needless to say, one should not smoke while sniffing.

The second disadvantage of a gasoline engine is its unreliability. Given the three essentials,—gas, a spark, and compression,—a gasoline engine must run, provided it is correctly timed. But it is very easy for the carburetor to become clogged, for dampness to penetrate the electrical system, for the distributor to work loose and get out of time. One main cause of unreliability is infrequent use. A gasoline engine on a cruising yacht should be run, if not every day, certainly every other day. It will then probably function reliably year in, year out. But when the engine is allowed to sit for any period of time, it is likely to be difficult to start.

Another disadvantage of a gasoline engine is the lack of fuel economy. Gasoline is expensive to begin with, and the fuel consumption of the gasoline engine, power for power, is probably double that of the diesel. Fuel tanks in a gasoline-powered yacht must therefore be much larger than they would be in a diesel-powered vessel.

Furthermore, the small slow-turning diesel is often strictly a marine engine. Major overhauls can be made without removing it from the boat, as the crankcase is equipped with inspection ports. Some gasoline engines (usually slow-turning) are truly marine, but most small gasoline engines are high-rpm automotive conversions which must be removed from the boat when bearings, rods, or what-have-you are to be changed; only minor overhauls can be done with the engine in place.

The great advantages of the gasoline engine over the diesel are its light weight, its smoothness, and its horsepower-weight ratio. The last of these is especially pronounced in the smaller engine, hence the popularity of the Universal Atomic 4. This model is widely chosen as the light, 20-h.p. engine for fast, small racing sailboats, though I much prefer the Gray Sea Scout, which is slightly heavier, slower turning, and more reliable. The comments about weight, rpm, slow versus fast turning made about the diesel hold true for the gasoline engine as well.

From 40 h.p. up, the gasoline engines no longer have a weight advantage over the diesels. They are about equivalent in this respect except that for any given horsepower, diesels always seem to have more torque. Probably in the near future a similar equivalence will exist between small 10- and 20-h.p. diesels and gasoline engines, but at present, the latter still have a substantial weight advantage.

Petrol Paraffin

The petrol-paraffin engine starts on gasoline (petrol), and once running, can be switched over to kerosene (paraffin). The kerosene is vaporized by being preheated in the manifold. This type of engine, practically unknown in the United States, was popular in Europe in the 1920's and 1930's, but is seldom seen today, as it has all the disadvantages of both the gasoline engine and the diesel. It is prone to explosions, since it must be started with gasoline like a gasoline engine, and it is heavy, so it has the disadvantage of the diesel. It uses about as much fuel—and therefore requires as much tank space—as a gasoline engine, rather than a diesel. Some economy results from the fact that the fuel is cheap, but the amount of time the engine is run on a sailboat is so small that the saving does not warrant the expense and weight of this type of engine. I advise against it.

STARTING

Hand–Starting

A few of the slow-speed diesels, notably those in the smaller sizes—such as the Volvo Penta MD 1 and MD 2, and the Saab HS models—and almost all small gasoline engines, can be hand started. One need only open the compression release, get the flywheel turning over, and when it is really spinning hard, close the compression release, and off she goes. Larger engines, of three or four cylinders, are usually too heavy for hand starting, but there are exceptions: the big old Gardners, even up to six cylinders, can be hand started.

High-speed diesels must have some sort of mechanical starting device.

Electric Starters

Electric starters are standard; they work fine and give little difficulty. However, it must be remembered that when a diesel is started, the compression ratio is high, so the starter itself, and more important, the batteries, must be in good shape, to turn over the diesel against compression. It is absolutely necessary to have two separate batteries, one for starting, and one for the ship's equipment, and these should be so wired that the engine can be started off the starting battery, off the house battery, or off both, in parallel. Similarly, if worst comes to worst and both batteries are low, by means of jumpers they can be connected in series to double the voltage. So connected, even almost dead batteries will usually turn over the engine. Throwing double voltage onto a starting motor certainly does not do it any good, but if only done briefly, so that the starter does not heat up, it is an acceptable emergency starting procedure. As has been noted (Drawing 176), a switch can be installed to put batteries in series.

Dyna Start

The dyna start was popular for a number of years in Europe as an attachment for the small hand-starting engine. It was usually easy to add, since it was belted off the flywheel. Another advantage was that this piece of equipment acted as both a starter and a generator: essentially it was a generator, motorized so it could start the engine; once the engine was started it automatically switched to functioning as a generator. Since it was usually mounted high on the engine, it was out of the bilge and dampness. Its great disadvantage was that it only generated minimal amperage—6–8 amperes—and so was definitely inadequate if any amount of electrical equipment was installed.

Hydraulic Starting

There are many methods of hydraulic starting. Usually a hydraulic pump, operating off the engine, pumps hydraulic pressure into a hydraulic accumulator. This in turn supplies the power to the hydraulic starter. This system is expensive, but usually foolproof. If for some reason the engine does not start, and the accumulator runs down, hydraulic pressure can be built up with a hand pump, so that one can try again. On large engines, if the hydraulic starting system is ordered as original equipment, it costs little more than an electric starter.

Inertia Starters

Inertia starters are not too popular. Originally made to start aircraft engines, and available as surplus after World War II, they are now hard to come by, and they are not easily adapted to marine engines. Basically, the inertia starter consists of a gearbox and a small flywheel. The handle is rotated as fast as possible, the small flywheel spins at high speed, the clutch is engaged, and the engine is turned over. The device is fairly foolproof, as long as one's arm holds out; and one is not depending upon batteries. It has its advantages for cruising in out-of-the-way places.

Air Starting

Air starting is almost always used with the larger diesels, but seldom with the small ones, so it is not usually seen on the cruising yacht. Air starting is generally reliable, but if something goes wrong and the engine does not respond, once the air bottles become deflated, there is usually no hope of pumping them up, though occasionally one runs across a setup which can be pumped up by hand when necessary. The other disadvantage of air starting is that the number of times one can stop and start the engine is drastically limited, a serious handicap for a boat with direct-reversing diesels. The German E-boat skippers in World War II developed great skill at handling their craft in tight waters, because with their direct-reversing diesels, unless they got alongside the dock in three bells, they had to call for a tow. They had no margin for error.

Quick Start

What is referred to as "quick start" is actually just an aerosol can filled with ether. Since it is usually a great help in starting a recalcitrant diesel, it should be kept on board any diesel-powered boat. However, most diesels have their own cold-weather-starting device, and before using quick start on a particular engine, one should check on what type of device it has. If it is a glow plug that takes ten or fifteen seconds to warm up, quick start can be used. But if—as on the ever-popular Westerbeke—the cold-starting aid is a heating element in the air intake, *under no circumstances should quick start be used.* Many a person has tried—with the result being a hell of an explosion, and the loss of his moustache, his eyebrows, and most of his hair.

ENGINE MOUNTINGS

For years, engines have been firmly bolted to the engine beds, with everything carefully lined up, and where they have been well secured, they have produced relatively little vibration. However, now that boats have become lighter, in many cases the engine beds have insufficient mass, and vibration becomes a problem.

Many manufacturers now attempt to eliminate this difficulty by using flex mountings on their engines. These also require flex coupling. The idea is that though the engine may vibrate, the flex mountings will prevent the vibration from being transferred to the vessel. If the installation is correctly done, it does seem to accomplish its purpose. But even with flex mountings, the engine bed must be heavily constructed and well braced. All too often, bad bearings, excessive vibration, and misalignment can be traced to an inadequate engine bed.

Even with proper installation, when flex mountings are adopted, various problems arise from the vibration of the engine. One should make sure that flexible hose is used for the water intake from the sea cock, and for the fuel line, and most important, that there is a flexible connection between the engine and the exhaust pipe. For if rigid piping is used for any of these lines—and all to frequently it is—the day will come when the flange will break, the exhaust manifold will crack, the exhaust pipe will crack, or some other major catastrophe will occur. Indeed, if the engine is flex mounted, everything connected to it must also be flexibly mounted, so that the vibration is not transferred from the engine to other parts of the boat. Flex couplings arc available in various grades of flexibility. Some manufacturers provide extremely flexible mountings. These make it most difficult to attach the exhaust pipe and fuel and water lines in such a fashion that the great vibration of the engine does not cause them to fracture. Flex mountings should allow the engine to vibrate freely but not shake around to excess.

One cause of weakness in flex mountings is the flex coupling. This may fail because of age or more important, abuse—such as the wrapping of a dock line around the prop, an occurrence more common than most of us like to admit. It is advisable to carry spare flex coupling.

ENGINE COOLING

On small gasoline and diesel engines, there is usually a raw-water cooling system. On large diesels, cooling is almost always done with fresh water by means of a heat exchanger. In the past this was usually an outside keel cooler, extending along the outside of the hull so that the heat in the circulating fresh water would be dissipated into the sea. But anything outside the hull is prone to damage, and these keel coolers have gone into disrepute.

A heat exchanger is mounted on or near the engine, and seawater is circulated through the heat exchanger and then overside, while fresh water runs through a closed system from the hot engine through the heat exchanger and back to the engine. The result is much more efficient heat control and more uniform cooling; the engine is not subjected to cold water at one end and hot water at the other. Also, the fresh water is so much better for the engine block than salt water that it is well worthwhile on a large diesel to install fresh-water cooling for this reason.

One advantage of salt-water cooling is that if a bypass system is installed (Drawing 180), once the engine has been shut off, a small electric pump can be turned on which will pump seawater through the engine for fifteen to twenty minutes, cooling it down to water temperature

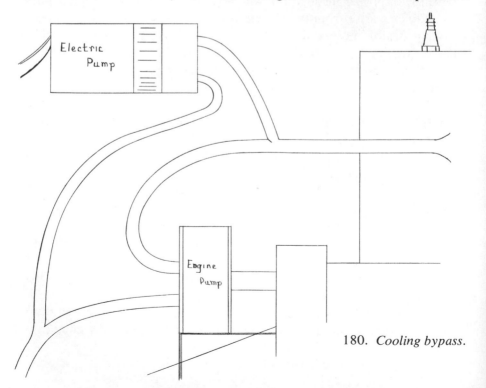

180. *Cooling bypass.*

in a matter of minutes rather than hours. On smaller boats with salt-water-cooled engines this installation is worthwhile, since in most cases on such boats the engine is located close to the living quarters. Once the engine is shut off, if water is not circulating, the temperature rises drastically, and the engine may take as much as twelve or eighteen hours to cool down. This warm engine may be acceptable in northern climates, but it makes belowdecks an oven in the tropics.

ENGINE MAINTENANCE

Engine maintenance is no better than the person who does it. Since one is not likely to have on board the type of skilled mechanic who knows the engine by heart and can recognize at a glance what is wrong, the manufacturer's service manual—not just the owner's manual, but the one published for the use of dealers, who may wish to rebuild the engine from scratch—should be kept on the boat at all times.

Before sailing, one should discuss with a mechanic who is familiar with the particular engine the list of spare parts to be carried. In addition to the parts normally recommended, one should always carry a spare set of bearings. Rod and main bearings are not excessively expensive, but if a bearing goes, it sometimes takes many weeks or months to obtain a replacement. If a set is carried on board, changing the bearings and getting the engine running again is relatively simple.

In general, before going to sea, one should visit the nearest discount house and buy the biggest tool kit one can afford. A boat seldom has too many tools, and any excess items can always be stowed low and used as ballast.

Whenever one buys a boat, or changes an engine installation, one should sit down with the mechanic, and using the tools in the ship's kit, do the normal jobs which the particular engine will require. This procedure has two purposes. It develops familiarity with the various operations of the engine, and it serves as a means of checking that the necessary tools are on board. One may discover that for one operation or another a special tool is needed—a particular extension wrench to remove the starter, a specially bent wrench to adjust the tension of the water pump. There is no use making this discovery two hundred miles away from the nearest hardware store.

ENGINE ROOMS

LOCATION

The location of the engine must be carefully considered. Most engine installations in yachts leave much to be desired.

With the advent of the fiber-glass boat, and the emphasis today on racing, designers place the engine in the depths of the bilge. Continually in the various yachting magazines one can read design-evaluation comments on how nice it is to have the engine well down below where the weight is doing the most good and giving the boat extra stability. But it must be remembered that according to both the Cruising Club of America rule and the new I.O.R. rule, stability is an important part of the rating formula. If an engine is placed in the depths of the bilge, and the boat gains stability, its rating goes up. Further, in the depths of the bilge, only a few gallons of water may put the engine out of commission. The reading of a few accounts of rough-weather ocean races will indicate how often boats do indeed lose their engines and/or all electrical equipment in these circumstances.

I remember once being on a boat, with the engine mounted in the bilge, which was leaking through a stuffing gland that we could not reach. We were very careful to pump the bilge every watch, to keep the water level down, but about the fourth night out, it began to blow, the leak increased, and we did not immediately realize what had happened. The bilge was pumped out at midnight. At 2:30 A.M., I lashed the helm and went below to wake my relief, discovered a good deal of water in the cabin floor, and lifted the engine-room hatch. All I could see was four spark plugs; the engine was completely under water!

Deep down in the bilge is not a good place for an engine in a racing boat, much less a cruising boat. An engine should be located so that the average person can get into the engine compartment without too much difficulty, change the oil filters, remove the carburetor and check the points on a gasoline engine, reach the fuel pump and injectors on a diesel engine, reach the water pump, adjust the belt tension for equipment belted off the engine, and most important, get to the starter. If these functions cannot be easily performed, the engine will suffer continually from lack of maintenance, and will therefore be unreliable.

The midship-cockpit boat has a wonderful location for the engine. It can be placed underneath the cockpit. There is easy access to both sides of the engine by way of the sail lockers, and an absolutely watertight hatch can be installed in the cockpit sole, so that if the engine ever needs to be removed, one can undo a dozen or so bolts, move the cockpit floor, and lift the engine out.

Furthermore, in a steel, aluminum, or fiber-glass boat, even one that is comparatively small, it is simple to put watertight bulkheads fore and aft of an engine which is under the cockpit. The boat is then divided into three watertight compartments. This arrangement increases the safety of the vessel, as in most cases if any single compartment is punctured, the engine, generators, and electrical system, in their own watertight compartment, will not be flooded. Another advantage of the installation of these watertight bulkheads is that the cubic content of the engine room is so reduced that an automatic fire-extinguishing system may be easily installed.

VENTILATION

One reason engines are not maintained as they should be is that the engine room is universally hot and stuffy. One method of making the engine room more bearable to the mechanic is to have a small electric fan, similar to the type used on cars, fitted on a clamp so that it can be put in an appropriate spot and plugged in to give the mechanic a good cool breeze. On a large cruising boat with a sit-down engine room which is likely to have generators, a workbench, and so on, such a fan is not enough, for the engine room should be one of the coolest places in the boat. Therefore, one or two ventilators should lead into the room; a good blower can operate whenever the generator or engine is run, without depleting the batteries, and can be run for half an hour or so after the engine is shut off, to cool the engine compartment.

If an exhaust blower is installed in the engine room, the intake of the exhaust blower should be directly over the hottest part of the engine. Whether hot air should be exhausted from the engine room and the cool air brought in by induction, or cool air blown in and the hot air exhausted through conduction and convection currents, seems to be unimportant. Both arrangements appear to work equally well.

A good big blower, belted directly off the engine, can do more than ventilate the engine room. It can pull cool air through the boat whenever the engine is being run. Also, without too much difficulty, ducting can be arranged so that in a northern climate the hot air from the engine room can be run through the boat, while by changing baffles, one can have air pulled from the various parts of the boat in hot weather and forced into the engine room. Cool air sucked through the entire boat by the engine blower will make the belowdecks area much more habitable in the tropics.

SHAFTS AND DRIVE SYSTEMS

For many years the location of the engine was drastically limited by the fact that it had to be connected directly to the propeller. But recently many new types of drives have come into use, so that now an engine can be mounted almost anywhere. Of course, if one can place the engine so that it drives the propeller through a four-foot shaft, and is still accessible for maintenance, one has by far the simplest, most reliable, and cheapest mounting of all. If such an arrangement is not feasible, various other methods of placing the engine in relation to the propeller must be considered.

In yachts built prior to World War II, the engine was frequently mounted in the forecastle, in the middle of the galley. As a result, a shaft of anywhere from thirty to fifty feet was required. The shaft of course had a number of universals, as keeping a shaft of this length lined up in a wooden boat which was continually changing shape was absolutely impossible. Some of these arrangements have lasted very well through the years, but there are difficulties.

V DRIVE

In other cases, in boats with the cockpit aft, the engine has been mounted with a V drive, which makes it possible to adjust the angle of the drive as desired (Drawing 181). This type of drive seems to work quite well, and has been frequently used in big high-speed powerboats, but it is expensive and difficult to align.

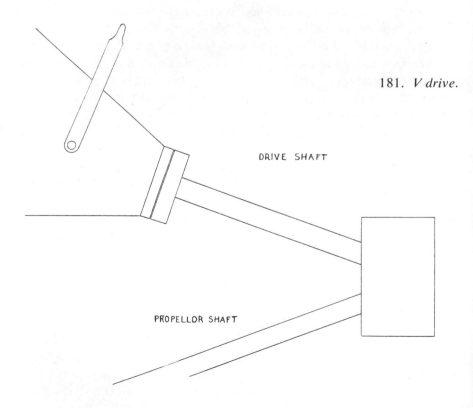

181. *V drive.*

DRIVE SHAFT

PROPELLOR SHAFT

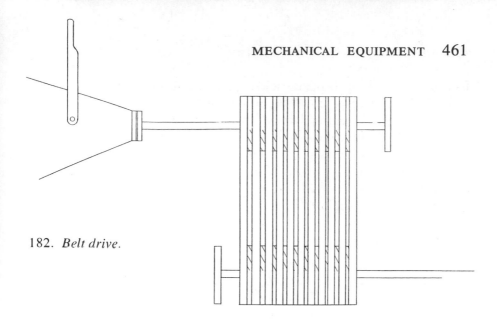

182. *Belt drive.*

BELT DRIVE

In still other cases, boats have belt drives (Drawing 182). This is a very old method; it was used in *Maruffa* back in the late 1930's. Since it is very difficult to transmit more than 5 h.p. per belt, this type of installation requires several belts, their number depending on the size of the engine. The great problem with belt drive is to maintain accurate tension on the belts. As the engine is run over a period of time, the belts stretch and therefore the distance between the engine pulley drive and the shaft drive must be adjusted. It is necessary to have the engine on adjustable mountings, so that it may be raised or lowered to regulate the tension, or to have an adjustable idler pulley on the side. Adjustable belting will also solve the problem. If the tension can be regulated easily, belt drive is an excellent system of propulsion, since there is no probelm of minor misalignment. However, if poor design or space limitations make tension adjustment difficult, there will be continual problems.

My own engine installation has been described as resembling squirrels in a squirrel cage, with six rubber bands to drive the shaft. Space prevented installing an idler, but the engine is out of the bilge and located where it is very easy to service. For belt-tension adjustment we have had to rely on link belting. The old type, with numerous short links clipped one to the other, was unsatisfactory because it stretched too much. The newest type of adjustable link belting, referred to simply as adjustable belting, has been more than adequate, and should be carried on all boats. It is bought in a continuous length, with holes every inch or so. Two metal plates held together with two screws secure the ends of the belt together. Thus, any time a belt is needed, a piece of this belting may be cut and installed, and the length can be adjusted if a mistake has been made (Photo 128). The new wire-cored heavy-duty belts have almost negligible stretch.

The disadvantage of belt drive is that a really good installation may cost as much as a good reduction gear. Hence belt drive is usually preferred only for specialized and odd-ball installations.

128. Adjustable belting and link. (West Products)

Geared Belt Drive

The newest thing in belt drive is the geared belt. This is not as strong and efficient as a chain drive, but it is strong and efficient. It can transfer much more horsepower than the older types of V-belt. In some applications, a number of belts are used in the same fashion as conventional V-belts, while in other applications the total horsepower is figured and a single belt—six, eight, twelve, sometimes as much as eighteen inches wide—is used. The installation must be correctly engineered, and a spare belt must be carried.

Like the conventional belt, this one should be easy to change, so that a broken belt will not mean a disabled vessel, and the tension should be readily adjustable.

HYDRAULIC DRIVE

The newest type of drive is the hydraulic drive. A hydraulic pump is mounted on the end of the engine in place of the gearbox, and a hydraulic motor is attached to the forward end of the propeller shaft. The whole unit is tied together by three hoses (Drawing 183). Some people swear by this system. It is popular on the brooks and rivers of England, and a few ocean racers have used it. This method of propulsion presents wonderfully intriguing possibilities. For one thing, the engine can be mounted all the way up in the forecastle if desired. Another advantage is that if correctly designed, the entire hydraulic unit can be pulled on board, either to minimize drag, or for overhauling. This was the arrangement on the Gurney-designed, light-displacement ocean racer

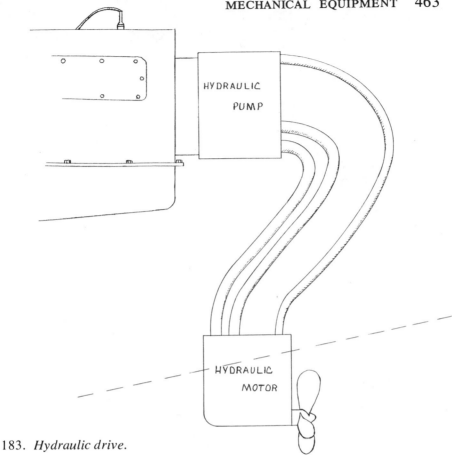

183. *Hydraulic drive.*

Windward Passage. She was powered by a 30-h.p. Westerbeke driving a hydraulic unit which was completely retractable (Drawing 184). With this arrangement, much power is lost to heat and friction, a significant disadvantage where horsepower is as low as 30, but larger units are now available, taking engines up to about 100 h.p. The latest news is that Volva Penta is actively selling three different sizes of hydraulic drive. If a large producer such as Volva Penta is promoting this type of drive, the bugs must have been eliminated.

FUEL

FUEL TANKS

Fuel tanks have been made out of many different materials. In the past, the tinned-copper gasoline tank was standard. As it got old, the

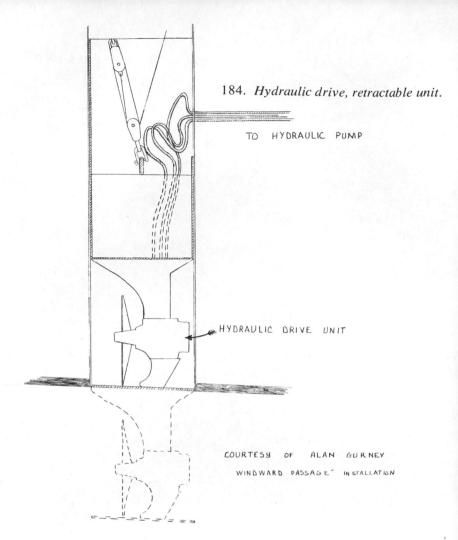

184. *Hydraulic drive, retractable unit.*

TO HYDRAULIC PUMP

HYDRAULIC DRIVE UNIT

COURTESY OF ALAN GURNEY
WINDWARD PASSAGE" INSTALLATION

tin came off, the gasoline broke down, became gummy, and caused great difficulties with the carburetors. Diesel tanks are frequently made of black iron, which seems to stand up very well with diesel fuel, but they must be kept as full as possible at all times to minimize oxidation on their inside walls. Such tanks should not be galvanized, since the zinc is dissolved by the diesel fuel, and contaminates both the tank and the fuel.

Iron gasoline tanks leave much to be desired, and should be avoided if possible. Tanks of stainless steel and of Monel are often used, but they are expensive, and these metals are very difficult to weld.

Fiber-glass fuel tanks have become increasingly popular, especially since the fire in Essex, Connecticut, in 1967. After the fire, just about nothing was left of the boats in the yard except for the fiber-glass tanks, their fuel intact. Fiber glass is usually very flammable, but it can be made fireproof, or almost so, by means of a suitable additive.

Integral Versus Conventional Tanks

Steel ships with double bottoms have for years relied on integral fuel tanks, and certainly there is much to be said for tanks of this type in boats built of aluminum or steel. Since these tanks can be welded across the deepest part of the bilge, the fuel can be kept down low, where it contributes appreciably to the stability of the boat, as long as the tanks are full or nearly full. Integral tanks must be very well baffled; otherwise as the boat rolls, the fuel sloshes from side to side, contributing nothing to stability and making noise. Further, as was pointed out in Chapter X, the center of gravity of a half-filled tank moves appreciably to leeward when the boat is heeled. Therefore, integral tanks should be divided fore and aft or athwartships into completely separate compartments. Then one compartment of the tank may be used while the remaining portions remain full and contribute to the vessel's stability.

With integral tanks a tremendous amount of fuel may be carried. On *Mariann,* a forty-two foot aluminum Sparkman and Stephens ocean racer, we carried 70 gallons of fuel below the cabin sole, which with 320 gallons in her water tanks gave her unbelievable stability.

Integral tanks should have good large manholes to facilitate periodic cleaning of the tanks.

In my view, fiber-glass boats should not be equipped with integral fuel tanks. Fiber-glass boats presumably do not leak, but all too frequently in such boats a tiny quantity of salt water seeps through the hull and into the integral tank. One cup of salt water in a hundred gallons of fresh water will have no effect, except to make the coffee a little better. But any water in the fuel will interfere with the engine's performance, perhaps bring it to a standstill. Therefore integral fuel tanks should be used only in steel or aluminum boats.

FUEL SYSTEMS

Probably no two mechanics agree on the correct design for a fuel system. The simplest fuel system consists of a line coming directly off the bottom of the tank, with, needless to say, an accessible shutoff at the bottom of the tank. This arrangement is less than perfect: if sludge gets into the tank, it comes out in the fuel line; if someone forgets to turn off the fuel on a gasoline engine, there is a possibility of flooding the carburetor. Most insurance companies much prefer the fuel to come from the top of the tank (Drawing 185), with the fuel line going down to within an inch or so of the bottom. This is a rather standard arrangement, but the tank itself is very difficult to clean unless it has a

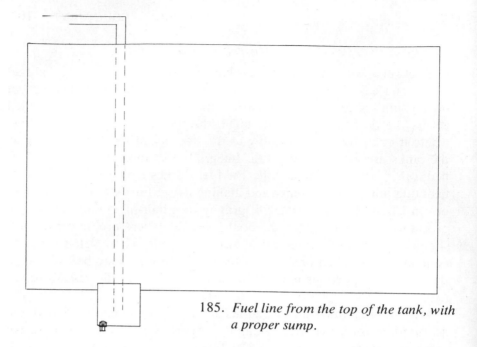

185. *Fuel line from the top of the tank, with a proper sump.*

sump, as shown in the sketch. If a fuel line from the bottom is acceptable, a good possibility is to have a sump in the center of the bottom of the tank, holding about a quart of fuel (Drawing 185). The sump is six inches deep, and the fuel-intake line extends up about four inches from its bottom. All the sludge settles in the sump, and it may then be removed in one of two ways. The bottom of the sump may be constructed as a plate, fastened in place with five or six machine screws, which can be removed when the tank is empty so that the entire sump can be cleared out. Or a one-inch pipe with a valve at the end can be inserted in the bottom of the sump; this can be opened and the sludge dumped into a coffee can and thrown overside.

Fuel tanks must be vented—and vented adequately. All too often vent pipes consist of ⅛-inch copper tubing bent over outside the cockpit coaming. Vents this size are so narrow that they are easily clogged. Also, they are much too small to facilitate rapid filling of the tank. Indeed, these small-diameter vents are actually hard on the tank, as pressure builds up during filling, causing a flexing effect that is harmful to welds, rivets, and so on. Much better are vents of ½-inch or ¾-inch plastic hose, brought up on deck as high as possible. Engineers claim that ideally the vent pipe should be 75 percent of the diameter of the fill pipe, but I have never seen tank vents this large on any yacht.

When the fuel-tank vent pipe emerges at deck level, salt water may work its way in, even if the vent is shielded. This happened in 1960 when we were taking *Iolaire* south. We left New York in a temperature of 25 degrees, with our fuel tank absolutely full. The next day the weather turned warm and the fuel expanded and came pouring out of the fuel-tank vent; that night, when the temperature dropped, the fuel evidently contracted and sucked into the tank the water sloshing around on deck, so of course the engine would not start. Not until we reached Bermuda did we discover·that we had two gallons of salt water mixed with twenty gallons of fuel.

To eliminate this problem, I ran my vent hose four feet up the mizzenmast. There has since been no difficulty of this sort.

Filtering

The greatest cause of trouble in both diesel and gasoline engines is bad fuel. In out-of-the-way areas most fuel is delivered in old rusty fifty-five gallon drums that may or may not have water in them, and almost certainly do contain rust and dirt. Hence the need for filtering. With a gasoline engine one should have a big funnel and a good filter, and in addition the fuel should always be filtered through a chamois. Furthermore, to guarantee completely clean fuel, one or more filters should be placed in the fuel line. The fuel filters themselves must be drained when necessary to remove accumulated water, and the filter elements must be changed as frequently as the manufacturer recommends.

With a diesel engine there are usually three filters in the line, as well as a filter on the engine. With this arrangement one gets clean fuel, and engine problems are minimized.

Some boats have a double fuel-filter system (Drawing 186). The feed line comes off the tank, then goes to a tee, which splits it into two sepa-

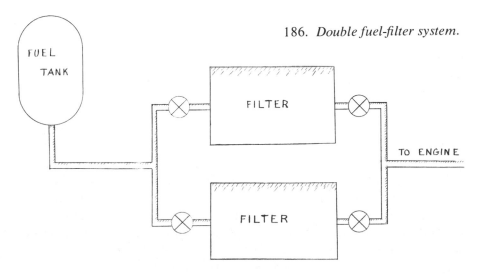

186. *Double fuel-filter system.*

rate lines, each with a shutoff valve and with several filters. Then the individual lines rejoin at another tee, to form a single line feeding the engine. Fuel for the engine normally runs through one of the two lines. If the filters being used get clogged and need cleaning, one need only shut off the valve on the line being used and open the valve on the other line. Since the clogged filters are disassembled and cleaned while the engine runs off fuel fed through the opposite set of filters, one does not have to turn off the engine and bleed the system every time the filters are being cleaned. This arrangement is particularly useful in heavy weather, when the sludge is stirred up in the tanks and is especially likely to clog the filters.

FUEL FILLING PUMPS

The fifty-five-gallon drums in which fuel is delivered in many remote areas weigh roughly four hundred pounds when full, so they are rather difficult to handle. Often they are brought out to the boat in a dinghy or small barge, and then unless the drum is held up in the air on the main halyard, it is impossible to siphon the fuel into the boat's tanks. For that reason, anyone intending to cruise seriously in out-of-the-way places should have his own transfer pump.

If gasoline is to be transferred, one can shop in the surplus stores for an old bronze wobble pump which will screw into the bunghole of the standard fifty-five-gallon drum. For diesel fuel, one can purchase a small 12-volt pump and mount it on a board with appropriate hoses and long wires to plug in to the ship's 12-volt system, and the pain will be taken out of fuel transferring.

PROPELLERS

TYPES OF PROPELLERS

Solid Propellers

The propeller most commonly found on yachts is the solid propeller (Photo 129). Indeed, until recently it was almost universally installed on American yachts.

The great disadvantage of the solid propeller is that it creates drag under sail. This effect is especially serious for the heavy cruising boat or motor sailer with a big three- or four-bladed propeller. Often a heavy cruising boat is repowered with a larger engine and propeller because she does not sail well and therefore reliance must be placed on motor power. The removal of weight from the after end of the keel, or the addition of ballast forward, or changes in stowing, may compensate

129. Center-line solid propeller. (Robberson)

for the added weight of the new engine, but with the bigger propeller, drag is inevitably increased, and the performance under sail falls off still more. It is notable that boats like *Creole,* Niarchos' fabulous big schooner, and the replica of *America* are not outstanding sailers: *Creole* is dragging two big solid wheels, and *America* is dragging one big four-bladed wheel; in effect, both of these yachts have big sea anchors.

Adjustable-Pitch Propellers

Propellers with adjustable pitch (Photo 130) are not a new development. The *Randihil,* a trading cutter from the west coast of Sweden which is still chartering out of St. Thomas, has a diesel engine and an adjustable-pitch propeller installed shortly after the turn of the century. The propeller works beautifully and the company that made it still exists and can supply parts. With such a propeller, efficiency is high under all conditions, not just one condition, because the engineer can alter the rpm and pitch as desired for a flat calm, a moderate sea, or heavy weather.

Furthermore, on some of these propellers, the blades can be turned straight fore and aft, for minimal drag under sail. When we delivered the Garden-designed forty-nine-foot ketch *Pixie* to the United States, we discovered that feathering the blades straight fore and aft increased our speed by almost a full knot, making her a full-power auxiliary, rather than a motor sailer.

130. Center-line adjustable pitch propeller. (Charles Booz)

The adjustable-pitch propeller is available in Europe in sizes varying from the smallest, for use with 5-h.p. one-lung diesels, through large ones suitable for harbor tugs. For some reason or other it is not popular in the United States. American yacht designers are not familiar with this type of propeller and seem to view it with suspicion, even though it seems clear that not only *America* but also many of the big modern motor sailers would really sail if they had adjustable-pitch propellers.

The adjustable-pitch propeller is expensive, but not as costly as it first appears, since it eliminates the need for a reduction gear, a complicated clutch, and a reverse gear. On the smaller sizes no clutch is needed; on the larger sizes a straight-dog clutch is sufficient. If the engine and the propeller are purchased as a package, the total cost is little different from that of an engine with a reduction gear and a reverse gear. If I were to repower, I would insist on an adjustable-pitch propeller.

Feathering Propellers

In the 1930's the Hyde self-feathering propeller (Photo 131) was very popular in the United States for use with an offset mounting. This propeller automatically feathers its blades when the engine is not running. Its disadvantage is that the hub is quite large, and occasionally the blades jam and will not reverse themselves. It is unnerving to approach a dock and discover that there is no reverse, though a good seaman should come slowly enough so that the boat can be stopped with the spring line alone. If every time the boat is hauled, the plugs in the hubs of the propeller are removed, and the gears are well flushed and repacked in grease, the chances of failure are minimized.

Folding Propellers

In the 1930's the folding propeller too was popular for use in off-center mounts. (Center-line mounting, as shown in Photo 132, became

131. Offset feathering propeller. (DeFontaine)

132. Center-line folding propeller. (D. M. Street)

possible somewhat later, when the rudder was removed from the back of the hull and set either independently or on a skeg.) A folding propeller cannot be placed in an aperture, as the blades will foul the rudder. The first folding propeller had clam-shaped blades held open by centrifugal force and water pressure when the engine was being run in the ahead position. In neutral, water pressure folded the blades; reverse did not exist. However, just after World War II the South Coast Company (which has since gone out of business) made a folding propeller that would work in reverse. The tips were heavily weighted, and if the engine was placed in reverse and revved up hard, centrifugal force would open the blades and hold them out against water pressure.

The disadvantage of the South Coast propeller was that the center hub was quite large. A few years ago, Martec and others eliminated this difficulty, developing a propeller with a small center hub, the bases of each propeller blade heavily weighted, and the pivot between the base and head. When the engine is revved up in either forward or reverse, the weights are swung at right angles to the shaft by centrifugal force. The result is a folding propeller that will operate in both directions and that has practically minimal resistance since it is only a little larger when folded than the diameter of the shaft.

PROPELLER SIZE

There is wide disagreement concerning what size propeller should be installed in a boat. When building a new boat, one can sit down with the designer, listen to his recommendations, and discuss the possibilities. Some guidance can also be obtained from engine manufacturers, who normally specify the type of propeller correct for various engines, and there are numerous rules for determining proper propeller size. However, some factors seem to be beyond the scope of any rule. The only sure way to find the correct propeller is to obtain not only the propeller which promises to be most suitable but also a few propellers slightly larger and slightly smaller, slightly more pitched and slightly less pitched. Then one should grease the shaft thoroughly, have a few spare keys made, in case one is dropped during propeller changes, and experiment with the different sizes. Once the model has been found that performs best under varying conditions, a new propeller of that size should be purchased.

Some propeller shops will lend an assortment of secondhand propellers for this type of experimentation. If this arrangement cannot be made, the alternative is to buy a group of secondhand propellers and sell them back to the dealer when they have served their purpose.

When an old vessel is being repowered, the amount of horsepower to be provided may be limited by the propeller size, which in many cases cannot be changed without drastic alterations of the boat. In more than one case the substitution of a 150-h.p. engine for a 50-h.p. engine in a large yacht has resulted in no increase in speed because the yacht had an offset propeller, so its diameter could not be increased. The bigger engine turned the propeller faster, but without any real gain in speed.

In determining engine and propeller size, one should consider the circumstances in which the engine is most likely to be used. The normal auxiliary engine is rated in terms of flat-calm power. On an average forty-footer, a Perkins, Westerbeke, or Mercedes-Benz 40-h.p. diesel, with a 2-to-1 reduction gear, can usually achieve 7½ knots in calm flat water. But when one is pushing into a head sea with an engine of this type, the small propeller normally accompanying it is not really effective. All it does is cavitate, and the boat slows down to three or four knots. In the Caribbean there is little use for the engine in flat calm, but it may be needed when it is blowing hard, the sea has built up, and everyone is tired and desires to motor sail to the nearest anchorage. With a 3-to-1 reduction gear, the standard diesel can turn a really large propeller; it will not give a great performance in a flat calm, but will give excellent performance in a seaway.

PROPELLER LOCATION

The standard installation, found on most yachts, consists of a two-bladed solid propeller mounted on the center line, in an aperture; the aperture is either in the deadwood forward of the rudder or partly in the deadwood and partly in the rudder (Drawing 187). This arrangement gives maximum performance under power, but leaves something to be desired under sail because it gives rise to a significant amount of drag. To reduce this effect, when the engine is shut off, the propeller should lock in the vertical position; if the shaft has been marked, the blades can easily be lined up behind the deadwood.

The aperture in itself also creates considerable drag. More than one boat has shown a dramatic change in performance when the engine was removed and the aperture plugged. It is therefore advisable to avoid mounting the propeller in an aperture, if possible. One alternative method of center-line mounting is to place the propeller above the rudder (Drawing 188). This method eliminates the aperture and makes possible the use of a folding propeller. However, the boat is then far

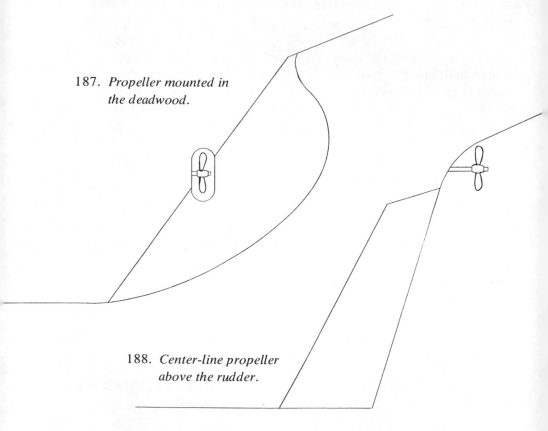

187. *Propeller mounted in the deadwood.*

188. *Center-line propeller above the rudder.*

less maneuverable under power than it would be with the aperture mounting. The recently introduced scimitar-shaped keel, with a separate rudder, makes possible the mounting of the propeller in an excellent position—directly aft of the keel and forward of the rudder. This arrangement gives maneuverability under power equal to that of the aperture mounting, but does away with the drag caused by the aperture. A two-bladed solid propeller lined up with the keel gives little drag, and a folding propeller gives practically no drag.

Off-Center Mounting

Before World War II, yacht designers almost universally preferred an off-center engine mounting with a feathering propeller. Fortunately, these mountings are seldom seen today. The drag of the hub of a feathering propeller is appreciable, and with the off-center wheel, many boats will turn in only one direction. If such a mounting is used, to counter the off-center propeller effect, one should be sure to install a right-hand-rotating engine to port, and a left-hand rotating engine to starboard. If the boat should be subsequently repowered with an engine rotating the opposite way, a real problem is at hand. *Iolaire* originally had a left-hand-rotating engine mounted on the starboard side; this was replaced by a right-hand-rotating engine in the same place. The result is that she will pivot sharply to port, but turning her to starboard is almost an impossibility; it can be accomplished only by revving up until the boat picks up speed, then putting it into neutral, and putting over the helm.

WINDMILLING

Innumerable articles have been written to prove that the propeller should, or should not, be permitted to turn when a boat is under sail. In my experience, a boat traveling at hull speed will slow down as much as a knot when the propeller is allowed to windmill. One explanation for this effect is that as the propeller spins, it pulls up a ball of water, and hence the drag is that of a solid sphere the diameter of the propeller. If the propeller is fixed, there is only the drag of the area of the propeller, plus of course the turbulence that it creates. Therefore, even if a propeller cannot be lined up behind the keel (because it has more than two blades, or is mounted off center), it should be kept in a fixed position when the boat is under sail.

On boats with hydraulic gearboxes, windmilling creates an additional problem: most of the manufacturers do not recommend allowing the hydraulic gearbox to turn free, since it receives no lubrication when the engine is not running. On one boat this difficulty was met with a small hydraulic pump belted off the shaft, so that when it did windmill, hydraulic fluid was pumped through the gearbox, keeping it lubricated.

Shaft Brakes

Because the amount of drag on a spinning propeller is considerable, it is preferable, in my view, to construct for any installation with a hydraulic gearbox a really good brake that is easily operated and is effective in stopping the propeller from spinning. One of the best I have seen was designed by Cis Roper of California and installed on *Caroline*. Basically it is an automotive hand brake with a hydraulic pump, which may be pumped up to clamp the brake tight on the shaft. When the engine is to be run, the pressure is released and the shaft is allowed to turn freely before the engine is started (Drawing 189).

On many a boat, the brake on the engine has been ruined when the engine was started while the brake was on. The simplest and most effective method to prevent this occurrence was devised by Olle, of *Djinn*. He always placed an old glove over the throttle control immediately upon stopping the engine and clamping the shaft, and never started the engine without first releasing the brake and removing the glove.

The shaft lock devised by Cis Roper is not commercially available, but from Hobco Marine Systems can be obtained a hydraulic shaft lock that is directly connected to the engine. This is so devised that the

189. *Cis Roper's shaft brake; the drum may be mounted anywhere on the shaft, and the brake may be mounted on any place convenient to the drum.*

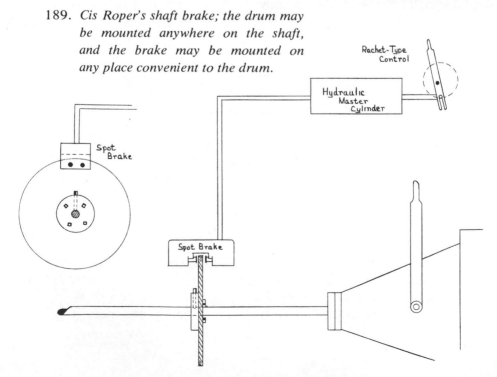

clutch cannot be engaged while the lock is on. Hydraulic pressure created by starting the engine opens the lock automatically. When the engine is turned off, a reduction in hydraulic pressure causes the lock to close.

SINGLE-SCREW VERSUS TWIN-SCREW INSTALLATIONS

On the smaller vessel, of thirty to thirty-five feet, especially in view of the difficulty of obtaining a small diesel, the single-screw installation is ideal. However, on boats of fifty-five feet or more, it leaves something to be desired. The engine is very big and hard to handle. It is difficult to get in and out of the boat unless special hatches have been built and special arrangements made. Further, a large engine is usually fairly long.

A single 100-h.p. engine is likely to be a big lump of iron about six feet long. Two 50-h.p. engines require only about four feet of engine-room space. Together, they may be wider than the single large engine, but the engine room usually takes up the width of the boat in any case, whether occupied by one engine or two.

Two engines, driving adjustable-pitch propellers, can yield the ultimate in efficiency. Maneuverability too is greatly increased. When motor sailing, the lee engine only can be used. When powering in a flat calm, and fuel economy is desirable, one engine can be used, but when powering into a head sea, the pitch can be adjusted and both engines put on the line. For maximum flexibility, the right-hand-rotating engine should be to port and the left-hand to starboard; otherwise maneuvering under a single screw will be very difficult; for example, if the right-hand engine is to starboard, the boat will try hard to go into a left-hand circle when operating under the starboard engine only.

A 50-h.p. engine is relatively light and in the event of a breakdown can be removed from the vessel and put on the dock by the ship's crew, using the ship's gear. Further, only one complete set of spare parts need be carried, for both engines. If in an out-of-the-way spot both engines should break down, by utilizing the usable parts from each, one should be able to get one operating engine.

A twin-engine installation also adds flexibility to the use of auxiliary equipment. A jackshaft can be put in the forward end of each engine to take a belt drive to another shaft, at the center. It is inefficient to run a 100-h.p. engine just to charge batteries, and run the bilge pump, the refrigeration, and so on. A diesel should not be run in a no-load condition. However, when a small 40- or 50-h.p. engine is used to charge batteries and the rest, it uses up a fair amount of its power and it runs at least under a small load. If the jackshafts are correctly set up, the engines are still available for propulsion, and when full power is desired the jackshafts may be disconnected and full power put on the propeller shafts.

A twin-engine installation does require two gearboxes, two shafts, two propellers, but they are much smaller units, and much more easily serviced than those for a single engine of equivalent horsepower. The expense is certainly greater, but the added reliability and maneuverability, and the saving in space, make the twin-engine installation worth considering for a new boat. In addition, the drag of twin engines and two small, adjustable-pitch propellers is less than that of one engine at the center, with the propeller in an aperture.

A number of skippers do not like the twin-screw installation because a sailboat has only a single rudder and the propellers are quite close together, giving insufficient twisting action. For example, they feel that one cannot go ahead on starboard, then go back on port and twist to port, especially if the wind is from the port side. Some thought should be given to accompanying a twin-screw installation with twin offset rudders. Since these could be angled out, with placement similar to the toe-out angle of twin keels, they might function with a total area smaller than that of the single individual rudder, and provide the desired twisting action. To be sure, sailboats for centuries have had a single on-center rudder, but that is no reason for the designer not to try other ideas in future tank testing.

CLEANING THE PROPELLER

Frequently when a boat has been sitting in the tropics for a few weeks or months the propeller will become very badly fouled with marine growth. When the engine is put into gear, it will smoke like mad but be unable to rev up, and the boat will move only slowly, or not at all. To keep the propeller clean even when the rest of the bottom gets foul, one should put on a face mask and snorkel and go down and scrub it. One of my sport-fishing friends, when he hauls his boat, always removes the propellers, polishes them, warms them with a blowtorch, and rubs hot wax into them. At full throttle these polished propellers give 200 rpm more than the normal clean propellers. If there is this difference between the loading on polished and on clean propellers, one can imagine the decrease in efficiency in a dirty or really fouled propeller.

EXHAUST SYSTEMS

In the past, almost universally the exhaust has been fed into the muffler through a dry line wrapped with asbestos tape to keep it from burning the woodwork; then the exhaust pipe is run aft all the way to the stern. This is usually a copper pipe with two jackets, the outer for cooling water, the inner for the exhaust gases; it is most difficult and expensive to make. When sailing downwind in heavy weather, one must close the valve in the stern to prevent the sea from driving up the exhaust pipe, and flooding the engine.

This type of exhaust pipe has other serious disadvantages as well. Once it becomes old, the inner jacket usually leaks, allowing the cooling water to run into the exhaust pipe proper and down into the engine. Today this problem is more serious than ever. For some strange reason, builders insist on using copper pipe even with diesel engines. The diesel exhaust is full of sulfuric acid, which eats through copper rapidly, soon leaving holes which result in flooding.

With a diesel, galvanized-iron pipe should be used for the exhaust system. It is cheap, and more acid-resistant than the copper pipe. Of course, galvanized-iron pipe cannot be as readily bent around corners as can the softer copper pipe, but in most applications the long twisting and turning around cockpit and stern can be avoided cheaply.

Another disadvantage of the traditional exhaust system is that if an exhaust pipe is longer than twelve feet, back pressure builds up and drastically reduces the efficiency of the engine. Also, difficulties may arise if the exhaust pipe is rigidly attached to both the hull of the boat and the engine. Even an engine bolted directly to a heavy bed, without a flex mounting, will have some vibration. If there is no flexibility in the exhaust-pipe mounting, sooner or later the pipe or the exhaust manifold will fatigue and fracture.

STANDPIPES

In my view, one of the simplest and most efficient exhaust systems is made with a standpipe coming directly off the forward or after end of the exhaust manifold (Drawing 190). It should be noted that the hot spot is only an inch or so long. Water, introduced through the top of the standpipe, fills the pipe, and cools and mixes with the exhaust gases, which are then brought overside by means of a steam hose. If the engine is mounted well forward of the stern, alternative outlets for the exhaust can be installed port and starboard, so that one can always use the lee exhaust, and avoid having fumes and water splashing on board over the windward side. If outlets on both sides are not practical, the exhaust gases can be released on one side close to the waterline, where there should be relatively little trouble with their flowing back on board. Since the head of the standpipe is brought up to the deck level, and is either amidships or close to amidships, the standpipe cannot fill up and flood the engine. A gate valve is needed on the through-hull fitting only for use in case the exhaust pipe should fail.

This type of exhaust pipe can be made in any good welding shop in a matter of hours. If eventually the inner jacket does corrode through, replacement of the whole unit is very simple, and does not require a major yard operation. If desired, this same system can be used to exhaust out the stern, since the discharge from the standpipe is a steam hose, which can be bent around corners and go all the way aft. With this arrangement, the chance of the standpipe being flooded is still slight, but it does exist, so the standpipe should have a shutoff to be used in heavy weather.

AQUALIFTS

The Aqualift, now used on generators made by Onan, and also available as a separate unit, is a combination muffler and exhaust sys-

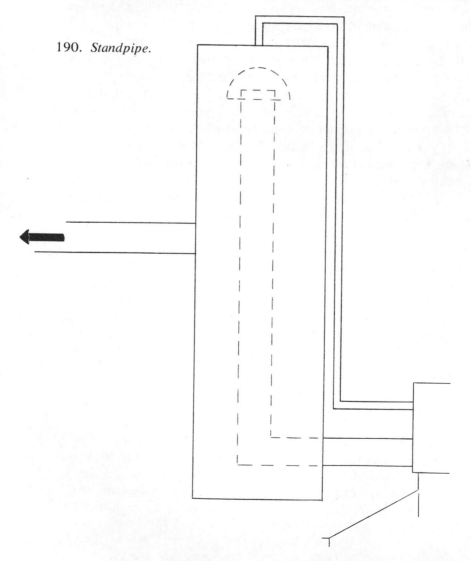

190. *Standpipe.*

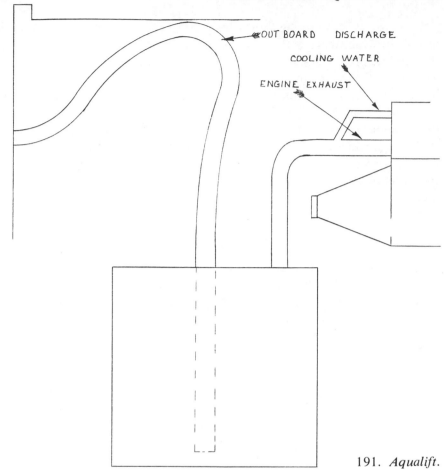

OUT BOARD DISCHARGE

COOLING WATER

ENGINE EXHAUST

191. *Aqualift.*

tem. It is nothing more really than a big tin can with a steam hose coming from the engine to the top of the can, bringing in a combination of water and exhaust gases. A pipe ending four inches above the bottom of the can comes to the top of the can and is connected to an exhaust pipe, which again can be a steam hose (Drawing 191). The Aqualift is mounted slightly lower than the exhaust pipe of the engine. Immediately after the exhaust gases come out of the exhaust manifold, water is added to them, cooling them enough so that the steam hose can carry them to the Aqualift. As pressure builds up inside the Aqualift, the mixed exhaust and water is forced into the second steam hose and blown out through the hull. An Aqualift will lift this mixture as much as four feet; indeed, it can raise it even higher, but at the expense of engine efficiency.

If the steam hose to the hull is looped against the deckhead as shown in the drawing, there is little chance of water backing up and flooding the engine. Again, a gate valve should be installed for emergency use. The Aqualift is made in one size—twelve inches high and twelve inches in diameter—which will handle anything up to a four-cylinder 107 Perkins or Mercedes diesel engine. For larger engines one can have this type of system made to order at the nearest sheet-metal shop. Before such a homemade unit is installed, the interior should be cleaned and coated with epoxy paint. This can be done by pouring the paint into the Aqualift, rolling it around, and shaking it until the surface is covered.

The large cubic content of the Aqualift in comparison to the diameter of the exhaust pipe gives a very quiet engine exhaust, making it ideal for use with generators, especially the rubber-mounted generators, which tend to dance around in a circle, thereby fracturing their stainless-steel exhaust pipes over a period of three or four months. Being rubber, steam hose will take infinitely more flexing than even the most flexible metal exhaust pipes.

DRY EXHAUSTS

Dry exhausts are occasionally found, especially on boats with two-cycle engines, or with air-cooled engines. Shrimpers and other commercial boats operating with General Motors two-cycle diesels, which lose efficiency as a result of back pressure, love dry exhausts. On board a cruising yacht, a dry exhaust is an absolute abomination, not only hot but noisy.

DRIP PANS

At one time, oil drip pans were seldom used, and through the years the entire bilge became smelly with crankcase oil, gearbox oil, and so on. When building a new boat, repowering an old boat, or having the engine lifted out for overhaul, one should install a good drip pan. Traditionally, these have been made of copper and secured to the engine bed. The simplest of the older type is merely a flat pan in which drippings from the engine collect. Periodically, with the aid of old rags, paper towels, or what-have-you, the pan is scrubbed clean. This sort of pan is always a bother at sea; when the boat is heeled well over, the contents of the pan overflows into the bilge. One can improve this type of pan by cutting out a hole in it of the proper size so that a can may be soldered into place, forming a small sump (Drawing 192). A small plastic dinghy pump can be kept stored by the engine. Periodically, the

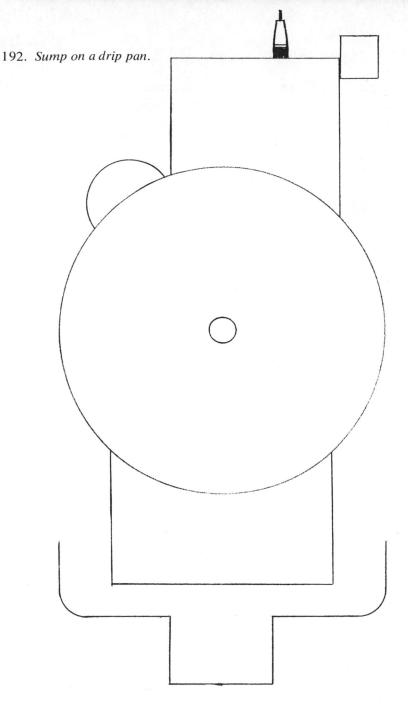

192. *Sump on a drip pan.*

dinghy pump can be placed in the sump, and oil, crud, and corruption pumped out.

The sides of the drip pan should be at least six inches high, so that when the boat is heeled over in heavy weather, the oil will not splash over into the bilge. To keep the pan itself clean, one can occasionally dump diesel fuel into it, allow it to splash around, and pump it out. On boats that have a wine-glass section under the engine, often a one-inch stopcock can be put into the side or the bottom of the drip pan (Drawing 193). Then to clean the pan one need only hold a coffee can under

193. *Drain cock on a drip pan.*

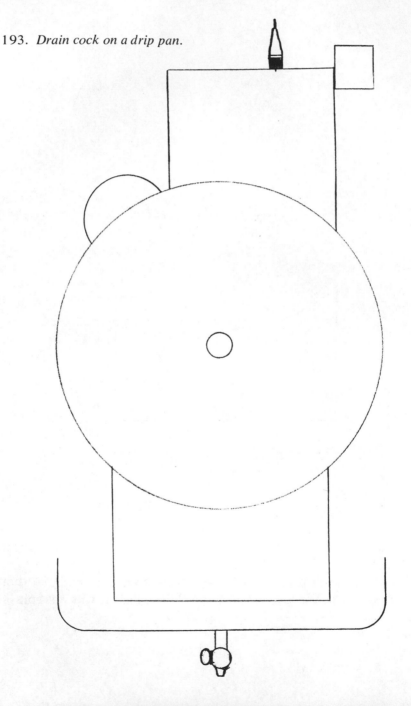

it, open a valve, and drain it. Another advantage of this arrangement is that it makes changing the oil very simple, requiring only that one run the engine, let the oil warm up, and pull a drain plug at the bottom so that everything drains out. Good engine maintenance is easy if the oil is easily changed, for then it will be changed as frequently as necessary. Also, if the oil is drained from the bottom of the engine instead of being pumped out, all the heavy dirt that settled to the bottom of the engine will also be removed.

ENGINE CONTROLS

Engine controls vary from the most simple to the most complicated. When an engine was installed in *Iolaire* it had a most reliable set of controls. The throttle was held closed by a rubber band secured to a tack in the engine mount; to open it, one pulled on a piece of string secured to two other tacks, which acted as a cleat. The gear-shift lever was operated by a member of the crew stationed in the companionway hatch and responding to hand signals: one finger held in the air meant "ahead," two fingers meant "neutral," three fingers meant "reverse."

DIRECT MECHANICAL LINKAGE

Direct mechanical linkage is by far the best method of engine control. However, one must be careful not to store anything where it can fall and jam either the throttle or the clutch. More than one boat has suffered a badly bent pulpit after canned goods fell down and jammed the gear lever in the "ahead" position. If throttle and choke controls are run through Boden cable, the appropriate type must be chosen. In particular, the old-fashioned Boden brass casing, with brass wire inside, must be avoided, as it is bound to freeze up sooner or later. Much to be preferred is the outboard-motor-control casing of hard plastic, over stainless-steel wire. Oiled frequently, it should work almost forever.

The one disadvantage of direct mechanical linkage is that it is very difficult to install unless the engine is relatively close to the helm.

VACUUM GEARBOXES

Not often seen today, vacuum gearboxes worked off the vacuum side of the exhaust manifold. They usually worked very well, and were especially suitable for boats with the engine mounted at a distance from the helm, but what failures they had invariably occurred at the worst time—when the boat was coming in alongside the deck. Despite its advantages, this system should be viewed with suspicion.

MORSE SINGLE-LEVER CONTROLS

The Morse controls are very well made, and are obtainable in many different varieties. Though usually used only with hydraulic gearboxes, they can be adapted to mechanical gearboxes.

HYDRAULIC CONTROLS

Hydraulic controls are not seen very frequently. They can be good, but are expensive, and seem to be unreliable if not constantly used.

GAUGES

The engine manufacturers usually provide a set of gauges showing rpm, temperature, oil pressure, and battery charge or discharge in amperes. These should be mounted, if at all possible, where visible to the helmsman, and every helmsman should remember the importance of continually looking at the gauges. However, this is easier said than done. Almost every experienced yachtsman has at some time suddenly discovered that the engine was overheating, oil pressure was low, or the battery was not charging, and has wondered if the difficulty began one minute ago or twenty. I had one such experience when the oil line to the pressure gauge broke. How long it had been broken was unknown; there was still a quart of oil in the engine, but there were three quarts all over the engine room.

Since at one time or another we all do forget to watch the gauges, an oil-pressure and temperature alarm should be connected to the engine. As soon as the engine overheats, or oil pressure drops below the safety level, the alarm goes off and appropriate action can be taken. Oil-pressure gauges should be connected to the engine by flexible rubber hose; rigid tubing tends to fracture because of the fatigue caused by engine vibration.

XV

Refrigeration

By Jon Repke, with comments by Donald M. Street,
literary critic and devil's advocate.

Any yacht doing extensive cruising must have some method of keeping
things cool. The days of the cruising yachtsmen who existed on salt
beef, rice, and warm beer, have thankfully departed. Those brave souls
merely existed, they did not live. To be sure, some people today eat
canned goods throughout a voyage. But the result is a diet which is not
only very boring but also expensive and not very healthful. Many
world cruisers complain of cuts and bruises that do not heal, and of de-
clining health. These problems appear to be the result of a steady diet
of canned food. Because of the monotony of this diet, there is danger,
especially in the tropics, of eating too little. Furthermore, canned food
is low in vitamins. Some fresh food, which must be kept cool, is essential.

It has been claimed that in such areas as northern Europe and Nova
Scotia, the water is cold enough for food to keep adequately without
refrigeration. However, even in these areas, meat will tend to go bad in
a warm summer, such as England had in 1969. And whenever one
cruises southward in the Northern Hemisphere, one eventually reaches
an area where refrigeration of some sort is necessary. Cooling may be
accomplished by a number of methods: the old-fashioned icebox, mechanical refrigeration, or heat refrigeration. In making a choice, one
should consider one's particular plans and needs, the mechanical capability of the boat, and one's financial capability; the important thing is
to come to a decision carefully, and do it right the first time.

The latest magic words have been "holding plates." Many an individual has an indistinct notion that any unused locker or storage place

fitted with holding plates will suddenly turn into a magnificent freezer or refrigerator. After such a person has spent a lot of money and time on some do-it-yourself refrigeration kit, advertised as maintaining 0 degrees on just a few minutes of power a day, he may discover that he is refrigerating at the expense of four or five hours a day of engine or generator operation. He likes to sail, but because he is now saddled with a badly designed and badly insulated installation, he suddenly finds himself in effect the operator of a full-time motorboat not a sailing yacht. Situations such as this can be avoided by proper planning.

Living in the tropics, where throughout the year the temperature reaches 80 or 90 degrees by day and 75 degrees at night, and being primarily in the business of marine refrigeration, Jon Repke sees an ever-expanding collection of so-called marine refrigeration units. Some of these units get by passably well in the northern latitudes, but when they reach the Caribbean, suddenly they do not work as they did in Maine, and Repke is usually the first to be called.

Here follows Jon Repke's analysis of the cooling problem, with suggestions that will meet many needs and inclinations.—D.S.

REFRIGERATION METHODS

Since we must "keep our cool," we come to the most important question of all. How are we going to get the cooling effect? Perhaps ice seems to be the most logical answer, but it may not always be practical, for ice is difficult to obtain in some tropical areas.

HEAT REFRIGERATION

Kerosene and gas refrigerators for use on boats are available. Frequently they work satisfactorily in the northern climates, but in the tropics, where the air temperature is in the 80's, and the heat in an enclosed space (even well vented) will probably reach 100 to 120, heat refrigeration is inefficient. It may cool the food, but the likelihood of ice being produced is minimal.

Furthermore, though an installation of this type may work in port if it is well vented—and it must be vented outboard or it will heat the interior of the boat—once one goes to sea and the boat heels over and starts rocking back and forth, causing the flame to rise and fall, this kind of refrigerator frequently will not work at all. Some boat owners have managed to overcome this difficulty. On one boat the gas refrigerator has been mounted on gimbals, and it appears to run satisfactorily, although it uses a large amount of bottled gas. On another boat, the fuel tanks of a kerosene refrigerator have been filled with nylon scouring pads. These decrease the fuel capacity of the tank by only about 30 percent, and provide a perfect baffle which prevents the flame from going up and down as the boat rolls. The owner claims that the refrigerator works well, providing as much ice as is needed. However, I am doubtful, since I have owned a kerosene refrigerator ashore, and it produces very little ice. A further disadvantage is that it must be cleaned out once a week.

Another disadvantage of both gas and kerosene refrigerators is that there is an untended flame belowdecks. It is true that the gas refrigerator is equipped with a heat switch which turns off the gas automatically if the flame goes out. However, if gas from another source—a leaking burner from the gas stove, improperly stowed paint thinner, gasoline vapors, or anything of that type—should reach the flame, which is located low in the refrigerator—no more boat. I know of two instances where this happened. Both times, luckily, no one was hurt. In one case, the crew was ashore; in the second, the crew was having early-morning coffee in the cockpit when the forecastle blew off.

MECHANICAL REFRIGERATION

Mechanical refrigeration is perhaps the most practical method. The system basically consists of a compressor which is driven either by an electric motor or by a V-belt directly coupled to the main engine or to a small auxiliary generator. The energy is stored either in batteries or in holding plates.

Battery Refrigeration

With the battery system, the energy is produced by a generator, alternator, or battery charger, and stored in batteries until cooling is required. Then the batteries release the power to turn the compressor and cool the box by means of an evaporator and cooling coils, as found in a normal household refrigerator.

The advantages of the battery-driven unit are its low initial cost, ease of installation, and the fact that it is the type of refrigeration with which most repairmen are familiar. But there are a number of disadvantages. In this type of box, it is difficult to prevent the water in the icetrays from spilling as the boat heels over. The batteries are expensive and must be replaced every two to four years, and on boats under forty feet there is rarely sufficient battery capacity to maintain refrigeration in the tropics. Also, the long chain of components—generator, battery, motor, compressor—means there are many possibilities for failure.

In the tropics, even in a good installation, the compressor will probably run fifteen minutes of each hour. If the 12-volt ¼ -h.p. compressor motor draws 26 amps, that means a total of 156 ampere hours per day for refrigeration alone. If to this are added another 40 ampere hours for lights, fans, blowers, and the like, the total is 196 ampere hours. Even a 50-amp alternator will produce 50 amps only when the batteries are dead flat. The charge tapers off as the batteries build up. At the end of a few hours, the alternator is putting out only 10 or so amps. Thus, to produce 196 usable ampere hours in a day, a boat will need massive batteries to absorb large amperage from the alternator. Depending on the size of the batteries and the size of the alternator, the engine is going to have to run anywhere from three to six hours a day to keep the refrigeration working efficiently.

Holding Plates

With holding plates the energy is stored as ice, formed inside the plates during the period of power application. Then, when the engine is not operating, the ice melts. In doing so, it absorbs heat, cooling the box.

Holding-plate units have several advantages. If properly designed, they generally require very short operating periods. There is plenty of extra capacity to make ice or cool down food as necessary. Holding plates occupy a relatively small space, and a holding-plate system will produce better than double the effect obtainable with batteries of the same weight. Also, holding plates are good almost indefinitely.

Most people think these units somehow provide "something for nothing." But they have to be cooled before they will do any cooling. The holding plate consists of a steel tank filled with a solution of calcium chloride, water, and a little alcohol. Through this liquid runs a pipe which carries the refrigerant. While the plant is in operation, the refrigerant freezes the solution. During the "off" part of the cycle the ice that has been formed melts, and in doing so absorbs heat. The temperature maintained by the plate at this time depends on the amount of calcium chloride in the solution inside. If the plate were filled with pure water, it would maintain a temperature of 32 degrees, which would result in a box temperature of about 50 degrees (the exact figure depends on the plate size, box insulation, and a few other factors). For a refrigerator, the plate is set to maintain about 24 degrees, while for a freezer it is set to maintain about 10 degrees.

In any case, the change of the state of the water is what produces the refrigeration effect. When a one-pound piece of ice at 32 degrees is melted, becoming a pound of water at 32 degrees, it absorbs 144 BTU. The same 144 BTU would be required to warm a one-pound piece of ice from -112 degrees to 32 degrees, but not melt it. Clearly, it is much easier to obtain refrigeration by forming ice and then allowing it to melt than by lowering the temperature of ice to -112 and then permitting it to rise to 32. The same principle explains the relative inadequacy of pure ethylene glycol, which is sometimes used to fill holding plates. The specific heat of ethylene glycol is .602, and since it does not change state when cooled, it is only $\frac{1}{300}$ as effective as melting ice.

Other factors also enter into the design of the holding plates, such as the diameter of the internal pipe, and the effect on the heat transfer of the velocity of the refrigerant. Most plates are made for a pull down or freezing in the neighborhood of eight hours. One supplier whose plates effect the pull down in the shortest possible time is the Carlsen Kolevognsfabrik in Denmark. The more quickly all the solution in the plate is frozen, the more efficient will be the system.

Compressors

BELT-DRIVEN OFF THE MAIN ENGINE: These units are quite cheap but have certain disadvantages. For one thing, they have built-in possibilities for trouble—such as failure of the crankshaft seal. Also, while the boat is at the dock, the engine must be run every day to keep the box cool, and this running of the engine is likely to make one unpopular with the neighbors. The alternative is to connect the unit to an electric motor, and to do this one must either use an over-running clutch, or change belts.

BELT-DRIVEN WITH ELECTRIC MOTOR ATTACHED: Some units can be belt-driven off the main engine from one end or connected to an electric motor from the other. This arrangement eliminates belt changing, but the shaft seal, the main source of trouble, still remains. The unit does have the advantage that one can plug in at dockside to run the 110-volt motor to cool the box.

BELT-DRIVEN FROM ELECTRIC MOTOR: Some holding-plate systems driven by an electric motor are set up so that they will operate only when the main engine is running. If the battery system is large enough, a refrigeration system can be allowed to run directly from the batteries, which must then be recharged from the main engine when it is operating. But with a holding-plate deep-freeze system, it is usually necessary to operate the electric motor when the engine is running and to keep the batteries fully charged. On the holding-plate unit, the compressor is of such a size that the electric motor would run the batteries down if allowed to pull directly from the batteries, rather than from the alternator or generator.

SEALED UNITS: The best type of system is the sealed unit, similar to the one used in a household freezer, in which a compressor and an electric motor are coupled together and sealed inside a steel cylinder. The advantage of such a system is that it has no brushes, no belts, no crankshaft seal to cause trouble. However, it must be run by alternating current, which cannot be stored in batteries. Therefore, one must have an auxiliary generator. Onan produces all sizes and types of marine generators, for both gas and diesel engines. It is possible to belt a 110-volt AC generator off the main engine and run the engine at a constant speed, but the engine speed must be carefully monitored to keep output within fixed limits. For this purpose, relays can be used which will disconnect the generator if the voltage goes above or below certain limits. A system of this type is manufactured by Onan. Or a variable-speed clutch can be used, as noted in Chapter XIII.

When reliability is of prime importance (there aren't many refrigeration experts in the South Pacific), the very best arrangement consists of two hermetically sealed compressors, cooling their own holding plates in the box, and actually constituting two entirely separate systems. Then should either system fail, which is very unlikely, one could carry on with the other unit, though it might have to run for twice the normal length of time.

This setup has only two drawbacks. It is expensive, and it is not too satisfactory for boats of less than thirty-five feet because an AC generator is necessary.

COMPRESSOR SIZE: There is no hard and fast rule regarding the size of a compressor unit. So much depends on how well the box is made, insulated, and kept up. However, a ¼-h.p. motor and a compressor of ¼ ton or less will take care of any well-designed box on a boat of up to fifty feet. If a unit runs more than 25 percent of the time on a normal summer day, it is getting near the border line, and probably will not be able to keep the box cold when the weather gets really hot. In this situation, a larger compressor should be installed.

With a holding-plate system too the day's work should be done in as short a time as possible, so a fairly large unit is desirable. Claims for the effectiveness of converted air-conditioning compressors which are rated at 2 h.p. for an air-conditioning system are often exaggerated. In a system doing low-temperature work, such as a freezer, the gas is much less dense than in an air-conditioning system. Therefore, less gas is drawn into the cylinder at each revolution. The same compressor will not be likely to need more than ¼ or ½ h.p. for refrigeration and freezing. For large systems one needs high rpm, with, if possible, large displacement as well. There is no substitute for cubic inches! Getting a monster compressor is only part of the job; all the other components —the condenser, lines, valves, and so forth—should be correspondingly large.

A suitable compressor for a holding-plate system on a forty-foot boat will be in the neighborhood of 1 h.p. and 1 ton. For larger boats a 1½-ton or 2-ton compressor is necessary. The problem is that a big compressor needs a large surge of amperage to get started. Therefore, on a sixty- or seventy-foot boat, it is advisable to switch to a double system, with two completely independent small compressors operating what are essentially two separate cooling systems. This arrangement reduces the starting surge and increases reliability (Drawing 174).

Condensers

AIR-COOLED CONDENSERS: The purpose of the condenser is to cool the refrigerant and get the heat out of the boat. The air-cooled condenser, while cheap, is not very efficient, and under tropical conditions it is particularly unsatisfactory. In the tropics, the air temperature on deck during the day will run to 85 degrees or above. In any locker, even a well-ventilated one, the air temperature will be 95 degrees or more. Once the air-cooled condenser starts to operate, the temperature will rapidly rise to well over 100. The fan will merely recirculate the hot air through the boat—heating up the boat and not cooling the condenser.

An air-cooled unit mounted on deck quickly turns into a ball of rust. Streaks and leaks follow soon after.

WATER-COOLED CONDENSERS: The water-cooled condenser is generally preferable. In the tropics, water is always cooler than air, and will remain at a constant temperature when the engine is running. Therefore, water is an infinitely more efficient cooling agent than air, especially since air being recirculated in a restricted compartment gets steadily warmer.

The main objection to the water-cooled condenser is that it requires a pump, which is one more thing to go wrong. But though a pump is necessary for a refrigeration system that runs intermittently throughout the day, it is not necessary if the refrigeration system is run only when the main engine is operating. In this case, the cooling water for the engine first is pulled through the condenser, cooling it; so a separate pump is not required.

A water-cooled unit should be made of cupronickel. Otherwise, in a few years the salt water may eat a hole in it.

Magnetic-Drive Pumps   As has been mentioned, the one disadvantage of a water-cooled condenser is that it may necessitate the maintenance of an additional pump and pump-shaft seals. In the newest pump on the market, the problem of pump seals is eliminated. The electric motor turns a magnet, and this turns another magnet, attached to the impeller and the electric motor. Pumps of this type are produced by the March Manufacturing Company.

This kind of pump has its limitations. Since it is a centrifugal pump, it must be mounted below the waterline. Also, at present it is only available wired for AC. In the future, the manufacturer will undoubtedly develop models wired for DC.

KEEL COOLERS: Some people make what is known as a "keel cooler," by running a copper tube outside the hull. This will work, but there is a risk that oil from the compressor will be deposited in the tube. Also, it is susceptible to damage from the salt water, or from anything, like an anchor, that may be dragged across the bottom of the boat; marine growth, too, may make the tube most inefficient.

Location of Compressors and Condensers

Compressors and condensers need not be immediately adjacent to the cooling units. They can be remotely located—in the engine room, lazaret, or other convenient place. Excessively long suction lines should be avoided. If they must be used, they should be one size larger than normally specified. Tables showing the relationships between footage, pressure drops, and tonnage requirements can be found in standard refrigeration manuals.

Construction Details

TUBING INSTALLATION: Copper tubing is by far the best. Some systems use rubber hose with clamp-on fittings, as in some air conditioning. But while this hose is cheap, and easy to push together, it lacks reliability, and definitely lacks a finished look. A freezer is for storing food, not for miles of rubber hose. Only a certain amount of refrigeration can be effected with a certain size of tube. This is true for both the in and the out lines. The line on the high-pressure side, or the liquid line, can be of ¼-inch copper, but that size is marginal. The next size up, ⁵⁄₁₆-inch, is not used as refrigeration tubing. So one is left with ⅜-inch copper, which is a little larger than necessary but does add to efficiency. The tubing for the suction lines of a holding unit should be even larger—at least ⅝ inch. Even ⅝ inch is a little restrictive. New, clean, dehydrated refrigeration tubing should be used exclusively. The larger suction lines will sweat. On a wooden boat, they should be covered with an insulating tube, made by splitting foam-plastic sleeving, to prevent condensation. Otherwise, water dripping into the hull and frames will cause rot.

For assembling copper tubing, forged flare nuts of the long type should be used. These will add some support to the tube. With short nuts, the tube will tend to break at the flare. The so-called "refrigeration nuts," which are of the short type, should be used only where there is frosting or the likelihood of frost getting between the nuts and the tube.

Short sections of hose should be placed on both lines to absorb the vibrations of the compressor. The hose ends should be the factory-swaged, medium-pressure type of screw-on ends, such as the Aeroquip Corporation manufactures. These will never blow off or split at an inconvenient time.

DRYERS: Almost any good-quality dryer can be used. I prefer the unit made by Virginia Chemicals because it is easy to change. It is so constructed that one can change it without disconnecting the copper lines. Also, a sight glass on the top enables even the inexperienced to charge the system without losing Freon, since one eye can be kept on the sight glass and one on the Freon. When the liquid becomes solid, the glass if full.

FREON: "Freon" is the trade name for a group of refrigerants produced by Du Pont. There are many types, and when recharging, one must be careful to use the right Freon for the particular design. Freon 12 is the cheapest, most available, and most common. Freon 22 is the gas most suitable for low-temperature systems, but because of the higher pressures involved, it tends to be a little hard on the valves of the compressor. Therefore it must be used only in compressors or systems designed for it. Freon 502 is the best gas for freezer systems. Most things being equal, at low temperature, a Freon-502 system will remove heat at almost twice the rate of a Freon-12 system. It does need a compressor and tubing of larger size to remove this extra heat.

Cost of Mechanical Refrigeration

On a forty-foot boat, a good system using battery refrigeration and an evaporator rather than holding plates can be installed for about $700. The same type of system on a sixty-foot boat should cost $900 to $1,200. A good hermetically sealed 110-volt freezer or refrigerator unit could be installed in a forty-foot boat for about $1,200; a similar system suitable for a sixty-foot boat would probably run to about $2,500.

Repair of Mechanical Refrigeration

Anyone intending to do serious cruising must be sure to understand fully the refrigeration system of his boat. He should know the purpose of every component, every valve, and be able to adjust the valves, change the dryers, recharge the system, and so on. Refrigeration experts are few and far between in the middle of the ocean.

BOX CONSTRUCTION

TESTING CONSTRUCTION OF AN EXISTING BOX

The first step in testing a mechanical refrigeration unit is to fill it with food. Then, if there is a freezer, the unit should be run until the freezer temperature is down to 0 degrees. If there is only a refrigerator, the unit should be run until the box temperature is about 35 degrees. The box should next be kept closed for twelve hours, and then checked. If the temperature has risen more than five degrees, the box should be discarded.

A good test for an icebox is to fill it with block ice and see how long it takes to melt. A good box will hold ice for two weeks in the tropics and perhaps three weeks in temperate waters. If the box fails this test, it should be rebuilt. Chances are that it needs better insulation. The run-of-the-mill fiber-glass popouts produced in the United States (with insulation consisting of a thin sheet of styrofoam) and in the Far East are completely inadequate, and should be replaced.

BOX LOCATION AND DESIGN

In planning a refrigeration unit one should consider where the box is to be placed, what space is available, and what type of box will be most useful—icebox, refrigerator, freezer, or a refrigerator-freezer combination.

On some new boats, notably those constructed of steel, aluminum, or fiber glass, the refrigerator and freezer are placed in the bilge. In a modern boat, in which the bilge can be expected to remain dry, this location is excellent, since it makes use of space which is usually wasted. Also, in rough weather, it is much easier to sit on the cabin sole and dig around than it is to chock oneself into place and disappear headfirst into the freezer, which always seems to be on the windward side.

The refrigeration units should be made as large as possible. In planning the galley one should remember that some of the space given to these units will be taken up by insulation and by the evaporators or holding plates. A good way to determine if the box is going to be large enough to take care of all requirements is to make a mock-up of the inside. The thickness of the insulation depends on how much space can be spared. Insulation should be two to three inches thick for a refrigerator, and four to six inches thick for a freezer. If the given thickness of insulation is doubled, the operating time of the unit—and the resulting noise of the generator—is essentially cut in half.

Should the box open at the top or from the side? Many people prefer the top-opening type, because with it, air does not spill out when the door is opened. Sometimes a top opening is inevitable on a small boat because of space limitations. However, the side opening also has advantages. Access, especially to the bottom of the box, is much easier with a side door. One doesn't have to move everything off the counter just to get out a cold beer. Also, contrary to popular opinion, a side opening does not really seem to cause a great loss of efficiency. What loss does occur may be compensated for by the additional convenience. However, on a sailboat, the side-opening door must be on an athwartship axis. If it is on a fore-and-aft axis, on a tack, everything will try to fall out.

Whatever its location, the door may be a source of unnecessary heat loss if it is not properly designed. A top that fits flat on an icebox, merely clamping down against a gasket, is not as effective as one that is tapered or fits into notches in the icebox walls as well as against a gasket (Drawing 194). Further, it should be remembered that frequently iceboxes are right next to the companionway hatch, where for long periods of time the sun will be blazing down on the top of the box. For that reason, the insulation in the top of the icebox should be substantial.

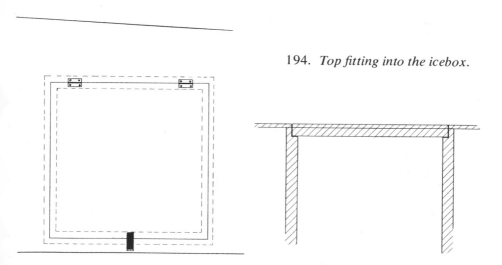

194. *Top fitting into the icebox.*

If one wants both a freezer and a refrigerator, they should be placed side by side (Photo 133) or one above the other. The main advantage of keeping these units close together is that a separate cooling mechanism for the refrigerator becomes unnecessary. The cooling of the refrigerator is accomplished in one of two ways. The best way is to place a small thermostatically controlled fan between the units. When the re-

133. Completed refrigeration unit. (Repke)

frigerator warms up to a predetermined temperature, the fan turns on and blows cold air from the freezer into it. When the refrigerator temperature has dropped sufficiently, the fan turns off.

The second way is to place between the refrigerator and freezer a wall providing a degree of insulation which has been calculated to admit just enough leakage from the freezer to offset the losses through the other refrigerator walls. The leakage keeps the box cold. This can be augmented by manually operated flaps over holes between the boxes. However, with the latter arrangement, the system will be warm if a large amount of warm food is put in at once. Furthermore, if the box is left closed overnight, the contents may freeze. The best dividend of side-by-side, or one-above-the-other placement, is that as the freezer warms, the refrigerator cools. Almost a something for nothing.

BOX MATERIALS

Anyone who is at all handy with tools can easily undertake the construction of the box (Photo 134). The best material for the box itself is ⅜- or ½-inch plywood. Something thinner would leave more space for insulation, but with the heavier material, appropriately braced, the box can be expected to retain its shape when the insulation is poured in. Adequate bracing is essential. Many a novice, even after repeated warnings, ends up with a box that has badly bulged sides. Under restraint, insulating foam can exert a force of up to seven pounds per square inch; that works out to over ten thousand pounds on the side of a 3-by-4-foot box. Besides providing bracing, one should cut a few holes in the top of the box, or better yet, leave the entire top of the box off, until the insulation has been poured and has solidified. Then one can simply saw off the excess foam, and install the top.

Lining Materials

METAL: Metal, generally stainless steel or Monel, is the most commonly used lining material—and it should be avoided. Metal linings are expensive, difficult to construct, and very rigid. When the foam insu-

134. Building an icebox. (Repke)

lation is poured, they usually bulge and buckle. Further, a split or crack in a welded seam, such as might be caused by someone dropping a heavy block of ice into the box, is almost impossible to repair, since it cannot be welded in place. Finally, metal is an excellent conductor of heat and cold, and usually the metal liner conducts all the cold out of the box. It is for this reason that the tops of most stainless-lined ice-boxes and refrigerators sweat and are cold to the touch. They are great for keeping the beer one is drinking cool, but only because the box it-self is not being kept cool efficiently. To be acceptable, a metal liner must end at the gasket for the lid or door, and be completely insulated from the outside air. Then it will not conduct all the cold out into the cabin.

FIBER GLASS: If properly made, and of adequate thickness to prevent bulging when foam insulation is poured, fiber-glass liners can be excel-lent. They are most suitable for production-line boxes; if the box is not of a standard size, a special mold for the liner must be made.

FIBER-GLASS-COVERED PLYWOOD: Another method of making a lin-ing is to fiber-glass the plywood on the inside. This job requires some skill, for unless the surface of the fiber glass is absolutely smooth, it is most difficult to keep clean. To prevent the fiber-glass taste from pene-trating the food, one should pour five or six gallons of boiling water into the box, close it tightly, and allow it to stand for a few hours.

FORMICA-COVERED PLYWOOD: Formica is in every way as acceptable as plywood and in addition is simple to clean. In some areas, plywood may be purchased with the Formica already attached. If this is not ob-tainable, the Formica must be glued to the plywood.

Insulation

Freon II foam insulation should be used. It is the best insulation now available. Also, it forms a one-piece vapor barrier, preventing the box from collecting a lot of moisture from the air. Freon II is some-times difficult to find, but can be ordered from Reichhold Chemicals, which can also furnish technical literature covering the mixing and handling of the material.

It comes in the form of two liquids, or rather semiliquids, like thick syrup. The two components are combined by means of a mixing pro-peller attached to an electric drill. After perhaps thirty seconds—the exact time depends to some extent on the temperature—the material turns white and foamy. At that point it must be used in a hurry. We once tried to pour several gallons of it, which we had mixed below-decks, into what turned out to be too small a hole. The end result was four or five cubic feet of foam all over everything—arms, legs, decks, counters. It adheres to all surfaces, even Formica, and is almost impossible to remove. To avoid this kind of situation one should mix the foam on deck and then hand it down to a helper who can pour it into the box. Then if things get out of hand, the whole works can be pitched overboard.

One other word of caution. The gas released by the mixing of the two components is pretty smelly and can make one sick or even worse. The working area should have plenty of ventilation, and after the foam has been poured into the box, one should leave the area for about half an hour. Better yet, if an aqualung, or similar diving gear, is available, it can be used by the person pouring the foam.

MAKING ICE

Ice can best be made in empty plastic ice-cream containers, in the quart or half-gallon size; these are filled with water, covered with their special lids, and deposited on the bottom of the freezer. When frozen, the ice is easily chipped out with an ice pick. Plastic is not a good conductor, so to speed up the ice making, one can drill a number of holes in the top of the container, insert brass bolts through the holes, and set them up tightly with nuts and washers (Drawing 195). The bolts conduct the cold to the water and speed up the freezing process markedly.

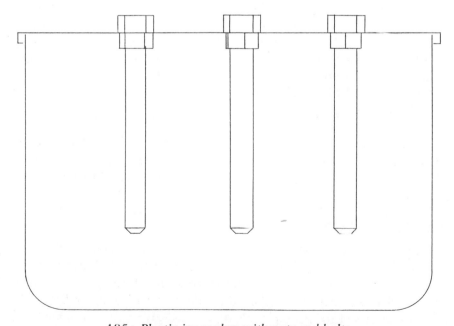

195. *Plastic ice maker with nuts and bolts.*

The covers keep the moisture from being drawn to and deposited on the plates as frost. All moisture, whether in a liquid or frozen form, tends to be deposited on the plates as frost. The more quickly this frost accumulates, the more often the box must be defrosted. Therefore, one can save a lot of extra work, and have a more efficient box, by keeping all liquids, ice, and foods well wrapped in plastic.

The lovely vertical ice-cube trays on the market should be avoided. Generally, on the first using, they swell so badly that the ice must be half melted before it can be removed from the container. By the third or fourth use, such a tray is likely to split and be totally finished.

AIR CONDITIONING

While air conditioning is not necessary on boats at all times, it is nice to have on a very hot night in a quiet anchorage or at a marina where there is not much air. There are a number of systems on the market, of varying quality. One should be sure to select a unit which is well made and has a quiet water pump, since otherwise one will be kept awake all night by the noise. In most systems each fan-coil unit has its own small compressor. While these are inexpensive, they are generally placed where they can't be reached when they need service. One can avoid this problem by having the several cooling units run off one remotely located compressor-condenser unit. However, this type of installation is limited in that the temperature can be controlled at only one station. Hence, there will be variations in temperature from cabin to cabin.

The best type of air conditioning is the chilled-water type, in which water is chilled and then pumped through the boat to the various cabins. This is a little more expensive, but very quiet and very reliable. A further advantage is that with the addition of a heater to warm the water, the same system can be used for heating the boat.

One other point should be kept in mind. Even a boat that is completely air-conditioned should have plenty of hatches. Otherwise, if for any reason the air conditioning fails, the boat will become uninhabitable.

CONDENSATION

Because it dehumidifies the air, the cooling unit of an air-conditioning system causes condensation. The resulting water, if allowed to drip onto a wooden hull, will rapidly cause rot. Therefore, it is imperative that an adequate drip pan be installed under every unit, and that the fresh water be led to a sump tank or directly overboard, by way of a sink drain, cockpit scupper, or whatever you have. For the same reason, as has been noted, lines from the cooling units in air conditioners, refrigerators, or freezers should be insulated with foam plastic.

Here follow the comments and criticisms of Donald Street.

ICEBOXES

The author of this chapter, Jon Repke, lives in the wrong end of the islands. I, Don Street, live in the southern end of the islands, and always manage to have ice. The normal routine in the southern islands is to find a small boy with a dinghy, and give him a dollar, along with the money for the ice and a couple of ice bags. Then one can sit back and relax, have a couple of rums, and in no time, the ice arrives. Ice bags should be made of good heavy Dacron, and should be capable of holding a hundred pounds. To get the ice on board one can simply attach the handles of the bag to the main halyard, heave away, and swing the bag aboard and down the appropriate hatch.

On *Iolaire,* in southern waters, ice lasts ten to twelve days in an icebox that is less than perfect. In cold-water areas, ice should last three or four weeks in a well-designed icebox. Maintaining a cold box should therefore be no problem, for in northern waters one seldom goes for as much as three weeks without reaching a port where ice is readily available.

The great advantage of an icebox is that it is foolproof. One just fills it with ice, and everything gets cold. There is nothing to break down. Mechanical refrigeration on the other hand, can break down, but can also be wonderful. The original installation is expensive, and mechanical refrigeration is like a chain, the links being the starter motor, the engine, the generator, the water-cooling pumps, the compressor, the condenser, the holding plates, the expansion valves, and so on and on. Failure of a single link renders the whole system inoperable. Then one must revert to ice, but a box made for plates is not large enough to hold a decent quantity of ice, so one has the choice of letting some food spoil, or of putting the crew on a steady diet of steaks and roasts three meals a day in a mad race against spoilage.

ICEBOX DESIGN

Iolaire has two independently insulated hundred-pound boxes, standing side by side. At the start of a trip, these boxes are almost filled with ice, but there is still ample room on top of the ice for fresh food and drinks for as many as six people. The forward icebox is kept closed as much as possible, and the after one is used for soft drinks, cold beers, and the like. At the end of perhaps six days, both boxes are about half filled with ice. This is the point at which ice begins to disappear rapidly, because of the excessive and unnecessary area to be cooled. We therefore move all the ice from the after box to the forward box, in effect starting at the end of six days with a hundred-pound box filled to the top. Since heat loss is directly proportional to surface area, halving the area to be cooled, by means of this transfer, practically doubles the life of the ice. *Iolaire*'s individual boxes are much smaller than the one old box she formerly carried. Thirty pounds of ice in the bottom of a hundred-pound icebox will keep the box cool, and food will not spoil. Thirty pounds of ice in the bottom of a huge icebox will melt rapidly, but will not sufficiently cool the box to keep food from spoiling.

There is no reason why an icebox, even in the tropics, will not hold ice for about two weeks. In many boats it should be possible to stretch the supply over three weeks. On *Iolaire,* while on charter, the ice lasts for ten to twelve days. This is with six people on board having evening cocktails, beer continually during day, and large quantities of fresh food on the ice. I am not wasteful, but I do not stint. I cool tremendous quantities of beer each day. Cruising with just my wife and little daughter, I actually stretched the ice supply one time to seventeen days. Furthermore, *Iolaire*'s iceboxes are less than efficient. She is so narrow forward that there is room for only two inches of Freon foam insulation. According to Jon Repke, the optimum thickness for icebox insulation is four inches.

These figures are drawn from experience in the tropics, where the water temperature is 77 degrees and the air temperature 88 degrees. In the north, where the water temperature is 65 degrees and the air temperature in the 70's, ice could probably be kept for the better part of a month, especially with insulation a full four inches thick.

ICEBOX DRAINS

If the ice is to last, water must not be allowed to stand in the bottom of the icebox. On some boats an open hose running directly from the bottom of the box to the bilge drains the water as the ice melts. On a wooden boat, this arrangement is guaranteed to cause rot: ice water and wood provide a juicy bed for fungi. Even on a fiber-glass, aluminum, or steel boat, this method of draining the water is likely to create a smelly bilge.

On some boats, the water is pumped directly overside. One must then remember to pump five or six times a day, to keep the box dry. The method I find simplest and least expensive is to run the drain hose into a one-gallon Clorox bottle chocked in the bilge. Three times a day the bottle is removed, emptied into the sink, and then replaced in the bilge.

Still another method is to drain the icebox into a sump tank. If a sump tank already is present, this arrangement is satisfactory; to install a sump tank just for this purpose seems unnecessarily complicated in most cases. However, on some boats with a deep wineglass section, the addition of a sump tank may make possible almost completely efficient utilization of the ice. The tank, insulated with an inch or so of styrofoam, is installed in the bilge. It has a large opening in the top through which beer and soft drinks may be inserted. Cold water cools beer faster than ice, and here the excess water from the icebox, which is ordinarily just discarded, is put to good use.

Drain Construction

The drain pipe must not lead directly down from the icebox, since the cold air would then drop out of the box and enter the bilge. Instead, inside the insulation the drain line should be looped slightly above the level of the bottom of the box (Drawing 196), to produce a water trap.

Builders frequently install drains that are very small, sometimes consisting of copper tubing no more than ¼ inch in diameter. After much experimentation, I find that nothing smaller than ¾-inch plastic hose should be used as an icebox drain. A strainer should be placed over the outlet at the bottom of the box, and every effort should be made to keep the drain open. If it clogs—as it will—plastic hose usually can be blown clear by lung power. Failing that, a small dinghy bilge pump can

196. *Water trap in a drain line; in the incorrect installation, cold air falls down through the hose* (left), *while in the correct installation, water is trapped in the U section and keeps the cold air in the box* (right).

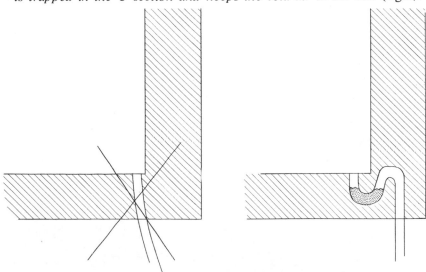

be used; the end of the hose is placed over the pump outlet, and water is discharged into the icebox, clearing the hose.

ICEBOX SIZE

An icebox for a small boat should hold at least fifty pounds of ice (which, cut to fit, will occupy about nine hundred cubic inches), and still have two cubic feet of stowage space for food. If it is a good box, the ice will last six to eight days. On a larger boat, two fifty-pound boxes side by side will have sufficient capacity for two or three people. If the crew consists of four, the boxes should each hold seventy-five pounds of ice, and have two to three cubic feet of stowage space. On large boats, three side-by-side boxes, carrying a hundred pounds each, should serve for a month or more without replenishment. In some people's estimation, this system is more desirable than mechanical refrigeration. Jon Repke does not agree, despite the fact that mechanical refrigeration usually costs a thousand dollars or more, but of course he is biased—he is in the refrigeration business.

XVI

Navigation

The needs of the navigator vary drastically, depending on the area the boat is to be cruising and the extent of the cruising to be done. I know people who have successfully made their way from Bequia to St. Thomas, a distance of over seven hundred miles, equipped only with an Esso road map and a boy scout compass. But of course they were sailing in an area of crystal-clear water and no fog. Similarly, on vessels along the east coast of the United States, where buoys and lighthouses are closely spaced and weather conditions are generally good, frequently the navigational equipment consists of a portable direction finder, a parallel rule, pencils, dividers, and charts, all used in the middle of the cockpit or on top of the icebox. By contrast, Europeans spend much more time navigating than we do, and have more elaborate equipment. Weather conditions in European waters are more extreme, and tidal conditions are violent, to say the least. The tidal range may be anywhere from fifteen to as much as thirty-five feet, and the resulting currents make good navigation imperative. Hence most European cruising boats, even those as small as 30 feet LOA, have a good chart table. To most Americans this seems a tremendous waste of space, but for anyone contemplating serious cruising, a good comfortable chart table is well worth the time and money spent in building it and the space it uses. If the navigator can have all his tools in one place right in front of him, a comfortable seat, and a good light, navigation will soon become a rather interesting game instead of a tiresome chore.

Navigational equipment can be as simple as that used by Josh Slocum, who sailed around the world with his nautical almanac, sextant, book of tables, and an alarm clock that had only one hand, or as elaborate as that of a modern yacht which may have 25 percent of the total value wrapped up in electrical gear, much of which has to do with navigation. Modern electronic and electrical aids to navigation are wonderful, but one should remember that the money poured into expensive electronic devices might instead finance additional cruising. Furthermore, electrical and electronic gear is not only expensive to purchase and install, but also expensive to maintain, and in out-of-the-way areas it may be impossible to repair.

There is a happy medium between Slocum's minimal gear and the overload of electronic equipment which frequently no one on board quite knows how to use. Slocum was able to get along with as little navigational equipment as he had because he was a superb navigator. He knew his mathematics. Indeed, he found his longitude by utilizing lunar distances. Today this method is only mentioned in the navigational manuals; it is so complicated that with the advent of reliable chronometers, the lunar-distance tables were dropped from nautical almanacs.

Many excellent books have been written on piloting and navigation. For piloting, it is very difficult to beat the famous old standby Charles F. Chapman's *Piloting, Seamanship and Small Boat Handling,* periodically revised, and published by Motor Boating. When the art of piloting has been mastered, and one begins to think of celestial navigation, one should turn to the superb *Celestial Navigation for Yachtsmen,* by Mary Blewitt. She treats navigation as something any idiot can master, provided he has a basic knowledge of piloting. Anyone who can add and subtract can learn celestial navigation—as countless yachtsmen have —by carefully studying Mary Blewitt's book.

Having climbed the first hill, and realized that celestial navigation is not black magic, but is relatively easy to understand, one should study George W. Mixter's *Primer of Navigation.* It is much more detailed than Mary Blewitt's book, and discusses many different methods of solving the spherical triangle. In fact, it covers everything to do with navigation in a clear and concise manner. However, it should not be tackled until one has learned the fundamentals with Mary Blewitt.

Any but the smallest boats on which it will take up too much space, should carrry an edition of "Bowditch"—*The American Practical Navigator,* originally by Nathaniel Bowditch, published by the United States Naval Oceanographic Office, formerly the Hydrographic Office. This is the standard reference work, useful whenever a problem in navigation arises. Bowditch discusses not only celestial navigation but also piloting and dead reckoning, electronic navigation, oceanography, weather, and charts. The volume also contains 550 pages of appendices and tables, so it is very valuable to have on board a serious cruising yacht. Furthermore, since it has a tremendous amount of background historical information, it makes an excellent book to be read leisurely, perhaps when one is sitting under the awning late in the afternoon, having a sundowner.

THE NAVIGATOR— TREAT HIM WELL

The navigator is frequently neither the skipper nor the owner of the boat, but merely a willing member of the crew. If he is to spend hour after hour navigating, his accuracy depends upon how well he is treated. There is nothing difficult about navigation; it is merely tedious. An uncomfortable position, bad lights, fatigue, all increase the tedium and consequently the chance of error. One well-known navigator has described the art of navigation as "checking continually, and finding one's errors before the vessel has been placed in a dangerous position."

In its most primitive form, the chart table is a piece of plywood which the navigator holds on his lap as he sits in a bunk and tries to navigate. His results, unless he is very brilliant, are likely to be less than good. Also a poor substitute for a proper table is the old American standby, the top of the icebox. Just when the navigator is involved in solving a problem, the cook will have to open the icebox, disturbing the navigator's trend of thought, stepping on his feet, and dropping his parallel rule and dividers down under the ice. Furthermore, there is no room over the icebox for the books and other equipment needed for navigating, so each time he prepares to get to work, the navigator must retrieve his bits and pieces of gear from the far corners of the boat.

The first improvement in arrangements for the navigator came after World War II, when he was given his own chart table. However, usually it was mounted fore and aft, with the navigator expected to stand in front of the table. On one tack he had great difficulty maintaining his stance, and was likely to be pitched across the cabin to fetch up in the middle of the stove, icebox, or what-have-you. In the last ten years, yacht designers have taken pity on the navigator and have given him a chart table mounted athwartships, so that he can sit on a seat or on the forward end of his own quarter berth while he works. If the navigator sits on the forward end of his quarter berth, he must face forward, since the quarter berth extends out under the cockpit. In some boats this arrangement is unavoidable. However, where alternatives exist, the chart table should, if possible, be placed so that the navigator faces aft. He can talk directly to the helmsman and those on deck without turning around, and both parties can more easily hear each other's orders.

The chart table should be as large as possible. A good guide to minimum size is provided by the dimensions of British Admiralty charts. While American Oceanographic Office charts are of all sizes and shapes, the British charts come in two standard sizes—28 by 42 inches and 28 by 21 inches. A table of at least 28 by 21 inches will therefore accommodate the British charts, either spread out or folded once.

The chart table must have fiddle rails around the edges to prevent pencils, pens, dividers, and the like from skidding to the cabin floor, but since at times the navigator will desire to lay a chart down with the edges over the side of the table, the fiddle rails must be removable.

All too often a chart table which appears excellent at first turns out to be less than perfect. The edge of the table should come fairly close to the waist of the navigator, and there must be ample room under the table for his legs (Drawing 197). Furthermore, all the gear he needs should be within his reach, so that he doesn't have to get up and search

197. *At the chart table, the navigator needs leg room.*

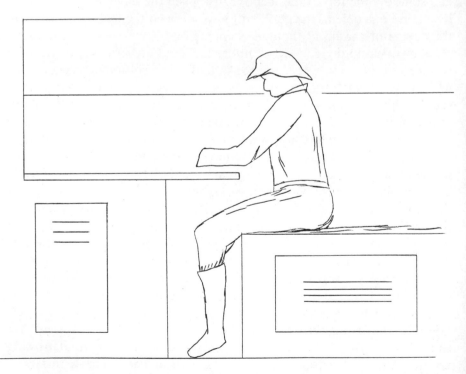

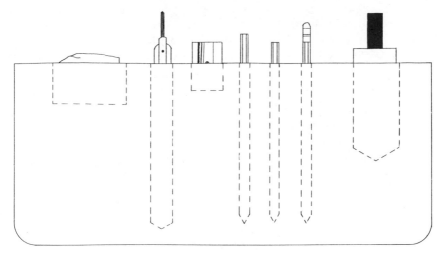

198. *Rack to hold the navigator's everyday tools.*

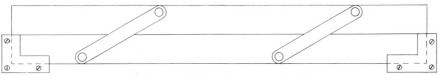

199. *Rack for the parallel rule.*

elsewhere for books and equipment. Books on navigation, the sextant, and as much electronic equipment as possible should be directly over the chart table. Everyday tools—pencils, pens, an eraser, a pencil sharpener—should all be stowed in a wooden block screwed to the bulkhead (Drawing 198). Often these wooden blocks are made without a place for the eraser and pencil sharpener. The parallel rule is best stowed in a rack (Drawing 199); if triangles are used, they can be kept in a small wooden box screwed to the bulkhead.

A clock with a second hand should be provided, placed where it is easily visible to the navigator. Similarly, if a chronometer is carried, it should be mounted so that the navigator can see it without difficulty. On one well-equipped boat, where I have often served as navigator, the chronometer is a real pain in the neck. It is in a case with a wooden cover, and is stowed alongside the charts in the chart table. To get a look at it, one must move the charts back, open the chart table, pick the chronometer up, and open the case, and then of course everything must be put back. If the wooden cover were removed from the chronometer case and a section of Lucite let into the top of the chart table, the navigator would only have to move aside the charts and take a quick look. The radio too should be readily accessible to the navigator.

As was noted in Chapter X, the navigator needs various kinds of light. At night he may require a dim red light so that he can take a quick look at a chart, note down a log entry, or do some basic navigation, without losing his night vision. At other times he will have extensive calculation to do while everyone else is sound asleep. Therefore, a chart-table light with a bright but small beam is very useful; the navigator can focus it on his work and obtain adequate illumination without disturbing anyone else. Finally, for much of his work, the navigator will want a big, bright light, encompassing his entire chart area, with no shadows or dim places. For this purpose a good fluorescent light is desirable; since it draws much less current than does a normal light, it can be used for long periods of time without draining the batteries.

NAVIGATIONAL EQUIPMENT

The most basic equipment, used by the navigator of even the smallest boat, will consist of a parallel rule, dividers, writing materials, a timepiece, a depth finder, and a compass. What other items will be necessary will depend on where one is going and how extensive the cruising is to be.

PARALLEL RULES

Parallel rules range in quality from very cheap plastic rules, held together by two thin pieces of aluminum, to very expensive heavy brass rules such as are found on *Djinn* and *Antilles* (Photo 135). The latter are not only wonderful pieces of navigational equipment but also, espe-

135. Antilles' parallel rules. (D. M. Street)

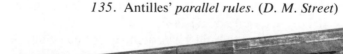

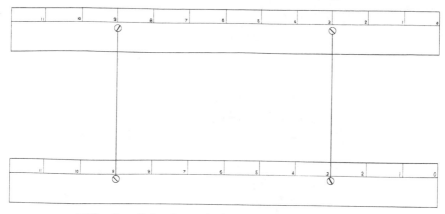

200. Parallel rule made from two rulers and string.

cially when polished, practically works of art. With a little care, one can make a very good, very cheap, and easily stowed parallel rule. The method is to take two wooden rulers, carefully position screws equidistant from the ends of each, and join the two rulers at each end with cords of equal length between the screws (Drawing 200).

There are various other methods of transferring a line of direction across a chart. One method is to use a plexiglass rod with a black line etched in it, and rubber tips at each end. This can be rolled across the chart, and is simple and accurate if well handled. It can also be used as a magnifying glass. Another device for this purpose is a clear sheet of plastic upon which parallel lines are marked. This is especially practical on very small boats, in which the equipment may be used in the cockpit.

A final method, and the one I much prefer, requires two right triangles (Photo 136), which, because they are marked out in degrees, can also serve as protractors. By placing one triangle against the other, one can draw parallel lines. Also, with a triangle, a right angle may be drawn directly from an azimuth bearing. I find it much quicker to plot out a line of position with two triangles than with a parallel rule. Further, a navigator who sails on various boats will find two triangles much easier to transport in his briefcase than a cumbersome parallel rule.

DIVIDERS

Dividers come in all shapes and sizes, ranging from the simple draftsman's dividers to the more elaborate bow dividers. All are satis-

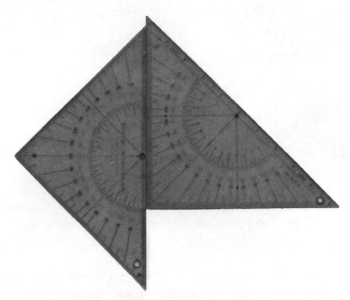

136. Two triangles used instead of parallel rules. (D. M. Street)

factory, as long as they are kept well oiled; there is nothing worse than trying to plot with a pair of stiff dividers. An extra pair of dividers should always be kept on board, for use if someone succeeds in losing the first pair.

WRITING MATERIALS

A good supply of writing materials is important; it should include hard pencils, soft pencils, conventional pens, and also a few of the big felt-tip pens and indelible marking pens. The latter are very useful for writing in good big letters the names and numbers of charts on the outsides of the envelopes in which they are stowed, so that members of the crew with bad eyesight need not rush for the magnifying glass or their reading glasses.

TIMEPIECES

A method of measuring time accurately is essential to the navigator; without it he cannot calculate the distance traveled and determine his present position. Celestial navigation is of course impossible without knowledge of the exact time. However, a stopwatch, while good to have on board, is not actually indispensable to the cruising yachtsman. For timing lights, counting by thousands is usually more than accurate enough. Some people do like to time their sights with a stopwatch, or to use it while correcting the chronometer from radio time. And a stop-watch is necessary for anyone doing any racing. Until the 1930's, a really good chronometer was essential, as there was little or no chance to correct a watch once the ship had sailed. However, the situation has now changed, as between WWV, CHU, and the BBC broadcasts from London, it is usually fairly easy to obtain accurate time. WWV broadcasts on 25.0, 20.0, 15.0, 10.0, 5.0, and 2.5 megacycles twenty-four hours a day. When WWV was in Washington, D.C., it was audible even down as far as Trinidad during the day. Now that it has been moved to Colorado, it is almost inaudible in the lower latitudes and in the eastern Atlantic and is also very difficult to pick up when one is nearing Europe. WWV announces the time verbally every minute and also broadcasts reports of important storms. CHU Canada, broadcasting on 3330 kilocycles (90 meters), announces the time in plain language, both in French and English, every minute. During various periods of the day, the BBC rebroadcasts news through its colonial and former colonial stations. The time given by the BBC is accurate enough for normal navigation.

Further, if listings of radio aids for navigation are consulted, it will be found that most nations broadcast time signals, so that large portions of the world are covered. Thus if one has a good radio, one can sail around the world with a five-dollar pocket watch. But one should be sure to take along a spare watch and a spare radio! Similarly, a United States Navy deck clock with a second hand, or one of the good marine clocks with a sweep-second, is usually good enough for navigation, since with a radio it can be corrected every day. As has been noted, whatever clock is chosen should be mounted so that it is accessible to the navigator.

If a wristwatch is to be used for navigation, it should be stowed in a safe place at the chart table, wound every day at the same time, and checked each night. Many people prefer a very good pocket watch. A gold watch originally given to my father fifty-five years ago has served as my chronometer on every trip. It has a good constant rate, is easy to read, is stowed conveniently in a dry spot in the chart table, and works fine.

Investing in a chronometer for the average small yacht is generally a waste of time and money. Universally, it arrives from the maker with a rate sheet attached. As long as the weather is calm and the temperature does not vary drastically, the rate remains fairly constant. However, when very heavy weather develops, the rate goes completely haywire. Temperature changes and violent motion affect a chronometer much more drastically than they do a wristwatch or a pocket watch.

Many firms now advertise chronometers, such as the Accutron, in which a tuning fork replaces the mainspring. These are tremendously expensive and supposedly almost perfectly accurate, with a maximum error of less than a second a day. My only experience with a chronometer of this type would have been disastrous but for the radio. The chronometer stayed accurate for several days, suddenly went haywire for two days, was less than accurate for another ten, and then became accurate once more. Had we not had a radio, we could have found ourselves in serious trouble, since at one point the chronometer was almost a minute out.

One way to make the skipper light his coal stove and keep the boat nice and warm is for the navigator to point out that while the crew can stand the cold, his watches can't, and malfunction if they get too cold. Even if the skipper is skeptical, he may be unwilling to take chances.

DEPTH FINDERS

A depth finder of some kind is essential; it may vary in type from the half-pound fishing sinker tied to a marked piece of string which is used by the man in the fourteen-foot dinghy to the recording Fathometer carried on the hundred-foot yacht. All cruising boats, no matter what their size, and regardless of whether they have an electronic Fathometer, should carry a plain old-fashioned lead line, if only for use in case the Fathometer fails. Whether or not a Fathometer should be carried as well as a lead line depends largely on the area in which one plans to sail. In most northern waters, the Fathometer is of great value, but in tropical waters, it is often useless. For example, in the Lesser Antilles, in many areas the Fathometer will record ample depth until suddenly one is aground; for the bottom may shoal from thirty feet to a foot in twenty yards, and the Fathometer cannot give enough warning of such a rapid change.

Sounding Poles

In deep water, of course a lead line or Fathometer must be used. However, in ten feet of water or less, it is much quicker, and more accurate, to take the depth with a sounding pole. The length of the pole should be appropriate to the size of the boat. The cruising boat of 42–45 feet LOA can easily carry for this purpose a fifteen-foot boathook, appropriately marked, stowed outboard of the spinnaker pole. Depths of up to twelve feet can be accurately measured with much greater speed and ease with a sounding pole of fifteen feet than with a lead line, even when the boat is sailing along at five or six knots. A word of warning—if sounding with a pole while moving at five or six knots, one should be sure to attach a light lanyard from the pole to the boom, so that it will not be lost if it sticks in the mud and is pulled from the leadsman's grasp.

Smaller boats will of course carry shorter boathooks, but in view of their shallow draft they will need a sounding pole only in correspondingly shallow water. Thus a boathook of reasonable length on a thirty-footer still can be used as a sounding pole.

If one does a large amount of shoal-water cruising, and dislikes the long boathook, one can make a pole by joining lengths of aluminum tubing or bamboo with wooden plugs. Then when the pole is not in use, it may be pulled apart and stowed.

COMPASSES

It goes without saying that a compass will be required. This should be mounted so that it is easily visible to the helmsman and not obstructed by other persons who are in the cockpit. This is often difficult to do, as someone is always sitting in front of the compass, leaning on top of it, or sticking a leg across the helmsman's line of vision. On a boat with wheel steering, the compass is normally mounted in the binnacle, an arrangement which is not always perfect. On some boats, the helmsman finds that when he is seated, the top edge of the wheel is directly in his line of sight to the compass, making him cross-eyed. Similarly, when he is standing, the light on the top of the compass obstructs the lubber line. Why the light is not instead mounted on the side, or at the after end, of the compass is a mystery to me. Furthermore, the compass is usually mounted so high that a person sitting on the side of the cockpit cannot see the main fore-and-aft lubber line, or cannot see the compass at all.

The problem of compass visibility is further aggravated when steering is done with a tiller, for then one is almost always sitting off center. When steering is done with a tiller and there is only one lubber line, the error in bearing may be as much as 10 degrees, which certainly will not improve the navigator's dead reckoning. For this reason, if one can afford it, one should purchase a compass with beam bearings and also quarter bearings. These are desirable also on a boat with wheel steering, for when sitting alongside the wheel, the helmsman will have the beam bearing directly in front of him. The presence of these extra lubber lines makes the taking of bearings across the top of the compass much easier.

The compass should be lit with a red light, focused as much as possible directly on the lubber line. A rheostat should be provided, if possible, since various helmsmen will desire different degrees of intensity in the compass light. Also, the compass-light switch should be easily accessible to the helmsman. Then on long passages on starlit nights, the light can be turned off, saving that much electricity.

Compass lights are very prone to failure because they are out in the wind and the spray continually. The bulb is likely to burn out all too quickly, and the standard bulb that fits in the socket in the binnacle of many compasses is difficult, and in some places impossible, to obtain. For this reason, when going offshore one should be sure that there are a number of spare bulbs on board. Furthermore, frequently the socket becomes so corroded because of its exposure to the salt spray that it disintegrates when one tries to change the bulb. Therefore, a spare compass-light assembly should be carried. Then the entire compass light may be changed when necessary. On some boats, among them *Iolaire,* the compass light can be removed and stowed belowdecks during the day. If this arrangement is possible, it should be adopted, for then the compass light is exposed to the salt and spray only when absolutely necessary. A further precaution is to check the compass-light wires inside the steering stand; many a boat has lost her compass light because slack in the wires became entangled in the gears.

Compass Adjustments

Most compass adjustments are done only when the boat is under power. On a modern wooden, fiber-glass, or aluminum yacht with bronze and stainless-steel fittings, there is relatively little chance of large heeling errors. However, if the yacht is made of steel, or is generously equipped with galvanized-iron deck hardware, lifeline stanchions, and the like, the heeling error in the compass should be carefully checked. This is not an easy job; it should be done with the boat under sail, at various angles of heel. When compass adjustment is necessary, a professional should be called in. However, if one is in a jam with an erratic compass, one can consult Mixter or Bowditch for directions on compass adjustment.

Before leaving shore, one should also make sure that the electrical fields caused by the running of the boat's equipment are not affecting the compass. To this end, while the boat is alongside a dock, or on a mooring where she is not swinging, the generators, engines, compressors, and so on, should be turned on individually and all together, so that any resulting aberration can be caught and corrected.

Every navigator should remember that as long as the sun is visible it is relatively simple to check the compass on the course one intends to average while at sea. Most sailboats today are provided with spherical compasses. When the sun is low in the morning or in the afternoon, the center post casts a shadow across the card. By noting one's approximate—not exact—location, and the correct time, one can easily check the azimuth from the sun and thereby check the compass. If it seems to be wrong, the first step is to ascertain whether anyone has left beer cans, pliers, a knife, or perhaps a small transistor radio near the compass. This is an all-too-frequent but easily remedied cause of compass errors. If a deviation exists for which no obvious cause can be found, I would advise against trying to correct it; instead one should just note it in the log and compensate for the error.

Hand-Bearing Compasses

Hand-bearing compasses have recently become very popular. In former years, the good ones were very expensive and cumbersome, but now some compasses are hardly larger than a large pocket watch, so the navigator can carry a compass on a lanyard around his neck. Furthermore, a new method of using this type of compass has been developed recently. Until World War II or sometime after, most bearings from yachts were taken either across the top of the compass, or by a separate pelorus. The latter method leaves much room for error, since when the bearing is taken, the navigator must call to the helmsman to mark his course. Additions or subtractions are made and it is hoped that a decent bearing has been taken. By contrast, the latest hand-bearing compass—a real navigator's delight—is mounted inside a pair of 7 by 50 binoculars. At a touch of the button a transparent scale becomes visible, giving a precise bearing day or night on marks unseen by the naked eye. These binoculars are made in England by Offshore Instruments. However, in many areas, navigators still do merely sight across the top of the compass; this procedure is practical but not too accurate. Whether a hand-bearing compass is suitable depends largely on the size of the boat and the skill of the navigator. Also, how accurate the compass must be is determined by the area in which one is sailing; some areas demand much more accurate bearings than others.

NAUTICAL SLIDE RULES

The nautical slide rule, consisting of a square plastic board with adjustable circles (Photo 137), is a great asset to the navigator. Time-and-distance problems that normally require several minutes to work out are solved almost instantly with the aid of the nautical slide rule. One should never go to sea without one of these as part of the navigational equipment.

COURSE CORRECTORS

It is relatively simple for the navigator to sit down and draw out a diagram of current, direction and velocity, and the desired course, and

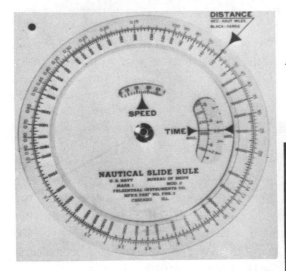

137. *Nautical slide rule.*
(*Land's End Catalogue*)

138. *Young's Course Corrector.*
(*Malchom Mills*)

then determine the actual course to be steered. But this plotting operation does take four or five minutes, and tools are available which enable the navigator to solve the problem almost instantly. Numbers of these plotting machines have been manufactured at various times. Probably best known today is Young's Course Corrector (Photo 138), manufactured by Coastal Navigation Aids; it costs sixty-five shillings and is well worth the investment.

TIDAL ESTIMATORS

At least once a year an article appears in *Yachting World* or *Yachting Monthly* explaining how to figure the depth of the tide for the hours before and after high water. Obtaining this information is especially important if one is sailing where there are great tides—say twenty or

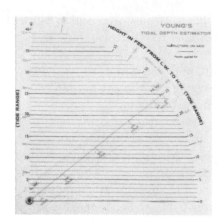

139. *Young's Tidal Depth Estimator.*
   (*Malchom Mills*)

twenty-five feet—and particularly if one is trying to save distance in an area where long sandbanks extend out from points on land. In the period from half high water to high water and back to half high water, one can frequently save many miles by dodging across the banks. However, to do so successfully one must carefully figure out the actual depth of the water at the time one will be bank jumping. One must know not only the average range of tide for the area but the actual range for the particular day. The problem is further complicated by the fact that during a six-hour tide, the height of the water does not increase by one-sixth during each hour.

The methods presented in the many articles in British cruising guides on this problem are too complicated to be dealt with here. Much of the difficulty can be avoided by the use of Young's Tidal Depth Estimator (Photo 139), available from Coastal Navigation Aids. This is of tremendous value to anyone who does much sailing in areas of great tides, and who is inclined to take shortcuts across the banks. A quick look at the tide tables to ascertain the tidal range for the day, a check on the time, and a minute with the estimator are all one needs to determine how much above low water the tide will be.

BINOCULARS

The importance of binoculars as navigational equipment is often not recognized. There are times when one's life may depend upon having a really good pair of binoculars. They are essential at night for picking up lights and unlit buoys, identifying shapes, and so on. Yet in making deliveries of yachts, I have sometimes felt that the quality of the binoculars provided was inversely proportional to the cost of the yacht.

Cheap, twenty-five dollar binoculars may work fine in a store, or be suitable for bird-watching in the backyard, but the first time one takes them out on a hot, sunny day and a cold wave douses them, they fog up, and one can never see decently through them again. If they escape fogging up, the prisms get knocked out of line—everything happens to cheap binoculars.

By contrast, expensive binoculars can be grossly misused and still remain in good shape for many years. The binoculars on *Iolaire* were given to me as a college-graduation present seventeen years ago, and have been at sea twelve months of the year ever since. They are Bausch and Lomb 7 by 50 binoculars made to United States Navy specifications. After this long period of use and abuse they are still in good shape.

Many articles have been written on the selection of binoculars. The standard choice the world over for seagoing use is the 7 by 50. The light-gathering capacity of 7 by 50 binoculars makes them excellent for use as a night glass, and they have the correct magnification for use on a small yacht. If the power is increased, the field of vision and the light-gathering capacity are reduced; also, glasses of power over 7 cannot be held steady enough, so everything seems to be blurred. Among 7 by 50 binoculars, those with the built-in compass, previously mentioned, are especially well worth the investment.

PRINTED MATERIAL

Along with Chapman and some of the other books mentioned early in this chapter, certain additional publications will be necessary, their nature and extent depending upon the type of cruising to be done. Cruising yachtsmen will require tide and current tables, cruising guides, possibly nautical almanacs, light lists, radio aids, and for offshore work, navigation tables. One should obtain lists of the publications available from the British Admiralty Printing Office and the Oceanographic Office of the United States Navy.

Tide and Current Tables

On all alongshore cruises, if the piloting is to be at all accurate, tide and current tables for the waters to be visited must be on board. For some areas, the necessary information can be obtained from government publications. For other areas, single volumes containing all the relevant tide and current tables, and current charts, are available. For example, *Reed's Nautical Almanac* supplies almost all the information one needs when cruising the British Isles. American yachtsmen have to buy different publications for different areas.

Guides

Standard coast pilots for various parts of the world are produced by both the British and the American governments. For many areas they are obviously unnecessary, and those for some other areas are so terrifying that if one reads them first one will never go to sea. Their great disadvantage is that they are written for large commercial vessels. Hence, they are extremely detailed, and spend page after page warning of shoals that will not bother a yacht drawing seven or eight feet. Accordingly, unless one is going to a completely or almost completely unfamiliar area, these coast pilots are not particularly useful.

Instead, when a long voyage or a cruise in waters seldom visited is planned, one would do well to try to obtain a set of eighteenth- or early-nineteenth-century sailing directions for the area in question. These sailing directions are often unbelievably good. They were written in the days of commercial sailing, when most of the vessels of the world had no auxiliary power.

For example, a pilot book for the West Indies, printed in 1867, has taught me a great deal about sailing in and around the islands of the Lesser Antilles. Indeed, much of the information on wind and weather found in my *Cruising Guide to the Lesser Antilles* is actually lifted from the old sailing directions in this book.

Also obtainable for the various popular cruising areas of the world are modern directions, written by individuals or offered by commercial organizations, such as fuel companies. These are well worth obtaining, since they tell much more than can be discerned from the charts; however, some of them, like the government publications, are directed to large commercial vessels, rather than to yachts.

Almanacs

Nautical almanacs, air almanacs, or the equivalent should be carried even in coastal cruising. With the aid of the almanac, the time of sunrise, sunset, twilight, moonrise, moonset, can be figured. This information will frequently influence the course of the cruise. With the aid of the almanac one can determine whether one will arrive in daylight, twilight, pitch dark, or moonlight.

Light Lists

Light lists covering the entire world are obtainable from both the British Admiralty and the United States Naval Oceanographic Office. If requested, the United States government will also send free of charge the fortnightly "Notice to Mariners," which includes corrections for all the books, light lists, and radio aids. Even temporarily disconnected and temporarily installed lights are listed. Thus one need only keep one's records up-to-date—as we all too seldom do—to have a light list which is always accurate. It is particularly important to obtain all the recent issues of the "Notice to Mariners" and correct the light list before entering an area where marine construction is in progress.

Radio Aids

Both the Admiralty and the Oceanographic Office issue listings of various radio aids to navigation, including all direction-finding stations, transmitting stations, communication stations, and the like, throughout the world, and again corrections can be obtained from the "Notice to Mariners."

Comprehensive Almanacs

The individual who plans to do all his sailing in the vicinity of the British Isles is very lucky in that for this area practically all of the information found in the above-mentioned publications is compiled each year in a single volume—*Reed's Nautical Almanac*. Similarly, a person who does not expect to venture outside Long Island Sound may purchase *The Eldridge Tide and Pilot Book,* by Robert Eldridge White, which also comes out yearly. Anyone going further afield will need the others, for the information supplied by *Eldridge* concerning the waters beyond the Sound is not detailed enough to be sufficient by itself.

Navigation Tables

At the back of Mixter, a copy of HO 211 is provided. However, while the method of using HO 211 is essentially simple, it involves so much adding and subtracting that there are many chances for error. Therefore, it is much safer to use HO 214 or HO 249. By and large, for the yachtsman these are equally satisfactory. Both are easy to use. The advantage of HO 214 is that if one takes a sight of an unknown star, by reading the directions carefully one can work the problem backward, identify the star, and obtain a position line from it. On the other hand, HO 249 lists only selected stars—the most brilliant ones to be found at the specified locations at various times of the year. HO 249 is more popular among yachtsmen because it consists of only three volumes, while HO 214 consists of eleven volumes and therefore costs a good deal of money and takes up much more space.

Star Identification

Many books have been written on the stars. Nautical almanacs, navigational books, and the like include numerous star-finding charts and diagrams of the stars. However, I have found these of little use because all of the really good ones concern the northern latitudes, where both sailing and visibility are poor during much of the year. If someone could come up with a good book describing the major stars and constellations visible in the tropics, many sailors would be appreciative. Some of this material was available in a star finder, HO 2102-D. This is no longer published by the Oceanographic Office, but the privately produced Weems star finder is similar. In any event, the star finder only identifies individual stars; it unfortunately does not lay out the constellations or the bearing of one star to another, in such a fashion that the major stars can be easily committed to memory.

Plotting Sheets

Some people plot their position lines directly on the chart. This method wears out charts rapidly, and often on long passages a chart is used with a scale such that the thickness of the pencil line is three miles; one thus loses in the plotting any accuracy that may have been achieved through careful calculation. I therefore advise doing all celestial navigation on plotting sheets. For small-boat use the best obtainable are the United States Navy universal plotting sheets (VP.OS), originally printed in 1942, and available in pads of a hundred. They measure 13 by 14 inches, and the scale is three inches to one degree of latitude.

The plotting sheets used on big steamships all over the world are too large for convenient use on yachts. Also, each sheet covers only a limited number of degrees of latitude; hence on a north–south voyage one will end the trip overloaded with plotting sheets, though there is no such problem on an east–west trip. If the universal plotting sheets are not available, one can make do with these larger sheets by obtaining those covering the latitudes where one plans to cruise and cutting them to a convenient size.

It is also possible to make up one's own plotting sheets, as described in Mixter. However, this is one more tedious job for the navigator.

Charts

Almost every nation in the world prints its own charts. However, most hydrographic chart work has been done in the past by the ships of Great Britain and the United States. A large part of the chart information provided by other nations has been compiled from the basic data supplied by these two sources. At present, Japan, Russia, and many other countries are getting into the hydrographic-survey business, but for the average yachtsman the American and British charts are still sufficient. While the British charts are published by the Admiralty, the American charts come from two sources. Overseas charts arc under the control of the Oceanographic Office. Charts covering the territorial waters of the United States and overseas possessions are under the control of the United States Coast and Geodetic Survey.

The individual planning a cruise in his own country can simply get charts from his local chart agent. For other areas, he should deal with a reputable firm that specializes in handling charts. Just about every major port has a chart supply house, with charts covering practically every part of the world. Two of the leading chart supply houses are New York Nautical Instrument and Service Corporation, in New York, and Kelvin Hughes, in London. Both of these carry a tremendous stock of charts, instruments, nautical publications, everything to do with navigation. Their staffs are very friendly, and willing to help in any way they can. Each company can arrange to order both American and British charts.

Anyone planning to cruise off the usual track should consult both the American and British chart catalogs, as some areas are well covered by one nation's charts and largely ignored by the other's. Furthermore, while the chart information is supposedly cross-referenced and cross-checked, the British and the American charts for some areas are diametrically opposed, with the British being correct in some cases and the American in others. Where the two sources supply contradictory information, the yachtsman will doubtless wish to sail with extra caution. The British charts are considerably more expensive than the American. However, they are printed on better paper, and come in standard sizes, so that all of them can be folded to fit in a 28-by-21 inch folio. Most important, if ordered from Kelvin Hughes, they are sure to be absolutely up-to-date. In the Kelvin Hughes chart office, six or eight draftsmen devote all their time to correcting charts. Indeed, shipping companies periodically send the charts from their ships to Kelvin Hughes, and as long as the returned charts are in good condition, corrected ones are immediately sent out in exchange.

By contrast, charts purchased from the Oceanographic Office cannot be assumed to be up-to-date. The Oceanographic Office expects the purchaser to read the "Notice to Mariners" and make his own corrections. A date-stamp at the corner of a chart means nothing, apparently. A few years ago, I brought to the Lesser Antilles a new set of charts purchased directly from what was then the Hydrographic Office, only to find by cross-checking on the spot that lights discontinued many years previously were still listed on the charts, while lights that had been installed in recent years were still unlisted. This inaccuracy was especially annoying in that in large part these charts were concerned with United States waters.

For certain areas of the world, notably the overseas possessions of European nations, foreign charts should be used. The French charts of the French West Indies are absolutely superb, much more detailed than the American or British charts, probably because the French were blockaded there for two years during World War II, and the young naval officers, with nothing else to do, surveyed Martinique, Guadeloupe, and Les Saintes in great detail. Similarly, probably in years gone by, Indonesia was well charted by the Dutch, and parts of Africa by the Portuguese.

It is seldom possible to have too many charts. Many people sailing from one place to another take along charts only for the ports they plan to visit and not for intermediate ports. To be sure, when making a trip from Halifax to Trinidad, one cannot afford the money or the space for charts of the whole east coast of the United States. But certainly general charts could be carried, and also detailed charts for harbors that might be ports of refuge in an emergency.

CHART STOWAGE: A nice big chart table with a lift-up top and space inside to stow thirty or forty charts is wonderful, but even this will frequently be overloaded, if one is going on a really extensive cruise. Some chart tables do have drawers below which make it possible for all charts to be stowed right at the table, but most do not.

In the days of the old sailing ship, and chart tables that were four feet square, charts were always rolled for stowage, and held down by weights when in use. However, on a modern yacht these arrangements are impossible; hence they are almost universally folded. I recommend folding American charts in four, information side in, clean side out, and writing the chart number and a description of the chart in one corner. Then the charts can be grouped according to the areas they cover, and stacked under the lower bunks in the main cabin.

When we delivered *Mariann* south, she had by far the best chart-stowage arrangement I have ever encountered. Mrs. Gibbons, the owner's wife, folded the charts in four and labeled them in the manner I have suggested. Then she classified them according to the areas covered, and stowed each group of charts in a clear-plastic envelope. On the inside of each envelope, she taped a list of the charts it contained, giving the number and description of each. Finally, she compiled a master list, showing exactly which chart was in which envelope. Her efforts certainly made the navigator's life easier and pleasanter.

The stowage of British charts is simpler in that all of them can be folded, printed side in, into 28-by-21-inch rectangles. Also, these charts do not have to be labeled by hand, as each one comes with its name, description, and number already on the back.

LOGS

A log is merely a method of measuring speed. The old-fashioned wood-chip log was a triangular board attached to a line with spaced knots, which was pitched overside. At the exact time the log was cast, the timing glass was turned. At the call "mark," the line was held. When the line was hauled back in, the number of knots run out was counted. With this indication of the distance traveled during a measured interval of time, the speed of the vessel could be ascertained. I actually saw a variation of this method used, on a small scale, on the little ketch *Donau*. It worked perfectly, but each casting of the log required the attention of three men.

Some good navigators who are very familiar with the boat on which they are sailing can merely look overside and give a close estimate of the vessel's speed. For greater accuracy, a taffrail log may be towed. The old standard log is the great big "walker" (Photo 141), which is very expensive and causes appreciable drag on a small yacht. I prefer the Negus log (Photo 140), as it is much smaller and the drag is minimal. The rotor is only seven inches long and a half inch in diameter, not including the fins. It is normally towed on a fifty-foot length of line, and with a little adjustment will work almost perfectly. But while the Negus log seems to be almost universally accurate under sail, under

140. "Walker" log—and Negus log rotor. (D. M. Street)

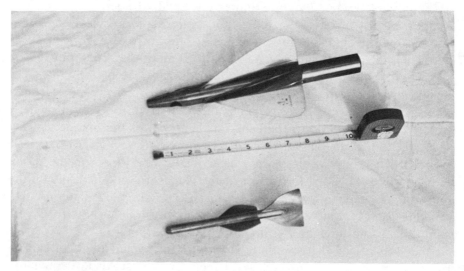

power the extra water shoved astern by the propeller causes it to over-register. A further disadvantage is that sharks love it. When traveling offshore, one should be sure to carry spare log line, spare lead weights, and spare rotors; we have had more than three consumed in one ten-day trip to the United States.

Another disadvantage of the Negus log is that someone must go back aft to read it. The larger "walker" log is obtainable with a re-peater that can be mounted on the chart table. This of course is the navi-gator's delight; he just has to look up to see the distance run.

Nowadays, many types of "steam" gauges are available. They vary from the old Kenyon through the modern electronic instruments cost-ing thousands of dollars. All racing boats have a steam gauge of some sort. For the average cruising man, it is a nice toy, but by no means es-sential. Unless perfectly tuned, it can only be regarded as a compara-tive speed indicator. It is wonderful for guidance in trimming sails, but not so useful for the navigator calculating distances. Some of the steam gauges do have a cumulative distance indicator, and a repeater which can be mounted at the navigator's chart table. This arrangement is fine as long as everything is working accurately.

However, continued reliability over even two seasons is unusual. The various steam gauges are prone to damage, fouling, and what-have-you, and suffer from inaccuracy or complete failure if they become fouled with marine growth. For this reason I feel that the only ones worth the investment are those that are so designed that they may be retracted into the hull for cleaning, repair, or adjustment. If the sensor head is removed and stored inside the boat except when it is actually being used, the repair and maintenance costs will be greatly reduced and accuracy will be vastly increased. Even so, because of the long-term unreliability of the steam gauge, and the difficulty of repairing it in out-of-the-way places, one should always carry a taffrail log as well.

ELECTRICAL AND ELECTRONIC AIDS

Electrical and electronic aids include devices of many degrees of complexity, varying from the radio receiver which provides time signals to the most expensive and complicated radar, loran, and the like. The radio is a basic piece of equipment that all cruising yachts must carry; the others are rather expensive toys. Today there is an increasing ten-dency to overload boats with costly electronic equipment which in many cases serves only as a status symbol. The money required for the elaborate electronic accessories could be better spent on food, sails, and gear to enable the boat to do more cruising. Also, one would then be able to spend less time on shore waiting for electronic gear to be re-paired.

Radio Receivers

The basic shortwave transistor radio, battery powered, is a great boon to the yachtsman. Various makes are on the market, many of which are good. Some are more expensive and better than others, but as a group they never cease to amaze. I recall buying a $12.95 transistor radio as an emergency spare, for use on a delivery trip. It brought in WWV much better than did the expensive set on board, and lasted for many years, until finally it was dropped down the hatch—a noble death! Two separate transistor radios, with spare batteries for each, should be carried, as sooner or later one will be drowned, dropped, left on, or what-have-you. Also, an earphone for the radio is advisable. Wearing it, the navigator can obtain his time tick or use the radio as a direction finder without disturbing the rest of the crew. Similarly, the watch on deck in the middle of the night can listen to the radio without waking anyone.

Direction Finders

Often, a small transistor radio will have a quite accurate direction finder at the top. Correspondingly, many portable, battery-powered transistorized DF's can also be used as radios. A more old-fashioned type of DF, often found on older boats, has a big loop antenna mounted on the deck. All these types of DF suffer from the same disadvantage: they provide no real direct-reading compass for the navigator. He must take his bearing, call "mark" to the helmsman, add or subtract, and obtain his true bearing. There are many chances for error; the course called out by the helmsman may not be exactly right, the boat is swinging while the course is called, and the time lag is such that a few degrees of error inevitably creep in.

The British developed an answer to this problem not too many years ago. Their DF is tuned into a small antenna incorporated into a hand-bearing compass. The navigator can stand up on a cabin top clear of all the rigging, take his DF bearing, and read the magnetic bearing directly from his compass. With this type of DF set, the chances for error are reduced and some quite accurate guessing can be done.

One must say "guessing," for DF sets have very drastic limitations. The first and most fundamental is the one that most people completely ignore. The basic null as broadcast by a DF station is two degrees wide. Thus, if one obtains a perfect bearing on two separate DF stations many miles apart, the width of the null is many miles. To this must be joined the additional miles resulting from human error, which may increase the null by five or ten degrees. At best one is somewhere in a two-degree cone. If one then takes a bearing on still another station, a hundred miles away, one again places oneself somewhere in its wide cone. Especially when human error is taken into account, it is clear that the DF bearing merely gives a good approximation of a boat's position. However, the cone narrows as one approaches the station. One can home in on a DF bearing with a considerable degree of accuracy.

The DF should be regarded as a good method of getting a close approximation of one's position, but not an accurate fix.

OMNI: This is a line-of-sight direction finder, consisting of two small antennas at the top of the mainmast. In the region of an airport, one can turn on the omni, tune to the correct station, fiddle with a few buttons, and obtain a direct true bearing on the station. Since its range is very short, it is only useful in areas where airport radio beacons are numerous. Furthermore, it is expensive, so though it is a very good piece of equipment, one may wish to think twice before installing it.

Consolan

Consolan is excellent in that the signals may be received on a normal portable radio that receives the correct frequency. It is very popular in Europe, and numerous stations cover most of the waters of western Europe. However, in the Western Hemisphere, the one east-coast Consolan station, at Nantucket, is no longer operating as this book goes to press—a pity, since from the yachtsman's point of view Consolan is the cheapest long-range method of radio navigation.

Like other electronic aids, Consolan is not as accurate as yachtsmen seem to assume. The navigation books, and the information on the chart, indicate the margin of error; it can be considerable under certain circumstances.

Loran

Loran, the long range aid to navigation, is universally acclaimed. It is used extensively for navigation by aircraft and by the navies of the world. Loran sets today, though still expensive, are small and compact, and one of them can easily be fitted on a boat of 40 feet LOA. Whether it should be purchased depends largely on one's pocketbook and on the area to be traversed. The chapter in Bowditch on loran includes a chart showing loran coverage. This is definitely not worldwide; there are various large gaps where loran would be totally useless.

The early loran sets were difficult to use, as one had to line up the waves, count the microseconds mentally, change scales, count, again change scales, and count again; somewhere along the line one was likely to make an error, so the result was somewhat variable. All this is now ended; today one simply turns the set on and lines up the waves, and the numbers pop up as if in a pinball machine. Like other methods of electronic navigation, loran is not absolutely accurate, and its results vary according to the boat's position in relation to the master and the slave station. A good discussion of the functions and accuracy of loran can be found in Bowditch.

Few people bother with loran tables, because using them, although not difficult, is very tedious. If accurate results are to be obtained from a loran set, one must have a pair of proportional dividers, to aid in plotting position lines between the various lines on the loran chart. One of the major sources of error in the use of loran is slightly inaccurate or sloppy plotting, which can move the position appreciably, especially on a large-scale chart, perhaps covering the whole of the Atlantic. Employment of the individual coastal charts, with their numerous division lines, is likely to result in a greater degree of accuracy. A loran chart should not be used under a red light, since some of the lines are red, and will be invisible with this illumination.

Decca

Decca is a navigational system which is usually found only in large steamers. It is popular in Europe, not in the Western Hemisphere, where coverage is limited to parts of eastern Canada.

Radar

Radar is of course regarded as absolutely essential for modern high-speed ocean-going commercial vessels. Also, commercial fishermen, coasters, and the like, rely very heavily on radar, and frequently the result is a collision: everyone sits glued to the radar set, not realizing that it is not functioning as it should, and the vessel crashes into something that could perfectly well have been seen visually. Furthermore, wooden boats, unless they have hoisted a radar reflector, do not show up very well on radar.

Radar is seldom seen on yachts of much less than 60 feet LOA. Usually, it is mounted on the mizzenmast, about halfway between the deck and the masthead. In a seaway, the weight of the radar tries to tear the mizzenmast out of the boat. One yachtsman on a comparatively small boat, about 50 feet LOA, conceived what seems a much better system. He managed to get from the company an antenna small enough to fit under his fiber-glass 7½-foot Dyer Dink, and mounted it on the cabin top. This mounting of course reduced his range to five or six miles, but as he pointed out, his navigation could always place him within five or six miles of the headland he was endeavoring to reach. He needed help when visibility was reduced to ten or fifteen yards, in Maine fog. With the aid of his radar set he could leave the harbor and enjoy a wonderful day's sailing, without being able to see a thing. Since he kept careful track of his position by dead reckoning, he could then make his landfall, and pick out the buoys with the radar set before he was close enough to shore to get into any trouble. Thus, for the individual who can afford the expense, and plans to do a large amount of sailing and piloting in areas of poor visibility, the right radar set is a great asset.

Getting the Most Out of Electronic Gear

Electronic navigational gear is good, really good when correctly handled—but no better than its operator. In some cases people have the equipment on board but never try to use it until they really need it —and then discover that they don't know how to make it work. When installed, electrical and electronic gear should be checked out completely by the operator. He should read the manuals and make sure he completely understands how to use his instruments. Then, on a nice clear day, he should go to a known position and verify that he can indeed operate the equipment, and that it is working correctly. For example, if an individual is sitting in Long Island Sound and can take a bearing on Stepping Stones Lighthouse, Execution Rocks, and both pillars of the Throgs Neck Bridge, he knows exactly where he is. If his electronic navigational equipment places him in the same position, everything is fine. If not, either he or the equipment is in error. The nature of the fault should be ascertained, and the difficulty corrected, before any reliance is placed on the equipment.

The performance of radio direction finders, like that of Consolan and loran, is very sensitive both to human error, as has been noted, and to disturbances of the equipment. When a DF is installed, the boat must be taken out near a DF station so that the equipment can be checked and corrected, in the same way as a compass is corrected, both under sail and under power. There may be a heeling error, and sheet leads, especially if they are of wire, may drastically affect DF performance. An error exceeding 45 degrees has been found in more than one DF installation.

The British, who use DF more frequently than we do, have spent more time studying the causes of these errors. In the days of galvanized rigging, they were likely to be extreme. Now that stainless-steel rigging, which is usually almost nonmagnetic, is in general use, the errors have

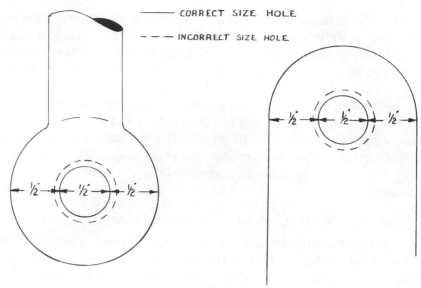

——— CORRECT SIZE HOLE

— — — INCORRECT SIZE HOLE

201. *Bushing weakens fitting.*

been reduced, but they still exist. The British DF experts are very positive in their view that there should be no continuous loops in the rigging, lifelines, and the like. To break the loops, insulators should be placed where the lifelines join the pulpit, and plastic bushings should be installed between the shroud endings and the turnbuckle pins. This is well and good from an electronic point of view, but they may cause difficulties with the rigging. When drilling the end fittings to receive the plastic bushings, one must be very careful not to remove too much meat from the fittings, thereby dangerously reducing their strength. The accurate DF set will not help if the rigging has been lost overside because the end fittings were weakened by the installation of plastic bushings (Drawing 201).

Electronic navigation aids are excellent, but navigation should not be entirely dependent on them. On a boat, anything electrical is prone to failure—batteries run down, generators fail, short circuits blow the works. Furthermore, it goes without saying that for every piece of electronic equipment, the manual and the schematic should be carried on board, so that when failure does occur, repairs can be attempted. In many an out-of-the-way port a good electrician will be found who can fix even unfamiliar equipment, if he is provided with a complete schematic. Similarly, a crewman who is a good electrician can fix the equipment even at sea.

The importance of having the schematic at hand was once demonstrated on *Antilles* in a quite amusing fashion. Bob Lamson, officially the cook but formerly a coast-guard chief engineer, and Viv Snow, the long-time skipper of *Antilles,* were bringing her home from the Virgin Islands one spring. Halfway between Norfolk and Padanaram, in a thick fog, they decided to take a loran fix. Viv went below, turned on the set, and started to get a signal, but suddenly there was the smell of something burning, and a cloud of smoke came out of the set. Viv quickly turned it off and waited. Although the faint aroma of something that had burnt lingered in the main cabin, nothing more happened. He turned the set on again, but it did not work at all. Viv called to. Bob, who left the helm and came below, and the two of them scratched their heads. After a while, Bob remembered how a rat had once shorted the leads on some high-priced electrical equipment on a lightship he was on. He thought perhaps something similar might have happened. They unbolted the loran set, placed it on the cabin floor, laid the schematic alongside, and began to track the circuits. After about half an hour, they came to a burned relay, and in it were the remains of a fried cockroach. They dusted out the remains of the cockroach with a paintbrush, cleaned the relay with some fine dry sandpaper, and reassembled the set. Three years later, when we crossed the Atlantic in 1969, it was still working perfectly. Moral—manuals for equipment should be kept on board at all times.

PILOTING

Since many books on piloting and coastal navigation are available, we will not discuss the actual methods of piloting here. However, it should be pointed out that the individual who wishes to become a good pilot must do more than read; he must practice regularly. To begin with, he should try piloting in good weather, and attempt to develop accuracy in running from one point to another. If he becomes so proficient that he continually hits every buoy right on the nose in good weather, the chances are that when the weather turns bad, the skill and confidence he has built up will serve him well, and he will have no problems. If one has the necessary equipment, practicing piloting can be fun, and something to pass the time on the nice quiet sails.

NAVIGATION TECHNIQUES
CELESTIAL NAVIGATION

Some people are content with a very rudimentary knowledge of celestial navigation, believing that it is too complicated to master. More than one boat has been guided across the Atlantic from the Cape Verde Islands to Barbados by individuals who know only how to take a noon sight, and nothing more. Such individuals get an idea of their longitude by timing the rising and setting of the sun, and interpolating from the nautical almanac; latitude they estimate, just steering due west from Cape Verde. Sometimes they do indeed reach Barbados; on other occasions they pass through the Antilles and end up in South America. In any event, this method of navigation is not very accurate and of course will work only in areas such as tropics, where one always has a good clear horizon at dawn and dusk.

When I first started to learn to take sights, my instructor, the navigator on *Arabella* in her 1955 transatlantic crossing, refused to help me at all with star sights. He was a master mariner, had raced yachts all his life, and had been around Cape Horn and the Cape of Good Hope four times each. He pointed out that while taking star sights from the bridge of a steamer is relatively simple when it is done every day, taking star sights from the deck of a small yacht is most difficult. He pointed out also that only the individual who continually practices taking star sights is likely to obtain accurate results. Further, he maintained that if the weather is good enough so that one can get a star sight, one could doubtless have obtained a sun sight during the day, making the star sight unnecessary.

As the years go by, I find myself more and more in agreement with him. On numerous trips north and south, I have taken very few star sights: during the northern half of the trip the weather is usually so overcast that there are no stars; during the southern half of the trip the weather is so good that star sights are unnecessary; and in the tropics the twilight is so brief that there is scarcely time to get a round of the stars.

Once when sailing from New York to Cork on *Antilles,* I firmly resolved to become very proficient in taking star sights, but could get only five sun sights in seventeen days, and no star sights, as it was continually foggy, overcast, or raining.

Anyone who has the inclination, time, energy, and proper weather conditions, and is willing to work at it, can become proficient enough to take a complete round of the stars, obtaining a good fix. But the average yachtsman is too busy being captain, sailing master, engineer, and so on to spare the time every morning and evening to take a round of the stars and work out the results. However, even if one does not become proficient enough to obtain a complete round of the stars, one may find it worthwhile to learn to take star sights, and more important, planet sights. Just one sight on an individual body gives a line of position, which when crossed with a D.R., DF, loran, or afternoon-sun line, can provide a very good running fix. Among the planets, Venus is especially useful, as frequently it enables one to get an early-morning longitude. The moon is of most value when it is visible during the day, since then one can take simultaneous moon and sun sights and obtain a fix at once. Similarly, when sailing along a coast, one can frequently cross a sun line with a visual bearing on shore, a DF bearing, a loran line, or what-have-you.

Although sighting on the sun provides only a line of position, often one can gain a surprising amount of information just from a series of sights on the sun. For this reason, a careful check should be kept on the sun's azimuth during the day in relation to the course being sailed. For example, the course from St. Thomas to the southern part of the United States is normally about northwest. A sight in the morning when the sun is directly over the stern will give a line of position at right angles to the course. Another sight the following day, again when the sun is at square to the course line, will enable one to calculate the exact distance traveled during the previous twenty-four hours, so that the log can be checked for accuracy and the speed of the current verified. Further, an afternoon sight when the sun is exactly beam on to the vessel will give a line of position parallel to the course line. By quick inspection one can then ascertain whether one is to the right or the left of the rhumb line.

Taking the noon sight, which is discussed in the various navigation books, is of course the standard method of determining latitude. It is also possible to obtain a three-line running fix over a short period of time by taking sights shortly before noon, at noon, and after noon. In view of the leisurely pace of a sailboat, when all three observations are made within an hour, this can be regarded for all intents and purposes as an exact fix. Further, in the tropical latitudes the sun goes from east to west very rapidly. It does this whenever its declination is approximately the same as the yacht's latitude. Thus it is possible at noon to get a five- or six-line position fix in a matter of ten or fifteen minutes. Under these conditions, the noon sight should not be missed; until the following noon there will be no way of determining latitude except by the North Star, since the sun is always almost due east or due west when its declination is about the same as the observer's latitude.

The most important part of celestial navigation is practice. One should not wait until sailing offshore to take sights; one should try taking them while along the coast, so that their accuracy can be verified during a practice period.

Many navigation books suggest taking a series of sights and recording them on a graph. This method is excellent for beginners, except that it is slightly complicated. I have a system which I find easier, but it does require the help of another person. The procedure is to take a sight, have the assistant write it down, noting also the time, and have him then give warning when forty-five seconds have passed since the sight was made. At that point, another sight is taken. The process is repeated until a series of seven or eight sights about a minute apart has been obtained. While the intervals between sights will not all be exactly a minute long, they will not vary by more than two or three seconds. A survey of the series will rapidly indicate what the change in altitude per minute should be at the particular time of day. Any incorrect sights will stand out clearly, as they will not fit the general pattern of the increase or decrease in altitude.

Those who are very eager navigators, and really wish to become efficient at their sun sights, will find that a pan of oil in the backyard works excellently as an artificial horizon, especially if a small glass skylight is placed over it so that the wind does not disturb the oil. Or one can carry navigational equipment, and the pan and oil, in the trunk of the car, stop the car along the highway, take a sight, make a notation, and do the calculations later at home. An advantage of this method is that one can continually check on one's accuracy, since the shooting is done from known positions.

Numerous navigators take a sight and call it out to someone else, who writes it down, also noting the time. This procedure is permissible for beginners, but except during extremely heavy weather, it is not really acceptable on a cruising boat for an experienced navigator. There are just not enough people around. To have one man at the helm, one man taking the sight, and one man recording the sight and the time, is to keep the whole crew busy on a small yacht.

Other navigators use a stopwatch. Their method is to take a sight, start the stopwatch, go below, note the time, stop the watch, and subtract the seconds recorded by the watch from the chronometer time to obtain the time of the sight. The objection to this method is that the stopwatch is just another thing to keep dry. Most experienced navigators prefer to take the sight and then keep track of the passage of time by counting by thousands until they reach the chronometer. It is impossible to make an error of more than one or two seconds during the fifteen seconds required to go below, and an error of one second will not affect navigation on the average small yacht.

The navigator must find a comfortable, steady place where he can chock himself, leaving both hands free for the sextant. For example, he may choose to lean against the mizzenmast or the boom gallows.

In very rough weather, the navigator will find it necessary to take a series of sights, and pick the best one. In this case, he will have to have someone else to note the time and record the sights. With a big sea running, it is important to take the sights while at the top of the sea. To do so, he may have to stand on the main boom, mizzen boom, winches, or the like. It is then essential that he tie himself to the mast with a sail stop, so that if thrown off balance by a sudden jump of the vessel, he can still hang on to the sextant with both hands and not worry about going overboard.

PLOTTING

Taking correct sights is of little use if the plotting is not also done properly.

A good accurate log and a continuous plot must be kept. Even when the boat is well offshore, an accurate plot is necessary; otherwise, especially when running downwind, the watch on deck may not realize how far from the rhumb line the boat is being sailed in the attempt to avoid jibing. This situation arose on one trip in which I participated. We suddenly found ourselves well north of the course, and instead of being broad off, we had to come on a close reach to get back on the rhumb line and avoid some icebergs. This predicament developed because though the navigator (myself) knew we had altered course, he did not realize how fast we were traveling. The watch on deck had noted the course changes in the log, but had not plotted them. After this experience, we decided that the watch on deck should be responsible for plotting their course at the time they turned over their watch.

Few navigators like to have the entire crew playing with the charts, as too many pen scratches merely confuse matters. However, the navigator can easily keep on the chart table a plotting sheet of a convenient scale, marked with the latitude and longitude of the vessel. Then the watch captains can keep a continuous running plot. The navigator, by transferring information from the plotting sheet to the chart, can maintain a close watch on the boat's actual position, and the issue is not confused by everyone's hen tracks across the chart.

Traverse Tables

Some navigators eliminate the need for complicated plotting by using—and training everyone to use—traverse tables. They were commonly employed years ago in sailing ships and small fishing vessels. They have now dropped into disuse, but can still be found in Bowditch. The actual method of working with traverse tables is too long to be described here, but it should be mentioned that when using these tables, one can comfortably do all the work necessary for calculating latitude and longitude in a small notebook on one's lap, without rules, dividers, and the like. Then one need only mark the calculated latitude and longitude on the chart.

Hadrian

For those who can afford it, Hadrian, made by Brookes and Gatehouse, greatly simplifies the problem of calculating a D.R. position. This instrument, which is connected to both the log and the compass, automatically records all variations in speed and direction, and gives the result continuously in terms of distance traveled and course made good through the water. The effects of current must of course still be plotted by the navigator, but guesswork concerning the continual variations of course and speed is eliminated.

Useful Navigation Tables

TACKING DOWNWIND: Navigators frequently plot out tacking-downwind diagrams, i.e., alterations in course away from the rhumb line to increase speed. There is continual argument as to whether or not this pays off in day races. However, on a long ten- or twelve-mile leg, the navigator can sit down and work out the problem, telling the skipper what increase in speed he must have to compensate for the extra distance sailed. Table XIV (Appendix) shows the extra speed required to make worthwhile various deviations from a course dead downwind. BEATING TO WINDWARD: Similarly, going to windward two problems arise: how far, in distance through the water, one actually has to sail to get from one point to another when beating to windward; and how close one should point. The amount of distance traveled going to windward varies drastically with the tacking angle. If the tacking angle is 90 degrees, for every mile to be covered dead to windward, the boat must sail 1.4 miles through the water. If the tacking angle is increased to 120 degrees, which is not at all uncommon with a cruising boat offshore when a big swell is rolling in, for every mile to windward one must sail two miles. Thus, beating to windward in the open sea against a steady equatorial current is pretty much a dead loss unless one has a very large boat.

It is relatively simple to use Table XV to figure the distance one must sail when beating dead to windward if the course line and wind are of similar bearing. However, the problem becomes more complicated when the course is 090 and the wind is 080. Hence Table XVI (Appendix), which shows the lessening of distance for each five degrees if the wind is to the right or left of the course, is useful. This column is figured with a tacking angle of 90 degrees. Thus one can enter the table at the column representing the tacking angle and read across on the row that gives the closest number of degrees that the wind is right or left of the course (rhumb line). Figures at the intersection will give the distance to be sailed in relation to the rhumb line (A), the percentage of time to be spent on the long tack (B), and the percentage to be spent on the short tack (C). Having figured how many miles must be sailed to reach the objective on the basis of a tacking angle of 90 degrees, one can then enter Table XVI with the actual tacking angle, and immediately see the percentage of increase. Multiplying this percentage of increase by the number of miles to be sailed with a 90-degree tacking angle should give a good approximation of the distance that must be sailed going to windward, providing no wind shifts occur.

THE HUMAN ELEMENT

If he is to do a good job, the navigator must learn to know his boat and his helmsman. Some helmsmen always sail absolutely on course; others are optimistic, and when the boat is on the wind, always declare her direction to be five degrees higher than it actually is, and her speed to be two-tenths of a knot faster. Others are pessimistic. Also, on a shy reach all boats tend to kite high off the course; similarly, when sailing broad off, especially when the main-boom fore guy is not rigged, a helmsman will tend to sail to windward of the course.

Good navigation, like good cooking, requires a comfortable place to work, the necessary tools, and time for practice. The skipper who knows he has a competent navigator is relieved of a tremendous responsibility and can concentrate upon the actual running and sailing of the yacht.

If the skipper is himself the navigator, and is planning long cruises, he should teach someone else in the crew to navigate as well, for an assistant will prove very helpful. On many delivery trips, my first mate has been Dave Ellis. Being an excellent navigator, he has saved me tremendous amounts of effort. Especially in rough, wet weather, life is much easier for everyone on the boat if there are two navigators. Whoever is on deck can take the sight, pass down the sextant, and let the calculation be done by the one sitting comfortably below, free of the necessity of struggling into foul-weather gear.

XVII

Self Steering

We all like to sail, and most of us like to have the helm for a good part of the time. But to spend four, six, or eight hours straight on the helm can become a great bore—or worse—especially if one does it for weeks on end with no relief. John Barsdell, who sailed his *Pip II* across the Atlantic with his brother-in-law Jack McKittrich as crew, reported that the last few days at sea were pure torture, as they had been unable to get the boat to self-steer at all during their forty-five days at sea.

If enough thought is given to the problem, one can generally find a way to make a boat self-steer most of the time merely by trimming the sails. *Pip II* was a standard Folkboat, with a tall, narrow rig and a very short keel. This is the type of boat with which self steering is most difficult, for although she will be light on the helm, the keel is so short that the slightest bit of wave will throw her off course and she will not come back on course.

A more conservative cruising boat with a longer keel, especially if the sail plan is spread out fore and aft, can usually be made to self-steer as long as the wind is abeam or forward of the beam. Once the wind gets aft of the beam, self steering is very difficult until the wind gets dead aft. Then, with twin genoas, twin spinnakers, or twin staysails, it is comparatively easy to make a boat self-steer, without the aid of vane steering or an autopilot.

SELF STEERING WITHOUT MECHANICAL AIDS

Years ago, in the days when Josh Slocum was sailing around the world, and Claud Worth was doing his early cruising, self steering under sail was relatively easy. The boats had long keels, long bowsprits, and long booms. The leverage exerted by either the leech of the mainsail or the luff of the jib was very considerable, because of the long, low sail plan. Thus when going to windward, if the jib was trimmed a little bit flat it would always hold the head off; similarly, if the boat sailed below the course, the leech of the mainsail, trimmed well back aft, would bring her back up on course. With *Spray*, Slocum was even able to run downwind without rigging twins. He merely sheeted his little jib topsail, mounted on the head stay, so that it was absolutely flat, and whenever the boat tried to come up, the leverage of the jib topsail would pull her head back down. Similarly, with the fore guy rigged on the main boom, and a big, broad half-acre mainsail, it was very difficult for a boat of *Spray*'s type to bear off below the course. This type of heavy, plodding cruising boat is seldom seen today; more frequently the design of the cruising yacht falls somewhere between that of the traditional cruising boat and that of an ocean racer.

In the 1930's, ocean cruising either single-handed or with a small crew became very popular. The result was the advent of twin spinnakers, twin staysails, twin genoas, square sails, and so on, which could be rigged in one way or another to enable a boat to sail dead downwind, or with the wind on the quarter, without steering and with little or no danger of jibing. The great problem with these various twin rigs was that they required a tremendous number of blocks, tackles, fore guys, lifts, after guys, and the like. Now, with the advent of the electric and hydraulic autopilots and the vane self-steering gear, the complicated twin rig has been largely abandoned. Instead, the autopilot or the vane gear is set, and the boat sails downwind with a normal fore-and-aft rig, as discussed in Chapter XIX.

The methods used to make a modern boat self-steer without the aid of an autopilot or a vane gear vary with each individual boat. Where there is a long, narrow centerboard, self steering is relatively easy to achieve, as the center of lateral plane can be shifted for and aft by adjusting the angle of the board. Boats that have twin centerboards or a main board and a trimming board (whether aft or forward of the main board) are even easier to make self-steering. The approach here is to adjust the sails and the underwater profile of the boat to achieve balance. The person who is interested in doing serious cruising on a boat of this type will find it worthwhile to tabulate the center of effort of the sails under various rigs, and the center of lateral plane of the hull with the board or boards at various settings. Once he has studied this data, and has obtained a few weeks of experience on the boat, he should find it relatively simple to get a boat of this type to self-steer.

Self steering is rather difficult to achieve on the modern keel boats, with their short keels. The problem is further complicated by the fact that more and more boats are being steered by wheels. To be sure, with wheel steering, the helm can be locked, but it can only be locked firmly into position, with no come and go. If steering is by tiller, an arrangement of lashing line and shock cord in various directions can usually be devised which will enable the boat to self-steer, perhaps at the cost of a maze of jig lines, shock cord, snatch blocks, and the like.

We can seldom get *Iolaire* to self-steer by simply lashing the helm, but if the helm is lashed from the windward side and a piece of shock cord is placed around the lee cockpit winch and over the tiller, and tension is adjusted as necessary by the addition of extra loops of shock cord around the tiller, she can be made to self-steer for hours or even days at a time, as long as the wind is abeam or forward of abeam.

Once the wind gets on the quarter the problem is more complicated, though still not insoluble. The piece of shock cord from the tiller to the lee winch is retained, but the helm is not lashed from the windward side. Instead, a jig line from the genoa sheet goes through a snatch block on the windward side of the boat and then to the tiller, which is held in place by shock cord alone (Drawing 202). If the boat heads up too much, the extra strain causes the jib sheet to straighten out, pulling the jig line, which in turn pulls the tiller to windward against the shock cord, causing her to bear off. As the genoa tries to collapse, the shock cord to the lee winch pulls the tiller to leeward, heading the boat up until the genoa is full; thus she gets back on course. With this arrangement, and a fore guy on the main boom. *Iolaire* will just about sail herself for long periods. Admittedly, one cannot go below and sleep, but one can do jobs on deck, navigate, read, catnap etc. While she is not really self-steering, the helmsman is relieved of the minute-by-minute responsibility of steering. Going dead downwind or almost dead downwind, we can usually get her to sail herself by rigging the big genoa to

202. *Jib sheet to the tiller; shock cord on the tiller balances the jib.*

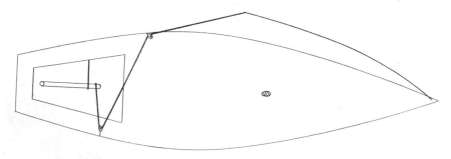

leeward to the main boom and the medium genoa to windward on the spinnaker pole, and shock cord on the tiller. Again the result is not absolute self steering, but certainly gives the helmsman relief.

On some boats, one can achieve self steering merely by trimming sails, while leaving the helm free. Guy Thompson, who designed the Calliope series, and the T 24 and T 31, excels in boats that are self-steering. He builds a sailing model of each boat, and unless the model can self-steer without a vane gear, he does not complete the design. He is probably the only designer in the world who actually sees models of his boats under sail before the boats are built. With a little knowledge of the laws of physics, one can estimate from a model the performance of a full-scale boat. The effect of a 10-knot breeze on a model is practically equivalent to that of a full gale on a full-sized boat. This must be taken into account when one judges from the performance of a small model what a projected full-scale yacht would do.

ELECTRIC AUTOMATIC PILOTS

Automatic pilots—iron mikes—have been known on power boats since the early 1920's. They were not used on sailboats until after World War II, and even now they are not often seen. Since the autopilot follows the compass, it works continually, and consumes a fair amount of amperage. The autopilot cannot anticipate that a yacht will usually come back on course of her own volition. However, if the sails are well trimmed, the wind is steady, and the coarse setting of the autopilot is used, on a well-balanced yacht the autopilot frequently does not do a tremendous amount of work. Accordingly, I have often wondered why instead of having just two adjustments—fine and coarse—an autopilot could not be fitted with a device, like the rheostat on a compass light, with settings at five-degree intervals—for deviations, let us say, of ten, fifteen, and twenty degrees. If the autopilot were then set so that it would be triggered only by the widest deviation, a boat could frequently be made to self-steer, with the autopilot cutting in only very occasionally.

Normally, an autopilot reads off the compass, and each time the wind shifts, the sails must be adjusted. But an electric autopilot can be made to operate in other ways. For example, autopilots that work off the wind indicator have been built.

In the late 1930's Arthur P. Davis, who was racing in the I.O.D. class in Long Island Sound, devoted a good deal of thought to this problem. He installed in an I.O.D. racing sloop, 33 feet 6 inches LOA, an autopilot running off a masthead wind indicator, powered by dry cells. He obtained the permission of the class to race his boat with this autopilot, although not to be counted in with the regular season's competitors. The autopilot running from the wind indicator was so successful that had he been included as a competitor, he would have won the season's point championship. In normal conditions, the autopilot was much better going to windward than a helmsman; the autopilot picked up lifts and headers much faster and more consistently than even the best helmsman. Its one failure—or rather, less than complete success—was in very light shifting winds. When a wind shift of thirty or forty degrees occurs, a helmsman will ease on around with the lift, but the autopilot slammed the rudder hard around, thereby stopping the boat.

It is also interesting to note that with his autopilot sailing for him all season, Davis was able to devote himself to studying wind shifts, racing tactics, and his rivals' tactics, and he put his time to such good use that the following year, when he raced without the autopilot, he won the season's championship, although hitherto he had been strictly a middle-of-the-road competitor. Davis' description of his experiment, in an article called "Automatic Helmsman for Sailing Yachts," may be found in *Yachting* for November, 1946.

ELECTRIC AUTOMATIC PILOT TIED TO TRIM TAB

One reason for the high consumption of amperage by electric autopilots is the force required to turn the main rudder. If the autopilot could be tied into a trim tab mounted at the back end of the rudder, or if the main rudder could be locked and the boat steered by a small auxiliary rudder run by the autopilot, a much smaller electric motor could be used and the amperage consumed could be considerably reduced.

In 1962, I discussed these possibilities with Captain Fred Lawton, of Raytheon, during the New York Boat Show. He felt that they were practical, and also that with the aid of a changeover switch and an electric wind indicator, an autopilot could be so installed that it would work off either the wind indicator or the compass. The electronics experts present agreed, but the marketing experts vetoed the proposals on the grounds that there was not enough interest to make them profitable.

However, in 1970 the gaff-rigged Caryl ketch *Coryphaena* arrived in Grenada with the autopilot rigged to the trim tab. The autopilot read off the compass, but the owner, John Mathias, an electrical engineer, was in the process of changing the installation so that it would work off either the compass or the wind indicator.

Very little power was required to operate the trim tab. The entire autopilot (compass excepted) was no larger than a shoe box; it was mounted directly on the rudderhead, and drew a tenth of an ampere per hour. Furthermore, it was built almost entirely out of standard auto parts, the main motor being a 12-volt windshield-wiper motor from a Simca car. An autopilot of this type would be practical for those who do not like to run the generator for hours on end.

PROBLEMS AND POSSIBILITIES OF AUTOPILOTS

Autopilots have a justifiably bad reputation for reliability. Also, they are commonly supposed to be very complicated, though actually they are not. When an autopilot is installed, the owner should learn to do the basic maintenance on it. Then he should make sure that a schematic diagram and repair instructions are kept on board at all times, along with a complete set of spares.

The biggest advantage of the electric self-steering gear is that even if it is tied to the wind indicator, there is no necessity for pieces of vane hanging out over the stern, such as are required for vane steering. If sailing engineers would investigate the possibilities mentioned above—for adjustable setting, tying into a trim tab rather than the main rudder, tying into the wind indicator rather than the compass (or installation of a changeover switch to make possible tying into either the compass or the wind indicator)—the suitability of the electric autopilot for the sailboat would become even greater.

HYDRAULIC
SELF-STEERING GEAR

Hydraulic self-steering gear has been home built and installed on both *Rena* and *Seva,* and has worked out very well on both boats. Such gear, running off a hydraulic pump which is powered by a free-wheeling shaft, is now available commercially in England from Sharp and Company. Stan Young, of *Solquest-Lunaquest* fame, has had it installed on *Lunaquest,* and is completely happy with the results, finding it to be much more reliable than the electric autopilot.

In the hydraulic self-steering gear (Drawing 203), a hydraulic pump is belted off the propeller shaft, which is allowed to turn freely. This pumps hydraulic pressure through two systems: one part of the pressure is utilized by the main hydraulic ram, or push-rod power transfer, attached to the tiller or rudder; the other part is delivered to a secondary hydraulic system, operating the changeover valves which give port or starboard rudder. This secondary system is activated in one direction or the other by an electrically operated valve responsive to a photoelectric cell reading off the compass. The only electricity needed—less

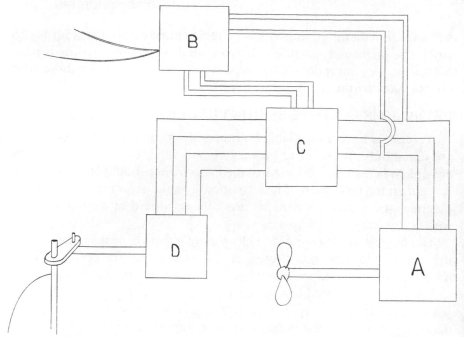

203. *Hydraulic self-steering gear: A, hydraulic pump worked by a free-turning shaft; B, valve electrically operated off the compass or wind indicator; C, hydraulically operated valve activated by B; D, push-rod power transfer connected to the rudder.*

than an ampere per hour—is for opening and closing this tiny valve. The electrical portion of the system is simple and easily repaired.

Once installed and functioning, the hydraulic system should last forever. Like the electric autopilot, it could be made to work off the wind indicator rather than the compass. This system is said to start operating when the boat is moving at between one and two knots. The only objection to it is that the turning of the propeller results in drag, but even this situation might be used to advantage. Since the propeller is allowed to turn to develop the hydraulic pressure, there seems to be no reason why a generator should not also be belted off the shaft. Then one could simultaneously operate the self-steering gear and build up reserves of electricity.

VANE SELF-STEERING GEAR

The appearance of the vane self-steering gear on full-sized yachts is relatively recent, though it has been used on model racing yachts since the early 1930's. In 1936 Marin Marie installed one on his forty-five-foot motor cruiser *Arielle*. With the aid of this gear he powered across the Atlantic single-handed, his being probably the only small yacht to make such a voyage.

Not until 1955 did the vane self-steering gear appear on full-sized sailing boats—Major Ian Major's *Buttercup* and Michael Henderson's *Mick the Miller*. Both boats had gears designed by, or with the aid of, Colonel H. D. (Blondie) Hasler, who should probably be regarded as the father of the vane self-steering gear.

Many types of this gear are now available (Photos 141–146). Some are strictly experimental; others are produced commercially. In its basic form, the vane self-steering gear is a relatively simple affair, oper-

141–146. Various vane self-steering rigs.

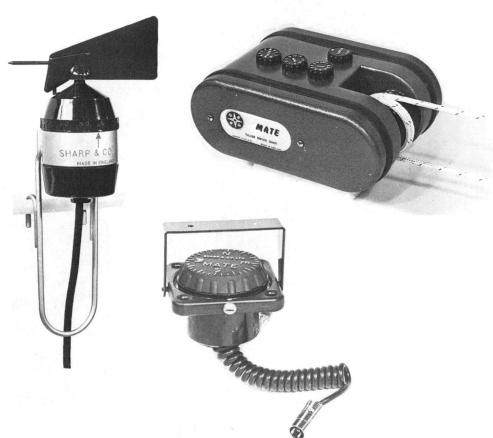

141. Sharp and Company automatic pilot: tiller drive unit (right top), *wind-vane* (left), *and magnetic sense unit* (below).

142. *Quantock Marine enterprises'
QME wind-vane gear.
(Quantock Marine Enterprises)*

143. *Automate self-steering gear. (Automate Co.)*

144. Mike Henderson gear designed
specially for Prout Ranger 31
cruising cat. (J. B. Moore)

145. Home-made
self-steering.
(D. M. Street)

146. *Hasler self-steering gear.*
(*D. M. Street*)

ating off a trim tab on the back end of the rudder (Drawing 204). The wind vane turns the small trim tab to one side, thereby causing the rudder to be sucked to the other. Relatively little force is required too turn the trim tab, but a rather complicated linkage is necessary to keep the rudder from slamming from hard starboard to hard port; credit for figuring out this linkage must go to Colonel Hasler and the friends who helped him.

The amount of force necessary to turn a trim tab is minimal. In fact, once having seen how easy it is to steer a boat with a trim tab, one wonders why, fifteen years after the first trim-tab self-steering gear was installed, we are still fighting the whole rudder instead of connecting our steering linkage directly to the trim tab.

The first self-steering gear could be used only with an outboard rudder, but the seed had been planted and ideas grew from it. For boats with inboard rudders, Hasler designed a pendulum gear (Drawing 205). This type of gear too is activated by a wind vane, which turns the pendulum in the required direction. Water flowing past the pendulum twists it up to the surface of the water, thereby tightening the tiller lines and

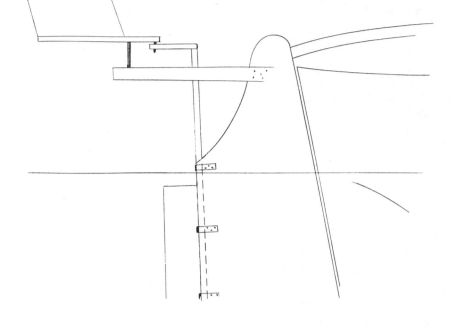

204. *Basic vane self-steering gear.*

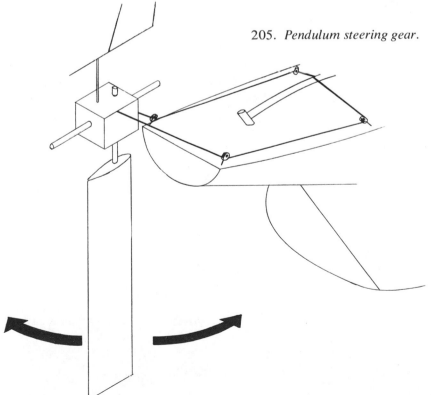

205. *Pendulum steering gear.*

causing the rudder to swing. This type of gear can be rigged to yoke across an inboard tiller or to run around drums and operate a wheel-steering installation.

There are wind-vane gears that operate the rudder directly, but they are suitable only for the boat that has a balance rudder and is not particularly heavy. Still other types of gears operate on an auxiliary rudder clamped on the stern; when the boat is self-steering, the main rudder is fixed at an appropriate angle.

Because pieces of vane hang out over the stern, the wind-vane gear is practically impossible to mount on the sailing ketch or yawl unless the boat has been specifically designed for that type of gear. However, there are some varieties of vane gears that have no underwater projections. Quantock Marine Enterprises' QME is a horizontal-axis wind-vane gear which is reported to be able to steer boats of up to about fifty feet. Having no underwater projections, it can be mounted on any type of boat (Photo 142; Drawing 206).

All these rigs are prone to failure. Pendulums break, pins in the steering gear sheer, frames warp, as they are put under tremendous and constant strain. When ordering or installing self-steering gear, one should be careful to obtain a complete set of spares. Replacement of parts as necessary during a cruise is easy, but improvising parts from odds and ends may be slow and difficult, perhaps impossible.

Having self steering is like having on board an extra hand, available day or night. Watches must still be kept and a good lookout must be maintained, but instead of spending all his time at the helm, the watch on deck can check matters every few mintues and in the intervals do the navigation, ship's chores, and so on. Without self-steering, long trips with a two-man crew get to be a great trial, but many a boat with good self-steering gear has arrived at the Antilles, after crossing from England, with her two-man crew in fine shape—happy, healthy, and well rested.

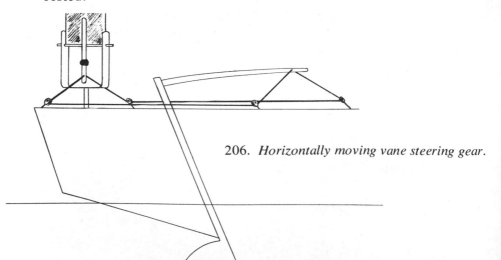

206. *Horizontally moving vane steering gear.*

XVIII

Seamanship

There are people who have raced small boats all their lives, are most competent sailors, are unbeatable in round-the-buoy racing, but cannot be regarded as seamen. They have had little or no experience outside their own small boats. For them, such skills as splicing wire to rope are black magic. Similarly, the crew member on an ocean racer is not necessarily a complete seaman. He knows how to crank winches, set spinnakers, change jibs, tack, and jibe. But his proficiency too often depends on the fact that he is operating perfect gear and has a large crew to support him.

By contrast, a seaman, in my estimation, is a man who can cruise over long distances with a relatively small crew. He can repair his own sails, and is something of an electrician, carpenter, plumber, and mechanic. He can cope with calms and hurricanes. He can jury rig and keep going. When he reaches a destination in his boat, he takes up food, fuel, and water, has a shower at the local yacht club or marina, and then returns to his boat, living aboard.

A seaman is a man who cruises fast and far with his small crew, and enjoys it. There are many seamen who know much more than I, but they are too busy sailing, or preparing to sail, to take time to sit down and put their knowledge into writing. From men like these I have gained quantities of odd bits of information, which I hope I have compiled into readable form.

Seamanship is seldom really well learned unless a person has sailed on various boats with various people. Many single-handers have done all their sailing on their own boats, with no one to point out their errors, and with no exposure to other people's methods. As a result, they have often been doing the same thing wrong—or the hard way—for many years. They drift, as it were, around the world. They think they know how to sail, but often really do not.

Frequently, an individual of this type may be recognized by the appearance of his boat. For example, his headsails and mainsails, when furled, may be secured to the boom by a line continually spiraled around them. This is the hard way; it takes much more time, and the sails don't look as neat, and take much longer to unfurl. The good seaman is likely, instead, to secure his sails with nice flat sail stops (which I prefer) or to use shock-cord furling. One can also judge the competence of a seaman by observing the gear on deck, how the lines are coiled, whether or not there are gilguys on the halyards; one can note the set of the sail covers, the set of the awning, or the securing of the dock lines.

An obvious indicator of good seamanship is the ability to handle one's vessel under sail in restricted waters. Many a person who considers himself a good seaman starts up the engine, drops off the hook, powers out of the harbor, and once outside, sets the sails. He sails to his heart's content until he is ready to return to restricted waters; then down come the sails and on goes the engine, and he drives the boat home. For this individual an engine failure will completely ruin a cruise, as he does not have the ability to sail on and off the hook, into and out of crowded harbors. I am not advocating that one should come into a harbor with a 180-percent low-cut genoa set—such a sail is hard to handle and completely obstructs vision—but certainly any seaman should be able to handle his boat in restricted waters with a three-quarters genoa or a working jib.

Watching a yacht sail in restricted waters is always a good way to judge the seamanship of the members of the crew. Some manage this kind of sailing only with much shouting, screaming, and running around; others come in with the minimum amount of fuss and furor— they are the seamen.

The most obvious element of good seamanship is the ability to sail long distances at a respectable speed without breaking down any gear. The ocean racers continually turn in fabulous runs, but they are raced on a coast-be-damned basis. It is often said that ocean racing is like standing fully clothed in a cold shower, trying to smoke a cigar, and tearing up fifty-dollar bills—all at the same time. On an ocean racer everything is likely to be left up much too long; a sail may stay up till it blows out, a split spinnaker being easier to take down than one full of wind. The ocean-racing sailor continually takes chances. On a cold, dark, rainy night he will run into harbor, with his spinnaker set, in order to cross the finish line a few seconds sooner. He will duck across sandbanks on a falling tide to save three minutes, which may mean the race. He always has a big crew on board to bail him out if a mistake is made, plenty of spare gear, and repair facilities. Frequently the prize goes not to the seaman but to the man who has the biggest checkbook. Perhaps at the end of an ocean race a special trophy should be presented to the boat that comes in first on corrected time with no gear damage at all. This is the trophy I would be happier to win than any other.

Though the cruising sailor is not seeking to break speed records, he does not sail slowly or sloppily. The good seaman does the hard thing: heaves to for the night and waits for the dawn instead of running in, tacks off short to clear all shoals, shortens down in heavy weather— but still turns in good runs. During the innumerable trips I have made on *Antilles* as navigator, helping to take her south in the winter and back north in the summer, we have pushed her hard. I can remember one trip where we took off from St. Thomas with everyone a little under the weather and not really concentrating. Two days out, I discovered we were moving very well indeed, and urged everyone to push a little harder. Under a strictly cruising rig, we did 920 miles in five days, which I thought was tremendous going for a vessel of 46 feet LOA without the aid of any racing sails and little or no assistance from the current.

On the very next trip, we took off from Morehead City for St. Thomas, close reaching across the Gulf Stream, with the wind blowing very hard out of the northeast against the northeast-running Stream. Needless to say, everyone was most uncomfortable. Two of the crew were violently seasick, the skipper, Viv Snow, was not sick but was eating saltines by the bushel basket, and I felt so bad I was eating beef stew out of the can—but *Antilles* enjoyed it. After two days, the wind shifted to the northwest. In five days, we sailed 960 miles.

Between 1960 and 1970, *Antilles* made ten round trips between the east coast of the United States and St. Thomas, and in addition sailed across the Atlantic to Ireland, down to Portugal and Madeira, and back to the islands. During this entire period there was no damage except that a very tired working jib finally gave up the ghost, and three or four feet of genoa track lifted off. We used cruising sails rather than racing sails most of the time. This absence of damage was the result of having a well-built boat, with good-quality gear, and a first-rate skipper who kept the gear in top order and signed on a fine crew of experienced seamen.

DOCKING

HANDLING UNDER POWER

Handling under power is an art which can be mastered only by constant experience, though reading the articles in the various yachting magazines on this subject is certainly advisable. Individual boats have their own idiosyncrasies; some back down to port, some back down to starboard, and some won't steer at all when backing down. Many centerboarders won't handle well with the board up, and most sailboats are very difficult to turn into the wind when moving slowly; hence, on a yawl some seamen will suddenly set the mizzen, to swing the bow into the wind. When handling under power, a good seaman does not need a large crew to throw lines, fend off, or heave the bow in by force. He remembers that a spring line rigged amidships is the most effective line in the boat. If a spring line is correctly rigged and the engine is set to slow ahead, most boats can be brought to lie alongside the dock with no other line over. The great rush to get the bow line across and secure usually results in nothing but a bent pulpit, panic, a call for fenders, and scraped topsides. Coming alongside or leaving a dock should not require muscle power for fending off; it should all be done mainly with the spring line, aided by bow and stern lines, and a few appropriately placed fenders.

EQUIPMENT

Heaving Lines

Two items that are of great help when one is maneuvering alongside a dock are a good long boathook and a heaving line.

It is presumed that every good seaman can throw a ¾-inch or ⅝-inch dock line a moderate distance, and a ½-inch line quite a distance. But in some circumstances—when maneuvering alongside a dock, or trying to get a tow line onto a freighter or pulling a man out of the water—these kinds of line are not suitable, and a good heaving line is essential.

Having line consists of light line, of ¼- or 5⁄16-inch diameter, with a monkey's fist at the end. On commercial steamers, such as freighters, a weighted monkey's fist is not used, since the line is always thrown from the height of the deck down onto a dock. If a longshoreman finds a weighted monkey's fist at the end of a heaving line, he cuts it off and tosses it into the harbor. However, on small yachts a weighted heaving line is essential, since the line is commonly heaved upward onto a dock or freighter deck. The monkey's fist can be weighted with a fishing sinker of suitable size, or an old nut.

On some boats a heaving line is kept always ready; on others, one or two monkey's fists, each with an eye splice in the end, are kept on hand, and if a heaving line is needed, a light line is secured to the monkey's fist with a sheet bend, and it is ready to go.

THROWING HEAVING LINE: Learning to throw a heaving line properly requires continual practice. To see some really good line throwing one should go to a submarine base. Since a submarine on the surface is relatively unmaneuverable, a good berthing is frequently dependent on the ability of a couple of old-timers who can straighten out two heaving lines tied together.

In preparing to throw a heaving line, one first coils the line neatly in the open palm of the left hand. Then half of the coil, including the weight, is transferred to the palm of the right hand. The final step is to stand with feet apart, swing the right arm back, and heave. The normal person heaves sidearm, and can get good direction and distance by that method. However, the real expert throws overarm, with a stiff arm, in the manner of an Englishman throwing a cricket ball. This technique is very difficult to master and is seldom seen except among professional seamen who have had long experience.

MAKING A MONKEY'S FIST: Many people cannot remember how to make a monkey's fist and do not have on hand a book such as *The Ashley Book of Knots,* by Clifford W. Ashley, but all is not lost for them. They can easily make a substitute by taking some leather or heavy Dacron (8- or 10-ounce will do), sewing it into an envelope, filling the envelope with a suitable amount of bird shot, gravel, or what-have-you, sewing it closed, and inserting a No. 3 tooth grommet. The result is a weight that can be secured to the end of a line in place of a monkey's fist, and is much less likely to do damage if it hits anyone.

Boathooks

An honest boathook is seldom seen on yachts today. Usually one finds a little six-foot Tinkertoy not good for much of anything. In my estimation, the boathook should be just slightly shorter than the spinnaker pole; then it can be stowed in chocks alongside the pole, and being of smaller diameter, can be placed so that it takes up no extra space (Drawing 207). The boathook should be made either of light spruce, about 1¼ inches in diameter, or of aluminum tubing.

A long boathook has many uses. As has been noted, with proper markings it can serve as a sounding pole, being much faster and more accurate than a lead in shallow water. Second, if the boat is being set down on the dock by the tide, a long boathook can be placed against the piles and used as a fend off, keeping arms, hands, and legs clear of danger. Further, when leaving shore, with a good long boathook one can make an easy exit by either pushing the bow or the stern well away from the dock, or by hooking onto something and walking down the deck to get way on the boat.

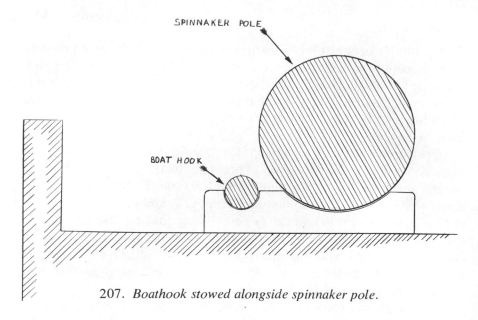

207. *Boathook stowed alongside spinnaker pole.*

If the boathook is of wood, a groove should be cut along its length, in line with the hook on the tip, so that in the dark one can always tell in which direction the hook is facing.

BOATHOOK TIPS: Normally, on boathooks on yachts one sees only polished bronze tips. However, if any sailing is to be done on inland waterways or canals, I would strongly advise the pointed, galvanized-iron barge-pole end. Because its slips and slides, the rounded, polished-bronze hook is most difficult to use for fending off from a piling; however, the sharp spike of the barge-pole end will remain in place against the piling, and the crew can therefore lean on the other end of the pole and effectively fend off. Of course, care must be taken not to use the sharpened boathook on one's neighbor's varnished topsides.

SAILBOATS WITHOUT ENGINES

In some areas of the world, it is possible to cruise extensively without the aid of a permanently installed engine. However, two things are likely to improve drastically one's ability to do so comfortably.

The first of these is a Seagull outboard. I recommend the Seagull because the person sailing without a permanently installed engine is likely not to be a particularly good mechanic. The Seagull is the nonmechanic's motor; it has one spark plug, one cylinder, one condenser, and one coil, and is relatively easy to disassemble and repair. Further, with its one large-diameter piston, the Seagull has low rpm but plenty of torque. Even a small Seagull on a dinghy will push *Iolaire* in flat, calm water—not very fast, to be sure. A big Seagull, with the big 2-to-1 reduction gear, will swing a four-bladed propeller twelve inches in diameter. It turns a dinghy almost into a tugboat. With a Seagull equipped with a 2-to-1 reduction gear and a clutch, a dinghy can maneuver *Iolaire* in a harbor in all but the worst weather, undisturbed by even 10 or 12 knots of wind.

The second thing that makes sailing without a permanently installed engine much easier is long light line made up for use in maneuvering alongside docks.

For this purpose nylon, with its great strength, is most suitable. The breaking strength of ⅜-inch nylon is four thousand pounds, so it is amply strong for warping even a comparatively large boat, of forty-five or fifty feet. Yet six hundred feet of ⅜-inch nylon can easily be carried even on quite a small boat, since it can be stowed on a reel eight inches wide between the faces and twelve inches in diameter. And nylon has elasticity as well as strength; it stretches 50 percent before reaching its breaking point. Because it can therefore absorb sudden shocks, ⅜-inch nylon is amply strong for maneuvering a heavy boat. Admittedly, it is not too easy to haul—the old rule applies, that any line smaller than ½ inch in diameter is harder on the hands—but if a few turns are taken on a winch, it is not too difficult to hold. Once some way is obtained, it is amazingly easy to warp a boat with a long length of nylon.

SEAMANSHIP AT SEA

A good seaman is easily recognized on a cruising yacht by the way he handles sails. He is very careful about chafe, adjusting his sheets to every change of the wind, arranging his vangs and guys so that the sails do not flog as the yacht rolls in a swell. He rigs pieces of shock cord to the snatch blocks so that they don't try to beat the deck and the bulwark apart and drive everyone belowdecks crazy.

I have seen boats that have sailed around the world and are still using the sheets, halyards, and guys with which they started the trip. Since nylon and Dacron do not rot and are affected only by chafe, if the sheets and guys are the correct size and are kept properly adjusted, it is almost impossible for them to wear out. Similarly, the good seaman does not suffer from split sails. He keeps an eye on his sails, and when a seam appears weak, repairs it at once. He knows that at sea, especially with Dacron sails, "a stich in time" usually saves not just nine, but nine hundred.

It is interesting to go on board any of the new boats and observe how completely the plastic age has taken over. In years gone by, on a good boat one would see double-sewn whippings at the end of every line, and neatly tucked eye splices. These beautiful splices were works of art. The artistry was not absolutely necessary for strength, but the person who did an artistic job of splicing was also the one who knew how to splice really well. He was sure his work was not going to pull out. Double whipping was not a status symbol; it was used because then if the outer whipping worked loose and fell off, only two inches of unraveled line were lost, instead of two or three feet.

Today, we see plastic whippings, line that is knotted rather than spliced, and wire halyards going to the drums, so that making a tail splice is rapidly becoming a lost art. The new Norseman, Nicopress, and swage fittings are wonderful, and in many cases superior to a splice, but there comes a time when the fitting is not available and if an eye is to be put in a wire, someone must sit down with a spike and splice. It is in a situation of this kind, when repairs must be made under adverse circumstances, that the experienced, well-trained seaman comes into his own.

On one trip across the Atlantic on which I was navigator, with two thousand miles to go, we pulled the clew out of the light genoa. With the aid of the skipper and a little hand-powered sewing machine, we were able to build a whole new clew, which lasted perfectly not only for the remainder of the crossing, but also for our trip to the Canaries and back across the Atlantic. I was glad I was enough of a seaman to justify my existence by repairing the sail, for we had not seen the sun for the past six days and the others in the crew were ready to drop their navigator overboard as not very useful.

Many a good sailor knows his own boat very well but if thrown on another boat finds himself completely adrift because he lacks seamanship. A good seaman recognizes the truth of the old adage "different ships, different long splices." The first thing he does upon arriving on board a strange boat is to survey all the gear, both on deck and below decks. He may seem like a pest, asking where everything is and where everything goes, but he makes sure he will not mis-stow anything. Similarly, he recognizes that different people coil line in different ways, and wherever he is, he coils line the skipper's way.

The good seaman arrives on board well equipped, with his seaboots, foul-weather gear, and other clothes, and with his knife, spike, and pliers. He stows his clothing where he is told, and carries his tools with him at all times, along with bits and pieces of line, which make his pocket seem like an old junk shop. He can give no good reason why he carries these, but they do come in handy. Furthermore, he comes prepared to do not just what is required of him, but much more. A ship crewed by a group of seamen each pulling more than his own weight is a happy ship.

By contrast, the poor seaman is a pain in the neck. He is the one who is always borrowing your foul-weather gear, so you get wet, or using your knife for a moment, so he can drop it overboard; sitting at the end of the bowsprit changing sails, he says to the man at the halyard, "Lend me your pliers, mate."

The average small-boat sailor, when he is part of the crew on a large boat, never bothers answering commands. He doesn't realize that the old navy routine of repeating every order makes life much more bearable on a boat. A skipper shouts, "Douse the genoa," and nothing but silence comes from the foredeck. He doesn't know whether his crew members haven't heard, or have heard and are having difficulty getting the halyard laid out, or have heard and are busy assigning stations, or what. So for the next two minutes he sits frustrated, wondering what is happening, until suddenly the genoa comes down. Or after five minutes he shouts again, to discover that no one heard him the first time. It is essential that a seaman always answer commands, so that the person giving the orders knows exactly where he stands.

All too often these days a good sailor is not a good seaman in that he cannot tie knots quickly and efficiently. To be sure, one can spend a tremendous amount of time learning all sorts of useless knots—I have never figured why boy scouts are taught to tie the sheepshank, for which there seems to be no possible use. But a seaman should know the bowline, figure eight, square knot, reef knot, sheet bend, double sheet bend, clove hitch, and rolling hitch. These are the knots normally used on a modern yacht. In my view, the rolling hitch is probably the most useful knot of them all, and the most often mis-tied. It is used to put a stopper on a line under strain so that it may be uncleated, removed from the winch, and moved elsewhere. The rolling hitch works beautifully on manila or linen line. It will work on Dacron, but care must be exerted in tying it; the soft spun Dacron is better for this purpose than filament Dacron—a good reason to keep a few lengths of spun Dacron on board.

SAIL REPAIR

The man who wishes to consider himself a real seaman should be fairly good at sail repair. To gain proficiency requires practice and also some reading on the subject. Three books written in the days of cotton sails provide a tremendous amount of information that is still of use today. These are *Yacht Sails, Their Care and Handling,* by W. H. de Fontaine and Ernest A. Ratsey; *Sailmaking Simplified,* by Alan Gray; and *Make Your Own Sails,* by R. M. Bowker and S. A. Budd. They are small and easily stowed in a seabag, handy for study at leisure or for consulting when repairs must be made in an out-of-the-way place. With the aid of these books, one can, without too much difficulty, make one's own sails or recut another boat's sails to serve in an emergency.

Operating a sewing machine is supposedly a lady's job, but the good seaman will sit down and learn how to use that machine, and then will find a hand-powered straight-stitch Singer to carry on board. This is not a sail-making machine, but since it will chew its way through two layers of 8-ounce Dacron, it can be used for repairs, about an hour being required for a ten-foot tear in a sail that would take half a day to sew up by hand.

Anyone with a friend in the sail-making business should take every available opportunity to watch the operators at work. Indeed, I would even suggest offering to pay for a lesson or two in restitching sails on one of the heavy-duty machines. On properly restitched old Dacron sails, a tear or an opened seam seldom occurs. In out-of-the-way corners of the world one may not be able to find a sailmaker, but one can almost always find an upholsterer who has a heavy-duty zigzag sewing machine. He may not be accustomed to stitching Dacron, but the person who has a supply of cloth of the correct weight and plenty of Dacron twine, and knows how to operate the machine, can probably get the use of it to stitch his own sails—for a fee, of course.

Yachts are usually equipped with sail-repair kits and gear, but my advice is always to carry one's own palm, as a great crop of blisters may be rapidly raised if one sews for long periods of time with a poorly fitting palm.

BOATSWAIN'S CHAIRS

The boatswain's chair is an essential piece of equipment on any yacht. In its simplest form it is merely a solid wooden plank with rope threaded through it and spliced with a shackle at the top to be attached to the halyard. This has been the standard means of going aloft, with tools usually being carried in a bucket tied to the chair. However, it has serious disadvantages. Because one can slip out of a boatswain's chair, many people find it necessary to tie themselves in with a lanyard while working aloft; one's bottom gets very sore from hours on a wooden seat; often, while being hauled aloft or lowered, the bucket catches on a spreader, dumping all the tools down on the people below; and it is difficult to tie the bucket at a height where it can be reached conveniently.

These problems are eliminated in an expensive but practical boatswain's chair now produced by sailmakers. The wooden board is sewn inside an envelope of Dacron, and an inch or so of foam-rubber padding is provided; instead of line, heavy Dacron panels support the chair; a strap across the front, and a backrest, make falling out almost impossible. Pockets for holding tools are provided on each side. Some boatswain's chairs even have at the bottom a large D ring to which a downhaul may be shackled to eliminate excessive swing when a man is going aloft in rough weather.

Anyone planning to do serious offshore cruising should purchase or make a boatswain's chair of this type.

EMERGENCIES

A good seaman anticipates emergencies. Though he may be sitting idly in the cockpit drinking coffee, his mind is not idle. Instead, he is thinking, for example: If the after guy on the spinnaker pole were to let go, what could we do to minimize the damage and repair it in a hurry? Or he begins to speculate with his mates about how the boat could be jury-rigged if the steering system were to pack up or the rudder to fall off. If a main boom broke, how might it be repaired? He considers whether the cabin floorboards could be used, and finds out if there are two-by-fours lashed up under the deckhead in the sail lockers. Again, what could a sea anchor be made of? Matters such as these continually occupy the mind of the seaman. Consequently, what may appear at first to be a brilliant maneuver improvised under emergency conditions may turn out to be a plan of action figured out two or three years previously, on another boat. Just as there is no substitute for experience, so there is no substitute for an inquiring, inquisitive mind.

A good seaman does not rely merely on the weather forecast provided by the daily map or newspaper (which in any event he probably does not see) or by the government weather broadcast. In his own area, where he is familiar with conditions, he can quite frequently make more accurate predictions than the weather bureau. How often has a boat been flat becalmed when the official forecast promised 15-knot breezes? The seaman realizes that though there may be a 15-knot southwester on Great South Bay, it will not break through the light northerly blowing in Long Island Sound until later in the afternoon—if at all. Because he has an eye for weather, he is never caught completely unaware by a squall. He may misjudge its strength, but he knows it is coming.

HEAVY-WEATHER SAILING

There is a tremendous variety of opinion concerning what should be done in the ultimate storm, or indeed in just a heavy gale. In the early days of flying, it was often said that any landing the pilot could walk away from was a good one. In the same way, it sometimes appears that any man who sails through a hurricane successfully must have done the correct thing; otherwise he would be dead.

A boat must be prepared to survive the kind of heavy weather that can be expected in the area being traversed. The yacht used for week-end cruising along the east coast of the United States will certainly not require as a matter of course the storm trysails, sea anchors, and so on that would be carried by a boat rounding Cape Horn.

Anyone heading south offshore in the fall should be prepared to en-counter some really heavy weather. For example, the yachtsman who is cruising from England or northern Europe down to the coast of Spain, and must cross the Bay of Biscay, has a good chance of being caught in a gale and having to spend days on end either trying to make his way to windward or lying to a sea anchor and hoping that the gale will end before he is driven up on the coast.

Preparing the Boat

Extremely heavy weather very seldom comes on unnanounced. The ground swell tends to build up, the wind shifts, the color of the sky changes, the barometer falls—the exact signs vary from area to area, but the experienced seaman can usually tell when he is in for a blow. As soon as it is evident that a blow is coming, preparations should be made. Double lashings should be placed on the dinghy and any other deck gear that might go overboard. In some areas, to reduce the chances of the ventilator boxes being torn loose, the ventilators should be removed and replaced by caps. In moderately heavy weather, it is of course convenient to keep weather cloths around the cockpit, but in a very heavy gale, leaving them there is likely to result in bent stanchions and torn weather cloths, so they should be removed. If the storm shut-ters are easily put in place (some storm shutters are merely for emer-gency use, to replace broken doghouse windows) they should be mounted. If there is a likelihood that a sea anchor will have to be streamed, the anchor rope should be removed from the forepeak before the weather becomes very rough, and neatly coiled down in the cock-pit, or lashed on the stern, where it can be reached without great diffi-culty when needed.

Preparing the Crew

Along with the ship, the crew must be prepared. If a gale seems im-minent, the best thing to do, in my view, is to give everyone a seasickness pill, and a good big dinner. A pot of good stew should be cooked up, and tied to the stove. The safety belts should be put in order, the snaps checked to be sure they are in good condition and work easily; rubber bands for the seaboots, towels for the neck, should be placed where they will be handy. When everything is ready, all unnecessary personnel should be sent below to get some sleep. A well-rested crew is in a better position to fight a gale than is a tired or partly tired crew. Further, a person who is warm, dry, full of food, and comfortable in his bunk seldom gets seasick.

Tactics

One must, of course, listen to the weather reports and try to ascertain on which side of the boat the low is passing, and how soon it will arrive. The weather predictions which are broadcast are not always accurate, but in certain circumstances yachtsmen can develop their own predictions, on the basis of a series of weather reports. In this respect sailors on the east coast of the United States are in a better position than their European cousins. When sailing a boat along the coast at night, or coming in from offshore, if the watch listens to the radio broadcasts from the Midwest he can follow the course of a cold front, with its temperature drop and gale-velocity winds, as it comes across the continent. When the radio reports a sudden fall in temperature, the front has just passed through the city from which the broadcast comes. As the front approaches the coast, the watch can switch to the coast stations. When they report a drop in temperature, he knows that in only a few hours the gale will reach the boat.

Most gales coming offshore from the center of the continent follow a definite pattern; the wind normally comes in hard from the northwest, blowing like mad, and then slowly shifts around to the north and then the northeast. As it shifts toward the east, it moderates and dies. These gales last roughly two to three days. Tactics can be planned accordingly. While the wind is from the northwest, the situation is bearable in the Gulf Stream, but when the wind goes to the north or northeast, so that it is against the current, the Stream is definitely not the place in which to lie ahull, not even in order to heave to. Indeed, *Doubloon* was capsized twice trying to heave to in the Stream by lying ahull. Since one cannot heave to in the Stream, and a northeast gale makes many of the ports in the east coast of the United States, from Charleston to Norfolk, difficult to enter, it is advisable to duck inshore and enter an inland waterway before the wind gets around to the northeast. Discretion is the better part of valor.

In the Bay of Biscay, shipping forecasts give a good indication of the approach of a gale. At the onset of a gale, sails should of course be shortened, and if there is doubt about when a gale is coming, the shortening down should be done safely in advance. Often the attempt is made to carry on too long, and then shortening down becomes a major project, resulting in the destruction of gear, and an exhausted and perhaps injured crew.

If the gale is a fair one, blowing in the direction in which the boat is heading, a modern yacht can carry on for an amazingly long time. When the wind is abeam, or aft of abeam, on ketches and yawls the mizzen should be the first to come off; similarly, on schooners the main, which is the aftmost sail and gives the worst weather helm, should be the first to come off. All the aft sails should be removed very early in the game, because when reaching or running in heavy weather, there is always a tendency to broach.

If the course is dead downwind, or almost downwind, the jib should be swung out on a pole. Otherwise, if the boat gets the least bit by the lee, the headsail will flop over with a bang and try to tear out the mast. It also tends to shake the hanks open, and if one is not careful, one may find oneself running with the jib attached to three points only, and not hanked to the stay. One should not try to clip the pole directly into the clew of the sail, as the slogging of the sail makes it difficult to clip the pole into the clew and even more difficult to get the pole into the bell on the mast. Instead, if the pole is to be set to port, one should broad reach on port tack, with the jib sheeted of course on the starboard sheet. Next, one should drop the weather sheet through the pole jaws, rig the pole to port with topping lift and fore guy, and place the pole in the mast socket. Then, swing dead downwind, sheet the jib with the port sheet, and winch in, slacking the starboard sheet. The port sheet will run through the jaws of the pole. If the pole jaws are not large enough to do this, a new pole end fitting should be obtained.

With the working jib rigged to a pole, the average medium-sized yacht can carry on in almost any weather.

How Long To Carry On: How long one should carry on will depend on the crew, the weather conditions, and the size of the boat. A ninety-footer, having tremendous stability, can carry on under reduced canvas even when the winds reach 45 or 50 knots. However, a fifty-foot boat will probably have to heave to at this point. Whether a large boat should carry on is usually determined not by wind velocity, but rather by the boat's own speed and the size of the waves. For example, at the point when the big ninety-footer rises up on a large wave and drops twenty feet into the next trough, something is bound to break, so it is time to shorten sail and slow down.

On a boat of any size, the extent to which one can run downwind is strictly limited by one's ability to steer and by the configuration of the quarter wave. Once a certain speed is reached, even the best-designed boat in the world will tend to pull her own stern wave aboard. When this happens, the time has come to start taking off sail and slow down.

On a reach, the limiting factor is usually the speed of the boat. If she is going too fast, she slams into the odd sea as if hitting a wall, and the result may be cracked frames, a broken mast, or the like. Even a good well-built yacht is not indestructible.

HEAVING To: How heaving to should be done will depend on the boat and the rig. My own *Iolaire,* with her good, deep forefoot, heaves to beautifully with the mizzen sheeted flat and about four feet of the roller-furling jib rolled out and sheeted flat. But some boats just cannot lie bow on to the sea. This inability is caused by a variety of factors; a cutaway forefoot, a bow higher than the stern, extra windage of the pulpit, lashed-down headsails, and so on, all tend to throw the bow off despite the best efforts of the mizzen.

When it is blowing so hard that a yacht cannot beat to windward any longer under storm trysail and spitfire jib, the time has come to head downwind. A sloop or cutter will usually head dead downwind under bare poles fairly well. A yawl or ketch usually has enough windage back aft, even under bare poles, to make steering dead downwind somewhat difficult. It is better to keep the boat heading downwind, or almost dead downwind, sometimes slightly quartering the seas, than to go absolutely dead before it. A small spitfire jib can be set and sheeted flat to hold the head off. I have talked to some people who have made boats perform beautifully going dead downwind by merely lashing a couple of sail bags to the bow pulpit. The resulting windage tends to keep the bow dead downwind.

If one is caught on a lee shore or if the gale is blowing the boat away from her destination, one will wish to slow her down. The old dodge was sea anchors.

Sea Anchors   The sea anchor was very highly regarded in years gone by as a method of heaving to. It was usually streamed from the bow. In the days of Claud Worth and the plumb-stemmed cutter this arrangement was practical. But with the modern yacht, that tacks around her anchor in the harbor, the chances of a sea anchor off the bow working are I think minimal. Also, if the sea anchor is streamed off the bow, the yacht will tend to slide backward down the wave as the very large seas strike the bow. This movement of course puts tremendous strain on the rudderstock, rudderpost, and steering gear. Therefore, I feel that the sea anchor should be streamed from the stern.

A good sea anchor is a large and bulky object. A normal sea anchor suitable for a forty-foot boat is cone-shaped, about fifteen feet long, with a mouth about five feet in diameter, and it has a heavy steel hoop to hold the mouth open, and a heavy bridle shackled to a heavy swivel which is then shackled to the anchor rope. In former years the anchor was made of the heaviest canvas obtainable, which of course tended to mildew when stowed wet in the forepeak. Further, it seems to have lasted for only a relatively short time before coming apart, often because of chafe. Therefore, the canvas cone-shaped sea anchor is in my estimation not worth carrying.

Fritz Fenger has designed a plank sea anchor which is virtually indestructible. It is made of two 2-by-8-inch planks, each about four feet long (the exact dimensions depend on the size of the boat) and has iron braces and a chain bridle. It is not easily stowed, but could be made up in pieces which could be stowed and then assembled when needed. Like the canvas anchor, it must be secured to a swivel, and the swivel must be secured to the anchor line or chain. The line must be fed through a good, heavy, smooth, well-parceled chock. Since there is tremendous strain on a sea-anchor rode, it must be firmly secured either to a big cleat or, preferably, to a big winch. With a winch, one can adjust the length of the anchor rode without too much difficulty. Then, if the chafing gear begins to wear out, one can parcel the line between the chock and its securing point, veer a few more feet of line, and end up with a new piece of chafing gear in the chock.

The average cruising yacht does not carry a sea anchor, and unless one is visiting an area where numerous gales are to be expected, and where space is so restricted that a sea anchor is necessary to slow down a vessel and keep it from being blown to a lee shore, there seems to be no good reason to both with one. Most yachts do have plenty of dock lines, anchor rodes, and the like, which can be employed in slowing the progress of the boat in very bad weather. The most effective method of using rope for this purpose is to stream it in a bight run: the anchor line is run out through the port chock under the stern and back through the starboard chock, and the bitter end is secured to a cleat; then the line is veered through the port chock, so that a bight of line is being dragged astern. When feeding out the line, one should make sure it is first secured around a strong cleat or big winch, as at six or seven knots the strain on a bight of line thrown over the stern is unbelievable.

Construction Features Desirable for Heavy-Weather Sailing

As we know, compromise is necessary everywhere. Thus, heaving to or running before stern first does reduce the strain on the rudder, but makes the cockpit less safe than it would be if the bow were facing the sea. Any waves breaking aboard tend to sweep and fill the cockpit. For this reason, a yacht should have good, big cockpit scuppers. A good bridge deck is also desirable, as without it water from the cockpit will pour down through the doors into the cabin. The cabin doors may be closed, but they are seldom robust enough to withstand the blow of a sea breaking on board. If a yacht does not have a bridge deck, it should certainly have two good 2-by-4 strongbacks to be placed behind the cabin doors to prevent them from bursting if a wave comes aboard.

Running downwind before a gale, the center-cockpit boat comes into her own. In this type of boat the after cabin affords great protection, and the cockpit is unlikely to be flooded. A center cockpit may be wet going to windward, but it is certainly dry and comfortable running before a gale.

XIX

~~~~~~

Passage Making

Planning for a long cruise is best started in a main cabin over rum and coffee, or in a living room with charts spread out before the fire as a winter gale tries to shake the shutters from their hinges. The use during this stage of appropriate books and charts can save much grief, and in some cases change what would have been a rough, miserable trip into a pleasant, comfortable one.

Probably the first and most important book for this purpose is an edition of *Ocean Passages of the World,* issued by the British Admiralty. For long passages, this gives the recommended routes, with their distances, for fast steamers, low-powered steamers, and sailing vessels. The older the edition of this book, the better. The editions which appeared prior to World War I deal with sailing to a great extent. The later ones give little attention to the problems of a sailing vessel.

The second item is a selection of the wind charts put out by the United States Naval Oceanographic Office and the British Admiralty. These charts cover the entire world month by month. By carefully studying the charts for the areas to be visited, one can learn the prevailing wind direction during each month, the percentage of calms and of gales, the average ice conditions, and so on. These will indicate, for example, that although big freighters and liners cross the North Atlantic every month of the year, only the yachtsman with an overactive suicidal instinct would try sailing the North Atlantic during the winter months—even in order to head south for the Lesser Antilles. From mid-November to mid-April, the North Atlantic, including the waters of the northeast coast of the United States, is no place for a small yacht.

The third item, extremely useful but probably the most difficult to obtain, is a volume of sailing directions for the area under consideration, printed prior to 1900, when most of the world's commerce was carried by sailing vessels. As was noted in the chapter on navigation, such a volume can frequently save large amounts of time and energy for the sailing yachtsman.

John Hazelhurst gives two illustrations of how he was helped by his old sailing directions when he was sailing around the world on *Paisano*. In the first case, he was a few days out of Panama, heading for the Galápagos, when the wind came in light from the southwest. The normal response to this situation would be to tack south toward the South American coast. But he discovered that this phenomenon was discussed in his sailing directions, and following the recommendations of the book, he held on the port tack. The wind gradually went more to the south, and brought him to the Galápagos in eight days in one tack. This was substantially less time than was taken by other vessels, which following the modern accepted practice, had tacked over toward South America.

Similarly, when beating up the Red Sea, *Paisano* made a faster passage than expected, because Hazelhurst learned from the sailing directions that the wind drew (lifted) on the Arabian shore. Accordingly, he had *Paisano* hug the reefs, and every time she was driven the least distance offshore, tacked back inshore, thereby obtaining favorable lifts and smooth water.

Other yachtsmen, too, have found the old sailing directions very useful. Major Roberts, who has cruised the equivalent of twice around the world in his little thirty-six-foot sloop *Hiada Sea,* reports being helped on numerous occasions in his Pacific cruising by following the old 1890 sailing directions rather than the advice of "common sense" and modern yachtsmen.

Hence any serious cruising yachtsman should try to obtain the old sailing directions for the area he plans to traverse, even at some expense.

Also essential for planning a cruise is a gnomonic (great-circle) chart of the area in question. It must be remembered that a great circle, not a straight line, is the shortest distance between two points on the surface of the globe. A straight line drawn across a Mercator chart does not show a correct course, but on a gnomonic chart, the arcs of great circles are represented by straight lines (Drawing 208). As can be seen in Drawing 208, a true great-circle course cannot actually be taken from New York to England because followed exactly, it would carry one up into the ice fields and across the bottom tip of Nova Scotia. Therefore, there must be a bend in the line to clear Nova Scotia.

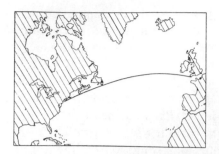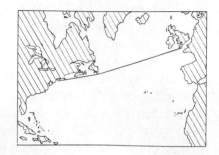

208. *Great-circle route appears as curve on standard Mercator chart* (left)
but as straight line on gnomonic chart (right).

Thus, to lay out a cruise across the ocean one must consult wind
charts, great-circle charts, sailing directions, and *Ocean Passages of the
World*. As a result of such a study, for example, the yachtsman wishing
to go from the United States to England is likely to decide to leave in
mid-June, because during this month Atlantic gales are at their least
frequent, and it is late enough in the year for some chance of warmth
in the North Atlantic and still too early for hurricanes, which occasionally come up from the Caribbean even in July. Further, since the longest day in the year is June 21, for most of the trip the nights will be
quite short. The course is laid to "point A," as the approximate southeast corner of the ice field is called. Since this varies in position from
year to year, a check on its actual location should be made immediately before departure. This information may be obtained from the
Coast Guard weather ship; also, Coast Guard radio broadcasts indicate
where icebergs are to be found. From this point on, the great-circle
course to England is followed.

LONG CRUISES

Everyone dreams of cruising on his own yacht to the Pacific and visiting such romantic-sounding islands as the Tuamotus, Tahiti, and
Samoa, but the force of circumstances—earning a living, raising a
family, and other considerations—usually keeps the yachtsman closer
to home. Some yachtsmen cannot stand this restricted cruising, and
suddenly sell everything, pull up stakes, and leave to wander around
the world. Others, who cannot make such a violent and complete
break, do the next best thing, arranging their affairs so that they can
leave for six months, a year, or longer, get the wanderlust out of their
system, and then return to life in civilization. With correct planning, it is

possible in a period of eight to twelve months to take a really long, exciting, and varied cruise, covering vast areas, without too much difficulty.

The usual cruise from England to the West Indies begins in the fall, just early enough to avoid the worst of the winter gales. Typically, the yacht sails down the Bay of Biscay, down the coast of Portugal, and on to the Canaries. Here the boat waits for the winds to settle down after the end of the hurricane season, then leaves for the West Indies in late November or early December, and cruises slowly across the Atlantic, arriving in the islands just before Christmas or New Year's, depending on the departure date. Passage during this period is likely to be slow because during November, December, and January the trades have not settled down from the instability of the hurrican season.

Arriving in Barbados in late December, the yacht may cruise on to Grenada, perhaps sail the length of the Lesser Antilles, then go from St. Thomas to Bermuda, and from Bermuda to the Azores, and arrive back in England in late June or early July. A boat with the necessary time might continue westward from St. Thomas, cruising to the Bahamas and the east coast of the United States, and finally leaving New York or New England for the return to England sometime in May or June. A cruise on this schedule takes the better part of a year.

With a different timetable, the same area can be covered in a much shorter period. A yacht which leaves England at the beginning of April, and cruises to Madeira, the Canaries, the Cape Verde Islands, and then west to Barbados, crosses the Atlantic at a time when the trades are as reliable as clockwork, and should make a very rapid passage, arriving perhaps by mid-May. A month of cruising through the islands (and June and July are the best time for cruising in the Lesser Antilles) would permit departure in mid-June, and a crossing by way of Bermuda and the Azores would put her back in England in time for Cowes Week, in early August. Thus in four months she would have had some wonderful ocean passages under ideal circumstances, and fabulous cruising in the Lesser Antilles under perfect conditions.

Some people who arrive in the Lesser Antilles cruise for a few months and then take off downwind for Panama and points west, usually continuing on around the world. These are the lucky people we all envy.

The Lesser Antilles are easily accessible from the east coast of the United States, but except in the spring there are only a few weeks in the year when the winds are suitable for the trip to the islands. And yachts seldom come to the Bahamas or the Lesser Antilles in the spring because they would then be arriving just before the hurricane season. Also, most American yachtsmen want to use their boats in the north during the summer.

Hence most yachts head south after the completion of their summer season. But to try to depart in September or October is to play with fire, since these are the months of the hurricane season. And by the end of November or early December, the winter gale season has begun—year in and year out, the winter gales sink one or more yachts en route from the United States to the West Indies. All that is left is the two-week period from November 1 to November 14—a small breathing space between the hurrican season and the winter gales.

With a little planning, the east-coast yachtsman can take advantage of this period. For example, during the early fall he can bring his boat down to Morehead City on weekends by easy stages, as the weather permits. Then he can leave the boat there, have a crew meet him the last weekend in October, and if conditions are right, take off at high water on Saturday and be in St. Thomas seven to ten days later. With a good boat and a good crew, that is a glorious passage. He can then continue cruising in the islands throughout the winter, flying back to the United States when necessary to take care of business. In the spring he can make the long offshore passage from St. Thomas direct to Charleston, Morehead City, or New York, or he can sail leisurely through the Bahamas and then head north along the coast.

The yacht taking one of the cruises so far described, at the time of the year specified, will have largely fair wind, with some heavy weather thrown in. Though the wind may temporarily turn foul, there will be no long slog against the prevailing wind.

The yachtsman from the west coast of the United States is not so lucky as his eastern counterpart. The California yachtsman loves to cruise south to Lower California, Acapulco, and other romantic spots along the west coast of Mexico. However, when he starts heading north to return home, he faces a dead muzzler and a long hard slog. Many yachts continue on south, along the coast of Central America, and arrive in Panama after a glorious cruise, though admittedly there are extensive patches of calm along the way which necessitate a good engine and large fuel capacity. At Panama, they can make a right turn, off to the Galápagos and the classic Pacific cruise, but many of them head eastward into the Caribbean.

To the men who can embark on this trip, I take off my hat; once they come out of the Panama Canal, they have a beat of perhaps a thousand miles dead to windward to reach the Lesser Antilles, whether they work their way along the coast of South America, stopping at

Cartagena, Aruba, and Curaçao, and then moving on to Grenada, or stand north to Jamaica and then make their way eastward along the south coast of Hispaniola and Puerto Rico. But most yachtsmen agree, once they reach the Lesser Antilles, that the trip was worth the effort.

A very few west-coast yachtsmen, instead of slogging all the way out to windward to the Lesser Antilles, explore the east coast of Central America, a poorly charted and seldom visited area, usually entered only by transient yachts en route to or from the east coast of the United States. Recently, however, yachtsmen from Tampa have begun to frequent these waters. A check of the wind chart shows that for the boat from the west coast of Florida, given a decent break in the wind, the trip can be a reach down and a reach back. Thus the islands along the eastern shore of Central America may in the future become to Gulf yachtsmen what the Lesser Antilles are to European and American yachtsmen.

Another favorite cruise for yachtsmen from the west coast of the United States is out to the Hawaiian Islands and then across the trades to the South Pacific. Or they may sail down the west coast of the United States and out to the Galápagos, from which it is a sleigh ride to the Pacific islands. The difficulty with both of these trips is that a direct return requires much beating to windward.

For that reason, many yachtsmen choose instead to sail on west, and continue around the world. A few sail south from Tahiti to the area of the prevailing westerlies, go with the westerlies to the west coast of South America, and there pick up the Humboldt Current; they then have light variable winds but a strong current all the way to Panama. However, thereafter they are faced with the long haul from Panama to Los Angeles—three thousand miles of calms, windward work, and irregular fuel stops.

Another method of returning to the United States is to stand north from Tahiti to Hawaii, then continue well north to get around the Pacific high before turning eastward for San Francisco and other west-coast ports. But this too is a very rough trip, with the latter part in cold and fog.

Australians and New Zealanders are wanderers. Once they decide to go cruising, they are likely to turn up halfway around the world. Frequently, they fly home to do business, and then fly back again to rejoin their boat. Or they may fly home, and have friends come out to sail the boat on the return voyage.

South Africans, if they sail at all, are enthusiastic yachtsmen. With their lack of harbors and their weather conditions, they have to be enthusiasts to enjoy sailing. They often prefer long cruises, and their sail to the Caribbean is probably one of the nicest in the world. Once they leave Cape Town, they head northwest to pick up the southeast trade, which can be carried all the way to Ascension Island. After the stop at Ascension Island, there is a jump of 3,500 miles to Trinidad or Grenada, again with the trades and currents. Along the Guiana coast, the Guiana current will frequently give a boat a lift of fifty to sixty miles a day. Once they arrive in the Lesser Antilles, a great number of them remain permanently, enjoying the wonderful sailing, which is among the best in the world.

South African sailors certainly are wanderers. In view of how few people in their country know one end of a boat from another, the number of South African yachts cruising the Antilles at any one time is amazing.

To the person attracted by long-term cruising, I would say, go ahead and make the jump. The preparation and equipment of the boat is likely to be expensive, but once the cruise begins, bills become minimal for anyone capable of doing most of his own work. There are no entertainment costs while one is at sea, and living expenses at the various areas to which a yacht cruises are likely to be low, as long as one stays away from the big hotels and casinos. In fact, if one decides to live on fish, rice, and whatever fresh food can be purchased in the islands, outlays can be reduced to practically nothing; ten pounds of rice in the islands costs very little and will feed a crew for a long time! Food costs can be kept low, too, if one is willing to find out what the local people eat, and to buy that. In the backward areas of the world food is relatively cheap, but not for the individual who insists on seeking out his home diet no matter where he is.

Those with only limited time for cruising should remember that in most areas of the world, arrangements can be made to leave a boat laid up with a yard, a local yachtsman, or some other reliable person. With air transportation as frequent and as inexpensive as it is now becoming, one can cruise for a month or two months in foreign ports, leave the boat, fly back home, and return the following year to continue cruising. Frequently a boat can be laid up and maintained in a foreign port for far less than in the United States. The saving often compensates for the air fare, and this method of operation certainly broadens one's cruising range.

PASSAGE SAILING

Prior to World War II, almost all ocean cruisers had twin spinnakers, twin staysails, or square sails, because the only way for them to achieve self steering when running broad off was with a rig of twins or square sails set up with lines attached to the tiller. These rigs were always complicated, requiring numerous fore guys, lifts, after guys, sheets, jig lines, and what-have-you.

The deficiency in twins or square sails, which probably accounts for the slow passages common in the past, is that often they do not provide sufficient sail area to be spread for moderate weather. Having lived in the trade-wind belt for the past fifteen years, I have observed that although the trades may on occasion blow up to the 30-to-35-knot range for a week at a time, as a rule, they are somewhere between 12 and 18 knots. When the wind is at this level, to achieve a decent turn of speed with the wind on the quarter or dead aft, one must be able to spread sails whose area equals that provided by a full main and large genoa. With twin staysails it is absolutely impossible to get sufficient area to sail fast in a normal trade-wind passage. With twin jibs it is possible, but the poles become very long, and the sails are large and can be used only going downwind, not going to windward. Also, the center of effort is very high.

Furthermore, with twin sails there is the problem of rolling. Because these sails dip the poles when rolling, people who cruise with twins advise cutting them so the poles are high. But the result is a vicious circle. When the twins are cut higher, the center of effort goes up, the rolling tendency becomes greater, and the poles still dip.

Today, as has been pointed out in Chapter XVII, it is no longer necessary to rig square sails or twins with lines to the tiller in order to achieve self steering. One may use normal fore-and-aft sails and a vane self-steering gear or an electric or hydraulic autopilot.

CHOICE OF RIG

When close-hauled or reaching, the normal rig of course is best. When broad off, there is of course the problem of chafe, with the mainsail rubbing against the shrouds. However, a good fore guy and vang rigged to keep the boom sheeted hard down will reduce the amount of movement of the sail against the stays and shrouds. If, in addition, the spreader and the spreader tip are covered with soft chafing gear, relatively little chafe damage will be caused to the stitching of the main.

When broad off, a spinnaker may be set, but this is generally not done on cruising boats because it is really not safe to set a spinnaker at sea in anything but the lightest conditions unless there is a big competent crew on board. A cruising boat seldom carries a crew of sufficient size to allow the spinnaker to be used regularly.

In cruising, where top speed is not essential, it is possible to sail broad off or dead downwind with absolutely minimal chafe. The rig used on *Iolaire* with great success for many years has consisted of the three-quarters roller-furling genoa to windward on the spinnaker pole, and the big genoa hanked to the head stay and sheeted to the end of the main boom (Photo 14). This rig provides enough area to move the boat nicely in all but the lightest conditions, and is very easy to handle —and there is nothing to chafe. Even if a boat does not have any roller-furling headsails, it is still possible to avoid use of the mainsail, and the accompanying chafe problems. The simplest approach is to replace the normal spinnaker halyard block with a becket block. A wire shackled to the becket and lashed temporarily to the stemhead can act as a jackstay for the three-quarters genoa. This wire can be fairly light, since all the strain on the sail comes on the halyard; the jackstay just keeps the sail from blowing all over the place when it is being downed.

I have used the rig consisting of three-quarters roller-furling genoa and big genoa for many years on *Iolaire*—35 feet LWL, with a 10½-foot beam and a slack bilge—the worst type of yacht to sail downwind, and have had no difficulties. Similarly, this rig was used by Stan Young on *Lunaquest,* again a long narrow boat, when he sailed from the Canaries to Barbados in 15 days, 20 hours. He turned in fabulous runs and at no time had difficulty with the poles dipping. I have also used this rig successfully in many delivery trips to the United States, and it served *Antilles* well when she crossed the Atlantic in 1969.

This rig will stand with the wind anywhere from the weather quarter to dead aft. Once the wind begins to shift to the lee quarter, the course must be altered, or one must jibe. Admittedly, when the time comes to jibe, the boat can become like a spaghetti factory. However, the situation is somewhat improved if the medium roller-furling genoa is set back three or four feet from the head stay when off the wind. Then when jibing the big genoa can be passed between the roller-furling jib and the head stay instead of being unhanked and rehanked on the other side.

The great advantage of this rig is that no extra gear need be carried except for the jackstay. The center of effort is low, especially in comparison to that of twins (Drawing 209). This rig gives appreciably more sail area than do twin staysails or twin jibs, and when coupled with a mizzen staysail it provides ample area for all but the very lightest conditions. Furthermore, since the sails being used are standard working sails, they can remain set in all but the heaviest weather. Hence, I think that the money paid for twins is poorly spent, and could better be used for other sails.

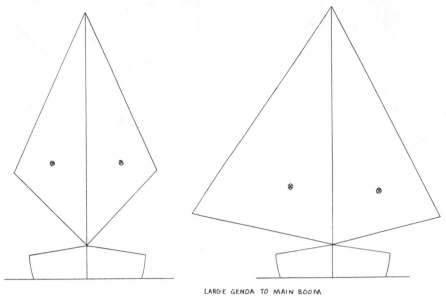

LARGE GENOA TO MAIN BOOM

TWIN STAYSAILS WITH BOOMS

SMALL GENOA TO SPINAKER POLI

209. *Twin staysails versus genoas.*

It must be remembered that at times, no matter how carefully a passage has been picked, one must go to windward. Then the pole may be rigged in, the genoa sheeted flat, and the main set, and the cruiser is ready to beat to windward without all the windage caused by the extra rigging needed for twins.

SQUARE SAILS

The square sail, often found on the so-called character boats, is functional as well as picturesque. It is especially useful on a gaff-rigged boat, since unless such a vessel has a good tall topmast, it is almost impossible to set twin genoas large enough to give the sail area necessary for a decent passage. Further, the square sail has a place on boats of sixty feet and over, for in yachts of this size, the spinnaker poles used to wing out the genoa or twins become large and hard to handle; a square sail, permanently rigged, is probably much easier to manage.

Everybody has his own way of rigging square sails, and many of the older methods are worth reviewing. A discussion of square sails and the raffees set above them would itself fill a book.

Many people believe that square sails can be used only when the wind is dead aft or slightly on the quarter. This is not true, unless there has been a bad installation. When square sails are rigged, the shrouds

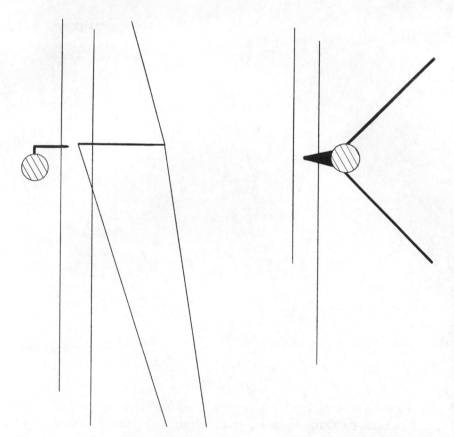

210. *Proper way to rig spreaders so that a square-sail yard may be braced forward for close reaching.*

must be led well aft, to allow the yard to be braced well around (Drawing 210). This is one reason why the modern fore-and-aft rig with spreaders mounted square to the mast does not lend itself to the square-sail rig. If the yard can be braced well around, the square sail can be carried with the wind abeam. Also, for a square sail to be effective, the boat must have sufficient beam to allow a wide yard and adequate spread to the foot of the sail. Under proper circumstances, the square sail is not only a good running sail but also a superb reaching sail.

REACHING

In offshore passages, the most useful sail on the boat is the high-cut three-quarters genoa. This sail is likely to set well in any sort of moderate breeze, and is cut high enough so that it does not pick up the bow wave. When it begins to blow very hard, the main can be dropped and the boat can continue reaching under the three-quarters genoa. Since this sail is of heavy material, there is little danger of its being damaged by the high wind.

On long offshore passages, the main should be equipped with a roll reef (Drawing 84), so that the tip of the boom will not dip in the water when the boat is reaching in heavy weather. Further, even when reaching, a fore guy to the bow should be used. There will undoubtedly be a boom vang with rubber snubber in the middle of the boom. If the end of the boom dips into the sea and is pushed aft by the water, the strain imposed on the middle of the boom is sometimes great enough to cause it to break. If the outer end of the boom is held forward by a fore guy, it cannot swing aft when it dips, and the strain on the middle of the boom is minimized.

BEATING

The most important thing to remember when beating to windward is that when one headsail has been set on the stay, another headsail, the one most likely to be next used, should be hanked on the stay and stowed in its bag. What sail is likely to be needed next depends on which one is up and what the weather appears to be doing. If the three-quarters genoa is up and it appears likely to blow harder, the working jib should be snapped onto the head stay and secured there in the pulpit in its own bag. If the three-quarters genoa is up and the weather appears likely to moderate, the big genoa should be hanked on the stay, ready to go up. Similarly, the minute the big genoa is set, the three-quarters genoa, or the next size down, should be on the stay, ready to be set in case the weather blows up. If at all in doubt about whether the big genoa should be used, one should take it down and switch to a more manageable headsail.

When beating, the main must be reefed early in the game, before the wind is blowing so hard that reefing is difficult. On ocean racers, the main is often reefed before the headsail is changed, a practice which is hard on the largest genoa. By contrast, the cruising man will probably switch to his medium genoa before reefing his main, but once the medium genoa is set, at the first sign of overpowering, his main should be reefed. Then if it blows still more, the medium genoa must be doused, and the working jib set, but the main requires no further attention. Should heavy weather necessitate switching to the trysail, a reefed main is much easier to douse than a full main.

Similarly, on a schooner with its mainsail way aft, the very first adjustment for heavy weather should be reefing the main. All too often, when it begins to blow up, the jib is doused, with the result that the center of effort is thrown too far aft, leaving the whole rig out of balance, and consequently there is too much weather helm to permit the boat to handle well. The clew earing of a schooner's main is always well aft or outboard—none too easy to reach in the best of times, and difficult to get to in heavy weather. This situation is avoided if a schooner has really efficient reefing gear on the main, the main is reefed first, and the change to smaller headsails is then begun. In all but the heaviest weather, a schooner will handle well with a storm trysail, a foresail, and a staysail; these are relatively small, easily handled sails that will keep the boat in balance.

Beating in Heavy Weather

The well-designed yacht with modern rig, winches, and Dacron sails should be able to beat to windward and make progress in all but the most extreme conditions. When beating in heavy weather, all working jibs and storm jibs should be kept stopped with the aid of rubber bands. Then when the wind is at 35 or 40 knots and the sails are to be set, there is no need to expend great effort cranking up a badly flogging headsail; the headsail can be bent on and the halyard set up tight very easily by one person, and the sail can be broken out with minimal flogging and little danger of anyone being struck by either sail or sheet.

Given good stitching, modern Dacron sails are practically indestructible. However, jib snaps are frequently too light and snap off, or pop open when the sail is flogging in heavy weather. For this reason, heavy-weather jibs, and especially storm jibs, should be geared to the stay with Abeking and Rasmussen or Merriman snaps, as noted in Chapter VI. Also, since the working jib and storm jibs are likely to lie forgotten in the lazaret for long periods, the snaps in those headsails tend to corrode. Therefore, periodically they should be checked and oiled. There is nothing worse than trying to fight a jammed snap on the bow at two o'clock in the morning in a heavy gale.

In my view, storm trysails are generally too small. They are usually about the right size for heaving to in the ultimate hurricane, but practically useless for anything else. With the advent of Dacron and of roller reefing, the practice in recent years has been to reef the main down to a handkerchief instead of switching to a trysail. There are serious objections to this procedure. It leaves exposed to the gale the portion of the mainsail that has had the most wear and tear, and is most likely to fail. And if a seam does open up in a gale, the sail will undoubtedly tear itself half to death before it is doused. I therefore believe that a storm trysail, the same size as a double-reefed main, should be set instead. Since the storm trysail is of heavy material and is seldom used, its seams are unlikely to open. If a full gale or hurricane blows up, reefing the trysail is relatively simple, provided it has a set of reef points. Also, the large trysail makes a good heavy-weather mainsail. *Iolaire* has often had hers up for days at a time when going to windward in heavy weather.

STORM CONDITIONS

When one reads of the terrible storms weathered by small yachts, one must remember that the smaller the yacht, the higher the waves appear. Also, a large wave is not in itself dangerous; what is destructive is the breaking crest of the wave. Ocean swells, no matter what their size, will do no damage as long as they are not breaking.

It should not be assumed that the larger the yacht the greater its safety. In fact, experience indicates that a boat of forty-five to fifty feet may be the safest of all. On a smaller boat the motion can be so violent that the crew tires quickly. On a larger yacht, the gear is so big that it is hard to handle and in case of failure is most difficult to jury rig.

Exactly what should be done when the ultimate storm is encountered is a subject of much disagreement, even among those who have weathered such a storm. In my view, if it is necessary to heave to, and sail can still be carried, the yacht should heave to facing as close to the wind as possible, using mizzen and spitfire jib, or storm trysail and storm jib sheeted slightly to weather, to whatever rig balances the boat best. I suggest facing into the seas because on most boats the bow has more buoyancy than the stern; the forward end of the cabin trunk is low and strong, well able to take the strain of breaking seas; and the cockpit is well aft, where it is unlikely to be filled.

There can come a time when conditions make it impossible to carry any sail and still face the wind. At this point, some sailors like to lie ahull, However, in my judgment this is not the wise thing to do. Lying ahull exposes the entire side of the vessel to the destructive force of the breaking sea. Indeed, a breaking sea coming aboard a boat lying ahull has been known to smash in the cabin sides, demolish the doghouse, tear lifeline stanchions out, and throw the boat on her beam-ends. Each sea tries to roll the sticks out of the boat; if it is blowing 60 or 70, the windage against the mast may take out the worse of the motion but it is still quite violent.

In my view, once it is blowing so hard that no sails can be shown, the right thing to do is to run dead downwind. The average yacht, with the mast forward and a high bow, has enough windage forward to be able easily to run dead downwind on bare poles. As previously mentioned, a sail bag, awning, or other small cloth can be lashed to the bow pulpit to increase wind resistance forward if the need arises.

How fast to run downwind is a subject of great debate. Certainly no one should know better than Bernard Moitessier, who has had much experience with the ultimate storms in the high latitudes. His view, after much experimentation, is that the vessel should be allowed to run at the maximum speed, and should not be slowed down by drogues. However, William Robinson, who also has had experience with storms in the high latitudes, advocates streaming warps in order to slow the vessel down and help keep her head off the wind. Which method should be adopted probably depends on the particular circumstances, the individual sailor, and the type of vessel.

XX

Safety

Whether an offshore cruise will be free of trouble depends largely upon the ability of the crew. And the ablest crew will be the one whose members are well fed, warm, dry, and rested. Some of the requirements for keeping them that way have been discussed in Chapter X ("Accommodation") and Chapter XI ("Galley"). Other aspects of this subject will be considered here.

CLOTHING

Some people who have gone out in ocean racers in bad weather equipped with a wet suit swear that it keeps one warm and dry. This may be true, but I think that anyone who wears a wet suit day after day will soon have a good crop of salt-water blisters. Also, a wet suit is very difficult to put on in rough weather. For long-term wear, foul-weather gear over some warm clothing seems to be best.

Fabrics should be chosen with a view to the special needs of the yachtsman. For him, cotton is useless. Cotton trousers, socks, and sweat shirts do not provide much warmth for their weight and bulk. Once wet, they are very cold. The modern quilted fabrics of Dacron or similar fibers, now used for underwear and other garments, are excellent in that they keep one warm. However, once wet, they are absolutely frigid.

By contrast, wool, for its weight is one of the warmest materials available, and it retains a tremendous amount of warmth even when soaking wet. Further, wristlets, sweaters, and caps of unbleached wool, if they are not put through a washing machine, will stay waterproof. Admittedly, after many years, they will not smell too good, but they will keep one warm and dry. The occasional spray that drips down one's neck or comes over the rail when one is not wearing foul-weather gear will not soak the oily wool.

For extreme conditions, I would advise wearing woolen underwear against the skin, quilted Dacron clothing on top of that, then woolen trousers and a woolen sweater, and finally, of course, foul-weather gear.

FOUL-WEATHER GEAR

In northern climates, the gear used to stay warm, dry, and comfortable in heavy weather will be quite different from the light gear suitable for a race on Long Island Sound on a summer afternoon. In spring and fall the temperature frequently will be 55° F. and below, with rain and fog, and the crew must be clothed accordingly. British yachtsmen have much more experience than their American counterparts in keeping warm and dry at sea. Significantly, British magazines carry few advertisements for sunglasses, but many for foul-weather gear; in American and French magazines the situation is just the opposite.

For offshore work, heavy foul-weather gear is needed. Whether to use a sou'wester hat is a matter of personal preference—and violent personal prejudice—so the decision is best left to each individual. In any case, towels of suitable size should be available to put around the neck and the wrists. While any old towels will serve, if possible they should be fitted with snaps or buttons to keep them firmly in place. I do know one experienced offshore sailor who never uses towels; he prefers a good silk scarf because, he says, it is warm even when wet!

The jacket should be selected carefully. The old-fashioned pullover jacket is just too difficult to put on and take off, aboard a boat, and impossible to take off if one falls overside. The single-breasted jacket with a front zipper is apt to leak even when the zipper is closed. However, today a good double-breasted, front-opening jacket is available. It has a zipper closing sealed with a flap held down by Velcro tape; there are no buttons to come adrift or buttonholes to tear. The jacket should be at least long enough to cover the hips. Some people like it so long that it covers one's bottom when one is seated. Also, it should have a drawstring or belt at the waist so that when one bends down, the wind does not blow it up around one's armpits.

In the past, the pockets of foul-weather jackets soon filled with water, as they were very difficult to seal. Today, they can be kept closed with Velcro tape, so that they stay dry in almost any weather. Nevertheless, jacket pockets must have drain holes.

Trousers

The trousers commonly worn for day sailing along the coast, with their elastic or drawstring waists, are useless offshore. One cannot get one's hands comfortably into the pockets, and spray driving up under the foul-weather jacket can easily get one's midsection soaked. This problem is eliminated by foul-weather trousers that are cut high, under the armpits, and held up by suspenders.

Further, they should have a fly. There is nothing more uncomfortable than sitting completely encased in foul-weather gear, warm and dry, and then realizing, halfway through a watch, the impossibility of relieving oneself without taking everything off. During World War II, United States Navy foul-weather trousers were made with a zippered fly; however, immediately after the war, the manufacturers of foul-weather gear for yachtsmen dropped this feature. Even today, trousers with a fly are hard to find, but the type is slowly making a comeback. In the modern version, the fly is sealed in the same way as the front· of the double-breasted foul-weather jackets—the zipper closing is protected by a flap held down with Velcro tape.

Occasionally one can find foul-weather trousers with a double seat. This is a good feature, keeping the bottom really dry.

Boots and Shoes

At one time, the deep-water sailor wore a knee-length slicker and hip boots. Those days are now gone, and by and large the offshore yachtsman, whether amateur or professional, wears a foul-weather jacket, trousers, and knee boots. However, a few people do still wear hip boots, insisting that when they work in the lee scuppers in heavy weather, water floods up above the tops of the knee boots and fills them. This difficulty can be avoided. Years ago, Norris Hoyt showed me how to secure foul-weather trousers outside the boots with heavy rubber bands. In more than a dozen trips across the Atlantic I have still not had wet feet.

In choosing among the various types of boots available, one should be sure first of all that they have good, nonskid soles. Farmers' or icemen's boots which have soles that are heavy and not nonskid, are guaranteed to put the wearer in the water.

The question arises as to whether shoes should be worn inside the boots. One theory is that boots should be used without shoes because by the time the boots are needed the shoes are likely to be soaked. However, leather topsiders are fairly well waterproofed and will not absorb water. No matter how wet they get, one need merely pour the water out, put on a dry pair of socks, and replace the shoes, and they can then be worn inside boots if desired. By contrast, canvas topsiders take a tremendous amount of time to dry. They cannot be worn inside boots, and if dry socks are put on with wet canvas shoes, the socks soon become soaking wet. For these reasons, I prefer leather to canvas.

Those who do not wish to wear shoes with the boots should be sure to use the felt innersoles that absorb some of the dampness always present inside rubber boots. Felt innersoles, like socks, keep the feet warm, but I prefer to wear shoes inside boots, as I feel they keep my feet warmer than boots and socks.

CLOTHING FOR NORTHERN WATERS

Sweaters

"Old Harry," of *Yachting Monthly* fame, recommends having sweaters so long that reef points are needed. He may be going too far, but he does make sense. There is nothing worse than a short sweater that exposes one's skin to the cold breezes every time one bends over. When I have a sweater made, I see that it hangs almost to the knee, to protect my back and give me something nice and warm to sit on. Also, a turtleneck is essential, and the sleeves must be long enough so that the cuffs can be folded back two or three times to keep the wrists really warm.

Although the pullover is the most popular type of sweater, I believe that one fastened with a zipper or buttons in front is far better, as it is much easier to get on and off. Further, if both the foul-weather jacket and the sweater can be opened at the front, one does not have to go to the trouble of removing them to avoid overheating when going below for a short while.

Trousers

Trousers should be of heavy wool. The best I have ever worn for offshore work are icemen's trousers, available at Fulton Supply. These are made of wool so heavy and stiff that they almost stand up by themselves.

Underwear

For offshore work, long underwear is a must, and it should be of wool, not cotton. Further, the undershirt should have long sleeves and should reach well below the hips, to eliminate any expanse of bare skin between the tops and the bottoms. For really cold climates, one can cut the legs off one set of long johns, making shorts. Worn over the long underwear, these provide warmth where needed without adding bulk at the legs.

Socks

For heavy-weather use, one should always have on board several pairs of socks made of unbleached wool, so that if water does chance to get into one's boots, the socks will still remain almost dry.

Wristlets

As long as the wrists are kept warm, the fingers will function even in the coldest weather. A pair of knitted wristlets is therefore essential. They should be about seven or eight inches long, and should take the form of a straight sock, with holes for the thumb and the fingers. Even if they get damp or in fact soaking wet, wristlets of this kind, especially if made of unbleached wool, will still keep the wrists, and therefore the hands, quite warm.

Mittens

Waterproof mittens are not really necessary for every member of the crew, but certainly a few pairs should be carried on board every yacht cruising offshore in northern waters. These should not be ski mittens, but really good, solid waterproof mittens such as those made for fishermen. Inside of these, mittens of unbleached wool should be worn. Thus the helmsman, and anyone else remaining on deck for a long period of time, can keep their hands warm and dry. To be sure, they will have to remove the mittens when they wish to crank winches, trim sheets, or what-have-you, but their hands will have been kept dry, warm, and comfortable for the greater part of the watch.

Extra Gear

The boat cruising in northern waters should carry one or two warm coats, big enough to fit the largest member of the crew. These should be alpaca lined, and have a waterproof or water-repellent outer shell. It is impossible to walk around on deck while wearing a coat of this type, but wonderful to be inside one when on the helm at three in the morning. These coats can be purchased quite cheaply at army-surplus stores, and are well worth the investment.

TROPICAL CLOTHING

Except in one or two major yachting centers, foul-weather gear is virtually unobtainable in the tropics. Even the best foul-weather gear seems to last no more than eighteen months in the tropics, so one must carry several sets of gear for each person on board, or make arrangements to have additional items shipped out when needed.

Most people in the tropics discover that even in the worst weather, during the day they need only a sweater and a long foul-weather jacket; wet bottoms are not generally minded in tropical climates. Or one can have the jacket specially made, of sufficient length so that one can sit on it, and in this way remain dry without wearing foul-weather trousers. At night, a sweater is needed even in fine weather, and usually one likes a foul-weather jacket and trousers as well. The weight of foul-weather gear is important in the tropics, the stiff, heavy garments worn in the north being much too hot. Light gear such as that favored by small-boat sailors in round-the-buoy races is ideal.

Similarly, woolen socks and sneakers are all that is needed to keep the feet warm, in an area where the temperature gets down as far as 65 degrees only at three or four in the morning. Many people in the tropics prefer short boots, usually discarding them altogether when working on deck; those who find barefoot work painful stick to socks and sneakers.

FOOD

In rough weather, the boat will generally take a much greater beating than the crew. Frequently vessels get into trouble because the crew is exhausted and makes mistakes in judgment. To help prevent this situation, hot food is essential in rough weather, even in the tropics. For some reason, an uninterrupted diet of cold food for two or three days drastically saps a man's strength. Therefore, every cook must have some menus that can be prepared no matter how rough the weather becomes.

If, in the ultimate storm, cooking real meals is impossible, hot soup, cocoa, tea, or the like should be supplied. Coffee is less desirable. It is not too easily digested, and although a good stimulant, has absolutely no food value. Hence while it does keep one awake, frequently it also makes one hungry. In bad weather I prefer, like the British Navy, to give the crew cocoa or hot chocolate; these provide nourishment as well as warmth. Another possibility, if the galley facilities break down completely, is chocolate bars and hot tea loaded with honey. Honey is practically predigested, and tea is easy on the stomach. A large supply of chocolate bars should be stowed for emergencies, and be used only when necessary, so that they will not be eaten as snacks, and be all gone when needed.

SEASICKNESS PILLS

Before going offshore, the skipper should ascertain from each member of his crew what seasickness pill he finds most effective. Then he should make sure that each individual, even if he claims he is never seasick, has an adequate supply of the pills. Everyone should start taking the pills at the onset of bad weather, before it gets really rough, as they are only effective if they have time to operate. Once people begin getting seasick, they cannot hold a pill down long enough to benefit from it.

If there is someone on board experienced at giving shots, he may be able to give either intravenous or intramuscular shots for seasickness.

SAFETY DEVICES

SAFETY LINES

Many years before anyone ever thought of making a safety harness, it was considered normal operating procedure to tie a bowline around one's waist when going forward in rough weather. Many boats have a full complement of safety harnesses; if these are not available, a bow line around one's waist is certainly better than nothing. However, much gear has been broken, and many people have been lost, because of an inability to tie a good tight bow line rapidly around the waist. The skipper should therefore make sure that every member of his crew can tie a line around himself in a matter of seconds.

SAFETY BELTS

Every serious offshore cruising boat should have safety harnesses on board. Originally these were merely heavy belts around the waist; now they are almost universally chest-high harnesses with shoulder straps. Almost all of the many on the market are very good; the one complaint is that all too often a nicely made harness has at the end of its lanyard a snap made of cadmium-plated steel, with a steel spring. Rusting soon occurs, the spring jams, and the harness loses a good part of its effectiveness. Snaps should be of solid bronze, with bronze springs.

The next question concerns the length of the safety line on the harness. Many people prefer a very short line, clipping it to whatever is handy and unclipping it when they move to another part of the deck. However, more than one man has gone overside during the interval when his line was unclipped. Similarly, many people have gone overboard, their line unclipped, while attempting to pass through the main companionway hatch on their way to or from the deck. I therefore feel that the safety line should be long enough so that when it has been clipped onto a strong point in the cockpit, the wearer can reach all the way to the bow pulpit and all the way aft without unclipping it. Further, the individual coming up in rough weather should first pass up the end of the line, to be secured before he goes out on deck. When going below, he should reverse the process, having the safety line unclipped and passed down after he has left the deck.

One problem with a safety harness is that it is one more thing to put on; getting into all the heavy clothes, then the foul-weather gear, then the safety harness, is a long, time-consuming operation. Now in England there is available what looks like a good solution to the problem —a heavy foul-weather jacket with safety harness attached. Thus one need only put on the foul-weather gear and snap a lanyard to the built-in harness. Furthermore, the jacket has built-in buoyancy, so that the individual unfortunate enough to fall overboard will remain afloat. There is then a good chance of retrieving him, even at night if he has clipped to his jacket one of the new small, very efficient, individual strobe lights.

MAN-OVERBOARD EQUIPMENT

Prior to World War II, if a man went overboard, a life ring was thrown, the boat was turned around, and a search was made—all too often unsuccessfully, as an object as small as a life ring or a man's head is all but impossible to see in any sort of seaway. Today, ocean racers are required to have a dan buoy, a life ring, and a strobe light, secured to one another by a light line and kept in readiness where they can be thrown overboard instantly.

Dan Buoys

The dan buoy, which functions as a marker, consists of a fiber-glass or bamboo pole, weighted at one end, with a float near the weighted end and a flag on the upper end. The flag should be of high-visibility orange, and a minimum of eighteen inches on the hoist, two feet being even better; it should remain at least eight feet above the water.

There are various ways of stowing a dan buoy. The method shown in Drawing 211 is simple, cheap, foolproof, and effective. Two lengths of plastic tubing, at an appropriate distance apart, are secured to the backstay. The end of the buoy with the lead weight stows in the bottom tubing, the furled flag in the upper. To release the buoy, one just raises it out of the bottom tubing; it is then ready to be thrown overboard.

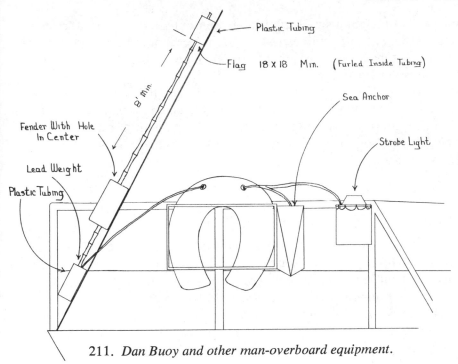

Plastic Tubing

Flag 18 X 18 Min. (Furled Inside Tubing)

Sea Anchor

8' Min.

Strobe Light

Fender With Hole In Center

Lead Weight

Plastic Tubing

211. *Dan Buoy and other man-overboard equipment.*

Life Buoys

The old-fashioned round life ring is now a thing of the past; almost universally one sees the horseshoe-shaped life ring, as it provides more buoyancy and support. A drogue, or small sea anchor, should be attached to it, since otherwise it will drift off to leeward in heavy weather faster than a man can swim.

Strobe Lights

At one time, it was customary to attach to the life buoy waterproof man-overboard lights that were activated by gravity. These were not very reliable, and since they were powered by flashlight batteries, they were not visible for more than a mile or so. In 1960, Guest Products introduced the strobe light. It is a flashing light of such great intensity that it reflects off low clouds. It proved its worth in the first race in which it was used: *Scylla,* Charlie Ulmer's Block Island 40, lost a man overboard under the worst circumstances—at night, during rain and a full gale—yet he was retrieved, as the strobe light attached to the life ring was visible even under such conditions.

Now on the market are numerous different types of strobe lights, by various manufacturers. Some consist simply of the light; others have attached to the light a small transmitter that automatically broadcasts on both 2182 and 500 kilocycles. This enables both the yacht and any other ships in the area to home in on the man in the water even if he is not immediately found.

INDIVIDUAL STROBE LIGHTS: Individual strobe lights, which are small enough to clip onto a foul-weather jacket, are now manufactured. A man overboard who cannot reach the life buoy, with its attached strobe light, can still be found if he has one of these, since it should be visible for several miles.

SHIP SAFETY

COMMON SENSE IN PLANNING

Every serious offshore cruising boat should be equipped to weather a full gale. However, even though a vessel is well prepared for emergencies, precautions should be taken to avoid gales and impossible weather. Common sense should be used in mapping out a voyage. There are certain times of the year when a yacht just should not go to sea. The aforementioned planning sessions held before a log fire are invaluable in this respect.

COLLISONS

One of the greatest hazards for a yacht is the possibility of being run down by a big vessel whose crew never even realizes that she has collided with a sailboat. As the years go by, ships become larger and larger, faster and faster, and less and less maneuverable. It is therefore essential when at sea to keep a good lookout at all times. Even offshore, five hundred miles from the nearest land, an amazing number of near misses have taken place.

To minimize the danger of collision at sea, a few basic rules should be observed. A radar reflector should be exhibited at all times in crowded waters such as the entrance to New York Harbor, Bristol Channel, or the English Channel, and in any waters where fog has closed in, or there is heavy rain. Some cruising yachts mount a radar reflector permanently, since a yacht's running lights are visible for only a few miles. A freighter traveling at twenty knots has little or no chance of spotting a yacht in time to avoid a collision. Indeed, the likelihood is that the yacht's lights will not be spotted at all. For the modern freighter operates with a very small crew, and few lookouts. The officer on the deck is usually back in the pilothouse catching up on paper work concerning pay records, cargo handling, or the like. Every ten minutes or so he takes a look at the radar set. Even if one does carry a radar reflector, to avoid colliding with a steamer one must always assume that one has not been seen, and alter course to get out of the way.

Running Lights

Once boats started using genoa jibs, the old-fashioned running lights on the light boards in the main or fore rigging became useless. The lights were then moved to the bow pulpit; this location was better, but they were too low. Now, under the new International Regulations for Preventing Collisions at Sea, running lights can be mounted on the masthead, where they are high enough to be seen from a steamer even with a large sea running. These regulations are in the process of revision, and much experimentation is being done by Bernard Hayman, editor of *Yachting World*.

Perhaps the best source of guidance in the placement of running lights is to be found in the reglations of the Royal Ocean Racing Club. The danger of collision while racing in the Channel at night is very great. Hence, the RORC leads the yachting world in its rather stringent regulations concerning running lights. I would recommend that the running lights on every cruising yacht be mounted in accordance with RORC regulations, for then an efficient mounting is assured.

GROUNDING

Grounding on a soft bottom, in a protected spot, may be just a good joke, but if a boat grounds on coral, rock, or hard sand, especially with a swell picking her up and dropping her down hard enough to do serious damage, the situation is dangerous. It may even cause the loss of the vessel.

In former days, when a yacht went aground, an anchor was run out, and a line was taken to the anchor windlass. If the windlass proved not powerful enough to heave the vessel off, one had to wait for extra help. However, today, the sheet winches installed in the ocean racer and in many an ocean cruiser, even of comparatively small size, are so powerful that the boat is almost like the man strong enough to lift himself by his own bootstraps.

Four cockpit winches, each with a mechanical advantage of 48 to 1, and a few big men cranking, can yield vast power. A hundred pounds of pressure can easily be placed on each winch handle, and even if friction reduces the mechanical advantage to 40 to 1, the result is a line pull of 4,000 pounds. If all four winches are used simultaneously, a total line pull of 16,000 pounds can be realized. If two men are available for each winch, the line pull can probably be doubled—to 32,000 pounds. Thus, given four good winches and sufficient manpower, practically any boat can heave itself off a reef. The procedure is to carry out and firmly embed a heavy anchor, run the anchor line back to the boat, tie a bow line to the anchor line forty or fifty feet away from the boat, and have individual genoa sheets secured to the winches and run out from the bow line and tied to the anchor line. In this situation, good strong chocks in the stern and the bow are worth their weight in gold, as the pressures generated will tear loose any poorly secured chocks.

Carrying out the anchor is best done in a good, easily rowed, easily launched dinghy. It is most difficult to do this job with an outboard and just about impossible with a rubber dinghy. The big Dell Quay dories, Boston Whalers, and the like can seldom be launched in short order. Therefore, as I have already indicated, I believe the small yacht should carry a rigid dinghy. The large boat, which has a big launch, should carry an easily launched eight- or ten-foot rowing dinghy as well.

CARRYING OUT AN ANCHOR

Good men have been drowned while carrying out anchors in adverse conditions. Care and thought should be given to the project. If a fisherman-type anchor is being carried and the dinghy has a sculling hole, as all dinghies should, the arm of the anchor can be hooked into the sculling hole, and the anchor rowed out and dropped at the appropriate place.

However, if a really heavy anchor is carried out, a line should be secured to the stern of the dinghy, taken down through the anchor shackle, and secured back to the ringbolt with a slip hitch. Then at the appropriate time, all that is required to drop the anchor is a quick yank on the slip hitch. Heavy Danforths should always be carried in this manner.

If a Danforth is being carried out, ten or fifteen feet of chain should be shackled to it. This chain should be piled in the dinghy and the anchor line secured to the dinghy with stopping twine or light, easily broken marline. The anchor line should not be fed from the dinghy, but should be paid out by the skipper, as he stands by on the yacht, giving directions to the rowers.

Line Versus Chain

One reason why every yacht, even a large one that carries both anchors on chain, should have at least one nylon anchor rode is that it may be required for use in taking out an anchor in an emergency. To row out an anchor when trying to drag the chain along behind is practically impossible. Rowing out an anchor and a chain at the same time requires superb seamanship and is really a salvage operation, done with the aid of many people and many boats rather than just by the yacht's own crew.

FIRE AT SEA

Since earliest times, fire at sea has been the seaman's greatest fear. Even on today's boats of steel or aluminum, fire at sea can be disastrous, for there is still so much wood in the interior of the vessel that a fire allowed to get out of hand can cause complete destruction. Hence, every boat should have adequate fire-fighting equipment. Just which fire-fighting facilities are advisable will depend on the type of boat, the equipment on board, and other variables.

Fire Extinguishers

A fire extinguisher, easily reached, should be kept in each compartment. In addition to the extinguisher in the engine room, one should be placed right outside, for use if a fire becomes so intense that the engine room cannot be entered.

On the larger boat it was formerly common to have an automatic CO_2 system, with a remote pull for use in case the automatic trigger did not work. This system did increase the vessel's safety, but was big, heavy, and expensive. Insurance underwriters still allow a discount when a boat is fitted with this type of equipment.

CO_2:   The CO_2 extinguisher is the old standby—good, and inexpensive. It is the ideal extinguisher for the galley, since if a galley-stove fire is put out with CO_2, the meal on the stove may still be eaten. If the galley fire is put out with dry powder, the meal is ruined, and the powder is hard to clean up. The disadvantage of a CO_2 system is that in out-of-the-way areas it is difficult to get recharged.

FREON: There is now available a newer and lighter type of equipment, originally invented for aircraft use—the Freon fire-extinguishing system, based on Freon manufactured in the United States by Du Pont and in England by Intercontinental Equipment Corporation. The Freon system has a number of advantages. It is compact, light, and inexpensive. Also, the entire compartment does not have to be flooded with gas to extinguish a fire, as is necessary when CO_2 is used.

DRY POWDER: Dry-powder extinguishers are becoming more and more popular. They are effective, they are light, and they can be recharged right on board the vessel, provided a recharge kit is carried. In the tropics, dry-powder extinguishers must be checked every few months, as the humidity sometimes penetrates and turns the dry powder into a solid mass, which will not blow through the nozzle.

CARBON TETRACHLORIDE: Carbon-tetrachloride extinguishers were formerly used to put out electrical fires, but they probably killed many people, as the gases they release are deadly poisonous. They have been illegal in the United States for many years and have recently gone off the marine market in Europe. Under no circumstances should carbon tetrachloride be used to extinguish a fire on board a boat.

WATER: Water, the real old standby, has put out innumerable fires. A bucket of water will take care of most small fires on a yacht, except, of course, for electrical fires. Many larger yachts have an arrangement by which the deck pump can be used as an emergency fire pump.

Fire Control

When fire breaks out, the most important thing is not to panic. While the flames are being extinguished, someone should attempt to ascertain the cause of the fire. The main causes of fire on yachts are broken fuel lines and short circuits.

If a fuel line has broken, the fuel supply should be cut off immediately. For this reason, a fuel-line shutoff outside the engine room—all too frequently missing on yachts—is desirable.

When a short circuit has occurred, one must pull the main disconnect, cutting off all electric power in the vessel. Unfortunately, few yachts have a battery disconnect that isolates the entire circuit. One should be installed in an accessible location, for use in case of an engine-room fire.

Galley fires, too, are likely to be frequent. Alcohol stoves are the main offender. In lighting such stoves, one must bleed fuel into the burner, turn off the valve, ignite the fuel to preheat the burner, then turn the valve back on. Leaking valves, forgetful cooks, all add up to numerous fires on alcohol stoves. Nevertheless, these stoves are listed as safe by Underwriters' Laboratories because the fires are easily put out with water, and do not result in explosions. Boats may burn, but seldom are people killed.

Since all stoves are subject to fire, if only from grease or fat overheating in the oven or frying pan, a CO_2 extinguisher should be kept in the galley. Also, as I indicated in the chapter on the galley, the shutoff valve should be so placed that even with fire blazing in and around the stove, the fuel line may be cut off. If, as occurs all too often, the builder has located it behind the stove, where it is impossible to reach in case of fire, it must be moved.

DISMASTING

In recent years, many yachts have been rebuilt and rerigged with Dacron sails and big, modern winches. The result has been the overloading of the wooden spars, which consequently fall down with alarming frequency. This happened so often among the 8 meters racing on the Clyde that the skippers got together and formed a broken-mast club, its insignia being a blue tie on which a broken mast was embroidered in gold. Some senior members had two broken masts on their ties, and one actually had three. I believe I have topped them all, with seven: that is, I have been on board seven boats—not all of them my own—when they lost their rigs.

Sometimes, when the rig goes overside, it is possible to hang onto the bottom end of the mast, lash it on board, get the sails off, get the boom on board, and heave the rig on board or tow it in. In other cases, one must disconnect everything and let it float away, in order to save the boat. Exactly what should be done will depend on the size of the crew, the condtion of the sea, and the type of rig. However, a few general rules can be stated.

First of all, everyone must be secured with safety lines or the end of a jib sheet. As the mast goes overside, the motion of the boat will change violently, and the roll period will be down to two or three seconds. It will be almost impossible to stand up in rough weather. Unless precautions are taken, the boat will soon be minus a crew as well as a mast.

Second, under no circumstances should the engine be started until a really careful check has been made to ascertain that all rigging is clear of the propeller. Next, if the butt end of the spar is still on deck, it should be secured there, so that it can be kept somewhat under control while all rigging—halyards, and the like—is disconnected. Serious cruising boats should always carry on board bolt cutters big enough to cut the largest rigging on the vessel.

However, even these may not do the job. In the old days of galvanized turnbuckles and wire, the turnbuckles were likely to be frozen or almost frozen, and hence impossible to disconnect, but the soft 7 by 7 wire was easy to cut. Trying to cut today's ⅜-inch or ⁷⁄₁₆-inch 1 by 19 wire is more of a project, and on modern turnbuckles the bronze is so hard that cutters don't make much headway; often it is quicker to disconnect the turnbuckles than to try to cut the rigging.

Once the rigging has been removed, either the spar should be cast loose, or preparations should be made for taking it on board, as conditions dictate. I never had the misfortune to be on a boat that lost an aluminum spar, but I imagine that since an aluminum spar (unless foam filled) would most likely sink instantly, salvaging anything would be very difficult, except in the most favorable circumstances. The situation is different with a wooden spar, since it will float. On a ketch or a yawl, if the sail can be taken off and the butt end of the spar is still on board, there is a good chance of rigging a tackle to the mizzenmast head and heaving the spar back on board. However, it should be remembered that the safety of the entire vessel is much more important than saving the sails, spars, and other gear.

Methods of jury rigging after a dismasting vary with the boat, and every skipper should have his own ideas. Even if there is adequate fuel on board for powering to a port of refuge, some sort of jury rig is of value to slow down the motion of the boat and steady her up. If the boom or spinnaker poles can be saved, there is a good chance with a competent crew to set up a jury rig. Moreover, on a ketch or a yawl, if the masts are independently stayed, it is almost impossible to lose everything. If the mizzen is still up, some sort of sail can be rigged to the spinnaker pole, set up as a mast. A working jib or small genoa hoisted ninety degrees out (Drawing 212) will tend to balance the mizzen and mizzen staysail, making it possible to maintain a fairly decent speed even on a reach. Downwind, practically anything will work. Many a boat has finished quite far up in the Transpac race despite a jury rig. However, a jury rig is seldom capable of driving a boat to windward; a close reach is about the best that can be hoped for.

212. *Jury-rigged yawl.*

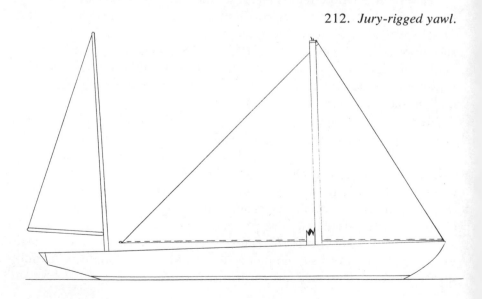

In summation, while each dismasting will present its own problems and possibilities, one should always remember not to start the engine until every single piece of line is clear of the propeller, and not to jeopardize the safety of the boat in salvage efforts.

RADIOS

Although at first glance it may seem like a good idea, the splicing of a radio antenna into a stay or shroud is actually the height of folly. First of all, if the splice pulls out or insulators collapse, the usual result is the loss of the spar. At the same time, the yacht is then without a radio until an emergency antenna can be rigged. For the safety of a vessel after a dismasting, it is essential that the radio antenna be independently rigged. On a sloop or cutter the antenna can be rigged permanently off the stern. On a yawl or ketch the antenna can either be removable or be mounted parallel to the mizzen rigging, on an adjustable bracket which can be swung outboard when the radio is to be used. On some yawls and ketches the antenna is rigged on the top of the mizzenmast, on the assumption that even if the main is lost, the mizzen will still be there, and radio transmission will be possible. If the mizzen is lost, use of the radio is interrupted, but the boat is not disabled, since she still has the mainmast. But if both masts are lost, the yacht is in real trouble.

When the boat is well offshore or in an out-of-the-way area, the normal radiotelephone is of little use. Its range is limited, and in many parts of the world the standard ship-distress frequency of 2182 is very poorly monitored. An emergency transmitter which will trip the automatic SOS alarm on the radios of commercial ships or aircraft is therefore desirable. The advantage of broadcasting on an aircraft frequency is that the planes are so high that the range of even a small distress radio will be quite wide. The international distress frequencies are as follows:

2182 kilocycles—voice, ships;
500 kilocycles—code and voice, ships;
1805 kilocycles—new experimental emergency frequency;
121.6 megacycles—code and voice, aircraft.

Some of the manufacturers who build marine distress sets of one type or another are listed in the Appendix.

FLOODING

All cruising yachts should be equipped with two reliable hand bilge pumps. If major flooding occurs, these pumps should be able to cope with the situation, or at least minimize the rising of the water. As soon as a leak of large proportions is discovered, steps should be taken to ascertain the cause. Often this will turn out to be very simple—a broken water line on the engine, a broken cockpit-scupper line, a head discharge line come adrift, or something similar. These are all relatively easy to correct.

However, in certain situations, as when leaks are caused by seams or butts working loose, drastic action may be required. In the first Bermuda race after World War II, one of the most famous big ocean racers almost sank. She started leaking so badly that it appeared that she would have to leave the race, although she was in an excellent position. Finally, the leak was traced to behind the icebox. The owner said, quite justifiably, "To hell with the icebox and the joiner work." Using wrecking bars and fire axes, the skipper and the mate demolished the icebox, tore out the ceiling, and found a number of leaking seams, which they sealed with bedding compound and heavy canvas.

Other methods have also been used to stop leaking through seams. In one case, *Paisano* almost sank. Finally, sheets of cork were jammed down on top of the leaking seams, and firmly wedged in place with wooden wedges. By this means, the leaking was cut to a bare minimum, and the boat remained in the water for many months before being hauled and repaired.

The old faithful combination of lead sheeting and bedding compound has kept innumerable boats afloat in emergencies. Since lead sheeting is most difficult to obtain, some should be kept on board at all times. Recently, an underwater epoxy has become available. The two components of the epoxy must be combined in a bucket of water, so that the mix is not exposed to air. Then one dives overside to apply the epoxy to the leaking seam; water pressure pushes it into the seam, and it hardens underwater, sealing the leak. This repair has been accomplished offshore under the most adverse circumstances. It is therefore very worthwhile to carry a few tins of epoxy.

Disastrous Flooding

Often when disastrous flooding occurs, all those on board panic, or at least do not use their minds to their full capacity. But there are methods of coping with this flooding. Hand pumps will remove a lot of water. Some boats have electric pumps or pumps belted off the engine or generator. These will of course dispose of a tremendous quantity of water, and are especially desirable for the larger yachts. It should also be remembered that it is very simple to improvise a pump if one has substituted for the normal engine intake valve a tee valve with one of its lines going to the deepest part of bilge. This must of course be equipped with a large-capacity strainer. When flooding occurs, one can then close off the normal engine overboard intake and suck directly from the bilge.

If this emergency bilge-pumping arrangement has not been prepared in advance, it can be jury-rigged. The engine water intake is turned off at the sea cock, and the intake line is disconnected and placed in the bilge, preferably in a coffee can with holes punched in it, which acts as a strainer. Large quantities of water will be moved by the engine. A diesel engine will continue pumping until the air intake goes under water. A rubber hose fastened to the air intake with a clamp will enable it to keep running until the boat sinks.

It should also be remembered that if the galley sink is on center and has a big two-inch straight-through drain, emptying directly overside, the fastest way to bail the boat is with a bucket directly to the sink rather than with a pump.

LOSS OF STEERING

Loss of steering is the most common emergency afloat, especially for the boat with a wheel. Most ocean-racing rules require an adequate emergency tiller which can be shipped promptly. How "adequate" is defined, I do not know. I have delivered numerous boats with what I consider grossly inadequate emergency steering.

The placement of the steering stand just forward of the rudderhead is the primary cause of difficulty (Drawing 213). Since this design leaves little room for an emergency tiller, we wind up with either a very short tiller or a tiller that comes up over the binnacle and curves forward. Tillers of the latter type are usually so high that they are most difficult to use. They may work all right in Long Island Sound, with a 5-knot breeze, but they are impossible offshore with a swell running. Here I believe the inspection committees for the various ocean races should be much more strict, for the racing boats usually set the style for the cruising yachts as well.

If the emergency tiller is long enough, and can be operated from a sitting position, there should be no difficulty in handling a boat when the wheel steering fails. If the tiller is short, control can be achieved by rigging blocks and tackles to its end; provisions for an arrangement of this kind should be made before going offshore, and the emergency tiller should be tested in heavy weather.

I was once the victim of a failure to make these preparations. Delivering a yacht to the United States, we were 150 miles from St. Thomas when the steering system failed. We managed to rig block and tackle to

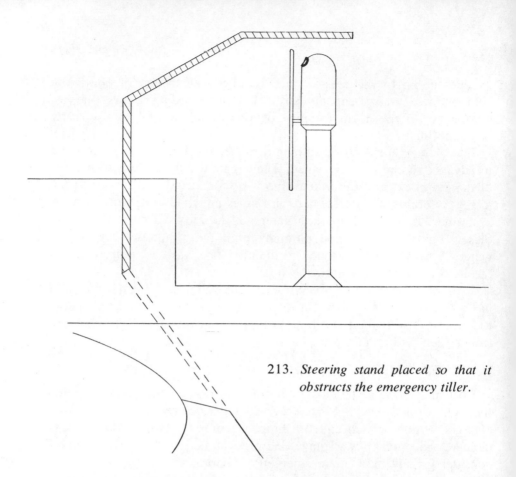

213. *Steering stand placed so that it obstructs the emergency tiller.*

the end of the tiller, which was very short, but fifty miles later this emergency tiller broke off. We then clamped a monkey wrench to the base of the broken tiller, rigged a block and tackle from the wrench to the base of the binnacle, and thence to a winch, balanced the boat by trimming the sails as best we could (Photo 147). The main problem was that occasionally the monkey wrench dropped off, and then there was fun and games for a few minutes, until we got the boat back under control. Finally, we discovered that the largest socket wrench just fitted the rudderhead, and we completed the trip under socket wrench and block and tackle (Photo 148).

Rudder Failure

The situation becomes more serious when the failure involves not just the steering but the rudder itself, as when the rudder comes completely off, when the rudderstock breaks off short, or when, in a fiber-glass boat, the rudderstock turns back and forth loosely inside the fiber-glass shell, and the rudder does exactly what it wishes. In situations like these, an emergency rudder of some sort must be mounted.

147. Monkey wrench with tackle as emergency tiller. (D. M. Street)

148. Socket wrench with tackle as emergency tiller. (D. M. Street)

Various solutions to this problem have been developed, for the loss of a rudder has become all too common in recent Transatlantic and Transpac races, where the boats are driven so hard that everything is straining and almost inevitably something goes.

Preparations for rigging an emergency rudder should be carefully considered before leaving port. The transom-sterned boat has few difficulties with the rudder, and in any event, since the rudder is outboard it usually can be repaired even with the boat under way. The inboard rudder causes more difficulty. If the boat has the square, deep stern so popular among the ocean racers a few years back, rudder pintles can be bolted to the stern and an emergency plywood rudder can be kept ready for shipping when needed (Drawing 214). If the boat has an overhanging stern, the stern pulpit can be used as a rudderpost (Drawing 215). With a rudder rigged in this way, *Aura II* managed to finish in the Transatlantic race to Germany. Hers was an excellent performance and a demonstration of why a serious cruising yacht should have a very strong pulpit, possibly with the necessary fittings attached in advance to enable this type of rudder to be rigged without too much difficulty.

On occasion, all sorts of ingenious rigs have been used. One of the most common is made by nailing boards to the end of the spinnaker pole, weighting one end of the pole with the anchor and dropping it overboard, and securing the inboard end to a fitting on or near the stern. Lines from the outer end of the pole are then rigged to a spar lashed across the boat, and thence to winches which control the spar and rudder.

The first and most important thing to remember when working under a jury rudder or jury steering system is that the rig of the boat should be balanced out to make her as easy as possible to steer. Going to windward or close reaching, one should be able to steer a well-designed boat simply by adjusting the sails. When the wind gets on the quarter, or the boat is heading downwind, the difficulty starts. At this point, one should douse the mizzen and main and work with different combinations of headsails. This procedure was followed with *Dyna*, and she was sailed right across the Atlantic with no rudder and no really effective emergency steering system, her direction being controlled largely by the balancing of the sails. With main and mizzen down, the danger of the boom breaking in jibing is removed. One may get caught back with a headsail out on a pole, but that is not likely to do any damage, whereas a jibing boom will.

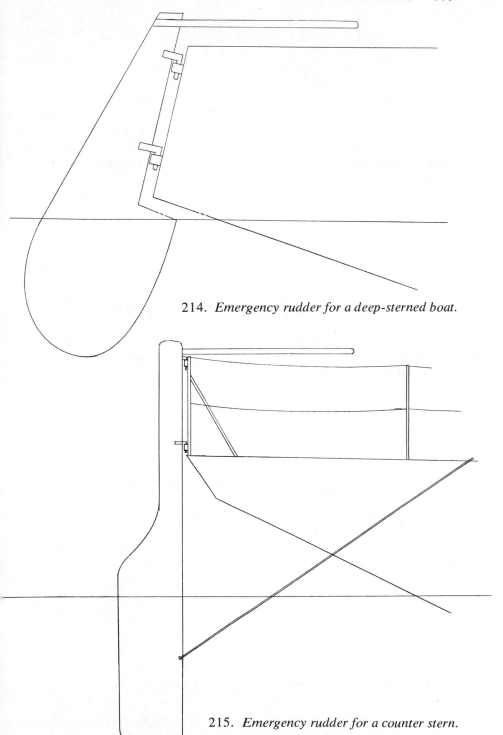

214. *Emergency rudder for a deep-sterned boat.*

215. *Emergency rudder for a counter stern.*

MEDICAL EMERGENCIES

A good book on the handling of medical emergencies—Dr. Paul Sheldon's *First Aid Afloat,* for example—should be carried on board for reference. A work of this sort will also specify what medical supplies should be stocked. For a long-distance trip, these should include enough pain-killer to keep a badly injured person comfortable for as long as a week. A broken hand may be immobilized with an old-fashioned wooden splint, or better, one of the new inflatable splints, but still hurts a great deal. If the patient is in pain, his suffering will get on the nerves of the rest of the crew. Hence, making the patient comfortable with pain-killers will not only bring him a long way toward recovery but also help maintain efficiency on board the yacht. There is usually a good chance of obtaining medical assistance within the week by means of the radio, by stopping a passing ship, or by reaching port.

ABANDONING SHIP

Of course we hope that none of us will ever have to abandon ship, but preparations should be made. At one time, yachts cruised the far corners of the world with no emergency craft except a dinghy. This was seldom large enough to carry the entire crew even for a day, much less for a long drift in the open ocean. The chances of survival if the yacht sank were slight.

However, today the situation has changed. Capacious life rafts are available, with canopies which provide protection from the sun in the tropics and from the cold up north. On a well-equipped life raft, a crew in fairly good physical shape should be able to float in semicomfort for a week. Survival studies show that if one can get through the first twenty-four hours at sea after abandoning ship, one's chances of survival increase. After forty-eight hours, one's chances start rising appreciably; and finally, if one manages to last a week, the likelihood of not being rescued is slight. The mental attitude of the persons adrift may be even more important than the gear on board. With good gear and a good mental attitude, those who are floating around in a life raft can justifiably expect to live to tell the tale.

CLOTHING

While food, drink, and equipment can be prepacked in the life raft, clothing is assembled when the decision has been made to abandon ship. On a life raft, the crew's comfort, and perhaps even survival, may depend on what clothing is available. In the colder climates one should of course have foul-weather gear, and all the clothing one can possibly put on. Even in the warmer climates foul-weather gear and sweaters are necessary, along with some light clothing to prevent sunburn during the day. In the tropics, during the day the heat on a raft is nearly unbearable, but in the evening, when the temperature drops to the low 70's or upper 60's, one almost freezes, and the foul-weather gear and sweaters are welcome.

WHEN TO ABANDON SHIP

After all is said and done, and all the preparations have been made to abandon ship, it should be remembered that a ship is much more easily spotted than is a life raft. Furthermore, all too many yachts are abandoned when it appears to the crew that there is so much water on boat that sinking is inevitable, and then three or four days later are found still afloat. Therefore, a yacht should not be abandoned until there is absolutely no question that the vessel is going down.

When *Curlew,* a seventy-two-foot schooner, was supposedly sinking off Bermuda, a ship answered the SOS, and the crew managed to scramble aboard by means of a cargo net, fortunately without anyone being crushed between *Curlew* and the rescue ship. The foremast was pulled out against the sides of the rescue ship, and *Curlew* was abandoned. Three days later, she was found drifting, still afloat, by a salvage tug from Bermuda. Had the crew stayed on board, undoubtedly the mast would not have been lost, lives would not have been jeopardized in the transfer to the rescue ship, and the cruise would not have been ruined.

Similarly, in the fall of 1970, *Integrity,* going south, was abandoned supposedly in a sinking condition. Again the rig was lost alongside the rescue ship, again lives were endangered in the process of abandoning ship, and weeks later, despite the fact that she was thought to be in a sinking condition when she was abandoned, she was found afloat and was towed in by another yacht.

Insurance underwriters can repeat stories like these by the hundreds. But two should be sufficient to demonstrate that the only way to abandon ship is to tie the life raft down on deck, inflate it, sit in it until the vessel physically goes down, and then cut loose.

LIFE RAFTS

The life raft should be well equipped, and the gear should be kept prepacked either inside the life raft, or in a sail bag which is tied into the life raft, so that there is no possibility of leaving it behind when the vessel is abandoned. The life raft should be firmly tied down before inflating. More than one crew has inflated a life raft and watched it drift off to leeward as they stood on the sinking deck.

The raft should be tested according to the manufacturer's recommendations, by the manufacturer's agent, every year. In some out-of-the-way areas, the manufacturer's agent is not available, and more important, frequently there is no way to have the CO^2 bottles filled. Therefore, the person testing his own life raft should not use the CO^2 system, but rather should pump it up with the foot pump provided, or blow it up with a diver's air bottle, or a vacuum cleaner. If the raft is then left for forty-eight hours, any leakage will become apparent.

Before repacking, all the air must be removed from the raft. This is a difficult job, but once again a vacuum cleaner can be used. If the suction end of the vacuum cleaner is attached to the raft, all the air will be sucked out. The raft should be repacked with five or ten pounds of talcum powder, and all the surfaces should be carefully dusted with it to prevent them from sticking together and deteriorating.

Lights

BUILT-IN LIGHTS: Most life rafts today have a small white light on the top of the canopy. However, the batteries in this unit must be changed very frequently; otherwise they deteriorate, explode, and ruin the light. Other disadvantages are that this light will not last for long, and is visible for only a mile or so.

STROBE LIGHTS: As has been pointed out, the flashing strobe light can be seen over great distances. Its high-intensity flash is often so bright that it is reflected off low clouds. I therefore feel that the life raft should have its own strobe light; if it does not, those attached to the life buoys should be taken along when the vessel is abandoned.

FLASHLIGHTS: All available flashlights should be thrown into the life raft when the vessel is abandoned, for use as signal lamps and as a source of spare batteries.

Radar Reflectors

A radar reflector is an essential piece of equipment, since without it, a rubber raft is all but impossible to spot on radar.

Flares

HAND-HELD FLARES: Hand-held flares are almost worthless. The raft is so low that the light from the flare cannot be seen unless both the raft and the searcher are on top of a wave at the same time. Therefore, Very-pistol flares or rockets are essential.

VERY PISTOLS AND ROCKETS: The old standby was the Very pistol. A red flare fired from the Very pistol is visible for a great distance, but remains aloft for only a matter of seconds; hence the parachute flare is infinitely preferable. Also, while the little kit containing a Very pistol and three or four flares is fine, a good many flares may be needed to attract attention. A dozen is the absolute minimum that any raft should carry, with half being parachute flares, and two dozen is better. Further, the dates on the flares should be checked periodically; overage flares rarely work.

Now available in England are rockets with parachutes. I have seen one demonstration of the comparative effectiveness of Very flares and rockets which was most impressive. At the celebration of the 250th anniversary of the Cork Water Club, each yacht, as she passed the original home of the club, fired a salute. Most of the American boats fired flares. These were spectacular and effective, but they were far outshone by the rockets released by the British boats. The height reached by the Very flares was only one-third that reached by the rockets. Since a rocket goes three times as high, it is visible over nine times the area— an advantage certainly worth the extra cost.

Radios

As has been pointed out, the average yacht's radiotelephone does not have sufficient range to alert other vessels offshore, and in any event, the 2182 frequency is poorly monitored. I have frequently been unable to raise passing freighters, passenger liners, and the like on 2182 even when they were clearly visible. In 1969, when cruising across the Atlantic in *Antilles*, we had tremendous difficulty raising the ocean weather ships on 2182. We were told that they had it turned on, but since they were receiving and transmitting on other frequencies, they kept 2182 so low that it was almost impossible for them to pick up a normal call on it. So as a safety feature on a life raft, the normal radiotelephone is not worth the expense.

There are two other possibilities. The first is a marine radio which transmits on an international frequency of 500 kilocycles. An SOS on this frequency will automatically trigger an alarm on every large vessel within range of the set.

The second type of radio which should be considered is a small VHF transmitter, no bigger than a cigar box, which broadcasts on the frequency continually monitored by all aircraft (121.6 megacycles). A call on this frequency will almost certainly bring a reply. The planes are likely to be flying at altitudes of from twenty thousand to forty thousand feet, and at these heights, the range of this type of radio will probably be a circle at least three hundred miles in diameter. To be sure, a jet cannot land on the sea, but it can alert rescue services. The FCC formerly regarded this type of transmitter as absolutely illegal, but no one would know it was being carried until it was used in a rescue, and having been rescued, who cares about a jail sentence! Now these sets are legal and commercially available.

Drogues, or Sea Anchors

The life raft should be equipped with a drogue, or sea anchor. If the prevailing wind is moving the raft in the desired direction, that's fine; a speed of as much as three knots may be reached in the trade-wind area. But if the raft is being pushed away from shore, the drogue will help minimize the drift.

Water

Cans of water for use as the emergency supply on a life raft are available. However, over the years the cans will deteriorate and begin to leak, and one may discover all too late that the water is gone. For that reason it seems better to pack beer cans in the emergency bag or inside the raft before each trip. Beer will provide both food value and liquid.

Food

Many people prefer to stock the life raft with the packaged emergency rations manufactured for this purpose. These have the advantage of being specially assembled for the job, but having seen West Indian cockroaches eat through everything, including aluminum foil, I suspect that after the life raft had been launched, when nothing could be done, one might discover the emergency rations spoiled. For this reason it is best to pack canned foods—and a can opener!—in the emergency bag before each trip. The amount and type of food to be taken will depend on the nature of the particular cruise.

In summation, anyone wondering about his capacity to survive in a life raft should read the story of Eddie Rickenbacker adrift for three weeks in the Pacific. He and his companions had little equipment, and the raft was without a canopy, but they survived. Certainly the chances of surviving on a well-equipped life raft until rescued are excellent.

APPENDICES

GLOSSARY

Aback   A sail is aback when so sheeted to windward that it exerts a braking force on the yacht's forward motion, or when the wind comes on what should be its lee side.

Abaft   Toward the stern; to the rear of.

Abeam   At right angles to the fore-and-aft center line amidships.

Aboard   On board or in a vessel.

About   A vessel is said to go, come, or put about when she swings her bow through the eye of the wind, i.e., tacks.

Accelerator   A chemical (usually put in the resin mix by the manufacturer) which is used in fiber-glass construction and in the preparation for use of polyurethane paint to speed up the rate of curing. It is dangerous to mix the accelerator and the catalyst (*q.v.*) because there may be an explosion. The accelerator should be mixed with the resin, and the catalyst then added.

Accommodation Ladder   A ladder or flight of steps enabling one to climb up the topsides from a dinghy to a vessel's deck.

Accommodation Plan   A drawing showing the internal arrangements of a vessel.

Acockbill   An anchor is said to be acockbill when it is hung in an up-and-down position, ready to be let go. Yards are said to be acockbill when they are topped at an angle with the horizontal.

Aft   Toward the stern; behind.

Aground   With the keel resting on the bottom; "on the putty" to the British, "parked" to some Americans.

Ahead   Toward the bows; in front of.

All Standing   To bring up people or things all standing is to bring them to a sudden and unexpected stop.

Aloft   Up above; up the mast or in the rigging.

Ambiguous Sector   An area where signals from one particular Consolan station give inaccurate and deceptive readings.

Amidships   Generally, the middle part of a vessel, between the bow and the stern; sometimes, on the fore-and-aft line (hence, to put the helm amidships is to steer neither to port nor to starboard).

Anemometer	An instrument for measuring the strength of the wind.
Apparent Wind	The wind that is felt aboard a moving boat, consisting of a combination of the true wind and the wind caused by the boat's motion. The greater the speed of the boat, the more the apparent wind moves ahead.
Apron	A strengthening piece behind the stem, seldom found in American-designed boats.
Arming	Tallow held in the recess of a sounding lead to bring up a sample of the seabed.
Ashore	Aground, or on land.
Aspect Ratio	The relation of length to width in a sail, a wing, a rudder, a centerboard, or any other object.
Astern	Behind; toward the stern.
Athwart	Across; the opposite of fore and aft.
Awash	Just under, or washed over by, water.
Aweather	To windward; toward the weather side.
Aweigh	An anchor is aweigh when it has broken out of the bottom.
Backbone	The center-line fore-and-aft structure of the boat, consisting of stem, keel, rudderpost, horn timber, and the various knees and aprons that support these timbers.
Baggy Wrinkle	Chafing gear made of old rope ends secured to rigging.
Ballast Keel	The lead or iron bolted onto the wooden structural keel to give a yacht stability.
Ballooner	A light, high-cut genoa which may be used on a reach, sheeted to the end of the main boom.
Bear Away, To; Bear Off, To	To put the helm up (to windward) and turn the bow of the boat away from the wind.
Beat, To	To tack to windward, sailing hard on the wind.
Bee Block	British for cheek block (q.v.). Also, to the British, a wooden chock on the side of a boom near its after end, to take the standing part of a reef pendant, somewhat similar to a cheek block.
Belay, To	To make fast or secure a rope on a cleat or pin.
Belly	The fullness, or draft, of a sail.
Bend, To	To fasten, as one rope to another or to some other object, a sail to its spars, and so on.

Beneaped	See *Neaped*.
Bermudian Rig	See *Jib-headed Rig*.
Bermudian Sail	A triangular fore-and-aft sail without a gaff or yard, set on a boom on the aft side of a mast.
Berth	(1) A sleeping place on board. (2) The place ashore, in a dock, or at an anchorage, which is occupied by a vessel. To berth a vessel is to put her into such a place.
Bight	(1) A bend or loop in a rope. (2) An open bay formed by a bend in the coast.
Bilge	(1) The curve of a vessel's bottom where it merges into the side. (2) The space in a vessel beneath the sole.
Bilge Keel	(1) A rubbing-piece fastened to the outside of the bilge of a dinghy to protect it from chafe when taking the ground or being dragged up a beach. (2) An actual keel on a larger boat with twin keels; it allows the boat to dry out upright and provides the necessary lateral plane to enable the boat to work to windward.
Bill	A certificate or a written agreement, as in "bill of health," "bill of lading," "bill of exchange."
Binnacle	The case in which a compass is fixed.
Bitt	One of the posts fitted in the foredeck to take the heel of the bowsprit and to which the anchor cable is made fast.
Bitter End	(1) The extreme end. (2) The inboard length of a ship's cable (from the fact that the cables of ships at anchor used to be belayed to specially fitted center-line bollards called "bitts").
Blade	The flat part of an oar or propeller.
Bleed, To	To drain, usually slowly. To bleed a buoy is to empty it of water. To bleed a fuel system is to loosen a connection and pump until all the air is exhausted from the system. To bleed the monkey is to extract the contents of a rum barrel by boring a small hole in it.
Block	Pulley.
Block and Block; Two-Blocked	The state of a tackle when its standing and moving blocks are hauled close together. Colloquially, the terms can be used to describe the position of any two

objects which are close together.

Board	The distance covered in one tack, or leg, when beating to windward.
Boathook	A pole with a hook at one end, used for picking up a mooring buoy, holding onto a dinghy, and the like.
Boatswain's, or Bosun's, Stores	Spare rigging materials carried on board.
Bobstay	A chain, wire, or rod from the stem to the end of the bowsprit, to support it against the upward pull of the jib.
Body Plan	A drawing which shows the shape of the athwartship sections of a vessel.
Boier	A type of shoal-draft Dutch yacht.
Bollard	(1) A post, usually on a pier or quay, to which mooring or warping lines are made fast. (2) A metal fitting with two heads, on a vessel's deck at the bow or quarter, to which mooring lines are secured.
Boltrope	A rope sewn along the edge of a sail to strengthen it and take the strain off the material.
Bonnet	(1) Any small cover or hood, of canvas or metal, used to close or protect a small fitting or opening. (2) Historically, an extra piece of canvas, laced to the foot of a sail to increase its area.
Boom	A horizontal spar for extending the foot of a sail.
Boot-Top Line	The line just above the load waterline, where the bottom paint joins the topsides paint.
Boot Topping	A strip of specially hard paint around the waterline, which can be scrubbed without damage. It is less used nowadays since hard racing copper antifouling paint can be scrubbed. Boats with high topsides often look better with the boot topping carried up a little way, to reduce the apparent height of the topsides.
Bottle Screw	(1) An adjusting screw fitted at the bottom of a wire stay; "closed-body turnbuckle" to Americans. Bottle screws are solid and internally tapped; they are often used aboard sailing dinghies. (2) Cruising boats usually use open ones, more correctly called "rigging screws," in which the threads can be more easily inspected.

Bottomry	A system of pledging the hull of a ship as security for a loan.
Bouse Down, To	To haul down taut.
Bow, Bows	The entire forepart of a vessel; also the sides of the forepart of a vessel, from the stem to the midship section.
Bow-and-But-tock Line	A line showing the shape of a fore-and-aft vertical section of a vessel. It is seen as a curve on the sheer plan.
Bower	The principal anchor, which is generally used with a chain cable, in England, as opposed to a kedge, which is lighter, and is used with a rope cable; also called a "working anchor."
Bowsprit	A spar on which the jib is set projecting horizontally from the bow.
Brace	A rope by means of which the yard of a square sail is controlled in a horizontal plane.
Brail	A rope which encircles a sail for the purpose of gathering it in to the mast, sprit, or yard.
Brail, To	To take in a sail by the brails.
Breaker	(1) A sea which is breaking, i.e., the water of which is in forward motion. (2) A small barrel for holding fresh water.
Breasthook	A wood or iron knee binding a pair of shelves, stringers, or gunwales to one another and to the stem.
Breast Rope	A rope from bow or stern made fast to the nearest point of a quay, a pier, or another vessel, when lying alongside.
Bridge Deck	Reinforcing beams and bulkheads, decked over, between the cockpit and the cabin. They strengthen a boat a great deal, and help to prevent water from going down the companionway in bad weather, but they restrict access to the cabin.
Brightwork	Woodwork which is kept varnished.
Bring Up, To	To anchor.
Broach, To	To lose control when running downwind and to round up, bringing wind and sea abeam.
Bulkhead	A partition belowdecks separating one part of a vessel from another.
Bulldog Grip	A screw fitting for temporarily clamping two parts of

wire rope side by side; also called a "wire rope clamp."

Bull Rope	A rope leading from the bowsprit end to a mooring buoy which is too large to be taken aboard, to keep the buoy from bumping the stem when wind and tide are opposed.
Bull's-eye	A round, hardwood thimble used for altering the lead of a rope.
Bulwarks	The solid protection built around the edges of a deck to prevent people or gear from being washed overboard.
Bumpkin	A spar, projecting horizontally from the stern, to which the mizzen sheet or permanent backstay is attached.
Bunk	A sleeping berth.
Bunk Board	A bulwark of wood to prevent a sleeper from being thrown out of his bunk by the motion of a vessel.
Bunt	The middle part of a sail.
Buntline Hitch	An excellent knot for attaching a dinghy painter made of synthetic line to a ring. It does not tend to come undone as two half hitches would. It is also used to attach a sheet to a sail, and takes up less space then a bow line.
Buoyancy Tank	An airtight tank fitted into a dinghy to maintain buoyancy should she become waterlogged.
Burden Boards	See *Floorboards*.
Burgee	A yacht-club flag.
Burton	A tackle used for lifting the anchor or dinghy aboard.
Butt	The place where two planks or other members touch one another end to end.
Butt End	The larger end of a spar, or any similarly shaped object.
Buttock Line	A line of intersection of a longitudinal vertical plane with the hull of a ship.
By the Lee	Running with the wind on the same side as the boom.
Cable	A chain, or a fiber or wire rope, by means of which a vessel rides to her anchor.
Cable-Laid Rope	Rope made by laying up three complete ropes with a left-handed twist; seldom seen today.

Call Sign	A combination of letters and perhaps numbers identifying a radio operator or station, for use in communication.
Camber	The athwartship curve of the deck; sometimes called the "crown."
Camel	A tank secured to the hull of a ship to provide extra buoyancy, used mainly in salvage work.
Canoe Stern	An overhanging stern with a pointed or rounded end.
Cant, To	To incline from the perpendicular.
Cap	The ring at the top of a lower mast, through which the housing topmast slides.
Capstan	A mechanical appliance with a vertical barrel, used to obtain increased power when hauling on a rope or chain.
Carline	A fore-and-aft member at the side of a coach roof, hatch, or skylight, to which the ends of the half-beams and the coaming are secured.
Carry Away, To	To break or lose any spar or part of the rigging.
Carvel-built	Constructed with the skin planks lying flush with one another and presenting a smooth surface.
Cast, To	To take a sounding with the lead.
Catalyst	A chemical added to polyester or epoxy resin to start it curing, in fiber-glass construction and in the preparation of polyurethane paint for use. See also *Accelerator*.
Catenary	The curve, or sag, of the cable between a vessel and her anchor.
Cat Rig	A fore-and-aft rig with one mast far forward and only one sail.
Cat the Anchor, To	To secure the anchor for sea.
Caulk, To	To drive strands of cotton or oakum into a seam to make it watertight.
Ceiling	Planking laid fore and aft inside the frames; sometimes installed for appearance's sake, but on commercial and fishing boats, a part of the structure.
Centerboard	A hinged vertical plate or board which can be lowered through a slot in the keel of a shoal-draught yacht or dinghy to provide lateral resistance.

Center of Effort	The geometric center of a sail or sail plan where the lateral force of the wind is theoretically concentrated.
Center of Lateral Resistance	The geometric center of an underwater profile of a vessel's hull—the theoretic point at which one could push the hull sideways without it turning.
Chafe, To	To rub, or damage by rubbing.
Chafing Gear	Anything which is used to prevent chafe.
Chain Plate	A metal strap on the side of a vessel to which the lower end of a shroud or runner is secured.
Channel	One of the ledges sometimes built out from the sides of a vessel to increase the spread of the shrouds.
Chart Datum	The level from which all soundings on a chart are measured. It may vary with the chart, as indicated by the following: *Mean low water* (M.L.W.): the average of all low tides; used on charts of the United States Atlantic and Gulf of Mexico coasts. *Mean lower low water* (M.L.L.W.): the average of the lower of the two daily tides; used on charts of the United States Pacific coast, Alaska, Hawaii, and the Philippines. *Lowest normal low water* (L.N.L.W.): used on Canadian charts. *Mean low water, spring tides* (M.L.W.S.); also called *low water, ordinary spring tides* (L.W.O.S.): used on most Admiralty charts. *Lowest astronomical tide* (L.A.T.): the lowest tide that can be expected; used on the new British metric charts. This datum can sometimes be considerably below those previously employed.
Check, To	To ease.
Cheek Block	A block bolted to a mast or boom in such a manner that the spar forms its inner face; "bee block" to the British.
Chine	The junction in a deep-bottomed boat between the bottom and the topsides; often it can be a distinct, sharp corner.
Chock	A piece of wood cut to allow an anchor, spinnaker pole, or the like to be lashed firmly in place.
Chopped-Strand Mat	The commonest and most economical reinforcing material in fiber-glass construction. It consists of strands

of flexible glass, cut to a uniform length but running in every direction, which are held together in a mat by a binder that unites with the resin. The mat is made in various weights and thicknesses.

Clamp
A vertical timber bolted underneath the shelf at the junction of the frame and the deck beam.

Clap On, To
To attach one tackle to another or to a rope. "Clap on," is an order to man a fall or a halyard.

Claw Off, To
To beat away from a lee shore.

Clearing Line
See *Danger Bearing*.

Cleat
A fitting to which a rope may be secured.

Clevis Pin
A pin securing rigging to a turnbuckle, mast, tang, chain plate, or the like, and secured in place by a cotter pin (split pin) rather than a nut.

Clew
The lower after corner of a fore-and-aft sail.

Clinker-built
See *Lapstrake*.

Clipper Bow
A bow in which the stem has a forward curve and the sides have much flare.

Close, To
A pair of leading marks are said to be closing when a vessel approaches their line, so that they draw closer together. A vessel is said to close with another or with the shore when she is approaching it.

Close-hauled
A vessel is said to be close-hauled when she is sailing as close to the wind as she can with advantage, and her sails are trimmed more nearly fore-and-aft than on any other point of sailing.

Close to the Wind
With the head of the ship directed as nearly as possible to the point from which the wind is blowing.

Clumbungay
A boat old in design and in years, but usually well loved and cared for.

Coach Roof
A part of the deck raised to give increased headroom.

Coaming
The side of a coach roof, hatch, cockpit, or the like extending above deck level.

Combination Rope
Fiber rope which has some wires buried in it.

Companionway
The entry from deck or cockpit to the accommodation area.

Compass Point
A division of the compass card; $1/32$ of a circle, or $11\frac{1}{4}$ degrees.

Compass Rose	A circle, marked like a compass card, which is printed on a chart.
Composite Method	A way of building in which iron framing and a wooden skin are used.
Consolan	A system of obtaining a fix by radio by counting the dots and dashes transmitted by a special station.
Constant Bearing	A constant bearing is said to exist when the bearing with respect to any other vessel remains unchanged such that if the course is not altered there is risk of collision.
Contline	The spiral space between the strands of a rope.
Cotter Key	A small metal pin used to keep a clevis pin in place or a nut from working loose; also called a "cotter pin"; "split pin" to the British.
Cotter Pin	See *Cotter Key*.
Counter	A stern which extends beyond the rudderstock and terminates in a small transom.
Course	(1) The direction in which a vessel is sailing, measured in degrees or compass points from her meridian. (2) The lowest and largest square sail, above which the topsail, the topgallant sail, and so on may be set.
Covering Board	The outermost deck plank, which covers the heads of the frames or timbers.
Crance Iron	The metal cap or band at the end of the bowsprit to which the shrouds, topmast stay, and bobstay are secured.
Crank	Said of a vessel that is unhandy, easily tipped; the opposite of "stiff."
Cringle	A rope eye formed on the outside of the boltrope of a sail and fitted with a metal thimble.
Crosstree	See *Spreader*.
Crown	(1) The part of an anchor where the arms join the shank. (2) See *Camber*.
Crutch	A wooden or metal fitting into which the boom fits when not in use. A well-designed boom crutch is of great help when reefing, but the often-seen scissors type is almost useless, and has an irritating way of collapsing and even falling overboard when the boom is lifted out. A permanent gallows is much more satisfactory.

Cuddy	A small cabin, usually in a day boat.
Cunningham Holes	Heavy grommets sewn in the luff and foot of the sail; they can be pulled, by means of lanyards, toward the tack to adjust the draft of the sail.
Cutter	A fore-and-aft-rigged vessel with one mast, a mainsail, and two headsails (staysail and jib).
Cutwater	The forepart of the stem of a ship. In sailing vessels with bluff bows it was a false stem.
Danger Bearing	A bearing from a fixed object leading clear of a navigational hazard. For example, "Little Tobago one finger open of Fota clears reef off Palm" means that when one can see Little Tobago open from Fota, one is safe from hitting the reef which is off Palm Island. Also called "clearing line."
Davit	A small crane used for hoisting a boat or large anchor aboard.
Deadeye	(1) A block of hardwood with one or more holes drilled in it to take the ropes of the fall or a simple purchase; the earliest form of block. Now used for standing rigging only.
	(2) A disk of wood with three holes through which a lanyard is rove for setting up the rigging.
Deadlight	A metal cover which can be clamped over the glass of a portlight.
Dead Reckoning (D.R.)	The determination of a vessel's position at sea, as indicated by the records of the course sailed, the distance run, the time spanned, and so on, without the aid of celestial navigation.
Deadwood	The solid wooden part of the fin keel at the aft end, where the rudder is hung.
Decca	A system of navigation widely used in Europe by large vessels. Since it requires heavy equipment, rented from the manufacturer (Kelvin Hughes), it is not usually found in yachts.
Deckhead	The undersurface of the deck.
Deck Light	A piece of glass let flush into a deck.
Deck Log	A small notebook in which all alterations in course, speed, and weather, and any other relevant matters, are recorded, with the time, so the reckoning can be worked up later by the navigator as desired.

Declination	The angle between a celestial body and the equinoctial line (the equator) as measured from the center of the earth.
Deep	(1) A depression in the seabed. (2) One of the fathom points on a lead line which is not marked, as in "deep six."
Depression	An area of low atmospheric pressure, bringing rain, wind, and generally bad weather. In the Northern Hemisphere, the wind blows counterclockwise around a depression. The severity of the weather, and particularly of the wind, depends on how low the pressure is.
Derrick	A spar rigged with a tackle, for use in lifting something.
Deviation	An error of the compass caused by the proximity of iron; it varies with the direction in which the vessel is heading.
DF Radio	A radio fitted with a direction finder.
Dip	The vertical angle at the eye of the observer between the horizontal and the line of sight to the visible horizon.
Dip, To	To lower partially and temporarily; to dip an ensign is to lower and rehoist it as a salute.
Displacement	The weight of water displaced by a hull when it floats, which is equal to the actual weight of the hull; also, in England, Thames measurement (*q.v.*).
Dodger	Canvas rigged on the lifelines to provide overhead shelter for the cockpit. Also, canvas secured along the lifelines to reduce spray in the cockpit; "weather cloth" to Americans.
Doghouse	A structure, usually provided with windows, built on deck over the companionway or cockpit.
Dolphin Striker	A strut rigged from the stemhead to the bobstay to give the bobstay a more favorable angle between the stem and bowsprit end; it performs the same job as the spreader on a mast.
Doubler Plate	One of the steel plates welded as reinforcement on top of existing hull plating which has become thin as a result of corrosion.
Douse, To	To lower or slacken suddenly.

Downhaul A rope used for pulling down a sail.

Down Helm, To To put the helm to leeward so as to bring the vessel's head toward the wind.

Downwind To leeward of a particular point.

D.R. See *Dead Reckoning*.

Draft The depth of water required to float a vessel.

Drag The amount by which a long straight keel is off the horizontal.

Drag, To An anchor is said to drag when it fails to hold the vessel in position.

Draw, To (1) A sail is said to draw when the wind fills it. To let draw is to let go the weather sheet of a sail and haul in the lee one, so that the sail may drive the vessel ahead.
(2) When her draft is specified, a ship is said to draw so many feet.

Draw Ahead, To; Draw Astern, To A ship is said to draw ahead if her relative position advances, and to draw astern if it drops back.

Dress Ship, To To run a string of code flags from stem to stern over the mastheads. The flags should terminate in the water at both bow and stern.

Dress the Mast, To A British expression meaning "to rig the mast"; to put on its standing and running rigging.

Drift (1) The distance between the blocks of a tackle; the distance forward or aft of the mast that a shroud or stay is attached to its chain plate.
(2) Direction of tidal current.

Drift, To To move with the tide or wind.

Dunnage Pieces of wood, matting, old rope, old canvas, and other similar materials when used for raising cargo off the bottom of a hold, for packing it to keep it from shifting, or for covering it to keep it dry.

Earing A hole in the sail, lined with a bronze ring sewn to the sail, for use in lashing the tack and clew in place while reefing.

Ease, To To slacken.

Echo Sounder An electronic device that determines the depth of water by measuring the time taken by a sound signal to go to the seabed and return; also known by the trade name Fathometer.

Ensign
A flag displayed by a vessel to indicate her nationality.

Epoxy Resin
A type of resin used in fiber-glass construction and for gluing where exceptional durability, strength, or adhesion is required. It is more expensive than the more commonly used polyester resins.

Eye
(1) A closed loop.
(2) The direction from which the wind is blowing.

Fairlead
A bull's-eye or metal fitting through which a rope is passed to alter the direction of its lead or to keep it clear of other gear.

Fake, To;
Fake Down,
To
To lay out line on deck in successive figure eights, so that it will run out freely without kinking; also called "to flake," "to flake down."

Fall
The hauling part of a rope.

Fall Off, To
A vessel is said to fall off when she shows a tendency to bear away from the wind.

False Keel
An addition to the main keel, its purpose usually being to fill in the space at the after end of the ballast keel.

Fashion Board
See *Splash Board*.

Fathom
A nautical measure of depth; six feet.

Fathometer
See *Echo Sounder*.

Feather, To
(1) To turn the blade of an oar so that it is parallel to the surface of the water, during recovery.
(2) To turn the blade of a propeller straight fore and aft, to minimize drag.

Fender
A cushion of cork, rubber, or rope, used to prevent damage when a vessel lies alongside another or at a quay.

Fetch, To
When a vessel is able to reach her objective without tacking, she is said to fetch it.

Fiber Glass
Glass spun into fine threads that are flexible and can be woven or treated like any other thread. In some form it provides the reinforcing in any fiber-glass hull, giving its name to the whole substance, which is correctly described as fiber glass and resin laminate.

Fiberglas is the trade name for the product of Owens-Corning, widely used in the United States. "GRP" (for "glass-reinforced plastic") is the term more commonly used in England.

Fid
(1) A large spike of wood.
(2) A short iron bar passing through a hole in the heel of a topmast or bowsprit to hold it in position.

Fiddle,
Fiddle Rail
One of the strips of wood fitted to a table or other surface to prevent crockery from sliding off.

Fiddle Block
A block having two sheaves, one larger and above the other.

Fiddlehead
A clipper bow.

Fife Rail
A rail in which belaying pins are inserted; also called a "pinrail."

Fisherman
A yachtsman anchor, an old-fashioned anchor.

Fisherman
Staysail
A four-sided sail set between the masts of a schooner.

Fit Out, To
To overhaul a vessel after she has been laid up.

Fix, To
To find a vessel's position by making observations of celestial or terrestrial objects.

Flake, To;
Flake Down,
To
See *Fake, To.*

Flare
The outward curve of a vessel's side.

Flattie
A dinghy with a flat bottom and chines.

Floor
A transverse member of wood or metal binding a pair of frames or timbers to one another and to the keel.

Floorboards
The boards in the bottom of a dinghy which distribute the weight of the load over the timbers; "burden boards" to the British.

Fluke
The pointed palm, at the end of the arm of an anchor, which bites into the ground.

Fly
The horizontal length of a flag.

Flying
See *Set Flying.*

Foot
The lower edge of a sail.

Fore
In or toward the front; opposite to "aft."

Fore and aft
In the direction of a line drawn from stem to stern, i.e. parallel to the keel.

Forecastle, Fo'c'sle	That part of the accommodation area which is beneath the foredecks; the forwardmost cabin in the bow, usually the crew's quarters.
Forefoot	That part of the bow which is between the load waterline and the fore end of the keel.
Forepeak	The triangular space belowdecks in the extreme forward part of the bow; now, loosely, the forecastle.
Forereach, To	To make headway when hove to.
Foresail	The fore-and-aft sail set on the aft side of a schooner's foremast. Also, on British cutters sometimes used to mean "staysail," with the result that confusion may occur when a cutter man sails on a schooner.
Foreshore	The beach below the high-water mark.
Forestaysail	See *Staysail.*
Fore-triangle	The area between the head stay, the mast, and the deck.
Foul	(1) Entangled. An anchor is said to be foul when its fluke catches on an obstruction; it is also foul when the cable twists around the arm or the stock. The bottom is said to be foul when there are rocks or chains which might foul the anchor. (2) Encrusted or clogged with a foreign substance. A vessel's bottom is foul when weeds or barnacles have grown on it.
Foul Hawse	An arrangement in which cables from different anchors become crossed or twisted. Compare *Open Hawse.*
Frame	A rib of a vessel.
Frap, To	To bind with lashing; to pass a rope around a sail or over an awning to keep it from breaking loose. Halyards are said to be frapped when they are held in to the mast by spiral turns of one of their number.
Frapping	The bracing together of ropes or lines with crosswise turns, to increase their tension.
Free	Not close-hauled.
Freeboard	The height of a vessel's side above the water.
Freeing Wind	A wind that tends to draw aft, making it possible to ease the sheets.
Freer	See *Lift.*

Front	The boundary between two unlike masses of air; the passage of fronts, usually associated with depressions, is characteristic of weather in temperate climates. A warm front, with warm air pushing colder air in front of it, is likely to result in continuous rain lasting some time; the passage of a cold front can be expected to be accompanied by squalls and followed by a drop in temperature and a dramatic clearing, with blue skies and a fresh northwest wind.
Full and By	Sailing with full sails and sailing by the wind, not by compass or mark.
Full and Change	Full and new moon. See also *H.W.F. & C.*
Furl, To	To fold up or roll up and stop a sail or an awning.
Futtock	One of the several pieces of timber which, overlapped and scarfed together, are used to form a frame which is to be of such size and shape that it cannot be made from a single piece of timber.
Gaff	The spar to which the head of a quadrilateral mainsail, foresail, or mizzen is bent.
Gaff Jaws	The fitting at the inboard end of a gaff which slides on the mast.
Gaff Sail	A quadrilateral sail fitted with a gaff.
Galley	A kitchen on a boat.
Galley Staysail	See *Windsail.*
Gallows, Gallows Frame	A permanent framework on which the end of a boom rests when the sail is lowered.
Galvanize, To	To coat iron or steel with zinc to protect it from corrosion.
Gammon Iron	The ring which holds a bowsprit to the stemhead.
Garboard	The plank which lies next to the keel.
Gasket	(1) A stop used for lashing up a furled sail or awning. (2) A piece of soft material placed between two metal surfaces to seal the joint.
Gatline	An extra line rigged aloft specifically for hauling a man up in a boatswain's chair, as distinguished from a spare halyard.
Gel Coat	The smooth outer skin of a fiber-glass hull.
Gel Time	The time taken for a resin to start to solidify after the catalyst has been added.

Genamaker	A cross between a spinnaker and genoa; it is set flying like a spinnaker, but is cut more like a ballooner, or reaching jib.
Genoa	A large triangular headsail which alone fills the entire fore-triangle and extends well aft of the shrouds.
Ghosting	A sailing vessel or boat is said to be ghosting, or ghosting along, when she is making good way in a very light breeze.
Gilguy	One of the lanyards tied around halyards and secured to stays to hold the halyards away from the mast when the boat is at anchor. Failure to secure halyards in this manner is what makes aluminum masts so noisy.
Gimbals	An arrangement of concentric rings and pivots for keeping a compass, lamp, stove, table, or other object level regardless of the movements of a vessel at sea.
Glass Fiber	See *Fiber Glass*.
Gnomonic Chart	A type of projection which is useful for plotting routes and calculating distances for long voyages because on it a great circle is represented as a straight line.
Golliwobbler	Technically, the main-topmast balloon staysail, a fisherman that extends from the masthead to the deck, overlapping the mainsail in the same fashion as a genoa. It is generally sheeted to the end of the boom.
Gooseneck	The universal joint which holds the boom to the mast.
Goosewinged	A two-masted vessel is said to be running goosewinged when her mainsail is extended on one side and her mizzen or foresail on the other.
Goosewinged Sail	A sail whose top part has caught on the spreader during jibing and remains on the opposite side of the boat from the boom and the lower part of the sail. The situation, also called a "Chinese jibe," is caused by the boom rising, and can be prevented by a kicking strap. Once it occurs, the only remedy is to jibe back and try again.
Grapnel	A small anchor with four or more arms.
Gripe, To	A vessel is said to gripe when she carries excessive weather helm and shows a strong inclination to round up into the wind.
Grommet	A ring made of rope; an eye made in the edge of a sail inside the boltrope.

GRP	See *Fiber Glass*.
Gudgeon	A metal eye on the after side of a sternpost into which the rudder pintle ships.
Gunter	A fore-and-aft rig used for small craft. Instead of a gaff, the mainsail has a yard which slides vertically on the mast.
Gunwale	The upper edge of a boat's side.
Guy	A steadying rope attached to a spar, holding it in the fore-and-aft plane.
Gybe, To	See *Jibe, To*.
Gypsy	A wheel on a windlass with recesses to hold the links of a chain, such as an anchor chain.
Half-beam	A deck beam which does not extend right across the vessel, but stops short at a carline.
Half-Breadth Plan	A drawing which shows the shape of the boat's water-lines and level lines.
Half-Tide Rock	A rock which uncovers when the tide is at half ebb.
Halyard	A rope used for hoisting a sail or flag.
Hambroline	Small three-strand rope used for lashings and lacings.
Hand, To	To lower, take in, or stow a sail.
Handsomely	Gradually and steadily.
Handy-billy	A tackle used temporarily to exert extra power on a rope.
Hang Off, To	To hold one rope temporarily with another while something is done with the end or bight of the first rope.
Hank	A clip used to hold the luff of a sail to a stay; a sail which is held to a stay by hanks is said to be hanked on.
Hard	A landing place, usually artificial, where the foreshore is hard.
Harden In, To	To haul in a sheet so as to flatten a sail.
Hardtack	Ship's biscuit, formerly very hard and tough.
Hard Up, Hard Down	The position of the helm—as far as possible to windward or to leeward, respectively.
Hatch	An opening in the deck provided with a cover.
Haul, To	To pull.

Hawsehole	A hole in the bulwarks or topsides through which the anchor cable runs.
Hawsepipe	A tube running diagonally from the deck to the bow slightly above the waterline and used as a fairlead for the anchor cable. Some types of anchor will stow in the hawsepipe.
Head	(1) The bow. (2) The top edge of a sail. (3) A ship's toilet (the "heads" of a sailing man-of-war were platforms on each side of the stem which were used as latrines by the men).
Headboard	A piece of wood or aluminum sewn to the head of a Bermudian sail or a spinnaker to increase the area of the sail slightly, to distribute the load on it, and to prevent it from twisting.
Header	A wind shift that forces one to bear off to keep the sails from luffing.
Headroom	The distance inside a vessel between the sole and the deckhead.
Headsail	A sail set forward of the forwardmost mast on the boat.
Headway	A vessel's movement ahead through the water.
Head Wind	A wind which prevents a vessel from laying the desired course, compelling her to beat.
Heart	A strand in the middle of a rope.
Heave Down, To	To careen.
Heave To, To	To trim the sails and helm in such a manner that the vessel lies almost stationary; heaving to is also called "lying to."
Heaving Line	A light rope, often with a small weight at one end, used for making the initial connection between a vessel and the shore or some other vessel, so that a stronger rope may then be hauled across.
Heel	The after end of a keel; the lower or inboard end of a spar.
Heel, To	To list.
Heeling Error	Deviation of the compass caused by changes in the relative position of nearby iron when a vessel heels.
Helm	The tiller or wheel used for steering.

Highfield Lever — A mechanical appliance used for setting up and letting go a runner or some other part of the rigging.

Hitch — (1) A method of making a rope fast to some object. (2) Sometimes, a short tack.

Hog-Backed — See *Hogged*.

Hogged — Said of a vessel which has been strained so that her sheer is convex instead of concave. Some craft are built with this conformation. "Hog-backed" to the British.

Hoist — The vertical edge or measurement of a sail or flag.

Hoist, To — To haul aloft.

Hold, To — (1) To stop the progress of a boat by holding the blades of the oars steady in the water.
(2) An anchor is said to hold when it gets a good grip on the bottom and does not drag.

Holiday — A gap left in a row or line; an unpainted patch in paintwork.

Holystone — One of the blocks of sandstone formerly used for scrubbing decks, so called because their use entailed kneeling down. Medium-sized holystones were called "bibles," and small ones "prayer books."

Hood-end — The end of a plank where it fits into the rabbet cut in the stem or sternpost.

Horn Timber — The fore-and-aft member at the bottom of a counter.

Horse — A bar or rope on which the sheet of a sail may travel athwartships.

Horse Latitudes — One of the two belts, located between the westerlies and the trade winds in the Northern and the Southern Hemispheres, which are characterized by light and variable winds and in which sailing vessels were often becalmed for some time. The name had its origin in the middle of the nineteenth century, when numerous horses who were being transported from Europe to America and the West Indies died from the heat and were thrown overboard. As a result, the belt in the North Atlantic became studded with dead horses.

Hounds — The chocks on a mast on which the eyes of the lower rigging are seated.

Hove Down — A vessel is said to be hove down when she has heeled excessively.

Hull	The body of a vessel exclusive of her masts and gear.
H.W.F. & C.	High water at full and change of the moon, i.e., at the time of the full and of the new moon.
H.W.O.S.	High water, ordinary spring tides.
Initial Stability	The resistance a vessel offers to being heeled, due to the shape of her hull and not to the effect of her ballast keel.
Inwale	The longitudinal strengthening piece inside the timber heads at the gunwale of a dinghy.
Irons	A vessel is said to be in irons when in attempting to come about she hangs stationary, head to wind, and will not pay off on either tack.
Jackstay	A rope holding the luff of a topsail or fisherman close to the mast.
Jackyard	A short yard used to extend the foot of a topsail beyond the end of the gaff.
Jib	The foremost headsail.
Jibe, Chinese	See *Goosewinged Sail.*
Jibe, To	When running, to bring the wind from one quarter to the other so that the boom swings across. Jibing is the opposite of tacking in that the stern rather than the bow passes through the eye of the wind. Also called "to gybe."
Jib-Headed	Said of any sail the upper part of which terminates in a point.
Jib-Headed Rig	A rig with a mainsail having three sides; also called a "Bermudian rig."
Jib Topsail	A jib set hanked to the topmast stay, with a high clew.
Jig Line	A light line attached to another line to allow for quick adjustment.
Joggle Shackle	A shackle with extra-long arms, used to hold two chains together, and made to fit between the links so that it cannot slip.
Jumper Stay	A stay which runs over a jumper strut; it is used to keep the upper part of a mast straight.
Jumper Strut	A spreader projecting from the forward face of the mast.

Jury Rig	A makeshift or substitute rig, such as may be improvised when the masts or gear have carried away.
Kedge	An anchor smaller than the bower, generally fitted with a line instead of a chain, and used to haul a vessel off when she has gone aground and to prevent her from fouling her bower; also called a "lunch hook."
Kedge, To	To haul forward by means of an anchor.
Kedge Warp	The line attached to a kedge.
Keel	The fore-and-aft member on which the whole structure of a vessel is built.
Ketch	Strictly speaking, a two-masted, fore-and-aft-rigged vessel with the mizzenmast stepped forward of the after end of the waterline; more loosely, a two-masted, fore-and-aft-rigged vessel with the mizzenmast stepped forward to the rudderpost.
Kevel	A type of cleat made by bolting a piece of wood across two bulwark stanchions.
Kicking Strap	See *Vang*.
Killick	A small anchor; hence, a slang term for a Leading Seaman, because the distinguishing badge he wears is an anchor.
King Plank	The center plank of a deck.
Knee	A piece of timber or iron with two arms, used for strengthening certain parts of a vessel. A hanging knee is one arranged in the vertical plane; a lodging knee is in the horizontal plane.
Knock Back	See *Rub Back*.
Knot	A measure of speed; one nautical mile (6,080 feet) per hour.
Laminate	A material built up in layers, such as fiber glass or plywood.
Land	The overlapping part of the planks in a clinker-built boat.
Lanyard	A short rope, especially one used for setting up a shroud or some other part of the rigging.
Lapstrake	Built with the type of construction where the skin planks overlap one another; also called "clinker-built."
Lash, To	To bind or secure with rope.
L.A.T.	See *Chart Datum*.

Latitude	Distance north or south of the equator, expressed in degrees.
Lay	Of a rope, the direction in which the strands are twisted together.
Lay, To	A vessel is said to lay her course when she can sail in the desired direction without tacking.
Lay Up, To	To dismantle a vessel and berth her for the winter.
Lazy Jack	A device, consisting of light lines from the topping lifts to the boom, which keeps sail under control when it is being lowered; usually found in gaff-rigged boats.
LBP	Length between perpendiculars, i.e., from the fore side of the stern to the after side of the sternpost, on deck.
Lead	A weight on a marked line, used for taking soundings.
Leading Edge	The forward part, as in the luff of a sail, or the front of the keel.
Leading Marks	See *Range Marks*.
League, Marine	An obsolete measurement of distance at sea, equivalent to three nautical miles.
Lee	(1) The side opposite to that toward which the wind is blowing. (2) When going dead downwind, the side of the boat that the main boom is on.
Leeboard	One of the boards, rigged outside the hull on each side of a shoal-draught vessel, which can be lowered on the lee side to prevent leeway by providing lateral resistance.
Lee-bow, To	To sail a boat against an adverse tide in such a way that the tide is on the lee bow instead of the weather bow, thereby pushing the boat to windward. If a slight degree of pinching brings the tide on the lee bow instead of the weather bow, it is worth doing.
Lee Canvas	A cloth strip secured to the bottom of a bunk, and overhead, to keep the occupant in the bunk.
Leech	The aftermost part of a sail.
Lee Helm	A vessel is said to carry lee helm when she has a tendency to turn her bow away from the wind, and the helm has to be kept to leeward to prevent her from doing so.

Lee Shore	A shore under a vessel's lee; one toward which the wind tends to drive her.
Leeward	The side away from the wind, i.e., the side of the boat that the main boom is on.
Leeway	The amount of sideways movement made through the water by a vessel, i.e., the difference between the course steered and the course made good, assuming there to be no tidal stream.
Leg	(1) A piece of wood or metal secured to a vessel's side to keep her upright on a hard when the tide leaves her. (2) When beating to windward, a tack is sometimes known as a leg.
Leg-o-Mutton Rig	A jib-headed rig with the main boom approximately as long as, or longer than, the mast, as seen in Tortola sloops and other West Indian workboats.
Level Lines	The fore-and-aft sections of a vessel above and parallel to the LWL, shown as curves on the half-breadth plan.
Lie Ahull, To	To heave to in a gale without setting any sail. The angle to the wind may vary considerably, depending upon the design of the boat.
Lie To, To	See *Heave To, To*.
Lifeline	(1) A rope passing through stanchions along the side of a vessel's deck to prevent the crew from falling overboard. (2) A line secured to a crew member as a safety precaution when he is working on deck in heavy weather.
Lift	A wind shift that allows the boat to head more to windward than previously; also called a "freer."
Lifting	When referring to sails, if someone calls "Lifting," he means the luff of the sail is lifting (i.e., the sail is luffing), and it is time to trim the sails or bear off.
Lignum Vitae	A hardwood of which fairleads, bull's-eyes, parrel balls, and the like, are often made.
Limber Hole	One of the holes in or beneath the floors through which bilge water runs down to the bilge-pump suction.
Line of Position	See *Position Line*.
Lines	The shape of a vessel, as shown in the set of drawings comprising body plan, sheer plan, and half-breadth plan.

L.N.L.W.	See *Chart Datum*.
LOA	Length over all, i.e., the extreme length of the hull.
Locker	A stowage place or cupboard.
Log	An instrument for measuring distance sailed.
Logbook	A record of a voyage.
Log Chip	A float attached to a marked line and tossed overboard, for determining a vessel's speed.
Long in the Jaw	A rope is said to have become long in the jaw when it has stretched considerably and the spiral of the strands is less steep.
Longitude	Distance east and west of the Greenwich meridian, expressed in degrees.
Longshoreman	A waterman who makes his living near the shore.
Loom	The part of an oar which one grips when rowing. Looms should be left free of paint or varnish, which makes them hard to grip.
LOP	Line of position. See *Position Line*.
Loran	A system of radio navigation utilizing signals emitted by stations of known position; it is becoming increasingly popular because scts are now coming down in size and price, and can be run off a normal 12-volt system (from *lo*ng *ra*nge *a*id to *n*avigation).
Lubber Line	The mark on the compass bowl which is aligned with the vessel's head. Also, on some compasses, similar marks set at 45 or 90 degrees from the main lubber line.
Luff	The forward part of a sail.
Luff, To	To put the helm down and bring the vessel's head closer to or into the wind.
Luffing	The flapping of sails which have been incorrectly trimmed.
Luff Rope	The boltrope sewn to the forward edge of a sail.
Lug	A quadrilateral fore-and-aft sail, the head of which is secured to a yard slung on, and projecting a short distance forward of, the mast.
Lunch Hook	See *Kedge*.
LWL	(1) Load waterline. The line on the hull which is reached by the water when a vessel is trimmed to float as the designer intended. (2) Length at waterline.

L.W.O.S.	See *Chart Datum.*
Mainsail	The fore-and-aft sail set on the aft side of the mainmast.
Make Fast, To	To secure a rope.
Making	Tides are said to be "making" during the period between the neap and the spring tide, when their height progressively increases.
Manifest	An official inventory of all cargo carried by a merchant vessel.
Manrope	A steadying rope, to provide a handhold for the person climbing up an accommodation ladder.
Marconi Rig	Generally, at present, the jib-headed rig; historically, the term refers to the rig characteristic of the big cutters just before World War I. They were gaff-rigged, but had an array of diamond struts, stays, and so on, reminiscent of the Marconi radio wireless towers.
Marine Glue	Not a proper glue, but a soft elastic compound used in deck seams; also called "seam compound."
Marl, To	To take turns around some object with small line at frequent intervals, each turn being half-hitched.
Marline	Tarred twine made of two loosely laid-up strands.
Marlinespike	A pointed instrument for opening up the strands of a rope and for tightening or loosening the pints of shackles.
Martingale	(1) A stay leading from the nose of the jibboom of a sailing vessel to her stem; in some ships it is passed through the head of a dolphin striker to give it a better downward pull on the jibboom. (2) Any stay which prevents a boom, spar, or strut from topping.
Masthead	The top of a mast.
Mast Step	The slotted member on the top of the keel or floors into which the lower end of a mast is shipped.
Matthew Walker	A stopper knot used on the standing end of a lanyard.
Mercator Projection	A method of representing the curved surface of the earth on a flat plane in which the meridians of longitude are shown as parallel, instead of converging. It is used for most charts.

Meridian	A true north-and-south line.
Miss Stays, To.	To fail to go about onto the other tack because conditions of wind or sea stop the boat; it can be embarrassing when one is heading for a nearby shore.
Miter	A seam, leading diagonally from the tack to the luff of the sail, on each side of which the weave of the sail's cloth runs in a different direction.
Mizzen	The fore-and-aft sail set on the aft side of the mizzenmast.
Mizzenmast	The aftermost mast in a ketch or yawl.
Mizzen Staysail	A triangular sail set from the mizzenmast head to the deck forward of that mast.
M.L.L.W.	See *Chart Datum.*
M.L.W.	See *Chart Datum.*
M.L.W.S.	See *Chart Datum.*
Molding	The dimension of a piece of wood between its vertical surfaces.
Mold Loft	The place in which a vessel's lines are laid down in full scale so that the size and shape of her various parts may be determined prior to cutting.
Moor, To	To make a vessel fast alongside a quay, or between two posts, buoys, or anchors, or to anchor her with two anchors from the bow so that she lies between them, occupying no more space than a circle whose diameter is approximately twice the length of the boat.
Mouse, To	To take turns with twine or marline around sister hooks to prevent them from opening, or across the open part of a hook so that it cannot become unhooked.
Muzzler	A gale blowing from right ahead.
Navel Pipe	The fitting in the deck through which the anchor chain passes to the chain locker.
Neaped, Beneaped	A vessel is said to be neaped when she has run aground at high water, and because the tides are taking off, the following tide fails to float her.
Neap Tide	A tide which occurs at the first and third quarters of the moon. It has a smaller-than-average range. Compare *Spring Tide.*

Night Effect

Inaccuracies in radio direction bearings, occurring at sunset and sunrise because the level of the ionosphere (off which radio waves are reflected) changes considerably at these times, and occurring at night because radio waves are reflected off the ionosphere more at night then during the day.

Nip

A sharp bend in a rope, as where it passes over a sheave or through a fairlead.

Nip, To Freshen the

To move a rope or wire, such as a halyard, so that a different part takes the heavy load and wringing effect at a sheave.

Oarlock

A device which supports an oar while it is used for rowing; called "rowlock" by the British, and "spur" by the Irish.

Offing

A position at a distance from the shore.

Offset

One of the measurements supplied by a designer to guide the builder in laying down a vessel's lines in the mold loft.

Off the Wind

Not close-hauled.

Omni

An aid to navigation based upon line-of-sight UHF radio direction bearings. It is used extensively in aircraft because the line of sight to an aircraft gives good range, but it is not very widely used on yachts because it is effective at sea only if the boat is close to an airport; also, the equipment is expensive.

On the Putty

See *Aground*.

On the Wind

Sailing close-hauled.

Open Hawse

An arrangement in which each anchor cable leads from the bow direct to its anchor, without crossing or being twisted up with the other. Compare *Foul Hawse*.

Opening

A pair of leading or clearing marks are said to be opening when, as the vessel leaves their line, they appear to draw farther apart.

Open Up, To

A vessel is said to open up when her planks shrink and her seams are no longer watertight.

Outhaul

The gear used for hauling a sail out along a spar.

Overhang

That part of a vessel at bow or stern which extends beyond her LWL.

Overhaul, To	(1) To overtake. (2) To examine carefully and repair where necessary. (3) To haul the blocks of a tackle apart to the full extent of the fall.
Painter	The rope attached to a dinghy's bow, by which she is made fast.
Palm	(1) A fitting worn on a sailmaker's hand for protection and for use in thrusting the needle through the sailcloth. (2) The flat part of the fluke of an anchor.
Paraffin	Diesel kerosene.
Parbuckle, To	To roll any cylindrical object upward by passing a rope beneath it, making one end fast, and hauling on the other.
Parcel, To	To bind canvas around a rope in a spiral manner to keep water out.
Parked	See *Aground*.
Parrel Ball	A small wooden ball with a hole for a lanyard.
Parting Agent	A coating of wax sprayed or painted inside the mold in which a fiber-glass hull is to be laid up, so the hull can eventually be removed from the mold; also called the "releasing agent."
Partner	One of the timbers forming the framework or pad which supports the mast where it passes through the deck.
Patent Log	An instrument for recording distance sailed, by means of a rotator in the water attached by a line to a recorder. Also called a "taffrail log."
Pay, To	To run marine glue (seam compound) into a seam after it has been caulked.
Pay Off, To	When the head of a vessel falls to leeward, she is said to pay off.
Pay Out, To	To ease away or slack out.
Peak	(1) The upper after corner of a gaff-headed sail. (2) The upper end of a gaff.
Pelican Hook	A jointed hook with a pivot pin, held closed by a ring; knocking back the ring causes the hook to release its hold even when it is under great strain. It is found frequently on mizzen backstays and gangway lifelines. "Senhouse slip" to the British.

Pelorus	A compass card without needles, fitted with sighting vanes and used for taking bearings.
Pendant	A hanging rope; for example, the reef pendant, which hangs from the reef cringle on the leech and is used to haul the sail down to the boom.
Pennant	A pointed flag.
Permanent Backstay	A backstay which is cleared by the boom end and therefore does not have to be cast off when tacking or jibing.
Pinch, To	To sail too close to the wind.
Pinrail	See *Fife Rail*.
Pintle	The fitting on a rudder which ships into a gudgeon so as to form a hinge.
Polyamide	The plastic from which nylon is made.
Polyester	The plastic from which Dacron, and certain other fibers, are made.
Polyester Resin	The plastic generally used in fiber-glass construction.
Polypropylene	The plastic used for a rope that has the advantage of floating but is not suitable for use on a yacht because it chafes easily, deteriorates in tropical sunlight, and is difficult to knot. Further, the rope from different manufacturers varies widely in quality.
Polythene	A nonrigid but strong plastic much used for water-proof bags, containers, and domestic gear, and also making a good buoyant rope.
Poop, To	An overtaking sea is said to poop a vessel when it breaks aboard over her stern.
Port	The left-hand side of a vessel, when one faces forward.
Portlight	A small pane of glass, sometimes made to open, fitted in a topside or coaming.
Port Tack	A boat is on the port tack when the boom is to starboard, and the wind is coming over the port side of the vessel.
Position Line	A bearing, obtained with the compass, sextant angles of shore objects, a DF, or other means, defining a line somewhere along which the vessel lies. Two or more position lines provide a fix. Also called "LOP," or "line of position."
Pram	A dinghy with a transom at the bow and stern.

Preformed Rope	Wire rope of which each strand is set to the linear shape it will assume in the rope before being laid up. Such rope shows no tendency to unlay.
Preventer	(1) Backstay. (2) Sometimes, fore guy. (3) Any rope, chain, or fitting backing up or limiting the movement of rigging, spars, cable, and the like.
Profile	The shape of a vessel as seen from the side. Compare *Sheer Plan*.
Proud	Said of an object projecting from an otherwise flat surface, such as the head of a rivet which is not countersunk; the term is also applied to a wooden shore which is cut slightly longer than the space into which it is to fit, so that it will have to be driven home, and thus jammed into place, when set up.
Pudding	A rope fender, cylindrical in shape and sometimes with the ends tapered; generally used on the bows of tugs and harbor launches, also on the griping spar of radial davits.
Puddle	Circular ripples made by the blade of an oar as it leaves the water.
Pulpit	A structure of tubing in the stem of a boat which provides a secure place where a man can work while changing headsails.
Pump Well	The lowest part of the bilge, from which the bilge pump sucks; also called the "well."
Purchase	See *Tackle*.
Pushpit	See *Stern Pulpit*.
Quadrant	A quarter of a circle; usually, a cast-bronze stock, of this shape, by means of which the rudder may be controlled.
Quarter	Strictly speaking, the point on each side of a vessel which lies midway between her midship section and her stern; also, frequently, the whole of each side from amidships to astern, just as the bows may be understood as all of the vessel lying forward of amidships.
Rabbet	A groove cut in a keel, stem, sternpost, or the like, to receive the edge or end of a plank.
Racking Seizing	A seizing made with figure-eight turns.

Radar	A method of obtaining ranges and bearings of objects by analyzing very high frequency radio waves reflected from their surfaces (from *r*adio *d*etection and *r*anging).
Raffee	A triangular sail set in one or two pieces above a square sail.
Rail	A narrow plank fitted to the edge of the deck or top of the bulwarks.
Rake	The fore-and-aft inclination of a mast, sternpost, or the like, out of the perpendicular.
Range	The difference in level between high and low water of a tide. See also *Range Marks*.
Range, To	(1) A vessel is said to range about if she does not lie steadily while at anchor or hove to. (2) To range a cable is to lay it on deck before anchoring.
Range Marks	Objects (buoys, headlands, or whatever) which when correctly lined up give an exact desired bearing, usually used to give a course in or out of a harbor clearing all obstructions; also called "leading marks."
Rating	A lineal number used to figure a yacht's handicap for racing. In American racing, the rating is used in conjunction with tables to determine seconds-per-mile handicapping. In the rest of the world, the rating is used to figure the time correction factor (*TCF*) by formula. Handicaps and results are figured on a time-and-time basis, with elapsed time multiplied by the *TCF* giving corrected time. The formula for converting rating in lineal feet to *TCF* is $$\frac{\text{Rating} + 3}{10} = TCF$$
Ratlines	Horizontal ropes or wooden bars seized to a pair of shrouds to form a ladder in the rigging.
Rat Tail	A reduction of a rope to a fine point, as in the termination of a boltrope.
Reach	A point of sailing at which the wind is abeam or forward of the beam, but not so far forward as to make the vessel close-hauled.
Reef, To	To reduce the area of a sail by tying or rolling down a part of it.

Reef Point	A short length of line permanently sewn through the reef eye and used to gather up the bunt of the sail when the sail is being reefed.
Reeve, To	To pass a rope through a block, fairlead, or hole of any kind.
Releasing Agent	See *Parting Agent*.
Releasing Fluid	A liquid that dissolves rust and enables rusted-up parts to be freed. Products much more effective than any oil or kerosene are now available for this purpose, probably the best known being Plus Gas A (in England) and Cabot's Liquid Wrench (in the United States).
Relieving Tackles	Tackles or ropes secured to the tiller of a vessel to assist her steering in a heavy sea.
Render, To	To run or slide freely, said of a rope.
Rhumb Line	A line cutting all the meridians at the same angle, represented on a Mercator chart as a straight line. (For short distances, a straight line between two points.)
Ribband	A flexible piece of wood used in yacht building.
Riding Light	A lantern hung up in the forepart of a vessel at anchor and showing a white light all around.
Rigging	See *Running Rigging; Standing Rigging*.
Rigging Screw	See *Turnbuckle*.
Rise of Tide	The height the water has risen above chart datum (*q.v.*).
Rising	A fore-and-aft member supporting the ends of the thwarts inside a dinghy's timbers.
Roach	The outward curve sometimes given to the leech of a sail.
Road, Roadstead	An exposed or offshore anchorage.
Rocker	The fore-and-aft curvature of a keel.
Roller Reefing	A method of reefing in which the boom is turned in a horizontal axis, rolling the sail around itself much in the fashion of a window shade, when the sail area is to be reduced.
Round Up, To; Round To, To	To bring a vessel head to wind from a run or a reach.

Roving	A bundle of continuous strands of fiber glass. Rovings are sometimes woven into a loose cloth, and are then known as woven rovings.
Rowlock	See *Oarlock*.
Rub Back	The distance between the point of attachment of the tack of the mainsail and a vertical line extending downward from the after face of the sail track; also called "knock back."
Rudder Box, Rudder Trunk	On older yachts, the housing in the counter through which the large-diameter wooden rudderstock passes. (On newer yachts the metal rudderstock is encased in a stuffing box.) The rudder box or trunk is brought up to deck level. It is large, cumbersome, and prone to damage on the inside by worms, but the arrangement is simple and foolproof.
Rudderstock	The part of a rudder which is closest to the sternpost, and which forms the pivot shaft of rudder.
Run	The upward sweep of a vessel's bottom from the point of greatest beam to the stern, as shown by the buttock lines on the sheer plan.
Run, To	To sail before the wind.
Run Before It, To	To run dead downwind before a gale or hard squall.
Runner	A movable stay whose purpose is to support the mast from aft against the pull of a headsail or the thrust of the gaff jaws.
Running by the Lee	Running with the wind on the same quarter as the boom.
Running Rigging	Sheets, halyards, topping lifts, and the like, by means of which sails are hoisted, trimmed, and controlled. Compare *Standing Rigging*.
Sag, To	(1) When the luff of a headsail curves to leeward instead of being straight, it is said to sag. (2) A vessel making excessive leeway is said to sag away.
Sail Off, To	To turn away from the wind.
Sail Stop	See *Stop*.
Sail Tie	See *Stop*.
Samson Post	A strong post in the foredeck to which the anchor cable is secured; also, a similar post fitted at the stern

	or on the quarter for use in mooring fore and aft or in towing.
Sawn Frame	A rib which is sawn rather than bent to shape.
Scantling	The dimension of a member used in the construction of a vessel.
Scarf	The diagonal joint between two planks which have been glued or bolted end to end.
Schooner	A fore-and-aft-rigged vessel having two or more masts, the mainmast being as tall as, or taller than, the foremast.
Scope	The length of cable by which a vessel is anchored.
Score	A groove to take a rope, such as is found on the rim of a sheave and on the shell of a rope-stropped block.
Screen	The board to which a sidelight is fixed to prevent it from showing on the opposite bow.
Scull, To	To propel a boat by working one oar from side to side over the stern or by doing likewise with a small-boat rudder.
Sculling Hole	A notch in the transom of a dinghy where an oar can rest, enabling one to scull.
Scupper	A hole in the bulwarks to allow water to drain from the deck.
Sea	A wave.
Sea Anchor	A conical canvas bag or other contrivance for reducing the speed of a vessel to the minimum in heavy weather.
Sea Cock	A valve which prevents sea water from entering a pipe passing through the skin planks.
Seam	(1) Of a sail, the stitching which holds two cloths together. (2) In yacht building, the space between two planks.
Seam Compound	See *Marine Glue*.
Section	Actually, the representation of a vessel as she would appear if cut through by a plane at any angle; unless otherwise defined, the word is assumed to refer to an athwartship section.
Seizing	A binding together of two ropes or of two parts of the same rope.
Senhouse Slip	See *Pelican Hook*.

Sennit	Rope made by plaiting instead of twisting the strands.
Serve, To	To bind tightly with marline or other small stuff, as a protection.
Set, To	To hoist or make sail.
Set Flying	Said of a sail whose luff is not secured to a mast or hanked to a stay.
Set Up, To	To tighten.
Seven-eighths Rig	A jib-headed rig in which the head stay meets the mast not at the masthead, but at a point located at approximately seven-eighths of the total height of the mast above the deck.
Shackle	(1) A metal U-shaped fitting with an eye in each of its arms through which a pin is screwed or driven. (2) A length of chain, usually fifteen fathoms.
Shake Out, To	To let out a reef.
Shank	The part of an anchor which joins the arms to the ring.
Sharpie	A vessel with a flat bottom.
Sheave	The wheel, in a block or spar, over which a rope runs.
Sheer	The curve of the gunwale or top strake in the vertical plane.
Sheer, To	(1) To move a vessel at anchor in a tideway to port or starboard of her anchor by putting the helm over. (2) A vessel which does not lie steadily to her anchor, but ranges from side to side, is said to sheer about.
Sheer Plan	A drawing showing the shape of a vessel as viewed from the side; also called a "profile."
Sheer Pole	A rod secured across the lower ends of all the shrouds at one side to prevent them from untwisting.
Sheer Strake	The uppermost plank of the topside.
Sheet	A rope by means of which a sail is trimmed, secured either to the clew of the sail or to the boom.
Shelf	A longitudinal member to which the ends of the deck beams are secured; it is placed with its width in the horizontal plane and its thickness in the vertical plane.
Shell	The outer casing of a block.

Shifting Backstay	A backstay which can be set up or let go according to whether it is to windward or to leeward.
Ship, To	(1) To put a thing in its proper position for working. (2) A vessel is said to ship a sea when a sea invades the deck.
Shroud	A wire rope giving athwartship support to a mast, bowsprit, or bumpkin.
Sidelight	Running light.
Siding	The dimension of a piece of wood in the horizontal plane between its flat surfaces when it is in position as a vessel's backbone.
Sight	An observation, by sextant or by compass, that gives a position line.
Sister, To	To double up, e.g., in the case of a frame, to install a duplicate of the frame.
Sister Hooks	Two hooks on a common eye or thimble.
Slab Reefing	The old-fashioned method of reefing the sail, by means of tack and clew earings and reef points.
Slack Water	A short period at the turn of the tide when there is no tidal stream.
Slick	The comparatively smooth patch on the surface of the sea which is left to windward of a boat drifting to leeward.
Slip	A sloping surface of concrete or stone, up which a dinghy may be dragged; also, a hard fitted with rails or skids, used for hauling a vessel out of the water.
Slip, To	(1) To haul a vessel out. (2) To let go the anchor chain instead of weighing the anchor.
Sloop	A fore-and-aft-rigged vessel similar to a cutter, but having one instead of two headsails.
Slot Effect	The flow of air through the area between two sails into which air is forced, greatly increasing the efficiency of the aftermost sail.
Smoke Head	The chimney for a stove, usually made of metal, and available in various different designs; anything that removes smoke from the belowdecks stove.
Snatch Block	A block with an opening in one side of the shell, so that one can insert a rope by its bight instead of reeving it.

Snub, To	(1) A vessel at anchor is said to snub when her bows lift to a sea and the cable is pulled taut with a jerk. (2) In line handling, to check slowly.
Snugged Down	Well reefed; under a small or comfortable area of sail.
Soft Eye	An eye made at the end of a rope without a thimble.
Sole	The cabin floor.
Sound, To	To measure the depth of the water with a lead line or by other means.
Sounding	The act of measuring the depth of the water; also, the figure so obtained, as marked on a chart.
Span	A rope, wire, or chain, the ends of which are secured at some distance apart to an object, such as a spar or boat, so that it can be lifted or carried.
Spinnaker	A large, light sail set flying on reaches and runs.
Spitfire Jib	A very small jib used in heavy weather.
Splash Board	A plank which can be slid vertically into grooves in a companionway to prevent water from entering, if doors have not been provided; "fashion board" to the British.
Splice, To	To join ropes or form eyes at their ends by interlacing the strands.
Spline	A thin strip of wood fitted into a seam in place of stopping.
Split Pin	See *Cotter Key*.
Spreader	A wooden or metal strut on a mast, which gives the rigging more spread; "crosstree" to the British.
Spring, Spring Line	A rope used to prevent a vessel secured alongside a dock from moving forward or aft.
Spring, To	To burst adrift a plank, or to damage a spar.
Spring Tide	A tide which occurs at the full and the change of the moon. It has a greater-than-average range. Compare *Neap Tide*.
Sprung	A mast or spar is said to be sprung when it is dangerously cracked or split.
Spun Yarn	A coarse kind of marline.
Spur	See *Oarlock*.
Square Sail	A sail set from a yard slung athwartships on the fore side of a mast.

Stanchion   A support for bulwarks, lifelines, or the like.

Standing Gaff   A gaff that is left aloft (with the sail brailed against it) when not in use, instead of being lowered or hoisted, as necessary.

Standing Part   That part of a rope which is made fast and not hauled upon.

Standing Rigging   Shrouds, stays, and the like which support the mast or some other spar, and are permanently installed and not manipulated in the sailing of the vessel. Compare *Running Rigging*.

Stand Off and On, To   To sail away from and then toward something, usually while waiting.

Starboard   The right-hand side of a vessel, when one faces forward.

Starboard Tack   A vessel is on the starboard tack when the boom is to port, and the wind is coming over the starboard side of the vessel.

Station Pointer   A protractor with movable arms used for taking direct visual bearings of two or more objects. The boat's position is then ascertained by placing the station pointer directly on the chart.

Stay   A wire rope giving fore-and-aft support to a mast.

Stay, To   A vessel is said to stay when she goes about from one tack to the other by turning her head to the wind.

Staysail   A triangular fore-and-aft sail, usually set on a stay; "forestaysail" to the British.

Steerageway   A vessel has steerageway when she is moving through the water with sufficient speed to answer her helm.

Stem   The member to which the plank ends are secured at the fore end of a vessel.

Stern Board   When a vessel that has been in irons moves astern fast enough to answer her helm, so that she can be made to pay off on one tack or the other, she is said to make a stern board.

Sternpost   The member to which the plank ends are secured at the stern and on which the rudder is hung.

Stern Pulpit   A structure of tubing, similar to a pulpit but located in the stern of a boat, whose purpose is to prevent people from falling overboard; "pushpit" to the British.

Stern Sheets	The part of an open boat which lies abaft the aftermost rowing thwart.
Sternway	A boat is making sternway when she is going backward.
Stiff	A vessel is said to be stiff when she does not heel readily; the opposite of "crank" and "tender."
Stock	The bar of an anchor which passes through a hole in the shank and lies on a plane at right angles to the arms.
Stop	(1) One of the weak bindings of easily broken cotton put around a sail which is to be hoisted but not broken out immediately. At the proper time, one need only give a stout pull on the sheet to break the stops and put the sail into use. Also called a "sail stop." (2) One of the strips of flat canvas, nylon, or Dacron used to secure furled sails to the spars; "sail tie" or "tier" to the British.
Stopper Knot	A knot worked on the end of a rope to prevent it from unreeving through an eye, block, cringle, or the like.
Stopping	Putty worked into a seam after caulking.
Stopwater	A soft pine plug inserted in a hole drilled at a right angle through a scarf joint. The stopwater swells up and prevents water from passing along the joint.
Strake	One of the skin planks of the hull of a vessel.
Strand	One of the lengths of wire or yarn twisted together in rope making.
Stranded	A rope is said to be stranded when one of its strands is broken.
Stretcher	A crossbar in the bottom of a dinghy against which the oarsman braces his feet.
Strike Over, To	To move a vessel off the cradle or slip on which she has been hauled up.
Stringer	A longitudinal strengthening member secured on the inner side of the frames or timbers of a vessel.
Strop	An iron or rope band used for securing rigging or a block to a mast or spar.
Strum Box	To the British, a kind of strainer on the end of a bilge-pump suction, used to prevent foreign matter from choking the pump.

Stud-Link Chain	Chain in which each link has a crossbar to prevent the sides from pulling together.
Surge	The lateral movement of a stationary vessel caused by a swell or by the wash of a passing ship.
Swashway	A channel across or between shoals or spits.
Sweat Up, To	To give an extra hard pull on a rope so as to eliminate every vestige of slack in it.
Sweep	A long oar, of the kind used to propel lighters, barges, and small sailing vessels.
Sweep, To	To drag the bight of a wire or chain along the bottom to locate or recover a sunken object.
Swell	Long, easy waves, the crests of which do not break.
Swig, To	To tighten a rope by holding its fall around a cleat or pin while the standing part is hauled away from the mast, the slack then being taken up around the cleat or pin.
Swing, To	(1) To turn the head of a vessel to the points of the compass, one by one, when checking or adjusting the compass. (2) A vessel at anchor is said to swing when she turns at the change of the tide or the wind.
Tabernacle	The housing on deck for the heel and pivot of a lowering mast.
Tabling	A doubling of cloth on the three edges of a sail.
Tack	(1) The lower forward corner of a fore-and-aft sail. (2) A point of sailing as close to the wind as a vessel will go with advantage.
Tack, To	To beat or work to windward in a zigzag manner, close-hauled first on one tack, then on the other, putting the bow of the boat through the eye of the wind.
Tackle	A device consisting of two blocks with line reeved through each, used to increase mechanical advantage; also called a "purchase."
Tack Tackle	A purchase applied to the tack of a fore-and-aft sail to get its luff taut.
Taffrail	The rail across or around the stern.
Taffrail Log	See *Patent Log*.
Tail	A short rope attached to a block so that it can be temporarily secured to something.

Tail On, To To clap on to a rope.

Tail Up, To To pull on a line.

Take Charge, To An inanimate object, such as a rope or a cable, is said to take charge when it gets out of control and runs out by its own momentum.

Take In, To To lower, take in, or stow a sail.

Taken Aback Surprised; a sailing vessel is said to be taken aback when the wind strikes her sails on the wrong side.

Take Off, To The tides are said to be taking off when they decrease progressively, between the spring tide and the neap tide.

Take Up, To (1) To make taut, as when one takes up the slack of a rope or nut.

(2) To absorb, to swell; thus, when a dry boat is placed in the water her planking will gradually take up and become tight.

(3) To buy, or acquire (in reference to supplies).

Tang One of the metal fittings, screwed or bolted to a mast or spar, to which a vessel's rigging is attached.

Taut Stretched tight.

Tender (1) Easily heeled, somewhat crank; the opposite of "stiff."

(2) Sometimes, a yacht's dinghy.

Terylene The British equivalent of Dacron.

Thames Measurement A "tonnage" formula, in general use in Great Britain. The formula is $\dfrac{(L-B) \times \frac{1}{2}B^2}{94}$, where B equals the extreme beam, and L equals the length between posts, i.e., the length between the stem and the sternpost at deck level. It is used by Lloyd's Underwriters in figuring premiums, to the great disadvantage of American boats, which usually are beamier than the British, as the Underwriters charge a certain amount of money per unit of Thames Measurement. Two boats can have the same displacement, i.e., weight, yet have a vastly different Thames tonnage measurement.

Thimble A round or heart-shaped metal eye or ring, concave on its outer surface so that a rope may be taken around it and spliced or seized; the thimble protects the rope from chafe.

Throat The upper forward corner of a gaff sail.

Thumb Cleat	A triangular piece of wood secured to a spar or spreader to keep some part of the rigging in place.
Thwart	An athwartship seat in a dinghy.
Tier	See *Stop*.
Tie Rod	A rod with a thread and nut, used, for example, to bind the carline of a coach roof to the shelf so that the side deck cannot open and leak.
Tiller	A wooden or metal bar, secured to the rudderhead, by means of which a vessel is steered.
Timber	A rib which has been bent to shape instead of being sawn.
Toggle	A short piece of wood which can be passed through the eye in the end of a rope to hold it without making a bend and in such a way that it can be cast off quickly.
Tonnage	Gross tonnage and net tonnage have nothing to do with the actual weight of a boat—they are custom-house figures; compare *Displacement, Thames Measurement*.
Top, To; **Top Up, To**	To lift a boom into or above its normal sailing position.
Top Off, To	To fill to capacity; i.e., water or fuel tanks.
Topmast	The upper part of a mast; sometimes, a separate spar.
Topping Lift	A rope or wire used to support the after or outboard end of a boom while the sail is being set or doused, or to take the weight of the boom in a seaway.
Topsail	(1) A triangular fore-and-aft sail set above a gaff-headed sail. (2) A square sail set above a course.
Topsides	Those parts of a vessel's sides which are above water when she is afloat but not heeled.
Track Chart	A small-scale chart on which a vessel's positions are plotted during a long passage.
Transom	A type of stern consisting of planks bolted athwartships on the sternpost to receive the after ends of the skin planks.
Traveler	A span across the deck which allows a block or carriage to slide from side to side; it may be made of wire, rope, or flat, heavy sail track, and is now available in the form of an X-shaped track with roller-bearing slides.

Treenail	A wooden peg split and wedged in place, formerly used instead of a rivet, nail, or screw; also called a "trunnel."
Trestletree	One of the pieces of wood on a mast which serve to support the heel of a topmast.
Triatic Stay	A wire rope connecting the mastheads of a schooner or a ketch.
Trim	The angle made with the water by the fore-and-aft line of a vessel, when she is afloat.
Trim, To	To adjust the helm, centerboard, leeboards, or sails; to sheet a sail so that it draws to the best advantage.
Trim Tab	A small adjustable portion of the trailing edge of either the rudder or the keel. When located on the rudder, it makes possible control of the total movement of the rudder with very little effort. When located on the keel, it serves mainly to give lift to the keel and to increase windward performance, but it may also be used to minimize weather helm.
Trough	A valley between two seas.
Truck	A wooden cap at the masthead or topmast head which has holes or a sheave for the burgee halyard.
Trunnel	See *Treenail*.
Trysail	A small sail of heavy Dacron sometimes set in place of the mainsail in heavy weather.
Tufnol	A material consisting of plastic reinforced with linen or paper, often preferred for blocks intended for nautical use; it has the great advantage of being lubricated by water.
Tumble Home	The inward curve that the sides of some vessels have above the load waterline.
Turnbuckle	A fitting with threaded ends screwing into a common body, used for setting up the rigging; "rigging screw" to the British.
Turn to Windward, To	To beat, tack, or work to windward, steering a zigzag course.
Turn Up, To	To make fast a rope on a cleat or pin.
Unbend, To	To remove a sail from its spars and other gear.
Under Bare Poles	Under way, but with no sail set.

Underrun, To	To weigh a kedge by hauling the dinghy along the warp (which slides in the sculling hole) until the dinghy is directly over the kedge.
Under Way	A vessel is said to be under way when she is moving over the ground or through the water.
Unreeve, To	To pull a rope out of a block, sheave, eye, or the like.
Unship, To	To remove something from its proper working position.
Up and Down	An anchor cable is said to be up and down when it has been hauled in until it is vertical and any further hauling will break out the anchor.
Up Helm, To	To put the helm to windward so as to make a vessel bear away.
Vang	A rope generally used to flatten a sail; with it, the main boom is hauled down and forward to take the twist out of the mainsail, or down and aft from the gaff end to take the twist out of the mainsail with respect to the gaff sail. To the British, the boom vang is a "kicking strap."
Variation	The difference between true and magnetic north at a particular place.
Veer, To	(1) To pay out anchor cable. (2) The wind is said to veer when it changes its direction in the same way as the sun moves—clockwise.
Wake	The path of disturbed water left astern of a moving vessel.
Warp	A strong rope attached to an anchor or dock. See also *Kedge Warp*.
Warp, To	To move a boat by hauling on a long line secured to a fixed object, such as an anchor or dock.
Waterline	One of the horizontal sections of a vessel's hull at and below the load waterline, seen as curves on the half-breadth plan.
Way	The movement of a vessel through the water.
Wear, To	The act of putting a vessel about onto the other tack by turning her away from the wind and jibing instead of staying.
Weather, To	A vessel is said to weather something when she is able to pass to windward of it without tacking.

Weather Cloth	See *Dodger*.
Weatherly	Said of a vessel which is capable of sailing close to the wind.
Weather Helm	A vessel is said to have a weather helm when she has a tendency to turn her bow into the wind, and the helm has to be kept to windward to prevent her from doing so.
Weather Shore	A shore to windward of a vessel; therefore, one which offers shelter.
Weather Side	See *Windward*.
Weigh, To	To raise the anchor from the bottom.
Well	See *Pump Well*.
Whip	A purchase in which only one block is used.
Whip, To	To bind the end of a rope with twine to prevent it from unlaying.
Whisker	One of the struts from the bows, which spread the bowsprit shrouds.
Whisker Stay	One of the stays supporting the bowsprit in the horizontal plane.
Winch	A mechanical appliance consisting of a drum on an axle, a pawl, and a crank handle with or without gearing, used to obtain increased power when hauling on a rope.
Windlass	A type of winch which has a horizontal drum and is fitted with a gypsy, for handling chain cable.
Windsail, Wind Scoop	A ventilation trunk of canvas slung from aloft with its mouth set to catch the wind and its foot led below to the space to be ventilated; also called a "galley staysail."
Windward, Windward Side	The side of the boat closest to the wind, i.e., always the opposite side of the boat from the main boom; also called "weather side."
Wire Rope Clamp	See *Bulldog Grip*.
Wishbone	A spar in two halves like a wishbone, between which a sail is hoisted, its clew sheeted to the outer end of the wishbone.
Working Anchor	See *Bower*.
Working Sails	Sails normally used when cruising, in contrast to racing or light sails, such as the genoa.

Worm, To   To fill in the contlines of a rope with small line or yarn before parceling and serving.

Yankee, Yankee Jib   To the British, a large, high-cut triangular headsail, used in light or moderate winds and set on the topmast stay, overlapping the mast only slightly. Unlike a genoa, it does not fill the whole fore-triangle, but is set in combination with the working or reaching staysail. Also, on a modern boat, a masthead jib, cut high in the clew, usually hoisted over a large overlapping staysail; referred to by most Americans as the number-one jib topsail.

Yard   A spar to which a topsail or square sail is bent.

Yarn   Fibers which are twisted together to form a strand of a rope.

Yaw, To   To wobble about on either side of the intended course. A good helmsman will prevent unnecessary yawing with minimum movement of the helm in good time, instead of waiting until the yaw has developed and heavy movement of the helm becomes necessary.

Yawl   A two-masted boat with the mizzenmast aft of the after end of the waterline (the position of the helm is irrelevant).

TOOLS AND SPARES

First of all, it is absolutely essential that the boat carry the manual for every piece of equipment on board. These manuals should be carefully filed away, so that when an item needs to be repaired the manual can be found readily and the repairs carried out correctly.

TOOLS

Hull

A small vise is essential; a large vise is very useful. The large vise should be bolted to a piece of one-inch plywood long enough to reach across the companionway hatch; then the whole unit can be clamped into place with wood clamps when heavy work is to be done.

Claw hammer; ball peen hammer; tack hammer.

Crosscut saw; small backsaw; hacksaw; keyhole saw with various blades.

Mallet.

Chisels, four sizes.

Six-foot tape.

Small plane; large plane.

Small square, with adjustable bevel.

Whetstone.

Brace.

Four sizes of screwdriver bits; wood bits in $\frac{1}{4}$″, $\frac{5}{16}$″, $\frac{3}{8}$″, $\frac{7}{16}$″, $\frac{1}{2}$″, $\frac{5}{8}$″, 1″ sizes; expansion bit.

High-speed drills in $\frac{1}{16}$″ through $\frac{3}{8}$″ sizes; flat high-speed wood bits in $\frac{1}{4}$″ through 1″ sizes.

Small eggbeater drill; large two-speed eggbeater drill.

Set of all-in-one countersinks for wood screws.

Plug cutters in $\frac{1}{2}$″, $\frac{3}{8}$″, $\frac{5}{8}$″ sizes.

End cutters.

Screwdrivers, short, long, fine, stubby, and so on.

Caulking irons, three sizes.

Wood rasps, flat, round, and oval.

Grinding stones, small hand-powered on most boats, electric on larger boats.

Electric drill. The standard $\frac{1}{4}$″ drill is generally too small. The $\frac{3}{8}$″ drill, though it costs a little more, is preferable, as it is much more powerful. The $\frac{1}{2}$″ drill is good for some uses but too large and cumbersome for most; hence it is valuable as a backup for the smaller drill, but should not be selected as the only one. A 12-volt drill which can be powered from the ship's supply is excellent, but expensive. A cordless drill too is excellent, but expensive; also, it is difficult to charge from the ship's supply, and impossible to charge in areas using 220-volt single-phase current, which is found extensively outside the United States. A 110-volt drill is cheap, and on a ship with a 12-volt system, the power can be stepped up by means of an inverter. However, the capacity of the inverter should be checked against the amperage needed by the drill under load. Further, if going abroad, one should be sure to purchase a transformer capable of converting from other voltages to 110. European 220-volt equipment needs a transformer if it is to be used with United States 110-volt equipment.

Saber saw. A small saber saw is useful; the comments about choice of an electric drill, above, apply to the saber saw as well.

Rigging

Special tools, as needed, to dismantle the winches.

For rigging wire up to $\frac{5}{16}$″, Nicopress. The small tool sold by S and F Tool Company is satisfactory. Or if it is not too expensive, one of the bolt-cutter types can be carried; these can sometimes be found with jaws for three or four different sizes of Nicopress. Also available are Nicopress jaws to be used with a standard bolt cutter.

For rigging wire above $\frac{5}{16}$″, hot sockets or Norseman fittings.

Splicing vise. For 7 by 19 wire up to $\frac{1}{4}$″ in diameter, the best splicing vise I know of is the one made by Herman Melin, head rigger at Ratsey and Lapthorn. For 1 by 19 wire, the best splicing vise available is made by Durko Marine (formerly Durkee).

Hollow fid, small, for tail splices. Again the best I know of is the one made by Herman Melin and available through Ratsey and Lapthorn.

Wire spikes (marlinespikes). There is a lot more than meets the eye to a spike. The flat-tipped spike is much better than the round type, as once it is spliced between the strands of wire it may be rotated ninety degrees, allowing room for wire to be passed through alongside the vertical spike. Excellent flat-tipped spikes of various sizes can be obtained from Topping Brothers. Herman Melin also makes special spikes for splicing small wire.

Block of lead, for smoothing wire splices.

Serving mallet. If a hole is drilled diagonally through the handle and the ball of marline is placed over the handle, the marline can be fed through the hole from the center of the ball; thus one person can serve, without needing a second person to pass the ball of marline.

A cold chisel and a piece of bronze, for cutting wire. (Cutting the wire on a piece of bronze protects the edge of the chisel.)

Sails

Palms, the number depending on the size of the boat. Two kinds, seaming palms and roping palms, should be carried. Normally, all palms are right-handed, though once in a while a left-handed one can be found. Most smart left-handed people carry their own palms.

Needles, various sizes, from the smallest (No. 21) up through the large ones. The exact sizes and quantities desirable will depend on the size of the boat; in any event, large supplies of small needles should be carried, as they are easily broken. A good method of stowing needles is to place them in a baby-food jar with coffee grounds; the coffee grounds absorb the dampness and keep the needles shining.

Bench hook.

Wooden fid, big enough to make the largest cringle on board the yacht. Making a cringle without a big fid is almost impossible. A small wooden fid is also useful.

Hollow fids, small, for line ½" or less in diameter; large, for line above ½" in diameter, up to the largest anchor rode carried.

Hollow tube for splicing braided line. This can be made from aluminum tubing, with a removable wooden plug at one end.

Sewing machine. A hand-powered machine will go through two layers of 8-ounce Dacron. It can be stowed in the ballast box of a gimbaled table. A boat 50 feet LOA, or longer, should carry a regular heavy-duty sewing machine on any long cruise. The machine and its table may be disassembled and packed in a box.

Plumbing

Tubing cutters.
Flaring tools.
Pipe wrenches, various sizes.

Electricity

Wire cutters.
Wire strippers.
Small screwdrivers.
Meter for checking out the electrical system.
Soldering attachment for the gas torch, or an electric soldering iron that will work off the electrical system.

Mechanical Equipment

The largest set of mechanic's tools that one can afford should be purchased. Sometimes they can be obtained on sale at a place like Sears, Roebuck or Montgomery Ward.

Files, round, flat, square, rattail.
A set of taps and dies in sizes to ½".
Impact wrench.
A set of "easy outs."
Adjustable open-end wrench, large enough to fit on stern gland and rudderpost stuffing box. On some boats, two may be necessary.
Pipe wrenches, one small, one 8".

Slip-joint pliers; vise-grip pliers.

Bottled-gas torch with various tips; the type that can be attached to a cooking-gas bottle is preferable.

Gasoline Engine

A check should be made as to whether any special tools are needed for the particular engine. For example, the boat with a valve-in-head engine should carry a valve lifter, since this tool is difficult to locate now that the overhead-valve engine has become popular.

Tappet wrenches, as many as are needed to adjust the valves. Some engines require the use of three tappet wrenches at the same time.

Ignition wrenches, to adjust the points.

Small wrenches and screwdrivers to dismantle the carburetor.

Feeler gauge.

Valve-grinding tool and compound.

Diesel Engine

Wrenches to dismantle the fuel system. Spares should be carried as well, since all too often a wrench slips and is lost in the bilge, and it is then impossible to bleed the system.

Large magnet to retrieve tools dropped in the bilge.

SPARES

Hull

Wood

Sheets of plywood, cut to fit under the bunks.

Two-by-fours and one-by-sixes, stowed wherever possible.

Lead sheeting and bedding compound. Lead sheeting is hard to find, but very useful on a wooden boat, since it can be cut up into strips, placed over the bedding compound, and nailed down, to seal a leaking seam. Without the aid of an aqualung, his breathing assisted only by a snorkel, Jim Crawford repaired *Dirigo II* in this fashion, and she was then able to sail from the Galápagos to Tahiti in record time.

Aluminum and Steel

For the hull itself nothing much can be carried in the way of spares. Most repairs will have to be done with quick-drying cement, epoxy, fiber glass, or the like; underwater epoxy is especially useful.

For aluminum hulls, a large supply of the correct type of welding rod.

Fiber-Glass

Mat.

Cloth.

Resin.

Underwater epoxy.

General Repairs

All boats should carry as generous a supply as possible of the following items:

Tapered wooden bungs, preferably with a coarse spiral thread, in various sizes to fit all through-hull fittings.

Bolts.

Bronze rods.

Nuts of various sizes.

Wood screws.

Self-tapping metal screws.

Galvanized nails, not very pretty but sometimes very useful in an emergency.

Rigging

Turnbuckles.

Toggles.

Thimbles.

Split pins; clevis pins.

Serving wire.

Shackles; snap shackles.

Blocks.

Spreader, usable as either upper or lower spreader if the boat is double-spreader-rigged.

Wire. At least one length of wire longer than the longest stay, with a fitting already in place at one end, and a spare Norseman fitting for the lower end. The boat's rigging book should give the exact length of each stay, so that the replacement can be made up on deck as necessary and then sent aloft.

End fittings of the type being used, along with the materials and tools necessary to install them.

Halyard, made up ready to go.

Plenty of line. For a long cruise, six-hundred-foot coils of various sizes of line should be bought from one of the discount houses, such as West Products or Defender Industries. Coiled down carefully, an amazing amount of line can be carried on a boat.

Winch springs; bronze wire for making springs.

Ratchets and pawls for all winches.

Roller-reefing handles; winch handles.

Steel tape, fifty or a hundred feet, depending on the size of the boat.

Sails

Rip-stop tape.

Cloth of various weights, the quantity depending upon the size of the boat and length of the cruise.

Leather—rawhide, elk, or the like—for chafing patches for the sails.

Sail twine; big balls of waxed nylon and Dacron; Dacron thread for the sewing machine.

Sailcloth, various weights.

Jib snaps.

Sail slides; shackles to secure slides to sails; plastic chafing patches to place between the shackles and the sails.

Toothed grommets (No. 3, standard); grommet tool.

Cringles of stainless steel or bronze, various sizes; Italian hemp, for making cringles.

Thimbles and the like, as needed for the boat's particular sails; the Howe and Bainbridge catalog should prove useful.

Commonsense fasteners, and tool for placing fasteners in dodgers.

Deck

Emergency shutters, or material to make shutters, for use if the cabin or doghouse windows are damaged, should be carried by all boats, no matter what material they are made of.

Mechanical Equipment

GASOLINE ENGINE

Complete gasket set.
Half set of valves.
Set of rods.
Set of main bearings.
Carburetor rebuilding kit.
Points.
Distributor cap and rotor.

High-tension leads.
Coil.
Condenser.
Water pump and spare belts.
Filters.
Gasket cement; O rings of various sizes.
Penetrating oil; light oil; engine oil; grease; CRC or equivalent.
Spray to protect the electrical system.
Spark plugs.
Set of piston rings.

DIESEL ENGINE

Gasket set.
Set of valves.
Set of rods.
Set of main bearings.
Set of piston rings.
At least two injectors.
Set of injector lines, if the engine is not absolutely new.
Fuel injector pump, if it can be afforded.
Filters.
Belts.
Water-pump impellers.
Gasket cement; O rings.
Penetrating oil; grease; CRC or equivalent.

AUXILIARY GENERATOR

Same as above, along with the necessary electrical parts—brushes, diodes, bearings, and so on, as advised by a good mechanic.

Plumbing

Complete parts for all pumps and heads.
Hoses, various sizes.
Hose clamps, stainless steel, not cadmium-plated.
Nipples.
Adapters.
Reducers.
Pipe fittings, various sizes.
Valves and/or stopcocks.
Tuflon tape.
Permatex.

Electricity

Wire.
Fuses.

Circuit breakers.
Junction boxes.
Bulbs; running-light glasses.
Gaskets, or material for making gaskets.
Electrical tape.
Silicone sealant.
Solder.
Rosin.
Fine sandpaper and emery paper for cleaning contacts.
Crimp-on fittings and tools.
Battery lugs.
Hydrometer.
Distilled water.
Brushes for starter motor and generator.
Diodes for alternator.
Complete starter, if possible.
Complete generator, if possible.
Voltage regulator.

SOURCES OF SUPPLY

Marine Equipment (General)

Brookstone Co.
Brookstone Building
Peterborough, N. H. 03458
(hard-to-find tools)

Camper and Nicholsons
Southampton, England

Defender Industries
384 Broadway
New York, N. Y. 10013
(discount house)

Thomas Foulkes
Lansdowne Rd.
Leytonstone
London E.11 3HB, England
(discount house)

M. S. Gibb
Warsash
Southampton SO3 6ZG, England

Goldbergs' Marine Distributors
202 Market St.
Philadelphia, Pa. 19106
(discount house)

Lewmar Marine
Southmoor Lane
Havant
Hants PO9 1JJ, England

London Yachting Center
9 Devonshire Row
London E.C.2M 4RL, England

Manhattan Marine and Electric Co.
116 Chambers St.
New York, N. Y. 10007

Merriman Holbrook
301 River St.
Grand River, Ohio 44045

Simpson Lawrence
St. Andrews Square
Glasgow, Scotland

South Western Marine Factors
43 Pottery Rd.
Poole
Dorset, England

Taselaar's Handel Mij.N.V.
Box 5030
Rotterdam, Holland

West Products
P.O. Box 707
Newark, N. J. 07101
(discount house)

Wilcox-Crittenden
Middletown, Conn. 06457

Yacht Tests
22 High St.
Burnham-on-Crouch
Essex, England

Cruising Hulls

STEERING SYSTEMS

Canpa Yacht Equipment
Mumby Rd.
Gosport
Hants, England

Edson
480 Industrial Park Rd.
New Bedford, Mass. 02745

Yacht Specialties Co.
1555 East St. Gertrude Pl.
Santa Ana, Calif. 92705

Spars and Standing Rigging

ALUMINUM SPARS

T. P. Hanna and Co.
859 West 18 St.
Costa Mesa, Calif. 92627

Sparlight
Southbourne near Emsworth
Hampshire PO1 O8PG, England

Zephyr Products
Wareham, Mass. 02571

METAL MASTS

Ian Proctor Metal Masts
Duncan Rd.
Swanwick
Southampton, England

NICOPRESS SLEEVES AND TOOLS

S and F Tool Co.
Box 1546
Costa Mesa, Calif. 92626

WINCHES

Abeking and Rasmussen
Lemwerder, Germany

Barient Co.
936 Bransten Rd.
San Carlos, Calif. 94070

Barlow
102 Seymour Pl.
London W.1H 5DG, England

Camper and Nicholsons
Southampton, England

M. S. Gibb
Warsash
Southampton SO3 6ZG, England

Lewmar Marine
Southmoor Lane
Havant
Hants PO9 1JJ, England

Paul E. Luke
East Boothbay, Me. 04544

Merriman Holbrook
301 River St.
Grand River, Ohio 44045

Taselaar's Handel Mij.N.V.
Box 5030
Rotterdam, Holland

Rigging

MATERIALS

Norseman Ropes
Bridge Rd.
Sarisbury Green
Southampton SO3 7EH, England

Wilcox-Crittenden
Middletown, Conn. 06457
   (*U.S. agent for Norseman Ropes*)

TOOLS

Durko Marine (formerly Durkee)
610 Commercial Ave.
Garden City, N. Y. 11530
   (*splicing vises*)

Ratsey and Lapthorn
E. Schofield St.
City Island
Bronx, N. Y. 10464
   (*small splicing vises, small hollow fids*)

Topping Brothers
159 Varick St.
New York, N. Y. 10013
   (*marlinespikes*)

Sail-Making Materials

Adix Manufacturing Co.
381 Park Avenue South
New York, N. Y. 10016
   (*Vivatex*)

Howe and Bainbridge
220 Commercial St.
Boston, Mass. 02109
   (*all sail-making supplies: sailcloth, battens, cringles, grommets, zippers, and so on*)

Deck Layout

VENTILATORS

Abeking and Rasmussen
Lemwerder, Germany

Moyle Marine Products
Afco Works
73 Walton Rd.
Woking
Surrey, England

Galley

STOVES

Fatsco
251 N. Fair Ave.
Benton Harbor, Mich. 49022
   (*coal stoves*)

Paul E. Luke
East Boothbay, Me. 04544

Manhattan Marine and Electric Co.
116 Chambers St.
New York, N. Y. 10007
(*Tiny Tot*)

Washington Stove Works
P.O. Box 687
Everett, Wash. 98201

GAS BOTTLES

Suburban Propane Gas Corp.
Mt. Pleasant Ave.
Whippany, N. J. 07981
(*steel cylinders*)

Worthington Cylinders
P.O. Box 29008
Columbus, Ohio 43229
(*aluminum cylinders*)

Plumbing

HEADS, VALVES, SEA COCKS

Blake and Sons
Park Rd.
Gosport
Hants, England

HOSE ENDINGS

Aeroquip
300 S. East Ave.
Jackson, Mich. 49203

PUMPS

Dart Union Co., Marine Division
134 Thurbers Ave.
Providence, R. I. 02905
(*Guzzler pump*)

Edson
480 Industrial Park Rd.
New Bedford, Mass. 02745
(*diaphragm pumps*)

Henderson Pumps and Equipment
38 Medina Rd.
Cowes
Isle of Wight, England

Jack Holt
The Embankment
Putney
London S.W.15, England
(*rubber hose pump, Wykeham Martin type*)

Munster Simms Engineering
Imperial House
Donegall Sq. E.
Belfast, N. Ireland
(*diaphragm pumps*)

RUBBER DRINKING-WATER TANKS

Taselaar's Handel Mij.N.V.
Box 5030
Rotterdam, Holland

West Products
P.O. Box 707
Newark, N. J. 07101

Electricity

ALTERNATORS

C. E. Niehoff and Co.
4925 W. Lawrence St.
Chicago, Ill. 60603

FUSE BOXES

Crouch Engineering Co.
Kings Rd.
Burnham-on-Crouch
Essex, England

C. W. C. Equipment
Maidenhead
Berks, England

Peter Smales
2 Bramble Rd.
Southsea
Hants PO4 ODT, England

West Products
P.O. Box 707
Newark, N.J. 07101

GENERATORS

Mercantile Manufacturing Co.
Box 895
Minden, La. 71055
(*110-volt generators, automotive generators*)

Onan
1400 73 Ave.
Minneapolis, Minn. 55432

SWITCH PANELS

Peter Smales
2 Bramble Rd.
Southsea
Hants PO4 ODT

Mechanical Equipment

ENGINE ACCESSORIES

Huber Industries
4960 Hillside Ave.
Cincinnati, Ohio 45233
(*oil sump pump working off electric drill*)

Research Enterprises
P.O. Box 232
Nutley, N.J. 07110
(*automatic fuel shutoff*)

PROPELLERS AND ACCESSORIES

Bird Engineering Products Co.
Upland Dr.
Greenwich, Conn. 06830
(*cable propeller locks*)

Hamble Foundry
Swanwick
Southampton, England
(*folding propellers*)

Hobco Marine Systems
Old Mill Rd.
Greenwich, Conn. 06830
(*hydraulic propeller locks*)

A/S Hundested Motor Fabrik
3390 Hundested, Denmark
(*adjustable-pitch propellers*)

Martec
2257 Gaylord St.
Long Beach, Calif. 90813
(*folding propellers*)

Michigan Wheel Corp.
1501 Buchanan Ave., S.W.
Grand Rapids, Mich. 49502
(*folding propellers*)

Refrigeration

EQUIPMENT AND DESIGN

Adler and Barbour Yacht Services
43 Lawton St.
New Rochelle, N.Y. 10801

Grunert
195 Drum Point Rd.
Osbornville, N.J. 08723

Jon Repke
Power Products
Box 2454
St. Thomas, U.S. Virgin Islands 00801

PARTS AND MATERIALS

Carlsen Kolevognsfabrik
Humlebaek, Denmark
(*holding plates*)

March Manufacturing Co.
1819 Pickwick Ave.
Glenview, Ill. 60025
(*magnetic-drive pumps*)

Reichhold Chemicals
523 N. Broadway
White Plains, N.Y. 10602
(*Freon II foam insulation*)

Virginia Chemicals
Portsmouth, Va.
(*dryer*)

Navigation

CHARTS AND NAVIGATIONAL EQUIPMENT

Kelvin Hughes
St. Clare House
Minories
London E.C.3, England

M. Low
110 Hudson St.
New York, N.Y. 10013

New York Nautical Instrument and
Service Corp.
140 West Broadway
New York, N.Y. 10013

NAVIGATIONAL EQUIPMENT

Coast Navigation School
418 E. Canon Perdido
Santa Barbara, Calif. 93102

PARTICULAR ITEMS

Channel Marine Factors
Westcliff Arcade
Ramsgate
Kent, England
(*Young's Course Corrector: Young's Tidal Estimator*)

Danforth Division, The Eastern Co.
501 Riverside Industrial Pkwy.
Portland, Me. 04103
(*circular nautical slide rule*)

Offshore Instruments
47 Upper Grosvenor St.
London W.1, England
(*small hand-bearing compass; compass inside binoculars*)

Weems and Plath
48 Maryland Ave.
Annapolis, Md. 21401
(*Weems star finder, similar to HO 2102-D*)

Self Steering

WIND-VANE SELF-STEERING GEAR

Automate Products
Pitts Lane
Binstead, Ryde
Isle of Wight, England

Bingley, Son, and Follit
50 Minerva Rd.
Cowes
Isle of Wight, England

M. S. Gibb
Warsash
Southampton SO3 6ZG, England

M. F. Gunning
Little Hawsted Steep
Petersfield
Hampshire, England

Quadrant
250 Kennington Lane
London S.E.11, England

Quantock Marine Enterprises
82 Durleigh Rd.
Bridgewater
Somerset, England

AUTOPILOTS

M. S. Gibb
Warsash
Southampton SO3 6ZG, England

Quantock Marine Enterprises
82 Durleigh Rd.
Bridgewater
Somerset, England

Safe Flight Instrument Corp.
Box 550
White Plains, N.Y. 10602
(*autopilots reading off wind indicator*)

Sharp and Co.
Richborough Hall
Sandwich
Kent, England
(*autopilots—hydraulic, electric and reading off wind indicator or compass*)

Safety

SAFETY EQUIPMENT (GENERAL)

Camper and Nicholsons
Southampton, England

Canpa Yacht Equipment
Mumby Rd.
Gosport
Hants, England

Frank Moore
Northam
Southampton, England

Nordby Supply Co.
Salmon Bay Terminal
Seattle, Wash. 98119

CLOTHING

Fulton Supply Co.
23 Fulton St.
New York, N.Y. 10007

FIRE EXTINGUISHERS

Intercontinental Equipment Corp.
Chobham Rd.
Comberley
Surrey, England
(*Noxfire Freon extinguishers*)

LIFE RAFTS

Avon Rubber Co.
Dafen, Llanelli
Carms, Wales

Beaufort Equipment
Beaufort Rd.
Birkenhead, England

The Winslow Co.
Box 578
Osprey, Fla. 33559

STROBE LIGHTS

Chromalloy American Corp.
ARC Electronics Division
160 Fifth Ave.
New York, N.Y. 10010
(*individual strobe lights*)

Derritron
Marine Division
24 Upper Brook St.
London W.1, England

Hoskins
Symbolic Displays
1188 Batavia
Orange, Calif. 92667
(*large strobe lights*)

Intronic Products
P.O. Box 1231
Huntington Beach, Calif. 92647
(*large strobe lights*)

National Instrument Co.
53 State St.
Boston, Mass. 02109

SPREADER LIGHTS

Engineering and Marine Products
(EMP)
67A High St.
Fareham
Hants, England

FLARES

Survival Systems
1830 S. Baker Ave.
Ontario, Calif. 91761

EMERGENCY RADIOS

Channel Marine
49 Ramsgate
Kent, England

Derritron
Marine Division
24 Upper Brook St.
London W.1, England

Direction Corp.
P.O. Box 5800
Grand Central Station
New York, N.Y. 10017
    (*small emergency radios*)

IRW Electronics
Forgehammer Industrial Estate
Cumbran, Mon., Wales

Nordby Supply Co.
Salmon Bay Terminal
Seattle, Wash. 98119

TABLES

Table I. Weights of Boat-Building Materials

Materials	Lbs. per Cubic Foot	Materials	Lbs. per Cubic Foot
Styrofoam	1.3	Spanish cedar	37
Cork	16	Cypress	40
White cedar	23	Elm	40
White pine	26	Walnut	40
Spruce	27	Mexican mahogany	41
Redwood	28	Ash	41
Port Oxford cedar	30	Longleaf yellow	
Alaskan yellow		pine (pitch pine)	41
cedar	31	Teak (or more, depending	
Douglas fir		on age and dryness)	45
(Oregon pine)	32	Black locust	49
African mahogany	32	Hickory	53
Honduras mahogany	35	White oak	53
Butternut	35	Greenheart (won't float)	66
Philippine mahogany	36	Fiber glass (70 percent glass,	
Fir plywood	36	30 percent resin)	96

Table II. Screw Sizes for Various Planking Thicknesses

Planking Thickness, in Inches	Screw Gauge Number
5/16	5
3/8	6
7/16	7
1/2	8
5/8	9
3/4	10
7/8	12
1	14
1 1/4	16
1 1/2	18
1 3/4	20
2	24

Table III(a). Periods and Lengths of Sea Waves

Velocity, in Knots	Length, in Feet	Velocity, in Knots	Length, in Feet
1	.56	16	142.4
2	2.23	17	160.8
3	5.01	18	180.2
4	8.90	19	200.8
5	13.90	20	222.5
6	20.0	21	245.3
7	27.2	22	269.2
8	35.6	23	294.3
9	45.0	24	320.4
10	55.6	25	347.7
11	67.3	26	376.1
12	80.1	27	405.5
13	94.0	28	436.2
14	109.0	29	467.8
15	125.2	30	500.6

Courtesy of *Practical Boat Owner*.

Table III(b). Maximum Wave Size for Given Fetch, Wind Velocity, and Time Duration

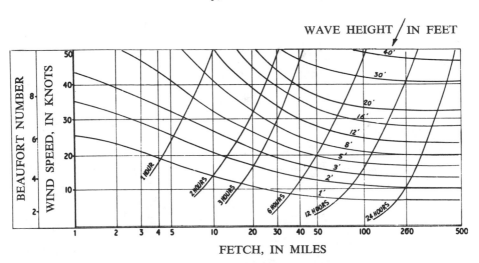

WAVE HEIGHT / IN FEET

FETCH, IN MILES

TO READ: *Enter wind speed (LHS) & go along sideways until you meet the line corresponding to the duration of the storm or the fetch, stopping at whichever comes first. At this point the wave heights can be read off.*

By permission of *Practical Boat Owner*, Tower House, London.

Table IV. Comparative Strength Table

| | ROPE | | | | | CHAIN | WIRE |
| Manila | Polypropylene | Filament Dacron | Nylon | Samson Braid | | | 1 x 19 Stainless |
Diameter, in Inches / Strength, in Pounds						Test	
¼ 690							
			3/16 850			3/16 966	
5/16 1,200	¼ 1,250	¼ 1,200	¼ 1,100				3/32 1,200
⅜ 1,600						¼ 1,680	
7/16 1,930	5/16 1,900	5/16 1,800	5/16 1,800				
				¼ 2,100			⅛ 2,100
		⅜ 2,600	⅜ 2,600			5/16 2,500	
½ 2,900	⅜ 2,700			5/16 2,700			
				⅜ 3,000			5/32 3,300
						⅜ 3,640	
	½ 4,500	½ 4,500					
⅝ 4,800			½ 5,000	7/16 4,900		7/16 4,950	3/16 4,700
¾ 5,900	⅝ 6,600	9/16 6,800	9/16 6,400			½ 6,600	7/32 6,300
⅞ 7,700	¾ 8,000		⅝ 8,000	½ 7,500		9/16 8,250	¼ 8,000
1 9,000		⅝ 9,300	¾ 10,500			⅝ 10,120	9/32 10,300
				⅝ 11,000			
		¾ 12,600					5/16 12,500
			⅞ 14,000				
		1 16,000	1 16,000	¾ 16,500			
							⅜ 17,600
				⅞ 22,000			7/16 23,400
							½ 29,700
							9/16 37,000
							⅝ 46,000

| WIRE | | | TURNBUCKLES | | SHACKLES | |
7 x 7 Stainless	7 x 19 Stainless	7 x 19 Galvanized	Merriman	Lewmar Superston	Merriman Bronze	Gibb Stainless
						5/32 750
					3/16 1,200	3/16 1,350
⅛ 1,700						
	⅛ 1,900	⅛ 1,800				
3/32 2,600	5/32 2,600	5/32 2,500				
			¼ 2,300			
					¼ 2,800	¼ 2,700
3/16 3,700	3/16 3,900	3/16 3,800	5/16 3,600			
					5/16 4,300	

WIRE			TURNBUCKLES		SHACKLES	
7/32 4,800						
	7/32 5,200	7/32 5,100	3/8 5,600	5/16 5,500		
1/4 6,100	1/4 6,600	1/4 6,500			3/8 6,000	
5/16 9,100	9/32 8,800	9/32 7,900	7/16 7,500		7/16 8,500	3/8 2,800
	5/16 9,000	5/16 9,700	1/2 10,500	3/8 9,300		1/2 10,000
					1/2 11,000	
3/8 12,600	3/8 12,000					
		3/8 14,300				
	7/16 16,300			7/16 15,300		
				1/2 16,100		
			5/8 17,500			
1/2 21,300				5/8 23,000		
			3/4 25,000			
	1/2 23,800		7/8 34,000			
				3/4 39,000		
			1 45,000			

Table V. Comparative Weights, Wire and Line

STAINLESS-STEEL WIRE

Diameter, in Fractions of an Inch	Construction	Weight per 100 Feet, in Pounds
1/8	1 x 19	3.6
3/16		8.0
1/4		14.5
5/16		22.2
3/8		31.8
7/16		44.0
1/2		58.0
9/16		73.0
5/8		90.0
	7 x 7	
Approximately the same as 1 x 19.		
	7 x 19	
1/8		2.9
3/16		6.5
1/4		11.0
5/16		17.3
3/8		24.3

DACRON OR NYLON

Diameter, in Fractions of an Inch	Approx. Weight per 600 Feet, in Pounds
3/8	20
1/2	40
5/8	67
3/4	90

Table VI. Dimensions of Norseman Fittings

EYE

Terminal size (Wire dia.)		H		D		B		L	
mm.	in.	mm.	in.	mm.	in.	mm.	in.	mm.	in.
3	⅛	5.6	.219	12.7	.50	4.7	.187	48	1.88
4	5/32	6.4	.250	16.0	.63	6.4	.250	54	2.13
5	3/16	8.0	.313	17.5	.69	7.9	.312	62	2.44
6	¼	11.1	.437	23.9	.94	9.5	.375	92	3.63
7	9/32	12.7	.500	23.9	.94	9.5	.375	92	3.63
8	5/16	14.3	.563	25.4	1.00	11.1	.437	95	3.75
9	⅜	15.9	.625	26.9	1.06	12.7	.500	121	4.75
10	13/32	15.9	.625	26.9	1.06	12.7	.500	121	4.75
12	½	19.1	.750	36.5	1.43	18.8	.740	140	5.50
14	9/16	22.2	.875	38.1	1.50	21.3	.840	165	6.50
16	⅝	25.4	1.00	50.8	2.00	24.6	.968	165	6.50

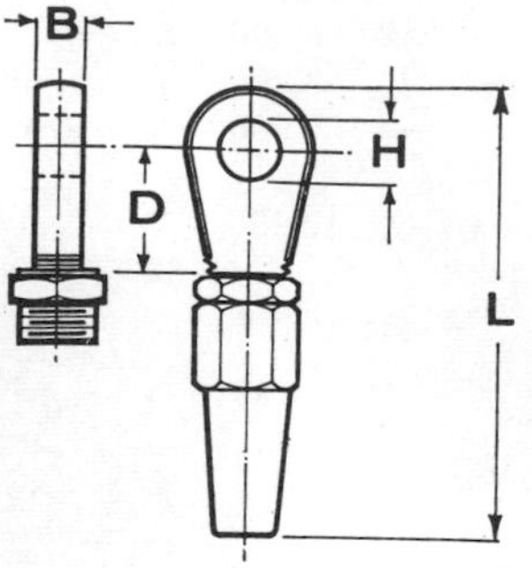

FORK

Terminal size (Wire dia.)		P		D		A		L	
mm.	in.	mm.	in.	mm.	in.	mm.	in.	mm.	in.
3	⅛	4.7	.187	12.7	.50	4.8	.189	56	2.19
4	5/32	6.1	.240	14.7	.58	6.9	.270	64	2.50
5	3/16	7.9	.312	16.3	.64	8.1	.317	73	2.88
6	¼	9.5	.375	21.3	.84	9.7	.380	98	3.88
7	9/32	9.5	.375	21.3	.84	9.7	.380	98	3.88
8	5/16	11.1	.437	22.2	.88	11.7	.460	102	4.00
9	⅜	12.7	.500	25.4	1.00	12.8	.505	130	5.13
10	13/32	12.7	.500	25.4	1.00	12.8	.505	130	5.13
12	½	18.8	.750	34.9	1.38	19.1	.750	147	5.75
14	9/16	22.2	.875	38.1	1.50	23.5	.925	178	7.00
16	⅝	25.4	1.00	44.5	1.75	25.7	1.010	190	7.50

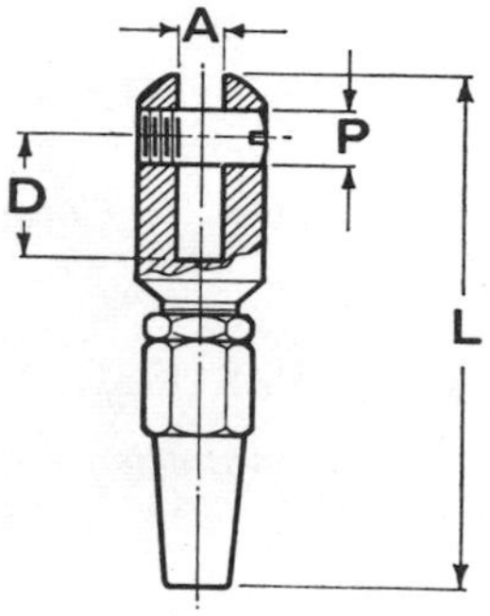

STUD

Terminal size (Wire dia.)		T	D		S		L	
mm.	in.	U.N.F.	mm.	in.	mm.	in.	mm.	in.
3	⅛	¼	48	1.88	2.4	.094	83	3.25
4	5/32	5/16	52	2.06	2.8	.109	95	3.75
5	3/16	⅜	64	2.50	3.2	.125	102	4.00
6	¼	7/16	73	2.88	4.0	.156	143	5.63
7	9/32	½	79	3.13	4.0	.156	147	5.75
8	5/16	½	79	3.13	4.0	.156	152	6.00
9	⅜	⅝	95	3.75	4.0	.156	187	7.38
10	13/32	⅝	95	3.75	4.0	.156	187	7.38

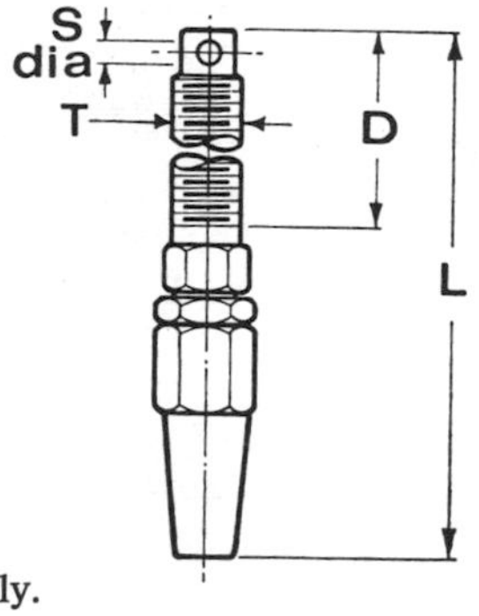

The above tables apply to the Mk. III stainless-steel versions only.

Courtesy of Norseman Ropes Ltd.

Wire Size (Diameter, in Inches)	7 x 19 A INCHES	B INCHES
1/16	1 1/8	.039
3/32	1 1/2	.056
1/8	2 1/4	.075
5/32	2 3/4	.091
3/16	3 1/2	.108
7/32	4	.124
1/4	4 1/2	.142
9/32	5	.160

Table VII. Dimensions of Standard U.S. End Fittings, and Recommended Sheave Dimensions

Wire Size (Diameter, in Inches)	Marine Eye D	Marine Eye J	MS-20668 Eye D	MS-20668 Eye J	MS-20667 Fork D	MS-20667 Fork G	MS-21259 AN-669 V	MS-21259 Y	AN-669 Y	Bs	As	Cs	Ls
1/16	.263	.218	.19	.088	.19	.093	6-40	1.045	.375	.19	.112	.156	.39
3/32	.263	.218	.19	.103	.19	.108	10-32	1.204	.5	.253	.143	.234	.578
1/8	.263	.218	.19	.19	.19	.195	1/4-28	1.376	.563	.315	.19	.313	.765
5/32	.325	.281	.25	.197	.25	.202	1/4-28	1.376	.625	.379	.222	.391	.953
3/16	.39	.359	.313	.255	.313	.26	5/16-24	1.453	.75	.442	.255	.469	1.14
7/32	.45	.406	.313	.291	.313	.296	3/8-24	1.625	.875	.505	.302	.547	1.328
1/4	.515	.468	.375	.307	.375	.313	3/8-24	1.75	.875	.567	.348	.625	1.515
9/32	.515	.468	.438	.322	.438	.327	7/16-20	1.875	1.	.632	.382	.75	1.719
5/16	.64	.593	.438	.343	.438	.348	1/2-20	2.	1.	.694	.413	.813	1.875
3/8	.64	.593	.5	.375	.5	.38	9/16-18	2.25	1.125	—	—	—	—
7/16	.765	.719	.562	.375	.562	.38	5/8-18	2.5	1.25	—	—	—	—
1/2	.89	.844	.625	.468	.625	.473	5/8-18	2.5	1.25	—	—	—	—
9/16	.89	.884	.75	.562	.75	.567	3/4-16	3.	1.5	—	—	—	—
5/8	1.015	.968	.875	.657	.875	.663	7/8-14	3.5	1.75	—	—	—	—

By permission of Merriman Holbrook, Inc., Grand River, Ohio.

Table VIII. Properties of Commonly Used Marine Alloys

Nickel Aluminum Bronze. A very high strength corrosion-resistant bronze, used for cast snap shackles, turnbuckles, and furling gear, that has a tensile strength of 115,000 lbs. per sq. inch. Yield 75,000 psi.

Everdur Bronze. A bronze widely used in forgings, such as turnbuckles, snap shackles, and toggles. Everdur provides an excellent combination of strength, corrosion resistance, and ductility, and has a tensile strength of 90,000 lbs. per sq. inch. Yield 55,000 psi.

Manganese Bronze. A high-strength corrosion-resistant bronze widely used where strength is important, in fittings such as large winches, winch handles, genoa and spinnaker slides, pad eyes, headboard shackles, turning blocks, and tiller fittings. Tensile strength is 80,000 lbs. per sq. inch. Yield 40,000 psi.

Navy Bronze. A very ductile, corrosion-resistant bronze used where great strength is not as important as lack of brittleness. Navy bronze is used for tee track, sail track, small winches, cleats, shackles, and some block sheaves. Tensile strength is 40,000 lbs. per sq. inch. Yield 18,000 psi.

Beryllium Copper. A super-strength copper alloy used in castings and forgings where 180,000 lbs. per sq. inch strength is needed. Yield 150,000 psi.

40-E Aluminum. A very strong and corrosion-resistant alloy used for cleats, spinnaker-pole fittings, track end stops, and all other aluminum castings. Tensile strength is 40,000 lbs. per sq. inch. Yield 31,000 psi.

6061 T-6 Aluminum. A wrought-aluminum alloy with excellent corrosion resistance and strength, used for tee track, block sheaves, and spinnaker poles, and in aluminum castings. Tensile strength is 45,000 lbs. per sq. inch. Yield 40,000 psi.

303 Stainless Steel. A free machining stainless steel with good corrosion resistance, used for shafts, axles, and pins. Strength is 90,000 lbs. per sq. inch. Yield 35,000 psi.

303 SE Stainless Steel. Very similar to standard 303 except that the addition of selenium makes it suitable for swage fittings. Strength is 90,000 lbs. per sq. inch. Yield 35,000 psi.

302/304 Stainless Steel. Very similar to 303 but used in the form of flat bar, strip, and sheet for block straps, clevis pins, pins and cotter pins, also in forgings for block swivels and life-rail eyes. Strength is 90,000 lbs. per sq. inch. Yield 35,000 psi.

316 Stainless Steel. Similar but more corrosion resistant than 303, used for precision castings such as headboard shackles, genoa cars, and spinnaker slides. Strength is 90,000 lbs. per sq. inch. Yield 35,000 psi.

22-13-5 Stainless Steel. A very high-strength corrosion-resistant alloy used for rod rigging and pins. This alloy is resis-

tant to stress corrosion cracking and intergranular corrosion, and has a tensile strength of 170,000 lbs. Yield 135,000 psi.

17-4 Stainless Steel. A super-strength stainless steel gives up some corrosion resistance for its tensile strength of 180,-000 psi. It is used for precision castings of winch pawls, gears, snap shackles, and pins. Yield 170,000 psi.

Monel Metal. An extremely stiff and corrosion-resistant nickel alloy used for plunger pins in snap shackles, has a tensile strength of 100,000 psi. Yield 80,000 psi.

MP-35-N Alloy. A very expensive alloy of nickel, cobalt, chromium, and molybdenum that is unequaled for strength and corrosion resistance. It is absolutely inert to corrosion by seawater and has a tensile strength of 300,000 psi. It is used for rod rigging and pins. Yield 290,000 psi.

By permission of Merriman Holbrook, Inc., Grand River, Ohio.

Table IX. Weights of Various Sailcloths

Weights of Various Sails

MAINSAILS

The rule of thumb of Sol Lamport (American Dacron manufacturer) is

$$\frac{\text{LOA} + \text{mainsail hoist in feet}}{10} = \text{weight, American measure.}$$

The rule of thumb of Howard Williams (Ratsey and Lapthorn, England) is

$$\frac{\text{Main hoist}}{4} = \text{weight, British measure.}$$

Very large mainsails, of over 550 square feet, can be slightly below weight to reduce the difficulty of furling. The amount below weight will be minimal on sloops and cutters (unless they have a very large trysail carried on switch track) as the main is used in heavy weather. On

yawls the mainsail weight can be reduced, as in heavy weather they should be able to sail on headsails and mizzen, or on headsails, trysail, and mizzen. On big ketches, the mainsail weight can be substantially reduced as the mainsail is seldom used in heavy weather.

Mizzens

On yawls, the mizzen should be the one weight less than the main; despite its small size, this sail needs heavy cloth as it will be used in heavy weather. Similarly, on ketches the mizzen should be the same weight as the main.

Working Headsails

The staysail, working jib, and large Yankee, should be the same weight as the mainsail; since the large Yankee is the sail that makes a boat go, the main should be reefed first, and the Yankee may remain up until the wind reaches 18 to 20 knots.

Storm Sails

Storm sails should be the same weight as working sails; if heavier, they become too hard to handle and to stow. The storm trysail on large boats (of at least 60 feet LOA) can be lighter than the main to facilitate ease of handling. The necessary strength can be achieved by Scotch cut, large head, tack, and clew patches, and roping all around.

Three-quarter Working Genoa

This most useful sail should be the same weight as the main; it will frequently be used in conjunction with a reefed main or no main. Since it is only used when the wind is at 10 knots or over, this weight does not create problems.

Light Genoa or Reaching Jib

On cruising boats this sail can be half the weight of the main, since it will be taken off early in the game when going to windward. On reaches, comparatively light Dacron will hold its shape with a hatful of wind. On cruising boats the light genoa or reacher must be light and easily stowed by a small crew, since space and manpower are limited.

Genoa Staysail

This sail should be one weight below the main. In heavy weather a working staysail the same weight as the main will be used instead.

Reaching Genoa Staysail

This sail is set under a high-clewed reaching jib (ballooner) or under a spinnaker. Since it is seldom used going to windward, it can be of very light cloth to facilitate stowage.

Equivalent Sailcloth Weights

	0	1	2	3	4	5	6	7	8	9	10	11	12	13	14	15	16	17	18	19	20
British measure (ounces per square yard)	0	1	2	3	4	5	6	7	8	9	10	11	12	13	14	15	16	17	18	19	20
American measure (ounces per running yard—28½ inches wide)		1	2	3	4	5	6	7	8	9	10	11	12	13	14						
Continental measure (grams per square meter)	0	50	100	150	200	250	300	350	400	450	500	550	600								

Table X. Chain Weights

Diameter, in Inches	Short Link, per Fathom	Stud Link, per Fathom	Formulas
$\frac{3}{16}$	3½ pounds		Weight per Fathom, Short Link $= \dfrac{D^2}{40}$ Tons.
¼	4½		
$\frac{5}{16}$	6½		Approximate Ultimate Strength $= 24D^2$ Tons.
$\frac{3}{8}$	9		
$\frac{7}{16}$	11¼	13½	Proof Test $= 70\% \times 24D^2$ Tons.
½	14¼	16½	
$\frac{9}{16}$	20	22	D is chain diameter. Tons are long tons.
$\frac{5}{8}$	24	26	

Table XI. Weights and Dimensions of Stores

Potatoes	40 lbs. per cubic ft.; 60 lbs. per bushel
Liquor	3 lbs. per quart
Beer, by the case, 9½-ounce cans	20 lbs.; 11¾″ x 4½″ x 16″
10-ounce bottles	34 lbs.; 10¼″ x 6½″ x 15″
Soda, by the case, cans	approximately the same as beer
6½-ounce bottles	38 lbs.; 11¾″ x 8½″ x 18″
Milk, by the 48-can	
case, 14½-ounce cans	54 lbs.; 12″ x 8″ x 18″
Consumable stores	5½ lbs. per man per day
Sea kit, temperate	
or cool climate	75–100 lbs.
warm climate	25 lbs.
Coal	47–58 lbs. per cubic foot
Charcoal	10–12 lbs. per cubic foot
Ice, 50-lb. block	approx. 1500 cubic inches
50 lbs. of cubes	approx. 1600 cubic inches

Gas bottles	Dimensions	Weight, empty	Weight, full
United States			
Horizontal, steel	10″ x 20″	20	40
Horizontal, aluminum	13″ x 19⅜″	9	29
Vertical, aluminum	10⅜″ x 14½″	4.5	12.5
British			
Vertical, steel	12″ x 21″	20	40

Well-equipped engine toolbox, with tools	
Well-equipped woodworking toolbox,	
with tools, including electric drill,	60 lbs.
saber saw, and so on	80 lbs.

Table XII. Nomograph for Determining Pounds Per Inch of Immersion in Salt Water

Design Waterline in Feet

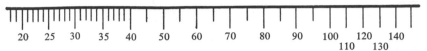

Pounds per Inch of Immersion

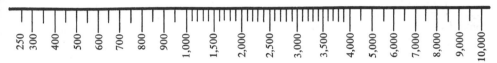

Beam on Design Waterline in Feet

If the points on the top and bottom lines are connected by a straight line, its point of intersection with the middle line gives the increase in displacement per inch of immersion.

Beam is measured at the waterline, not at the deck; the difference between these two dimensions is sometimes sizable.

Long-ended boats will have considerably different waterline lengths at 2, 4, and 6 inches of immersion; for these boats, interpolation is necessary to obtain an accurate answer.

From *Skene's Elements of Yacht Design*,
Revised by Francis S. Kinney, New York, Dodd, Mead, 1962.

Table XIII. Galvanic Series of Metals and Alloys

Sea-Water Corrosion of Galvanic Couples

Corroded End (Anodic or Least Noble)

Magnesium
Magnesium alloys
Zinc
Aluminum
Aluminum Alloys
Cadmium
Carbon steel
Cast iron
Stainless steel Type 410 (active)
Stainless steel Type 430 (active)
Ni-Resist
Stainless steel Type 304 (active)
Stainless steel Type 316 (active)
Corronel 240 (active)
Lead
Nickel (active)
Inconel (active)
Corronel 220 (active)
Brasses
Copper
Bronzes
Monel
Nickel (passive)
Inconel (passive)
Stainless steel Type 410 (passive)
Stainless steel Type 430 (passive)
Stainless steel Type 304 (passive)
Stainless steel Type 316 (passive)
Ni-o-nel
Titanium
Corronel 220 (passive)
Corronel 240 (passive)
Silver
Graphite
Gold
Platinum

Protected End (Catholic or Most Noble)

**Couple any
two items for
degree of reaction**
i.e. Magnesium+
Platinum=Max.
Reaction

Maximum Reaction

Courtesy of Norseman Ropes Ltd.

Table XIV. Tacking Downwind

A (in degrees)	B	C (in percents)
0	–	–
5	(Infinitesimal)	(Any increase in speed makes course alteration worthwhile.)
10	0.015	1.5
15	0.035	3.5
20	0.064	6.4
25	0.103	10.3
30	0.154	15.4
35	0.221	22.1
40	0.305	30.5
45	0.414	41.4
50	0.556	55.6
55	0.743	74.3
60	1.000	100.0

A gives course relative to true wind, in degrees.

B gives extra distance traveled by tacking downward, in miles per mile of direct course.

C gives minimum percentage of increase in speed over direct downwind speed required to justify change in course.

Courtesy of H. Marvin Berning, Virgin Islands Engineering and Surveying.

Table XV. Optimum Course to Steer When Beating to Windward

If your original tacking angle to TRUE wind is:	And you alter the tacking angle to:	You must increase your boat speed at least this percentage to make an improvement in your position to windward:	You may decrease your speed up to this percentage to make an improvement in your position to windward:
40°	30°	—	11.5%
	35°	—	6.5%
	45°	8.3%	—
	50°	19.2%	—
	55°	33.6%	—
	60°	53.2%	—
	65°	81.3%	—
45°	30°	—	18.4%
	35°	—	13.7%
	40°	—	7.7%
	50°	10.0%	—
	55°	23.3%	—
	60°	41.4%	—
	65°	67.3%	—
50°	30°	—	25.8%
	35°	—	21.5%
	40°	—	16.1%
	45°	—	9.1%
	55°	12.1%	—
	60°	28.6%	—
	65°	52.1%	—
	70°	87.9%	—
	75°	148.3%	—
55°	35°	—	30.0%
	40°	—	25.1%
	45°	—	18.9%
	50°	—	10.8%
	60°	14.7%	—
	65°	35.7%	—
	70°	67.7%	—
	75°	121.6%	—
60°	35°	—	39.0%
	40°	—	34.7%
	45°	—	29.3%
	50°	—	22.2%
	55°	—	12.8%
	65°	18.3%	—
	70°	46.2%	—
	75°	93.2%	—
65°	40°	—	44.8%
	45°	—	40.2%
	50°	—	34.3%
	55°	—	26.3%
	60°	—	15.5%
	70°	23.6%	—
	75°	63.3%	—
	80°	143.3%	—

Table XVI. Total Distance To Be Traveled When Beating to Windward at Various Tacking Angles and Various Wind Directions and Percentage of Time Spent on Each Tack.

Tacking Angle		90°	100°	110°	120°	130°	140°
Ship's course relative to the true wind* Δ, in degrees		45°	50°	55°	60°	65°	70°
0	A	1.41	1.56	1.74	2.00	2.37	2.92
	B	50	50	50	50	50	50
	C	50	50	50	50	50	50
5	A	1.41	1.55	1.74	1.99	2.36	2.91
	B	54	54	53	53	52	51
	C	46	46	47	47	48	49
10	A	1.39	1.53	1.72	1.97	2.33	2.88
	B	59	57	56	55	54	53
	C	41	43	44	45	46	47
15	A	1.37	1.50	1.68	1.83	2.29	2.80
	B	63	61	59	58	56	55
	C	37	39	41	42	44	45
20	A	1.33	1.46	1.60	1.88	2.22	2.74
	B	68	65	63	61	58	57
	C	32	35	37	39	42	43
25	A	1.28	1.41	1.58	1.81	2.14	2.64
	B	73	70	66	63	60	58
	C	27	30	34	37	40	42
30	A	1.22	1.35	1.51	1.73	2.04	2.53
	B	79	74	71	67	63	61
	C	21	26	29	33	37	39
35	A	1.16	1.27	1.43	1.64	1.93	2.39
	B	85	79	75	70	66	63
	C	15	21	25	30	34	37
40	A	1.08	1.19	1.34	1.53	1.81	2.23
	B	92	85	79	74	70	65
	C	8	15	21	26	30	35
45	A	1.00	1.10	1.23	1.41	1.67	2.06
	B	100	92	85	79	73	68
	C	0	8	15	21	27	32
50	A		1.00	1.12	1.28	1.52	1.87
	B		100	91	84	78	72
	C		0	9	16	22	28
55	A			1.00	1.15	1.36	1.67
	B			100	91	83	76
	C			0	9	17	24
60	A				1.00	1.18	1.46
	B				100	90	82
	C				0	10	18
65	A					1.00	1.23
	B					100	89
	C					0	11

A is total distance to be traveled in relation to one mile on the rhumb-line course.
B is percentage of time to be spent on the long tack to end up on the rhumb-line.
C is percentage of time to be spent on the short tack to end up on the rhumb-line.
Δ is wind direction in degrees right or left of the rhumb-line course.

* Ship's course relative to true wind is considered to be one-half the tacking angle and assumes no wind change and consistent sea conditions on each tack.

Courtesy of H. Marvin Berning, Virgin Islands Engineering and Surveying.

Table XVII. Simplified Laterals of Departure

Δ, *in degrees*	A	
1	0.17	Δ is course right or left of the rhumb line.
5	0.87	*A* is distance from the rhumb line after ten miles of sailing. A quick rule of thumb is that this distance is .17 miles, or 340 yards, in ten miles per degree of divergence from the rhumb line.
10	1.73	
15	2.58	
20	3.42	
25	4.22	
30	5.00	Courtesy of H. Marvin Berning, Virgin Islands Engineering and Surveying.

Table XVIII. Weights of Commonly Used Materials

Material	Pounds per Cubit Foot	Material	Pounds per Cubit Foot
Aluminum, cast	165	Zinc	440
sheet	168	Gasoline (6.19 pounds per gallon)	46.3
Brass	534		
Bronze, 7.9–14% tin	509	Kerosene (paraffin) (6.8 pounds per gallon)	50.9
aluminum	481		
phospor	537	Oil, diesel (7.13 pounds per gallon)	53.3
Copper	556		
Iron, cast	450	fuel bunker (8.09 pounds pcr gallon)	60.6
wrought	485		
Lead, scrap	700	lube (7.69 pounds per gallon)	57.5
virgin	712	Water, fresh	62.4
Mercury	849	Sea	64
Monel	556		
Steel, stainless	492–510		
structural	490		

Table XIX. Diameter–Circumference Equivalents

diam., in ins.	circum. ins.	nearest frac. circumference ins.	diam., in ins.	circum. ins.	nearest frac. circumference ins.
¼	0·785	¾ —	1½	4·712	4¾ +
5⁄16	0·981	1 +	1 9⁄16	4·908	5 +
⅜	1·178	1¼ +	1⅝	5·105	5⅛ +
7⁄16	1·374	1⅜ =	1 11⁄16	5·301	5⅜ +
½	1·570	1½ —	1¾	5·497	5½ =
9⁄16	1·767	1¾ —	1 13⁄16	5·694	5¾ +
⅝	1·963	2 +	1⅞	5·890	5⅞ —
11⁄16	2·159	2 3⁄16 +	1 15⁄16	6·086	6 —
¾	2·356	2⅜ +	2	6·283	6¼ —
13⁄16	2·552	2½ —	2⅛	6·675	6⅝ —
⅞	2·748	2¾ =	2¼	7·068	7 —
15⁄16	2·945	3 +	2⅜	7·461	7½ +
1	3·141	3⅛ —	2½	7·853	7⅞ +
1⅛	3·534	3½ —			
1 3⁄16	3·730	3¾ +			
1¼	3·926	4 +			
1 5⁄16	4·123	4⅛ =			
1⅜	4·319	4⅜ +			
1 7⁄16	4·516	4½ —			

To convert Diameter into Circumference, multiply by 3·14159.
To convert Circumference into Diameter, multiply by 0·3183.

Courtesy of Norseman Ropes Ltd.

Table XX. Conversion to and from Metric Measures

English Measures to Metric Measures

Pounds	To Kilograms	× 0·45357
Long Hundredweights (Cwts.) *	To Kilograms	× 50·80
Long Tons *	To Kilograms	× 1016·00
Lineal Inches	To Millimeters	× 25·3999
Lineal Feet	To Millimeters	× 304·7997
Lineal Yards	To Millimeters	× 914·3992
Lineal Fathoms	To Millimeters	× 1828·7984
Lineal Inches	To Meters	× 0·0254
Lineal Feet	To Meters	× 0·3048
Lineal Yards	To Meters	× 0·9144
Lineal Fathoms	To Meters	× 1·8288
Pounds per Lineal Foot	To Kilos per Meter	× 1·4881
Pounds per Lineal Yard	To Kilos per Meter	× 0·4960
Pounds per Lineal Fathom	To Kilos per Meter	× 0·2480
Long Tons per Sq. Inch	To Kilos per Sq. mm.	× 1·5748
Square Inch	To Sq. mm.	× 645·1549

One-eighth of an inch of Circumference = One mm. of Diameter.

Metric Measures to English Measures

Kilograms (Kilos)	To Pounds	× 0·039370
Kilograms	To Long Cwts.	× 0·003281
Kilograms	To Long Tons	× 0·001094
Millimeters	To Inches	× 0·000547
Millimeters	To Feet	× 2·204724
Millimeters	To Yards	× 0·019685
Millimeters	To Fathoms	× 0·000984
Meters	To Inches	× 39·370113
Meters	To Feet	× 3·280842
Meters	To Yards	× 1·093614
Meters	To Fathoms	× 0·546807
Kilos per Lineal Meter	To Pounds per Foot	× 0·671999
Kilos per Lineal Meter	To Pounds per Yard	× 2·015998
Kilos per Lineal Meter	To Pounds per Fathom	× 4·031997
Kilos per Sq. mm.	To Long Tons per Sq. Inch	× 0·634997
	To Square Inch	× 0·001550

Mm. of Diameter ÷ 8 = Circumference in inches.

*A long hundredweight equals 112 pounds; a long ton equals 20 hundredweights or 2240 pounds.

Fractions of an Inch to Decimals of an Inch and to Millimeters

Inches	Inches	Millimeters	Inches	Inches	Millimeters
1/64	0·015625	0·3969	33/64	0·515625	13·0969
1/32	0·03125	0·7938	17/32	0·53125	13·4938
3/64	0·046875	1·1906	35/64	0·546875	13·8906
1/16	0·0625	1·5875	9/16	0·5625	14·2875
5/64	0·078125	1·9844	37/64	0·578125	14·6844
3/32	0·09375	2·3812	19/32	0·59375	15·0812
7/64	0·109375	2·7781	39/64	0·609375	15·4781
1/8	0·125	3·175	5/8	0·625	15·875
9/64	0·140625	3·5719	41/64	0·640625	16·2719
5/32	0·15625	3·9688	21/32	0·65625	16·6688
11/64	0·171875	4·3656	43/64	0·671875	17·0656
3/16	0·1875	4·7625	11/16	0·6875	17·4625
13/64	0·203125	5·1594	45/64	0·703125	17·8594
7/32	0·21875	5·5562	23/32	0·71875	18·2562
15/64	0·234375	5·9531	47/64	0·734375	18·6531
1/4	0·25	6·35	3/4	0·75	19·05
17/64	0·265625	6·7469	49/64	0·765625	19·4469
9/32	0·28125	7·1438	25/32	0·78125	19·8438
19/64	0·296875	7·5406	51/64	0·796875	20·2406
5/16	0·3125	7·9375	13/16	0·8125	20·6375
21/64	0·328125	8·3344	53/64	0·828125	21·0344
11/32	0·34375	8·7312	27/32	0·84375	21·4312
23/64	0·359375	9·1281	55/64	0·859375	21·8281
3/8	0·375	9·525	7/8	0·875	22·225
25/64	0·390625	9·9219	57/64	0·890625	22·6219
13/32	0·40625	10·3188	29/32	0·90625	23·0188
27/64	0·421875	10·7156	59/64	0·921875	23·4156
7/16	0·4375	11·1125	15/16	0·9375	23·8125
29/64	0·453125	11·5094	61/64	0·953125	24·2094
15/32	0·46875	11·9062	31/32	0·96875	24·6062
31/64	0·484375	12·3031	63/64	0·984375	25·0031
1/2	0·5	12·7	1	1	25·4

Feet and Fathoms to Meters

Feet	6	12	18	24	30	36	42	48	54	60
Fathoms	1	2	3	4	5	6	7	8	9	10
Meters	1.8	3.6	5.5	7.3	9.1	10.9	12.8	14.6	16.4	18.3
1	0.3	2.1	3.9	5.8	7.6	9.4	11.3	13.1	14.9	16.7	18.6
2	0.6	2.4	4.2	6.1	7.9	9.7	11.6	13.4	15.2	17.0	18.9
3	0.9	2.7	4.5	6.4	8.2	10.0	11.9	13.7	15.5	17.3	19.2
4	1.2	3.0	4.9	6.7	8.5	10.3	12.2	14.0	15.8	17.7	19.5
5	1.5	3.3	5.2	7.0	8.8	10.6	12.5	14.3	16.1	18.0	19.8

Square Measure, Metric Equivalents

1 square inch	6.451 square centimeters
1 square foot	0.093 square meters
1 square yard	0.836 square meters
100 square feet	9.29 square meters

Liquid Measure, Metric Equivalents

United States		*Imperial*	
1 quart	0.946 liters	1 quart	1.136 liters
1 gallon	3.785 liters _ 1 gallon		4.545 liters

Courtesy of Norseman Ropes Ltd.

BIBLIOGRAPHY

Design

Baader, Juan, *The Sailing Yacht,* New York, Norton, 1965.

Beiser, Arthur, *The Proper Yacht,* New York, Macmillan, 1966.

Birt, Douglas H. C., *Sailing Yacht Design,* Southampton, Robert Ross & Co., 1951.

Chapelle, Howard I., *Yacht Designing and Planning,* revised, New York, Norton, 1971.

Fox, Uffa, *According to Uffa,* New York, St. Martin's, 1961.

—— *Crest of the Wave,* London, Peter Davis, 1939.

—— *Racing and Cruising Design,* New York, Scribner's, 1938.

—— *Sail and Power,* New York, Scribner's, 1937.

—— *Sailing Boats,* New York, St. Martin's, 1960.

—— *Sailing, Seamanship and Yacht Construction,* New York, Scribner's, 1934.

—— *Thoughts on Yachts and Yachting,* New York, Scribner's, 1939.

—— *Uffa Fox's Second Book,* New York, Scribner's, 1935.

Herreshoff, L. Francis, *The Common Sense of Yacht Design,* New York, Rudder Publishing Co., 1946.

Illingworth, John, *Further Offshore,* Chicago, Quadrangle Books, 1969.

Marchaj, C. A., *Sailing Theory and Practice,* New York, Dodd, Mead, 1964.

Skene's Elements of Yacht Design, revised by Francis S. Kinney, New York, Dodd, Mead, 1962.

Construction

Bell, Charles, *How to Build Fiberglass Boats,* New York, Coward-McCann, 1957.

Chapelle, Howard I., *Boatbuilding,* New York, Norton, 1941.

Cobb, Boughton, *Fiberglass Boats, Construction and Maintenance,* Third Edition. New York, Yachting Publishing Corp., 1969.

Gibbs and Cox, Staff of, *Fiberglass Marine Design.* New York, McGraw-Hill, 1960.

—— *Marine Survey Manual,* Tuckahoe, John de Graff, 1962.

Smith, Harvey Garrett, *Boat Carpentry,* Princeton, Van Nostrand, 1955.

Navigation

The American Practical Navigator, originally by Nathaniel Bowditch (issued by the U. S. Naval Oceanographic Office), Washington, U. S. Government Printing Office, periodically revised.

Blewitt, Mary, *Celestial Navigation for Yachtsmen,* Tuckahoe, John de Graff, 1967.

Chapman, Charles F., *Piloting, Seamanship and Small Boat Handling,* New York, Motor Boating, periodically revised.

Devereux, Frederick L., Jr., *Practical Navigation for the Yachtsman,* New York, Norton, 1972.

Mixter, George W., *Primer of Navigation,* Third Edition, edited by Donald McClench, Princeton, Van Nostrand, 1967.

——and Williams, Ramon, *Navigation Problems and Solutions,* Princeton, Van Nostrand, 1951.

Sails and Their Care

Bowker, R. M. and Budd, S. A., *Make Your Own Sails,* New York, Macmillan, 1960.

Gray, Alan, *Sailmaking Simplified,* New York, Rudder Publishing Co., 1932.

Howard-Williams, Jeremy, *Sails,* Third Edition, Tuckahoe, John de Graff, 1972.

Ratsey, Ernest A. and de Fontaine, W. H., *Yacht Sails, Their Care and Handling,* New York, Norton, 1948.

Passage Making

Bruce, Errol, *Deep Sea Sailing*, New York, D. Van Nostrand Comp. Inc., 1953.
Coles, K. Adlard, *Heavy Weather Sailing*, Tuckahoe, John de Graff, 1968.
Hiscock, Eric, *Cruising Under Sail*. London, Oxford University Press, 1967.
—— *Voyaging Under Sail*, London, Oxford University Press, 1959.
Worth, Claud, *Yacht Cruising*, New York, Yachting Inc., 1926.
—— *Yacht Navigation and Voyaging*, New York, Yachting Publishing Corp., 1927.

General Information

Boat Owners Buying Guide, New York, Yachting Publishing Corp., issued annually.
Sailboat and Sailboat Equipment Directory, Boston, Institute for Advancement of Sailing, issued annually.
Webb, Barbra, *Ready About*, England, W. & J. Mackay & Co. Ltd., 1965.

Periodicals

Boating, 1 Park Ave. S., New York, N. Y. 10016.
National Fisherman, Camden, Maine 04843.
Sail, Institute for Advancement of Sailing, 38 Commercial Wharf, Boston, Mass. 02110.
Yachting, Yachting Publishing Corp., 50 W. 44 St., New York, N. Y. 10036.
Yachting Monthly, Tower House, Southampton St., London W.C.2, England.
Yachting World, Dorset House, Stamford St., London S.W.1, England.

INDEX